GREAT DEBATES IN AMERICAN HISTORY

*From the Debates in the British Parliament on the
Colonial Stamp Act (1764–1765) to the Debates
in Congress at the Close of the Taft
Administration (1912–1913)*

EDITED BY

MARION MILLS MILLER, Litt.D. (Princeton)

Editor of "The Life and Works of Abraham Lincoln," etc.

IN FOURTEEN VOLUMES

EACH DEALING WITH A SPECIFIC SUBJECT, AND CONTAINING A SPECIAL INTRODUC-
TION BY A DISTINGUISHED AMERICAN STATESMAN OR PUBLICIST

VOLUME NINE

DEPARTMENTS OF GOVERNMENT

With an Introduction by WILLIAM HOWARD TAFT, LL.D.
Ex-President of the United States

CURRENT LITERATURE PUBLISHING COMPANY
NEW YORK

15749

CONTENTS OF VOLUME NINE

ILLUSTRATIONS IN VOLUME NINE

INTRODUCTION

THE PRIME OBJECT OF GOVERNMENT [1]

THE history of the world seems to show that our form of government is more enduring and satisfactory than any other. We began as a small Union of thirteen States strung along the Atlantic coast, of three million of people, and under the same Constitution we have enlarged to be a world power of forty-eight sovereign States, bound into one, of more than ninety millions of people, and with a humane guardianship of ten millions more—nine in the Pacific and one in the Atlantic. We have fought, beginning with the Revolution, four foreign wars, and we have survived a Civil War of the greatest proportions recorded in history, and have united the battling sections by an indissoluble tie. From our body politic we have excised the cancer of slavery, the only thing protected by the Constitution which was inconsistent with that liberty the preservation of which was the main purpose of establishing the Union. We have increased our business and productive activities in every direction; we have expanded the development of our natural resources to be continent wide, and all the time we have maintained sacred those inalienable rights of man, the right of liberty, the right of privote property, and the right to the pursuit of happiness.

For these reasons we believe in popular government. Government is a human instrumentality to secure the

[1] From an address delivered at Toledo, O., on March 8, 1912.

1

greatest good to the greatest number and the greatest happiness to the individual. Experience, and especially the growth of popular government in our own history, have shown that in the long run every class of the people, and by that I mean those similarly situated, are better able to secure attention to their own welfare than any other class, however altruistic the latter class may be. Of course this assumes that the members of the class have reasonable intelligence and capacity for knowing their own rights and interest. Hence it follows that the best government, in the sense of the government most certain to provide for and protect the rights and governmental needs of every class, is that one in which every class has a voice. In recognition of this the tendency from earliest times in our history has been the enlargement of the electorate to include in the ultimate source of governmental power as many as possible of those governed. But even to-day the electorate is not more in number than one-sixth of the total number of those who are citizens of the nation and are the people for whom the Government is maintained, and whose rights and happiness the Government is intended to secure. More than this, government by unanimous vote of the electorate is impossible, and therefore the majority of the electorate must rule.

We find, therefore, that government by the people is, under our present system, government by a majority of one sixth of those whose rights and happiness are to be affected by the course and conduct of the Government. This is the nearest to a government by the whole people we have ever had. Woman's suffrage will change this, and it is doubtless coming as soon as the electorate can be certain that most women desire it and will assume its burden and responsibility. But, even then, the electorate will be only a one-third part of the whole people. In other words, the electorate is a representative governing body for the whole people for which the Government was established, and the controlling majority of the electorate is a body still less numerous. It is thus apparent that ours is a Government of all the people by a representative part of the people.

Now, the object of government is not only to secure the greatest good to the greatest number, but also to do this as near as may be by securing the rights of each individual in his liberty, property, and pursuit of happiness. Hence it was long ago recognized that the direct action of a temporary majority of the existing electorate must be limited by fundamental law; that is, by a constitution intended to protect the individual and the minority of the electorate and the nonvoting majority of the people against the unjust or arbitrary action of the majority of the electorate. This made it necessary to introduce into the Constitution certain declarations as to the rights of the individual which it was the purpose of the whole people to maintain through the Government against the aggression of any temporary majority of the electorate and to provide in the same instrument certain procedure by which the individual might assert and vindicate those rights. Then, to protect against the momentary impulse of a temporary majority of the electorate to change the fundamental law and deprive the individual or the voting minority or the nonvoting majority of inalienable rights, the Constitution provided a number of checks and balances whereby every amendment to the Constitution must be adopted under forms and with delays that are intended to secure much deliberation on the part of the electorate in adopting such amendments.

I cannot state the necessity for maintaining the checks and balances in a constitution to secure the guaranty of individual rights and well-ordered liberty better than by quoting from Daniel Webster. He said:

The first object of a free people is the preservation of their liberty; and liberty is only to be preserved by maintaining constitutional restraints and just divisions of political power. Nothing is more deceptive or more dangerous than the pretence of a desire to simplify government. The simplest governments are despotism; the next simplest, limited monarchies; but all republics, all governments of law, must impose numerous limitations and qualifications of authority and give many positive and many qualified rights. In other words, they must be subject to rule and regulation. This is the very essence of free political institutions. The spirit of liberty is, indeed, a bold and fearless spirit; but it is also a sharpsighted spirit; it is a cautious, sagacious, discriminating, far-seeing intelligence; it is jealous of encroachment, jealous of power, jealous of man. It demands checks; it seeks for guards; it insists on securities; it intrenches itself behind strong defences, and fortifies itself with all possible care against the assaults of ambition and passion. It does not trust the amiable weaknesses of human nature, and therefore it will not permit power to overstep its prescribed limits, though benevolence, good intent, and patriotic purpose come along with it. Neither does it satisfy itself with flashy and temporary resistance to illegal authority. Far otherwise. It seeks for duration and permanence. It looks before and after; and, building on the experience of ages which are past, it labors diligently for the benefit of ages to come. This is the nature of constitutional liberty; and this is *our* liberty, if we will rightly understand and preserve it.

Every free government is necessarily complicated, because all such governments establish restraints, as well on the power of government itself as on that of individuals. If we will abolish the distinction of branches, and have but one branch; if we will abolish jury trials, and leave it all to the judge; if we will then ordain that the legislator shall himself be that judge; and if we will place the executive power in the same hands, we may readily simplify government. We may easily bring it to the simplest of all possible forms—a pure despotism. But a separation of departments, so far as practical, and the preservation of clear lines of division between them, is the fundamental idea in the creation of all our constitutions; and, doubtless, the continuance of regulated liberty depends on maintaining these boundaries.

Mr. Justice Miller, of Iowa, was one of the greatest jurists that ever adorned the Supreme Bench of the United States. Speaking for that great court in the case of Loan Association *v*. Topeka (20 Wall., 655), in a case presenting the question of the constitutionality of a law imposing a general tax on all citizens to pay for a factory to be run and owned by a private company, after referring to the act as "an invasion of private right," he said:

It must be conceded that there are such rights in every free government beyond the control of the State. A government which recognized no such rights, which held the lives, the liberty, and the property of its citizens subject at all times to the absolute disposition and unlimited control of even the most democratic repository of power is, after all, but a despotism. It is true it is a despotism of the many—of the majority, if you choose to call it so. But it is none the less a despotism. It may well be doubted if a man is to hold all that he is accustomed to call his own, all in which he has placed his happiness and the security of which is essential to that happiness, under the unlimited dominion of others, whether it is not wiser that this power should be exercised by one man than by many.

The theory of our governments, State and national, is opposed to the deposit of unlimited power anywhere. The executive, the legislative, and the judicial branches of these governments are all of limited and defined powers.

There are limitations on such power, which grow out of the essential nature of all free governments—implied reservations of individual rights, without which the social compact could not exist, and which are respected by all governments entitled to the name. . . .

To lay with one hand the power of the Government on the property of the citizen, and with the other to bestow it upon favored individuals to aid private enterprises and build up private fortunes, is none the less a robbery because it is done under the forms of law and is called taxation. This is not legislation. It is a decree under legislative forms.

I agree that we are making progress and ought to make progress in the shaping of governmental action to secure greater equality of opportunity, to destroy the undue advantage of special privilege and of accumulated capital, and to remove obstructions to the pursuit of human happiness; and in working out these difficult problems we may possibly have, from time to time, to limit or narrow by amendment the breadth of constitutional guaranties in respect of property and other rights. But, if we do it, let us do it deliberately, understanding what we are doing, and with full consideration and clear weighing of what we are giving up of private right for the general welfare. Let us do it under circumstances which shall make the operation of the change uniform and just, and not depend on the feverish, uncertain, and unstable determination of successive votes on different laws by temporary and changing majorities. Such a proposal as this is utterly without merit or utility and, instead of being progressive, is reactionary; instead of being in the interest of all the people and of the stability of popular government, it is sowing the seeds of confusion and tyranny.

CHAPTER I

THE PRESIDENT'S POWER OF REMOVAL

[TENURE-OF-OFFICE BILL]

Debate in the First Congress on the President's Power of Removal: Chief
Speakers, John Lawrence [N. Y.], James Madison [Va.]—President
Johnson Removes Radicals from Office—George H. Williams [Ore.] In-
troduces in the Senate Bill to Regulate Tenure of Civil Offices; It Is
Committed, and Reported Again by George F. Edmunds [Vt.]—Debate:
Timothy O. Howe [Wis.], Sen. Edmunds, Charles R. Buckalew [Pa.],
Sen. Williams, George G. Fogg [N. H.], William P. Fessenden [Me.],
Reverdy Johnson [Md.], Jacob M. Howard [Mich.], John Sherman [O.],
Thomas A. Hendricks [Ind.], Edgar Cowan [Pa.], Frederick T. Fre-
linghuysen [N. J.], Charles Sumner [Mass.], James A. McDougall
[Cal.], James R. Doolittle [Wis.]; Bill Is Passed—Thomas Williams
[Pa.] Moves in the House to Include Cabinet Among Officers Affected;
Motion Adopted, and Bill Passed—Senate Rejects House Amendment;
Conference Committee Reports Bill Continuing in Office President Lin-
coln's Cabinet Appointees Unless Removed with Consent of Senate; It
Is Passed; Vetoed by the President, It Is Passed Over the Veto.

I N organizing the departments of Government during the first year of Washington's Administration it became an important subject of inquiry in
what manner, or by whom, the officers of these departments could be removed from office. This was a question as new as it was important, and was applicable to
all other officers of Executive appointment. It depended on the construction of the Constitution itself,
and occasioned long and learned debates, as well as
great divisions in both branches of the national legislature. As the doors of the Senate were not open the
debates of that body on this and other questions are
not known. Some of the members in the House of Representatives were of opinion that the officers could not
be removed without impeachment. The principal ques-

7

tion, however, on which Congress was divided was whether they were removable by the President alone or by the President in concurrence with the Senate. A majority, however, in both Houses decided that this power was in the President alone.

When the question first came before the Senate, on the bill establishing the Department of Foreign Affairs [State Department] that body was equally divided, and the casting vote was given by the Vice-President. On a subsequent bill there was a majority of two in favor of the same construction. That it might not be considered a grant of power by Congress, the law was so worded as to imply a constitutional power already existing in the President, the expression being, "that whenever the Secretary shall be removed by the President of the United States," etc.

Timothy Pitkin, in his "Political History of the United States," presents the following summary of the debate in the House on the question:

THE PRESIDENT'S POWER OF REMOVAL

HOUSE OF REPRESENTATIVES, 1789

The opponents of the measure urged, in the first place, that it was improper for the national legislature in this manner to give a construction to the Constitution; that it should be left with the judiciary, another coördinate department of the Government; or it should remain to be decided by the President and Senate, whenever the occasion occurred in which a decision should be necessary. In the second place it was said that this great and important power, by a fair construction of the Constitution, was in the President and Senate. It was an established principle, its opponents said, that the power of removal necessarily rested with those to whom was entrusted the power of appointment, except when there was an express restriction, as in the case of the judges, who held their offices during good behavior; and that the Senate had, in effect, an equal voice with the President in the appointment of officers when their appointment was not by law vested in the President alone or in some other department of the Government, as no appointment could be made without the assent of that body. It was further said that, the Constitution being silent on the question, it was contrary to sound policy, as well as inconsistent with the principles of a free government, to give, by construction, such power to any one individual; and that it was liable to great abuses and would render officers entirely dependent on the will, perhaps the whim and caprice, of one man. Whatever confidence might be placed in the Chief Magistrate then at the head of the Government, equal confidence could not be expected in his successors. A concurrence of the Senate was as necessary and proper in the removal of a person from office as in his appointment.

The advocates for this clause in the bill agreed in its importance, and considered the genius and character of the Government itself, in no small degree, to depend upon it. In ordinary cases, they said, constitutional questions might be left with the Judiciary department without a legislative expression of opinion; but this case was of no ordinary character or magnitude—one which it would be difficult to bring properly before the courts. It was one on which it was highly proper that the legislature, particularly the House of Representatives, should express an opinion. This opinion, if assented to by the President and Senate, would put the question at rest. If left to be settled at a future time by the President and Senate a difference might arise between them which would create infinite difficulties and delays in the administration of the Government. They also contended that, by a fair construction of the Constitution, this power was in the President alone. It was a political axiom, they said, not to be disputed, that the legislative, executive, and judicial powers of government should be kept distinct, and blended as little as possible. By the Constitution the executive power was vested in the President; and the association of the Senate, in one executive function, was an exception to the general principle, and exceptions to general rules were taken strictly. So, by the Constitution, all legislative power was vested in Congress; and the qualified negative given to the President was only a special restriction to this general power.

The power of appointment, they also said, was substantially in the President alone. He was authorized to nominate, and by and with the advice and consent of the Senate, *to appoint*. The President was the agent, and the Senate had only a negative on his agency.

Other parts of the Constitution were referred to in support of this construction. The President, they said, was directed to take care that the laws be faithfully executed; and it must have been the intention of the framers of the new system to give him power to an extent necessary for the accomplishment of that object. If an officer, once appointed, was not to depend on the President alone for his official existence it would be difficult to see how he could be answerable for a faithful execution of the laws.

It was urged with great force also that if the power of removal was divided between the President and Senate responsibility would be destroyed and the benefits expected from its exercise, in a great measure, lost. Secrecy and despatch were often necessary to secure and preserve the public interest. Facts relative to the malconduct of an officer might come to the knowledge of the President, rendering an immediate removal indispensable, and the delay in convening the Senate might be fatal to the best interests of the community. In answer to the objection that this power would be liable to great abuse in the hands of an individual it was said that all power wherever placed was liable to this objection; but that the mode of choosing the Chief Magistrate would insure the election of an individual of integrity as well as talents; and that the tenure of office would be as secure, and the liberties of the people as safe, in the hands of a President thus chosen as with the President and Senate.

With respect to removals from whim, caprice, or any unworthy motive, it was alleged that sufficient checks were provided against such a wanton abuse of this power. The principal, if not the only, inducement for the removal of a meritorious officer would be to place some favorite in his room. The President, indeed, might remove, but he could not supply the vacancy without the assent of the Senate. The nomination of a successor would elicit inquiry in that body and produce a rejection of the favorite nominated to fill the vacancy.

It was also stated by some members, particularly by John Lawrence [N. Y.] and James Madison [Va.], that for such wanton abuse of power the President himself would be liable to impeachment and removal from office. Said Mr. Lawrence:

"If the President abuse his trust, will he escape the popular censure when the period which terminates his elevation arrives? And would he not be liable to impeachment for displacing a worthy and able man, who enjoyed the confidence of the people?"

"The danger, then," MR. MADISON observed, "consists in this: The President can displace from office a man whose merits require that he should be continued in it. What will be the motives which the President can feel for such abuse of his power, and the restraints to operate to prevent it? In the first place, he will be impeachable by this House, before the Senate, for such an act of maladministration; for I contend that the wanton removal of meritorious officers would subject him to impeachment and removal from his own high trust."

A majority in both Houses decided that the power of removal was in the President alone.

This decision of a debatable constitutional question, says Mr. Pitkin, was of great importance to the new Government, giving a tone and character to the executive branch not contemplated, it is believed, by the framers of the Constitution. It greatly increased the influence and patronage of the President, making him the center around which the other branches of the Government revolve.

The President's power of removal was not contested again until the Administration of Andrew Johnson, who had angered his opponents in Congress by his use of Government patronage to secure support for his reconstruction policy. It was feared by the radicals that he might build up a party united "by the cohesive power of public plunder"—in the classic phrase coined at this time by Representative Samuel L. Warner [Ct.]—which might prove a serious obstacle in the way of their own projects. During the recess of the Senate, in 1866, the President had appointed a number of Administration Republicans to office, and the belief became general that, so soon as Congress should again adjourn, he would remove all the Federal officers throughout the Union who were not faithful to the Administration.

Against the unbroken practice of the Government for seventy-eight years the Republican leaders now determined to deprive the President of the power of removing Federal officers. Many were induced to join in the movement under the belief that it was important to test the true meaning of the Constitution in the premises, and that this could be most effectively done by directly restraining by law the power which had been so long conceded to the Executive Department. To that end George H. Williams [Ore.], on the first Monday of December, 1866, introduced in the Senate a bill "to regulate the tenure of civil offices." It was referred to the Committee on Retrenchment, and reported back with amendment by George F. Edmunds [Vt.], who thenceforward assumed parliamentary control of the subject.

The first section of the bill provided that every person *except members of the Cabinet,* "holding any civil office to which he has been appointed by and with the advice and consent of the Senate, and every person who shall hereafter be appointed to such office, shall be entitled to hold such office until a successor shall have been, in like manner, appointed and duly qualified, except as herein otherwise provided."

The second section declared that "when any officer shall, during the recess of the Senate, be shown by evidence satisfactory to the President to be guilty of misconduct in office, or crime, or for any reason shall become legally disqualified or incapable of performing the duties of his office; in such case, and in no other, the President may suspend such officer and designate some suitable person to perform temporarily the duties of such office, until the next meeting of the Senate, and until the case shall be acted upon by the Senate: and in such case it shall be the duty of the President, within twenty days after the first day of such next meeting of the Senate, to report to the Senate such suspension, with the evidence and reasons for his action in the case and the name of the person so designated to perform the duties of such office. And, if the Senate shall concur in such suspension and advise and consent to the removal of such officer, they shall so certify to the President, who may thereupon remove such officer, and, by and with the advice and consent of the Senate, appoint another person to such office. But, if the Senate shall refuse to concur in such suspension, such officer so suspended shall forthwith resume the functions of his office, and the powers of the person so performing its duties in his stead shall cease."

TENURE OF OFFICE

SENATE, JANUARY 10-18, 1867

The bill came up for discussion on January 10, 1867. Timothy O. Howe [Wis.] wished to know why the Cabinet should be expected. Each of those offices was created by statute not for the personal benefit of the President but for the public service. The occupants should be independent of undue exercise of executive influence just as much as any other officer.

Senator Edmunds admitted the force of Senator Howe's contention, but said that the committee, after due consideration of the point, had concluded:

That it was right and just that the Chief Executive of the nation, in selecting these named secretaries, who, by law and by the practice of the country, and officers analogous to whom by the practice of all other countries, are the confidential advisers of the Executive respecting the administration of all his departments, should be persons who were personally agreeable to him, in whom he could place entire confidence and reliance, and that, whenever it should seem to him that the state of relations between him and any of them had become so as to render this relation of confidence and trust and personal esteem inharmonious, he should in such case be allowed to dispense with the services of that officer in vacation and have some other person act in his stead. It may happen that at some particular time—some people may suppose that it has happened now—the Chief Magistrate for the time being ought not to be invested with such powers; but the committee have recommended the adoption of this rule respecting the tenure of officers as a permanent, systematic and, as they believe, an appropriate regulation of the Government for all Administrations and for all time.

On the whole, it seemed best for the interest of the nation that the President should be allowed during a recess of the Senate to change his confidential advisers if it should appear to him to be fit, subject to that general responsibility which every officer must be held to to the public and to the Senate when they meet again.

Senator Howe insisted on his point. The greater the importance of officers the greater was the need that their tenure of office be regulated by law. He denied to the Cabinet the right to the designation of ''confidential advisers of the President.''

They are the servitors of the country; they are placed there for the benefit of the people; and it is no more necessary that they should be on confidential terms with the President than that they should be on confidential terms with the representatives of the people. It is very true it may happen at some juncture that the head of a department may be on unfriendly terms with the head of the executive department; it may make their personal intercourse disagreeable to one or the other; but such contingencies happen in the administration of public affairs in other countries. I believe no attention is paid to the question whether a minister of Great Britain is personally agreeable or disagreeable to the sovereign. He is put in office because he is agreeable to the people, and he holds office no longer than he is agreeable to the representatives of the people; and, whatever may be the personal inclinations of the sovereign, he leaves office whenever he proves dissatisfactory to the people. Shall American executive officers be less responsible to the people than British officers?

Senator Howe therefore moved to strike out the exception of the Cabinet officers from the provisions of the bill.

Charles R. Buckalew [Pa.] asked whether Senator Howe ''would have the head of the Executive Department hampered and worried by political enemies in his Cabinet, held there by a political opposition in the Senate?''

Senator Howe denied that the Cabinet was "the President's Cabinet" in law, and claimed that it should not be so in fact.

Its members are to serve the people, and every duty prescribed to each one of those officers is prescribed by law; and there is no duty prescribed by law to any one of them that they may not execute just as faithfully and just as ably when not in accord with the President as when in accord with the President; and, unless I am greatly mistaken, there is no duty devolved by the Constitution or by law upon the President that he may not discharge just as well whether his Secretary of State, or his Secretary of the Treasury, or any other member of the ministry, or all other members of the ministry disagree with him or not. It is to enable him to exert powers and influences not given to him by the Constitution or by law that it is thought to be essential that he should have control of the tenure of these heads of departments; and it is precisely because you cannot give him control of the terms of these officers without giving him powers and influences which the Constitution never designed that he should have that I object to leaving that control in his hands.

Senator Edmunds enforced his view that the President should have the power, during a recess of the Senate, to dismiss a Cabinet officer who opposed him, by the query that, if he have not this power, when Congress reassembles who is to be reproached for the derangement of public business?

Senator Howe submitted that the power of suspension granted in the bill fully covered the point.

Senator Williams thought the exception of Cabinet ministers from the general rule was of no practical consequence, since, according to the unvarying practice from the formation of our Government, the President had only to suggest the retirement of one of his council to bring it about. The chief reason why he had made the exception in the bill was because of the responsibility of the President for the acts of the departments.

This bill undertakes to reverse what has heretofore been the admitted practice of the Government; and it seemed to me that it was due to the exalted office of the President of the United States, the Chief Magistrate of the nation, that he should exercise this power; that he should be left to choose his own Cabinet, and that he should be held responsible, as he will be, to the country for whatever acts that Cabinet may perform.

George G. Fogg [N. H.] asked Senator Williams if he believed that the President could be impeached for an act of a Cabinet officer, except where the President personally directed it.

Senator Williams replied in the negative. However, he put this case to the Senator:

Take the condition of the country during the late war; suppose the orders of the President of the United States, upon whom devolved the responsibility of the prosecution of that war, who is made by the Constitution commander-in-chief of the armies, and is therefore responsible to the country, had been disobeyed by the Secretary of War; and suppose the Secretary of War had set up an independent government, if I may so express myself, and undertaken to manage the armies of the United States without any respect to the wishes of the President; then there would have been a difficulty at once; the efficiency of the Administration would have been practically destroyed.

SENATOR HOWE.—The President could suspend him under the second section.

SENATOR WILLIAMS.—That suggestion is sufficient, it seems to me, to answer the argument made by the Senator from Wisconsin. If any member of the Cabinet may be temporarily removed and another man put in his place to discharge the duties of the position until the next session of the Senate, why not let the President remove him?

SENATOR HOWE.—Why not in all cases?

Senator Williams replied that something was due to the dignity of the office.

Notwithstanding the office may not be administered as it ought to be, it is well enough for the American people to maintain some little respect for the office of President of the United States.

William P. Fessenden [Me.] supported Senator Williams's view. He thought that naturally no man of a mental and moral character which fitted him to become a member of the Cabinet would stay in it against the will of the President "unless he was controlled by a sense of overruling public duty in a very dangerous and peculiar time."

He regretted that it was necessary to legislate at all on the subject of removals from office. Some time ago he had opposed putting a "rider" of the nature of the present measure upon an appropriation bill.

I stated at that time that I thought action would be required on our part if the President should go so far as to disregard the power of the Senate: that is, if he sent a nomination to the Senate and that nomination should be rejected or not confirmed, and then, after the Senate adjourned, he should appoint the same man again, and this should be recognized as the practice, the result would be that the Senate would lose entirely the power conferred upon it by the Constitution to have a voice in the appointment of officers. If I am not much mistaken, the honorable Senator from Maryland [Reverdy Johnson] said that that would be a decided outrage on the Constitution.

SENATOR JOHNSON.—I say so still.

Senator Fessenden, concluding, said that, despite his former opposition to limiting the President's power of removal, he believed that a contingency had now arisen where such limitation should be made. He believed, however, that exception should be made in the case of removals of Cabinet officers.

Senator Howe, on the question of the "dignity of the presidential office," drily remarked that he had not found that the respect of the American people for that high office was very much affected by the manner in which the occupant handled the patronage which lay in his hands.

Senator Fessenden asked Senator Howe if he expected the present incumbent to remain in his place always.

IX—2

SENATOR HOWE.—I am not debating this bill, Mr. President, with the slightest reference to the person of the present incumbent.

SENATOR FESSENDEN.—The Senator will excuse me; he is just putting it precisely upon that ground, speaking of this President, as an argument, peddling offices.

SENATOR HOWE.—I beg the Senator's pardon. I made no allusion to the present President of the United States in the world. I do not undertake to say that the present President of the United States has not indulged somewhat in that habit which I call peddling offices; but I am very far from saying that he is the first one or the worst one who has done it. It is long since that became rather too much the habit of American Executives.

Senator Howe denied that the Constitution intended the Cabinet officers to be the President's "confidential advisers."

I think the whole practice of the President's consulting his ministers has grown out of this clause in the Constitution. Referring to the President, it says:

"He may require the opinion in writing of the principal officers in each of the Executive Departments upon any subject relating to the duties of their respective offices."

From which I understand, not that the President may convene all his Cabinet officers in secret conclave and hold a whispered consultation, from which the world is excluded, upon any measure of the Administration or of the Government; but that on any measure touching the interests of the country he may ask, not the private, but the written opinion of the secretary of the department particularly concerned.

Senator Williams asked Senator Howe if this clause of the Constitution did not assume that the President is responsible for the act concerned, and if asking for advice was not as to how he should *perform* the act, thus making the Cabinet officers his constitutional advisers.

SENATOR HOWE.—It does not follow that because he asks the opinion of the secretary he is bound to follow it. If his secretary is unfriendly to him, there is no reason in the world why he cannot criticize the advice the secretary gives. It does not follow because the secretary is personally unfriendly that he will advise in reference to a public measure dishonestly, for then he damns himself just as surely as he prejudices the President.

It is said that it is essential that there should be harmony, not merely between the President and his ministers, but between the different ministers. Essential to whom? Doubtless essential to the President that he should have the personal support of all his ministers; but is it more essential to the nation, I ask you, that there should be harmony between the ministers and the President than that there should be harmony between the ministers and the people? The Constitution did not provide any such thing. If it had wished any such thing, it would have said the President may select for his confidential advisers such men as he pleases. The Senate has no business to have any voice in the confirmation of Cabinet officers if it is the purpose of the law to make them the echo of the President.

If the view of the Senator from Maine is correct, it is not only fatal to my amendment, but it is fatal to the whole bill; it is fatal to the bill as originally introduced, and it is fatal to the whole amendment reported by the committee; for he insists not merely upon the right of the President to remove a Cabinet minister who is obnoxious to him, but insists upon the right of a Cabinet officer to remove every one of his subordinates for the same reason. It happens, Mr. President, that you have no officer in the public employment who is not either directly the subordinate of the President or directly the subordinate of one or the other of his ministers; and, if the Senator from Maine is correct in his theory, you ought to abandon this bill altogether and say, as the practice is, but as the law never was and never ought to be, that the President may remove his Cabinet ministers for such reason as is satisfactory to him, and that they may remove in turn every one of their subordinates; for this is a bill, not, as the Senator from Maine seems to suppose, to vindicate the right of the Senate to confirm the nominations—the main purpose of this bill is to regulate the tenure and to restrict the right of the President to remove from office men who have been confirmed.

It was said by the Senator from Oregon, it was repeated by the Senator from Maine, that in practice this will have very little effect, because in practice it is said if a Cabinet minister comes to know that he is distasteful to the President he will not wait for an act of removal, but will retire voluntarily. That such cases have happened in the history of the country I sup-

pose is true; but I suppose it is true because you have abandoned the protection of these offices and the protection of these
officers, because you have surrendered to the President of the
United States this control over them. I hold, on the contrary,
that the secretary who leaves an office created by law for the
public good, not for the President's good, to which he has been
appointed by the President and the Senate, and leaves that
post of duty merely because the President, one individual of
the great number that have to combine in making the appointment, intimates a wish that he should leave, is derelict to his
duty and cannot be recommended as a faithful public servant.
He has no more right to do it because the President may intimate such a wish than he has to do it because any one Senator
who voted upon his confirmation asks him to do it.

Senator Johnson explained his position on the President, during a recess of the Senate, reappointing an officer who had been antecedently rejected by the Senate.

By the very terms of the Constitution the commission which
the President is to issue in an appointment during the recess
continues until the last day of the succeeding session of the
Senate. The President, under this authority, may dispense with
the action of the Senate altogether; for, if the commission which
he gives to the officer continues until the last day of the session, there is then, when Congress adjourns, of course a vacancy
in that office happening in the recess which he is to fill; and
he may go on from time to time appointing during a recess so
as to avoid entirely the authority and the controlling authority
which the Constitution intended to give to the Senate of the
United States over such appointments as the President is directed to send in to the Senate for confirmation.

But it is only for the President to say—perhaps all the Senate are not aware of it—that in what he has done in cases of
this description he has but followed the example of his predecessors; and that example was in its origin supported, and,
in the cases where it has been followed since, it has been supported by the opinions of the several Attorneys-General who
happened to be in office at the time the instances occurred.
Those Attorneys-General were, I think—at least I only recollect those—Mr. Wirt, Mr. Taney, Mr. Cushing, Mr. Crittenden,
Mr. Mason, and I believe three or four others. The question
was not submitted to me when I was an incumbent of that
office; but I had occasion to say to the President [Taylor] at

that time that I certainly should not give that opinion, except upon the authority of the precedent, and, if I yielded to that authority, I should say that as an original question the law was really different.

The President has in some cases, I know—there are several nominations here that fall within that class—appointed during the recess persons whom he had before appointed during an antecedent recess, and who, upon being nominated to the Senate at the last session, were rejected. There may be cases in which the President would be justified in doing that, because of the particular circumstances of the case. He may be satisfied that the propriety of confirming the nomination was not brought entirely before the Senate, because all the facts which might exist in relation to the appointee were not before them. What I mean to say is that, in my judgment (and it is not a judgment recently formed, and it is one having no reference to the conduct of the present President for the time being, but it is an opinion long since formed), that a practice of that kind is altogether at war with the spirit of the Constitution, because it enables a President to avoid entirely the authority which the Constitution intended to give the Senate of the United States over such appointments as are to be made only by their consent.

But, upon the question of the power of removing officers, different considerations govern me. I believe it was at the first session of the first Congress—certainly at the time when the Treasury Department and the State Department were organized—that it became a subject of controversy in both branches of Congress whether the President had a right to remove without first consulting the Senate. A great many of the best men of that day thought that he had not; a great many of the lights that have adorned this Chamber since then thought that he had not the power; but, from the time it was settled by a majority of one, I believe, that majority being the casting vote of the Vice-President, up to the present time, it has not been seriously questioned that the President has the right to remove under the Constitution. Mr. Webster discussed the question during the presidency of General Jackson with the ability which marked all his efforts on this floor or anywhere else; but he offered no remedy; and every President from the time of General Washington up to the present time has exercised the power as one in his judgment clearly vested in him. I think he has the power.

But Mr. Madison, in the debate when the question was originally settled to which I have referred, stated, and I think stated very properly, that that power to remove, which he held to be a clear power, might be so abused as to furnish a just cause for impeaching the President; but in after times a removal for such a purpose as Mr. Madison intimated would be a just ground for an impeachment was held to be no ground for impeachment at all, or not ground of censure. The most striking cases that have occurred during our existence as a nation were those that occurred, or one particularly which occurred, during the presidency of General Jackson. The Senator will remember that under the charter of the Bank of the United States the public moneys of the United States were to remain on deposit with that institution unless they were removed by the Secretary of the Treasury. I thought then, and think now, that it was the purpose of Congress in passing that charter to take from the President the power in that case to interfere with the duty which the section imposed upon the Secretary of the Treasury; but the President decided otherwise, and he actually removed the incumbent [Louis McLane]. The Senate will see that that case presented the strongest one that can be imagined upon which to bring before Congress and bring before the courts of the country the question of the President's power to remove. The bank had an interest so deep that her safety depended upon the reversal of that authority. The public moneys being withdrawn from her vaults, the credit of the institution almost at once fell, or everybody saw that it must fall in a very short time, as in the end it did.[1]

SENATOR HOWE.—Did not the Senate concur in that change?

SENATOR JOHNSON.—No, sir; or, rather, it concurred in the way I am about to state. The bank, therefore, had a remedy, a clear remedy, provided she had a case, and she had a clear case if the President had no authority to force a removal of the deposits by the Secretary. She might have refused to pay over the deposits, and that would have brought the question immediately before the tribunals. There was no military law in force then, and the only way in which the moneys could have been recovered from the bank by the Government would have been by a suit, and, if there was under the charter a contract between the bank and the Government which entitled the bank to hold on to the deposits until they were removed under the authority conferred upon the Secretary of the Treasury, it would have been a **complete** defence to the removal which was actually ordered, **provided** it was true, and had been so adjudged, that the President had no control over the deposits;

[1] See Volume XIII, chapter IV.

but the bank acquiesced, and I have every reason to believe that they took counsel of the ablest lawyers in the country.

The President removed the Secretary of the Treasury during the recess, and he appointed his then Attorney-General [Roger B. Taney]. Mr. Taney was nominated to the Senate and rejected; and, if I had been in the Senate, I should have voted to reject him, upon the ground that, according to the opinion I held at that time and still hold, the President of the United States was guilty in that instance of a usurpation, of a violation of what I believed to be a contract between the Government and the bank in ordering himself his Secretary of the Treasury to remove the deposits, and, having removed him because he failed to comply with the order, appointing anyone to carry that out, or to act upon his own opinion of the propriety of that removal.

SENATOR HOWE.—I ask if the statute creating the office of Secretary of the Treasury does not make the term dependent upon the pleasure of the President.

SENATOR JOHNSON.—That is so; but, if my friend will turn to the debates, he will find that it was said in a report made by Mr. McDuffie in the other House, and I think in a speech made by Mr. Adams, and in several of the speeches made upon the floor of the Senate upon the question, that, notwithstanding that the character of the bank constituted the Secretary of the Treasury the agent of Congress, and took him, therefore, out of the removing power of the President, Congress had the authority to place the public funds wherever they thought proper, and in the exercise of that admitted power they had placed the funds in the hands of the Bank of the United States, and had, with a view to secure themselves against loss, authorized the Secretary of the Treasury as their officer, not the officer of the President, if he should discover at any time that there was any danger of the Government losing the deposits to remove them.

I thought then that the President had no authority whatever over the subject, and that the ground assumed by McDuffie and others, and particularly in the debate in the Senate, was the sound one, that the Secretary of the Treasury was selected merely by virtue of his office as the most convenient and reliable person that Congress could select to watch over the funds of the Government, so as to see that at no time they should be endangered by the misconduct of the bank.

From that time until the last session the authority of the President to remove has never been questioned. The abuse of that authority is an entirely distinct question. The President is not above Congress or above the people during his continuance in office. He is as liable to impeachment as any other officer. The only limitation upon the power of impeachment is that he shall be impeached only for high crimes and misdemeanors. If he commits a high crime or a misdemeanor in the sense in which those terms are used in the Constitution, the other branch of Congress may bring his case before the Senate in form of an impeachment, and this body has to act upon it.

The question whether the President has the power which he exercises in relation to removals from office or the power which he exercises in relation to the reappointment of officers who have been rejected by the Senate is one question. Whether he abuses either power is quite another question. And the question whether that abuse, if it be an abuse, is a high crime or a high misdemeanor is another question also upon which sooner or later, perhaps, if we are to be visited by such an affliction, the Senate may have to pass.

In my judgment, the President does go beyond the power conferred upon him when he reappoints a party whose nomination has been presented to the Senate and rejected, provided the case stands there and stands there alone. If he thinks proper to reappoint such a person, I think it is his duty to inform the Senate, when he sends that nominee in a second time for approval, what were the peculiar circumstances which caused him to disregard the opinion of the Senate. Any newly discovered facts, any evidence which he supposes would operate upon the judgment of the Senate, not in their possession at the time they voted upon the nomination in the first instance, he may produce; but to disregard the opinion of the Senate upon the exact case on which the Senate acted, in my judgment, is a clear abuse which must be remedied in some way or other, and the only way to remedy it is to reject those who may be nominated again.

JOHN B. HENDERSON [Mo.] and JOHN SHERMAN [O.].—And he may reappoint again.

SENATOR JOHNSON.—I know it, and it is for that reason that I said to him, and said to his Attorney-General at the last session, that cannot be justified by me or by the Senate, and certainly will not be by me, because that would be to avoid altogether the authority of the Senate; and, if he in the case supposed persevered in nominating and appointing again after one or more rejections, it would be, in my judgment, a very serious question whether that of itself would not constitute a ground for impeachment. If Mr. Madison was right in saying that an abuse of the power of removal was a subject for an impeachment, *a fortiori* is the abuse of the power of appointment in a case in which, if it is submitted to, the whole authority of the Senate becomes a nullity and is set at defiance.

Now, a word upon the particular amendment offered by my friend from Wisconsin. I shall vote against the bill whether that amendment succeeds or not; but the effect of that amendment on the Government would be pretty much the same as the proposition which John C. Calhoun more than once advocated, and the late Senator Robert M. T. Hunter on this floor advocated, of a dual President.[1] It was said, and said with a force that must be obvious to us all, that the Executive, to be at all competent to the duties of such an office, must be a unit. There can be no divided executive. The proposition fell. It hardly received a vote.

Now, what is to be the result of the amendment suggested by my friend from Wisconsin? The President—you cannot get clear of that obligation; you cannot take from him that duty, and he cannot absolve himself from that duty—is to see that the laws are faithfully executed. How is he to do it? He cannot do it alone. This is a great Government of ours. Its transactions are not the ordinary transactions of a common counting-house. They extend not only over all our limits, but they go beyond the limits. We have negotiations with the rest of the world and transactions with the rest of the world, and we are likely to be called into a conflict, as we may discharge our duty properly or not toward the other nations of the world, at any moment.

Suppose he has a Secretary of State whom he does not trust, either because of some suspicion of want of integrity or a belief that he is incompetent to the duties, or a belief founded upon good evidence that he is for pursuing a foreign policy that will entangle us with other nations, and perhaps involve us in war and affect our commercial marine; what is he to do with him? Leave him in, says the honorable member; suspend him. What then? What is to become of the negotiations in the meantime? What will foreign nations say? "We have been negotiating with the United States upon the assumption that they had a policy; we have acted in good faith; we can only know the President; we know that under the Constitution the Secretary of State is but his mouthpiece; we know, and we have been taught to believe, that it is in his power to shape the foreign relations of the country; and now, when his secretary

[1] See Volume V, page 423.

has been shaping them, and he discovers that he is about, by the shape which he has caused them to assume, to involve us in trouble, he turns him out, and the whole negotiation is to begin again.'' And when he sends to the Senate his reasons for the suspension under this bill, as he will be obliged to do, and the Senate declares that they are unsatisfactory, this suspended officer becomes again the Secretary of State. What is the effect of that upon the President so far as the negotiation of which I have spoken is concerned? He ceases to have any control of it; he is a mere cipher; you might as well not have him. The organ, then, with foreign nations will be a Secretary of State of the Senate of the United States, and not the Secretary of State appointed to be an adviser of the President, and to carry out the policy which the President may think proper and may suppose should be adopted as between ourselves and foreign nations.

The observations which I have thus cursorily submitted to the Senate are equally applicable to any of the other departments. Take the office of the Attorney-General. The President finds he has made a mistake; he has appointed a man to that office who has proven his incompetency. What is he to do? Suspend the Attorney-General? Whom is he to get to take the place? I do not believe any man could be found fit for the place who would take the office which he is to hold only during the suspension of the previous incumbent, which may be for but three or four weeks, for the miserable consideration of the proportion of the salary of the office that he would get during those few weeks. Then what will the President do? He cannot get a competent officer under the provisions of this bill if my friend's amendment prevails. Then the public suffers, suffers sadly. Everything is placed in confusion. Nobody knows officially what the rights of the United States are; nobody knows officially what are the interests of the United States, and how they are about being sacrificed.

Then what becomes of the President? Why, in relation to that officer as well as in relation to the Secretary of State in the case supposed, he is made a cipher.

SENATOR FESSENDEN.—As the Senate is now.

SENATOR JOHNSON.—That is all wrong. I am not for making ciphers of any department of the Government, and, for the reasons which I stated just now, as far as concerns the reappointment of rejected officers, I am against it, because that is a practice which makes ciphers of us, and I am for claiming the whole of the power which the Constitution confers upon the

Senate or upon the Congress of the United States. All that I mean to say, in conclusion, is that it is all-important that the Executive shall be a unit. If he fails to perform his duty criminally, the remedy is in our own hands. If we unfortunately elect a man who is incompetent, not from wilfulness, but from incapacity, the remedy which the Constitution confers is in the succeeding election, and in no other way.

Senator Howe's amendment was rejected. Senator John Sherman [O.] then moved an amendment forbidding under penalty the Treasurer of the United States to pay the salary of an officer who had been rejected by the Senate, and punishing by heavy fine or imprisonment the signer of the reappointment of such officer.

Senator Edmunds said that this was impracticable.

They seem to have a system in the Treasury Department by which either it is everybody's business not to know whether any money is illegally paid out or else it is nobody's business in particular to know. Each officer in the routine takes the particular paper that he has as *prima facie* evidence of the propriety of the person receiving the money who is named in it.

Now, all that must be provided for. All that was considered by the committee who reported this bill with the amendment. It appeared to them that, inasmuch as the subject of this bill was one which was working a great practical change in the administration of the Government, one the propriety of which would be greatly doubted by many men, one the constitutionality of which would be greatly contested by many persons in the country, it would be better on the whole to report the simple proposition, first determining whether Congress should take any action on the subject, and provide simply by this bill for regulating the tenure of these offices and the method of removal and the substitution of other persons to the administration of them; and, if the Senate should think it fit to pass the bill and to provide for this general change in the administration of the Government, we would then prepare and report to the Senate immediately, and I promise the Senator that I will devote the skill I possess with his aid to such further legislation in the way of penalties and in the way of guarding the treasury against any evasion as should be necessary, when we decide that we will enter upon what may be called an experiment. Therefore it is that I hope my friend from Ohio will for the present withdraw his amendment and let the sense of the Senate be taken upon the general question which is involved in the simple bill which we have submitted.

SENATOR SHERMAN.—I do not think the object of the Senator will be accomplished by this bill. There are no terms in it to enforce its provisions. There is nothing in this bill that is not already enacted with regard to other matters. Take the case I will put: we passed a law in February, 1863, declaring that no money should be taken from the Treasury of the United States to pay an officer who had been once rejected by the Senate. That is utterly disregarded, to my personal knowledge.

The attention of the executive officers was called to the law, and the President submitted it to the present Attorney-General, and the Attorney-General has given his opinion that the law is unconstitutional and that the President has the power. My amendment is so framed that if the President should make such an appointment, and authorize the payment of money under those circumstances, he would be guilty of a declared offence, a high crime and misdemeanor. If he should violate that law once or twice, the Senator from Maryland says that he would be willing to impeach him. I think it is important for us to declare this offence beforehand in a law fully considered, that we may punish him for its violation.

SENATOR EDMUNDS.—I will mention to my friend that that is precisely what the whole joint committee on full consultation thought it desirable should be done in supplementary legislation.

SENATOR SHERMAN.—It ought to be done in this bill.

SENATOR EDMUNDS.—We thought it more desirable, as a matter of expediency and convenience, to bring forward first the main measure as a separate proposition, and, if the main measure should meet the approval of the Senate, we would then immediately bring forward those additional measures which should completely protect it.

The committee adopted the suggestion of Senator Sherman and affixed to the bill the penalty which he advocated, and other penalties calculated to enforce the provisions of the measure. The amendments came up for discussion on January 11, 1867, and were adopted by a vote of 23 to 9.

Thomas A. Hendricks [Ind.] opposed the bill limiting the power which the Constitution broadly gives the

President to fill vacancies in his Cabinet occurring during the recess of the Senate.

Many have thought that that language means such a vacancy as takes place or begins during the recess; but the construction has obtained, and I suppose it is as settled as any construction well can be, that the words mean vacancies that may exist or be during the recess of the Senate. Where a vacancy exists during the session of the Senate, and is not filled before the adjournment, it has been understood and construed as a vacancy happening during the recess, and the President has uniformly filled such vacancies. If this be the proper construction of the Constitution, then there is no power to pass the section as it now stands.

But, sir, suppose that the Constitution does not forbid the legislation which is proposed; is it good policy to adopt it? Here is a period perhaps of some months during which the Senate may not be in session. The appointee of the President may not be agreeable to the Senate for that time; yet that appointee can only hold the office until the close of the next session; it is but a temporary appointment, and no great harm can take place or be suffered because a person holds office whose political views are not agreeable to the Senate for that length of time. What may be the consequences of the adoption of this section of the bill it is difficult for us to tell.

This section is framed as if, in case of a vacancy in any office, there is always provided by law somebody who may discharge the duties of the position; but I think, in point of law, that is not the case. It would be a very serious matter if in some of the districts the revenues, for instance, should not be collected.

Jacob M. Howard [Mich.].—I agree with the Senator from Indiana that the practical precedents of the Government lead to this interpretation of the Constitution, that it is competent for the President, during the recess of the Senate, to turn out of office a present incumbent and to fill his place by commissioning another. This has been, I admit, the practice for long years and many generations; but it is to be observed at the same time that this claim of power on the part of the Executive has been uniformly contested by some of the best minds of the country.

What is it, sir, to fill up a vacancy? The President and the Senate make the officer—give him his appointment. It is very true that the last act is to be performed by the President, which is the issuing to the officer of a commission. Now, is it in accordance with the language used in the Constitution that one branch of the appointing power may create a vacancy? Is it according to the just and fair usage of language to say that the agent making the appointment may remove the incumbent and thus create the vacancy which by the terms of the Constitution is to "happen"? I suppose that when the framers of the Constitution used this language they used it in reference to the common law of England; and how by that law does a vacancy in an office "happen"; in other words, take place, come into existence? It happens, as we all know, by resignation, by death, by absolute inability to discharge the functions of the office; but it never is spoken of as happening in consequence of a removal from office by the executive power.

Then, sir, it is not in the power of the President to create such a vacancy by the appointment of a successor. The right of the Senate and the duty of the Senate is plain. An appointment proper cannot be made without consulting them and obtaining their consent. The country looks to them for their advice, for their opinion, for their interference, in order to secure suitable qualifications and to restrain the wayward exercise of this assumed power by the Executive whenever such a case shall exist; and it is beyond doubt that during the last year this power of removal has been exercised most wantonly and most injuriously in multitudes of cases, and greatly to the detriment of the true interest of the country. And the cases are almost innumerable in which the names of persons have been sent to us and put in nomination for offices, and those nominations rejected, and still, after the adjournment of the Senate, the President, in utter contempt of the opinions of the Senate, has proceeded to issue temporary commissions to persons thus rejected.

Sir, I believe there is no member of this body who will rise in his place and declare that under the Constitution it is competent for the President, after the rejection of such a nomination and during the succeeding recess of the Senate, to issue to that person a temporary commission; and why? Because it is too plain to every mind that in reference to the particular individual, the Senate having passed an unfavorable judgment, it was virtually forbidden that person to hold the office, and such a temporary appointment by the President is a complete contempt of the opinion of the Senate expressed in constitutional form.

Now, sir, I believe Congress have full power over this subject, and that it is our duty now to enact some statute which for the future shall restrain this wanton exercise of the power claimed by the President, and which, in my judgment, is forbidden by the Constitution. The country expects it and will not be content if we leave our seats at the present session without passing some such law.

The Senator from Indiana discovers an inconvenience arising from the construction of the Constitution for which I contend. Not only that inconvenience but a thousand others may possibly arise from this construction for which I contend; but the great question before us is: what does the Constitution itself mean, what is the true interpretation of its language?

If the power of the President in making these temporary appointments is, by the fair construction of the Constitution, confined to this particular period of time, then we must be content with it, and so must he. He cannot constitutionally issue a commission to fill a vacancy which did not occur during that exact period of time, mathematically ascertainable. If the vacancy occurred at any other time, it is not to be filled in that way; and I reject entirely the doctrine under which the Executive at present seems to be practicing, that it is perfectly immaterial at what time a vacancy takes place or occurs. That doctrine leads to the complete divestiture of the Senate of all its power over the question of appointments to office.

As to the broad, practical construction that has been given to the clause of the Constitution empowering the President to fill vacancies, I admit its force in legislation as well as law; but it is to be observed that this question of the power of removal has never been considered as completely at rest. The best minds in the country have all along doubted and disputed the unlimited right of the President to turn incumbents out of office in the recess. The example was first set to the country under the administration of General Jackson, who made an indiscriminate removal of all officers who were opposed to his policy, he going upon the ground, first probably suggested to him by the Albany regency, that "to the victors belong the spoils"; and I am free to say that I think no fact in our history has tended so strongly and effectually to corrupt the public mind, and, if I may so speak, the political morality of the nation, as this doctrine that "to the victors belong the spoils." It makes almost every man who gives a vote a scrambler and an aspirant for office, and "office," "office," from the dawn of day to the setting of the sun, is the cry of the hungry crowd besetting not only us here but every man throughout the country who is supposed to exercise some influence in the bestowment of these precious articles. I hope this Congress will do something toward checking this spirit of office-seeking, fostered and upheld as it has been by this misconstruction and misuse of the Constitution of our fathers.

SENATOR JOHNSON.—There may be, as was the case during the War of 1812, negotiations going on between our minister and the minister of the nation with which we have been at war, upon which hangs the peace of the country, which is to decide whether the war is to be continued or is to terminate. We have a minister there to represent us upon that grave question, that vital question. He dies. On the 4th of March we hear for the first time of his death. The Senate has adjourned. As the law stood originally it could not meet again until the following December; so that during the whole period that is to elapse from the 4th of March in the year when we are advised of the death of our minister abroad and the succeeding first Monday in December that vacancy cannot be supplied.

SENATOR EDMUNDS.—I should like to ask the honorable Senator from Maryland whether the President has it not in his power to call the Senate together without a regular meeting of Congress, to advise him in respect to the filling of that very vacancy which may occur?

SENATOR JOHNSON.—Of course he can call the Senate together; but is he to call the Senate together on the happening of each such contingency as I have stated? The very provision of the Constitution which gives him the power to fill a vacancy necessarily shows that, in the judgment of the convention which framed the Constitution, it was not necessary to call the Senate together for any such purpose.

SENATOR EDMUNDS.—The Senator from Indiana [Mr. Hendricks] has stigmatized this measure as being one pushed forward for partisan purposes, reversing the settled construction of the Constitution, exposing the public service of the Government to great injury and inconvenience, in order that the political friends of the party in power may be protected or may be avenged if they have suffered anything, as the case may be. Now, sir, speaking for myself, and, I think, speaking for a majority of the party to whom I belong, I repudiate totally and absolutely any such accusation. The functions which we are endeavoring to protect will belong as much to the Senate (if that singular millennium should ever happen to come) when it shall be composed of a majority of the friends of the Senator from Indiana as they do as it is now constituted. We are not legislating for men; this is a Government of laws, not of men. We are merely protecting the functions of a body to whom the Constitution has intrusted in part the execution of the laws in being a coördinate branch with the President and a concurring branch in the selection of all the agents of the Government. The bill is an attempt to restore the practice of the Government to its true original theory, and to preserve to this body, which Mr. Madison, one of the authors of the Constitution, declared to be the great anchor of the Government, some of those high powers and duties of which practically it has been stripped.

On January 14 Senator Williams, in the absence of Senator Edmunds, brought forward the bill again.

Edgar Cowan [Pa.] spoke:

I should like to ask the honorable Senator from Oregon how the Government is to get along in case the Senate refuses to confirm any of the President's nominations. I ask whether the purport of this bill is that the Government shall stop, cease to be, because of the want of concurrence between the two coördinate powers who have these appointments?

SENATOR WILLIAMS.—Mr. President, I hope the honorable Senator does not indulge in the supposition that the Senate of the United States will be more likely to act in a manner to overturn the Government than the President of the United States. There is nothing of that kind to be apprehended. Are the Senate to act upon the assumption that they themselves will arbitrarily and without reason reject nominations made by the President so as to prevent the administration of the Government? Are we not responsible to the people of the United States? Are we not as competent to decide upon the qualifications of a candidate for office as the President? Are we not as competent to determine whether a certain course will promote or prevent the administration of the Government as the President? Are we to surrender our power as the Senate of the United States and put it all in the hands of the President, upon the apprehension that we are incompetent to discharge our duty as Senators upon nominations made by the President? If the nominee be an unworthy or an incompetent man he will be rejected, and it will be the duty of the President to make another nomination in the place of the one rejected; and if he makes another nomination it is not at all probable that in many cases there will be a disagreement between the President

and the Senate; but, if it should so happen that in some few
cases they should disagree and the duties of the office should
devolve upon a deputy, or if the office should possibly be vacant
for a short length of time, I say it is much better for the whole
country than that this absolute and unlimited power over all
the officers of this Government should be in the hands of any
one man.

SENATOR COWAN.—The responsibility of the Senate to the
people is not so direct as that of the President. If my honorable friend from Oregon has read very closely the history of
the past he has found that the danger is far greater from a
body irresponsible, because of its numbers, than it is from a
single man. It also unfortunately happens for his theory here
in this case that the President has the initiative. The office of
the Senate is secondary; the office of the Senate is not to do
good, it is to prevent mischief. It is not exactly in its nature
active, but rather negative. The President appoints officers;
the Senate advises and consents to those of them which are
good; but it by no means follows from that that, if there is a
disagreement, the President is to be deprived of his power
of appointing officers, and it is too late in the day now to
attempt to reverse the practice of seventy-five years, when the
Government has gone upon an entirely different theory and one
which I may say resulted from the necessity of the case.

I think myself that this is revolution. I think this passion-
ate conflict between two departments of the general Government, neither one willing to trust the other, neither one willing
to abide upon the original foundation on which the Government
was laid, is revolution. If it be revolution, the bill of the honorable Senator is perfectly in keeping. If it be so, and if it
be necessarily so, that one or the other of these two powers or
two parties or two factions (if you please to call them so) is
to have the appointment of the officers and the regulation of
the offices, revolution will bring about that result; but, if we
are to remain where the Constitution put us, the President has
that right, and the honorable Senator and his friends will have
to submit to it. If you think you have the power to overturn
it and have your way, where are you going to stop? The very
moment you take that step you are obliged to take another
and another and another; and what is the end of it? The
end of it is that the Government will be crushed between the
upper and nether millstone, and nothing else.

FREDERICK T. FRELINGHUYSEN [N. J.].—The other day the
President commended to the Senate a long extract from Mr.

Justice Story against usurpation on the part of the legislature. Consequently he approves of the writings of that distinguished jurist. Now, I desire to read the Senate what that authority says on this very subject.

SENATOR COWAN.—What book does the honorable Senator read from?

SENATOR FRELINGHUYSEN.—I read from Story's "Commentaries on the Constitution"; not his extended commentaries, but a work based upon them and prepared for colleges:

"The power of appointment, one of the most important and delicate in a republican government, is next provided for. Upon its fair and honest exercise must, in a great measure, depend the vigor, the public virtue, and even the safety of the government. If it shall ever be wielded by any executive exclusively to gratify his own ambition or resentment, to satisfy his own personal favorites or to carry his own political measures, and still more if it shall ever interfere with the freedom of elections by the people, or suppress the honest expression of opinion and judgment by voters, it will become one of the most dangerous and corrupt engines to destroy private independence and public virtue which can assail the Republic. The framers of the Constitution were aware of this danger and have sedulously interposed certain guards to check, if not wholly prevent, the abuse of the power. The advice and consent of the Senate is required to the appointment of ambassadors, public ministers, as well as other high officers."

Then the learned jurist goes on to speak of the power of removal:

"If we connect this power of removal with another power, which is given in the succeeding clause, to fill up vacancies in the recess of the Senate, the chief guards intended by the Constitution over the power of appointment may become utterly nugatory. A President of high ambition and feeble principles may remove all officers and make new appointments in the recess of the Senate: and if his choice should not be confirmed by the Senate he may reappoint the same persons in the recess, and thus set at defiance the salutary check of the Senate in all such cases. The clause to which we have alluded is the clause giving the power to appoint in the recess. This is a provision almost indispensable to secure a due performance of public duties by officers of the Government during the recess of the Senate, and, as the appointments are but temporary, the temptation to an abuse of the power would seem to be sufficiently guarded if it might not draw in its train the dangerous consequences which we have before stated."

This is the opinion of one of the greatest jurists of this country—one commended to us as Senators by the President in his veto message vetoing the suffrage bill for the District of Columbia. [See Vol. VIII, p. 37.] I think we may safely be controlled and guided by what Mr. Justice Story says.

SENATOR COWAN.—Mr. President, I have a very high respect, not only for the memory of Judge Story, but also for his teachings, and I have read the same argument which has been quoted by the honorable Senator from New Jersey, and I think I have felt its force. But the honorable Senator should have informed us at the same time that the question has been decided the other way. I admit that a very strong and very forcible argument can be made upon this side of the question; but the difficulty about it is that it has been for seventy-five years the uniform rule of the Government of the United States to allow the President this power, and, as I think, from the very necessity of the thing. The power heretofore has never been deemed dangerous. The power may have been annoying, just as the power is now annoying to a dominant party who cannot have themselves all control of the offices. But why should the President appoint bad men to office? He may not appoint a member of your party; but he is interested as much as anybody can be to appoint a member of his own party who will creditably execute and perform the duties of the office, and that has been the safety of the country always.

I have another thing to say: that, whenever one or the other of the two parties of this country are afraid to trust the other, then the Government is in the throes of dissolution. The whole of its strength heretofore depended on the fact that the one party in this country was always willing to trust the other party. It is true they said it will not administer the Government as well as we would do if we had it; it will not appoint as good officers as we would do if we had the appointment of them; but still being in the same boat, interested in the same way, there is no reason to suppose they should desire the destruction of the Government.

But if you proceed upon the supposition that the President is a traitor, that the President is a destructionist, that he is given over body and soul to the devil, and that all his adherents and all those who believe as he does are likewise given over, what then? Then, of course, you must end this Government in order to correct that mischief. If, however, honorable Senators and everybody else were to come back to the common-sense view of this matter, rid themselves of their prejudices, rid themselves of their passions, and come to the conclusion to be patient and abide the regular normal working of our institutions, there would be no difficulty. But it is from this war of factions, roused passions, terrible prejudices, that the danger to all free governments has come. Parties cease to be parties; parties become factions; and, over the ruins of the very fabric they intend to save, both have occasion to lament.

What will you gain by this crusade upon the President? What do you expect to achieve by curtailing him of his power? If the President abuses his power of appointment, how is that to be corrected? Heretofore it was corrected at the next election, and the next time you come to an election you correct it by electing a new President—a man who will not abuse his power; and why so? For the most obvious reason in the world that it was far better to endure all the ills which you can conceive of from bad and maladministration than that you should overturn the Constitution of the country—overturn its settled law and introduce revolution. I put it to any Senator on this floor whether, suppose you have the very worst President in the world, a man who is disposed to do all the mischief he possibly can do within the scope of his not only legal but possible power, is not that better than revolution?

Mr. President, this Government has existed for a long while —seventy-five years—under this rule. Annoyance, to be sure, heart-burnings, to be sure, grumblings everywhere there have been by those who had not the distribution of the "plunder" and the "spoils"; but nevertheless the Government was preserved; and upon looking back over its history I think that you will find that they all got about their share. If we preserve our tempers, and if we preserve our trust in the people (because trust in the people, as a matter of necessity, implies trust in the opposite party, in the other half of the people to which you belong), we shall secure the perpetuity of our institutions; but nothing else will do it. I wish to say here that I have the firmest conviction in the world that, if you take a single revolutionary step now in these excited times, if you overturn any well-settled principle of this Government, any well-settled principle of its Constitution, or I may say any well-settled item in its theory, you are on the brink of a precipice, and when you go over it you will have no Union, no Republic; you will have no free Government left.

SENATOR SHERMAN.—Mr. President, the Senator seems today to be in a mood not to do much business, and perhaps that may justify the honorable Senator in threatening us with revolution and all the dire woes unnumbered that may spring from it. In this bill Congress does not propose to do anything that is not sanctioned by the Constitution. It proposes to prevent the violation of the Constitution, that is all. And now we are threatened by those who have violated the spirit of the Con-

stitution with woes unnumbered, with revolution, with being on
the brink of a precipice! Let me say to my honorable friend
from Pennsylvania that the Senate of the United States is not
the place for threats like these. We have already been placed
on the brink of a precipice by a different set of antagonists
whom we have overthrown by war. They attempted to revolutionize this Government, but they were met and subdued by
the American people. Let me say to him that, whenever any
other power in this Government or outside of this Government
shall undertake to carry on a revolution or to carry the American people over the brink of a precipice, that power will be
ground between the upper and the nether millstone.

Senator Williams gave a legal exposition of the question. He first referred to *ex parte* Hennen, 13 Peters,
where the Supreme Court maintained the doctrine that:

"In the absence of all constitutional provisions, or statutory
regulations, it would seem to be a sound and necessary rule to
consider the power of removal as incident to the power of appointment."

He then took up the case of Marbury *vs.* Madison.

During the administration of John Adams there were five
justices of the peace appointed for the District of Columbia.
Their nominations were consented to by the Senate; but before the commissions were issued James Madison became President and refused to issue commissions to these five justices of
the peace, and application was made to the Supreme Court of
the United States for a *mandamus* upon Mr. Madison to compel him to deliver to these justices their commissions. The court
granted the *mandamus* upon Mr. Madison, compelling him to
give to these men so appointed their commissions, upon the
ground that, after these men had been nominated by the President and confirmed by the Senate, under that law they were
beyond the reach of executive power and were entitled to hold
those offices for the five years, and that Mr. Madison had no
right to withhold their commissions.

SENATOR HOWARD.—If the Senator will permit me, in the
case to which he refers he will discover that Mr. Adams had
made out and signed the commission of Marbury, but that the
commission had never been formally delivered, but was retained.
Mr. Adams signed the commission just as he was going out

of office, and Mr. Madison refused to deliver it. I think it was made out and left on the President's table, but never formally delivered. The question was, in the first place, as to the power of the court to compel by *mandamus* the delivery of the commission to Marbury, and that was really the whole question before the court.

Senator Williams gave the opinion of Chief Justice Marshall in the case:

"Where an officer is removable at the will of the Executive the circumstance which completes his appointment is of no concern, because the act is at any time revocable; and the commission may be arrested if still in the office. But when the officer is not removable at the will of the Executive the appointment is not revocable and cannot be annulled. It has conferred legal rights which cannot be resumed."

The Senator continued his account of the case.

Mr. Madison's manifest object was to keep these men from having their offices, and he undertook to effectuate that object by withholding their commissions; but, if the doctrine that is now practiced upon had then been recognized, instead of doing that he would at once have removed those officers and appointed others in their places.

The Supreme Court of the United States, with Chief Justice Marshall at its head, was of the opinion that the President of the United States could not exercise the unlimited power of removal. Sir, you may bring on the opinions of your Attorneys-General and the arguments and speeches of your politicians, and I overwhelm them all with the authority of the Supreme Court of the United States, with Chief Justice Marshall at its head, a court that towered in its wisdom and purity above the partisan clamor and strife by which it was surrounded, as Teneriffe towers above the noisy and impotent waves that break around its base.

Now, sir, it is admitted by honorable Senators who contend for the existence of this power that there is no express provision for it in the Constitution. But the great argument that has been offered time and again and repeated here from day to day is that it would be inconvenient for the President not to have and to exercise this power. Sir, can a power of this magnitude be incorporated into the Constitution upon the argument *ab inconvenienti,* because it is inconvenient that such a power should not exist? It is inconvenient very often that other powers which do not exist cannot be exercised by different departments of the Government. Take, for instance, if you please, the election of a Representative from any State, the State in which I live, where the law requires a candidate to have a majority, and suppose no man at the election receives a majority. It is inconvenient for the State not to be represented in Congress; but does it therefore follow that the Governor has a right to appoint a member of Congress?

It is very inconvenient, when we pass bills here by a large majority, in accordance with the wishes and interests of the people, to have the President interpose his veto; but the Constitution gives him that right; and can we, because it is inconvenient, because it is contrary as we believe to the will of the people for him to exercise his power in that way to defeat our legislation, disregard the veto and treat it as a nullity?

Sometimes it is argued that this power belongs to the President because the Constitution declares that the executive power shall be "vested" in a single person who shall be called the Executive of the United States. I answer any argument that may be derived from that source by saying that the clause of the Constitution referred to was evidently intended simply to create the office and not to confer power, because it is followed by other provisions defining and describing the powers of the office, and similar phraseology is employed as to this as is employed in creating the other departments of the Government; and, besides that, I find by reference to the proceedings of the convention that this portion of the Constitution when it was reported was in these words: "That there should be instituted an executive department to consist of a single person, which was referred to the Committee on Style," and that this committee changed the phraseology, substituting the word "vested" for "instituted," and it was passed without question, showing that the convention understood the word "vested" in that connection to be equivalent to the word "instituted," and did not understand it to convey any other or greater power than was conveyed by words necessary to create the executive department of the Government.

All executive powers are defined and described in the Constitution, and I claim, therefore, that a new and independent power cannot be drawn to the Executive by mere inference or by some imaginary reason for its existence. Beyond question, the men who framed the Constitution determined to restrict and control the President, for Benjamin Franklin is reported to have said, notwithstanding the provisions which the Constitution contains, that the country was about to try an experiment with an Executive that would end in monarchy.

I know that in common parlance it is said that the President appoints an officer, but the Constitution does not give him that power. The President transmits a name to the Senate; but whether or not that person so named shall fill the office for which the President designates him is the province of the Senate to determine. I say that the Constitution of the United States, not in phraseology perhaps as explicit as might be employed, practically constitutes the Senate an electoral body, and so the power over the appointment is in the Senate of the United States.

Now, sir, if it is claimed that the Constitution confers upon the President the power of appointment in any of its general clauses, I will ask the honorable Senator from Pennsylvania what it means when it provides that "the Congress may by law vest the appointment of such inferior officers as they think proper in the President alone"? Does not the Constitution clearly convey the idea that the President alone has no power to appoint unless that power is conferred by Congress? To assume that under the Constitution the President has the absolute power of appointment in all cases is to make the Constitution, so far as this clause is concerned, perfect nonsense; for, if all power to appoint was conferred upon the President by the Constitution, it would be absurd to confer such power in specific cases.

It is to be remembered, too, that the President is authorized to fill vacancies that may happen during the recess of the Senate. I argue that, if entire power of appointment was in the hands of the President, it would not be necessary to specify these particular cases in which he should exercise the power, and the inclusion of these cases is the exclusion of all others.

To concede the power of removal to the President is to concede the absolute power of appointment. Assume that the President of the United States may, without the advice and consent of the Senate, remove a man from office, and you *ex necessitate rei* assume that he may make an appointment to fill the vacancy so created.

Let us illustrate this view by the course of the present Executive. During the recess of the Senate he removed good men from office upon party grounds and then appointed his own creatures to fill the vacancies so made by granting to them commissions that would expire at the end of the next session of the Senate. The nominations of some of these creatures were rejected by the Senate and thereupon the President, instead of nominating other persons, waited until the Senate adjourned, and then reappointed the persons so rejected, thus at his own will displacing good men and perpetuating his own creatures in office in spite of all efforts of the Senate to prevent it.

Sir, if the President can exercise the power in one case he can in all cases. I object, therefore, to this right of removal on the part of the President, because it necessarily involves the right of absolute and unlimited appointment, and I am confident that the Senator from Pennsylvania will not contend that the Constitution contemplates that the Executive should possess any such power.

I say that there are two noticeable ideas in this clause as to vacancies. One is that this filling up is to be temporary; and the other that it is to be exercised within a given time; and it is in disregarding this last idea that the President pretends to find his power to fill an office at any time that is not filled by a person appointed by and with the advice of the Senate. What is the use of taking the advice of the Senate as to an officer if as soon as the advice is taken that officer can be removed by the President and another appointed in his place without consulting the Senate? Such a power in the Senate is a shadow and a mockery. I understand this clause as to vacancies of the Constitution to be intended simply to bridge over that space of time which may intervene between different sessions of the Senate; but when this designation, or appointment if you choose, is made during the recess, then when the Senate convenes the control of the President over that vacancy ceases, and it then becomes a question between the President and the Senate as to whether the vacancy shall or shall not be filled.

The Senator from Maryland [Mr. Johnson] suggested that this clause ought to be construed as though it read, "vacancies that happen to exist." Now, sir, can it be said with any propriety that when the President of the United States, for personal ends or party objects, deliberately removes a man from office, and so makes a vacancy, that the vacancy has *happened?* Whenever an office during the recess of the Senate is made vacant by any power over which the President has no control, then a vacancy happens as to him; but when he proceeds and by his own deliberate act creates a vacancy, then it does not happen, but it is made. Sir, you might as well argue that when the husbandman plants his seed and cultivates his crop the harvest which follows "happens" to him.

I do not understand that this absolute power of removal has ever been contended for until within a late period. If I am not mistaken as to the history of the country, removals without cause averaged about two for each Administration for the first forty years of the Government; and General Washington, instead of removing an officer during the recess of the Senate when he was found to be unfit to discharge its duties, suspended him, as this bill provides that the President shall now suspend in such a case. He did not claim this extraordinary power of removal; it was not claimed by his successors until within a comparatively late period; and in the discussions of 1789 it was not contended by Mr. Madison that the President had the unlimited power of removal; but it was argued that if an officer was incompetent or dishonest he might be removed by the President. When there was good cause the President, it was said, might remove; but it was admitted then by the advocates of this power that if the President of the United States, for any other purpose than to subserve the public interests, displaced a good officer it would be ground for impeachment.

Now it is claimed that the President has the unlimited control of all the officers in the Government, and that he may remove any or all of them at his pleasure and without any reason or any cause. This bill only undertakes to control what has been confessed by the advocates of this power to be an abuse of the executive authority. What does it propose to do? Take it altogether and it amounts practically to this: that the President shall not remove persons from office without cause; but, whenever an officer should be dismissed from the performance of his duties and another person put in his place, this bill provides that it may be done. It provides for every case where the public necessities or interests demand a change, and it only prohibits the abuse of executive power. I presume that no Senator will contend that Congress cannot prohibit by law the abuse of his authority by any officer of the Government.

Acknowledge, if you please, that the President has the power of removal, then cannot Congress by legislation declare and provide that he shall not abuse that power? It was admitted by Mr. Madison, and, for forty years after the Constitution was formed, by everybody, that a removal from office for personal ends or party purposes was an abuse of executive authority, and was a violation of the spirit if not the letter of the Constitution.

Now, sir, all we propose to do is simply to prohibit and prevent the abuse of that power. I referred to the case of *ex parte* Hennen, where the power of removal was held to be an incident of the power of appointment. All respectable authorities sustain that position, and I say that unless gentlemen can overthrow the opinion of Alexander Hamilton, the opinion of the Supreme Court in the case of Marbury *vs.* Madison, the opinion of the Supreme Court in the case of *ex parte* Hennen, they cannot escape from the conclusion that the consent of the Senate is necessary to the removal of an officer to whose appointment it was necessary to have the advice and consent of the Senate.

Congress has power to create an office; Congress has power to define the tenure of that office; and I ask why Congress has not power to say that when a man is appointed to an office which it has created, and the tenure of which it has fixed, he shall not be removed before the expiration of his term?

Sir, this bill is only intended to vindicate the constitutional power of the Senate. We have more light on this subject than the men who made the Constitution. Sir, they were good men and patriots, but they were born and educated under a monarchical form of government. Some of them had certain ideas about the executive power derived from their education. I do not intend to impeach their wisdom, but they lacked our experience. We have seen the operation and effect of this power; we have seen how dangerous it can become in the hands of a bold, bad man; we have seen how it can be used to debauch the public mind. When the mischief is so great and obvious it is our duty, regardless of precedents, to apply the remedy. Believing that there is nothing in the provisions of this bill which is in conflict with the Constitution, I hope that it will become a law. I trust it will not be regarded as any mere party measure, but as an honest effort to bring back the Government to the purposes and views of the men who made it.

Senator Johnson spoke on January 15.

The reasoning in support of the proposition that there is danger in clothing the President with the power of appointment is that he may use it for the purpose of rewarding favorites and continuing party ascendency to accomplish his reëlection. That is all true; but it requires no particular foresight to see that each one of these motives may operate upon the Senate, if not collectively, individually.

There are now in the Senate but very few who concur in what has been called "the policy" of the President, which was neither more nor less than the policy of his immediate predecessor, in the steps which have been taken to restore into the Union for all purposes the States which attempted to escape from it. A large majority of the Senate are of a different opinion, and they think that that is a subject vital to the interests and to the safety of the United States.

The Senate, supposing that under the administration of his immediate predecessor nearly all the offices of the Government were held by men who favor what is termed the congressional as distinguished from executive policy, will, if the President removes men of that description, not only not confirm those whom he appoints to take their places, but, if he removes and appoints as successors those who have been nominated and rejected by the Senate, says that these shall not receive any salary, and that every officer of the Government, through whose hands the money is to pass from the treasury in the payment of the obligation of the Government, who pays the salary to such a man is to be punished criminally.

Why does the Senate desire to take to itself that power? Why does the Senate charge as against the President an abuse of the power of appointment, founded upon the fact that he appoints those who concur with him instead of those who concur with Congress and differ from him? It is only because the Senate think proper to exercise the power of appointment which is in them to attain some political end or some party end, and to secure the continuance in power of the political party in the country to which they belong. And if my friend from New Jersey [Senator Frelinghuysen] would, if he has not already done so, recur to what has been said by some of the lights who carried the Government through in the beginning of its existence, he would see that there is such danger to be apprehended from the conduct of the Senate in this particular as from the conduct of the President. In this connection I wish to read from a letter written by the older Adams to Roger Sherman, a member of the convention from Connecticut:

"A Senator of great influence will be naturally ambitious and desirous of increasing his influence. Will he not be under a temptation to use his influence with the President as well as his brother Senators to appoint persons to office in the several States who will exert themselves in elections to get out his enemies or opposers, both in Senate and House of Representatives, and to get in his friends, perhaps his instruments?"[1]

[1] See Pitkin's Political History of the United States, Vol. II, p. 285.

I beg leave to say to my friend from Oregon, with all respect, that he has entirely misapprehended the case in the Supreme Court to which he referred. He cited the case of Marbury *vs.* Madison, reported in 7 Cranch, which I understood him to say decided that it was not in the power of the President to remove. There is no such doctrine in that case. The court went beyond the mere question of their power to issue a *mandamus* in that case, and for so doing were not censured as the Supreme Court in modern days has been; I mean the judges who decided the case of Dred Scott. The opinion in the Marbury case has never been assailed by either lawyer or judge upon the ground that that part of it was extrajudicial, and yet it was just as extrajudicial as was the opinion in the Dred Scott case. Marshall had been baptized in the blood of the Revolution; [1] he had served his country as diplomatist and as Secretary of State; he had illustrated the Constitution in judgments that challenged the admiration of the whole country; and no one ventured to assert, as against an officer of that description, that any improper motive, any desire to trench upon the legitimate power of the Executive, entered at all into the consideration of that judgment.

But, says my brother and friend from Oregon, that case decided that the President had no right to remove. Surely that is an entire misapprehension. The Constitution gives to the President the authority to appoint, by and with the advice and consent of the Senate, to certain high offices, but gives to Congress the power to vest the appointment and to give the removal of inferior officers to anybody they think proper; and these justices of the peace were inferior and not high officers within the meaning of those two terms in the Constitution. Congress, therefore, by providing that such an officer should hold his commission for four years, removed the officer from the power of removal of the President, as they could have taken from him the power to appoint. Nobody doubts that, if they were inferior officers, as they were, Congress might have given the power to appoint those officers to the people of the District by election, or to any individual that they might think proper, or to any tribunal other than the executive department of the Government. They had a right, although they thought proper to give it to the President himself, to provide that it should endure for four years as against any such power of removal. That is all the case decided upon that question.

On the same point I take occasion also to refer to the case

---

[1] Marshall fought at Brandywine, Germantown, and Monmouth.

of *ex parte* Hennen, 13 Peters, 250. Mr. Justice Thompson, delivering the opinion of the court in that case, said:

"This power of removal from office was a subject much disputed, and upon which a great diversity of opinion was entertained in the early history of this Government. This related, however, to the power of the President to remove officers appointed with the concurrence of the Senate; and the great question was, whether the removal was to be by the President alone, or with the concurrence of the Senate, both constituting the appointing power. No one denied the power of the President and Senate jointly to remove, where the tenure of the office was not fixed by the Constitution: which was a full recognition of the principle that the power of removal was incident to the power of appointment. But it was very early adopted as the practical construction of the Constitution that this power was vested in the President alone."—13 Peters, p. 259.

A word more, and I shall cease to trouble the Senate. My friend from Pennsylvania [Mr. Cowan] was supposed by some of the Senators to threaten another revolution if this bill or bills of a like character were passed. He disavows any such purpose; and those who know his frankness will have no hesitation in believing in the sincerity of that disavowal. I do not anticipate and do not fear any such revolution as that; but there may be a revolution of a different kind, the kind of revolution which changed the whole political destiny of the country for a time, and which was successfully brought about in 1800. The Congress of the United States, acting with the assent of the then President, Mr. Adams, because he approved of the bills, had passed the Alien and the Sedition laws. The country became alarmed. No force was threatened of a physical kind; but the subjects of the alleged usurpation of power by Congress became matters of political speculation and discussion in the papers of the day. The people of the country came to the rescue of the Constitution thus, in their opinion, invaded, and swept from power those who had adopted such measures. I am no prophet, Mr. President. I may not live to see the day when it shall occur, if it occurs at all, when the same revolution will be seen condemning many of the measures of the present day precisely upon the same ground that the people in 1800 censured and condemned what had been done at that time. A latitudinarian construction of the Constitution, the absorption of nearly all power into the legislative department of the Government, an unwillingness to submit to the judiciary, an interference with what have heretofore been considered the legitimate powers of the President—I do not say from any bad motive—these are the symptoms of the times.

We have just emerged from a war without example in the annals of civil strife or any other strife. Every house in our broad land is filled more or less with mourning for the departed dead who, upon one side or the other, have died in support of what they believed to be the principles of liberty. The angry passions have been excited. They more or less affect us all, for members of Congress are but men. They lead to a claim for power that would not have been thought of in the beginning of the Government. When everything becomes quiet and settled; when the particular circumstances to which the party who are now dominant owe their present condition shall cease to exist; when they shall have a President of their own choice (if that is to be the result of the present state of things), who will carry out what they believe to be the true policy of the country, reason then with them, and with the opposition (if it does not control us now) will control, and a better day will dawn upon a now distracted land. But, sir, that is not to be done through the instrumentality of a civil war. Its desolation; the affliction with which it has visited individual men and women; the loss of material wealth; the danger to which our very Government was subjected during its existence, and must be more or less subjected during any such strife—all are warnings to keep us again from entering into any such conflict. The conflict into which alone the people will enter will be that which the ballot will decide, for which that weapon alone will be used; and when, as I believe in my existence, the time shall come when the excitement of the day shall have terminated and the judgment of the people shall be what it was from the beginning of the Government up to the commencement of this strife, the Constitution will be restored in all its integrity and each department of the Government be permitted to exercise every power which the Constitution as construed in the past vests with it.

Charles Sumner [Mass.] moved an amendment to the bill, providing that all agents and officers now appointed by the President or by a head of a department be appointed only with the consent of the Senate, and that all such appointments made in the recent recess be vacated.

Is there any one who doubts, after what we have seen on a large scale, that the President, for the time being at least, ought to be deprived of the extraordinary function which he has exercised? He has announced openly in a speech that he meant to "kick out of office" present incumbents, and it was in that proceeding, "kicking out of office," that on his return to Washington afterward he undertook to remove incumbents wherever he could. Now, sir, it seems to me that we owe our protection to these incumbents so far as possible. It belongs to the duty of the hour.

Why postpone what is in itself so essentially good? Why put off to some unknown future the chance of applying a remedy to an admitted abuse? Is there any one here who insists that this is not an abuse, that here has not been a tyrannical exercise of power? No one. Then, sir, let us apply the remedy. This is the first chance we can get. Let us take it.

One of the finest sentiments that has fallen from one of the most gifted of our fellow countrymen was that verse in which he says:

"New occasions teach new duties."[1]

We have a new occasion now teaching a new duty. That new occasion is the misconduct of the Executive of the United States, and the new duty which this occasion teaches is that Congress should exercise all its powers in throwing a shield over our fellow citizens.

On January 17 Senator Sumner continued his remarks in the same vein. At the close he said:

I return, then, to my proposition that the duty of the hour is protection to the loyal and patriotic citizen. But when I have said this I have not completed my proposition. You may ask, protection against whom? I answer, plainly, protection against the President of the United States. There, sir, is the duty of the hour. Ponder it well, and do not forget it. There was no such duty on our fathers; there was no such duty on our recent predecessors in this chamber, because there was no President of the United States who had become the enemy of his country.

Senator James A. McDougall [Cal.] rose to a question of privilege, but Senator Sumner refused to yield the floor.

[1] James Russell Lowell, in "The Present Crisis."

IX—4

SENATOR McDOUGALL.—I do not ask you to yield the floor. I rise to a question which gives me a right to be heard—a question of privilege.

THE PRESIDING OFFICER [Henry B. Anthony in the chair].— The Senator from California rises to a question of privilege; he will state his question of privilege.

SENATOR McDOUGALL.—It is that no Senator on this floor has a right to make use of such remarks of or about the Executive of the United States as those the Senator from Massachusetts has just uttered, when that Senator may be a judge upon a question of impeachment, if an impeachment should be preferred against the President. It has been held so always as the law of parliament. It was the law of the Senate in its better days, always maintained by the gentleman from Vermont, now called to his long home, who for so many years graced the chair [Mr. Foot].

If a remark or an accusation like that were made against a Senator it would be a grave offence and would deserve the condemnation of the Senate unless there was good cause why. But it is not within the courtesy of the Senate to assault a person not present on the floor who cannot defend himself. To assault here a judge of the Supreme Court on the bench would be a violation of parliamentary rules. If the Senator from Ohio should go into the Supreme Court to-morrow morning and should say a rude thing of the President of the Senate, he would be immediately told by the presiding justice to take his seat. It is not within the courtesy and the law that a person absent, belonging to an independent branch of government, should be assaulted by being accused of being an enemy of his country. Why? Because it is accusation of treason, if you please, substantially. When that question shall come here and the Senator from Massachusetts shall be its champion, it being brought up here by its promoters from the House of Representatives, then he may discuss it as carefully and well as he can as a member of the high court of impeachment, if he chooses to be one of the impeaching parties. Otherwise, it is not within the license of a Senator to say of the President things of that kind that involve his integrity as a public officer.

The Presiding Officer [Henry B. Anthony] decided that the words of Senator Sumner, to which exception was taken, did not exceed the latitude of debate which prevailed in the Senate.

Senator McDougall acceded to this decision, but Senator James R. Doolittle [Wis.] appealed from it. His appeal was tabled by a vote of 29 to 10.

On the next day (January 18) Senator Sumner continued his remarks:

At last the country is opening its eyes to the actual condition of things. Already it sees that Andrew Johnson, who came to supreme power by a bloody accident, has become the successor of Jefferson Davis in the spirit by which he is governed and in the mischief he is inflicting on his country. It sees the President of the rebellion revived in the President of the United States. It sees that the violence which took the life of his illustrious predecessor is now by his perverse complicity extending throughout the rebel States, making all who love the Union its victims and filling the land with tragedy. It sees that the war upon the faithful Unionists is still continued under his powerful auspices, without any distinction of color, so that all, both white and black, are sacrificed. It sees that he is the minister of discord, and not the minister of peace. It sees that, so long as his influence prevails, there is small chance of tranquillity, security, or reconciliation; that the restoration of prosperity in the rebel States, so much longed for, must be arrested; that the business of the whole country must be embarrassed, and that those conditions on which a sound currency depends must be postponed. All these things the country now sees. But indignation assumes the form of judgment when it is seen also that this incredible, unparalleled, and far-reaching mischief, second only to the rebellion itself, of which it is a continuation, is invigorated and extended through a plain usurpation.

I know that the President sometimes quotes the Constitution and professes to carry out its behests. But this pretension is of little value. A French historian has used words which aptly characterize an attempt like that of the President. I quote from the history of M. Thiers, while describing what is known as the resolution of the 18th Brumaire:

"When any one wishes to make a revolution or a counter-revolution it is necessary always to disguise the illegality as much as possible, and to this end to use the terms of the constitution in order to destroy it, and also the members of a government in order to overturn it."

In this spirit the President has acted. He has bent Constitution, laws, and men to his arbitrary will, and has even invoked the Declaration of Independence for the overthrow of those equal rights which it so grandly proclaims.

In holding up Andrew Johnson to judgment, I do not dwell on his open exposure of himself in a condition of beastly intoxication while he was taking his oath of office; nor do I dwell on the maudlin speeches by which he has degraded the country as it was never degraded before; nor do I hearken to any reports of pardons sold, or of personal corruption. This is not the case against him, as I deem it my duty to present it in this argument. These things are bad, very bad; but they might not, in the opinion of some Senators, justify us on the present occasion.

But there is a reason which is ample. The President has usurped the powers of Congress on a colossal scale, and he has employed these usurped powers in fomenting the rebel spirit and awakening anew the dying fires of the rebellion. Though the head of the executive, he has rapaciously seized the powers of the legislative and made himself a whole Congress in defiance of a cardinal principle of republican government that each branch must act for itself without assuming the powers of the other; and, in the exercise of these illegitimate powers, he has become a terror to the good and a support to the wicked. This is his great and unpardonable offence, for which history must condemn him if you do not. He is a usurper, through whom infinite wrong has been done to his country. He is a usurper, who, promising to be a Moses, has become a Pharaoh. Do you ask for evidence? It is found in public acts which are beyond question. It is already written in the history of our country. And now in the maintenance of his usurpation he has employed the power of removal from office. Some, who would not become the partisans of his tyranny, he has, according to his own language, "kicked out." Others are left, but silenced by this menace and the fate of their associates. Wherever any vacancy occurs, whether in the loyal or the rebel States, it is filled by the partisans of his usurpation. Other vacancies are created to provide for these partisans. I need not add that just in proportion as we sanction such nominations or fail to arrest them, according to the measure of our power, we become parties to his usurpation.

The question then recurs, are you ready to apply the remedy, according to the measure of your powers? The necessity of this remedy may be seen in the rebel States, and also in the loyal States, for the usurpation is felt in both.

If you look at the rebel States, you will see everywhere the triumph of presidential tyranny. There is not a mail which does not bring letters without number supplicating the exercise of all the powers of Congress against the President. There is not a newspaper which does not exhibit evidence that you are already tardy in this work of necessity. There is not a wind from that suffering region which is not freighted with voices of distress. And yet you hesitate.

The bill now before the Senate arises from this necessity. Had Abraham Lincoln been spared to us there would have been no occasion for this bill. But it does not meet the whole case. Undertaking to give protection, it gives it to a few only, instead of the many. It provides against the removal, appointment, or employment of persons whose offices, according to existing law and Constitution, are held by and with the advice and consent of the Senate. Its special object is to vindicate the power of the Senate over the offices committed to it according to existing law and Constitution. Thus vindicating the power of the Senate it does something indirectly for the protection of the citizen. In this respect it is a beneficent measure, and I shall be glad to vote for it.

The amendment which I have moved goes further in the same direction, so as in a certain measure to arrest the recent process of "kicking out." This proposition is simple enough; and I insist that it is necessary, unless you are willing to leave fellow citizens without protection against tyranny.

We are told, with something of indifference if not of levity, that it is not the duty of the Senate to look after the "bread and butter" of officeholders. This is a familiar way of saying that these small cases are not worthy of occupying the Senate. Not so do I understand our duties. There is no case so small as not to be worthy of occupying the Senate; especially if in this way you can save a citizen from oppression and weaken the power of an oppressor.

The effect of this amendment is to take from the President a large class of nominations and bring them within the control of the Senate. The old resolution of the House of Commons, moved by Mr. Dunning, is applicable here: "The power of the Crown has increased, is increasing, and ought to be diminished." In this spirit we must put a bit in the President, who is now maintaining an illegitimate power by removals from office.

We are in the midst of a crisis. On one side is the President and on the other the people. It is the old question between prerogative and Parliament which occupied our English fa-

thers. But the form it now takes is grander than ever before.
In this controversy I am with the people and against the President. I have great faith in the people, but I have no faith in
the President.

Senator Sumner's amendment was rejected by 16
yeas to 21 nays. Senator Howe's amendment to include
Cabinet officers in the provisions of the bill was rejected by 13 yeas to 27 nays. The bill was then adopted
by 29 yeas to 9 nays.

When the bill reached the House, on February 1,
every provision of it was readily agreed to except that
which excluded Cabinet officers from its operation. An
amendment offered by Thomas Williams [Pa.] to strike
that out was at first defeated—ayes 76, nays 78. On
February 2 the vote was reconsidered—75 ayes, 66 nays,
and the amendment was at once adopted. The bill was
then passed by a party vote—ayes, 111; nays, 38. When
it was returned to the Senate that body refused, on February 6, by a vote of 17 yeas, 28 nays, to concur in the
amendment which placed members of the Cabinet on the
same basis with other officers respecting the President's
power of removal.

Upon a conference between the two branches on the
disagreement, a substitute was adopted, on February 18, declaring that the members of the Cabinet "shall
hold their offices, respectively, for and during the term
of the President by whom they may have been appointed,
and for one month thereafter, subject to removal by and
with the advice and consent of the Senate." The alleged
violation by President Johnson of this provision was
the direct cause of his impeachment by the House of
Representatives a year later.

The President vetoed the bill on the 2d of March. In
reviewing the measure he said:

"In effect it provides that the President shall not remove
from their places any of the civil officers whose terms of service
are not limited by law, without the advice and consent of the
Senate of the United States. The bill conflicts, in my judgment,
with the Constitution of the United States. The question, as
Congress is well aware, is by no means a new one. That the

power of removal is constitutionally vested in the President of the United States is a principle which has been not more distinctly declared by judicial authority and judicial commentators than it has been uniformly practiced upon by the legislative and executive departments of the Government. The question has often been raised in subsequent times of high excitement, and the practice of the Government has nevertheless conformed in all cases to the decision thus made. Having at an early period accepted the Constitution, in regard to the executive office, in the sense in which it was interpreted with the concurrence of its founders, I have found no sufficient grounds in the arguments now opposed to that construction, or in any assumed necessity of the times, for changing those opinions.

For these reasons, I return the bill to the Senate, in which house it originated, for the further consideration of Congress which the Constitution prescribes. Experience, I think, has shown that it is the easiest, as it is also the most attractive, of studies to frame constitutions for the self-government of free states and nations but I think experience has equally shown that it is the most difficult of all political labors to preserve and maintain such free constitutions of self-government when once happily established.''

"The veto message," says Mr. Blaine, "was a very able document. In all official papers of importance the President appeared at his best, having the inestimable advantage of Mr. Seward's calm temper and of his attractive and forcible statement of the proper argument. Few among the public men of the United States have rivaled Mr. Seward in the dignity, felicity, and vigor which he imparted to an official paper. No one ever surpassed him. In the veto message under consideration his hand was evident in every paragraph; and if it had been President Johnson's good fortune to go down to posterity on this single issue with Congress, he might confidently have anticipated the verdict of history in his favor."

The bill was promptly passed over the veto—in the Senate by 35 ayes to 11 nays; in the House by 133 ayes to 37 nays.

CHAPTER II

IMPEACHMENT OF PRESIDENT JOHNSON

James M. Ashley [O.] Moves in the House to Impeach President Johnson; Resolution Committed—James F. Wilson [Ia.], Chairman of Committee, Presents Majority Report to Investigate President's Conduct; Andrew J. Rogers [N. J.] Presents Minority Report against Investigation— Debate: In Favor of Investigation, Mr. Ashley, Benjamin F. Butler [Mass.], George F. Miller [Pa.]; Opposed, Samuel J. Randall [Pa.], Benjamin M. Boyer [Pa.], Rufus P. Spalding [O.], James Brooks [N. Y.], John V. L. Pruyn [N. Y.], John W. Chanler [N. Y.]; Investigation Ordered—Gen. Ulysses S. Grant Testifies in Favor of the President—Committee Presents Majority Report in Favor of Impeachment, and Two Minority Reports against It—Debate: In Favor of Impeachment, George S. Boutwell [Mass.]; Opposed, Mr. Wilson; Majority Report Defeated—The President Suspends Edwin M. Stanton, Secretary of War, and Appoints Gen. Grant Secretary *ad interim*— Senate Reinstates Stanton—Grant Resigns Office, Leading to Quarrel with the President—The President Appoints Adj.-Gen. Lorenzo Thomas Secretary *ad interim*—Senate Declares He Had No Power to Do So— John Covode [Pa.] Moves in the House to Impeach the President for His Action; Resolution Committed; Thaddeus Stevens [Pa.], Chairman of Committee, Reports the Resolution—Debate: in Favor, John A. Bingham [O.], Gen. John A. Logan [Ill.], Ebon C. Ingersoll [Ill.], Mr. Ashley, Burton C. Cook [Ill.], George W. Julian [Ind.], Gen. Butler, Mr. Boutwell, Mr. Stevens; Opposed, Mr. Brooks, George W. Woodward [Pa.]; Impeachment Ordered; Mr. Bingham, Mr. Boutwell, Mr. Wilson, Gen. Butler, Thomas Williams [Pa.], Gen. Logan and Mr. Stevens Chosen Managers of Impeachment—The President Nominates Thomas Ewing, Sr. [O.], as Secretary of War; Senate Refuses to Confirm, Declaring No Vacancy—Trial of President Johnson before Senate, Chief-Justice Salmon P. Chase Presiding; Articles of Impeachment; Answers by President's Counsel (ex-Attorney-General Henry Stanbery, Judge Benjamin R. Curtis, Judge Thomas A. R. Nelson, William M. Evarts, Esq., William S. Groesbeck, Esq.); Addresses by the Prosecution, Including Brief on Impeachment by Representative William Lawrence [O.]; Addresses by the Defence; Additional Briefs Presented by Senators; Senate Refuses to Impeach on Articles XI, II, and III, and Adjourns *sine die* without Voting on the Others—Mr. Stanton Returns to Private Life; His Subsequent Career—Gen. John

56

M. Schofield Appointed Secretary of War—Senate Refuses to Confirm Renomination of Mr. Stanbery as Attorney-General, and Mr. Evarts Is Appointed to the Place—Gen. Benjamin F. Butler [Mass.] Introduces Bill in the House to Repeal Tenure-of-Office Act; Carried—Debate in the Senate: In Favor of Repeal, Allen G. Thurman [O.], Oliver P. Morton [Ind.], Richard Yates [Ill.], William P. Fessenden [Me.], Carl Schurz [Mo.]; In Favor of Suspension, Lyman Trumbull [Ill.], Jacob M. Howard [Mich.], George F. Edmunds [Vt.]; Bill Withdrawn— Sen. Trumbull Reports Substitute for the Act; Adopted by Senate and Refused by House—Conference Committee Reports New Act Virtually Abolishing the Old; Adopted; President Grant Unsuccessfully Tries to Have the Old Act Entirely Abolished.

A RESOLUTION was introduced in the House on January 7, 1867, by James M. Ashley [O.], impeaching Andrew Johnson of high crimes and misdemeanors.

"I charge him," said Mr. Ashley, "with an usurpation of power and violation of law: in that he has corruptly used the appointing power; in that he has corruptly used the pardoning power; in that he has corruptly used the veto power; in that he has corruptly disposed of the public property of the United States; in that he has corruptly interfered in elections and committed acts which in contemplation of the Constitution are high crimes and misdemeanors."

This resolution was referred to the Judiciary Committee (James F. Wilson of Iowa, chairman), who were empowered to make a thorough investigation by examining papers, witnesses, etc.

On March 2, on the eve of the session's close, the majority of the committee, being all Republicans, reported that they had entered into such an investigation, and found justification for its continuance. The one Democrat upon the committee, Andrew J. Rogers [N. J.], submitted a minority report declaring that the evidence was mostly of a secondary character, such as could not be admitted in a court of justice, and that none of it sustained the charges against the President. He therefore advised that the investigation be discontinued, since it served only to keep the country in a state of political agitation.

ON CONTINUING INVESTIGATION OF PRESIDENT'S ACTS

DEBATE IN THE HOUSE OF REPRESENTATIVES, MARCH 7, 1867

On the 7th of March, in the new Congress, Mr. Ashley introduced a resolution in the House directing the Judiciary Committee to pursue the investigation. The President, he said, had aggravated his offences by his message of March 2, 1867, in which he gave his reasons for vetoing the Reconstruction Bill.[1] This was, he said, "an invitation to revolution and civil war."

Sir, a man of Mr. Johnson's antecedents, of his mental and moral caliber, coming into the presidency as he came into it— and I say nothing now of the dark suspicion which crept over the minds of men as to his complicity in the assassination plot— I say such a man ought to have walked with uncovered head and very humbly before the loyal men of this nation and their Representatives in the American Congress.

Self-protection and a proper respect for the honor of the nation demand that the Representatives of the people shall declare, in a manner not to be misunderstood, that no man hereafter elected President or Vice-President shall present himself at his inauguration drunk; that no man discharging the duties of the office of President of the United States shall be permitted to turn the White House into a den of thieves and pardon brokers, nor shall he be permitted with impunity to address in vulgar, seditious language a drunken, howling mob from the steps of the executive mansion.

Sir, unless this committee take charge of this matter and proceed with it, this Congress might as well lay down its powers. If, however, nothing more should be done, I am sure that, when the evidence which has been already taken is published, it will operate as a deliberate and solemn protest against a repetition in the future of another drunken electioneering tour such as last year mantled the cheek of this nation with shame; that it will be a protest against the unpardonable attacks which the acting Executive made upon the national Congress, a protest against his usurpations and crimes and misdemeanors.

Sir, his crime is not, as many suppose, the mere perfidy of which he has been guilty to the men who in an evil hour elected

[1] See Volume VIII, page 62.

him Vice-President of the United States, black and infamous as it is; his crime is the highest known in our country, a crime against the Republic itself.

The nation cries out in its agony and calls upon the Congress of the United States to deliver them from the shame and disgrace which the acting President has brought upon them. They demand that the loathing incubus which has blotted our country's history with its foulest blot shall be removed. In the name of loyalty betrayed, of law violated, of the Constitution trampled upon, the nation demands the impeachment and removal of Andrew Johnson.

On the Speaker remarking that Mr. Ashley was exceeding the large license permitted in debate on impeachment, Samuel J. Randall [Dem.] of Pennsylvania, inquired, amid the laughter of the House, if there was "any insane asylum near here." Benjamin M. Boyer [Dem.] of Pennsylvania asked that Mr. Ashley be permitted to continue, "on account of the service he is doing to the President of the United States."

Mr. Ashley continued:

Mr. Speaker, I know, on this question, that the timid among the loyal hesitate, that the late rebels and their Northern allies are defiant, and that the camp followers of the President alternately threaten and supplicate, and that all unite in prophesying war and revolution, and in any event financial ruin to the country, if Congress shall undertake to arraign and depose the President as provided by the Constitution. Sir, I hope this Congress will not hesitate to do its duty, but that it will proceed with dignity and deliberation to the discharge of the high and important duty imposed upon it, uninfluenced by passion and unawed by fear. If, as has been happily suggested by one of our able and true men, the nation could stand the shock occasioned by the assassination of a beloved President by the hand of an assassin, it surely can stand the shock caused by the removal of one so detested as the acting President, if done in pursuance of law.

And, sir, has he not done enough? Before he had been one month in the presidency he entered into a combination with the enemies of the nation to usurp in their interest the prerogatives of Congress, and sought to bind hand and foot the loyal men of the South, who had aided us in putting down the rebellion, by putting the governments of the South in the hands of their mortal enemies and ours. This with me is enough. When you add to this his other acts, which have become public history, the case for me is complete.

The duty of the President of the United States is to execute, not to make laws. His oath requires him to see that the laws are faithfully executed. That the President has neglected or refused to execute many of the laws of Congress no man ques-

THE BAD BOY [ANDY JOHNSON] IN THE NATIONAL SCHOOL
Cartoon by Frank Beard
From the collection of the New York Public Library

tions. That he has failed to execute the Civil Rights bill, nay, that he has not even attempted to execute it the whole country knows. On the other hand, he has not only failed to execute it, but in most indecent and offensive language he has assailed and denounced the law as unconstitutional.

Sir, in his failure to execute this just and most necessary law the crime of the President becomes perfectly colossal. Since the surrender of Lee and Johnston more than five thousand American citizens, guilty of no crime but love of country, have been murdered by men lately in arms against this country. Thousands more have been driven from their homes into exile.

Sir, there never was a nation on this earth guilty of the infamy of treating its loyal citizens as the President of the United States has treated the loyal men of the South.

I know how easy it is for the President and his co-conspirators to deny his guilty knowledge. I know also how difficult it is to prove by technical rules the guilt of a man occupying his position, although the whole country may know him to be guilty.

Why, sir, when the rebellion broke out, no conspirator, however flagrant his crime, could have been arrested, tried, and convicted before a court and jury in this District. It is much more difficult in a case of this kind, where the rebellion is not an open, armed rebellion, but a negative rebellion. In this rebellion the President is the recognized leader, and it is well known that he has coöperating with him nearly all the late rebels of the South.

Mr. Ashley declared that, if the trial of the President were not proceeded with, the section of the Constitution providing for impeaching the President was valueless.

Sir, if this man is not impeached, if he is not tried and deposed from the high place which he has disgraced, then no man who may succeed him need ever fear trial and conviction, no matter what his crime.

Rufus P. Spalding [O.] differed "the whole heaven" from his colleague. He denounced the scheme of impeachment as "consummate folly." Not one act amounting to a crime or misdemeanor had been proved against the President.

And I say more than that. It is not expected by some of those who charge the Executive with high crimes and misdemeanors that proof will be obtained. It is only necessary, as has been said in high places within the last week or ten days, that it should be known that the President is an "obstruction" in the way of what my friend from Ohio calls "progress," and the Radical party of the country will feel it to be their duty to remove him from office.

Sir, I hold to no such doctrine, and I say to my associates of the great Union party that they are mistaken if they suppose that the intelligent people of the United States are going to uphold them in a practice based upon any such principle.

Sir, we are bringing our republican institutions, our popular form of government, to a test such as no free nation ever yet imposed upon its government with impunity. I trust we are not yet called to exhibit the same temper with those who lived in the days of Oliver Cromwell in England, or with Robespierre and Marat in France, when men who one day advocated the most extreme measures of the Radicals were the next day brought to the block or the guillotine because they were not far enough in the advance in the line of progress.

I have voted for every radical measure of reconstruction proposed in this House, and yet we have not adopted measures radical enough to suit the purposes of some gentlemen who are around me. They now cry for the head of the Executive.

FERNANDO WOOD [N. Y.].—They want more blood.

MR. SPALDING.—And for what good purpose? Is it to make way for some other man or set of men? Is this whole nation to be convulsed; is our public credit to be trifled with; are our stocks to be brought down to forty, thirty, twenty, or perhaps ten cents on the dollar, just to gratify this eagerness to remove the executive head of the nation? I can, in conscience, support no such policy.

BENJAMIN F. BUTLER [Mass.].—I hold this Congress would be false to itself, false to the country, false to the principles of the American Government did they shrink from the investigation.

If a bare quorum of the Representatives elected to the first Congress of the United States, and only a majority of the States composing the Union, could make George Washington President, cannot this House unmake Andrew Johnson? [Laughter.]

GEORGE F. MILLER [Pa.].—Give the President an impartial trial; wait for the evidence and report of your committee, and then, if evidence sustains the charges as to his guilt, do not hesitate to impeach him; and, on the other hand, if insufficient, dismiss the subject, and let the country understand that he escapes for want of proper evidence. But until the committee shall report let us forbear making any allegations as to his guilt or innocence.

We are told that if we impeach the President our governmental securities will depreciate in the market, and that it will bring upon us bankruptcy. I have no such fears, and Congress ought not to be intimidated by any suggestions of the kind. But, even if it would have that effect, it is no reason for shrinking from duty.

Had Andrew Johnson been true to his friends he had an opportunity of making himself popular, and been an honor to himself and his country. After the assassination of the much-lamented Lincoln, the mantle of that great and good man, at whose death the nation still mourns, was thrown on the shoulders of Mr. Johnson; but, alas! in an evil hour he was induced to partake of the forbidden fruit in the form of modern democracy, which seemed pleasant for him to look upon, hence his great fall. His course will be a warning to all those in future that may occupy the presidential chair not to forsake the party that elected him.

James Brooks [N. Y.] scouted the charges brought by Mr. Ashley against the President as demagogic claptrap, entirely unsupported by evidence. He denied, in particular, that five thousand Union men had been killed in the South since the war, and adduced testimony of generals in charge of the Southern military districts to the contrary. Crime existed in all the States, but only in the South was political significance imputed to it. Every sort of an outrage occurring, or alleged to have occurred, in that outlawed region was garnered up and spread before the people to inflame their minds and induce them to support military reconstruction and the impeachment of the President.

The opposition to impeachment by the conservative Republicans, he said, would be unavailing.

History tells me that the destructive work of the revolutionists—the architects of ruin—must go on. And I appreciate also the fact that I and those who are politically associated with me must be prepared to endure our share of the disastrous future now opening on the country.

Mr. Brooks denied the expediency of impeachment, even if a great crime had been committed. The courts of law afforded a complete remedy.

Let me appeal to my Republican friends on the other side to consider what a precedent this is that they are called upon to establish as law. At some future time they will be in the minority; another party will be in the majority; and if the President of the minority stands in the way of the party of the majority that majority can suspend, impeach, and if he stands in their way remove him. If such a precedent, therefore, is established, this is no longer a constitutional government. Let it go to the country, then, that the chief leader of impeachment here has avowed, in substance, that no matter as to "the crimes or misdemeanors" of the President, whether he be guilty or not, so long as he stands in their way that is enough—he must be taken off and stricken down.

The first movement of the honorable gentleman from Ohio [Mr. Ashley] has already cost the merchants, capitalists, manufacturers, and farmers of this country over a hundred million dollars by the decline in the stocks, obligations, and property of this country. And now he proposes to keep up this agitation for months and months longer.

What is the proposition which we are called upon to adopt? It is to provide the Committee on the Judiciary with an unlimited amount of money and means to enable them to go about the country hunting up scandals, drumming up witnesses, employing detectives, informers, spies, and the like to suborn perjury, informers of all classes and kinds, in order to recreate this agitation and reëxcite the people. Sir, we have already approached, if we are not in the midst of a financial crisis. The wages of labor are already being cut down in the State of Rhode Island; hundreds of operatives are being discharged from the factories of Massachusetts and Connecticut; thousands of laborers are stalking unemployed through the streets of New York; and elsewhere throughout the country the demand for labor is made by thousands who are dependent upon it for their daily subsistence.

Like operations will extend from the great heart of New York through all the country if this agitation is encouraged to go on. No more railroads can be built in the West, no more bonds of Western States can be sold, no more capital can be profitably employed in those States.

It is proper, therefore, that this impeachment should go on this very day, or it should stop this very day. Agitation, revolutionary agitation, financial agitation, is death to the commerce, the trade, the agriculture, the capital of this country. If the President of the United States is to be removed or deposed, take him now from the White House, and install there your newly elected President of the Senate [Benjamin F. Wade]. Do it forthwith, immediately; and then go on with no longer delay in this work of destruction and death.

John V. L. Pruyn [N. Y.] declared that, if the President were guilty, the members of his Cabinet were equally so, being accomplices. Would you impeach these also?

He counseled deliberation.

Look at the deliberate and orderly proceeding of the British Parliament in the impeachment of Warren Hastings, and contrast them with the hot haste in this Congress this day if this resolution be passed.

JOHN W. CHANLER [N. Y.].—The Committee on the Judiciary have reported progress, and in that report they have given assurance that the impeachment of the President upon the charges of the gentleman from Ohio [Mr. Ashley] never will take place. They have deserted the ground they took. They now ask for a continuance of the investigation to cover the impotency of their efforts and the fallacy of their charges. So far as revolution is concerned, if ridicule could stop revolution the speceh of the gentleman from Ohio [Mr. Ashley] would. He would put the mask of Laughter on the Muse of Tragedy.

This investigation has lost all the magnitude it had. It has dwindled into contemptible proportions. There is no fear now of the country from this agitation. They understand how weak and silly it is. There is no danger that the stock jobbers will consider it at all. My colleague [Mr. Brooks] has given too much importance to the gentleman and his agitation. There is no danger that the stock jobbers of Wall street will reward the gentleman from Ohio [Mr. Ashley] even with a leather medal.

My colleague has alluded to the suffering in our commercial, manufacturing, and agricultural interests. It is not because the impotent resolutions of this Congress are flaunted before the country. The prostration of the country is the result of an inflated currency.

So far, then, from this question of the impeachment being the cause, I look upon it as dead. It is dead—and stinketh.

Mr. Ashley's resolution was carried without a division, and the committee proceeded with their investigation, reporting on November 25, 1867.

The prophecy of Representative Brooks that the committee would employ itself in investigating wild rumors was borne out by the fact that it examined General Ulysses S. Grant upon the question of whether the President had ever sounded him upon securing the support of the army in the event of the President's admitting members from the ex-rebel States into Congress. General Grant's testimony was positively in the negative.

Three reports were submitted by the committee:

IX—5

(1) a majority report [George S. Boutwell of Massachusetts, spokesman] directing impeachment; (2) a minority report by James F. Wilson [Ia.], the chairman, and Frederic Woodbridge [Vt.], asking simply that the committee be discharged from further investigation, and the subject be tabled; and (3) a minority report by the two Democratic members, Charles A. Eldridge [Wis.] and Samuel S. Marshall [Wis.], to the same effect, but in language denunciatory of the charge.

By agreement Mr. Boutwell spoke for the majority of five, and Mr. Wilson for the minority of four.

On Impeaching the President

House of Representatives, December 5-6, 1867

Mr. Boutwell admitted that the immediate interests of the country would not suffer by continuing the President in office for the fifteen months remaining of his term, since Congress could, and would, override his vetoes, and held power over the officers of the executive department. But it was the duty of Congress to furnish an example for the future.

He argued that impeachable offences were not necessarily those indictable in a court of law. The seventh paragraph of the third section of the first article of the Constitution provides that the party convicted by impeachment might be liable subsequently to indictment in a court, and the Fifth Amendment to the Constitution declares that no person for the same offence should be put twice in jeopardy of life or limb. Therefore, in order that these two provisions do not conflict, the Constitution provided as a penalty for impeachment only removal from office and inability to hold office. "Impeachment is not in this country, as in England it is a mode by which crimes are punished." Accordingly English precedents of impeachment are valueless.

But the meaning of English common law terms is, on the contrary, an absolute guide to the interpretation of legal terms used in the Constitution. So the Supreme Court has decided. "Treason, bribery, and other high crimes and misdemeanors," which the Constitution (Article II, section 4) declares impeachable offences, therefore must be interpreted by the common law.

Blackstone has specified the acts which are "crimes and misdemeanors" under the general head of public wrongs: (1) crimes against justice, such as bribery and perjury; (2) crimes against peace, such as riots; (3) crimes against trade, such as smuggling; (4) crimes against health, such as selling unwholesome provisions; and (5) crimes against the police or public economy of the State, such as bigamy and nuisances.

Can there be any doubt that when our ancestors went to the common law of England as it was laid down by Blackstone and selected treason and bribery as two great public political crimes, thus indicating the nature of the crimes which by the Constitution they intended to make impeachable, and drew from Blackstone, or even older authorities than Blackstone, the intelligible and well-understood phrase, "other high crimes and misdemeanors," they intended to include those crimes which were as well known to the common law of England as were the crimes of treason and perjury.

If it be said that the circumstance that treason is defined in the Constitution has deprived Congress of the power to legislate upon this branch of the subject, and that its authority is therefore limited to "bribery and other high crimes and misdemeanors," it may be stated in answer that the Constitution did not create the crime of treason, but simply limited the definition of the crime to a single offence; while by the common law of England it included several distinct offences. It should be observed, however, that by the English law every form of treason was a crime or misdemeanor, and while by the Constitution of the United States only one of these forms is declared to be treason and other acts still rest in the class of crimes and misdemeanors.

Bribery was an offence as well known to and as well defined by the common law of England at the time the Constitution was framed as was the crime of treason. The phrase "high crimes and misdemeanors" had been in use in the courts and in the books of England for centuries.

Legislative wisdom is and ever must be incapable of rendering the meaning of these words more certain than it is when subjected to the principles which lie at the foundation of the

English common law. The Constitution makes the President and all civil officers liable to impeachment if guilty of bribery; is it to be assumed that this power in the Constitution was to remain dormant until Congress by law should declare what bribery is, and what acts are acts of bribery; and also provide that bribery as defined by law shall be an indictable offence? Be it remembered that, although bribery is named in the Constitution, it was not, when the Government was organized in 1789, an indictable offence, which the minority of the committee say it must be before it can be impeachable. The Government was in existence from the 4th day of March, 1789, to the 30th day of April, 1790, before a crimes act was passed, and during that time neither treason nor bribery was indictable by law in any court of the United States. Will anybody say in view of this provision of the Constitution that our fathers would have sat silently and submitted to the administration of a man who was elected by bribery, but whose offence was by no law of the land indictable?

Still further, it is constitutionally impossible for Congress to declare that certain offences are crimes and misdemeanors everywhere and under all circumstances within the territory of the United States. For example, the power of Congress to provide for the punishment of the crime of murder is limited to the forts and arsenals, to the District of Columbia, and to the Territories of the Union. Upon the theory that those offences only are impeachable which are made crimes by the laws of the United States a civil officer might be guilty of murder within the jurisdiction of a State where the crime is not and cannot be punishable by any law of Congress, and the House and Senate would have no power to arraign, try, and remove him from office. Practically it would be found impossible to anticipate by specific legislation all cases of misconduct which will occur in the career of criminal men. At the present moment we have no law which declares that it shall be a high crime or misdemeanor for the President to decline to recognize the Congress of the United States, and yet should he deny its lawful and constitutional existence and authority, and thus virtually dissolve the Government, would the House and Senate be impotent and unable to proceed by process of impeachment to secure his removal from office?

The theory that we must look to the statutes of the United States alone, and that the President and other officers, as long as they do not violate the criminal statute laws of the country, may do any act or thing, however detrimental to the public interests, however contrary to the public morals, however heinous in its nature, and still retain their offices, is a theory so at variance with civilization, with the principles of law, and with the existence of the Government, that it ought not to receive our support or countenance unless the language of the Constitution imperatively requires us to yield to its authority.

I rest firmly in the conclusion that the phrase "bribery or other high crimes and misdemeanors" is used in the Constitution in accordance with and subject to the rule of reason, which lies at the foundation of the English common law. This rule is that no person in office shall do an act *contra bonos mores,* contrary to good morals; and subjecting the provisions of the Constitution concerning impeachment to that rule the result is that neither the President, the Vice-President, nor any civil officer of the United States can lawfully do any act, either official or otherwise, which in a large, a public sense is contrary to the good morals of the office he holds. Misconduct in office, misbehavior in office, misdemeanor in office, are equivalent terms. The principle of the English common law furnishes not only the foundation for the cases which have arisen, but for others that may arise and to which the same great principles of law must be applied.

This principle has been elucidated by the most eminent writers of England and of this country, and it is especially recognized, applied, and elaborated by one of the great jurists of modern times. I refer to Chief Justice Shaw, of the supreme court of Massachusetts.

By the Constitution this House may determine the rule of its proceedings, punish its members for disorderly behavior, and with the concurrence of two-thirds expel a member. But are we to sit here without authority to protect ourselves until those acts which amount to disorderly behavior are enumerated in the laws of the country or by the rules of the House? Our security is first in the reason and conscience with which we are individually guided and warned; and then in the reason and conscience of our judges applied in the light of the principle which lies at the foundation of the common law, municipal, public, and parliamentary. Upon the view of the Constitution which I present and maintain honest public officers are safe in all their rights. In the nature of the case, a civil officer, guided by his conscience and judgment, will do no act which the Senate of the United States upon its conscience and judgment, and by a two-thirds majority of the members present, will pronounce a high crime and misdemeanor. On the other hand, the theory that I

aim to refute seems to me to be fraught with danger to civil officers and with peril to the Government.

With this view of the law I turn now to the authorities, and
then I shall pass briefly over the precedents which the history
of this country furnishes.

Here the speaker quoted Wooddeson, the first
English authority on impeachment, Alexander Hamilton
in "The Federalist," No. 65, and Nathan Dane in his
"Digest of American Law," chapter 222, articles 8
and 9.

It follows from these authorities that those acts are especially impeachable offences which affect the welfare or existence
of the State, or render the officer unfit for the discharge of his
duties. It does not follow that every act which is a crime at law
is therefore impeachable, or that impeachable offences are indictable.

Justice Joseph Story, writing about the year 1830, when the
cases of Blount, of Chase, and of Pickering were before him
and known to him, says that no one of the cases of impeachment which had then been tried rested upon statutable misdemeanors.

The speaker then discussed the cases of impeachment in the United States.

William Blount [Tenn.], a Senator, was impeached
by the House on July 3, 1797, for inciting the Indians
of the Southwest to rise against the Government. The
Senate discussed the case, holding that a Senator was
not a civil officer, but dismissed Blount from the Senate
because he was guilty of a high misdemeanor. Yet
Justice Story said that he had not committed a statutable offence.

Samuel Chase [Md.], a justice of the Supreme Court,
was impeached in 1804 by the House, of high crimes
and misdemeanors, and on one count (haranguing the
grand jury against the government of Maryland) a majority of the Senate, though not the requisite two-thirds
majority, found him guilty. Yet he conducted his own
case, and did not venture to risk it on the question
of law.

John Pickering [N. H.], judge of the district court

of his State, was successfully impeached for being drunk and blaspheming upon the bench, which were not statutable offences under the law of the United States. It was pleaded in Judge Pickering's behalf that he was insane, and not that his offences, if they had been committed by a sane man, would not be high crimes and misdemeanors.

West H. Humphreys [Tenn.], judge of the district court of his State, was successfully impeached in 1861 for declaring in a public speech that Tennessee had the right to secede.

"No lawyer will maintain that Judge Humphreys could have been indicted for treason or for any other crime under the laws of the United States because of what he did say, or of anything that he could have said in a public speech at Nashville at that time."

Mr. Boutwell then discussed the facts in the case of President Johnson. At the end of his summation Mr. Boutwell admitted that the offences which he charged against the President were not in themselves "high crimes and misdemeanors," but "tributary" to the accomplishment of the great object he had in view—the treasonable seizure of the Government. In other words, he indicted President Johnson for "constructive treason."

Mr. Wilson in reply said that Mr. Boutwell had spent the major part of his speech in demolishing an unimportant point which the minority had made as a suggestion rather than an affirmative declaration of law —namely, that only crimes and misdemeanors indictable under the statutes of the United States will justify the impeachment of a civil officer. Nevertheless, though the matter was of no consequence, the minority of the committee adhered to their view.

Mr. Boutwell, he said, held that impeachment looks merely to a removal of an officer who may have conducted himself in a manner which the conscience of the House disapproves; that a trial on impeachment is not a trial for crime in its technical sense. I commend to him as an answer to his most singular suggestion that part of section two of article three of the Constitution, which says:

"The trial of all crimes, except in cases of impeachment, shall be by jury," &c.

Can a non-indictable offence be tried by a jury? The gentleman from Massachusetts will not so affirm. Then, are not trials in cases of impeachments trials for indictable crimes, at least at common law? How will the gentleman avoid this conclusion except by rejecting the Constitution and affirming as its superior the conscience of this House, which may be Republican now and Democratic at no distant day?

The gentleman says, again, that impeachments look not to the punishment of persons, but to the removal of officers. Let this be granted for the sake of the present argument. What follows? The Constitution answers that for whatever purpose an impeachment may be instituted it must be based on "treason, bribery, or other high crime or misdemeanor." Now, sir, if this proceeding is not for punishment, if it is for something else, still it is plain we cannot put its machinery in motion unless we have the force of a crime or misdemeanor to move it.

And here we are told that for the meaning of the terms "high crimes and misdemeanors" we must resort to the common law of Parliament. If this be true what comes of the declaration that "English precedents should not influence the action of this House in its exercise of the power of impeachment"? Authority upon authority based on parliamentary law is presented by his report made to the House in this case, and yet we are told that English cases should not influence our action.

Sir, I accept the umpire offered by the gentleman. I am willing to go with him to the common law of Parliament to ascertain what the terms "high crimes and misdemeanors" mean. I have presented in the report of the minority two well-considered and thoroughly digested cases made up by this umpire. Both of these affirm that the terms "high crimes and misdemeanors" mean offences indictable by the common law of England or the statutes of Parliament.

I refer to the cases of Macclesfield and Melville—two of the best considered of all the English cases. Macclesfield was convicted upon the express ground that his offence was indictable under the act of Edward VI; Melville, on the contrary, was acquitted upon the ground that the case did not show, as committed by him, an offence which would support a presentment or indictment in any court of the realm.

These cases follow the current authority of England, and I ask the gentleman to cite a single case in opposition thereto entitled to the respect of this House.

The gentleman asserted with an air of triumph that the crime of murder might be committed by the President or any other civil officer of the United States in places and under circumstances which would not bring the crime within the jurisdiction of the courts of the United States, and demanded to know whether in such a case an objection would be interposed to an impeachment of the offending officer.

I answer this question by quoting the language of the gentleman's own report, as follows:

"The legitimate causes of impeachment can have reference only to public character and official duty. In general, those offences which may be committed equally by a private person as a public officer are not the subjects of impeachment. Murder, burglary, robbery, and, indeed, all offences not immediately connected with office, except the two expressly mentioned, are left to the ordinary course of judicial proceeding, and neither House can regularly inquire into them except for the purpose of expelling the member."

This answers the gentleman's inquiry. It very plainly declares that the supposititious case stated by the gentleman would not sustain an impeachment of a civil officer, and this is sufficient for my present purpose. It might be difficult for the conscience of this House to determine which rule of conduct to follow in such a case—the one presented by the majority report or the one stated in the speech to which we have listened.

The gentleman has told us that the power of impeachment vested in this House is subject to no revision or control, and that its exercise is to be guided solely by the conscience of the House. Correctly interpreted, this doctrine, as it seems to me, comes to this: that whatever this House may declare on its conscience to be an impeachable offence, reduce to the form of articles, and carry to the Senate for trial, that body is only to be allowed to declare whether the officer impeached is guilty of the facts presented against him, but is not to be permitted to say that such facts do or do not constitute a crime or misdemeanor. For, if this conscience is not subject to any control or revision, having determined that a given state of facts constitutes a high crime or misdemeanor, it would seem to follow, logically, that the House must demand judgment of conviction on proof of the facts charged, regardless of the opinions of the members of the Senate respecting the presence or absence of those elements which alone can constitute any act a real crime.

This doctrine may carry this case to the determination desired by the gentleman. But can he not see that it may return to plague him and the country? He admitted that if the minority of the committee are right on the law the majority have no case whatever. And I may here say that if he is right in his views of the power of impeachment no law is needed, for the law might control the conscience of the House.

I agree with him in the statement that Congress cannot declare and punish as a crime an act which does not involve the elements of crime as they are known to and established by the common law. But this doctrine is fatal to his argument and destructive of his case; for if it be true the conscience of this House is as much bound by it when exercising the impeaching power as it is in matters of ordinary legislation. You cannot bind the ordinary legislative power of this House by the principle here laid down and then, when you come to exercise the impeaching power, brush it out of the way in order that the obnoxious officer may be removed without the presentation of some act involving the well-known elements of crime.

The position which the minority of the committee occupy in this case may be summed up in these words: that no civil officer of the United States can be lawfully impeached except for a crime or misdemeanor known to the law; that this body must be guided by the law, and not by that indefinite something called its conscience, which may be one thing to-day and quite a different one to-morrow. If the case now before us, tested by the principles of criminal law, discloses high crimes or misdemeanors coming within the rule I have stated, then the gentleman is right in demanding that the President of the United States be impeached; and I here throw open to the gentleman the range of both statutory and common law impeachable crimes. If these cannot be found in the record of this case, then no amount of conscience in House and Senate can justify us in proceeding further with it.

The gentleman quoted from Wooddeson to show that nonindictable offences may justify an impeachment of a civil officer, but he did not read far enough. The principles of which Wooddeson is treating in the lecture from which the passage read by the gentleman is taken involve more than the power of impeachment: they involve the power of attainder and the power to pass bills of pains and penalties. These powers have been confused and confounded by many of the elementary writers. Wooddeson has been more fortunate than most writers in presenting the lines which divide these powers.

Impeachments were for offences known to the law; were founded on the laws in being; for other offences the sharp and unlimited powers of attainder and bills of pains and penalties were used. These extraordinary powers are denied to us by the Constitution. We may provide for crimes and misdemeanors known to the law when the acts constituting them were done. "No bill of attainder or *ex post facto* law shall be passed."

The gentleman also referred to Story. But how loosely Judge Story wrote on this subject may be seen by reading a few lines from one of the sections of his "Commentaries":

"The object of these prosecutions in America, as well as in England, is to reach high and potent offenders, such as might be presumed to escape punishment in the ordinary tribunals, either from their own extraordinary influence or from the imperfect organization and power of these tribunals."—*Story's Commentaries*, Section 688.

Does this present a correct idea of the power of impeachment vested in this House by the Constitution? Sir, send out your committee upon charges preferred against some petty postmaster who has not influence enough in his neighborhood to change the result of an election for a justice of the peace, and he, within the contemplation of the Constitution, is one of these "high and potent offenders" who must be punished by an exercise of this grand power lodged in the House of Representatives, for he is a civil officer of the United States. Why, sir, it is simply ridiculous, and it only tends to show how loosely the text writers have written on this subject.

But the gentleman found in Story an authority to the effect that we may impeach for "political offences." What is a "political offence"? That is a broad and a very significant term in this country. Is it the doing of something that the dominant political party in the country do not like? That, in one sense, is a political offence. Are we to impeach for that? We did not like the removal of our own friends from office by the present President. Are we to impeach for that? He has done many acts of political littleness, meanness, and treachery. Are these impeachable political offences? Sir, it is unsafe for us to wander into the field of political or party action for offences upon which to rest the impeaching power of this House. Disaster alone could result from such a course of procedure.

The gentleman referred to cases which have occurred in this country. We have had, as he stated, the case of Blount, of Chase, of Pickering, of Humphrey. Blount's case was decided, as the gentleman informed us, upon a plea to the jurisdiction of the court. Certainly, then, that case established no precedent beyond that involved in the one point passed upon by the court. In Chase's case the gentleman says he finds an approval of the doctrine he has argued here to-day, that something less than an indictable offence may be the subject of an impeachment. How is that ascertained? I have always supposed that before the action of a court can be treated as authority it must decide something in such a manner as to disclose the principle underlying its action and guiding its conduct. Chase was tried. What was the result? He was acquitted. Why? The record does not disclose the reason; but it must have been because the court did not believe him guilty of high crimes and misdemeanors. The proof of the facts charged was very strong, and an acquittal certainly does not tend to establish the doctrine that an impeachment may be properly had for a non-indictable offence. In what did the case originate? In the partisan feelings and excitements of the times. And this case of Judge Samuel Chase has gone into American political history as a partisan impeachment.

Then we come to the Pickering case. As the minority have said in their report, that case is a disgrace to the court that tried it. It is very manifest from the report of the case that, like the impeachment of Judge Chase, this was a partisan case. Notwithstanding the court permitted Judge Pickering's counsel to set up the plea of insanity, the case was disposed of without regard to that plea, although, if anything was proved in the case, it was that Pickering was insane. And if it is authority for any purpose or thing, it is that an insane man may be held criminally liable, and be punished for acts done by him in the midst of his insanity and caused thereby. Such a doctrine is monstrous. The Constitution has provided another remedy for such cases.

The Humphrey case, it is said, was not based, so far as the first article was concerned, on any act for which he could have been indicted. What are the facts? The South Carolina convention passed the ordinance of secession on the 17th day of December, 1860. The criminal act laid to the charge of Humphrey, and on which the first article rested, was alleged to have occurred on the 29th day of the same month, at which time he, being a judge of the district court of the United States, urged in a public speech the people of Tennessee to secede and make common cause with the people of South Carolina in the war which they had levied against the United States. This was an act of treason. War having been levied, his conduct made him a traitor.

Mr. Wilson then took up the charges against President Johnson and argued that either they were unfounded or they related to non-impeachable offences. He said in closing:

When the gentleman from Massachusetts, in commenting on one of the alleged offences of the President, stated that we could not ''arraign him for the specific crime,'' he disclosed the weakness of the case we are now considering. If we cannot arraign the President for a specific crime for what are we to proceed against him? For a bundle of generalities such as we have in the volume of testimony reported by the committee to the House in this case? If we cannot state upon paper a specific crime how are we to carry this case to the Senate for trial?

On the following day (December 7) the resolution of impeachment was put to vote and defeated—57 ayes, 108 nays. All the affirmative votes were Republican, but a still greater number of that party voted in the negative.

Removal of Secretary Stanton

The question seemed decisively settled. However, the President himself soon brought it forward again by engaging in a conflict with the Senate over his removal of Edwin M. Stanton from his position as Secretary of War.

The President and the Secretary had long been incompatible associates. The Chief Executive of the nation had plainly intimated to his military adviser that his resignation would be acceptable, but Secretary Stanton refused to act on the hint, and stuck to his post, because, believing the welfare of the country demanded that a man in sympathy with the anti-administration policy of military reconstruction should be in charge of the War Department, he feared that he would be replaced by one who would be opposed to this policy. Finally, on August 5, 1867, the President formally asked the secretary to hand in his resignation. Mr. Stanton refused, giving his reason for doing so. On August 12 the President suspended him from his office until the next session of Congress under the power conferred by the Tenure-of-Office Act, and appointed General Ulysses S. Grant in his place.

On the 12th of December President Johnson reported his actions in the matter to the Senate, giving his reasons therefor.

On January 13, 1868, the Senate, by a party vote, violated assurances which had been made by leading members at the time the Tenure-of-Office Act was passed, that no Cabinet officer obnoxious to the President would be forced upon him, and reinstated Mr. Stanton. In a characteristically discourteous fashion Mr. Stanton took immediate possession from General Grant. The President was incensed at the General for his acquiescence in the order of the Senate, having trusted that he would resist it and so bring the Tenure-of-Office Act before the Supreme Court for adjudication, and wrote him an angry letter to which General Grant replied in kind, leading to irreconcilable enmity between the two— a state which was inestimably valuable to the General in restoring him to the good graces of the Republican party, which had become suspicious of the quality of his "radicalism" because of the trust imposed in him by the President.

On February 21 the President brought the issue with Congress to a head by informing it that he had designated Lorenzo Thomas, adjutant-general of the army, to act as Secretary of War, *ad interim*. The Senate went into executive session and passed a resolution that the President had no constitutional power to perform this action. When this action was reported to the House John Covode [Pa.] offered a resolution to impeach the President of "high crimes and misdemeanors." The House referred the communication of the President and the resolution of Mr. Covode to the Committee on Reconstruction.

On the following day Thaddeus Stevens [Pa.], chairman of the committee, reported the resolution.

ON IMPEACHING THE PRESIDENT

DEBATE IN THE HOUSE OF REPRESENTATIVES, FEBRUARY 22, 1868

Mr. Brooks characterized the measure as "the ghost of impeachment," which had been successfully laid, stalking forth again from its grave at the strange spell exercised by the dominating radical minority of the Republican party. He realized that the familiar formula, the adjuration by the Constitution to begone, would not be effective this time—that proceedings to impeach the President would certainly be carried through. He therefore solemnly warned the opposition, amid its derisive laughter, that these proceedings must be conducted in strict accordance with law, that if any other process was adopted to throw the President out of office, "millions of the people of this country" would "never, never, so help me God! never, never submit."

The attack, he said, upon the President's constitutional power over the army had injected a new element into the contest: four-fifths of this army were Democrats, "and if you proceed to introduce politics into the army the Democratic soldier will follow the Democratic instinct, and stand by the Constitution and laws of his country," for in this matter Congress was the usurper.

Sir, all the offices of the departments of this Government are trusts. Congress has a high and august trust reposed in it; the judicial tribunals have also high and august trusts reposed in them. So, also, has the President of the United States an equally high trust reposed in him to maintain his constitutional powers, and to act and adjudicate upon those powers, subject to appeal to the Supreme Court of the United States. If he should throw away that trust; if he should abandon the powers and prerogatives given with that trust; if he should allow the executive department of the United States to be overthrown or disorganized, he would be guilty, not only of a high offence against the Constitution of the United States, but a high crime against the people of this country in not maintaining all the powers which the Constitution has given him.

You make a rule violating the Constitution, and you then impeach the President because he wishes to test the constitutionality of your rule. In other words, you claim the right to throw the President out of office, to abrogate or change the executive department of the Government, to strip it of its prerogatives and power, whenever, by a mere act of Congress, you can overrule a veto; and when you have thus done, unless the Executive obeys your act implicity, without any investigation or legal adjudication, you claim the right to snatch the case in contest from the Supreme Court of the United States and adjudicate it here in this House and in the Senate through the impeachment power, which destroys that Executive, even if he could afterward rule that all that has been done is right. You have a right, you contend, to pass any illegal and unconstitutional laws; you have a right to disfranchise all of the people of the United States, if you so choose, that are not of your party; you have a right to eject every Democratic member upon the floor of this House by some disqualifying law that you have passed; and if the President of the United States maintains and executes the laws as they have been adjudged by the courts hitherto you have a right then to impeach and depose him because in the exercise of this trust he has been executing what he deems to be the laws and the Constitution of the United States.

Sir, in my judgment, these doctrines and these principles are not maintainable, or if they are then we have ceased to have a written Constitution, and the whole Government which we have is an arbitrary majority on this floor or some arbitrary majority in the Senate. What is the Government? What is the Constitution? What is the law? What is the beauty of our free institutions? The arbitrary rule of a temporary House of Representatives or a temporary Senate? The mere will, the caprice, the tyranny of a majority of members of Congress elected two or four or six years ago?

Sir, these illimitable, uncontrollable forms of legislative government have been tried elsewhere, and everywhere they have been found to fail. A mere majority is often more tyrannical than a king or a despotism. An oligarchy such as you are creating is the worst form of government man ever devised. The worst of all tyrannies ever created, far more odious than any one-man despotism in history, was the illimitable, uncontrollable will of a legislative majority in the French revolution, acting from passion and caprice, beyond any law or written constitution whatsoever. Yet here, in this House, overriding our written Constitution, paying no regard whatsoever to its provisions, overthrowing the whole executive authority to-day, and but yesterday destroying an august tribunal of the judiciary—the last resort of conflicting opinions short of arms—here, on this floor, in this House, misrepresenting the people in point of fact—for you do not represent the majority even of the people of the North, as the votes will show hereafter—representing now but the passion, the caprice, and the power of the past, not of the present—you are attempting to concentrate here in a majority uncontrollable and illimitable that absorption of power which destroys the two other branches of the Government, the Supreme Court of the United States, and the Executive of the United States, and which thus makes you not only supreme, but the worst sort of an oligarchy and despotism that ever cursed, unhappily, men.

Sir, the history of all such acts as this has been written by many historians and illuminates many pages of the past; but here, for the first time in the history of our country; here, on the natal day of Washington, whose farewell address invokes peace, quiet, forgetfulness of party, and devotion to the public good, whose very presence should inspire us on a great occasion like this, you, by a mere party majority, in order to obtain possession of the Executive of the United States and to have the distribution of a few offices—you propose to depose the President of the United States and to substitute a President of your own, the present president of the Senate [Benjamin F. Wade].

Go on; go on, if you choose. If I were your trusted adviser and wished to accomplish your overthrow I would hurry you on. Andrew Johnson has no power now as President of the United States. He is without authority or influence or patronage, you have so manacled whatever influence or patronage that he has. By your violent acts, by your unconstitutional proceedings, by your revolutionary overthrow of executive rights, you may succeed, if not in reëlecting him to that office, at least in immortalizing him on the pages of history as the most glorious defender of liberty that ever lived under any constitutional government. You may strip him of his office, but you will canonize him among those heroic defenders of constitutional law and liberty in whose ranks it is the highest glory of human ambition to shine. You may sacrifice him as a President, but long, long after the very name of President—a free President—shall have been forgotten in the clouds of the past his will be blazoned forth in the foreground of the present as the pole star of liberty and law to be reverenced among men.

But why is this attempted? Because it is believed that the
IX—6

Northern people of this country are now with the Democratic party; because it is believed now, previous to a presidential election, it is necessary so to manipulate and control the executive and judicial departments of the Government, by the annexation of some African states of the South, that the so-called Republicans of the North, in spite of the majority of the Northern people, shall obtain control and possession of this Government. The sacrifice of two of the three branches of government is deemed indispensably necessary to keep the Republican party in power.

I beg the party upon the other side to consider the fatal danger of establishing such a precedent as this. Suppose you succeed, suppose you make the president of the Senate President of the United States, you settle that hereafter a party having a sufficient majority in the House and the Senate can depose the President of the United States. You establish a precedent which all future parties in all time to come will look to. The curse of all other countries, the curse of France, the curse of the South American republics, has been that they have followed such a precedent as you call upon us to establish here—the overthrow of their executive, not by law, not by Constitution, but by the irregular and arbitrary and revolutionary exercise of power, in order merely to obtain a temporary possession of the Government. Is the possession of the Government, the possession of these offices from now until March, 1869, worth the sacrifices of our country, the sacrifice of our institutions we are called up to make by the report of the Committee on Reconstruction? I beg you, then, to desist from that precedent with more than common earnestness and with a horror of the future if you follow on in this wild, revolutionary course. In the name of all history as well as all right, in the name of the present, in the name of the future, in the name of your children and of mine and of our children's children, I implore you to respect the institutions of your country and to fly from and beware of this terrible, fatal precedent of the deposition of the executive branch of the Government.

John A. Bingham [O.], who had formerly opposed impeachment, replied to Mr. Brooks.

The issue involved is whether the supremacy of the Constitution shall be maintained by the people's representatives. The President of the United States has assumed, sir, to set himself above the Constitution and the laws. Heretofore I have kept myself back and have endeavored to keep others back from making any unnecessary issue between the President and the representatives of the people touching the manner in which he discharged the duties of his great office. So long as there was any doubt upon the question of his liability to impeachment within the text and spirit of the Constitution I was unwilling to utter one syllable to favor such a proposition or to record a vote to advance it.

I stand here, however, to-day, filled with a conviction as strong as knowledge that the President of the United States has deliberately, defiantly, and criminally violated the Constitution, his oath of office, and the laws of the country in the removal of Secretary Stanton.

The gentleman tells us to beware, beware, beware. Beware of what, sir? To beware of rendering a faithful obedience to our oaths as the Representatives of the people? To beware of taking the steps authorized by the Constitution and demanded by the public safety to put this usurper of authority and criminal violator of public trusts on trial before the only tribunal on earth authorized to try him for his crimes?

The gentleman assumed—and I thank him for the assumption; his warning would have been wholly unintelligible without it—that this is not the House of Representatives. He ventured to say, in order to find some justification for his significant words of warning, that this was but a partial Congress. And yet he affects to be the friend of the Constitution. I aver, and I challenge contradiction of any man living whose opinion is entitled to any respect, that a partial Congress can neither impeach anybody nor pass any law. It is a Congress composed of a Senate and House of Representatives of the United States, which alone, by the Constitution, is vested with legislative power under that great instrument. A partial Congress is unknown to the Constitution. I protest against the gentleman's pretended affection for the Constitution when he stands here before the country warning us against the discharge of our duty, and in the next breath, in order to justify himself in his strange position, telling us that we have no Congress. If we have no Congress— if this be not the House of Representatives of the United States —of course our legislation is void. If there be no Congress to impeach and remove this recusant President, there is no remedy left but for the great people themselves to come to the rescue.

I undertake to say that there is enough in the facts already disclosed in the correspondence between the President and the Secretary of War and his appointee as Secretary *ad interim* to justify this House in drawing the inference—and inference is for the grand inquest of the nation—that the President of the United States was by that act guilty of another crime under another act of Congress additional to that defined in the sixth section of the act of 1867. I refer to the act of 1861, which makes it a high crime, punishable by fine and imprisonment, for two or more persons to conspire together by force or by intimidation or by threat to attempt to prevent any person from accepting or holding any office under the United States. I undertake to say that, upon a full investigation of this case, the President of the United States will be found to have been guilty, in conjunction with Lorenzo Thomas, of attempting, by threats, by intimidation, and, if need be, by force, to prevent the Secretary of War from holding or executing the duties of the office to which he had been appointed under the Constitution, and to which he was entitled by the solemn judgment of the Senate.

And I go a step further: I undertake to say, not upon any fact proved before the committee, but upon knowledge that has been communicated to me through original sources, that this appointee of the President was giving it out in the streets of your capital on yesterday that on this day he would demand a surrender of the war office, and if it were refused and the doors closed against him he would take it by force.

The President now comes in here and tells us, and tells the country that he is to construe the Constitution for himself; and his advocate takes his place upon this floor and reiterates the offensive assumption of the President, declaring that it is the right of the President to determine for himself the constitutionality of every act we pass, and to reject, disobey, or repeal it at his pleasure, and in defiance of the power of Congress. The lawmaking power is the supreme power of the Republic, and its acts may only be reviewed by the civil tribunals of justice. Your Constitution nowhere gives to the President the power claimed to defy and repeal the laws of Congress at his pleasure.

I insist, sir, that the President himself is as much the subject of law as the humblest citizen of the Republic; and God save the Republic when he may assert the prerogative of declaring what is law and what is not law at his own pleasure, and defy the power of the people to call him to account for it.

For one, sir, I would be willing to delay indefinitely, if you please, the final action of the House upon this question, if I were fully assured that the President from this time forth would have respect to the obligations of law, and not undertake to usurp the authority of this Government in defiance of the people's Constitution and the people's laws. But, sir, I have had evidence enough in the transaction, as it is spread upon your record, to satisfy me that the President of the United States is so bent upon his own destruction, or upon the destruction of the peace of this great country, that he is capable of rushing to any extreme of madness whatever. I propose to curb him at the threshold. I propose to do it, not in the spirit of a partisan, but in the spirit of a Representative of the people, acting under the obligations of his oath, and having due regard to the requirements of the Constitution and the laws.

No one in this land would rejoice more than myself to know that when this case shall have been presented to the Senate of the United States as a high court of impeachment it shall become clear to the satisfaction of that body that the President of the United States has only erred in judgment, and has not intended to invade the Constitution or to defy the authority or set aside the supremacy of the laws. I would rejoice at his acquittal thus honorably, for his own sake and for the sake of the Constitution of my country. But, sir, in the light of what he has already declared and placed upon the record, I am precluded from the conclusion that he meant anything else than to defy your power.

The gentleman talks about liberty. I stand here to-day for that liberty which is regulated by law, that liberty which belongs alike to us all, and which is not the exclusive right of those who hold high official station.

There was surely nothing in this statute that operated oppressively upon the President of the United States. It was simply a statute under the Constitution of the United States, enabling the people of the United States to exercise their own powers as to the mode and manner of executing their own laws. I ask the President to submit to it, to submit to it gracefully, to submit to it decently, to obey it, and to set the example to all the people of the land that the first duty of the citizen is obedience to the people's laws, as it is the first duty of their Chief Magistrate to see that they be faithfully executed.

I leave the final issue where it belongs under the Constitution —with the Senate—to determine whether the President has been guilty of a violation of the law, of wilfully, deliberately, criminally violating it, and violating as well the Constitution of his country, and disregarding as well the obligation of his oath.

General John A. Logan [Ill.], answering those who feared that the impeachment might lead to revolution, said that:

A country which in time of war and excitement can stand the assassination of so good and just a President as Abraham Lincoln can and will stand the impeachment of as bad a President as Andrew Johnson.

Ebon C. Ingersoll [Ill.] read a telegram from Richard Oglesby, Governor of Illinois, saying that the people of that State demanded the impeachment, and would heartily sustain Congress in such action.

MR. INGERSOLL said that this telegram was "but the voice of the people of the whole country. I know of no man who loves his country more than party who will not pronounce a verdict against the President. And I shall for one be grievously disappointed if, within ten days from this time, honest old Ben Wade (president of the Senate) is not President of the United States."

The Democrats attempted in vain to have Washington's Farewell Address read as a rebuke to the factious spirit of the Republicans.

Sunday intervened before the House reassembled (on February 24). Mr. Ashley reopened the debate with a characteristic bitter attack upon the President.

Burton C. Cook [Ill.] followed with a short, incisive legal argument in favor of impeachment.

George W. Julian [Ind.] expressed his gratification that the President, by removing Secretary Stanton, had brought his contest with Congress to a clear issue, "beautifully consolidating into a unit all the friends of the country in the House and throughout the nation." He admitted, however, that in itself this removal "would be regarded as scarcely sufficient grounds" for impeachment, but that it was so when "considered in the light of far greater previous offences," such as the President's action in regard to the New Orleans "Massacre."

Benjamin F. Butler [Mass.] recited the acts of the President which rendered him liable to impeachment, and said in conclusion:

"For a tithe of these acts of usurpation, lawlessness, and tyranny our Fathers dissolved their connection with the government of King George; for less than this King James lost his throne, and King Charles lost his head; while we, the Representatives of the people, adjudge only that there is probable cause shown why Andrew Johnson should be deprived of the office he has desecrated and the power he has abused, and if convicted by the court to which we shall send him, be forever incapable of filling that office—the ambition to be again nominated to which has been the moving spring of all these crimes.''

George W. Woodward [Dem.], of Pennsylvania, formerly Chief-Justice of the Supreme Court of his State, urged the legal reasons against impeachment. He said that, since all the States were not represented in the House and Senate, there was no competency in the former chamber to impeach an officer, nor in the latter to try him.

''If I were the President's counselor I would advise him, if you preferred articles of impeachment, to demur to your jurisdiction and to that of the Senate, and issue a proclamation giving you and all the world notice that, while he held himself impeachable for misdemeanors in office before the constitutional tribunal, he never would subject the office he holds in trust to the irregular, unconstitutional, and fragmentary bodies who propose to strip him of it.''

Mr. Boutwell stated what in his opinion was ''the plot in which the President is engaged.''

He desires, first, to get control of the war department, in order that, as in 1861, the munitions of war, arms, and material might be used for the purpose of enabling him to succeed in his aspirations to be President of the United States. He knows that if he can corrupt the officers in charge of the Southern military departments these ten States will be in his control, and that he can send to the Democratic convention, on the 4th of July next men who would sustain his claim for the presidency. Then he can secure the electoral votes of those ten States by excluding the negroes whom we have enfranchised from all participation in the election. If by fortune he should receive a sufficient number of votes in the North to make a majority, then, with the support of the army which he had corrupted he has determined to be inaugurated President of the United States at the hazard of civil war. To-day we escape from these evils and dangers.

Later in the day Mr. Stevens [Pa.] closed the debate, which had broken all previous records in the number of speeches made in a single day, these, together with the speeches not delivered, but printed, filling more than 200 columns of the *Congressional Globe*.

Mr. Stevens prefaced his remarks by adverting to the importance of the issue.

The charge, if falsely made, did a cruel wrong to the Chief Executive of the nation; if true, proved him guilty of so atrocious usurpation as was "ever perpetrated by the most detestable tyrant who ever oppressed his fellow-men. The question, therefore, should be discussed in no partisan spirit, but with legal accuracy and impartial justice. The people desire no victim, and they will tolerate no usurper."

In order to sustain impeachment under our Constitution I do not hold that it is necessary to prove a crime as an indictable offence, or any act *malum in se*.[1] I agree with the distinguished gentleman from Pennsylvania [Judge Woodward], on the other side of the House, who holds this to be a purely political proceeding. It is intended as a remedy for malfeasance in office and to prevent the continuance thereof. Beyond that it is not intended as a personal punishment for past offences or for future example

The speaker then recounted the "official misdemeanors" of the President, beginning with the latest, the removal of Secretary Stanton. In connection with this removal he admitted to the quarrel which had arisen between the President and General Grant. In this recrimination, he said, if the President told the truth, "he is guilty of a high misdemeanor, for he avows his effort to prevent the execution of the law." If the General tells the truth, the President is again proved guilty, for the General corroborates the President's avowal, but denies complicity in the effort.

We propose to prove on the trial that Andrew Johnson was guilty of misprision of bribery by offering to General Grant, if he would unite with him in his lawless violence, to assume in his stead the penalties and to endure the imprisonment denounced by the law. Bribery is one of the offences specifically enumer-

[1] "Evil in itself."

ated for which the President may be impeached and removed from office.

The speaker then reviewed the course of the President beginning with the inauguration of his reconstruction policy, and asserted that it was in defiance of the Constitution.

If Andrew Johnson escapes with bare removal from office, if he be not fined and incarcerated in the penitentiary afterward under criminal proceedings, he may thank the weakness or the clemency of Congress and not his own innocence.

I trust that when we come to vote upon this question we shall remember that, although it is the duty of the President to see that the laws be executed, the sovereign power of the nation rests in Congress, who have been placed around the Executive as muniments to defend his rights, and as watchmen to enforce his obedience to the law and the Constitution. His oath to obey the Constitution and our duty to compel him to do it are a tremendous obligation, heavier than was ever assumed by mortal rulers. We are to protect or to destroy the liberty and happiness of a mighty people, and to take care that they progress in civilization and defend themselves against every kind of tyranny. As we deal with the first great political malefactor, so will be the result of our efforts to perpetuate the happiness and good government of the human race. The God of our fathers, who inspired them with the thought of universal freedom, will hold us responsible for the noble institutions which they projected and expected us to carry out. This is not to be the temporary triumph of a political party, but is to endure in its consequence until this whole continent shall be filled with a free and untrammeled people or shall be a nest of shrinking, cowardly slaves.

The resolution that the President be impeached was then adopted by a strictly partisan vote of 126 yeas, 47 nays, 17 absent or not voting. Of the absentees and non-voters, only one was a Democrat.

The speaker appointed Mr. Boutwell, Mr. Bingham, Mr. Wilson, General Logan, Mr. Julian, and Hamilton Ward [N. Y.] as a committee to draw up the articles of impeachment.

On February 29 the committee made its report, which was adopted on March 2 by a party vote. The House then elected the following managers of impeachment. There were, in the order of number of votes received: Mr. Bingham, Mr. Boutwell, Mr. Wilson, General Butler, Thomas Williams [Pa.], General Logan, and Mr. Stevens. The Democrats refused to vote.

On February 22 the President had sent to the Senate the nomination of Thomas Ewing, Sr. [O.], as Secretary of War. The choice of this distinguished statesman, who was known as a staunch Republican, was a shrewd challenge to the Senate, but that body refused now to accept as the issue the qualifications of the appointee, and insisted that it was whether or not a vacancy existed. To uphold their contention that Edwin M. Stanton was still Secretary of War, the Senate, on February 24, refused to accept the nomination of Mr. Ewing. Nevertheless the action of the President in making so unexceptionable a nomination tended to impress the country that he was standing upon his rights and not seeking a partisan advantage.

The trial of President Johnson before the Senate began on March 5, 1868. As the report of it belongs more properly to a work entitled "Great Trials" rather than "Great Debates" in American history, only a bare account of it will be given here. Besides, the Government published the full proceedings in a separate volume, which may be obtained by those interested as a public document.

The Trial of President Johnson

Chief-Justice Salmon P. Chase presided. Mr. Bingham, chairman of the managers, read the articles of impeachment. They related chiefly to the President's removal of Secretary Stanton, though minor offences, such as the President's harangues against Congress, in which he stated that the Thirty-ninth Congress was illegitimate, were also charged.

At the conclusion of the reading of the articles the Senate adjourned to March 13. On this day Henry Stanbery, who had resigned his position as Attorney-General to become counsel for the President, asked for

THE SMELLING COMMITTEE

From the collection of the New York Historical Society

91

a further adjournment of forty days to prepare his answer. The Senate granted him only ten days (until March 23). Associated with Mr. Stanbery as the President's counsel were Benjamin R. Curtis [Mass.], Thomas A. R. Nelson [Tenn.], William M. Evarts [N. Y.], William S. Groesbeck [O.]. Judge Curtis and Mr. Evarts took the leading part in the conduct of the case. The managers of impeachment from the House were assisted by Judge William Lawrence [O.], another Representative, who prepared a brief of the authorities upon the law of impeachable crimes and misdemeanors.

The proceedings were opened on March 13 by counsel for defence reading an answer to the articles of impeachment. The answer defended the removal of Secretary Stanton on the ground that the President was acting in the matter within his constitutional rights, and within the latitude permitted him by the Tenure-of-Office Act. The answer denied the minor charges, pointing to the President's official recognition of the Thirty-ninth Congress, etc.

On March 30 General Butler opened the case for the prosecution. While his carefully prepared agreement covered the entire ground, it dwelt upon the removal of Secretary Stanton as the impeachable act in comparison with which all the others were insignificant. By such a declaration he established this removal as virtually the only issue in the case.

At the conclusion of General Butler's argument, the managers submitted their testimony in support of the charges brought by the House. The President's speeches attacking Congress were put in evidence. The managers concluded their testimony on the fourth day of April and the Senate took a recess for five days.

On the 9th of April Judge Curtis of the President's counsel opened for the defence. He went directly to the argument, supporting *seriatim* the answers to the articles of impeachment.

Although his speech occupied two days, it was notable for precision and directness of logic and clearness and economy of expression. It made a profound impression upon the Senate and the country.

"SPOONS" [GENERAL BUTLER] AS FALSTAFF MUSTERING THE IMPEACHMENT MANAGERS

From the collection of the New York Historical Society

At the close of the judge's address, witnesses were called for the President. The defence sought to introduce evidence to prove that the President, when the Tenure-of-Office bill was before him for approval, had submitted it to the Cabinet for their advice; that these ministers had declared the bill unconstitutional, and that Secretaries Seward and Stanton had prepared the message to Congress accompanying the President's veto.

Chief Justice Chase decided that the evidence was admissible for the purpose of showing the President's intent in his subsequent actions wherein it was claimed that he violated the Tenure-of-Office Act.

Manager Wilson objected to this as "immaterial, incompetent, and irrelevant." The advice which the President may have received, and the belief which he may have formed touching the constitutionality of said act, cannot be allowed to shield him from the consequences of his criminal acts.

Senator Jacob M. Howard [Mich.] called for the yeas and nays on the decision, and the Senate, by a vote of 20 yeas and 29 nays, overruled the chair and decided that the evidence was inadmissible.

This action of the Senate, says Mr. Blaine in his "Twenty Years of Congress," impressed the public most unfavorably, offending their desire for "fair play."

When the evidence on both sides had been submitted General Logan of the prosecution, on April 22, filed his argument. In addition to being a well-prepared legal presentation of the position of the prosecution, clear in analysis of the evidence and forcible in logical deductions therefrom, it was also highly rhetorical.

Mr. Boutwell followed General Logan, speaking also for the managers of impeachment. He concluded his address on the next day, April 23. His long argument covered every point of the case, and was presented with an earnestness which gave evidence of deep personal conviction.

Judge Nelson, who hailed from the President's State and was his close personal friend, having stood with him for the Union in the trying days at the outbreak of the war and during its continuance, made a moving plea for the man who had fought his way from poverty to the chief position of the nation from which it was now purposed to hurl him into ignominy and disgrace.

Mr. Groesbeck, who followed Judge Nelson, appeared also for the defence. He particularly attacked the position taken by Mr. Boutwell that the President cannot prove nor plead the motive by which he professes to have been governed in violating the laws of the country, the necessary legal presumption being that he acted with a bad motive.

Mr. Groesbeck said that under this construction President Lincoln ought to have been convicted for suspending *habeas corpus* in the loyal States and making military arrests there, since this was without authority from Congress, and the Supreme Court had decided that it was against the express provisions of the Constitution. Lincoln, however, pleaded that his motive was to save the Union, and the Senate and House of Representatives had accepted this as a sufficient warrant, and had validated the action.[1]

Mr. Stevens of the managers was ill (he died a few weeks after the trial), and, after addressing the Senate a short time, he handed his manuscript to General Butler, who completed the reading. The address dwelt chiefly upon the attempted usurpation by the President of the powers of Congress in the matter of reconstruction, and his use of patronage and illegal attempt at the removal of officers, chiefly Secretary Stanton, to effect the same.

Mr. Williams, one of the managers, then spoke. His speech, which occupied parts of two days, introduced few new arguments of the prosecution, but materially strengthened the old ones, as well as tended to stagger the chief arguments of the defence.

In closing, Mr. Williams made what was considered by Mr. Blaine, in his account of the impeachment, to have been an "imprudent" appeal to the Senate to do what the country expected of them—not that which, regardless of popular demand, justice required of them.

Mr. Evarts, of the defence, followed. His argument

[1] See Volume VI, page 61ss.

was a long and exhaustive one, occupying three days. With the opening address of ex-Justice Curtis it was considered the strongest presentation of the President's case, and established Mr. Evarts as without a superior in the American bar. Indeed, in the combination of convincing logic and chaste rhetorical style, he probably was unequaled by any lawyer of his generation. He logically brought the charge against the President to an issue, not of political, but of personal guilt.

Mr. Stanbery, Attorney-General, who closed the argument of the defence, was suffering from illness, and delivered his address only in part, the remainder being read by a friend. Like Judge Nelson, he spoke not only as counsel of the President, but as his close personal friend. His chief legal argument was that the office of Secretary of War was not included within the Tenure-of-Office Act, and, if it were, there was still no removal of Mr. Stanton from the office.

Mr. Bingham closed for the prosecution. He spoke for three days, devoting himself to rebutting the points of the defence, especially as advanced by Mr. Evarts. He presented his argument in clear and forcible fashion, and with marked sincerity of personal conviction which profoundly impressed the Senate. By close analysis of the positions of the defence and powerful logical deduction he assembled the questions before the court of impeachment into one great issue: Has the President the right to construe for himself the Constitution and judicially to determine for himself as a guide to his actions the validity of the laws of Congress? This was for the Senate to decide, and not the Supreme Court.

At the conclusion of Mr. Bingham's address (on May 6) a certain period of time was permitted in which Senators should be allowed to prepare and record opinions on the case. Twenty-nine Senators did so, and, being eminent lawyers, their arguments compare favorably with those of the managers of impeachment and the President's counsel.

The Senate was ready to vote on May 11. Public interest in the result was intense, since the opinions of a deciding number of the Senators, who had maintained strict secrecy in regard thereto throughout the trial, could not be inferred, save from their votes on excluding testimony favorable to the President, and these were not sure indications of what would be their final determination of the case. The Senate floor was crowded by the admission to it of Representatives. Correspondents of all the great newspapers of the country were in the space allotted to the press. The diplomatic gallery was filled with representatives of foreign governments "eagerly watching," says Mr. Blaine, "the possible and peaceful deposition of a sovereign ruler"; and the galleries open to the public were packed with citizens, not only of Washington, but of States near and far, so profound was the interest of the whole nation in the decision of the unique and, next to secession and slavery, the greatest constitutional question that had arisen in the history of the nation—the conviction or the vindication of a chief magistrate charged with usurpation of the Constitution and laws which he had sworn to support.

Article XI was first voted upon. As the name of each Senator was called he arose in his place and spoke his answer "Guilty" or "Not Guilty." Thirty-five votes were in the affirmative and nineteen in the negative; this fell short by one vote of the two-thirds majority required to convict. The anti-Administration Senators who voted in the negative were William P. Fessenden [Me.], Joseph S. Fowler [Tenn.], James W. Grimes [Ia.], John B. Henderson [Mo.], Edmund G. Ross [Kan.], Lyman Trumbull [Ill.], and Peter G. Van Winkle [W. Va.].

The friends of impeachment then fought for delay in voting upon the other articles, and, by the parliamentary device of moving to rescind the resolution in regard to the order of presenting these, secured an adjournment until May 26. In the intervening time rumors were afloat that pressure was bringing to bear on Senators who had voted in the negative, but that these rumors were baseless, or, if not, that the pressure had been ineffectual, was shown, when the Senate reconvened, by the vote on Article II, which was next taken,

the result being the same as before. The fifth Senator
from the last to vote in the negative was Senator Ross
of Kansas, who, rumor had it, would change his vote
to the affirmative on this and the subsequent articles.
On Article III the vote still remained the same. Thereupon George H. Williams [Ore.] moved that the Senate,
sitting as a court of impeachment, adjourn *sine die*. The
vote upon this was 34 yeas, 16 nays, 4 Senators not voting. So the Senate adjourned. It was never reconvened
as a court of impeachment on the case of Andrew Johnson.

The impeachment having failed, Mr. Stanton returned to private life. He was appointed Associate
Justice of the Supreme Court by President Grant on
December 20, 1869, but, broken in health by his devoted
official labors during the Civil War and the strain of his
contest with President Johnson, he died four days thereafter.

President Johnson nominated General John M.
Schofield as Secretary of War a few days after the close
of the trial, and the Senate confirmed the nomination.
The General served until the close of Johnson's Administration, March, 1869.

Immediately after the trial the President renomi-
nated Mr. Stanbery for his former position as Attorney-
General. The Senate refused to confirm the nomination, and gave no reason for their action. Thereupon
the President nominated William M. Evarts, another of
his counsel, for the position, and the nomination was confirmed. Mr. Evarts served until the close of Johnson's
Administration.

As President Grant had shown in his military career,
he was not a man to submit to interference with his
subordinates. Consequently, when at the beginning of
the short session of Congress following his inauguration he realized that after its close and until the Senate
should meet again he would have his hands tied with
respect to his removal and appointment of Federal
officers by the Tenure-of-Office Act, he used his influence
with Republican leaders in the Senate and House to have
the act repealed.

AMENDMENT OF TENURE-OF-OFFICE ACT

CONGRESS, MARCH 9-31, 1869

Accordingly, on March 9, 1869, General Benjamin F. Butler [Mass.], one of the managers who had prosecuted President Johnson for violating the very act obnoxious to President Grant, introduced a bill in the House absolutely repealing the act. His demand for the previous question on the bill was granted, and the bill was passed by a vote of 138 to 16, the minority being composed entirely of Republicans.

The Senate refused to act in such haste, and referred the bill to the Judiciary Committee. On March 16, Lyman Trumbull [Ill.], chairman of the committee, reported the bill with an amendment changing the repeal into "suspension until the next session of Congress."

Allen G. Thurman [O.], a member of the minority of the committee, scouted this "cowardly evasion" of the issue, which, he said, was whether or not the power of removal is vested in the President alone.

Oliver P. Morton [Ind.] was in favor of absolute repeal of the Tenure-of-Office Act. The act was unconstitutional. It had been passed for a special purpose, which now did not exist. If it were not on the statute books no Senator would think of proposing it.

"I am of the opinion that the country gained nothing by the operation of the law even during the administration of President Johnson; and as a party man I will say that the Republican party has gained nothing by it. It was a mistake from the first."

Richard Yates [Ill.] said that he had voted for impeaching President Johnson and would do so again, for the reason that he deserved a bill like the Tenure-of-Office Act to restrain him in his conduct. It was imposed on him for a special reason: for his treachery to his party and his treason to the Government. But the case of Grant, the favorite of the people, the victorious general, the chosen administrator of Republican principles, was altogether different.

William P. Fessenden [Me.], who had voted against both the Tenure-of-Office Act and the impeachment of President Johnson, was in favor of its repeal. He expressed his weariness at hearing fulsome adulations of the new President.

Jacob M. Howard [Mich.] was not prepared to swallow his words of two years before when he supported the act. Therefore, while he would vote for its suspension, he would never vote for its repeal.

George F. Edmunds [Vt.] also favored suspension and opposed repeal. The act was a good one and ought to have been passed many years before it was, in order, at need, to restrain the abuse of executive patronage.[1]

Carl Schurz [Mo.] opined that an independently thinking man might well be in favor of the repeal of the Tenure-of-Office Act without the least inclination of prostrating himself at the foot of the throne, or without any desire to betray the constitutional prerogatives of the Senate into the hands of the Executive. He confessed that he had an ulterior purpose in the vote which he should give upon the bill: the reform of the civil service.

Senator Edmunds, fearing that the majority of Senators would vote for repeal instead of suspension, withdrew the bill, and it was recommitted on March 23. On the next day Senator Trumbull reported a substitute for the Tenure-of-Office Act which left the President free

---

[1] Upon this admission of his purpose by Senator Edmunds, Mr. Blaine, in his "Twenty Years of Congress," remarks:

"Coming from a Senator of the United States, this declaration was regarded as extraordinary. The 'bad men' to whom Mr. Edmunds referred were the appointees of President Johnson, and every one of them had been confirmed by the Senate of the United States when the Republicans had more than two-thirds of the body. If these appointees were 'bad men,' why, it was pertinently and forcibly asked by the aggrieved, did not Mr. Edmunds submit proof of the fact to his Republican associates and procure their rejection? He knew, the accused men declared, as much about their characters when their names were before the Senate as he knew now when he sought, behind the protection of his privilege, to brand them with infamy. To permit them to be confirmed in the silence and confidence of an executive session, and then in open Senate, when their places were wanted for others, to describe them as 'bad men,' seemed to them a procedure not to be explained on the broad principles of statesmanship, or even on the common law of fair dealing."

to suspend any officer without assigning a cause, and to nominate his successor. If the Senator should refuse to confirm this nominee, the President might present one nominee after another until one was reached who was satisfactory to the Senate. If the session should end without a confirmation of any, the suspended officer should be restored.

This was adopted by 37 votes to 15. The House refused to accept it, desiring to give the President a free hand in appointments. A joint conference committee was thereupon appointed, which proposed a new amendment. It was passed on March 31—in the House by a vote of 108 yeas to 67 nays, and in the Senate by 42 yeas to 8 nays. The President approved the amendment on April 5.

This amendment provided that the President, during recess of the Senate, might suspend until the end of its next session any civil officer, approved by consent of the Senate, except a Federal judge, and that he might designate, subject to removal by similar designation of another person, some suitable person to perform in the meantime the duties of the suspended officer. Thirty days after the beginning of each session of the Senate the President should present to that body a list of vacant offices, and, if the Senate refused to advise and consent to appointments for these offices, he should make nominations to fill them.

The law virtually repealed the old act, although by its involved language it could be construed as a retention of some authority by the Senate in regard to removals, thus "saving the face" of that legislative body which has ever been jealous of its dignities.

President Grant, equally insistent upon his official rights, was displeased that the act had not been wiped entirely off the statute books. In his message to Congress at the opening of the next session he presented his objections to the act and made a plea for its repeal, which, however, was not granted.

CHAPTER III

THE ELECTORAL COMMISSION

[HAYES-TILDEN ELECTION]

Disputed Contest for the Presidency in 1876—Electoral Commission Appointed to Decide It; It Reports in Favor of the Republican Candidates; Report Adopted by Congress—Speech in the House against the Seating of Hayes and Wheeler by Benjamin A. Willis [N. Y.]: ''The Basest of Conspiracies''—Reply by Simeon B. Chittenden [N. Y.]: ''Who Are the Conspirators?'' and by John R. Tucker [Va.]: ''The Fruitlessness of Fraud''—Debate in the House on the Constitutionality of the Electoral Commission: Affirmative, George F. Hoar [Mass.]; Negative, Gen. James A. Garfield [O.]—Clarkson N. Potter [N. Y.] Introduces Bill in the House to Create Commission to Investigate Hayes's Southern Vote; It Is Passed; Investigation Finds Democratic Attempts at Bribery, and Is Discontinued.

IN the Presidential campaign of 1876 the Democratic candidates, Governor Samuel J. Tilden [N. Y.], and Thomas A. Hendricks [Ind.], carried New York, New Jersey, Connecticut, and Indiana, and the Republican candidates, Governor Rutherford B. Hayes [O.], and William A. Wheeler [N. Y.], the other Northern States. The contest depended on the vote in the South. Governor Hayes's manager, Senator Zachariah Chandler [Mich.], declared on the morning after election that he had information that South Carolina, Louisiana, and Florida had gone Republican, giving Governor Hayes 185 electoral votes—a majority of one.

It was charged by the Democrats that Senator Chandler's announcement was not based on information, but was a mere claim, preparatory to an endeavor to have the votes of these States counted for Governor Hayes, even though Governor Tilden had won them. It was pointed out that the three States named were likely

FIRE AND WATER MAKE VAPOR

[Caricature of Henry Watterson and Murat Halstead]

Cartoon by Thomas Nast in "Harper's Weekly"

103

to have given a Republican majority, since in South Carolina and Louisiana there were more negroes than whites, and in Florida, where the whites were slightly in the majority, a number of these were Northern settlers, and, therefore, if the cry of fraud were raised in the event of Hayes being declared the winner in these States, the presumption would be against the cry.

The legal convassing boards gave the electoral votes of the three States to Hayes and Wheeler. The Democrats at once declared that these were false returns and that the Tilden and Hendricks electors had really been elected, but "counted out." Committees of investigation were sent to the States by both parties, the members of the Republican one being named by President Grant, who later submitted their report to Congress.

On December 6, 1876, the day prescribed for the meeting, the Electoral College sat, and declared Hayes elected by a vote of 185 to 184 cast for Tilden.

The indignation of the Democrats was at boiling point. Henry Watterson [Ky.] declared that one hundred thousand Democrats should assemble in Washington in protest against the usurpation. Joseph Pulitzer, then editor of the St. Louis *Post-Dispatch,* followed this with the declaration that they should come armed. Watterson was credited, however, with Pulitzer's proposal.[1] Against the possibility of the fulfillment of this declaration, President Grant took military precautions.

By a joint rule of Congress, adopted in February, 1865, it had been agreed that "no electoral vote objected to shall be counted except by the concurrent votes of the two Houses." The Democrats, with the intention of objecting to enough Republican votes to leave Tilden with a majority, claimed that this rule was still in force. The Republicans held that it was applicable only to the occasion of its adoption, and that the Vice-President had resumed his constitutional right to open the returns of the Electoral College and declare the result. Finally (on December 14, 1876) the House passed

[1] See Mr. Watterson's article on the Hayes-Tilden contest in the *Century* for May, 1913.

abounded with exultant expressions of joy, hope, and thanksgiving. Republican editorials were crowded with philosophic reflections counseling acquiescence and submission. All save basest partisans indulged in a sigh of relief that the ordeal was over. American securities became buoyant and advanced in value. Confidence sprang into life. Joy and prosperity were, seemingly, just ahead.

But, gentlemen, when unprincipled party leaders recovered from the shock of their defeat they conjured up a fiend in their hearts. Audacious assertions that Tilden had been defeated were made and persisted in. Though the people disbelieved, apprehension and distrust came, and with them a period of gloom and depression which veils us in the black darkness of night. The people seized the meaning of these reckless assertions. They knew by sad experience that the authors of them were men wholly wanting in scruples, wholly strangers to honor. They knew instinctively that a conspiracy was determined upon involving the overthrow of popular government by the inauguration of a defeated candidate as President. They know it to-day, and ere long those plotters will realize the existence of a power before which their conspiracy will break away as do unstable dams when overridden by a flood—a people terribly in earnest to avenge their wrongs.

They who but a few weeks before declared that the South was a solid unit for Tilden and Hendricks now vociferously proclaim that South Carolina, Florida, and Louisiana have voted for Hayes.

Why South Carolina, Florida, and Louisiana? Palpably because they cast just enough votes to give Hayes and Wheeler a majority of one in the electoral college.

Does any man, knowing the conspirators, familiar with their methods and their desperation, doubt that, had it been necessary for their purpose, they would have insisted just as emphatically that North Carolina or Mississippi, or both, had voted the same way?

But those three States were sufficient for the end in view; they abounded in apt agencies, in men who could escape righteous retribution only by a continuance of this administration in power. Election laws were in force there, enacted for the express purpose of perpetuating their authority. Returning boards were there whose crimes, already exposed and denounced by honest men of all parties, by the voice of honorable committees appointed by both Houses of Congress, were such as to give assurance to their masters that they were equal to any infamy;

even to that infamy which towers above all others, as does the giant peak above the surrounding earth: the murder of American liberty. They had a Chief Magistrate already practiced in assaults upon the rights of his countrymen, who had already caused every honest cheek to blush with shame and every honest heart to throb with madness by the use of bayonet and cannon in suppressing the voice of the people. Could not the men who had perpetrated the foul crime against Louisiana in 1874 perpetrate anew the same crime in 1876? So they, instigators of this conspiracy, believed, and so they trusted not vainly.

Armies were hurriedly forwarded to the States in question, with orders to sustain the criminal returning boards and uphold the tottering wretches who misgovern and oppress their peoples; sent sometimes on a plea of suppressing domestic violence, as in Louisiana, where no violence occurred; sometimes, as in Florida, without any pretext whatever, where no justification is even claimed; sometimes, as in South Carolina, for the pretended reason that the National Government had been called upon to secure to the people a republican form of government. Where no outbreak had occurred the army has—shame—a shame human lips cannot express—upon its officers!—overthrown republican government by stamping upon the mandates of its highest courts.

Oh, how American manhood is debased, how American soldiership is sullied by the example of a Ruger! Unhappy Republic, when the defenders of its people become their oppressors! This is no novel experience. Strange these soldiers have such poor memories! After Sheridan had by his cold-blooded, heartless crime against the people of Louisiana oppressed the people with sadness and shame, provoking a feeling of wrathful resentment in the heart of every honest man, Democrat or Republican, the President in his annual message denounced the wrong and declared its commission to be without his authority.

He evidently had learned a lesson from Cæsar Borgia, who, after conquering Romagna, appointed Ramiro d'Orco as governor and gave him limitless authority. He oppressed the people by his baseness and cruelty; when Cæsar Borgia, who had instigated all, intent only upon his schemes, with a view of escaping the reproaches which were justly his due, caused Ramiro to be massacred in the market-place, before the eyes of all the people.

Our President did not massacre Sheridan, nor even cashier him, but he did not hesitate to do that which to a soldier of honor should be deemed a punishment more disgraceful than death. He made him the scorn of his countrymen.

In Gen. Thomas H. Ruger he found another Ramiro, and soon poor Ruger will be abandoned and disowned; at least so soon as the purposes of the Executive or of his party can be subserved thereby.

The President then, to resume the narrative, issued an order, in language which justly inspired the whole people with pride and confidence, insisting that a fair count should be had, and called upon certain gentlemen to proceed to New Orleans and elsewhere, and supervise the action of the returning board.

The President assumed the boards were dishonest, or wherefore have them watched? Why shoot arrows at the stars?

Then, indeed, very many believed that the President, a man who had carved through hostile legions a pathway to victory; whose brow had been laureled with glory by a grateful people; who had been honored, even as he who was first in war, first in peace, and first in the hearts of his countrymen, by a reëlection as Chief Magistrate, would in the hour of supreme peril have a proper consciousness of duty, and once more place his countrymen under an obligation which would cause him to be glorified in remembrance by after-generations. They dared, in a moment when hope was in the ascendant, to be oblivious of his political offences and to think that he might agreeably disappoint the country by asserting an honorable manhood as he did so unexpectedly before when he vetoed what was known as the inflation bill. By satisfying a hope so just the President could have climbed upon the heights of Olympus. He chose rather to descend.

The committee then sent to those States, as I have remarked, refused to confer with political opponents who were there in the interest of justice; they encouraged the returning boards in their work of infamy; they gave the plotters to understand that the military arm of the Government was behind them and would sustain them in any crime they might commit against a bleeding and oppressed people; they entered into conclave with conspirators, and, so well assured were they of the result already agreed upon, that weeks before any adjudication upon the returns was had, and when they showed *prima facie* an acknowledged majority for Tilden electors, telegraphed over the North that a given number of parishes would be thrown out sufficient to secure the electoral votes of those States for Hayes. What I have said everybody knows to be true; every step taken by this election board, either through the Administration or its agents, gives indubitable proof of a conspiracy to overthrow popular government.

Now, let it be understood, when I say the American people will never submit to the overthrow of self-government by conspirators.

There lives not an honest, patriotic citizen, Democrat or Republican, but would, if he could, suffer death a hundred times rather than behold the wreck of liberty, wrought by a scoundrelly returning board, upheld and spurred on by unworthy rulers. Such a conspiracy under the auspices of a Cæsar or a Napoleon might be borne; but submission to a conspiracy under the auspices of a returning board composed of scalawags and Federal officers would imply a moral degradation disgraceful even in a South American republic. Anglo-Saxon manhood will never fall to such a depth in the world's scorn and contempt.

This conspiracy has exposed the nation to a peril mightier than any it has ever encountered. It has aiders and abettors in every branch of the Government. Foreign war means expenditure of blood and treasure and the glory and shame consequent upon victory or defeat. Rebellion meant a Union saved or a divided Republic; in either case liberty would not perish. Today we are staggered by an unhallowed attempt to blight and destroy, utterly and forever, the divine right of the people to govern themselves. How to avert this peril, how to rescue this people from a destiny the contemplation of which curdles the blood and palsies the lips, is the fearful problem to be solved, wisely, if at all, by the sworn Representatives, not of a party, but of a people.

If we fall not far short of our obligations the toils will be speedily broken; the chains forged by conspirators will melt in the hot wrath of the people; it is our especial province to right every wrong, to pursue every fraud, until a just result is reached and self-government made triumphant. Some gentlemen seem to doubt our power, and to regard with nonchalance the fraudulent manipulation of canvassers and returning boards, because they are State officers, subject only to State laws, beyond the reach of Federal interference or Federal authority. Such a shallow pretence cannot stand alone or be supported for an instant. It only occurs to them as a convenience, as a dodge. It is belied by their own acts!

Why did Federal troops proceed to the State of South Carolina, and there, under the direction of an unprincipled and insignificant man by the name of Dennis, interfere with the organization of a State legislature and give moral support to Chamberlain and his confederates?

Why was a Federal judge dispatched there to spit upon the

mandates of the highest State court and to give impunity to the men who were in contempt for a disregard of its orders?

Why were troops hurried to Florida to overawe Democrats and encourage fraud? Why were United States bayonets and cannon put at the service of unconscionable partisans; and why were they sheltered by United States authority?

Why were partisans commissioned to go to Louisiana and elsewhere, on the plea of securing an honest count and in consummating a conspiracy?

Why all these things, I inquire, if those counts were State matters, with which the people had nothing to do?

This reasoning was not employed until villainy had done its worst, until the popular result in three States had been reversed by Federal interference, Federal intimidation, and Federal support. Now you want to profit by the fraud, it becomes necessary to abandon old tactics. You say a wrong done by the Federal Government the Federal Government cannot undo.

To the winds with such false logic. You may urge the troops were sent to secure a republican form of government. If no republican form of government existed in these States, assuredly they could not participate in that sovereign duty which implies a free exercise of choice on the part of electors, the election of President and Vice-President of the United States, and it follows their votes cannot be counted. If republican government was not overthrown the army had no business there, the rights of the people were invaded and trampled upon without possible justification.

In any case the result of the elections in those States would not have been reversed but for the interposition of Federal authority. What has been done by Federal authority will be undone by Federal authority.

The President is a mere agent of the people; the Constitution and laws made pursuant thereto are together the letter of his authority.

What he has done in the South is outside of the Constitution, is in defiance of the Constitution, and must be disowned and made of no effect by us. The product of this unconstitutional interference is, the people of the United States have had their will nullified and their sovereignty usurped.

Some justify the conduct of the Executive by the assumption that those States are naturally Republican. Distinguished party leaders have asserted that they will never permit the electoral vote of a State where negroes are in a majority to be counted for Tilden and Hendricks. The same men who assert this to-day before the election endeavored to rekindle the furious hates of a struggle ten years ago well ended by the cry of a solid South.

Gentlemen, this will not do. Ten years of misrule and oppression have brought starvation and sorrow to the freedmen!

Wherever Republican rule has obtained, chaos still presides —social order and security are unknown.

Wherever virtue and intelligence have dominated over carpet-bag rule business has revived and peace reigns.

The colored men have been robbed of their earnings by fraudulent savings-banks; they have been stuffed with lying promises; they have been deceived until deception no longer availeth.

The negroes are intelligent beings. Why wonder, then, that they are undeceived? Why wonder that they prefer peace rather than tumult; plenty rather than want; honest Democrats rather than dishonest Republicans; their old friends and masters rather than adventurers, who have proved to them devouring vultures.

Gentlemen, no man in this country detested slavery more than I; no man welcomed the proclamation of emancipation more than I; and therefore do I, for humanity's sake, protest against the attempt to bind the black man with chains more galling than those which, by God's providence, were snapped asunder in war.

The colored men understand all this; they are turning away with a sense of loathsomeness from their deceivers, and when the arm of Federal power is withheld, under the auspices of a benigner rule, they will overthrow the last vestige of carpet-bag rule on this continent.

Gentlemen, dismiss all thought of further prosecuting a conspiracy against the people, forego your plans of insisting that the President of the Senate shall count the vote, or that a decision shall be delayed until after the 4th of March; abandon any project which will result in an interregnum, and meanwhile expose the country to the terrors of revolution and blast with ruin the industries of the land; by one grand sacrifice suffer your ambitions, your plans, your prejudices, your hates, to be lost in a devotion to country which is as much beyond the fealty to party as the religion of Christ excels the creeds of the heathen.

Do not suppose you will profit by the conspiracy. Whether it fails or wins it will be the same to you. You will find all the comfort you are entitled to in the words Addison causes Sempronius to speak when urged to wrong:

Know, villains, when such paltry slaves presume
To mix in treason, if the plot succeeds
They're thrown neglected by, but if it fails
They're sure to die like dogs.

No trifling can be borne. Depart from precedents, trample on the Constitution, you defy the will of forty millions of freemen; you proclaim revolution.

Why, a crime of such tremendous magnitude as that contemplated has not been committed in the world's history. It might be tolerated were it of temporary consequence, but it involves the destruction of all confidence, all hope. If a party can prolong its authority for four years, why not for forty years? Why not for all time?

We are to-day standing face to face with a monster peril which must be met now if ever. The conspirators who threaten with rebellion our laws and liberties are criminals indescribably base; but infinitely more guilty will we be if by indifference, neglect, or cowardice we permit the success of the conspiracy. We shall have no excuse to urge. We have the power; what we need is the inclination to use it. The Constitution of our fathers is all-sufficient; wise precedents all along our history light our pathway.

Public opinion, burning with indignation at the commission of unequaled frauds, is urging us to be firm and constant. If we waver or betray, may Omnipotence crush with the thunderbolts of His wrath the walls of the Capitol, for they are hallowed by memories too sacred to survive such awful sacrilege!

The sovereign prerogative, the exalted duty of vindicating the right of the people to govern themselves, is ours. That prerogative, God helping us, we will assert; that duty we will piously perform. If we fail we will blacken our souls with cowardice, perjury, treason; we will permit and connive at the most unhallowed conspiracy ever planned against liberty and civilization. We will summon from the depths of hell the red demon war, and unchain his furies over this fair land.

But, Mr. Speaker, let us have a clear and accurate sense of what our duty is and resolutely determine to do it. All will then be well. We will cause the centennial year to surpass in glory all other years, for we will secure all through the coming ages a Government based upon the law of equal freedom. Despite the corruptions of our latter years, the reign of vice and profligacy which has poisoned as the blight of death; despite false notions of government, false sense of duty and responsibility engendered by war, there is a reserve force of virtue in this land; there is a moral consciousness in the minds of our people which will evoke from chaos a reign of peace, purity, and plenty.

Simeon B. Chittenden [N. Y.] replied to his colleague.

WHO ARE THE CONSPIRATORS

SIMEON B. CHITTENDEN, M.C.

Two hundred and one of the two hundred and ninety-two members of this body have studied law. I do not doubt that the legal members of this House are entirely competent and equipped to discuss the great constitutional questions which now agitate the country, including the status of the Louisiana returning board and the horrible conspiracy which my colleague, Mr. Willis, this morning so vividly revealed to us on this side of the House.

I have no doubt that the legal members of this body are fully prepared to discuss these questions to the end of the session or the century without coming to any practical conclusions thereon. It is the easiest and most natural thing in the world that lawyers should love to discuss such questions. But I say, Mr. Chairman, that the people of this country at this hour do not enjoy these eternal diatribes. Scourged by war and debt, sunk to the deepest pit of commercial and political demoralization, by reason of a genuine conspiracy, which culminated in the wickedest rebellion in all history, to which my friend did not allude, the people of this country cry to-day for wise and temperate counsels, for patriotic and practical statesmanship to lift them from a horrible pit to a better national life.

I wish to say to my colleague that, if I understand the popular thought and heart of the country, the priceless boon which the people craved in those hours and days of supreme peril, now in my judgment happily passed forever, were voices of genius and patriotism, which, ringing through these halls, should be heard in every hamlet and city in the land, speaking light and peace to the dark currents of party spirit.

Sir, let us not deceive ourselves. The people thank God for the report of the joint committee made the day before yesterday. The mass of the people will confirm that report with a unanimity which has scarcely been matched since the election of Washington to the presidency in 1789. The spirit and con-

THE PIRATES UNDER FALSE COLORS—CAN THEY CAPTURE THE SHIP OF STATE?

Cartoon by Thomas Nast, in campaign of 1872

From the collection of the New York Public Library

clusion of that report will, unless I am entirely mistaken in regard to the popular sense, sweep and control the popular judgment of the people of this country as fire driven by the wind sweeps and burns the browned and parched prairies of the West in autumn. I hope, Mr. Speaker, that the voice of the people will be listened to. It must be listened to, or our institutions are gone. We have descended as far as we can go. We have to look upward, to act upward, not in the spirit of partisans. I say it without any disrespect—not in the uncharitable spirit my good friend and colleague [Mr. Willis] manifested this morning, in broadly intimating that the party of this side of the House and all who believe as I do in the election of Hayes and Wheeler are conspirators. Let us have done with all such stuff. Let all hard words be dropped. We have had partisanship enough. The people of the country will not be misled by such nonsense. They think and act, and will expect and compel us to act, on principles of eternal justice in regard to this matter, now soon to be settled.

Corrupt elections are no new thing under the sun. From the time of the consular republic of Rome to the last election in New Orleans it has been so. Everybody knows that corrupt elections are as old as the history of republics. Why, then, all this howling about corrupt elections at the South? Was there no such thing ever heard of before? My colleague knows perfectly well that never on the face of the earth, since the name of republic was heard, have there been more shamefully corrupt elections than he and I have both submitted to in the State and city of New York. Every attempt to make the American people or the world believe that there was anything exceptional in the corruptions which have happened in this last presidential election, when made by an intelligent man, is insincere and untruthful, and designed to mislead.

I believe that the latest elections in at least three of the Southern States were an absolute farce. I do not think there is any other word to express it. I believe that must be the final conclusion of every fair-minded man. I believe that the leaders of both parties did all they could to carry their tickets, and the result was what I have stated, and according to the forms of law Hayes and Wheeler have been elected President and Vice-President of the United States. And I claim and sincerely believe that all the advantages of fair consideration are in favor of their inauguration; the cheating on both sides having been so absolutely universal that it is impossible for anybody to determine where the real truth lies. I venture to say that there is not a candid gentleman on either side of the House who, sitting by my fireside, will not admit most, if not all, that I claim.

It is a crime for us to threaten to tear this country to pieces or to mar or to destroy its material interests under such a condition of things for either party. I moreover wish to confess myself, according to the doctrines preached by my colleague this morning, a conspirator. I am a conspirator, if his conspiracy exists, and, while I do not court anything disreputable, I think I can stand his indictment. If I understood him, he included among the conspirators those who believe that the President of the Senate has a right to count the electoral vote in case of need. But it will forever remain in the archives of the Government that the framers of the Constitution, when they came to interpret their own words in regard to counting the electoral vote for the first time, elected a president of the Senate, there being no Vice-President, for the sole purpose of counting the vote, and it was in that way that the first president was elected.

On January 23 John R. Tucker [Va.], at the close of a long and learned discussion of the power of Congress in regard to the election of the President, said:

THE FRUITLESSNESS OF FRAUD

JOHN R. TUCKER, M. C.

If the chicanery and false devices of the day shall succeed in placing in the presidency one whose title is tainted with fraud, then may we, in the language of an unpublished poem of a half century ago, follow the method therein described in respect to our children:

> Hence, if you have a son, I would advise—
> Lest his fair prospects in the State you spoil—
> If you would have him in the State to rise,
> Instead of Grotius, let him study Hoyle!

> And if he show
> A turn for petty tricks, indulge the bent;
> A dextrous cut may rule some great event,
> And a stocked pack may make a President!

God forbid, Mr. Speaker, on the threshold of our second century, a President should ascend the chair of state with hands stained with blood or begrimed with fraud. His triumph would be fruitless. A people's wrath would

Hurl the wretch from high;
To bitter scorn a sacrifice,
And grinning infamy!

A title to the presidency fifty years ago tainted with the mere suspicion of fraud consigned a great son of Massachusetts [John Quincy Adams] to comparative retirement and barred the doors of the executive department forever against the favorite son of Kentucky [Henry Clay]. God in His mercy grant that we may start our second century with the noble purpose to elevate and purify our public morals; to return to the simple virtues and principles of our fathers; to cherish mutual respect, where self-respect has not been violated; to repair the breaches in our Constitution, by subordinating the military always and everywhere to the civil power; and so to reduce the army that, while it shall shield our borders from the invader and the savage, it can never be a sword to pierce the vitals of our liberties; to check expenditures; reduce taxation; and diminish the patronage of the purse, twin foe, with the sword, of a people's freedom; to forget the troubles of our civil strife, except as admonitions to the practice of forbearance, justice, and truth, and as an incentive to deeper devotion to our federative Republic of self-governed commonwealths; and, clearing the deck of the old ship Constitution of the *débris* of civil convulsion and of the corruption of maladministration growing out of the war, may we, with one heart, as a gallant crew of brother-patriots, trusting with simple faith in the God of our Christian land, spread again her sails, direct her course by the chart of our free institutions and by the pole star of honor to the haven of an enduring peace, with our freighted liberties safe, and the true happiness and glory of the people of these sister States, in one common and united country, assured to them and their posterity forever!

On January 25 George F. Hoar [Mass.] spoke in the House in support of the bill to appoint the Electoral Commission.

CONSTITUTIONALITY OF THE ELECTORAL COMMISSION

GEORGE F. HOAR, M.C.

MR. HOAR.—Mr. Speaker, the danger which our wisest writers on the Constitution years ago predicted and dreaded now confronts the American people. The Constitution contains no express provision for that determination of disputed questions of law or fact which it terms counting the electoral vote. The wisest students of its complicated mechanism have expressed their fear that it would give way, not in resisting foreign force or civil dissension, not even by decay or corruption, but because of its vague and imperfect provisions for determining that most vital of all questions, the title to executive power. With that peril, under circumstances of special difficulty, we have now to deal.

In estimating this danger I am not affected by any fear of civil war or any menace of violence. Such threats, if made in the spirit of empty bluster, deserve nothing but contempt; if serious, the swift and indignant scorn and condemnation of the whole people.

I do not dwell upon any apprehension of violent resistance to the lawful authority of the Government. The evil of civil war—so great that even to threaten it is a grievous crime—is only surpassed by the greater evil of yielding one jot of lawful authority to menace. But I do hold that nothing could be more injurious to the whole Republic, nothing more destructive to the principles that I myself hold dear, than that a man holding them shall be placed in the presidential office whom at least one-half of the American people will regard as an usurper by an act of power which at least one-half of the people will regard as an usurpation.

I shall not attempt to add another to the arguments of the constitutional question: With whom is the power to determine those grave questions of law and fact which may arise in determining what votes have been lawfully cast for President and Vice-President by the electoral colleges? I admit that those persons who believe that the Constitution requires the president of the Senate in all cases to perform that office must deem this bill unconstitutional. I do not expect the votes of such persons for the bill, unless they think that the recent almost unanimous acquiescence of Senate and House in a different construction, supported by a current of great authorities, including John Marshall, Daniel Webster, and Abraham Lincoln, may induce them to treat the question as concluded, or at least so far to yield their individual judgment as to deal with it as one of doubt.

This consideration may perhaps especially commend itself to those gentlemen who in the presence of a great temptation have honestly changed their opinions on a grave question of constitutional law. Fortunate is that statesman to whom

long-settled and matured convictions are sufficient for the solution of the ever new and various problems of his public life,

> Who in the height of conflict keeps the law
> In calmness made, and sees what he foresaw.

For myself three considerations make me deem it incredible
that the framers of the Constitution, or the people who accepted
it, ever meant or could mean to intrust the power of deciding
these vast questions to the president of the Senate, subject to no
control of the two Houses of Congress or of the law-making
power.

First.   They were a generation of men that dreaded above
all other things the usurpation of executive power.

Second.   They expected that the president of the Senate
would ordinarily be one of the candidates whose claim to the
office was to be decided.   They provided that two persons should
be voted for for president, of whom that one having the second
highest number of votes was to become Vice-President, and
President of the Senate.   The President of the Senate, therefore, must within four years have been a leading candidate for
the presidency.   The habit of continuing the same persons in
public station doubtless led them to anticipate that he would be
a leading candidate for the succession, as has first happened
when Adams succeeded Washington, when Jefferson succeeded
Adams, when Van Buren succeeded Jefferson, and in many cases
of unsuccessful competition.   The same suggestions apply to all
cases where the Vice-President is a candidate for reëlection.

Third.   As in Great Britain, from which our institutions
were derived, Parliament for centuries has regulated the inheritance of the Crown and determined all questions of right
to the succession, so, in every American State in existence when
the Constitution of the United States was adopted, the legislature, at that time, either itself elected the governor or counted
the votes of the people and decided all disputes as to the popular choice.

As the Vice-President—

Says Alexander Hamilton—

may occasionally be a substitute for the President, all the reasons which
recommend the mode of election prescribed for the one apply with great,
if not equal, force to the manner of appointing the other.

There are three other theories, with none of which is this bill
in conflict:

First. That the President of the Senate must count the vote in the absence of concurrent action by the two Houses, or of other provision by the law-making power.

Second. That under the power expressly conferred by the Constitution upon Congress to make "all laws which shall be necessary and proper for carrying into execution the foregoing powers, and all other powers vested by this Constitution in the Government of the United States, or in any department or officer thereof," the law-making power may provide a method for counting the vote.

Third. That the power of counting the vote is vested by the Constitution in the two Houses voting separately. The two Houses of Congress are the tribunal which, according to this bill, is to execute this grave authority. If they have it by the Constitution it is left undisturbed. If it needs the forces of the law-making power to confer it this bill confers it. The only case when any other aid comes in is when the two members of which the final tribunal is composed differ in their judgment. Certainly it is within the law-making power to provide what shall happen when the members of a constitutional tribunal composed of even numbers are equally divided in judgment. We may surely provide by law that, if the Supreme Court, composed of six or ten members, be equally divided in opinion, the judgment of the court below shall stand, or a report of a reference shall be accepted. The commission is not an umpire. It is not an arbitration. It is an agency inferior to the two Houses, reporting to them, its action wholly subject to theirs, but only to stand when the two Houses are divided. The warmest advocate of the constitutional powers of the Houses must concede that this bill comes within the very letter of the definition of the law-making powers of Congress; a "law necessary and proper for carrying into execution the powers vested in the Government and in every department thereof." Unless this power exist in Congress of providing by law for the case where the two members of this tribunal composed of an even number, House and Senate, stand divided on any question one to one, the advocates of the power of the two Houses to count the vote must believe that the framers of the Government meant it should perish when the not improbable case should arise of a division in sentiment between two political bodies on any question of law or fact which should arise in counting the vote.

Some gentlemen have spoken of this as a *compromise* bill. There is not a drop of compromise in it. I do not mean that, after it was found that the principle of securing an able and

impartial tribunal conformed to the opinions and desires of all
the committee, there was not some yielding of individual views
as to detail. But how can that man be said to compromise who,
having a just and righteous claim, asserts it, maintains it, en-
forces it by argument and proof, yields no jot or tittle of it
before a tribunal so constituted as to insure its decision in accordance with justice and righteousness so far as the lot of
humanity will admit? I think justice and right are compromised when they are submitted for their decision to force. They
are compromised when they can only be maintained by doubtful
disputed exercises of power. They never can be compromised
when they are permitted to stand before a tribunal clothed with
judicial powers, surrounded by judicial safeguards, invested
with legal authority by the law-making power of the country.

Let it not be said that this reasoning implies that truth and
error stand on an equality; that it makes no difference whether
matters be settled right or wrong provided only they be settled.
It is precisely because truth and error differ; it is because of the
vast difference between the righteous result and its antagonist,
that we propose to submit the differences between them not to
force, not to heat and passion, but to that tribunal which, among
all mechanisms possible to be executed by law, is least liable to
be diverted from the truth.

But it is charged that this commission is in the end to be
made up of seven men who of course will decide for one party,
and seven men who of course will decide for the other, and who
must call in an umpire by lot, and that therefore you are in
substance and effect putting the decision of this whole matter
upon chance. If this be true, never was a fact so humiliating
to the Republic confessed since it was inaugurated. Of the
members of our National Assembly, wisest and best selected for
the gravest judicial duty ever imposed upon man, under the
constraint of this solemn oath can there be found in all this
Sodom not ten, not one to obey any other mandate but that of
party? Far otherwise was the thought of Madison when with
exultant aspiration he commended the Constitution to his countrymen:

In cases where it may be doubtful on which side justice lies, what
better umpires could be desired by two violent factions, flying to arms and
tearing the State to pieces, than the representatives of Confederate States
not heated by the local flame? To the impartiality of judges they would
unite the affection of friends. Happy would it be if such a remedy for its
infirmities could be enjoyed by all free governments; if a project equally
effectual could be established for the universal peace of mankind.—*James
Madison, in "The Federalist," No. 43.*

But I especially repudiate this imputation when it rests upon those members of the commission who are to come from the Supreme Court. It is true there is a possibility of bias arising from old political opinions even there, and this, however minute, the bill seeks to place in exact equilibrium. But this small inclination, if any, will in my judgment be overweighted a hundredfold by the bias pressing them to preserve the dignity, honor, and weight of their judicial office before their countrymen and before posterity. They will not consent by a party division to have themselves or their court go down in history as incapable of the judicial function in the presence of the disturbing element of partisan desire for power, in regard to the greatest cause ever brought into judgment. Mr. Speaker, the act we are about to do will, in my judgment, be one of the greatest in history. Our annals have been crowded with great achievements in war and peace, in art, in literature, in commerce. But other countries, other republics have equaled us in these things. But in this great act we shall stand without a rival or an example. For a thousand years our children, with tears of joy and pride, will read that while in the fierce strife for executive power the sun of other republics has gone down in darkness and in blood, in their own country, too, the same great peril has arisen. Their sky has been darkened by the same cloud; their ship with its costly freight of love and hope encountered the same storm and was driven near the same rock; but in the midst of storm and darkness and conflict the august and awful figure of law rose over the face of the waters, uttering its divine, controlling mandate, Peace, be still! [Applause.]

General James A. Garfield [O.] replied to Mr. Hoar.

Unconstitutionality of the Electoral Commission

James A. Garfield, M. C.

I desire in the outset to recognize whatever of good there is in this bill. It has some great merits which I cheerfully recognize. It is intended to avoid strife in a great and trying crisis of the nation. It is intended to aid in tiding over a great present difficulty, possibly a great public danger. It will doubtless bring out a result. And, when it has brought out a result, it will leave the person who is declared to be the elect of the nation with a clearer title, or, rather, with a more nearly undisputed title, than any method that has yet been suggested.

These are certainly great results. At a time like this, no man should treat lightly a bill which may and probably will produce them all. Furthermore, I feel bound to say, if I were to speak of this bill only as a partisan—a word much abused just now—I should say that I am not afraid of its operation. The eminent gentlemen who are to compose the commission, eminent for their character and abilities, will, I have no doubt, seek to do and will do justice under its provisions. And, therefore, believing as I do that Rutherford B. Hayes has been honestly and legally elected President of the United States, I confidently expect that this commission will find that to be the fact and will declare it. Should they find otherwise, all good men everywhere will submit to their decision.

But neither the wishes nor the fate of Mr. Hayes or Mr. Tilden should be consulted in considering this bill. I presume no one here is authorized to speak for either of these gentlemen on the question. I certainly am not. It is our business to speak for ourselves and for the people whom we represent.

Before considering the bill itself, I pause to notice one of the reasons that have been urged in its favor.

We have been told to-day in this chamber that there is danger of civil war if the bill does not pass. I was amazed at the folly which could use such a suggestion as an argument in favor of this or any measure.

The Senate at Rome never deliberated a moment after the flag was hauled down which floated on the Janiculum Hill, across the Tiber. That flag was the sign that no enemy of Rome, breathing hot threats of war, had entered the sacred precincts of the city; and, when it was struck, the Senate sat no longer. The reply to war is not words but swords.

When you tell me that civil war is threatened by any party or State in this Republic, you have given me a supreme reason why an American Congress should refuse, with unutterable scorn, to listen to those who threaten, or to do any act whatever under the coercion of threats by any power on the earth. With all my soul I despise your threat of civil war, come it from what quarter or what party it may. Brave men, certainly a brave nation, will do nothing under such compulsion. We are intrusted with the work of obeying and defending the Constitution. I will not be deterred from obeying it because somebody threatens to destroy it. I dismiss all that class of motives as unworthy of Americans.

On this occasion, as on all others, let us seek only that which is worthy of ourselves and of our great country.

Self-reverence, self-knowledge, self-control—
These three alone lead life to sovereign power.
Yet not for power (power of herself
Would come uncalled for), but to live by law,
Acting the law we live by without fear;
And, because right is right, to follow right,
Were wisdom in the scorn of consequence.

Let such wisdom and such scorn inspire the House in its consideration of the pending measure.

What, then, are the grounds on which we should consider a bill like this? It would be unbecoming in me or in any member of the Congress to oppose it on mere technical or trifling grounds. It should be opposed, if at all, for reasons so broad and so weighty as to overcome all that has been said in its favor, and all the advantages which I have here admitted may follow from its passage. I do not wish to diminish the stature of my antagonist; I do not wish to undervalue the points of strength in a measure before I question its propriety. It is not enough that this bill will tide us over a present danger, however great. Let us for a moment forget Hayes and Tilden, Republicans and Democrats; let us forget our own epoch and our own generation; and, entering a broader field, inquire how this thing which we are about to do will affect the great future of our Republic; and in what condition, if we pass this bill, we shall transmit our institutions to those who shall come after us. The present good which we shall achieve by it may be very great, yet, if the evils that will flow from it in the future must be greater, it would be base in us to flinch from trouble by entailing remediless evils upon our children.

In my view, then, the foremost question is this: What will be the effect of this measure upon our institutions?

The creation of a President under our Constitution consists of three distinct steps: First, the creation of the electoral colleges; second, the vote of the colleges; and, third, the opening and counting of their votes. This is the simple plan of the Constitution.

The creation of the colleges is left absolutely to the States, within the five limitations I had the honor to mention to the House a few days ago: first, that it must be a *State* that creates it; second, that the State is limited as to the number of electors they may appoint; third, that electors shall not be members of Congress, nor officers of the United States; fourth, that the time for appointing electors may be fixed by Congress; and, fifth, the date when their appointment is announced, which must be before the time for giving their votes, may also be fixed by Congress.

These five simple limitations, and these alone, were laid upon the States. Every other act, fact, and thing possible to be done in creating the electoral colleges was absolutely and uncontrollably in the power of the States themselves. Within these limitations Congress has no more power to touch them in this work than England or France. That is the first step.

The second is still plainer and simpler, namely, the work of the colleges. They were created as an independent and separate power, or set of powers, for the sole purpose of electing a President. They were created by the States. Congress has just one thing to do with them, and only one; it may fix the day when they shall meet. By the act of 1792 Congress fixed the day as it still stands in the law; and there the authority of the Congress over the colleges ended.

There was a later act, of 1845, which gave to the States the authority to provide by law for filling vacancies of electors in these colleges, and Congress has passed no other law on the subject.

The States having created them, the time of their assemblage having been fixed by Congress, and their power to fill vacancies having been regulated by State laws, the colleges are as independent in the exercise of their functions as is any department of the Government within its sphere. Being thus equipped, their powers are restrained by a few simple limitations laid upon them by the Constitution itself; first, they must vote for a native-born citizen; second, for a man who has been fourteen years a resident of the United States; third, at least one of the persons for whom they vote must not be a citizen of their own State; fourth, the mode of voting and certifying their returns is prescribed by the Constitution itself. Within these simple and plain limitations, the electoral colleges are absolutely independent of the States and of Congress.

These colleges are none the less sovereign and independent because they exist only for a day. They meet on the same day in all the States; they do their work summarily, in one day, and dissolve forever. There is no power to interfere, no power to recall them, no power to revise their action. Their work is done; the record is made up, signed, sealed, and transmitted; and thus the second great act in the presidential election is completed. I ought to correct myself: the second act *is* the presidential election. The election is finished the hour when the electoral colleges have cast their votes and sealed up the record.

Still there is a third step in the process; and it is shorter, plainer, simpler than the other two. These sealed certificates of the electoral colleges are forwarded to the President of the Senate, where they rest under the silence of the seals for more than two months. The Constitution assumes that the result of the election is still unknown. But on a day fixed by law, and the only day, of all the days of February, on which the law commands Congress to be in session, the last act in the plan of electing a President is to be performed.

How plain and simple are the words that describe this third and last step! Here they are:

> The President of the Senate shall, in the presence of the Senate and House of Representatives, open all the certificates, and the votes shall then be counted.

Here is no ambiguity. Two words dominate and inspire the clause: They are the words *open* and *count*. These words are not shrouded in the black-letter mysteries of the law. They are plain words, understood by every man who speaks our mother-tongue, and need no lexicon or commentary.

Consider the grand and simple ceremonial by which the third act is to be completed. On the day fixed by law the two Houses of Congress are assembled. The President of the Senate, who, by the Constitution, has been made the custodian of the sealed certificates from all the electoral colleges, takes his place. The Constitution requires a "person" and a "presence." That "person" is the President of the Senate and that "presence" is the "presence" of the two Houses. Then two things are to be *done*. The certificates are to be opened and the votes are to be counted. These are not legislative acts, but clearly and plainly executive acts. I challenge any man to find anywhere an accepted definition of an executive act that does not include both these. They cannot be tortured into a meaning that will carry them beyond the boundaries of executive action. And one of these acts the President of the Senate is peremptorily ordered to perform. The Constitution commands him to "open all the certificates." Certificates of what? Certificates of the votes of the electoral colleges. Not any certificates that anybody may choose to send, but certificates of electors appointed by the States. The President of the Senate is presumed to know what are the States of the Union; who are their officers; and when he opens the certificates he learns from the official record who have been appointed electors; and he finds their votes.

The Constitution contemplated the President of the Senate

as the Vice-President of the United States, the elect of all the people. And to him is confided the great trust, the custodianship of the only official record of the election of President. What is it to "open the certificates"? It would be a narrow and inadequate view of that word to say that it means only the breaking of the seals. To open an envelope is not to "open the certificates." The certificate is not the paper on which the record is made; it is the record itself. To open the certificate is not a physical, but an intellectual act. It is to make patent the record; to publish it. When that is done the election of President and Vice-President is published. But one thing remains to be done, and here the language of the Constitution changes from the active to the passive voice, from the personal to the impersonal; to the trusted custodian of the votes succeeds the impersonality of arithmetic; the votes have been made known; there remains only the command of the Constitution: "They shall be counted," that is, the numbers shall be added up.

No further act is required. The Constitution itself declares the result.

> The person having the greatest number of votes for President shall be President, if such number be a majority of the whole number of electors appointed.

If no person has such majority, the House of Representatives shall *immediately* choose a President; not the House as organized for legislation, but a new electoral college is created out of the members of the House, by means of which each State has one vote for President, and only one.

To review the ground over which I have traveled, the several acts that constitute the election of a President may be symbolized by a pyramid consisting of three massive, separate blocks. The first, the creation of the electoral college by the States, is the broad base. It embraces the legislative, the judicial, and the executive powers of the States. All the departments of the State government and all the voters of the State coöperate in shaping and perfecting it.

The action of the electoral colleges forms the second block, perfect in itself and independent of the others, superimposed with exactness upon the first.

The opening and counting of the votes of the colleges is the little block that crowns and completes the pyramid.

Such, Mr. Speaker, was the grand and simple plan by which the framers of the Constitution empowered all the people, acting under the laws of the several States, to create special and select colleges of independent electors to choose a President, who should be, not the creature of Congress, nor of the States, but the Chief Magistrate of the whole nation, the elect of all the people.

Now, Mr. Speaker, contrast with the plan I have sketched the theory of this bill. I have studied its provisions in the light of the Constitution; and I am compelled to declare that it assails and overthrows, to its very foundation, the constitutional plan. Congress, finding itself excluded from every step in the process of electing a President until the very last, from the mere fact that its presence is deemed necessary at the opening of the certificates and counting of the votes, takes occasion of that presence to usurp authority over the whole process from beginning to end. Coming only as an invited guest to witness a grand and imposing ceremony, this bill makes Congress the chief actor and umpire in the scene, and, under cover of the word "count," proposes to take command of every step in the process of making a President.

Recurring again to the illustration I have used, Congress, having a simple part to play in reference to the little block that crowns the pyramid, proposes to reach down through all the others and supervise the whole from apex to base; or, rather, it proposes to overturn the whole pyramid and stand it upon its apex, so that it shall rest not upon the broad base of the people's will, but upon the uncertain and despotic will of Congress.

This is usurpation in every meaning of the word. Though the Constitution has sought to keep Congress away from all the process of making a President, this bill creates and places in the control of Congress the enginery by which Presidents can be made and unmade at the caprice of the Senate and House. It grasps all the power, and holds States and electors as toys in its hands. It assumes the right of Congress to go down into the colleges and inquire into all the acts and facts connected with their work. It assumes the right of Congress to go down into the States, to review the act of every officer, to open every ballot-box, and to pass judgment upon every ballot cast by seven millions of Americans.

I know the bill is not proposed as a permanent law; but I know equally well that if the Congress of our centennial year pass this measure they will destroy forever the constitutional plan of electing a President. Pass this bill, and the old constitutional safeguards are gone. Congress becomes a grand returning board from this day forward; and we shall see no

IX—9

more Presidents elected by the States until the people rebuke the apostasy and rebuild their old temple.

Gentlemen on the other side of the House have expressed their indignation that one or two States in the Union have established returning boards to examine and purge the returns from the ballot-boxes of their States; and I must say for myself that I would not tolerate such a board unless intimidation, outrage, and murder made it necessary to preserve the rights of voters. All the evils that have been charged against all the returning boards of the Southern States this bill invites and welcomes to the Capitol of the nation. It makes Congress a vast, irresponsible returning board, with all the vices of and none of the excuses for the returning boards of the States.

The radical and incurable defect of this bill is that it puts a vast, cumbrous machine in the place of the simple, plain plan of the Constitution; it adopts a method which invites and augments the evils from which we now suffer. That there are difficulties in the present situation I freely admit; that there may be doubt, honest doubt, in the minds of honest men as to who is elected President I admit. But I think the bill introduced by my colleague from Ohio [Charles Foster], which provides for submitting to the Supreme Court those questions of constitutional law about which we differ, would be far better. To the adjudication of that great and honored tribunal all would bow with ready obedience; but this novel, dangerous, and cumbrous device is, in my judgment, unwarranted by the Constitution. If we adopt it, we shirk a present difficulty, but, in doing so, we create far greater ones for those who come after us. What to us is a difficulty will be to them a peril.

Mr. Speaker, I have trespassed too long upon the indulgence of the House; but I cannot withhold from the gentleman from Massachusetts [Mr. Hoar] the tribute of my admiration for the earnestness and eloquence with which he closed his defence of this measure. I even shared his enthusiasm when, looking forward to the future of this nation, he pictured to our imagination the gratitude of those who may occupy these halls a hundred years hence, for the wisdom which planned and virtue which adopted this act, which my friend believes to be the great act of the century; an act that solves a great national difficulty, that calms party passion, that averts the dangers of civil war. Let us hope, Mr. Speaker, that they will not be compelled to add that, though this act enabled the men of 1877 to escape from temporary troubles, yet it entailed upon their children evils far more serious and perils far more formidable; that it transmitted to them shattered institutions, and set the good ship of the Union adrift upon an unknown and harborless sea. I hope they may not say that we built no safeguard against dangers except the slight ones that threatened us. It would be a far higher tribute if they could say of us: ''The men of 1876, who closed the cycle of the first century of the Republic, were men who, when they encountered danger, met it with clear-eyed wisdom and calm courage. As the men of 1776 met the perils of their time without flinching, and through years of sacrifice, suffering, and blood conquered their independence and created a nation, so the men of 1876, after having defended the great inheritance from still greater perils, bravely faced and conquered all the difficulties of their own epoch, and did not entail them upon their children. No threats of civil war, however formidable, could compel them to throw away any safeguard of liberty. The preservation of their institutions was to them an object of greater concern than present ease or temporary prosperity; and, instead of framing new devices which might endanger the old Constitution, they rejected all doubtful expedients; and, planting their feet upon the solid rock of the Constitution, they stood at their posts of duty until the tempest was overpassed, and peace walked hand in hand with liberty, ruled by law.'' [Applause.]

During the many calm years of the century our political pilots have grown careless of the course. The master of a vessel sailing down Lake Ontario has the whole breadth of that beautiful inland sea for his pathway. But when his ship arrives at the chute of the La Chine there is but one path of safety. With a steady hand, a clear eye, and a brave heart he points his prow to the well-fixed landmarks on the shore and, with death on either hand, makes the plunge and shoots the rapids in safety.

We, too, are approaching the narrows; and we hear the roar of angry waters below, and the muttering of sullen thunder overhead. Unterrified by breakers or tempest, let us steer our course by the Constitution of our fathers, and we shall neither sink in the rapids nor compel our children to ''shoot Niagara'' and perish in the whirlpool. [Great applause.]

INVESTIGATION OF THE PRESIDENT'S TITLE

On May 13, 1878, Clarkson N. Potter [N. Y.], at the instigation of Samuel J. Tilden and his advisers, had introduced in the House a resolution to appoint a select committee of eleven to inquire into the Presidential vote of 1876 in Louisiana and Florida. The resolution was adopted. Mr. Clarkson was made chairman of the committee, which consisted of seven Democrats and four Republicans. It entered upon its labors during the succeeding vacation.

A great number of cipher telegrams between Mr. Tilden's managers had been brought into the custody of an earlier investigating committee of the Senate by a subpœna issued to the Western Union Telegraph Company. Mr. William M. Grosvenor, of the New York *Tribune,* now turned his attention to these, and ingeniously deciphered them. They showed clearly that attempts had been made, though ineffectually, to bribe members of the election canvassing boards in the disputed States to count at least one of the electoral votes for Tilden and Hendricks, which would secure their election. These facts were proved before the House investigating committee during the Congressional session of 1878-9. Mr. Tilden appeared before the committee, and swore that at the time of the negotiations he knew nothing of them, and, when afterwards informed of them, had commanded such procedure to be stopped. Nothing transpired in the evidence to refute his statement, or to connect him in any way with the attempted fraud.

On account of these disclosures no further attempt was made to impeach President Hayes's title at this or a later time.

President Hayes adopted a conciliatory policy toward the South, appointing a Southern Democrat to his Cabinet (David M. Key, of Tennessee, Postmaster-General), and in other ways attempting to unite the sections. His appointment of Senator Carl Schurz [Mo.] as Secretary of the Interior was a similar offer to the Liberal Republicans, who had seceded in 1872, to come back into the regular Republican fold.

HAYES'S GREAT CABINET TRICK—UNCLE HORACE [GREELEY] MATERIALIZES

[*The Great Materialization Trick on the Platform. Medium Hayes tied in the Cabinet; when the door is opened by Schurz and Evarts, the Ghost of Horace Greeley steps forth and astonishes the Liberal Committee*]

H. G. [LOQUITUR]: "HA-HA! HOORAW, BOYS, WE'VE GOT 'EM! JEST AS I WANTED IT, ONLY YOU'RE FOUR YEARS TOO LATE. SAM BOWLES THERE, HOB-NOBBING WITH STANLEY MATTHEWS—IT ALWAYS DID TAKE HIM ABOUT FOUR YEARS TO TURN AROUND, BUT MURAT HALSTEAD, WHISPERING TO KEY, WAS GENERALLY ABOUT FOUR YEARS AHEAD OF TIME. BOYS, WE'VE GOT 'EM! LET US CLASP HANDS ACROSS THE BLOODY CHASM! THAT MY EYES SHOULD SEE THIS DAY! AIN'T THE OLD PARTY HACKS UNDER THE HARROW! HAW, HAW! LET US CAST BEHIND US THE WRECK AND RUBBISH OF WORN-OUT CONTENTIONS AND BY-GONE FEUDS. HURRAW FOR UNIVERSAL AMNESTY AND IMPARTIAL SUFFRAGE! IN VAIN DO THE DRILL-SERGEANTS OF A DECAYING ORGANIZATION FLOURISH MENACINGLY THEIR TRUNCHEONS; IN VAIN DO THE WHIPPERS-IN OF PARTIES ONCE VITAL——MY MAGNETISM IS GETTING WEAK; JOIN HANDS AND TURN OUT THE GAS. HAL-LELULAH! GOOD NIGHT!

From the collection of the New York Public Library

133

CHAPTER IV

CONGRESSIONAL COERCION OF THE PRESIDENT

[RIDERS ON APPROPRIATION BILLS]

The Forty-fifth Congress Fails to Pass Army Appropriation Bill—President Hayes Summons the Forty-sixth Congress [Democratic] in Special Session—William A. J. Sparks [Ill.] Introduces New Army Appropriation Bill with ''Rider'' Forbidding Use of Troops at the Polls—Debate: In Favor of the ''Rider,'' John G. Carlisle [Ky.], Alexander H. Stephens [Ga.], Samuel J. Randall [Pa.], Fernando Wood [N. Y.], John A. McMahon [O.], Joseph C. F. Blackburn [Ky.]; Opposed, Gen. J. Warren Keifer [O.], Omar D. Conger [Mich.], Harry White [Pa.], William P. Frye [Me.], George M. Robeson [N. J.], Thomas B. Reed [Me.], James A. Garfield [O.]; Bill Is Passed by House and Senate; It Is Vetoed by the President, with Reasons—''Riders'' on Civil Appropriation Bill (Payment in Pensions of Resumption Funds and Repeal of Federal Supervision of Elections)—Debate: In Favor, Mr. McMahon; Opposed, Gen. Garfield; Bill Is Passed by House and Senate; It Is Vetoed by the President, with Reasons.

THE elections of 1878 resulted in a reduction of the Democratic majority in the House, and in a change in the Senate from a Republican majority to a Democratic majority of six. Thirteen of the new Representatives were members of the Greenback party. On most questions these voted with the Democrats in the new (Forty-sixth) Congress, giving them a majority of about thirty.

The former Congress having failed to pass necessary appropriation bills, owing to a disagreement over the use of troops at the polls, President Hayes summoned the new one in special session. It sat from March 18 until July 1 1879.

On March 27, 1879, William A. J. Sparks [Ill.] introduced in the House a bill making appropriations for the army. It was substantially the bill disagreed to in the previous session with the repeal of the statute relating to the use of troops at the polls, on the retention of which the Senate (then Republican) had insisted. Upon this point the debate was concentrated.

Troops at the Polls

House of Representatives, March 28–April 30, 1879

On March 28 General J. Warren Keifer [O.] opposed the repeal of the statute in question.

This is not a work of repeal which we are engaged in. It is a work of making that which was hitherto a duty, made so by law, a crime; a crime entirely new, wholly new, in connection with officers of the army and officers of the navy and the civil officers of this Government. Never before, I believe, in the history of this country has it been attempted to make it a crime for an officer of the army or an officer of the navy, or a marshal of the United States, or a deputy marshal of the United States to keep the peace. This proposed legislation is intended to do that. Then this is not legislation that pertains to the army alone. It undertakes to make it a high crime, punishable by fine and imprisonment, for any civil officer of the United States to appear on election day at the polls with an armed body of men, not troops, not United States soldiers, but to go with an armed body of men to the polls to quell a riot. They may go with feathers in their hands without violating the law; but when armed force is to be resisted, when it becomes necessary to quell rioters with arms in their hands, persons gathered together for the purpose of murder, intimidation, or whatever else it may be, the marshals and their deputies, whose duty it is now by law to quell such disturbances and restore and preserve peace, must go without any armed men with them; otherwise under this proposed legislation they will be guilty of a high crime.

Now, when the marshal or deputy marshal comes, as it is his duty to come, to quell a riot, he has the right to summon the law-abiding citizens of the community to obey his orders, to go, if you please, armed—to become his *posse comitatus* in quelling such disturbances. But this proposed legislation takes away from the marshals and other civil officers of the United States who are charged with similar duties the power of putting down a riot on election day at the polls, and makes it a high crime punishable by fine and imprisonment if such an officer undertakes to do it. This does not relate to the army and navy alone, but to the civil side of the Government.

Hence, I insist that this proposed legislation is not germane to the army appropriation bill. It is not germane because it affects officers of the navy; and this is not a naval bill. It is not germane because it affects civil officers of the Government. If the legislation proposed as a whole includes anything not within the rule it must all fall together.

The gentleman from Illinois [Mr. Sparks] asked whether prior to the act of February 25, 1865, there was any law on the subject of the use of troops at the polls. Now let me say to him that was the first time in the history of the country that there was any restraining statute upon our statute-books at all in relation to the use of troops at the polls or anywhere else in the United States, and that legislation prohibited the use of troops and armed men at the polls by military, naval, or civil officers in the service of the Government, except for the purpose of repelling armed enemies of the United States or *to keep the peace at the polls*. Those two cases were excepted in this legislation passed by a republican Congress, and we propose that this legislation shall remain as it now is, so that it shall not be said as a reproach and a stigma upon this country that we have officers, military, naval, and civil, whose duty it is by law, under penalties, to keep the peace everywhere, save and except on one day at least in each year these officers shall be required to fold their arms and look on and witness riot, murder, intimidation, or anything else of an unlawful character, going on before their eyes, or be subject to severe penalties. By the second section of the second article of the Constitution the President is made commander-in-chief of the army and navy of the United States, and of the militia of the several States when called into actual service of the United States; and together with other powers given him he has the right to move the army whenever and wherever it is necessary. Such power cannot be taken away by law.

John G. Carlisle [Ky.] supported the provision.

I undertake to affirm, and I do it deliberately, that under the Constitution of the United States the President has no right to use the army or navy, or any part of the army or navy, to protect the States against domestic violence or to enforce State laws unless he is authorized so to do by act of Congress. I will read to the House that provision of the Constitution which is in point:

The United States shall guarantee to every State in this Union a Republican form of government, and shall protect each of them against invasion; and on application of the legislature or of the Executive (when the legislature cannot be convened), against domestic violence.

I appeal to my friends on the other side to tell me and the country whether they mean to say that this provision which simply makes it the duty of the United States to guarantee to each State a republican form of government and to protect it, upon the application of the governor or the legislature, against domestic violence, confers upon the President, a single officer of the United States, any such power. Are the gentlemen prepared to go before the country on the proposition that the President is the United States?

SEVERAL MEMBERS.—Oh, no!

OMAR D. CONGER [Mich.].—To whom does the application come which is referred to?

MR. CARLISLE.—It comes to the President. That is the constitutional provision making it the duty, not of the President, but of the United States as a government to protect the States against domestic violence on the application of the governor or the legislature. And I repeat the proposition that, under that provision of the Constitution, the President, without legislation on the part of Congress, did not possess one particle of power to use the army or the navy for this purpose. And the same authority which conferred the power on him by legislation can take it away from him. [Applause on the Democratic side.]

HARRY WHITE [Pa.].—Does my friend remember that in Mr. Pierce's administration, on the 12th of June, 1856, the Secretary of the Navy, under the order of the President of the United States, at the request of the mayor, sent a body of marines to the fourth ward in this city while an election for municipal officers was going on, and they shot down unoffending American citizens? That act was sustained by the gentleman's political friends. Does he know that?

MR. CARLISLE.—I do remember at that election the soldiers of the United States or the marines were used in this city, a district under the exclusive jurisdiction of the Federal Government, and that my friend's political party complained loudly and long of it.

MR. WHITE.—Did not Henry C. Burnett, a predecessor of the gentleman from Kentucky, defend on this floor the use of the troops to keep peace at the polls?

MR. CARLISLE.—The District of Columbia was not in a State.

MR. WHITE.—Had not the District of Columbia a municipal city government, a mayor, and police? [Laughter on the Democratic side.]

MR. CARLISLE.—The authority of the President to use the army or the navy in protecting the States against domestic violence, or in assisting the States to enforce their laws, is derived, not from the provision of the Constitution which I have read, but from an act of Congress which was passed on February 27, 1795; and it is under that act that the President proceeds in every instance to send the army or the navy into a State to protect it against domestic violence or to enforce its State laws.

There is the foundation and the only foundation upon which rests to-day all the authority the President has to use the troops, the army or the navy, for these purposes. And I submit to my friends on the other side if it is not entirely competent for the power which conferred this authority to take it away, to modify it, or to alter it. But I deny, sir, that under this authority, if left without any modification, the President can send soldiers into the States of this Union to stand around the polls on election day for the purpose of keeping the peace. I deny what has been asserted by my friend from Maine [Mr. William P. Frye], that the United States deputy marshals can call upon the army of the United States to assist them in keeping the peace. Up to the passage of the army appropriation bill in the second session of the Forty-fifth Congress that was true; but in that bill there was inserted a clause which provided that the army should not be used thereafter as a *posse comitatus*.

GEORGE M. ROBESON [N. J.].—I wish to ask the gentleman whether if the executive of a State, when the legislature cannot be convened, or the legislature itself, calls upon the President of the United States under the Constitution as it is written, and under the law as it now stands to suppress domestic violence, and that domestic violence be at a place where a general election is taking place, the President of the United States is not bound under his oath of office to comply with the request? And, if so, whether this amendment is not in derogation of his constitutional power and duty?

MR. CARLISLE.—If the application is made in the regular form under the act of Congress I admit that it is the duty of the President to send troops, but I say that when troops have gone into a State and have dispersed the mob or the insurrectionists or whoever else is acting in resistance to the State authorities, they have performed their duty and must stop; they cannot remain at the election precincts to keep the peace, or, in other words, to prevent outbreaks of violence.

MR. ROBESON.—I am not now disputing that point. The gentleman having answered that question so fairly, I now ask him whether or not this section of this bill, this proposed amendment of the law, would take away the power of the President to do that thing, if properly called upon?

MR. CARLISLE.—It certainly will not, as I have stated again and again.

MR. ROBESON.—If that be so, if this section does not take away his power in that respect, and if that contingency should happen, as it possibly may, then I would ask this question: is an officer of the army of the United States, who is sworn to obey the lawful orders of the President of the United States, bound to obey should he be ordered by the President to suppress a riot and to quiet domestic violence at a place where a general election is being held? And, if he does, what is to happen to him?

MR. CARLISLE.—The gentleman from New Jersey [Mr. Robeson] is asking me a question upon one subject and I am discussing another. [Laughter.] The gentleman from New Jersey asks me what would be the result in case an officer of the United States failed to perform his duty, where the President in giving him his order was acting in strict conformity to the law. I say that the officer is, of course, bound to obey the order.

We, however, are now discussing the question as to whether or not these soldiers shall be sent to a State for the purpose of keeping the peace at the polls, not for the purpose of suppressing domestic insurrection against the authority of the State or protecting the State against domestic violence. The two propositions are altogether different in their nature; they stand upon altogether different foundations. One is essential to the preservation, not only of the peace and integrity, but of the very existence of the Federal Government itself, because that Government cannot exist for a moment if the States are destroyed.

MR. ROBESON.—The amendment in effect says these troops shall not be there for any purpose. But one further question. Does the gentleman understand that the President of the United States is included in the scope of this section? In the fourth line of this section I find these words: "Other persons engaged in the civil, military, or naval service of the United States." I would like to ask the gentleman whether he considers that that expression includes the President of the United States? And, if it does, whether the President of the United States when called upon by the executive of a State in a proper manner—I assume all that—whether he would be liable to punishment under the provisions of this section if he acted upon that call of a State executive?

MR. CARLISLE.—My first answer to the gentleman's question is this: that the President cannot be properly called upon to do a thing which he has no power to do. In other words, he cannot be properly called upon to send troops into a State to preserve peace at an election.

MR. ROBESON.—But I understood the gentleman to say that he thought this section did not affect that power of the executive of a State to call upon the President, nor the duty of the President to respond to that call. If that be so, then he would be properly called upon and not improperly; and the troops would be there under his order.

MR. CARLISLE.—I am not prepared to say upon the instant exactly what the true construction of that portion of the section is, because my attention has not been previously called to it. But I undertake to say this much, that no provision of this law or of any other law can be so construed or so administered as to punish any officer or any private citizen for doing that which he has a lawful right to do.

Alexander H. Stephens [Ga.] supported the provision.

It is known that I was opposed to the policy of putting this provision on this appropriation bill. But the policy of doing it and the right to do it are different questions. The question now is, is the section excluded by the rule the accepted law of the House?

All laws penal in their character are to be strictly construed, but laws involving questions of public right, public liberty, public policy, are to be liberally construed. Rule 120 provides that any change in existing laws upon appropriation bills must not only be germane, but must be in the nature of retrenchment of expenditures.

There is no question this amendment is germane, none. Does it retrench expenditures? The gentleman from Maine [Mr. Frye] says it must appear on its face that it does reduce expenditures. That is strict construction. May it possibly reduce expenditures? Will it probably reduce expenditures? Will it most probably reduce expenditures? These are considerations which we should not neglect or overlook. If it does, if it probably may, if it possibly may, if it does not increase them, but possibly may reduce them and most probably will, then that liberal construction which I insist should be made of this rule would make us conclude the proposition is admissible under the one hundred and twentieth rule.

I think it will not only possibly and probably but certainly reduce expenditures. Our past history and experience show that enormous expenditures have attended the use of troops at the polls during elections.

It was not until 1807 that the organized army, the military force and the naval force, was authorized to be called out for a like purpose, to protect the States against domestic violence and insurrection. But the provision of the law for the use of the troops in civil cases is entirely a different matter. It is where provision is made for the execution of a mandate or judgment of a court. The generals are not to command the troops in such cases, but the marshals. The civil officers, as the sheriffs in our States, were authorized to call for the use of the troops, and the President was authorized to furnish them to the legislature or to the governor when the legislature was not in session or the marshals for the execution of the mandate of a court. That is what I call the execution of process in civil administration of the law. That is a very different thing from the other—the use of troops to suppress insurrection and domestic violence in a State upon the call of a legislature or the governor as provided by the Constitution.

Wherever the marshal calls for troops, as was decided by Attorney-General Caleb Cushing, it was as a *posse*, not as the army. The United States troops were under the command, not of the United States military officers, but under the command of the marshal who asked for them.

The whole of this amendment is simply this: all the new legislation it proposes, or change of legislation, is to repeal that clause which negatively affirms that the troops might be called out and ordered by military commanders to attend at elections under pretence of keeping the peace.

I am for law and order. I have witnessed the presence of soldiers at the polls. I have seen no good from their presence. We had gotten along for three-quarters of a century without it. I think the public sentiment is as much against the use of the troops to preserve the peace North as it is South. Let the relics and vestiges of the war be buried with the things of the past. I do insist that there will be no harm done, no unsettling of our institutions, no revolution in our matchless system of government, by the repeal of this law. It seems to me, therefore, this amendment being germane, regulating the use and the control of the army, and being also within the purview of a liberal construction of the rule, it is admissible on this bill.

Now, as to the use of the army, I wish in connection with some remarks which were offered yesterday on both sides upon this subject to state this: Congress has a right to raise armies. Congress has a right to designate the use to which the forces, naval or military, may be applied. But the President's right to control and direct the movements of those forces from one part of the country to the other, enlarging the declared function of Congress, is a clear executive right. We have no power to inter-fere with it, except by impeachment for the abuse of power conferred. But we can say that he shall not use the forces for any particular purposes. We have a right to say this—and I do not think the present Executive would desire it to be otherwise —we have a right to say the forces, land and naval, of the United States shall not be used for the purpose of controlling elections in the States, but that the elections shall be free and fair according to the laws of the land, State and Federal; and if any man violates the law, if there has been any violence at the polls, and a member of Congress has not been duly returned, we are to judge of it here on this floor, and we can set the return aside. Let the land and naval forces of our country be devoted to the objects for which they were raised by Congress. Let the army protect the frontier. Let the navy be afloat on the seas protecting our flag and our commerce everywhere. Let each branch of these forces be kept in that sphere they were created for, and in which in past years they have won such honor and glory to our common country.

THOMAS B. REED [Me.].—The tendency of the rules and the practice of the House has been for many years to concentrate an immense power in the hands of the Committee on Appropriations. So great has been that tendency that the gentleman who is now occupying the chair [Samuel J. Randall] seized the first opportunity to introduce a proposition to deprive them of a certain portion of their power. But an amendment like this in its principle goes further; it goes not only to increase the power of the Committee on Appropriations, but it also aggrandizes the power of the conference committee and leaves the decision of grave questions to six men, three appointed from the House and three from the Senate.

Whenever the House can propose an amendment which is germane to the bill and which repeals existing legislation simply because this amendment reduces expenditures they raise grounds of possible difference between the House and the Senate, and those questions must go to a conference committee, and every one who knows anything of the legislation of Congress knows that a large part of the most important legislation is decided by three men from the House and three men from the Senate. And the decision takes place in secret without any of the safeguards which ought to surround legislation.

Now, this thing is wrong. It is undemocratic; it is unrepublican. It is unsuitable for this nation and this people, and consequently any rule which allows an amendment of this sort ought to be construed strictly for the good of the country.

Rule 120 demands two things: first, that the amendment shall be germane to the bill; and, second, that it shall reduce expenditures. On the proposition as to the reduction of expenditures there has already been a decision by the first Speaker under whom this rule was adopted, Speaker Kerr, and his ruling, as I understand it, was that the amendment must upon its face show a reduction of expenditures. It is not a matter of argument or inference, or a question for discussion.

Why, this very case illustrates the necessity for this thing. This amendment contains two propositions: first, that no troops shall be employed at the polls; second, that men shall be punished if they have troops there. Is that last clause going to lessen expenditures in any way, or is it going to increase expenditures to punish men for being there? Your first clause may diminish expenses, but the last will certainly increase them. Who shall strike the balance? The thing is as broad as it is long. I say that the Chair ought to rule in such a fashion that an amendment shall not be admitted unless upon its face it shows affirmatively that it does reduce expenditures.

But I do not rest my objection so much upon the question of the reduction of expenditures as upon the question of whether the amendment is germane to the bill. I ask the attention of the Chair to some propositions I have to make.

Here is an amendment which embraces three statements and is to a bill to appropriate money for the support of the army, one which relates solely to the army appropriation. The largest extent that can be given to matters germane to it will only include matters that relate to the army, I should say myself to army expenditures alone, but, taking the widest and broadest limit you can put to it, it can only include matters that relate to the army, but not those that relate to naval and civil officers.

Here are three propositions in this amendment. The first is that no military officer shall have under his authority troops at polling places. Now, even if that could be construed as being germane to an appropriation bill, here is also a proposition that no naval officer shall have any armed men at the polls. How is that germane to an army appropriation bill? Here is a further provision that no person engaged in the civil service of the

United States shall have armed men there. How is that consistent with a bill which relates solely to the appropriations for the support of the army?

I say that so far from its being germane to the bill, as stated by the gentleman from Georgia [Mr. Stephens], it is, to the mind of any disinterested person, clearly not germane. You cannot mix up the naval and civil officers of the Government and drag them into an army appropriation bill simply because the proposed section refers as well to the army officers.

THE SPEAKER [SAMUEL J. RANDALL].—The point of order raised upon the pending section is this: that it changes existing law, that it is not germane to the pending bill, and that it does not retrench expenditures. Rule 120 provides that no proposition in an appropriation bill, or an amendment thereto, which changes existing law, shall be in order, except such as, being germane to the subject-matter of the bill, shall retrench expenditures. That the pending section changes existing law appears on its face. That it is germane to the pending bill there can scarcely be a doubt. It relates to the duties of the army, or the uses to which it may be put. The object of the bill is to provide a support for the army. A kindred subject to that would be the kind of service the army is expected to perform. The duties to be performed are closely allied to the matter of army support. "Germane" does not mean synonymous, but something "near akin," "closely allied," or "relevant" to the subject-matter to which it is applied. The Chair is therefore of the opinion that the section is germane to the pending bill.

But the most serious question involved is this: Does the section retrench expenditures?

Congress creates the army. It provides its support. It makes the rules for its government. And although the President is, by the Constitution, the commander-in-chief of the army, yet Congress must make all laws necessary and proper for carrying into execution the powers vested in him as such commander. Congress may therefore fix the places where troops may or may not be stationed, and may prohibit the President and all civil and military officers from using the army for any purpose deemed improper, or from interfering with the freedom of elections, or from doing any act dangerous to the liberties of the people. By existing law the army or any part thereof may now be used to keep the peace at the polls at any voting place, at any election, to which the President or any civil or military officer might see fit to order it. The official estimates and appropriations heretofore made show how much money has been expended for transportation and other expenses attending the use of troops at the polls. The pending section proposes to retrench such expenditures for the future.

If it were lawful to use troops as policemen in cities, as sheriffs and constables for serving civil processes, as guards for State prisons, or as messengers for carrying the mails or the transportation of merchandise for private individuals, would not such enlarged duties greatly increase the expense of supporting the army? As the enlarging of the duties of the army would necessarily increase the expenses of supporting it, so will the restricting of the uses to which it may be put reduce such expenses. In so far, then, as the services which may be required of the army, or any part thereof, are restricted by the pending amendment the expense necessarily attending such service is reduced, and to that extent the pending provision does retrench expenditures.

For these reasons, and others which might be assigned, the Chair overrules the point of order.

The decision of the Chair was sustained by a vote of 125 to 107.

James A. Garfield [O.] opened the debate proper by opposing the proviso.

Mr. Chairman, viewed from the standpoint of a foreigner, our Government may be said to be the feeblest on the earth. From our standpoint, and with our experience, it is the mightiest. But why would a foreigner call it the feeblest? He can point out a half dozen ways in which it can be destroyed without violence.

For example, if the people of the United States should say we will elect no Representatives to the House of Representatives. Does our Constitution provide any remedy whatever? In two years there would be no House of Representatives; of course, no support of the Government, and no Government. Suppose, again, the States should say, through their legislatures, we will elect no Senators. Such abstention alone would absolutely destroy this Government; and our system provides no process of compulsion to prevent it.

Again, suppose the two Houses were assembled in their usual order, and a majority of one in this body or in the Senate should firmly band themselves together and say, we will vote to adjourn the moment the hour of meeting arrives, and continue so to vote at every session during our two years of existence; the Government would perish, and there is no provision of the Constitution to prevent it. Or, again, if a majority of one of either body should declare that they would vote down, and did vote down, every bill to support the Government by appropriations, can you find in the whole range of our judicial or our executive authority any remedy whatever? A Senator, or a member of this House, is free, and may vote "no" on every proposition. Nothing but his oath and his honor restrains him. Not so with executive and judicial officers. They have no power to destroy this Government. Let them travel an inch beyond the line of the law, and they fall within the power of impeachment. But, against the people who create Representatives; against the legislatures who create Senators; against Senators and Representatives in these halls, there is no power of impeachment; there is no remedy, if, by abstention or by adverse votes, they refuse to support the Government.

At a first view, it would seem strange that a body of men so wise as our fathers were should have left a whole side of their fabric open to these deadly assaults; but, on a closer view of the case, their wisdom will appear. What was their reliance? This: the sovereign of this nation, the God-crowned and Heaven-anointed sovereign, in whom resides "the State's collected will," and to whom we all owe allegiance, is the people themselves. Inspired by love of country and by a deep sense of obligation to perform every public duty; being themselves the creators of all the agencies and forces to execute their own will, and choosing from themselves their representatives to express that will in the forms of law, it would have been like a suggestion of suicide to assume that any of these great voluntary powers would be turned against the life of the Government. Public opinion—that great ocean of thought from whose level all heights and all depths are measured—was trusted as a power amply able, and always willing, to guard all the approaches on that side of the Constitution from any assault on the life of the nation.

Up to this hour our sovereign has never failed us. There has never been such a refusal to exercise those primary functions of sovereignty as either to endanger or cripple the Government; nor have the majority of the representatives of that sovereign in either House of Congress ever before announced their purpose to use their voluntary powers for its destruction. And now, for the first time in our history, and, I will add, for the first time for at least two centuries in the history of any English-speaking nation, it is proposed and insisted upon that these voluntary powers shall be used for the destruction of the Government. I want it distinctly understood that the program announced to the American people to-day is this: that, if this House cannot have its own way in certain matters, not connected with appropriations, it will so use, or refrain from using, its voluntary powers as to destroy the Government.

Now, Mr. Chairman, it has been said on the other side that, when a demand for the redress of grievances is made, the authority that runs the risk of stopping and destroying the Government is the one that resists the redress. Not so.

Our theory of law is free consent. That is the granite foundation of our whole superstructure. Nothing in this Republic can be law without consent—the free consent of the House; the free consent of the Senate; the free consent of the Executive, or, if he refuse it, the free consent of two-thirds of these bodies. And yet the program announced two weeks ago was that, if the Senate refused to consent to the demand of the House, the Government should stop. And the proposition was then, and the program is now, that, although there is not a Senate to be coerced, there is still a third independent branch in the legislative power of the Government whose consent is to be coerced at the peril of the destruction of this Government; that is, if the President, in the discharge of his duty, shall exercise his plain constitutional right to refuse his consent to this proposed legislation, the Congress will so use its voluntary powers as to destroy the Government. This is the proposition which we confront; and we denounce it as revolution.

It makes no difference, Mr. Chairman, what the issue is. If it were the simplest and most inoffensive proposition in the world, yet, if you demand, as a matter of coercion, that it shall be adopted against the free consent prescribed in the Constitution, every fair-minded man in America is bound to resist you as much as though his own life depended upon his resistance.

Let it be understood that I am not arguing the merits of any one of the three amendments. I am discussing the proposed method of legislation! and I declare that it is against the Constitution of our country. It is revolutionary to the core, and is destructive of the fundamental element of American liberty, the free consent of all the powers that unite to make laws.

In opening this debate I challenge all comers to show a single instance in our history where this consent has been coerced. This is the great, the paramount issue, which dwarfs all others into insignificance.

I now turn aside for a moment from the line of my argument

to say that it is not a little surprising that our friends on the other side should have gone into this great contest on so weak a cause as the one embraced in the pending amendment to this bill.

Victor Hugo said, in his description of the battle of Waterloo, that the struggle of the two armies was like the wrestling of two giants, when a chip under the heel of one might determine the victory. It may be that this amendment is the chip under your heel, or it may be that it is the chip on our shoulder. As a chip, it is of small account to you or to us; but, when it represents the integrity of the Constitution and is assailed by revolution, we fight for it as if it were a Kohinoor of purest water. [Applause.]

The distinguished and venerable gentleman from Georgia [Mr. Stephens] spoke of this law, which is sought to be repealed, as "odious and dangerous." It has been denounced as a piece of partisan war legislation to enable the army to control elections.

Do gentlemen know its history? Do they know whereof they affirm? Who made this law which is denounced as so great an offence as to justify the destruction of the Government rather than let it remain on the statute-book? Its first draft was introduced into the Senate by a prominent Democrat from the State of Kentucky, Lazarus W. Powell, who made an able speech in its favor.[1] It was reported against by a Republican committee of that body. It encountered weeks of debate, was amended and passed, and then came into the House. Every Democrat present in the Senate voted for it on its final passage. Every Senator who voted against it was a Republican. No Democrat voted against it.

The bill then came to the House of Representatives and was put upon its passage here. How did the vote stand in this body? Every Democrat present at the time in the House of Representatives of the Thirty-eighth Congress voted for it. The distinguished speaker of this House, Mr. Samuel J. Randall, voted for it. The distinguished chairman of the Committee of Ways and Means of the last House, Mr. Fernando Wood, voted for it. Every Democrat of conspicuous name and fame in that House voted for the bill, and not one against it. There were but few Republicans who voted against it.

What was the controversy? What was the object of the bill? It was alleged by Democrats that in those days of war there were interferences with the proper freedom of elections in the

[1] See Volume VI, chapter xiii.

border States. We denied the charge; but, lest there might be some infraction of the freedom of elections, many Republicans, unwilling that there should be even the semblance of interference with that freedom, voted for it. This law is an expression of their purpose that the army should not be used at any election except for the purpose of keeping the peace.

Those Republicans who voted against it did so on the ground that there was no cause for such legislation; that it was a slander upon the Government and the army to say that they were interfering with the proper freedom of elections. I was among that number.

MR. STEPHENS.—I ask if the country is likely to be revolutionized and the Government destroyed by repealing a law that the gentleman himself voted against? [Laughter on the Democratic side.]

MR. GARFIELD.—I think not. That is not the element of revolution, as I will show the gentleman. The proposition now is that, after fourteen years have passed, and not one petition from one American citizen has come to us asking that this law be repealed; while not one memorial has found its way to our desks complaining of the law, so far as I have heard, the Democratic House of Representatives now holds that, if they are not permitted to force upon another House and upon the Executive, against their consent, the repeal of a law that Democrats made, this refusal shall be considered a sufficient ground for starving this Government to death. That is the proposition which we denounce as revolution. [Applause on the Republican side.]

FERNANDO WOOD [N. Y.].—I desire to ask the gentleman whether he wishes to make the impression upon the House that the bill introduced by Senator Powell, of Kentucky, and which resulted finally in the law of 1865, was the bill that passed the Senate, that passed the House, and for which he says the present Speaker of this House and myself voted?

MR. GARFIELD.—I have not intimated that there were no amendments. It was amended in the Senate. One amendment permitted the use of the army to repel armed enemies of the United States from the polls.

MR. WOOD.—So far as I am personally concerned, I deny that I ever voted for a bill except as a substitute for a more pernicious and objectionable measure. [Much laughter on the Republican side.]

MR. GARFIELD.—No amendments whatever were offered in the House, and there was no other bill on the subject before the House.

Mr. Wood.—I desire to submit another question to my friend.

Mr. Garfield.—Certainly.

Mr. Wood.—It is whether, in 1865, at the time of the passage of this law, when the war had not really subsided, there was not in a portion of this country a condition of things rendering it almost impossible to exercise the elective franchise unless there was some degree of military interference. [Great laughter.] And, further, whether, after the experience of fourteen years since the war has subsided, that gentleman is yet prepared to continue a war measure in a time of profound peace in this country?

Mr. Garfield.—No doubt the patriotic gentleman from New York [Mr. Wood] took all these things into consideration when he voted for this law; and I may have been unpatriotic in voting against it at that time; but he and I must stand by our records, as they were made.

Let it be understood that I am not discussing the merits of this law. I have merely turned aside from the line of my argument to show the inconsistency of the other side in proposing to stop the Government if they cannot force the repeal of a law which they themselves made. I am discussing a method of revolution against the Constitution now proposed by this House, and to that issue I hold gentlemen in this debate, and challenge them to reply.

And now, before I close, I ask the forbearance of gentlemen on the other side while I offer a suggestion which I make with reluctance. They will bear me witness that I have in many ways shown my desire that the wounds of the war should be healed; that the grass which has grown green over the graves of the dead of both armies might symbolize the returning spring of friendship and peace between citizens who were lately in arms against each other.

But I am compelled by the necessities of the case to refer to a chapter of our recent history. The last act of Democratic domination in this Capitol, eighteen years ago, was striking and dramatic, perhaps heroic. Then the Democratic party said to the Republicans: "If you elect the man of your choice as President of the United States we will shoot your Government to death"; and the people of this country, refusing to be coerced by threats or violence, voted as they pleased, and lawfully elected Abraham Lincoln as President of the United States.

Then your leaders, though holding a majority in the other branch of Congress, were heroic enough to withdraw from their seats and fling down the gage of mortal battle. We called it rebellion; but we recognized it as courageous and manly to avow your purpose, take all the risks, and fight it out in the open field. Notwithstanding your utmost efforts to destroy it, the Government was saved. Year by year since the war ended those who resisted you have come to believe that you have finally renounced your purpose to destroy and are willing to maintain the Government. In that belief you have been permitted to return to power in the two Houses.

To-day, after eighteen years of defeat, the book of your domination is again opened, and your first act awakens every unhappy memory and threatens to destroy the confidence which your professions of patriotism inspired. You turned down a leaf of the history that recorded your last act of power in 1861, and you have now signalized your return to power by beginning a second chapter at the same page; not this time by a heroic act that declares war on the battlefield, but you say if all the legislative powers of the Government do not consent to let you tear certain laws out of the statute-book you will not shoot our Government to death as you tried to do in the first chapter, but you declare that, if we do not consent against our will, if you cannot coerce an independent branch of this Government, against its will, to allow you to tear from the statute-books some laws put there by the will of the people, you will starve the Government to death. [Great applause on the Republican side.]

Between death on the field and death by starvation, I do not know that the American people will see any great difference. The end, if successfully reached, would be death in either case. Gentlemen, you have it in your power to kill this Government; you have it in your power, by withholding these two bills, to smite the nerve-centers of our Constitution with the paralysis of death; and you have declared your purpose to do this, if you cannot break down that fundamental element of free consent which up to this hour has always ruled in the legislation of this Government.

Touching this question of executive action, I remind the gentlemen that, in 1856, the National Democratic Convention, in session at Cincinnati, and, still later, the National Democratic Convention of 1860, affirmed the right of the veto as one of the sacred rights guaranteed by our Government.

The doctrine is that any measure which cannot be passed over a veto by a two-thirds vote has no right to become a law, and the only mode of redress is an appeal to the people at the next election. That has been the Democratic doctrine from the earliest days, notably so from the time of Andrew Jackson until now.

In leaving this topic, let me ask you what would you have said if, in 1861, the Democratic members of the Senate, being then a majority of that body, instead of taking the heroic course and going out to battle, had simply said: "We will put on an appropriation bill an amendment declaring the right of any State to secede from the Union at pleasure, and forbidding the President or any officer of the army or navy of the United States from interfering with any State in its work of secession"? Suppose they had said to the President: "Unless you consent to the incorporation of this provision in an appropriation bill we will refuse supplies to the Government." Perhaps they could then have killed the Government by starvation; but, even in the madness of that hour, the leaders of rebellion did not think it worthy their manhood to put their fight on that dishonorable ground. They planted themselves on the higher plane of battle and fought it out to defeat.

Now, by a method which the wildest secessionist scorned to adopt, it is proposed to make this new assault upon the life of the Republic.

We are ready to pass these bills for the support of the Government at any hour when you will offer them in the ordinary way, by the methods prescribed by the Constitution. If you offer those other propositions of legislation as separate measures we will meet you in the fraternal spirit of fair debate and will discuss their merits. Some of your measures many of us will vote for in separate bills. But you shall not coerce any independent branch of this Government, even by the threat of starvation, to consent to surrender its voluntary powers until the question has been appealed to the sovereign and decided in your favor. On this ground we plant ourselves, and here we will stand to the end.

Let it be remembered that the avowed object of this new revolution is to destroy all the defences which the nation has placed around its ballot-box to guard the fountain of its own life. You say that the United States shall not employ even its civil power to keep peace at the polls. You say that the marshals shall have no power either to arrest rioters or criminals who seek to destroy the freedom and purity of the ballot-box.

I remind you that you have not always shown this great zeal in keeping the civil officers of the general Government out of the States. Only six years before the war your law authorized marshals of the United States to enter all our hamlets and households to hunt for fugitive slaves. Not only that, it empowered the marshals to summon the *posse comitatus*, to command all bystanders to join in the chase and aid in remanding to eternal bondage the fleeing slave. And your Democratic

SHALL WE CALL HOME OUR TROOPS?

"We intend to beat the Negro in the battle of life, and defeat means one thing—EXTERMINATION."—*Birmingham (Alabama) News*

From the collection of the New York Public Library

Attorney-General [Caleb Cushing], in his opinion published in 1854, declared that the marshal of the United States might summon to his aid the whole able-bodied force of his precinct, not only including bystanders and other citizens generally, "but any and all organized armed forces, whether militia of the State, or officers, soldiers, sailors, and marines of the United States," to join in the chase and hunt down the fugitive. Now, gentlemen, if, for the purpose of making eternal slavery the lot of an American, you send your marshals, summon your *posse,* and use the armed force of the United States, with what face or grace can you tell us that this Government cannot lawfully employ the same marshals with their armed *posse,* if need be, to maintain the purity of our own elections and keep the peace at our own polls? You have made the issue and we have accepted it. In the name of the Constitution and on behalf of good government and public justice, we make the appeal to our common sovereign.

For the present I refrain from discussing the merits of the election laws. I have sought only to state the first fundamental ground of our opposition to this revolutionary method of legislation by coercion. [Great applause.]

JOHN A. McMAHON [O.].—I would ask my colleague from the State of Ohio, who constituted him the guardian of the Southern men on this floor? Who gave him the right to read them lectures, as if they were his subordinates and not his equals upon this floor? Does the gentleman assume to speak for the people of the North? He ought to have remembered the fact that his party is no longer in the majority. He ought to have recollected that, between its Southern policy and its financial management, Republicanism has been shorn of many hundred thousands of its followers. And, when he insists that Southern men shall be guided by Republican ideas as the price of the good opinion of Republican leaders, I would ask him what are they to follow? Shall they adopt the gentleman's teaching at the present time, or may they not adopt his practices in the past, when so many laws were enacted upon appropriation bills by him and his party?

And I want to say to gentlemen on the other side who talk as if they held this country in a sling and carried the Government around in their breeches pocket—I want them to know and to realize that in the last presidential election they were in a minority of over one million of the white voters of this country, and in a minority of over two hundred and fifty thousand of its whole voting population. They have a President in power, it is true; but we all know how he was put there. We all know he received neither a majority of the votes of the people, nor did he receive a legal majority of the electoral votes. We are here, sir, on this side representing the people, and in the other House we represent the people as well. If there had been fair play we would have had all the departments of the Government. Representing, as we do, the majority of the people of this country, we propose to exercise all the powers of legislation as men fully sensible of the responsibility resting upon us. The people have trusted us, and we are here to protect their rights, and he is no true Representative who will allow his judgment to be influenced by the line of argument adopted by my colleague from Ohio.

The course of my colleague [Mr. Garfield] is certainly extraordinary. He is unwilling to discuss the merits of the proposition. He will not say that our proposed amendment is not right. He admits that he voted against this section when it became a law, but he gives us no light about his present views. Surely, when so distinguished and intelligent a gentleman arraigns a large number of his colleagues as revolutionists because of their support of this measure, he ought to deign to give us an opinion as to whether, in his judgment, it is right or wrong. Does his party seek to evade this discussion and to find refuge under the worn-out "bloody shirt"?

Gentlemen upon the other side forget that, during the war, when it was popular, not only in their party, but with the people, to augment the executive power of the Government for the purpose of enabling us to put down the rebellion, almost every conceivable outrage was perpetrated upon the liberty of the people at the polls, under the so-called war power, the avowed pretext being to preserve the peace, but the real object being to secure a majority on the floor of this House and otherwise to control the elections in the various border States.

It is an old maxim, full of wisdom, that "a half loaf is better than no bread." This law did not meet the views of the Democratic members of either body; but it was better than no law. It was a step in the proper direction, and they trusted to the future, when the Union would be fully restored, to return to its proper channels the overgrown power of the executive branch of our Government.

But gentlemen on the other side plant themselves upon the position that we have no right to attach this measure to an appropriation bill. Why not? We are acting under the rules of the House and in strict accord with general parliamentary law. We have a right to put it there if we have the majority, and I would wish to recall to the gentleman's short memory the fact that he and his party have resorted to this method of enforcing their views upon many important occasions. It came into existence at an early day as one of the means by which the people of England saved themselves from tyrannical kings; and it is a power which we should never abandon under any circumstances, no matter how free our Government may seem to be at the present time. When our fathers conferred upon Congress the right to "raise and support armies," they intended to give Congress the absolute power to determine for what purposes these armies should be used.

If this was the first time this power had been exercised by either party, I would not be so surprised to hear our action denounced as "revolutionary." But it has been freely used in the past by the Republican party. And, in the last two Houses, all the economy, and it was great, which the Democratic House was able to accomplish it achieved by constant legislation upon the various appropriation bills presented to it.

Gentlemen assume that we are coercing somebody, some coordinate branch of the Government. By what right do they say so? How can we tell, or what difference ought it to make to us, what view the Senate or the President may take of this question? They may be as eager as we for this reform. As it is correct in principle, we have the right to suppose that it will be welcomed in any shape. Does the gentleman from Ohio speak with any authority when he assumes that our action will not receive the sanction of the President. I will not believe, and do not, that the President has been guilty of so gross a violation of the proprieties of the occasion.

Now, I am not in favor of constant general legislation upon appropriation bills. But, when we are voting money to support an army for the next fiscal year, have we not the right, and is it not our duty to say emphatically that these soldiers shall not be used for the purpose of intimidating voters or influencing the election? If the President of the United States can convince the country that we have no right to pass such a law, under any circumstances, because it invades his constitutional right as commander-in-chief of the army, the country will sustain him in refusing his assent to the bill. But, if his assent is withheld because he does not approve of the measure or of the manner in which it has been passed, the people will not approve of his action. The veto power was not given to the President, in my judgment, to make him a constant actor in legislation, but as a defensive or protective power, to prevent the invasion of the constitutional right of the other departments, or, in extreme cases, the passage of hasty and ill-advised legislation. I do not agree with my colleague in his statement that the President is a part and parcel of the legislative power of this country. He has become so, in practice, to a certain extent, but I believe the practice is wrong.

When I turn to the very first article of the Constitution, which speaks about the legislative power of the Government, I find it says:

All legislative powers herein granted shall be vested in a Congress of the United States, which shall consist of a Senate and House of Representatives.

It does not say it shall consist of a House and Senate and President of the United States. On the contrary, it says simply "a Senate and House of Representatives." When I then turn to that article of the Constitution which provides for the executive power, I find it says:

The executive power shall be vested in a President of the United States of America.

Therefore I say, Mr. Chairman, that, when certain vital measures concerning the purity and the freedom of elections are involved; when the question as to whether the people shall ever have the power, under the Constitution and under the laws, to rid themselves of a party in power which was not properly placed there, or whose policy makes it desirable that it should be turned out; when it comes to the vital question as to whether the people shall be permitted to have a fair opportunity to determine at the ballot-box who shall be their rulers, their representatives have a right to put upon any appropriation bill these measures, and say: "We want the jury-box pure and uncontaminated; we do not want the United States courts used as the machinery of a political party to intimidate whole sections of the country by political prosecutions with partisan juries for alleged election offences, thereby keeping one party in power; we do not want the President of the United States, under his pretended right as commander-in-chief, to move the troops to the polls to deter men from coming there to vote the opposite ticket, and we do not intend that it shall lie in the power of the marshals of the United States, the mere creatures of the President, to appoint any number of irresponsible and corrupt men to stand at the polls and to intimidate the honest voter in his exercise of the elective franchise."

These are measures upon which we stand. The gentleman has truly said that we have well weighed and considered them. We regard them all as vital. They concern the very foundation of free government, the right of the people to express an untrammeled will through the ballot-box, free from violence, corruption, and, above all, Federal interference. I believe that we have made up our minds fully to take all the consequences before the people of an adherence to our views. If the President of the United States prefers to "starve the Government," because the stalwarts of his party demand that he shall assist in raising the "bloody flag" once more, with him will rest the responsibility. If the party in power is determined to perpetuate itself in power by the retention, at all hazards, of all the political machinery by which they have hitherto suppressed the will of the people, and corrupted elections, the battle for an honest jury, the proper administration of justice, the purity and freedom of elections cannot begin too soon. The cry of the professional politician will not deceive the people. The appeal to war feelings will be laughed to scorn. A suffering nation wants peace, quiet, harmony, and relief from the burdens of taxation; and it no longer demands or desires the harassing legislation of the party in power.

Now, is the measure we are considering right and constitutional? This is the particular proposition which I propose to discuss at the present time. I could not follow, if I wished, my colleague in his eloquent and rambling discourse. I did not obtain the floor for that purpose. He has refused to discuss the merits of this question. I desire to discuss them. He indulged in a number of high-sounding phrases of a general character of which only the application was wrong. While he, as the leader upon that side, expressed his confidence in the people of the United States, I must be permitted to say that the statute-book is full of villainous laws which his party enacted, based on the idea that the people are without honest intelligence, full of depravity, ignorance, and corruption. A government of the people cannot last long if such be the fact.

Some of these laws we propose to repeal at the present time; others we propose to repeal at a future day, which, thank God! is not far distant. Then a greater "revolution" than the present will take place. Some gentlemen upon the other side seem to think that "revolution" is always going on when some Republican official is about to be put out of office. [Laughter and applause.] The Government is always in danger unless in the hands of Republican officeholders, and it is treason and disloyalty to pull down any machinery designed to perpetuate their exclusive reign!

Does the measure proposed infringe upon the constitutional right of the President as commander-in-chief of the army? And what are the respective powers of Congress and the President in regard to the army and navy? These are vital questions, and their exceeding importance is my apology for claiming the attention of the House to-day.

The country is under great obligations to the gentleman from Kentucky [Mr. Carlisle] who made so able an exposition yesterday of the extent of the right of the President to interfere, with the Federal troops, in the affairs of a State. It is the duty of every Representative to put himself on record against the wild claims for executive power put forward by gentlemen upon the other side, lest acquiescence in them may be presumed, and be cited as precedent at some distant day. I desire to speak more particularly as to the power of the President over the army, in connection with the powers of Congress.

I was surprised to hear the able member from Maine [WILLIAM P. FRYE] say that, even if we should pass this law, we would not thereby interfere with the President's power; that, as commander-in-chief, he would still possess the power to move the troops wherever he pleased; that he could take them from the Indian frontier and place them in New York, or order them from Galveston to a fort in Maine. If, by this remark, he only meant that, in the absence of any law, the President could exercise these powers, I make no objection. But the gentleman seemed to insist that he could do these things in spite of law; for he argued that, if we passed the measure, the President could yet transport troops where he pleased, and that our law would not reduce expenditures, because it would not control the President in his movements of the troops. Such a claim has been made in this House within my recollection more than once. Gentlemen who make it do not derive their ideas from the true sources of knowledge, the patriotic sources; they do not find such teachings in the writings of the Fathers. They derive their inspiration from the improper action of their own party in the days when it was popular, as I have said, and may have been necessary temporarily to permit the exercise of power by the Executive which it did not possess under the Constitution.

By the Constitution the whole power of declaring war, raising as well as supporting armies, providing and maintaining navies, organizing, arming, and governing the militia, and, above all, of making rules and regulations for the land and naval forces, and for calling forth the militia to execute the laws of the Union, suppressing insurrection, and repelling invasion, is confided in Congress—the representatives of the people. The President is the commander-in-chief of the land and naval forces and the militia when called into service; but, in the language of Alexander Hamilton, he is only the first general and the first admiral in the United States. Does that make him the first general in the land over the law or under the law?

Congress, having power to raise and support an army, may refuse to raise an army at all; or Congress may say that it will only have such an army as is necessary to maintain the peace on the Indian frontier. It may pass a law that ten regiments of cavalry shall constitute the entire standing army of the United States, to be stationed and used only upon the Indian frontier. Such a statute might not be a sensible one, but suppose it should be passed: does the gentleman from Maine contend that the President of the United States would have the right to withdraw these troops from the Indian frontier to the coast of Maine, or send them to harry the people of Louisiana or South Carolina on election day to perpetuate his party in power? I believe his party would act upon the theory that such a right exists.

I maintain that the whole subject of raising, providing, maintaining, and supporting an army and a navy is within the legitimate powers of Congress; that the purposes for which they are raised or provided may be lawfully stated in the statute; that their uses for certain purposes—for example, the maintenance of peace at the polls or use as a *posse comitatus*— may be denied. When such troops or naval forces have been constituted I do not deny that the President is the commander. But he is commander only under the law. Through him orders are conveyed. By him movements, not forbidden by statute, may be made at his pleasure. But, if he can violate the state, he is higher than the Constitution, and becomes at once our king, emperor, dictator, or what you will.

On April 3 George M. Robeson [N. J.] opposed the proviso.

My friend from Ohio warned us that it becomes us to look sharply and keenly to the use of military power, for by the military and through their means republics have always died. I beg to take some issue with him there upon his historic accuracy and fairness. The last final blow to the liberties of republics has usually come from the sword, but it has not been until some branch of the government has usurped to itself rights which it did not enjoy under the constitution and laws of the country, and has thus destroyed the unity and power of civil government. It has not been until some branch of the government, usually a branch claiming most especially to represent the popular will, has usurped to itself powers which did not belong to it and, absorbing or destroying the other branches, has broken down government and unsettled society. It was only after the Long Parliament of England had disgusted the people of England by their disregard of civil and of personal rights and by their assumption to themselves of everything which belonged to the government that that stern soldier, Oliver Cromwell, dared to invade that House and dissolve it with his military power. It was only after the assemblies and the councils of the French Republic had made France with its fair cornfields and its vine-clad hills run red with the blood of its best and noblest, not until Europe was appalled at the scenes of murder and of wrong which they perpetrated, not until the world stood aghast at the crimes which were committed in the name of liberty, that the young Napoleon with his armed soldiery was able to seize upon the government of the country and erect upon its ruins his military empire.

Now, Mr. Chairman, we belong to a system of government with coördinate and limited powers, all bearing relation to each other, each having its appropriate sphere, each clothed with its actual duty, each having, under the Constitution, its proper scope, power, and restraint. It is like the solar system in the heavens, each member of it dependent upon the other, each held in its place, each governed in its motions, each restrained in its orbit by the power and the attractions of the other members of that system. Let one of those spheres invade the orbit of the others, let it break loose from the influence of the laws of gravitation which move and direct it, and from the centripetal and centrifugal forces which hold and control it, what becomes of it and of the system of which it is a member? It wanders abroad not only to the destruction of its coördinate spheres, but an object of terror to the universe and of destruction to itself.

Now, we are here coördinate members of this Government, all held in harmonious accord by rights, privileges, powers, and restrictions of the Constitution of the United States; and, when one member of that system breaks loose from that attraction which holds and restrains it in its true relations to the other members, its old landmarks all swept away, its old traditions all forgotten, its old and safe attractions all gone, it will riot

IX—11

through the system, an object of terror and dismay, a mighty instrument of evil.

Mr. Chairman, it is on the ruins of disrupted systems of government that military power arises. It is in the confusion, the disorder arising from the loss of civil rights to be guaranteed and executed by the civil officers of the law; it is with the overthrow of constitutional law and amid the smoke of such a conflict which this occasions, that the "man on horseback" rises and liberty is sacrificed to order. So long as the civil process of the law may be properly executed by the civil officers in this country, so long there is no danger of military power. The strong arm, the clear head, the brave hearts of our people, North and South, would never yield to a military usurper, though backed by a standing army of a million of men, unless it became absolutely necessary under the pressure of the usurped and arbitrary power of some irresponsible assemblage to sacrifice liberty to order. That time will never come in this country unless we disregard the plain teachings of the Constitution which our Fathers gave to us and which we are sworn to preserve.

Mr. Chairman, the gentleman from Ohio took occasion to say, in allusion to the Executive of this country, that his title was in doubt and his tenure of office yet uncertain. I do not claim to speak for the Executive, but I cannot think the gentleman really meant all that. Certainly I hope he did not mean it as a threat, because, if he did, if that is the giant of revolution "whose baby fingers to-day we see" in the action of this House, let me say to the gentleman that the excitement which is apparent throughout the country to-day is but the mutterings of a storm which will increase in fury, will grow in strength and in resistless power, until the men and the party who endeavor to unsettle the title of the President of the United States will be swept forever from the political horizon. [Loud applause.]

Joseph C. S. Blackburn [Ky.] supported the proviso.

Mr. Chairman, it is generally true that the grave suffices to silence the tongue of detraction. It is not often that its darkened portals are invaded to pronounce severe criticism, even though richly deserved, if it is to be pronounced upon the dead. But the gentleman from Ohio [Gen. Garfield], forgetting himself in his speech on last Saturday, forgot also to observe this manly and magnanimous rule. By that speech he certainly must have sought, or, if not seeking, he was unfortunate in producing the impression that a distinguished dead Senator from the State of Kentucky had introduced into the Federal Senate chamber the bill which we, by this amendment, seek to repeal, and to send his name down to posterity to be blasted by the act. I hold in my hand the very bill which was introduced upon the 5th of January, 1864, by Senator Powell, of Kentucky. There lies before me on my desk the manly, statesmanlike, and patriotic, bold utterances that he delivered in the shape of a speech upon the consideration of that bill. I challenge the gentleman to find within the limits of this measure a single, solitary provision, line, sentence, word, or syllable that this amendment seeks to repeal.

Does not the gentleman know—if he does not, it is his fault —that the amendment incorporated upon this bill which we now seek to repeal was incorporated and ingrafted upon it, not when the Senate was in Committee of the Whole, but in open Senate, upon motion of Senator Samuel C. Pomeroy [Kan.], and, when the vote was taken upon that amendment by yeas and nays, every solitary Democrat in that Chamber voted against it and put the seal of his condemnation upon it, Mr. Powell among the number? Here stands Senator Powell's utterance, in which he explains how and why it was that the Democratic members in that body and this body at last accepted this as the best that could be had; notwithstanding, against their protest, the ingrafting of the Pomeroy amendment, because it was to be taken in lieu of what they charged was true, of what the President of the United States in an official communication to Congress had declared to be true, that, in the absence of even the limitations that amended bill would give, the military authorities and officers of the Government had arrogated to themselves the power in all the lately seceding States of declaring what should be the qualification of voters and what should be the qualification to hold office. It was as the least offensive of two offensive alternatives. It was not candid, it was not fair; the record rebukes the gentleman for seeking to place a dead statesman in such a false position.

But, Mr. Chairman, it is useless to follow these things further. It is not, sir, for me to waste the time and trench upon the patience of this committee by following out the tergiversations through which the Republican party has wound itself to this high plane of protest against revolutionary legislation. Why, sir, the gentleman from Ohio, in 1872, made a speech upon this floor which he will not deny. It was, as is always the case with his efforts, an adroit as well as an able speech. In that he declared that the minority to which we then belonged, but in which in God's providence we are no longer found—he declared that the minority were guilty of revolution. For what? Because they insisted that extraneous matter should not be put upon appropriation bills. He said that was revolution. [Laughter and applause.] We took him at his word, and now where does he stand? It was revolution then to resist the injection of extraneous matter over the protest of the majority. It is revolution now for the majority to resist that same protest of that minority; but, in the one case, it was his side protesting, in the other case, it was ours.

Ah, Mr. Chairman, let one take the darkened pages of his country's history for the last seventeen long years and read them carefully, and tell me, then, whether it lies in the mouth of that worthy leader of a once great but waning party to read lectures to anybody, either upon the score of revolutionary legislation or of extraneous introductions into appropriation bills.

Better far, in the face of the record that they have made, better to listen patiently to the confirmed inebriate as he dilates upon the virtues of temperance, better let the queen of the demimonde elaborate the beauties of female virtue, or let the devil prate of the scheme of universal redemption, than for homilies upon good morals and lectures upon revolutionary legislation to be delivered from such a source. [Applause.]

There is but one issue here, and I insist that neither this House nor the people of this country shall be allowed to wander from it. It is but this, and nothing more: whether the military power shall be allowed at your polls; whether the elections shall be guarded by the mailed hand of military power; whether the ballot-box, that last and safest shield of the freeman's liberties, shall be turned over to the tender mercies of the armies of your land. Or, to state it yet more tersely and probably more fairly, it is simply whether the spirit and the genius of this Government shall be reversed, and whether the civil shall be made subordinate to the military power.

Why, sir, among the most favored, the most cherished and precious principles ingrafted on our system of government from our old prototype, the English people, is that provision which would not tolerate not only the interference but the presence of the military at the polls. Over one hundred years ago an English statute [of George II] declared the will of Englishmen upon this vital question, ordering the troops to remain two or more miles from places of election.

From that time till now I do declare that it is not within the power of any man to find a single scion of the Saxon race that has not held in utter abhorrence the efforts of him or them who sought to control the freedom of the ballot by the employment of the military power. [Applause.]

The very army of this country protests against such a prostitution of its service.

I see before me the justly distinguished general-in-chief of our army [Philip H. Sheridan], and I do not believe that I overstate the fact when I say that from him down to the private in the ranks it is difficult to find one who has not recoiled from this service which they have been called upon to render. [Applause.]

It is this question, and it is none other, that I insist shall be kept before this House. We are declaring that the ballot shall be free. We are denying that it is either constitutional, legal, just, fair, or decent to subject the sovereign to the surveillance of the soldier.

Now, upon that issue the gentleman from Ohio and his associates tell us that they stand committed. I answer so do we. We are willing to discuss it, and, for my part, I shall oppose any limitation being put upon this debate. If we cannot stand upon an issue so broad, so constitutional, so catholic, so fair, so free as this, then tell me in Heaven's name where are there battlements strong enough for us to get behind? Let it go to the country that one party asserts that the manacles shall fall from the limbs of the citizen, and that the army shall not hold its mailed hand at the throat of the sovereign, and that the other party refuses to release the throttling grasp, and declares that it will block the wheels of the government and bring it to starvation.

I am willing, and those with whom I stand are willing, to accept this issue, and we go further, we tender it. We are the ones to make the issue and we are ready for you to accept it. Planting ourselves upon this broad ground, we welcome controversy. We seek no quarrel with you, but, for the first time in eighteen years past, the Democracy is back in power in both branches of this legislature, and she proposes to signalize her return to power; she proposes to celebrate her recovery of her long-lost heritage by tearing off these degrading badges of servitude and destroying the machinery of a corrupt and partisan legislation.

We do not intend to stop until we have stricken from the statute-book the last vestige of your war measures, which were born of the passions incident to civil strife and looked to the abridgment of the liberty of the citizen.

We demand an untrammeled election; no supervising of the ballot by the army. Free, absolutely free, right to the citizen in the deposit of his ballot as a condition precedent to the passage of your bills.

Now, sir, if the gentleman from Ohio is to be excused, for surely he cannot be justified, if he is to be excused for parading before this House the threat, the *argumentum in terrorem* of a veto that is already cut and dried to be placed upon a bill that is not yet passed; if he is to be pardoned for warning this House that the executive branch of this Government will never yield its assent to this measure in its present form, may I not be warranted and justified in employing equal candor, and may I not assure that gentleman and his associates that the dominant party of this Congress, the ruling element of this body, is also equally determined that, until their just demands are satisfied, demands sanctioned by all laws human and divine, protected and hedged around by precedents without number, demanded by the people of this land without regard to section, who are clamoring for a free, untrammeled ballot (not for the South, I beg you to remember, for, if there be sectionality in this issue, I cannot discover it); for Philadelphia as well as for New Orleans, for San Francisco and Boston as well as for Charleston and Savannah—that this side of the chamber, which has demonstrated its power, never means to yield or surrender until this Congress shall have died by virtue of its limitation. [Applause on the Democratic side.] We will not yield. A principle cannot be compromised. It may be surrendered; but that can only be done by its advocates giving proof to the world that they are cravens and cowards, lacking the courage of their own conviction. We cannot yield, and will not surrender.

Let me assure my friend, and it is a picture that I know he does not dwell upon with pleasure, that this is the restoration to power of a party as old as our Government itself, which, for almost a hundred years, has stood the boldest, fairest, freest exponent and champion and defender of the doctrine of constitutional limitations against the doctrine of the aggrandizement of power. It is this organization that has come back to rule, that means to rule, and means to rule in obedience to law.

Now, sir, the issue is laid down, the gage of battle is delivered. Lift it when you please; we are willing to appeal to that sovereign arbiter that the gentleman so handsomely lauded, the American people, to decide between us.

Standing upon such grounds, we intend to deny to the President of this Republic the right to exercise such unconstitutional power. We do not mean to pitch this contest upon ground of objection to him who happens, if not by the grace of God yet by the run of luck, to be administering that office.

I tell you here that if from yonder canvas [pointing to the picture of Washington] the first President of this Republic should step down and resume those powers that the grateful people of an infant republic conferred upon him as their first Chief Magistrate, if he were here fired by that patriotic ardor that moved him in the earlier and better days of this Republic, to him we would never consent to yield such dangerous and unwarranted powers, to rest the liberties of the citizens upon any one man's discretion, nor would he receive it.

It was not for the earlier but for the later Executives of this Government to grasp and seek to retain such questionable prerogatives. You cannot have it. The issue is made—it is made upon principle, not upon policy. It cannot be abandoned; it will not be surrendered. Standing upon such ground, clothed in such a panoply, resting this case upon the broadest principles of eternal justice, we are content to appeal to the people of this land. There is no tribunal to which we are not willing to carry this case of contest; and we are willing to allow Him who rules the destinies of men to judge between us and give victory to the right.

I do not mean to issue a threat. Unlike the gentleman from Ohio, I disclaim any authority to threaten. But I do mean to say that it is my deliberate conviction that there is not to be found in this majority a single man who will ever consent to abandon one jot or tittle of the faith that is in him. He cannot surrender if he would. I beg you to believe he will not be coerced by threats nor intimidated by parade of power. He must stand upon his conviction and there we will all stand. He who dallies is a dastard, and he who doubts is damned. [Great applause on the Democratic side.]

General Garfield replied to Mr. Blackburn on April 4.

The gentleman from Kentucky [Mr. Blackburn] evidently thought he was making a telling point against me when he cited the fact that in 1872 I insisted upon the adoption of a conference report on an appropriation bill that had a rider on it; and he alleged that I said it was revolutionary for his party to resist it. Let me refresh his memory. I said then, and I say now, that it was revolutionary for the minority party to refuse to let the appropriation bill be voted on. For four days they said we should not vote at all on the sundry civil appropriation bill because there was a rider on it, put there, not by the House, but by the Senate.

I was sorry the rider was put on, and moved to non-concur in the amendments when they came to the House. But, when the minority on this floor said that we should not act on the bill at all, because the rider was put upon it, I said, and now say, it was unjustifiable parliamentary obstruction. We do not filibuster. We do not struggle to prevent a vote on this bill. I will be loyal to the House that I am a member of, and maintain now as I did then the right of the majority to bring an appropriation bill to a vote.

You have a right, however unwise and indecent it may be as a matter of parliamentary practice—you have a perfect right to put this rider on this bill and pass it. When you send it to the Senate, that body has a perfect right to pass it. It is your constitutional right and theirs to pass it; for the free consent of each body is the basis of the law-making power.

When it goes to the President of the United States it is his constitutional right to approve it; and, if he does, it will then be a law which you and I must obey. But it is equally his constitutional right to disapprove of it; and, should he do so, then, gentlemen, unless two-thirds of this body and two-thirds of the Senate pass it, notwithstanding the objections of the President, it is not only not your right to make it a law, but it will be the flattest violation of the Constitution, the sheerest usurpation of power, for you to make it a law in any other way. Without these conditions you cannot make it a law.

What, then, is the proposition you have offered? You say that there are certain odious laws that you want to take off the statute-books. I say, repeal them, if you can do so constitutionally. But you declare that you will compel consent to your will by refusing the necessary support—not to the President, not to any man—but to the Government itself. This proposition I denounce as revolution, and no man has responded to the charge either by argument or denial.

You threatened the President in advance, before you allowed him an opportunity to say yes or no. You entered this hall fulminating threats against him in a high-sounding proclamation. You thundered in the index. It remains to be seen whether, in the body of your work and in its concluding paragraphs, your thunder will be as terrible as it was in the opening chapter. By adopting the program of the last House you have made it your own; but you have put the measures in their most offensive forms by tacking them all to the two great appropriation bills.

My distinguished friend from Virginia [John R. Tucker], who has come nearer meeting this case with argument than any other man on this floor, has made a point which I respect as an evidence of the gallantry of his intellect. He says that, under our Constitution, we can vote supplies to the army but for two years, that we may impose conditions upon our supplies, and, if these be refused, the army ceases to exist after the 30th of June next. In short, that the annual army bill is the act of reconstructing the army. He is mistaken in one vital point. The army is an organization created by general laws, and, so far as the creation of offices and grades is concerned, it is independent of the appropriation bills. The supply, of course, comes through appropriation bills. I grant that, if supplies are refused to the army, it must perish of inanition. It becomes a skeleton; but its anatomy was created by general law and it would remain a skeleton, your monument of starvation. The gentleman from Virginia says: "Unless you let us append a condition, which we regard as a redress of grievances, we will let the army be annihilated on the 30th day of next June by withholding supplies." That is legitimate argument; that is a frank declaration of your policy. Let us examine the proposition. What is the "grievance" of which the gentleman complains? He uses the word "grievance" in the old English sense, as though the king were thrusting himself in the way of the nation by making a war contrary to the nation's wish. But his "grievance" is a law of the land—a law made by the representatives of the people—by all the forms of consent known to the Constitution. It is his "grievance" that he cannot get rid of this law by the ordinary and constitutional methods of repeal. [Applause.] When he can get rid of any law by the union of all consents that are required to make or unmake a law, then he can lawfully get rid of it, whether it is a grievance or a blessing. But his method is first to call a law a "grievance," and then try to get rid of it in defiance of the process which the Constitution prescribes for the law-making power of the nation. I denounce his method as unconstitutional and revolutionary, and one that will result in far greater evil than that of which he complains.

If the party which, after eighteen years' banishment from power, has come back, as the gentleman from Kentucky [Mr.

Blackburn] said yesterday, to its "birthright of power" is to signalize its return by striking down the gallant and faithful army of the United States, the people of this country will not be slow to understand that there are reminiscences of that army which these gentlemen would willingly forget, by burying both the army and the memories of its great service to the Union in one grave. [Applause.]

We do not seek to revive the unhappy memories of the war; but we are unwilling to see the army perish at the hands of Congress, even if its continued existence should occasionally awaken the memory of its former glories.

Now, let it be understood, once for all, that we do not deny, we have never denied, your right to make rules for this House just as you please. Under those rules, as you make or construe them, you may put all your legislation upon these bills as "riders." But, we say that, whatever your rules may be, you must make or repeal a law in accordance with the Constitution by the triple consent to which I referred the other day, or you must do it by violence.

My friend from Virginia, whom I know to be a master and lover of mathematics, has formulated his argument into an equation: "Right equals duty plus power." His notions of duty lead him to tear down the laws which the Republic enacted to protect the purity of national elections and to authorize the army to be used to keep the peace while the national voice is finding expression at the polls. That, I say, is his notion of duty, of which he is sole arbiter; but when he comes to super-add power, in order to complete his "right" as a legislator, I hope he will not evoke that power out of his consciousness, but will seek for it in the great charter, the Constitution of the United States. According to his own algebra, he must have both these elements before he can claim the "right" to overturn these laws which he denounces as grievances.

The gentleman from Maryland [Robert M. McLane] said the other day there was nothing in the Constitution which empowered any officer of the United States to keep the peace in the States. A single sentence, Mr. Chairman, before your hammer falls. I ask that gentleman, when he rises to respond, whether the United States has no power to keep the peace in the great post-office in Baltimore City; so that the postmaster may attend to his duties; whether we have not the power to keep the peace along the line of every railroad that carries our mails, or where any post-rider of the "star service" carries the mail on his saddle; whether we have not the right, if need be,

to line the post-road with troops and to bring the guns of the
navy to bear to protect any customhouse or lighthouse of the
United States? And yet, if the gentleman's theory be correct,
we cannot enforce a single civil process of this Government by
the aid of an armed *posse* without making it a penitentiary
offence to be visited upon the officer who does it. [Applause on
the Republican side.]

The bill was passed on April 4 by a vote of 148 to
122. After still more extended debate in the Senate it
was passed on April 25 by a vote of 41 to 30. It was
vetoed by President Hayes on April 30. He submitted
the following reasons for his action:

Under existing laws there can be no military interference
with the elections. No case of such interference has, in fact,
occurred since the passage of the act last referred to. No soldier
of the United States has appeared under orders at any place of
election in any State. No complaint even of the presence of
United States troops has been made in any quarter. It may
therefore be confidently stated that there is no necessity for the
enactment of section 6 of the bill before me to prevent military
interference with the elections. The laws already in force are
all that are required for that end.

But that part of section 6 of this bill which is significant and
vitally important is the clause which, if adopted, will deprive the
civil authorities of the United States of all power to keep the
peace at the congressional elections. The congressional elections
in every district, in a very important sense, are justly a matter
of political interest and concern throughout the whole country.
Each State, every political party, is entitled to the share of
power which is conferred by the legal and constitutional suffrage. It is the right of every citizen possessing the qualifications prescribed by law to cast one unintimidated ballot and to
have his ballot honestly counted. So long as the exercise of this
power and the enjoyment of this right are common and equal,
practically as well as formally, submission to the results of the
suffrage will be accorded loyally and cheerfully, and all the departments of Government will feel the true vigor of the popular
will thus expressed.

The Supreme Court has held that the Fifteenth Amendment
invests the citizens of the United States with a new constitutional right which is within the protecting power of Congress.
That right the court declares to be exemption from discrimina-

tion in the exercise of the elective franchise on account of race, color, or previous condition of servitude. The power of Congress to protect this right by appropriate legislation is expressly affirmed by the court.

National legislation to provide safeguards for free and honest elections is necessary, as experience has shown, not only to secure the right to vote to the enfranchised race at the South, but also to prevent fraudulent voting in the large cities of the North. Congress has, therefore, exercised the power conferred by the Constitution, and has enacted certain laws to prevent discriminations on account of race, color, or previous condition of servitude, and to punish fraud, violence, and intimidation at Federal elections.

If the proposed legislation should become the law there will be no power vested in any officer of the Government to protect from violence the officers of the United States engaged in the discharge of their duties. Their rights and duties under the law will remain, but the National Government will be powerless to enforce its own statutes. The States may employ both military and civil power to keep the peace, and to enforce the laws at State elections. It is now proposed to deny to the United States even the necessary civil authority to protect the national elections. No sufficient reason has been given for this discrimination in favor of the State and against the national authority. If well-founded objections exist against the present national election laws all good citizens should unite in their amendment. The laws providing the safeguards of the elections should be impartial, just, and efficient. They should, if possible, be so nonpartisan and fair in their operation that the minority—the party out of power—will have no just grounds to complain. The present laws have, in practice, unquestionably conduced to the prevention of fraud and violence at the elections. In several of the States members of different political parties have applied for the safeguards which they furnish. It is the right and duty of the National Government to enact and enforce laws which will secure free and fair congressional elections. The laws now in force should not be repealed, except in connection with the enactment of measures which will better accomplish that important end. Believing that section 6 of the bill before me will weaken, if it does not altogether take away, the power of the National Government to protect the Federal elections by the civil authorities, I am forced to the conclusion that it ought not to receive my approval.

This section is, however, not presented to me as a separate

and independent measure, but is, as has been stated, attached to the bill making the usual annual appropriations for the support of the army. It makes a vital change in the election laws of the country, which is in no way connected with the use of the army. It prohibits, under heavy penalties, any person engaged in the civil service of the United States from having any force at the place of any election prepared to preserve order, to make arrests, to keep the peace, or in any manner to enforce the laws. This is altogether foreign to the purpose of an army appropriation bill. The practice of tacking to appropriation bills measures not pertinent to such bills did not prevail until more than forty years after the adoption of the Constitution. It has become a common practice. All parties when in power have adopted it. Many abuses and great waste of public money have in this way crept into appropriation bills. The public opinion of the country is against it. The States which have recently adopted constitutions have generally provided a remedy for the evil by enacting that no law shall contain more than one subject, which shall be plainly expressed in its title. The constitutions of more than half of the States contain substantially this provision. The public welfare will be promoted in many ways by a return to the early practice of the Government, and to the true principle of legislation, which requires that every measure shall stand or fall according to its own merits. If it were understood that to attach to an appropriation bill a measure irrelevant to the general object of the bill would imperil and probably prevent its final passage and approval, a valuable reform in the parliamentary practice of Congress would be accomplished. The best justification that has been offered for attaching irrelevant riders to appropriation bills is that it is done for convenience' sake, to facilitate the passage of measures which are deemed expedient by all the branches of government which participate in legislation. It cannot be claimed that there is any such reason for attaching this amendment of the election laws to the army appropriation bill. The history of the measure contradicts this assumption. A majority of the House of Representatives in the last Congress was in favor of section 6 of this bill. It was known that a majority of the Senate was opposed to it, and that as a separate measure it could not be adopted. It was attached to the army appropriation bill to compel the Senate to assent to it. It was plainly announced to the Senate that the army appropriation bill would not be allowed to pass unless the proposed amendments of the election laws were adopted with it. The Senate refused to assent to the bill on account of this irrelevant section.

Congress thereupon adjourned without passing an appropriation bill for the army, and the present extra session of the Forty-sixth Congress became necessary to furnish the means to carry on the Government.

Upon the assembling of this Congress, in pursuance of a call for an extra session, which was made necessary by the failure of the Forty-fifth Congress to make the needful appropriations for the support of the Government, the question was presented whether the attempt made in the last Congress to ingraft, by construction, a new principle upon the Constitution should be persisted in or not. This Congress has ample opportunity and time to pass the appropriation bills, and also to enact any political measures which may be determined upon in separate bills by the usual and orderly methods of proceeding. But the majority of both Houses have deemed it wise to adhere to the principles asserted and maintained in the last Congress by the majority of the House of Representatives. That principle is that the House of Representatives has the sole right to originate bills for raising revenue, and therefore has the right to withhold appropriations upon which the existence of the Government may depend, unless the Senate and the President shall give their assent to any legislation which the House may see fit to attach to appropriation bills. To establish this principle is to make a radical, dangerous, and unconstitutional change in the character of our institutions. The various departments of the Government, and the army and the navy, are established by the Constitution, or by laws passed in pursuance thereof. Their duties are clearly defined, and their support is carefully provided for by law. The money required for this purpose has been collected from the people, and is now in the treasury ready to be paid out as soon as the appropriation bills are passed. Whether appropriations are made or not the collection of the taxes will go on. The public money will accumulate in the treasury. It was not the intention of the framers of the Constitution that any single branch of the Government should have the power to dictate conditions upon which this treasure should be applied to the purposes for which it was collected. Any such intention, if it had been entertained, would have been plainly expressed in the Constitution.

That a majority of the Senate now concurs in the claim of the House adds to the gravity of the situation, but does not alter the question at issue. The new doctrine, if maintained, will result in a consolidation of unchecked and despotic power in the House of Representatives. A bare majority of the House will become the Government. The Executive will no longer be what the framers of the Constitution intended, an equal and independent branch of the Government. It is clearly the constitutional duty of the President to exercise his discretion and judgment upon all bills presented to him without constraint or duress from any other branch of the Government. To say that a majority of either or both of the Houses of Congress may insist upon the approval of a bill under the penalty of stopping all of the operations of the Government for want of the necessary supplies is to deny to the Executive that share of the legislative power which is plainly conferred by the second section of the seventh article of the Constitution. It strikes from the Constitution the qualified negative of the President. It is said that this should be done because it is the peculiar function of the House of Representatives to represent the will of the people. But no single branch or department of the Government has exclusive authority to speak for the American people. The most authentic and solemn expression of their will is contained in the Constitution of the United States. By that Constitution they have ordained and established a government whose powers are distributed among coördinate branches, which, as far as possible, consistently with a harmonious coöperation, are absolutely independent of each other. The people of this country are unwilling to see the supremacy of the Constitution replaced by the omnipotence of any one department of the Government.

The enactment of this bill into a law will establish a precedent which will tend to destroy the equal independence of the several branches of the Government. Its principle places not merely the Senate and the Executive, but the judiciary also, under the coercive dictation of the House. The House alone will be the judge of what constitutes a grievance, and also of the means and measure of redress. An act of Congress to protect elections is now the grievance complained of. But the House may, on the same principle, determine that any other act of Congress, a treaty made by the President with the advice and consent of the Senate, a nomination or appointment to office, or that a decision or opinion of the Supreme Court is a grievance, and that the measure of redress is to withhold the appropriations required for the support of the offending branch of the Government.

Believing that this bill is a dangerous violation of the spirit and meaning of the Constitution, I am compelled to return it to the House in which it originated without my approval. The qualified negative with which the Constitution invests the President is a trust that involves a duty which he cannot decline to

perform. With a firm and conscientious purpose to do what I
can to preserve, unimpaired, the constitutional powers and equal
independence, not merely of the Executive, but of every branch
of the Government, which will be imperiled by the adoption of
the principle of this bill, I desire earnestly to urge upon the
House of Representatives a return to the wise and wholesome
usage of the earlier days of the Republic, which excluded from
appropriation bills all irrelevant legislation. By this course you
will inaugurate an important reform in the method of congressional legislation; your action will be in harmony with the fundamental principles of the Constitution and the patriotic sentiment of nationality which is their firm support; and you will
restore to the country that feeling of confidence and security
and the repose which are so essential to the prosperity of all of
our fellow-citizens.

The House, on May 1, by a vote of 120 yeas to 110
nays (less than the requisite two-thirds affirmative vote),
failed to pass the bill over the President's veto.

Rider on Civil Appropriations Bill

The same attempt to coerce the President was made
in the case of the legislative, executive, and judicial
appropriations bill. Mr. McMahon introduced in the
House an amendment to the bill to the effect that, in
order to provide for the speedy payment of arrearages
of pensions, the Secretary of the Treasury be instructed
to issue $10,000,000 in legal-tender notes held as a special
fund for the redemption of fractional currency.

General Garfield raised the point of order that the
amendment proposed a mode of raising revenue and an
issue of obligations of the United States which were not
germane to anything in the bill, and, in this respect,
changed the existing law which limited the issue of legal
tenders. If permitted to stand, it and other similar
amendments would destroy the whole plan of resumption
of specie payments.

Mr. McMahon replied:

When we have ten millions of idle money in the United States
treasury which ought to be issued and paid out, money which is

doing the Government no good and the people no good—I say when the soldiers of this country have been notified there is, or will be, a deficiency in the United States treasury, so that they cannot get their arrearages of pension unless there be additional taxation or an additional issue of bonds, I am surprised to see the gentleman from Ohio get up and make the point of order against the soldiers of the country to prevent them from speedily receiving these $10,000,000, which is only a part of what is due to them. I supposed the gentleman owed an allegiance to them far superior to the allegiance he might owe to Wall Street or the capitalists of the country. I make use of this language advisedly, for there is no portion of the people of this country interested in keeping this money locked up in the treasury except those who are interested in mercilessly contracting the currency of the United States so as to make money dear and harder to get, and enhance thereby the extent of their wealth.

Why should this money continue to lie idle in the treasury? Why shall the poor soldier be compelled to wait for new bonds or new taxes? The Secretary of the Treasury tells us in this letter to the chairman of Ways and Means that for the coming fiscal year there will probably be a deficiency of $27,000,000. To meet that deficiency he says that new taxes must be imposed or more bonds be put out. Now at the present time we do not propose to impose any new taxes unless necessary. As Mr. Sherman says in this letter, no new taxes can be immediately productive. He therefore recommends that authority be given to him to raise the amount necessary by the sale of 4 per cent. bonds. Now I say instead of putting out these 4 per cent. bonds, which would be a crime while we have this money, we should put into circulation this money which is kept idle in the treasury, the purpose for which it was to be held in reserve having passed away. It should now be put into circulation as a part of the $346,000,000 which is authorized by law. I repeat that it is a crime against the people to keep it hoarded.

It never was in contemplation of the gentlemen who passed that law in 1876 that when that $10,000,000 was taken in it should be kept. That was a little private scheme of contraction of Mr. Sherman himself. Our order to him was to pay out in redemption of fractional currency. Instead of that he is redeeming constantly in silver coin and keeping the $10,000,000 in.

MR. GARFIELD.—I am not responsible for the secretary's execution of his duty under that law. But I should say if I were the secretary I was bound by the law and by the reason

IX—12

of the case to hold a sufficient amount of that fund to be an ample protection for all the outstanding scrip which would be likely to come in. Perhaps the secretary has kept more than he needed to; and, if he has, it is perfectly competent for this Congress to ascertain, after a fair examination, how much of that he can spare, and then let it out. I will agree to that at any time. But my colleague took no such method as that; he says simply let it all go, and he proposes to make this sweeping change of law and give up the whole reserve for that purpose, and therefore to that extent, or at least to some extent, breaks over the line of our reserve.

My colleague pained me by a single expression in his speech. When he said that I owed more allegiance to the soldier than perhaps to any other class, and when he said further that I appeared to act as though I owed my chief allegiance to Wall Street, he said what he had no more right to say on this floor, either as a matter of fact or a matter of fair inference, than I would have a right to say he owes his chief allegiance to the whisky-shops of Dayton.

MR. McMAHON.—If in all the discussions which have ever taken place in this House or this country on financial questions the gentleman can show one vote or one speech that was not based upon the idea of speedy resumption, no matter at what cost to the great mass of the people, even when his own party separated from him upon that question in the Forty-third Congress, when he was in a minority in his own party upon this question—if he can show one vote which he ever cast in favor of what was regarded then by the majority of his own party in the West as the interest of the people on this question, I will take my statement back.

MR. GARFIELD.—I will relieve my colleague upon that point. He could not certainly praise me any more according to my notions of legislative praise than to say what he has said. If I ever did cast a vote that was not in favor of the resumption of specie payments, that was not against all schemes to delay it unreasonably and prevent it, then I cast a vote that my conscience and my judgment disapproved of. [Applause.] And I do not know but I have cast as many votes as any man on this floor against Wall Street and the business of gold-gambling there which has been destroyed by resumption; that gold-gambling in Wall Street which locked up one hundred millions of the business capital of this country for fifteen years, away from all profitable investment, and converted Wall Street into a faro hell gambling with the business of this country up and down. And if every vote of mine in favor of honest money has not been a blow at gambling in Wall Street, then it has not had the effect I intended. [Applause.]

The Chair ruled against General Garfield's point of order. Mr. McMahon's amendment was agreed to. Other amendments were made modifying statutes authorizing the appointment of supervisors, etc., of elections, repealing their canvass of votes, etc. The bill was passed by the House on April 26 by a vote of 141 to 120. The Senate passed it on May 20 by a vote of 37 to 27.

President Hayes vetoed the bill on May 29. After referring to his former objections to "riders" on appropriation bills which were not germane thereto, he spoke in particular of the effect of the repeal of the election statutes.

If this bill is approved only the shadow of the authority of the United States at the national elections will remain—the substance will be gone. The supervision of the elections will be reduced to a mere inspection, without authority on the part of the supervisors to do any act whatever to make the election a fair one. All that will be left to the supervisors is the permission to have such oversight of the elections as political parties are in the habit of exercising without any authority of law, in order to prevent their opponents from obtaining unfair advantages. The object of the bill is to destroy any control whatever by the United States over the congressional elections.

The passage of this bill has been urged upon the ground that the election of members of Congress is a matter which concerns the States alone; that these elections should be controlled exclusively by the States; that there are and can be no such elections as national elections; and that the existing law of the United States regulating the congressional elections is without warrant in the Constitution. It is evident, however, that the framers of the Constitution regarded the election of members of Congress in every State and in every district as, in a very important sense, justly a matter of political interest and concern to the whole country. The original provision of the Constitution on this subject is as follows (section 4, article 1):

The times, places, and manner of holding elections for Senators and Representatives shall be prescribed in each State by the legislature therof;

but the Congress may at any time by law make or alter such regulations, except as to the places of choosing Senators.

A further provision has been since added, which is embraced in the Fifteenth Amendment.

The bill before me itself recognizes the principle that the congressional elections are not State elections, but national elections. It leaves in full force the existing statute under which supervisors are still to be appointed by national authority, to "observe and witness" the congressional elections whenever due application is made by citizens who desire said elections to be "guarded and scrutinized." If the power to supervise, in any respect whatever, the congressional elections exists under section 4, article 1, of the Constitution, it is a power which, like every other power belonging to the Government of the United States, is paramount and supreme, and includes the right to employ the necessary means to carry it into effect.

The framers of these laws have not been disappointed in their results. In the large cities, under their provisions, the elections have been comparatively peaceable, orderly, and honest. Even the opponents of these laws have borne testimony to their value and efficiency, and to the necessity for their enactment. The committee of the Forty-fourth Congress, composed of members a majority of whom were opposed to these laws, in their report on the New York election of 1876, said:

Whatever may have been the previous habit or conduct of elections in those cities, or howsoever they may conduct themselves in the future, this election of 1876 will stand as a monument of what good faith, honest endeavor, legal forms, and just authority may do for the protection of the electoral franchise.

The great body of all parties want free and fair elections. They do not think that a free election means freedom from the wholesome restraints of law, or that the place of an election should be a sanctuary for lawlessness and crime. So far from public opinion in any part of the country favoring any relaxation of the authority of the Government in the protection of elections from violence and corruption, I believe it demands greater vigor, both in the enactment and in the execution of laws framed for that purpose. Any oppression, any partisan partiality, which experience may have shown in the working of existing laws, may well engage the careful attention both of Congress and of the Executive in their respective spheres of duty for the correction of these mischiefs. But with my views, both of the constitutionality and of the value of the existing laws, I cannot approve any measure for their repeal except in connection with the enactment of other legislation which may reasonably be expected to afford wiser and more efficient safeguards for free and honest congressional elections.

The reading of the sentence, closing with the words "this election of 1876 will stand as a monument of what good faith, honest endeavor, legal forms, and just authority may do for the protection of the electoral franchise," was greeted with derisive laughter on the Democratic side, followed by applause on the Republican side.

CHAPTER V

A STANDING ARMY

Debate in the House on a Bill to Raise Provisional Troops in View of the Hostile Attitude of France [1798]: In Favor, Harrison Gray Otis [Mass.], Robert G. Harper [S. C.], John Rutledge, Jr. [S. C.]; Opposed, John Nicholas [Va.], Albert Gallatin [Pa.], Abraham Baldwin [Ga.], Joseph McDowell [N. C.], Gen. Thomas Sumter [S. C.]—In 1800 Mr. Nicholas Moves to Reduce the Army—Debate on His Motion: In Favor, Mr. Nicholas, Mr. Gallatin, Robert Williams [N. C.], John Randolph [Va.]; Opposed, John Marshall [Va.], James A. Bayard, Sr. [Del.], Gen. Henry Lee [Va.], Mr. Otis, Mr. Harper—Motion is Lost—Mr. Randolph Is Insulted by Army Officers—He Writes Derogatory Letter to the President—Debate on It as a "Breach of Privilege" Ends in a Deadlock.

D URING the strained relations between France and the United States in the closing years of the eighteenth century (Administration of John Adams) the party in power (Federalist) advocated a vigorous military and naval policy for the defence of the country.

In April, 1798, a bill was passed by the Senate to raise a provisional army of 20,000 men. Coming before the House on the 24th of the month it was vigorously opposed by the opposition (Republican).

ON THE PROVISIONAL ARMY

HOUSE OF REPRESENTATIVES, APRIL 24–MAY 10, 1798

John Nicholas [Va.] opposed the first reading of the bill because of its principle; it transferred to the Executive the highest act of legislative power, the raising of an army which the President was to use at his pleasure.

If an army was necessary the legislature ought to raise it; but he did not think it was necessary at present. Indeed, when

182

discussing the bill for providing a naval armament, gentlemen
had said that members had been willing to make preparations
for defence on the land, where there was no danger, but were
unwilling to do it at sea, where the greatest might be expected.
He did not believe there could be any necessity for going into a
measure of this kind at the present session. In case of pred-
atory attack the militia would be equal to repelling them. Mr.
N. said he lived in a part of the country perhaps more defenceless than any other; but, so far as he or his constituents were
concerned, he did not wish for a force of this kind. He was
willing to confide for defence on the militia of the country.

Harrison Gray Otis [Mass.] was of opinion that the
gentleman anticipated objections to the bill which did
not lie against it; he seemed to suppose that it proposed
raising a standing army.

It does no such thing; it only declares that, if existing circumstances shall make it necessary, then the President shall raise
an army not exceeding a certain number of men. It may happen
that the necessity may not exist; but the gentleman from Virginia must be able to fathom the intentions of France further
than he could pretend to do, if he could say that no such necessity would exist. If what was said by the agents of that government to our envoys could be relied on, there was a direct threat
to ravage our coasts. What is to prevent Victor Hugues [a San
Domingo adventurer] sending over two or three frigates? It
had been said that Hugues expected open war, and that he was
ready for it. In short, it would be the most disgraceful conduct
that ever was attempted in that House if the bill should be rejected without a second reading. It would be in vain to talk of
unanimity if a bill from the Senate was to be treated in this way.

ALBERT GALLATIN [Pa.] wondered that the gentleman from
Massachusetts should be so greatly surprised at a motion of this
kind, because, if he had attended to the rules of the House, he
would have found that it was a course expressly prescribed by
them. It had been acted upon before during this session. The
principle, he said, was well understood. When a member disapproves of the principle of a bill altogether, and does not wish
to go at all into a discussion of the detail, he moves to reject
it before it goes to a second reading.

This bill goes to authorize the President to raise an army.
He did not know what was meant by a provisional army. He
did not find anything said in the Constitution of the United

States relative to provisional armies, or of giving the President power to raise armies. He found mentioned there no other kind of defence than an army and militia. It says Congress shall raise and support an army, not provide for the raising of an army; but this bill is to enable the President of the United States to raise an army. The Constitution has declared that the raising of an army is placed in Congress, but this bill goes to declare that this power shall be vested by law in the President. That is the principle of the bill; and if Congress were once to admit the principle that they have a right to vest in the President powers placed in their hands by the Constitution that instrument would become a piece of blank paper. If it were to be admitted in one case, it would be admitted in another; and, if admitted in one department, it might be admitted in another. The power to raise taxes, he said, is contained in the same article of the Constitution which says Congress shall raise armies. And if they could delegate the power of raising an army to the President, why not do the same with respect to the power of raising taxes? He supposed the House would next hear of provisional taxes, to be raised if the President shall think fit. Mr. G., therefore, thought the principle inadmissible. If the circumstances of the Union required an army, let it be raised; if not, he wished to give no power to raise it—especially, as the President, if he saw necessity, could call Congress together, if he should find that the circumstances of the country required it.

ROBERT G. HARPER [S. C.] believed, notwithstanding what had been advanced by the gentleman from Pennsylvania [Mr. Gallatin], that this was a very unprecedented measure; because, however prepared the House may be on some occasions, at the first blush of business, to decide upon the abstract principle, yet it was perfectly novel in their proceedings to reject a bill on its first reading, which contains such a variety of propositions, and which is capable of such a variety of modifications as the present.

Gentlemen say this bill ought to be rejected, because it is unconstitutional. Could gentlemen be serious in making this objection? Were troops ever raised in a different manner? And if they had the power to authorize the President to raise troops immediately they could certainly do it under such contingencies as they thought proper. Did not Congress intrust the President with the discretionary power of borrowing money, of, in some cases, fixing salaries, etc., which powers were equally vested in them with the power of raising armies; and this must be the case, except gentlemen insist that Congress should itself do all the acts committed to it; and, if so, they must always be in session.

But the gentleman from Pennsylvania says that if this power be delegated to the President Congress may as well intrust the President with the power of raising provisional taxes. He had no hesitation in saying that he believed this might be done; that the House might determine upon a tax, and authorize the collecting of it only in case the President should find it necessary, or in case a certain event should take place.

With respect, then, to the expediency of the measure—what is the internal and external state of this country? Do we not know that the enemy have in view a plan upon which they place great reliance—of gaining over to their cause a certain class of men, who abound in the Southern part of this country, and by whose means they intend to subjugate or destroy the country? We do know this—gentlemen from the Southern States know it; yet they say it is impossible to raise any regular force to repel the enemy. He could not believe that, when we had to meet an enemy who has always fought by means of domestic insurrection, who is now subverting the most ancient government in the world by these means, it would be consistent with any maxim of common sense to be unprepared for the worst.

What, said he, is our external situation? Do we not see the nation with whom we are at variance find quarrels with every country who is not strong enough to resist her? Does she not injure us on every side? Do we not hear of depredatory threats, and the mischiefs she has the power of doing us, urged as reasons why we should submit to her? And yet, after being told of these designs, shall we sit with our arms folded and make no defence? For the measures already taken will be nothing without this. Fortifications would be nothing except supported by a sufficient number of infantry and cavalry.

What, he asked, is the situation of the West Indies? Were they not told that Victor Hugues, with 5,000 of his best troops, is ready to make a blow upon the Southern country whenever the word of command shall be given? They knew that these troops existed; they had been seen, and the desperate character of their leader was also known. Yet, with this enemy upon our threshold, within four or five days' sail of us, we still fold our arms and say we will make no defence.

When he reflected upon these things he could not help deploring that fatal blindness, that stubborn spirit of opposition, in certain gentlemen, which could hide from their view the danger of our present situation; that, at a period when the veil is rending from before the eyes of the community; when those who have been the most blind out-of-doors begin to see, that those gentlemen in this House who, from their ancient birth and fortunes, might be supposed to possess the true American spirit should still persist in their blind, their destructive, course was greatly to be lamented. And though he could not doubt the fate of this bill, yet that there should be a few men found supporting measures which tend directly to the destruction of the country he could not help lamenting.

ABRAHAM BALDWIN [Ga.] did not agree with the gentleman who had just sat down that the present motion was either unprecedented or improper. When it is proposed to make a law on any subject it presents itself to discussion on two grounds, the principles of the law and the details. The proper stages to debate the general principle on which the law is to be founded, by the rules of this House, are when it is proposed to introduce the law, and at the third reading, when it is considered as finished, and on its passage; the intermediate stages of the discussion are all supposed to be employed to settle and adjust the detail.

As to the principle of the bill, he must say it did not meet his approbation. If the House is convinced it is necessary to raise an army of twenty thousand men, as the bill now proposes, they ought to say so at once and let it be done; if they are not convinced that it is necessary the law ought not to pass, the army ought not to be raised till they are convinced it is necessary. The Constitution made the legislature the sole judge on this subject. The present bill says it is not necessary to raise this army now, but perhaps it may be before Congress meets again; it therefore proposes to transfer the right of judging on this subject to the Executive; he thought it a very improper transfer of legislative power. It has been said that all our troops are raised thus provisionally. If attention is paid to those laws it will be seen that they did not pass till the legislature was convinced that circumstances then required the troops to be raised; a clause is added that, if circumstances should alter so as to make the troops unnecessary, the President might forbear to raise, or discharge them; it gives him power to disband the army, but not to raise one.

JOHN RUTLEDGE, JR. [S. C.] adduced, as in point, the law enabling the President to call out troops in consequence of the Western rising [the Whisky Insurrection], and that making provision for the effectual protection of the frontiers of the United States.

JOSEPH McDOWELL was in favor of the motion for rejecting the bill, as it contained two principles which he thought inadmissible; the first, because it delegated legislative power to the President; the other, as it respects volunteer corps. The first, he believed, would be unconstitutional, and the last would go to the destruction of the militia of the United States.

It was well known that it had been the wish of the late President, that it was also the wish of the present President, of the heads of departments, and many members of Congress, to increase our military establishment, and to fix a standing army in this country. It has heretofore, however, been opposed with success, except in time of war. If we were to be involved in war an army must be resorted to in aid of the militia; but, in the first instance, the militia might be depended upon as a sure and safe defence of this country.

MR. GALLATIN said: If our danger be, as it is represented, likely to come from Victor Hugues and his troops, from an insurrection of the negroes, from disaffected persons, from our enemy being at the door, it is the duty of Congress to raise an army themselves, and not to give the President the power of doing it; but if it is not believed that this representation of danger rests upon any specific ground, but that it is merely imaginary, then there is no necessity for giving the President the power, as he can call Congress together whenever he thinks proper.

If any danger was to be apprehended from the negroes they would be best suppressed by the people in the States where they are. A militia is everywhere; whereas a standing army may be very distant from any attack which may take place. A standing army in Virginia, for instance, would do little good against insurgents in South Carolina; and if an insurrection of that kind was not immediately suppressed by the people the mischief would be incalculable.

General Thomas Sumter [S. C.] closed the debate.

This favorite scheme of raising a standing army must be pushed forward by every aid of fact and fiction, and that its success may be insured the Southern members are to be terrified into its adoption.

Here General Sumter eulogized at length the bravery of the Southern militia during the revolution.

Knowing the ardor and firmness of the Southern militia, and not doubting but the militia of the several States in the Union possess equal motives for their exertions, equal spirit and activity, I cannot but rely on them as the natural and main support of our national independence—a support fully effectual without a recurrence to a standing army. The instances which

THE NATION'S BULWARK—A WELL-DISCIPLINED MILITIA

Cartoon dated 1829

From the collection of the New York Historical Society

I have brought forward tend to show that the charges brought against the militia generally are as unfounded as they are cruel to their feelings; while, at the same time, they demonstrate that, if an invasion (which is a contingency by no means likely to happen) should actually take place, we may rely with confidence on the manly exertions of the militia to meet the attack, and to resist every effort, at least for such a period as until more effective aid shall be drawn down to their support, and more permanent measures adopted.

The bill passed on May 18 by a vote of 51 to 40.

Two years later, when negotiations for peace and amity were proceeding with France with high prospect of success, Mr. Nicholas brought forward a motion to reduce the army.

The chief supporters of the motion were: Mr. Gallatin, Robert Williams [N. C.], and John Randolph [Va.]; conspicuous among its opponents were: John Marshall

[Va.], James A. Bayard, Sr. [Del.], General Henry Lee,
[Va.], Mr. Otis and Mr. Harper.

REDUCTION OF THE ARMY

HOUSE OF REPRESENTATIVES, JANUARY 1-11, 1800

MR. NICHOLAS.—Sir, the finances of this country would be in
an alarming state if all the present expenses were necessary,
but my opinion is that they are not necessary, for that this additional army is in no wise useful. I cannot conceive for what
they are wanted. The idea of invasion, the only ground upon
which their necessity could be founded, is quite out of the question—an event of that sort in the present state of Europe is
absolutely impossible.

I suppose very little will be said about the usefulness of the
present army, but we shall hear more of the effects which a
measure of this kind would have on the state of our negotiation
in Europe. I suppose, therefore, that the question will turn on
the propriety of dismissing this army while our commissioners
are treating, and therefore this view of the subject may merit a
few remarks.

It is desirable, I should imagine, that at entering on a negotiation our country should be so situated as to be able to make
a firm and obstinate stand against unjust demands. If this is a
desirable situation, I ask gentlemen to say whether this army
does not lessen, instead of increasing, our importance with that
country to which we go to negotiate, when it is apparent to the
world that for its support we borrow money of more than one
half the amount of the revenue, and pay interest on that loan at
an enormous rate. This being known, will it not operate as a
strong ground for suspicion that you are forced to the negotiation from pecuniary considerations; that your present state of
exertion is greater than you can bear for any length of time,
and thus lessen your respectability with that nation? While
it may hurry you to submit to terms less advantageous than
could be wished, it may make the terms proposed for your acceptance harder than they would otherwise have been.

I do not hesitate to say if preference is due to one arm of the
Government it is to our naval preparations for defence. Sir,
if you part with one [the army], which has never proved useful,
will you not be better enabled to keep up the other [the navy],
which is certainly more favorable to your interest and local
situation?

MR. MARSHALL.—It has been urged, not only that the army is useless, but that there is in the United States a positive inability to maintain it. To prove this our revenue and expenditure have been stated. Suppose this had been the language of '75? Suppose, at the commencement of our Revolution, a gentleman had risen on the floor of Congress, to compare our revenues with our expenses—what would have been the result of the calculation? Would not the same system of reasoning which the gentleman from Virginia has adopted have proved that our resources were totally inadequate to the prosecution of the war? Yet it was prosecuted, and with success. If vast exertions were then made to acquire independence, will not the same exertions be now made to maintain it? The question now is whether self-government and national liberty be worth the money which must be expended to preserve them.

The reduction of the army would certainly diminish the expense of the present year; but if it should have any operation on the existing negotiation with France the present saving it would produce would bear no proportion to the immense waste of blood, as well as treasure, which it might occasion us. To determine in what manner this measure might, and probably would, bear on the existing negotiation, it became indispensable to take into our view what had preceded the actual state of things between the United States and France.

While prayers for peace were returned for indignities of every sort, while America was humbly supplicating for peace, and that her complaints might be heard, France spurned her contemptuously and refused to enter on a discussion of differences unless that discussion was preceded by a substantial surrender of the essential attributes of independence. America was at length goaded into resistance, and resolved on the system of defence of which the army now sought to be disbanded forms a part. Immediately the tone of France was changed, and she consented to treat us as an independent nation. What could have produced this change? Can any other motive be assigned than the defensive system which America had adopted? If no other did exist is it wise immediately to change the system which has alone been effectual? Is it not to be apprehended that this change may revive those sentiments which existed before that system was adopted?

In a few months the fate of the present negotiations will be decided. Should they terminate favorably the army expires by the law which gave it being, and the additional expense to be incurred will be very inconsiderable. Should they fail, and the

state of affairs then require even an augmentation of the existing force, the injury occasioned by our precipitation (in having
reduced the army) might be very considerable.

MR. NICHOLAS.—As usual, I fear that this wrong step (the
establishment of a provisional army) will never be got over.
Where is the end of it? In vain do we seek for it. The gentleman says that, on the moment of failure in the negotiation, an
army may be crossing the ocean, and then we shall want these
troops. Sir, this may occur at any period, and if we are never
to disband our army, under apprehensions of that event, it will
never be done, and our expense will be perpetual.

The gentleman considers this armament to be the measure
which extorted the overtures from France. But this is not so.
It is a little extraordinary that he should have ascribed an effort
to a measure that existed previous to the knowledge of that
measure; for the propositions, and the avowed willingness on
the part of the Directory to meet our complaints by an honorable adjustment, were made known to our ministers in August,
which was before the law of July, 1798, which created the army
we wish should be disbanded, could have reached that nation.

MR. BAYARD said he could perceive in the resolution a connection with a system which had long been pursued by a party
in the United States—a system which had for its object the de-
bilitation and degradation of the general Government. A knowledge of the party and a knowledge of their views prevented any
astonishment at the present measure they proposed. This
measure he did not regard as a single operation. It was part
of a general plan, which, if it were successful, would soon be
unfolded.

The conduct of France in relation to this country had compelled the United States to adopt a system of defence. The
nation had found that no reliance could be placed on the moderation or justice of the French Government. Their own energies were the only ground on which their independence could
be maintained. They did not hesitate as to the alternative of
defence or submission. Having resolved to resist the aggressions
and pretensions of the French Government, they found themselves forced into a state of hostility. The commercial intercourse with France was suspended, the treaty of alliance was
abolished, a navy was created for the protection of trade, and
an army ordered to be raised. Our ships of war were instructed
to seize and destroy the armed ships of the French Republic,
and a war, though deprecated, was expected without dread. The
national sentiment coincided with the temper of the Government,

and its measures were approved and applauded. The system which was adopted was connected in its parts, and the objection which went to one part applied with equal force to the whole. The naval hostilities authorized against France rendered an army necessary against invasion from Europe or the islands, which might reasonably be expected.

If gentlemen now said an army was not necessary it must be because they thought the French Government was not hostile, but friendly. If they thought that government friendly, surely there could be no occasion for the navy. The same reason would induce us to revive the treaty with France and open the commercial intercourse.

We are told that in case of invasion an army is not necessary, because we can rely on the patriotism of the nation. Sir, said Mr. B., I am not insensible to the melody of the word, but I must doubt of the efficacy of one thing. There was a time when everybody understood what was meant by patriotism; it indicated an attachment to our country. But a modern patriot was a character not so well understood. Patriotism has become a furious spirit of revolution; the ties of blood, the inspirations of nature, the principles of truth and honor are consumed by the devouring flame. The *natale solum* had lost its charm. To be a patriot you must forget your country, abjure your religion, suppress the impulses of nature, and maintain the equality of vice and virtue. He knew there were a sect of patriots who attributed to themselves exclusive merit. Was it on these patriots the country was to rely in case of invasion?

Sir, said he, let the French come with their cap of liberty mounted on their standards, singing *ça ira*, planting liberty poles, and denouncing the Government as an aristocratical and British faction, and I fear you would see some patriots forgetting their country, and, under the ardent impression of their political fanaticism, ready to imbrue their hands in their brothers' blood. Revolution was not confined to politics—religion and morals were revolutionized. The sacred love of country, once ranked among the best principles of man's nature, was now shamefully sacrificed to the very sound of equality.

It is not from any view of a possible operation of the army against France that the disbanding could influence the negotiation, but from the impression such a measure would necessarily make on the French Government, as to the state of affairs in this country. If, after having raised an army against them, without any change of conduct on their part, they were to, see us disband it, what would they infer? Either that extreme imbecility per-

vaded our councils, or that there was a want of means on the
part of the Government to maintain a small military force. Or,
perhaps they would make an inference still more, that those
whom they called and supposed their party in this country had
become more powerful than the Government. In either case
they would perceive less difficulty in the accomplishment of any
views which they had on the country than our plans of defence
may have caused them to apprehend; and, of consequence, the
inducements to an accommodation of differences would be diminished. It was a wise axiom in politics that a nation which
would negotiate to advantage should be prepared to fight. The
resolution was predicted on an opposite principle, and was repugnant to the plain evidences of experience and common sense.

MR. GALLATIN.—We are told by the gentleman from Delaware that the people of this country would pay fifty per
cent. for money rather than submit to a foreign invasion. I
admit that if the danger was imminent and real they would
agree to pay anything. We do not conceive there would be any
reluctance to pay taxes were such our situation, but, when it is
not, it will be difficult to convince them of the propriety of
additional taxation. Yet the confidence expressed by that gentleman in the willingness of the people to pay does not very well
comport with another part of his argument, wherein he insinu-
ated a want of confidence in a considerable part of the people,
whom he supposes so far as even to wish that our Government
should be overturned. In support of his opinion he alluded to
several legislative declarations and official addresses and answers [the Kentucky and Virginia Resolutions]. I am astonished at the palpable inconsistency of the gentleman—that the
people would willingly pay fifty per cent. of their property for
defence against an enemy, and yet no reliance is to be placed on
those very people when the enemy comes!

We are, however, told that any increase of debt that may be
created in consequence of our present situation is trifling in itself, and holds no proportion to the supposed increase of resources resulting from our growing population. But is this not
a most extraordinary and novel mode of calculating, not on the
present resources of the country, but on those which posterity
may have? Are we then so sure that our posterity will have
no dangers of their own to encounter, and no additional expenditures which will require every additional resource they may
possess? Let us provide, out of our own resources, for our own
wants, instead of mortgaging, not only our actual revenue, but
even that which may hereafter be raised by posterity.

GEN. LEE.—Gentlemen say regular troops are not necessary: militia, of themselves, are an adequate defence. This I deny; and much as I wish to see our militia placed on a respectable footing, much as I count on their aid whenever danger approaches, yet I never can be brought to trust the defence of the country solely to them. The experience of the last war justifies the opinion. Look at the battle of Long Island—braver men on the part of America were never brought into action, but vain was their courage. The best blood of America was prodigally and ineffectually expended during the war for want of the aid to be derived from discipline and skill. See what the same sort of men did at the close of the war when properly trained. The battle of the Eutaws is a distinguished example of the effect of discipline on the American soldiery. But really it is trifling with the committee to press farther this truth; the history of man, from the beginning of the world to this day, throughout maintains the folly of placing the defence of a nation on what we call militia only: economy, too, forbids it. But, because we firmly maintain this truth, insinuations go forth inculcating a belief that we are inimical to the militia and friendly to a standing army. This is untrue and unwarranted by our declarations. We hold no such sentiments. We wish for the best and cheapest defence, and that we believe to consist of an adequate regular force, calculated for the occasion, and dismissed as soon as the object is answered; to be seconded by seasonable reinforcements from the militia.

But, says the honorable member, let us reduce the army and use the saving in augmentation of the navy. I very much respect this last establishment; I prefer it, and will always be ready to cherish and invigorate it, but not now, in the way suggested, nor at the expense of the army. Until we are assured of peace we must hold both, and I doubt not we shall hold both.

MR. NICHOLAS.—The gentleman from Delaware [Mr. Bayard] supposes the French Government will think that we are either too poor to bear the expense, that we are foolishly versatile, or that there is a party in our country to support their views. I wish the gentleman would prove that the rejection of the resolution would not have the effect to prove our foolishness in continuing a great needless expense. Sir, is a nation never to alter its course? Is it never to determine whether it has done right or wrong, and change its system? Is it to persevere in doing the very work of its enemy, and never to retrench an expense, though ever so extravagant?

DISTINGUISHED MILITIA GENERAL DURING AN ACTION

From the collection of the New York Historical Society

Mr. R. Williams.—It is said that this army must be kept up for what may happen. I ask whether the same argument may not always hold good, with respect to any nation, between whom and us there may be but little friendship. When is the moment in which we might not be exposed to this danger? This argument will always apply to keep up a standing force in this country, greater than we ought to bear. When gentlemen use these arguments I take it for granted this is the force they mean to keep upon a permanent establishment, whatever name they may give it; for I can see no bounds to an argument of the kind, or line at which we are to stop; it goes, sir, too far to answer the purpose intended.

Mr. Randolph.—I oppose the establishment of a standing army in this country, not only as a useless and enormous expense, but upon the ground of the Constitution. The spirit of that instrument and the genius of a free people are equally hostile to this dangerous institution, which ought to be resorted to (if at all) only in extreme cases of difficulty and danger. Yet let it be remembered that usage, that immemorial custom, is paramount in every written obligation, and let us beware of ingrafting this abuse upon our Constitution. A people who mean to continue free must be prepared to meet danger in person; not to rely upon the fallacious protection of mercenary armies.

I am friendly to the resolution on your table, sir, on another ground. I believe that it will remove a considerable cause of irritation. The raising of these troops has had a deleterious effect upon the public temper. The military parade which meets the eye in almost every direction excites the gall of our citizens; they feel a just indignation at the sight of loungers, who live upon the public, who consume the fruits of their honest industry, under the pretext of protecting them from a foreign yoke. They put no confidence, sir, in the protection of a handful of ragamuffins; they know that when danger comes they must meet it, and they only ask arms at your hands. Gentlemen have talked of organizing the militia; I call upon them to make good what they have said. Instead of reducing this force I could wish to see the *whole* of it, reprobated as it is by our citizens, abandoned, and the defence of the country placed in proper hands, those of the people.

Our citizens are confident in their strength; they know themselves to be capable of protecting their own property and liberties; they do not want their noses held to the grindstone to pay protectors; the surplusage of their labor they wish to employ in increasing their property, in providing for their off-spring—that numerous and increasing population of which gentlemen have said so much; they do not wish to have money forced out of their pockets to pay hirelings, under the stale pretext of keeping off French invasion.

MR. OTIS.—Sir, I would ask gentlemen what right the people of this country have to expect to escape the conflagration in which the other three-quarters of the globe are involved without some pains and expense to erect barriers against its destructive progress? Are we chosen by heaven to live in a sequestered corner of the world, exempt from the troubles and distresses of other nations, to grow rich by their spoils, and to fatten on their misfortunes, without any additional burdens? While the Old World is wasted by fire and sword, while cities are sacked and unpeopled, their fields made desolate, and their commerce destroyed, are we privileged to count in quiet the gains of the counting-house and the produce of our acres without deduction or alloy? Do we presume that the Atlantic will open and swallow up an invading army, as the host of Pharaoh was swallowed up in the Red Sea? Confident as I am in the justice of our cause, I do not expect the assistance of miracles for our protection. We must rely, under Heaven, upon the arm of flesh. If we do not, if we neglect to make necessary preparation against natural accidents, we may be overwhelmed in the common fate of those nations which, lulled into a delusive security, have lost their liberties and perished in the general wreck of the social union.

This very year, for aught we know, our liberties may be required at our hands. Sir, we are told that the present establishment shows an annual deficit of five millions of dollars. But suppose, for the sake of the argument, the calculation to be just and the establishment certainly necessary; what are five millions of dollars? Or suppose that the price of our safety and independence should be twenty, forty, or, if you please, eighty millions of dollars, in addition to the present debt. This, indeed, sir, is money—as M. Talleyrand observed—is a great deal of money; but money is cheaper than blood, it is less precious than honor. Who would hesitate between the evils of doubling the national debt or relinquishing the rights of an independent nation?

This alarm relative to standing armies has been at least rung a thousand times a year since the first British army was landed in this country; and, if the objection is well founded, it goes to the destruction of the old regiments as well as of the new, and we must have immediate recourse to militia for every ordinary object. That gentleman further contends that this country cannot be defended by a standing army, but requires a force raised by requisition. Wherein lies the difference betwen a standing army and a force raised for a limited time by requisition? The gentleman may distinguish the first by the hard names of ragamuffins and mercenaries, if he thinks proper, I shall not dispute with him about terms. Yet, why troops raised according to his ideas of requisition, who are to be organized, disciplined, and compelled into service, to receive pay and march wherever they are ordered, are less ragamuffins and mercenaries than troops raised in any other mode is for that gentleman to explain. Sir, far be it from me to question the importance of the great national resource, the militia. I well know they are the palladium of the country, the fund on which we must rely for soldiers and defence.

But I contend that militia in itself is calculated only for sudden emergencies. They will fight bravely while they continue in the field. They will resist an invading army, but they will not endure a series of campaigns. I call on gentlemen to produce an instance wherein militia have been alone equal to cope with an army that had once got a footing in a country.

MR. HARPER.—On what do gentlemen rely when they say that France cannot invade this country? Do they rely on her want of troops? If so, let them remember that she found forty thousand men to send to Egypt. Do they rely on her having full employment for all her troops against the Austrians and Russians? Let them remember she may suddenly make peace with the Austrians and Russians, as she did with the Austrians in 1797; that such an event grows every day more probable; and should it take place she will have troops very fit for such an enterprise, and very ready to be employed in it. Do they rely on a want of ships? Let them remember that she found ships enough to transport forty thousand men to Egypt, and a fleet of thirteen sail-of-the-line to escort them, and that, having gained possession of the Spanish fleet, she has now a much greater naval force at her disposal than heretofore. Do they rely on the superior power of the British at sea, and on the vigilance of their fleets? Let them remember that when Bonaparte sailed from the ports of France on his Egyptian expedition he was watched by a superior British fleet, under the command of one of the ablest, most active, and most enterprising naval commanders that ever England could boast; that he eluded this fleet, arrived safe at Malta, and had time to conquer that important place before the British admiral could find out where he was, and come up with him; that he sailed from Malta, and, notwithstanding this fleet was in full pursuit of him, arrived in Egypt and made good his landing, without the least molestation; that his fleet might, after landing him, have returned safe to France, had not some unaccountable fatality induced the admiral who commanded it to remain for many days in a situation where it was exposed to the attack of the British. Do they rely, sir, on the distance? Let them remember that during our revolutionary war the French did find means, notwithstanding the distance and the naval superiority of England, to send fleets and armies to this country.

Sir, we must have a trained army to oppose this invasion. Where will be the reliance of this Government on the militia for the defence of the country if the militia, or considerable portions of them, should at length be induced, by the unceasing efforts which are employed, to regard the Government itself as their greatest enemy? Is there no danger that their efforts may be successful? Sir, I trust there is not. I have always relied on the good sense and prudence of the American people, and I have never yet been disappointed. But when we consider the greatness of the efforts, the increasing zeal with which they are renewed, the systematic form which they have assumed, and the hand whereby they are guided, can we say there is no danger of their success?

Shall I not speak of a most virulent manifesto [the Kentucky Resolutions][1] lately issued by a legislature of this country against the Government of the United States, under the name of instructions, where the highest sanction is given to the vilest calumny, and the Administration is plainly charged with laboring for the introduction of monarchy? If these persons should at length succeed by dint of repeated calumnies in persuading the people of America, or even certain portions of them, that the Executive of the United States, the whole Administration, and a majority of both Houses of Congress are embarked in a scheme for the gradual introduction of monarchy, and are pushing it with might and main, at every favorable opportunity, and under every plausible pretext; I ask what reliance could be had on the aid of the people, in resisting invaders who should declare, as the French never fail to do, that they come to rescue the people from oppression, to subvert aristocracy, and establish true liberty? When we see these artifices practiced, with increasing industry, and more extensive combination, ought we not to re-

[1] See Volume VII, chapter iv.

tain, in case our quarrel with France should continue, some force that may be more perfectly relied on?

MR. RANDOLPH.—The gentleman from South Carolina [Mr. Harper] has talked of modern patriotism, which he evidently thinks to consist in declamation against public burdens and a devotion to France. When it is recollected that those against whom these insinuations were thrown were supposed to have been peculiarly friendly to the mission to France, and to be highly anxious for its success, while the opponents to the resolution exhibited a great coolness with regard to a compromise of differences with that republic, he trusted that the alarm with respect to the effect of the measure under discussion upon that negotiation would wear off.

Mr. R. said that, although this army had been ordered into existence so long, yet scarcely 4,000 men were raised; and, if the recruiting went on, it would take a year perhaps to fill the regiments. Would not this be a stronger proof to France of our debility than the disbanding of them, which would indicate only a prudent application of resources to proper objects. But, in fact, sir, this circumstance is a proof the most decisive of the inutility of this force. In spite of the system of alarm, and the cry of danger from French invasion, the good sense of the country still prevailed. Our people knew that there was no immediate danger, nor can they hear it in every breeze; they therefore refused to enter a service into which the indolent and worthless had been allured by the potent consideration of being clothed and fed at public expense. Would this tardiness to defend their country, sir, be exhibited were the danger imminent, as gentlemen had alleged? He cautioned the members of the House, particularly from the South, against lavishing, by the smallest estimate which had any pretension to correctness, at least two and a half millions, perhaps four, upon so worthless an object.

The committee now rose and reported their disagreement to the resolution.

The question was taken that the House do agree with the Committee of the Whole in their said disagreement, and resolved in the affirmative—yeas 60, nays 39.

RANDOLPH'S BREACH OF PRIVILEGE

The speech of Mr. Randolph rendered him obnoxious to the officers of the army, who objected to his epithets

John Randolph

of "ragamuffins" and "mercenaries" applied to soldiers. Accordingly, a night or so afterwards certain of them insulted him publicly in a theater. Randolph seized the opportunity thus afforded, and wrote to the President an account of the incident, with incidental observations not at all complimentary to the policies of the Administration. He addressed the letter to "John Adams, President of the United States," without the customary title of "Your Excellency," and signed it, "Your fellow-citizen, John Randolph."

Mr. Adams sent the letter to the House, where the question of dealing with it as a "breach of privilege" was debated at great length, finally ending in a deadlock.

CHAPTER VI

THE NAVAL ESTABLISHMENT [1812]

Anti-naval Policy of Presidents Jefferson and Madison—Debate in the
House on a Naval Establishment [1812]: In favor, Langdon Cheves
[S. C.], William Lowndes [S. C.], Lyman Law [Conn.], Henry Clay
[Ky.], Josiah Quincy, 3rd [Mass.]; Opposed, Adam Seybert [Pa.],
Jonathan Roberts [Pa.], Samuel McKee [Ky.], Richard M. Johnson
[Ky.].

ONE of the chief issues between the Federalists
and Republicans during John Adams's administration was the navy, the Federalists desiring
to increase it greatly, in view of the offensive attitude
taken toward the United States by France and Great
Britain, and the Republicans wishing to maintain it at
a minimum strength, for fear that an increase would
too greatly augment the power of the Executive, and
so menace State rights and the liberties of the people.

Indeed, it was a part of the bargain made by James
A. Bayard, Sr. [Del.], the leader of the Federalists, with
the supporters of Thomas Jefferson, whereby the deciding Federalist votes were cast for Jefferson against
Aaron Burr [N. Y.] in the House contest for the Presidency, that Jefferson would at least not reduce the existing strength of the navy.[1]

While Jefferson fulfilled the letter of the bargain,
he did not go beyond it, but showed antagonism to every
measure which tended to the aggrandizement of the
naval power of the Government. Thus he made it a
pet policy to build little shallow "gunboats" to run
in and out of our shallow rivers, and so be available for
defence, though not for attack, instead of large and
powerful men-of-war which could strike the enemy on
the high seas and even in his home ports. Historians
are generally agreed that this was the chief, if not

[1] See page 400 ss.

indeed the only, blot upon an Administration that stands as a record of great achievement in increasing the territory of the country, in wiping out public debt and reducing public expenditure, and in generally promoting the prosperity and liberty of the people.

James Madison continued his predecessor's policies, including that in regard to the navy. However, as war with Great Britain became imminent, the Democratic leaders of the Administration responded to the popular demand for a great increase of the navy.

On December 17, 1811, Langdon Cheves [S. C.], as chairman of a special committee on naval affairs, reported that the committee advised the refitting of all vessels in the navy, the building of ten additional frigates, averaging 38 guns, the purchase of a stock of ship timber, and the establishment of a dock for repairing vessels. A bill was framed accordingly, and brought before the House on January 17, 1812. It was discussed from that day until January 29, when it was passed by a vote of 65 to 30. It had, however, been amended by the omission of the provisions for building frigates (vote, 62 to 59) and the dockyard (vote, 56 to 52).

The debate focused upon the question of building frigates, as this involved the establishment of a permanent navy and fixed the policy of the impending war as a contest by sea as well as by land. The chief speakers in support of the bill were the chairman of the committee, Mr. Cheves, William Lowndes [S. C.], Lyman Law [Conn.], Henry Clay [Ky.], and Josiah Quincy, 3rd [Mass.]. Those who opposed the measure were Adam Seybert [Pa.], Jonathan Roberts [Pa.], Samuel McKee [Ky.], and Richard M. Johnson [Ky.].

THE NAVAL ESTABLISHMENT

HOUSE OF REPRESENTATIVES, JANUARY 17-29, 1812

MR. CHEVES.—It has been said,[1] by a strong and lively figure of rhetoric, that this country is a great land animal, which

[1] By John Randolph.

should not venture into the water. But if you look at its broad high back, the Alleghanies, and its great sides swelling to the east and to the west, where do you find its immense limbs terminate? Not on some great plain which has been formed for their reception, but in two great oceans, the Pacific on the one side and the Atlantic on the other. The figure explains the true interests of the country, in the inseparable union and necessary dependence of agriculture and commerce. The God of nature did not give to the United States a coast of two thousand miles in extent not to be used. No; it was intended by this bounty to make us a great commercial people; and shall we ungratefully reject the enjoyment of His unexampled beneficence? No, it has not, and will not, be neglected. A great portion of our people exist but upon the ocean and its fruits. It has been eloquently, and not less truly than eloquently, said that "the ocean is their farm," and it must and will be protected.

But how is this protection to be afforded? No proposition appears to me more true or more obvious than that it is only by a naval force that our commerce and our neutral rights on the ocean can be protected.

But the adoption of a naval establishment is deemed improper on the grounds of the enormous expense which it will necessitate, and the inability of the nation, by any force which it can provide, to resist, with effect, the immense naval power of Great Britain. Is it not surprising that so much prejudice should exist against this establishment on account of its expensiveness, when it is ascertained that, during the whole eighteen years of its existence, from 1794 to 1811, inclusive, it has cost the Government only $27,175,695? The expense of the military establishment, from 1791 to 1811, inclusive, has been $37,541,669, giving an annual average of $1,700,000, or $200,000 per annum more than that of the navy. Compare, too, the services of the army with those of the navy, and it will be found that those of the latter have been most useful and most honorable to the nation. I know of no service of this character which the army has performed, except the defeat of the Indians by General Wayne, and the late gallant affair on the Wabash. The navy, in the contest with France in 1798, was victorious wherever it encountered an enemy, and probably laid the foundation of the subsequent accommodation with that nation. In the Mediterranean its exploits gave a name to the country throughout Europe, humbled, in an unexampled manner, the piratical and barbarous foe, and crowned itself with a reputation for intrepidity and heroism which had not been exceeded by the exploits of any nation, and which must go down to a distant posterity. Admitting that, from a variety of causes, the expense may have been unnecessarily great, an argument cannot thence be fairly drawn against its future use—the contrary is the fair conclusion. Past errors lay the foundation of future improvement. It was thus the greatest orator, and one of the greatest statesmen of antiquity, reasoned. The great Athenian orator, when rousing his countrymen, by his impetuous eloquence, to resist the ambition of Philip, declared that it was on their past misconduct that he built his highest hopes; for, said he, ''were we thus distressed, in spite of every vigorous effort which the honor of our State demanded, there were then no hope of recovery.'' So may we reason in this case; for, had these extraordinary expenses been the result of good economy, then, indeed, would their diminution be hopeless; but, as they have proceeded from a wasteful or unskilful expenditure, the remedy will be found in a reform of the abuse; to effect this reform is the duty of Congress. But it has not only been less expensive than the army, but it may be proved, as the committee have declared in their report, that ''a naval force within due limits and under proper regulations, will constitute the cheapest defence of the nation.'' This will be partly proved by a comparison between the expense of the permanent fortifications of our maritime frontier and that of an adequate naval defence. The experience of modern naval warfare has proved that no fortifications can prevent the passage of ships of war. The present fortifications of our maritime frontier, though they are more numerous and better than they have been at any other period in our history, cannot prevent an inconsiderable naval force from laying many of our towns in ashes. Indeed, it is believed that no fortifications which can be erected will afford a complete protection against such attacks, while their expense would be oppressive to the nation. The city of New York alone, if completely fortified, would require a further expenditure of three millions of dollars, and a garrison of ten thousand men, and then might be laid in ashes by four or five seventy-fours. But we have a coast of two thousand miles to protect, the expense of which could not be borne by the nation. A better defence would be furnished by such a naval force as would give you a mastery in the American seas, and at home much less expense.

But, while it is contended by some that it will not be in the power of the nation to establish an effective naval force, there are others who are opposed to it, lest we become too great a naval power. They fear that our fleets will cover the ocean, and, seeking victory on all the opposite shores of the Atlantic, involve the nation in oppressive expenses, and in wanton and habitual wars. Such objects are certainly not contemplated by the report of the committee; nor can such events possibly happen as long as we remain a free people. The committee have recommended such a navy as will give to the United States an ascendency in the American seas, and protect their ports and harbors. The people will never bear the establishment of a greater force than these objects require. The reasons which forbid Great Britain, or any other European power, to station large fleets on our seas will equally forbid us to cross the Atlantic, or go into distant seas, for the purpose of frequent or habitual wars.

We are told, also, that navies have ruined every nation that has employed them; and England, and Holland, and Venice, and other nations have been mentioned as examples. The vast debt of Great Britain is declared to be among the pernicious fruits of her naval establishment. This I deny. Her debt has grown out of her profuse subsidies, and her absurd wars on the land. Though the ruin which is supposed to threaten England is attributed to her navy, it is obvious that her navy alone has saved, and still saves, her from ruin. Without it she must, long since, have yielded to the power of France her independence and her liberties. We are told that the same wealth which she has expended in supporting her navies would have been employed more profitably for the nation in the improvement of its agriculture and manufactures, and in the establishment of canals and roads, and other internal improvements. But experience is better than theory. Let us compare England with nations which have no navies, or comparatively inconsiderable navies. The nations of the continent of Europe are without such overgrown and ruinous naval establishments, but do you there find the highest improvements in agriculture, the most flourishing manufactures, or the best roads and canals? No, it is in this nation, that has been ruined by her navy, that you find all these improvements most perfect and most extended. I mean not either to be the panegyrist of England; but these truths may be declared for our instruction, without suppressing the feelings excited by the wrongs she has done us. England has not, then, I conclude, been destroyed or impoverished, but preserved and enriched, by her navy. Was Holland ruined by her navy? No; surrounded by the great powers of the Continent, with a population not exceeding 2,000,000 of souls, she protected and secured her independence for more than a century against her powerful neighbors by means of her commercial riches, which were cherished and defended by her naval power. Did Venice owe her decline, or fall, to her navy? While the neighboring Italian states were subdued, year after year changing their masters and their tyrants, she long continued to ride triumphantly amid the storm, independent, and, in a great degree, free. It was her naval and commercial power which made her rich and great, and secured her existence as a state so long. Look even at the little republic of Genoa, whose inhabitants, but for its commerce and its navy, would scarcely ever have possessed ''a local habitation,'' or ''a name!''

MR. SEYBERT.—The gentleman from South Carolina has told us that when the war which we are about to wage shall be over our army will leave us. Sir, I am happy to hear that on such an event the military will be readily disbanded—a dread of the contrary gave much uneasiness to many a few days since—this is just what we wish should take place. On the other hand, said he, ''your proud navy'' will remain. It is for this, with many other reasons, that I am opposed to a navy. I wish he could have proved to us that with the end of the war the navy would also leave us; perhaps I should then agree with him in favor of its establishment: though the ''proud navy'' will remain with us, he has neglected to tell us at what rate of expense.

I will ask him, if it is to remain with us in times of peace with its numerous train of officers, may it not become a powerful engine in the hands of an ambitious Executive?

Sir, I deem it inexpedient to commence a permanent naval establishment at this time. We are quite unprepared for it— we are in want of all the necessary materials; though we have been told that our forests abound in all the necessary timber, it was said little of this material was to be found in our dockyards. The gentleman from South Carolina has told us that a sufficiency of seasoned timber to build four seventy-fours was now on hand, and that the proper authority deemed it advisable to be used for frigates. Sir, this timber is a portion of that which was purchased some years since for the purpose of building six seventy-fours. It now appears that of this timber as much as was sufficient for two of these vessels has been employed to build smaller vessels, or gunboats, I presume. This is all of a piece with our pretended economy. This mode of proceeding will not answer, sir. We are in the wrong from the commencement of our navy. I do not wish it to be understood that I have decided a navy will never be a proper mode of defence for this nation—but whenever it shall be determined on we should begin

right; this can only be done by following those nations who
have had most experience on the subject. Our first step should
be to store away the proper timber. This should be done in
times when we can best afford it—in times when our market is
glutted—in times when labor can be commanded at fair prices—
at a period when we enjoy peace, and surely not when we are
about to engage in a war. We have heretofore paid the highest
price for every article; we have given double wages for labor;
and instances might be mentioned when the workmen were
transported in stage coaches, at an enormous expense, from our
large seaport towns to the navy yard of this city. Contracts
for timber were made in haste and at a very advanced price.
As soon as it was obtained it was put together, and in a few
months we saw it floating in the form of a ship of war—*rotten*
ships, I may say, sir, for I believe, without exception, in the
frigates which were built by the United States the more important parts decayed and were rotten in two, three, or four
years. In many instances the expense for repairs was equal to
the original cost. A single frigate, the *Constitution*, has cost
for repairs, from October, 1802, to March, 1809, the enormous
sum of $302,582.21, or upward of $43,000 per annum for seven
years in succession.

Let us view this subject in a more extended sense—I mean
as regards our commerce generally—we shall still have cause to
entertain the opinion which we first adopted. We cannot protect our commerce on the ocean. Our ships have vexed every
sea—we trade to all parts of the world; of course, to protect
our commerce our ships of war must abandon our coasts and
encounter all the force of the enemy or those of Europe. The
ports we have in view are European. If your frigates, for convenience and safety, are to cruise only on your coasts, what will
be the fate of the millions which are embarked beyond the Cape
of Good Hope? By this management surely you cannot afford
it protection. France, Spain, and Holland, when combined and
backed by an armed neutrality in the north of Europe, could not
secure their commerce. The fleets of Great Britain now sail
triumphant over every wave of the deep. The Russians have a
navy far superior to that which it is proposed we shall establish,
and they cannot protect their trade in the confined limits of the
Baltic. They count fifty or sixty sail-of-the-line, besides many
frigates and smaller vessels.

Sir, the expenses which are incurred by a naval establishment far exceed the profits which arise from the commerce which
it is intended to protect. This proposition is warranted by the

experience of Great Britain, the most commercial nation of modern times. In the year 1798 the expenditure for her navy amounted to £13,654,013. In the year 1799 Mr. Pitt computed the profits on the commerce of Great Britain at £12,000,000, or one and a half millions less than the expenses for her navy the preceding year!

Sir, I further object to a navy because it will be the means of exciting many wars, which, without the establishment, may be honorably avoided. It is said nations are involved in war in proportion to the extent of their navies; and some assert (Lord Brougham) that a perpetual war is one of the two modes which are necessary to support a powerful naval establishment. Sir, a naval establishment will create a new and a dangerous interest in our country. Nothing is more common than to be told that such are the wishes of the naval interest of Great Britain, and that this or that war must be entered into to gratify them. For my part, sir, I shall be very sorry indeed if ever the period arrives in the United States when any particular interest or community shall direct the Government, whether it be naval, agricultural, manufacturing, or commercial. The general welfare should be the sole great ruling principle in the national councils.

Sir, I am deterred when I consider the fate of all those nations who at different periods have been famous for their navies. The naval strength of the Hanseatic League was such, two centuries past, as to excite terror on the part of England. These, sir, distant free cities, are now the appendages of mighty France, and have no political existence. Who has not heard of the once formidable fleets of Venice and Genoa? At one time England was indebted to the latter for officers to command her ships of war—alas; these republics are now consigned to oblivion. Denmark was at one time the mistress of the ocean; by means of her fleets she often invaded England, and held her in a state of subjection. The Danes heretofore burned London, Paris, and other great cities—they are now controlled by France, and they have had their Copenhagen defeat. Holland, with her Van Tromps and De Ruyters, occupied the British Channel at pleasure; this power defeated the navies of England and France. Where is Holland now? Incorporated as a part of the French empire. Spain boasted her invincible armadas; Elizabeth of England, by nature haughty, proud, and ambitious, trembled at the very mention of them, until they were dispersed and destroyed by storms at sea; Spain is now the vassal of France. Not very long since the navy of France sailed triumphant along the British coast, looked into Portsmouth harbor, and taunted British spirit. I ask you, sir, where is the strength of which these nations formerly boasted? All are inoperative, and dread the gigantic power of the British navy—they are in part sick in dry docks, or are blockaded in their ports.

Mr. Chairman, Great Britain, though at this time triumphant in every sea, if she persists in her expensive naval establishment, with her present debt of £800,000,000, which was chiefly created for her navy—Great Britain, sir, I say, with all this, must sink under the heavy pressure. She will hereafter derive very little satisfaction from her brilliant victories on the 1st of June off Cape St. Vincent, Camperdown, Aboukir, and Trafalgar.

Shall I be pardoned, sir, when I fear our vessels will only tend to swell the present catalog of the British navy? Of the 1,042 vessels which she possessed in July, 1811, one hundred and nine were captured from the French, forty-six from the Danes, twenty-five from the Spaniards, twenty-four from the Dutch, and three from the Italians; making a total of two hundred and seven captured ships, or one-fifth of her whole navy.

Small ships are proper for the service of the United States— by their agency we shall be able to annoy the convoys of an enemy. The privateers which were fitted out in every port during our revolutionary war destroyed much of the British commerce, even in the British and Irish Channels, while the frigates which were built by the Government did little or nothing—but two of them remained at the conclusion of the contest. The enemy will not watch your small vessels; they may enter all your small inlets, where heavy vessels cannot venture to approach them; and, at the conclusion of the war, they may be sold for the merchant service.

I shall vote against the bill, though it is my present intention to appropriate the sums requisite for the repairing and equipping our present ships of war. I will go no further. I tell you, sir, naval victories in the end would prove fatal to the United States; the consequences which have uniformly followed in other countries must take place here. If the United States shall determine to augment their navy, so as to rival those of Europe, the public debt will become permanent; direct taxes will be perpetual; the paupers of the country will be increased; the nation will be bankrupt; and, I fear, the tragedy will end in a revolution.

Mr. McKee.—Establish a navy and this country may bid farewell to peace; because you thereby organize a class of society who are interested in creating and keeping up wars and contention. Officers in the navy and army are mere cyphers in society in times of peace, and are only respectable in time of war, when wealth and fame may await their exertions. They are, therefore, interested in keeping up a state of war; and being invested with the management of an instrument of war, it is to be expected that it will be used in some degree to answer their own purposes? No man who will reflect for a moment but must be satisfied that the disgraceful and lawless conduct of the British naval officers on our coast originated in a desire on their part to bring on a war with this country, in which they looked forward to large dividends of prize money; and these acts were contrary to the wish and expectation of Great Britain; in one instance the act was disavowed; and it may be asked why were the officers not punished who acted contrary to the wishes of the government? The answer is obvious; because the influence of the navy in England is so predominant that the government are afraid to touch the subject, and the consequence is that the government are compelled to bear the odium of acts which they disapprove; and the same cause which has produced this effect in England, if permitted to operate, will produce a similar effect in this country.

Our little navy has already contributed much toward the irritation which exists between this country and England · and under any other President than Mr. Jefferson it would have brought on a war in 1807. And what real benefit has resulted from it to the Government? Has a picaroon or a buccaneer ever been chastised by them? If they have I have no recollection of the case; I have seen, indeed, paragraphs in the newspapers mentioning that the frigate *President*, or some one of the vessels, had sailed from the navy-yard to Norfolk, from thence to New York, and finally arrived safe at Boston; but for what purpose we are totally ignorant, unless, indeed, it was to sail back again, and furnish the materials for a new article for the newspapers; and for these eminent services the American people have already paid about $30,000,000.

MR. JOHNSON.—I will not vote one cent for a system of naval force which is destined to keep foreign nations in check in distant seas, and destined to entail upon this happy Government perpetual taxes and a perpetually increasing national debt. The people will not support such a naval establishment—they have the corrective in their hands; and build this fleet of twenty seventy-fours and forty frigates, and the people will in their turn put them down. But, sir, we are told that we are a commercial people, and that you cannot restrain a spirit of enterprise in our citizens which is limited only by the polar snows to the north and the icy mountains to the south. No person has attempted to damp that gallant spirit, that mercantile enterprise —such adventurous voyages have been fostered and cherished by every means in the power of the Government. But, sir, has this unparalleled enterprise, this gallant spirit, been carried on by a navy? Such a thing has never been thought of, which proves that this question of a navy has no connection with this commercial enterprise; and the existence of one without the other is positive proof of the fact. I am not prepared to give up our rights, whether upon the ocean or upon land, whether commercial or personal; but I may differ in the means of avenging these wrongs, and vindicating those rights, and I shall ever differ from those who wish a navy to ride triumphant in distant seas, and, under a pretext of protection to commerce, doom the nation to galling burdens too intolerable to be borne. But we are told, sir, that this question partakes of the character of a self-evident proposition. Indeed, sir, and in what respect is it entitled to this definition of self-evident? Unless, indeed, from every consideration of history, experience, and reason, it is evident that a navy is an engine of power and ambition, calculated to embroil a nation in quarrels and wars, and to fix permanent wretchedness upon the industrious class of the people. When we look to the delegation from each State we find a difference in sentiment upon this subject, whether lying on the seaboard or distant from it.

I defy history for an example of a single great naval power which confined its naval strength to the legitimate object of protecting commerce in distant seas. I will refer to Tyre and Sidon, Crete and Rhodes, to Athens and to Carthage. No sooner had these nations ceased to confine their naval strength to their maritime defence at home, to the protection of their seacoast, than they were engaged in plunder, piracy, depredations upon other nations, or involved in wars which certainly accelerated, if it did not produce, the downfall and destruction of those governments. Peace and tranquillity are not the natural state of a great naval power. A disregard of public law, sacred treaties, and bloodshed, would suit it better; it has been and ever will be the consequence of such force. These nations furnish another example and instructive lesson to the present generation—that, while their commerce and navy furnished a small part of the people with the luxuries of every country at that time known, the great mass of citizens at home were miserable and oppressed, their rights neglected, their burdens increased, and their happiness destroyed, while their fleets and external grandeur carried astonishment and terror to distant nations. When a nation puts forth her strength upon the ocean, the interior of the country will be neglected and oppressed with contributions. Ancient history does not furnish a solitary instance of any permanent good or long continuance of peace arising from a great naval supremacy; such overgrown power, such unnatural strength, must feed upon plunder at home and abroad.

Admit that Great Britain, with her thousand vessels, could protect her lawful commerce, let me ask if her navy has ever been confined to that object; whether it is confined to that object at this time; whether her navy has not fattened upon the spoils of Europe, Asia, Africa, and America, and the commerce of neutral nations, making war equally upon friends and enemies. Her navy, triumphant in every sea, is employed in a system of plunder against the world, and, notwithstanding this supremacy, we see her citizens groaning under a national debt of eight hundred millions of pounds sterling, more than all the nations of the universe could pay. We see her upon the precipice of bankruptcy—we see her people, her numerous subjects, loaded with taxes that would astonish any man who did not know the fact—notwithstanding this, the public debt is daily increasing, and it is now acknowledged by all the world that she is fighting for her existence—victorious at sea and safe at home from invasion, and still her very existence is at stake. Sir, I never wish to see the liberties of my country afloat upon the ocean and staked upon the strength of a navy. Look at France, separated from her enemy by a narrow channel, without vessels to meet the fleets of England on the water, and still she is unable to burn the seaport towns of France or invade the French territories, or in any way to make an impression upon her. Populous and powerful upon land, nothing but the imperial despotism that exists throughout that vast empire prevents the country from being the most enviable residence upon the globe, except our own favored land. Let not the Congress of the United States therefore stake their existence upon navies, let us not withdraw the protecting hand of government from the soil; let us not increase the burdens of the people, and weigh them down with a public debt to support external grandeur. Do not by this system destroy the affections and attachments of the solid and honest part of the community who support the government of the country.

But, I am asked, how will you contend with a maritime na-

tion without a navy? Sir, that question is as easily answered as
the first. I will ask how we succeeded in the Revolutionary
War? We were without any security upon our seacoast and
still we succeeded. But, to be more specific, I would grant letters of marque and reprisal, and authorize privateering. Give
scope to individual enterprise to destroy the commerce of the
enemy—which can be done effectually. I would fortify our
seaport towns; station our gunboats and frigates along our
coast to protect us at home. And, in this way, I would in war
avenge the infractions of our neutral rights.

MR. LOWNDES.—Although the honorable gentleman from
Kentucky [Mr. Johnson] is determined to defend commerce by some method which he will not fully disclose,
his arguments, like those of my honorable friend from
Pennsylvania [Mr. Seybert], appeared designed to show that
commerce was not worth defending. I hope to be excused for remarking that both these gentlemen have considered the profits of commerce as confined to the merchant.
They have forgotten that commerce implies a change of com-
modities, in which the merchant is only an intermediate agent.
He derives, indeed, a profit from the transaction—but so must
the seller and the buyer, the grower and the consumer, or they
would not engage in it. So must all those who are supported
by their own industry in commercial cities—the clerk, the ar-
tisan, the common laborer. But my honorable friend from
Pennsylvania says that Mr. Pitt estimated the profits of commerce in England at only twelve millions for a year, in which
the naval expense was fourteen or sixteen millions. I suppose
this estimate to have been made in relation to the income tax,
and it obviously must have referred only to the profits of merchants. The profits of merchants may be computed, but no
sober financier would attempt to compute the entire profits of
commerce. If it be desirable to form, not, indeed, an estimate,
but some conception of its importance, let my honorable friend
compute the value of New York, where a few square feet of land
are an estate, and then compare it with the value of the same
extent of ground for the purpose of the plow. But, is it in this
nation, and at this time, that it can be supposed that the profits
of commerce are confined to the merchant? Your trade was,
a few years ago, unrestrained and flourishing—did it not enrich
the most distant parts of your country? It has since been plun-
dered and confined. Does not the industry of the country languish? Is not the income of every man impaired? But, whatever may be the value of commerce, you have already determined

to defend it. Considerations of expense are not, indeed, to be neglected. We must employ, in the prosecution of the war, the cheapest and most efficacious instruments of hostility which we can obtain. The arguments of the honorable gentlemen on the other side are really directed against the war, rather than the navy. It would be absurd, say they, to protect commerce by a navy which should cost more than that commerce is worth. It must yet be more absurd, then, to protect it by an army which costs much more than the navy. In the comparison of the expenses and of the efficiency of an army and navy, instituted by my colleague, there is nothing invidious. The army is acknowledged to be necessary. It has had our votes. But, from the acknowledged propriety of raising the army, was fairly inferred the propriety of employing a navy, if it should be proved to be less expensive in proportion to its probable efficacy.

The honorable gentleman from Kentucky [Mr. McKee] offered objections to a navy which, if they were well founded, would supersede all further reasoning and calculation. He opposes a navy now—he will oppose it forever. It would produce no possible good and all possible evil. It would infallibly destroy the Constitution. Will the honorable gentleman tell us why? how? An ambitious general might corrupt his army and seize the Capitol—but will an admiral reduce us to subjection by bringing his ships up the Potomac? The strongest recommendation of a navy in free governments has hitherto been supposed to be that it was capable of defending but not of enslaving its country. The honorable gentleman has discovered that this is a vulgar error. A navy is really much more dangerous than an army to public liberty. He voted for the army and expressed no fears for the Constitution. But a navy would infallibly terminate in aristocracy and monarchy. All this may be very true. But are we unreasonable in expecting, before we give up the old opinion, to hear some argument in favor of the new one?

What is the nature of the defence which one of our large States may be supposed interested to obtain from the general Government? Is it a land force? We can scarcely expect an attack on land, to repel which the militia of New York or Massachusetts would be unequal. Were either of these States attacked the general Government would protect her by ordering out her own militia. To render the Union permanent you must render it the interest of all the States—the large as well as the small—to maintain it; you must show them that it will provide, not an army, which they can have without it, but what, without it, they cannot have—an adequate navy.

The honorable gentleman who anticipates the destruction of the Constitution, unless we shall neglect one of the great interests which it was intended to protect, considers the English Orders in Council as leaving our institutions firm and untouched. Regulations the effect of which is to give to a foreign power the complete disposition of the property of a large class of our people are, it seems, in their political result innocent. But let a navy be raised—let the Government which expects obedience provide protection, and the Constitution perishes!

But we have been referred particularly by my honorable friend from Pennsylvania to the experience of the world as having already decided the question which we are now discussing. It seems that Venice and Genoa, and every other naval power which can be named, have all furnished abundant proof of the ruinous effects which such a force is calculated to produce. Sir, the assertion is new. I do not pretend to an intimate acquaintance with the histories of those nations, but I have hitherto believed that the first great shock which the power of Venice received was given by the League of Cambray—a league formed to repress her ambition, not of maritime, but of territorial aggrandizement. But, while Venice has lost her independence after maintaining it for five or six centuries, may I ask my honorable friend whether the states of Italy, which were never oppressed by fleets, enjoyed a longer term of prosperity and freedom? As to Genoa—her naval power, her independence and glory, rose and sunk with the same man—Doria. But Holland, says the gentleman from Kentucky, affords an example of a nation whose commerce flourished greatly before it had a navy, and decayed while her navy continued powerful. If there ever were a people whose naval power has been employed to protect and almost to create their commerce, it is the Dutch. They fought their way at the same time to trade in the East Indies and America, and to national independence in Europe. The decay of their trade is to be attributed to the development of the resources of other nations; to the navigation act of England; and the similar measures adopted by other powers. As to France—the period of her greatest financial prosperity probably coincided with that of her greatest naval power; both were due to the administration of Colbert. But the evils of a navy (gentlemen tell us) have been concentrated in the case of England. With all her fleets she is destined soon to lose her independence. The expense of those fleets has crushed the industry of her subjects, and must soon reduce her to national bankruptcy. Let us suppose that these gentlemen, who have been so much mistaken in regard to the past, may be more accurate in their narrative of the future. Still England will have owed to her fleets her redemption from invasion for ages past. While every other considerable nation of Europe has been bankrupt over and over again, she is not yet bankrupt. While nearly every other government of Europe has been overset, hers yet rides out the storm. Should England fall to-morrow, it should seem impossible to deny that her navy will have prolonged her independence for at least two centuries.

MR. LAW.—Sir, in a country so blessed by nature; where the inhabitants have the greatest stimulus to industry, the fruits of their labor secured by just and equal laws; where the property cannot be taken from the owner without his consent, there will be a vast surplus beyond what the consumption of the country requires. Hence, commerce springs up as the daughter and handmaid of agriculture. Without commerce agriculture would languish. With it, wealth is consolidated and industry promoted. It diffuses its benign influence, discoverable in the splendid and delightful improvements which rejoice the eye of the traveler throughout the country. And it is as unnatural for the farming interest to oppress the commercial as it is for the parent to abandon its offspring. They mutually cherish and support each other; and, by natural sympathy, must be affected by the checks and disorders which each may receive. But commerce, being carried on abroad on the ocean, is subject to annoyance, interruption, and hazard. We must pass the common highway of nations to get to a market; and in this route the weak and defenceless must, and always will, be the sport and prey of the strong and violent whom they meet in the way. From the wretched state of those nations with whom we have intercourse we, from weakness, must fall victims to their violence. This is an evil which we shall always experience as a neutral coming in collision with belligerents. Shall we, then, abandon commerce, or shall we strive to support it? If we abandon it the evil will recoil on the agricultural part of the country, who, no longer than foreign commerce is supported, can find a vent for their surplus; and, without a vent for the surplus, a bare competency might be endangered. Internal commerce, being but a stream from foreign commerce, must dry when the fountain from whence it issues fails. Enterprise ceases and languor and poverty ensue. It is, then, for the interest of the nation to cherish commerce. But how can this be

done? Will a navy have this effect? I think it will. We are
now the defenceless prey of both France and England; deprived
of the common rights of nations and citizens of the world. I
verily believe, if this nation had fostered our infant navy from
the time it was commenced and had not, by a strange infatuation, abandoned and neglected it, it would now have been too
important to be despised by either France or England. Our
prosperity would have continued. Our strength would have
been dreaded, and our friendship courted by both nations.
While they have been contending for the mastery we, with such
naval force as we ought to have had, and a strict course of
neutrality, might have pursued a lawful and gainful trade.
We might have had a perpetual revenue of sixteen millions, instead of the pittance now received at the treasury. I believe
that, with the navy we might have had, and a correct strict neutral court, there would have been neither Berlin and Milan
decrees, nor Orders in Council, to annoy our lawful commerce.

MR. ROBERTS.—Soon after the Government came into operation it became a favorite object with one set of politicians to
form a navy. On the occasion of our commerce being depredated
upon by the Barbary corsairs the question first came up. It
became a matter of deliberation whether a peace should be purchased of them with money and presents; whether some European power should be subsidized to keep a few frigates on that
station, or whether a naval force should be equipped for the
purpose (as alleged) of enabling the President to negotiate to
better effect. The party with whom I have always found it my
duty to act opposed, on that occasion, the commencement of a
navy system when it was invited under circumstances so specious. They were, however, in the minority. The ships of war
were voted—with what effect on the Algerines he did not stop to
inquire. The question of increasing the navy was again discussed in the celebrated times of '98-9. The collisions with
France had raised the war fever very high. A navy was vociferously contended for as the most efficient means of defence. It
was when things were in this state that the President, in his
reply to the Marine Society of Boston, who had, with much
fervor, tendered him their approbation of his measures, hoped
to see the wooden walls of America considered as her best defence. Because Athens, when she was invaded by the hosts of
Xerxes, had chosen to interpret the oracle that promised her
safety in wooden walls, rationally, America must take the same
course, however dissimilarly situated. The people of Attica,
inhabiting a circumscribed territory, found safety in their fleet,

and they could have found it nowhere else. But such cannot be the case with America. Even the hosts of Xerxes could not make it necessary for the American people to quit their territory—the figure would not hold. On this occasion, too, the Republican party consistently opposed a navy.

History proves to us that maritime power has always excited national ambition to a spirit of conquest and plunder. A naval power will seek colonies and ports in distant places. The chance, nay, the certainty, of collisions with other nations is multiplied, and a corruption of morals is produced that cannot fail to make the first government on earth a tyranny by a course of events that the patriot can neither prevent nor divert to other consequences. A short time after Athens had found safety in her wooden walls one of her statesmen proposed she should burn the fleets of her neighbors, that she might thereby be rendered mistress of Greece. This project the virtue of the people resisted; but that virtue soon gave way in the expedition to the Cyclades, where her navy commited acts of violence that must indelibly fix the stain of the blackest perfidy and cruelty on the Athenian character. What could be a more unprovoked act of aggression than her crusade against Syracuse, a crime that visited her with a declension of power from which she never recovered? For a nation to believe her destinies fixed is in a great measure to fix them. Nothing, perhaps, contributed more to make Rome the mistress of the world than the oracles that promised it. Her heroes and statesmen were stimulated thereby to fulfil her destiny. The maritime supremacy of Britain is, perhaps, owing as much to the belief that she is the destined queen of the waters as to any other cause. Though such operations be calculated to bring about astonishing effects, how unfortunate is it when a nation's eyes are thus directed to improper attainments—it becomes a source of incalculable evil.

Athens and Rome were the victims of such a policy as Britain is at this time. Her marine puts the trident into her hands, but she can no longer shake the earth. Her monopolizing spirit has sealed the continent of Europe against her and interdicted her commerce with America. She has reduced the ocean almost to a desert; and she seems hastening to that destiny which has generally attended her predecessors in naval power through her ambition to rule the waves.

Yet the plunder of half the world has not sustained the British navy. A debt has been accumulated that almost baffles the power of figures to estimate. But debt and a prospect of government insolvency at home are of much less account than the wrongs this navy has wrought on the society of nations. And yet it is this government that is held up to Republican America as a model for imitation.

Need I remind you of the millions of victims sacrificed to commercial cupidity on the plains of Hindustan by means of this navy? A population thrice as great as that of the British Isles has been exterminated in this devoted region within comparatively but a few years by mercantile rapacity. Colonel Dowe informs us that the wealth of one of the cities of this wretched country had whetted the avarice of Clive and his associates, and that an offer was made to the government to pay the public debt for permission to sack it. It was too gross an act of infamy to assent to and the adventurers obtained their end by other means. A famine and pestilence was substituted for the bayonet and the spoils of the devoted city glutted the hands of rapine. In this exploit a shoeblack divided his £200,000. Need I remind you that the population of Africa has been drained to groan out a wretched existence in the West India colonies to prop up this naval and commercial power, or that the remotest corners of every sea have been visited with the scourge of blood and desolation for the same purpose? On general principles, does not past experience afford sufficient warning to these States to avoid those shoals on which so many nations have been wrecked?

MR. CLAY.—Gentlemen fear that if we provide a marine it will produce collisions with foreign nations, plunge us into war, and ultimately overturn the Constitution of the country. Sir, if you wish to avoid foreign collision you had better abandon the ocean; surrender all your commerce; give up all your prosperity. It is the thing protected, not the instrument of protection, that involves you in war. Commerce engenders collision, collision war, and war, the argument supposes, leads to despotism. Would the counsels be deemed wise of that statesman who should recommend that the nation should be unarmed —that the art of war, the martial spirit and martial exercises, should be prohibited—and that the great body of the people should be taught that national happiness was to be found in perpetual peace alone? No, sir. And yet every argument in favor of a power of protection on land applies, in some degree, to a power of protection on the sea. Undoubtedly a commerce void of naval protection is more exposed to rapacity than a guarded commerce; and, if we wish to invite the continuance of the old, or enaction of new, unjust edicts let us refrain from all exertion upon that element where they operate and where, in the end, they must be resisted.

For my part, I do not allow myself to be alarmed by those apprehensions of maritime power which appeared to agitate other gentlemen. In the nature of our Government I behold abundant security against abuse. I would be unwilling to tax the land to support the rights of the sea, but would draw from the sea itself the resources with which its violated freedom should at all times be vindicated. While this principle is adhered to there will be no danger of running into the folly and extravagance which so much alarm gentlemen; and, whenever it is abandoned, whenever Congress shall lay burdensome taxes to augment the navy beyond what may be authorized by the increased wealth, and demanded by the exigencies of the country, the people will interpose, and, removing their unworthy Representatives, apply the appropriate corrective. I cannot, then, see any just ground of dread in the nature of naval power. It is, on the contrary, free from the evils attendant upon standing armies. And the genius of our institutions—the great representative principle, in the practical enjoyment of which we are so eminently distinguished—affords the best guaranty against the ambition and wasteful extravagance of government.

I am far from surveying the vast maritime power of Great Britain with the desponding eye with which other gentlemen behold it. I cannot allow myself to be discouraged at the prospect even of her thousand ships. This country only requires resolution, and a proper exertion of its immense resources, to command respect and to vindicate every essential right. If we are not able to meet the wolves of the forest, shall we put up with the barking of every petty fox that trips across our way? Because we cannot guard against every possible danger shall we provide against none? I hope not. I have hardly expected that the instructing but humiliating lesson was so soon to be forgotten which was taught us in the murder of Pierce; the attack on the *Chesapeake;* and the insult offered in the harbor of Charleston, which the brave old fellow that commanded the fort in vain endeavored to chastise.

Gentlemen refer to the period of 1798, and we are reminded of the principles maintained by the opposition at that time. I have no doubt of the correctness of that opposition. The naval schemes of that day were premature, not warranted by the resources of the country, and were contemplated for an unnecessary war into which the nation was about to be plunged. I have always admired and approved the zeal and ability with

which that opposition was conducted by the distinguished gentleman now at the head of the treasury. But the state of things
is totally altered. What was folly in 1798 may be wisdom now.
At that time, we had a revenue only of about six millions. Our
revenue now, upon a supposition that commerce is restored, is
about sixteen millions. The population of the country, too, is
greatly increased—nearly doubled—and the wealth of the nation is, perhaps, tripled. While our ability to construct a navy
is thus enhanced, the necessity for maritime protection is pro-
portionately augmented. Independent of the extension of our
commerce, since the year 1798, we have had an addition of more
than five hundred miles to our coast, from the bay of Perdido
to the mouth of the Sabine—a weak and defenceless accession,
requiring, more than any other part of our maritime frontier,
the protecting arm of government.

MR. QUINCY.—Commerce is the leading interest of more than
one-half, and is the predoment interest of more than one-third,
of the people of the United States. The States north of the
Potomac contain nearly four millions of souls; and surely it
needs no proof to convince the most casual observer that the
proportion which the commercial interest bears to the other interests of that great section of the Union is such as entitles it
to the denomination of *leading interest*. The States north of
the Hudson contain nearly two and a half millions of souls;
and surely there is as little need of proof to show that the proportion the commercial interest bears to the other interests of
that Northern section of the Union is such as entitles it there
to the denomination of *predominating interest*.

If this commerce were the mushroom growth of a night—if
it had its vigor from the temporary excitement and the accumulated nutriment which warring elements in Europe had swept
from the places of their natural deposit—then, indeed, there
might be some excuse for a temporizing policy touching so transi-
tory an interest. But commerce in the Eastern States is of no
foreign growth, and of no adventitious seed; its root is of a fiber
which almost two centuries have nourished; and the perpetuity
of its destiny is written in legible characters, as well in the
nature of the country as in the disposition of its inhabitants.
Indeed, sir, look along your whole coast, from Passamaquoddy
to Capes Henry and Charles, and behold the deep and far-wind-
ing creeks and inlets, the noble basins, the projecting headlands,
the majestic rivers, and those sounds and bays which are more
like inland seas than anything called by those names in other
quarters of the globe! Can any man do this and not realize

that the destiny of the people inhabiting such a country is essentially maritime?

How is this commerce, this great national interest, to be protected? Is it by an army? Suppose that in every land project you are successful—suppose both the Canadas, Quebec, Halifax, everything to the north pole, yours by fair conquest—are your rights on the ocean, therefore, secure? Does your flag float afterward in honor? Are your seamen safe from impressment? Is your course along the highway of nations unobstructed? No one pretends it. No one has or can show, by any logical deduction or any detail of facts, that the loss of those countries would so compress Great Britain as to induce her to abandon for one hour any of her maritime pretensions. What then results? Why, sir, what is palpable as the day—that maritime rights are to be maintained only by maritime means.

With respect to the nature and extent of this naval force some difference of opinion may arise, according to the view taken of the primary objects of protection. For myself, I consider that those objects are first to be protected in the safety of which the national character and happiness are most deeply interested. And these are chiefly concerned, beyond all question, in the preservation of our maritime settlements from pillage and our coast from violence. For this purpose it is requisite that there should be a ship of war for the harbor of every great city of the United States equal in point of force to the usual grade of ships-of-the-line of the maritime belligerents.

But it is said that "we have not capacity to maintain such a naval force." Is it want of pecuniary or want of physical capacity? In relation to our pecuniary capacity I will not condescend to add any proof to that plain statement already exhibited, showing that we have an annual commercial exposure equal to six hundred millions of dollars, and that two-thirds of one per cent. upon this amount of value, or four millions of dollars, is more than is necessary, if annually and systematically appropriated, for this great object; so anxiously and rightfully desired by your seaboard, and so essential to the honor and obligations of the nation.

This objection of pecuniary inability may be believed in the interior country, where the greatness of the commercial property and all the tender obligations connected with its preservation are not realized. But in the cities and in the commercial States the extent of the national resources is more truly estimated. They know the magnitude of the interests at stake and their essential claim to protection. Why, sir, were we seriously to urge this objection of pecuniary incapacity to the commercial men of Massachusetts they would laugh us to scorn. Let me state a single fact. In the year 1745 the State, then the colony of Massachusetts Bay, included a population of 220,000 souls, and yet in that infant state of the country it owned a fleet consisting of three ships, one of which carried twenty guns, three snows, one brig, and three sloops; being an aggregate of ten vessels of war. These partook of the dangers and shared in the glory of that expedition which terminated with the surrender of Louisburg. Comparing the population, the extent of territory, the capital, and all the other resources of this great nation with the narrow means of the colony of Massachusetts at that period of its history, it is not extravagant to assert that the fleet it then possessed, in proportion to its pecuniary resources, was greater than would be, in proportion to the resources of the United States, a fleet of fifty sail-of-the-line and one hundred frigates.

As to respect abroad, what course can be more certain to insure it? What object more honorable, what more dignified than to behold a great nation pursuing wise ends by appropriate means; rising to adopt a series of systematic exertions suited to her power and adequate to her purposes? What object more consolatory to the friends—what more paralyzing to the enemies of our Union—than to behold the natural jealousies and rivalries, which are the acknowledged dangers of our political condition, subsiding or sacrificing? What sight more exhilarating than to see this great nation once more walking forth among the nations of the earth under the protection of no foreign shield? Peaceful because powerful—powerful because united in interests and amalgamated by concentration of those interests in the national affections.

CHAPTER VII

Flogging in the Navy

Flogging Is Abolished in the American Navy—Petition to Congress to Restore It—Debate in the Senate: In Favor of the Petition, George E. Badger [N. C.]; Opposed, Commodore Robert F. Stockton [N. J.].

DURING President Fillmore's Administration the ancient practice of flogging was abolished in the American navy. On January 7, 1852, a memorial was presented to the Senate by citizens of Philadelphia asking that the practice be restored.

Your memorialists most respectfully represent that on the high seas, where ready access to legal civil tribunals cannot be obtained for the prompt punishment of offenders against the laws of the naval and marine service, and where it is neither possible to discharge such offenders from the service nor to obtain others to occupy their places and perform their duties, it is of the highest importance that a power should be conferred upon commanders to compel the service of their crews by means and punishments which, under other circumstances, would not be required.

Good men, who do their duty, fear no punishment, and it is not inflicted upon them. The good men of the service, it is believed, desire the repeal of the late law. It imposes upon them the duty of bad men, who shelter themselves under it from the performance of their duty. It is not, in the opinion of your memorialists, punishment, whether it be of the lash, the dungeon, or the sword, that disgraces a man. It is the *offence* which merits such punishment that disgraces him. Lafayette was not disgraced by incarceration in the dungeons of Olmutz, Algernon Sydney by the axe of the second Charles, nor the great Apostle to the Gentiles by the repeated infliction on his person of the Mosaic law of "forty stripes to save one."

If a sailor be so lost to a sense of duty, feeling, and honor as to desert his post, or to commit crime, there is little danger

225

to be apprehended of his feeling disgraced by the infliction of punishment by the lash, the chain ball, or the treadmill.

And your memorialists would further add that the necessary power of moderate and prompt punishment for petty offences committed on board ship has been, and still is, conferred on commanders of British vessels, and was so upon commanders of American vessels until the last session of the Congress of the United States; and will only refer, in addition to the foregoing statements, to the high state of discipline and efficiency attained by these great maritime powers as a vindication of that practice, and an argument in favor of its reënactment.

A debate ensued on the subject between Commodore Robert F. Stockton [N. J.] who opposed the memorial, and George E. Badger [N. C.] who supported it.

FLOGGING IN THE NAVY

SENATE, JANUARY 7, 1852

SENATOR STOCKTON.—I am of opinion that the nation whose service is supplied with the best common sailors will excel in naval warfare as well as in all maritime pursuits. I am further of opinion that, in versatility, education, courage, and industry, our sailors in the whaling and coasting service excel those of all other nations. I am, furthermore, of opinion that the superiority of the American sailor has decided the battle in our favor in many a bloody conflict, when, without that superiority, it might have been otherwise. I desire to secure and preserve that superiority. To that end, and for humanity's sake, I am utterly and irreconcilably opposed to the use of the lash in the navy or anywhere else.

The longest, the most arduous voyages are made in the merchant service without the use of the lash. In the Polar seas among the icebergs of the Arctic and Antarctic Oceans, the intrepid New Englander pursues his gigantic game and hurls his harpoon; and, after a three years' voyage, returns with the oily spoils of his adventurous navigation. But he owes none of his success, his patient endurance, his exemplary discipline, and his indefatigable industry to the guarded ministrations of the lash. To say that men who can make such voyages and endure such hardships cheerfully and contentedly cannot navigate their own national ships without the infliction of the infamous lash is a libel. Is their nature changed the moment they step on the deck of a national vessel? Are they less men—less Americans—as soon as the custody of the American flag or the national honor is intrusted to their keeping? No, sir; it is one of those inconsiderate, thoughtless opinions which mankind seems to think they have a perfect right to express in regard to sailors. It was not long since, sir, that I had a conversation on this subject with a gentleman who had for several years commanded a fine ship in the merchant service, but who is now an honorable, active, and efficient man of business in one of our large cities, and to whose integrity, generosity, and humanity I would intrust anybody *but a sailor*. After he had heard my views on this subject he instantly replied: "Why, you mean to treat them like human beings." The theory that the navy cannot be governed and that our national ships cannot be navigated without the use of the lash seems to me to be founded in that false idea that sailors *are not men*—not American citizens— have not the common feelings, sympathies, and honorable impulses of our Anglo-American race.

I do not wonder, when I look back on the past history of the sailor, at the prevalence of this idea. His life has been a life of habitual, I will not say of systematic, degradation. The officers who command him—the oldest, the bravest, and the best—have been accustomed from their boyhood to see the sailor lashed about the ship's deck like a brute. He who, by the laws of the service in which he is engaged is treated, or liable to be treated, like a brute soon comes to be thought of as at least but little better than a brute. Who in social life respects a man whose back has been scarred at the whipping-post? Into what depth of contempt does such a punishment sink its victim? And here is one of the worst evils of the system: It destroys those feelings of respect and kindness which officers ought to entertain for the sailors under their command.

But this is only one of the worst evils of the system. It destroys those feelings of regard and respect which the sailors should entertain for their officers. The truth is, there are no relations of affection and regard between them. The one is the oppressor, the other the oppressed. Sir, a man may fear or hate; but he neither loves nor respects his tyrant. The worst government upon earth is that of fear; the best, that of love and affection. These sentiments, by a law of our nature, must be mutual sentiments. Bonaparte was the idol of the soldiers because the soldier was his idol. They loved him because they supposed he loved them. There is nothing that gallant and brave men will not do and suffer for a commander whom they love. Difficulties and dangers and death have no terrors for such men. In great battles, where the contest has been doubtful, those soldiers have always fought most desperately whose devotion to their commander was the greatest. It has always been considered as an essential element in the character of a successful commander that he should be able to excite and encourage the confidence and affection of the men under his command. But what confidence or regard can be expected under the government of the lash?

But more than this: the punishment destroys the sailor's own self-respect. What has honor—what has pride—what has patriotism to do with a man who may be, at the caprice of another, subjected to an infamous punishment, worse—aye, sir, in some cases worse a thousand times—than death? Can nobleness of sentiment or an honorable pride of character dwell with one whose every muscle has been made to quiver under the *lash?* Can he long continue to love his country whose laws degrade him to the level of a brute? The infamous "question" of torture now only remains as a blot on the page of Anglo-Saxon history. The whipping-post, where the worst vagrants used to expiate their offences, has been discarded from society. The worst offences in our State prisons are no longer punished by the lash. Why is all this? Why are those punishments now condemned as the shameful relics of a barbarous age? It is because the light of a better day has dawned. It is because the precepts of the Gospel of Christianity have ameliorated our laws. It is because society has made the discovery that, if a man is fit to live at all, he ought not to be divested of all the qualities which make a man by the infamous mutilation of his body. What is the answer which is given to all this by those who seek to restore this relic of barbarism to the navy? Why, they tell us we intend only to apply this system of punishment to seamen—we intend only to flog sailors. That is quite true. It is only sailors who are to be treated like brutes—aye, sir, worse than brutes. There is no man who hears me who would permit his dog to be thus treated. There is no spot on the habitable globe known to me where a man would be permitted to seize upon a dog and lash him until he cut the flesh from off his ribs, and the blood should be made to run down from his backbone to his heels. But, sir, it is only the sailor for whom this punishment is to be reserved.

Who, O Senators! is the American sailor that he is to be treated worse than a dog? He has been my companion for more than a quarter of a century—through calm and storm, privations, sufferings, and danger. In peace and in war I have lived with him and fought with him side by side, by sea and land. I have seen him in the northern ocean where there was no night to veil his deeds. I have seen him on the coast of Africa surrounded by pestilential disease. I have seen him among the West Indian Islands in chase of pirates with his parched tongue hanging almost out of his mouth. I have encamped with him on the Californian mountains and on the plains of the Mesa. I have seen the rays of the morning sun play on his carbine and his boarding-pike. I have seen him march one hundred and fifty miles through an enemy's country, over mountains and through rivers. I have seen his feet scarified by the projecting rocks as he hauled his cannon over the hills. I have seen him with no shoes on but those of canvas, made by his own hands, and with no provision but what he took from the enemy. I have seen him plunge into the Rio San Gabriel and drag his guns after him in the face of a galling fire from a desperate foe. And, finally, I have lain beside him on the cold ground when the ice has formed on his beard. Sir, his heart has beat close to my own. I ought to know him. I do know him. And this day— now, before the assembled Senate of the Republic, I stand up to speak in his behalf.

Mr. President, our sailors, as a class, have loved their country as well and have done more for her in peace and war than any other equal number of citizens. Passing by for a moment his antecedent glorious achievements, let me remind you that the American sailor has recently gained for his country an empire. Through perils by land and perils by water he has gained a golden empire which has added to his country's renown and greatness, and, perhaps, saved his fellow-citizens from almost universal bankruptcy and ruin.[1] And what has his country done for him? When the fighting was over you refused to give him "bounty lands," which you gave to the soldier—his comrade fighting by his side—and you have neglected to give him even your thanks. And now, to cap the climax of his country's ingratitude, these memoralists would have him scourged. They would scourge him for drunkenness when they put the bottle to his mouth. They would scourge him for inattention to his duty when injustice and wrong have made him for an instant discontented and sullen. Shame! Shame! You would scourge him while living and when dead consign him to a felon's grave.

Mr. President, to whom in time of peace are intrusted the

[1] California is referred to, in the conquest of which Commodore Stockton played an important part.

lives of the thousands who traverse the ocean? Whose energy and skill and hardy self-denying toil carry the products of your soil through the world, and bring back the rich return? It is the American sailor. By his superior qualities as a man he has enabled you to rival in commerce the boasted mistress of the ocean. Where is the coast or harbor in the wide world accessible to human enterprise to which he has not carried your flag? His berth is no sinecure. His service is no easy service. He is necessarily an isolated being; he knows no comforts of home and wife and children. He reaps no golden rewards for the increase of treasure which he brings to you. When on shore he is among strangers and friendless. When worn out he is scarcely provided for. Making many rich, he lives and dies poor; carrying the arts of civilization and the blessings of the Gospel through the world, he is treated as an outcast from the mercies of both. But look to your history—that part of it which the world knows by heart—and you will find on its brightest page the glorious achievements of the American sailor. Whatever his country has done to disgrace him and break his spirit, he has never disgraced her; he has always been ready to serve her; he always has served her faithfully and effectually. He has often been weighed in the balance and never found wanting. The only fault ever found with him is that he sometimes fights ahead of his orders. The world has no match for him, man for man; and he asks no odds, and he cares for no odds, when the cause of humanity or the glory of his country calls him to fight. Who, in the darkest days of our Revolution, carried your flag into the very chops of the British Channel, bearded the lion in his den, and woke the echoes of old Albion's hills by the thunders of his cannon and the shouts of triumph? It was the American sailor. And the names of John Paul Jones and the *Bon Homme Richard* will go down the annals of time forever. Who struck the first blow that humbled the Barbary flag, which for a hundred years had been the terror of Christendom, drove it from the Mediterranean, and put an end to the infamous tribute it had been accustomed to extort? It was the American sailor. And the name of Decatur and his gallant companions will be as lasting as monumental brass. In your war of 1812, when your arms on shore were covered by disaster—when Winchester had been defeated—when the Army of the Northwest had surrendered, and when the gloom of despondency hung like a cloud over the land—who first relit the fires of national glory and made the welkin ring with the shouts of victory? It was the American sailor. And the names of Hull and the *Constitu-*

tion will be remembered as long as we have left anything worth remembering. That was no small event. The wand of Mexican prowess was broken on the Rio Grande. The wand of British invincibility was broken when the flag of the *Guerrière* came down. That one event was worth more to the Republic than all the money which has ever been expended for the navy. Since that day the navy has had no stain upon its escutcheon, but has been cherished as your pride and glory. And the American sailor has established a reputation throughout the world—in peace and in war, in storm and in battle—for unsurpassed heroism and prowess.

Mr. President, I am no painter. I cannot draw with artistic skill the scene I would have you look upon. But it requires no artist. Picture it to yourself, sir. See the gallant, bold sailor who has served his apprenticeship with Hull in the *Constitution*, or one who helped to drag the guns across the San Gabriel, stripped and lashed worse than a dog. Can you stand it, sir? Yet your laws have authorized it to be done—it probably has been done. And now it is proposed to give authority to do it again. Will the American people stand it? Will this more than Roman Senate long debate whether, American citizen as he is, the sailor shall be entitled to all his rights as an American citizen or not; whether, freeman as he is, he shall be scourged like a slave? Cicero's climacteric, in his speech against Verres, is that, though a Roman citizen, his client had been scourged. And shall an American citizen be scourged? Forbid it, God of Humanity, forbid it. For my own part, I would rather see the navy abolished and the stars and stripes buried with their glory in the depths of the ocean than that those who won its glories should be subjected to a punishment so ignominious and brutalizing. Sir, if I had the power vouchsafed to others to impress my own feelings upon the hearts of those who hear me, I would rouse in the minds of Senators such a sense of national pride and human sympathy that they would with one voice demand that the memorial which seeks to rob the American sailor of his rights as an American freeman should be thrown under your table and trampled beneath your feet.

But it is said that the navy cannot be governed without the lash. As a general proposition I express my utter dissent to it. I admit that, among sailors, as among other classes, there will always be found some who are vicious and troublesome. That is the case in the army as well as in the navy; and they have abolished the lash in the army. It is as easy to get other and less offensive punishments for the navy as for the army;

and, if those punishments will not answer, the refractory person had better be driven in disgrace from the navy. He is not fit to be trusted in the hour of peril—he is unworthy to have the honor of the flag confided to him. Sufficient inducements should be offered to the better classes to enter the navy; and a part of those inducements should always be good treatment. A free use of the lash—nay, its probable use, its permission by law—has always been an objection urged by better classes to entering the navy. They prefer the merchant service, where they can at least select their own commander, while in the navy they know not into whose hands they may fall. Thus you see that the very necessity which is pleaded creates, in a great degree, the circumstances out of which it is supposed to spring. You flog because there are bad men in the navy, and the fact that you do flog excludes the better class of sailors from entering the service; so that the mischief is self-perpetuating. But, again, it is said that a large majority of the officers of the navy are of opinion that the lash is necessary and indispensable. Well, there are differences of opinion about it. We all know, however, that old notions and opinions are hard to be rooted out, and that men are very apt to love arbitrary power when they are to exercise it, and not be subject to it. It would seem, sir, that it is a part of man's nature to yield with great reluctance the smallest atom of power with which he may be invested. He is unwilling to admit that he can abuse it. Its safest depository he considers is his own hands. For these and similar reasons I think that the opinion of the officers of the navy on this subject should be taken with many grains of allowance.

The offence for which there seems to have been more lashes inflicted than for all other offences is that of drunkenness. Now, sir, the Government furnishes the liquor for the sailor and, if he gets drunk upon his allowance, the Government itself is responsible, and the sailor ought not to be flogged. If he procures it on board of a ship by theft or bargain, it is evidence of a laxity of discipline for which others are responsible, and for which the sailor ought not to be flogged. The lash, therefore, is not necessary to prevent drunkenness, not only for the reasons just stated but because it must be universally admitted that it never has and never can prevent the offence of drunkenness, if he who is habituated to it is permitted to have liquor.

The offence of disobedience of orders has also been punished by flogging. I will hazard the opinion that stopping the offender's allowance of tobacco, or rum, tea, sugar, and coffee would have been, in every case, a much more reasonable and a more efficient punishment. And now, sir, what has become of this plea of necessity?—I will not call it in this connection the tyrant's plea; the officers of the navy do not deserve such a reproach from any one, and especially from myself, because I did, when in the service, execute, and permit to be executed, the law of the lash as I hope I did all other laws of the service, which I had sworn to obey and to enforce. And this should be a sufficient answer to those who expect to escape from the grasp of argument and facts by indulging individual recrimination, and will be sufficient to remind them that there is some difference in the position of those who are called upon to make the laws and those whose duty it is to execute them.

The officers of the navy, in my judgment, are entitled to high commendation. They are, as a class, brave, noble, generous, and patriotic men; and, in all the elements of character which constitute valuable public servants, they have no superiors. But, however much respect I may entertain for them as a class, it is my duty, which I shall endeavor to perform, to deal without reserve or false delicacy with their arguments, and the errors which disgrace and paralyze the service to which they belong. It does appear to me, Mr. President, that the argument, from necessity, has resolved itself simply into this: that the lash is an easy and short way to settle a trifling difficulty with a sailor. And so were the thumb-screw and the rack an easy and short way to get a confession, and the Inquisition settled matters of faith easily and readily. But, sir, there has been a great change in the opinions of mankind on this subject, and I hope the change will go on until the last relic of barbarism shall be banished from the world.

SENATOR BADGER.—The views that have been submitted to the Senate by the Senator from New Jersey have in some respects struck me with surprise; and I think that, as I am a member of the Naval Committee, and as I entertain a very different opinion upon the subject of this petition from that which has been so forcibly and eloquently expressed by the honorable Senator from New Jersey, I could not think it right that remarks of this kind should go forth to the country without an instantaneous notice from some gentleman who belongs to that committee. In the absence of the chairman I have assumed that duty myself.

Now, what is the petition? It is simply a petition that the Congress of the United States will restore a discipline to the navy which had existed in it from its institution, and was discontinued only during the last session of Congress. It is an application to restore a discipline to the navy which went into operation under the sanction of the immortal Washington, and was continued under all succeeding administrations of the Government; and surely I need not say, sir, that asking us to restore such a discipline is not asking us either to restore or introduce into the navy a system of horrible, barbarous, and detestable exaggeration of punishment such as cannot be stated without making the heart turn sick with horror and detestation.

The Senator's objections to the punishment which it is proposed to restore to the discipline of the navy divide themselves into two heads. So far as I see my task will be a very easy one, for the honorable Senator himself has distinctly refuted both of them in the course of his remarks. The first is: that this punishment is positively mischievous; that to subject the sailor to the lash is to teach him to be a coward; that, if you expect him to maintain the glory of the country, to maintain possession of the public ships, to resist the enemy who assails him, if you do not wish to build ships, not for yourselves, but for your enemies, you must abolish the lash, for, by accustoming the sailor to that punishment, you deprive him of the principles of honor and make him a coward. Yet, in the very same breath, the honorable Senator reminds us of those gallant and noble achievements which distinguished the progress of the late war with England —of those victories upon the ocean and lakes which have made the names of the naval commanders immortal, and shed luster upon this country; and of which I would only say that I should be entirely satisfied if the successes of our naval commanders under this or any modification of the law would equal them. How were those sailors bred? Under what discipline were they trained? Was it not with this very discipline of the lash, which the honorable Senator says must be abolished in order to make them brave? Every victory which they have gained, every monument of naval renown which, at the day, was received with shouts of joy and gratulation from one portion of the Union to the other, and the memory of which is cherished by us all, was gained by sailors, noble, daring, courageous sailors, but sailors who were formed under the discipline of the lash.

The next objection of the honorable Senator was that this punishment is inexpedient and unnecessary. Let us see how that is. As I should have said, it is a punishment that obtains in every naval service on the globe. It obtained in ours from the establishment of our naval marine until the last Congress. It is said by the honorable Senator that nothing is urged, in the form of an argument, in support of the necessity and propriety of that punishment. He says the common course is to say that the punishment is necessary, that it cannot be dispensed with, and there leave the subject. What more does the honorable Senator say in reply but simply to make a strong and confident assertion; and what is that? That it is unnecessary. He says that no officer who is fit to command a ship needs the lash. Is that an argument, or is it not rather one assertion opposed to another? Certainly the opinion of the Senator is entitled to as much weight and consideration as that of any man in this country. But it is no more an argument than the opinion of any other man. And then, as I have said, the honorable Senator has refuted his own proposition by his own statements. What does he say? ''He that is fit to command a ship does not need the lash.'' The honorable Senator has certainly told us, in the eulogy he passed on the celebrated victory of Hull in the *Constitution*, that Hull was fit to command a ship. I suppose that Decatur, I suppose that Perry, the conqueror of the lakes, that Morris, that Warrington were all fit to command ships. Yet they all needed, they all used, the lash. They formed their men with the lash; and, in using that term, I do not mean to say that they were engaged in excessive flagellation. No one asks or contends for that; but that they used it as a means of discipline, as a means of coercing their authority and forming the sailor to habits of obedience. Then, if the honorable Senator has conceded the fact that these men actually needed the lash; if, as he has shown, they were fit to command ships, I ask if he has not repudiated all his objections?

But, again: the honorable Senator has repudiated them further, for he tells us, in anticipation of what he supposes may be a reply, by an *argumentum ad hominem*, that when he was in the command of ships he used the lash. And why? He says he acted in obedience to the law. What law? There never was a law in the United States that required the commander of a ship to use the lash. The law authorized him to use it when it was needful. It made him the judge, and the sole judge, of that necessity. He has no assessors in his tribunal. He has no jury to determine when the lash shall be used. He is the one supreme judge on his own ship. The law says to him, in fact, ''When you shall deem it necessary for controlling and directing your vessel and governing your men, for restraining misconduct, for giving a proper degree of order to the ship and efficiency to the service, you are at liberty to use the lash.'' Now, the honorable Senator says that when he was in command of a ship he used it. There is no man who knows him and who knows the kindliness of his heart who would suppose that ne ever used it except in a case of necessity in his judgment. Then he himself, being in the possession of a power, at liberty to use it at his own discretion when it was needful, and to forbear using it when it was not needful, actually used it. I suppose none of us here doubts for a single moment that he is fit to command a ship; he is eminently fit for it, at least he was while he was in the service. Thus I think I have a distinct refutation of the honorable Senator's own proposition. All the leading commanders in our service did need the lash as an instrument of authority, the honorable Senator himself included; they were fit to command ships, therefore the lash was needful.

The honorable Senator commenced his remarks by saying that that government is the best which rules by love and not by fear. I am a good deal in the habit of distrusting these abstractions. I do not know that we are exactly able to form an idea of what is the best government in the abstract. If we confine ourselves to the affairs of this globe on which we live, and on which our ancestors have lived before us, we will find that there never has been any such government in it, either human or divine, for one single instant of time. When that primeval pair from whom we have all sprung were placed in perfect and happy innocence in Paradise, with their affections all attuned in a harmonious disposition to love, to reverence, and to serve their great Creator, were they left without the influence of this principle of fear? Not at all. "In the day that ye eat thereof, ye shall surely die." However agreeable and pleasing it may be to us to imagine a state of society in which all men shall do exactly everything that is right and nothing that is wrong merely because of a spontaneous disposition to do it, it is very certain that no such government ever has existed, or ever can exist, until there is a total renovation of man's character. All governments, that is all wise and just governments, act by the double influence of hope and fear, by the application at one time of reward, at another of punishment. Is not that the rule in the domestic circle? We encourage and lead our children; but, if they will not be encouraged and led we punish them. We endeavor to induce them to do right from love to us; but, if they will not do it from love, they must do it from fear. It is the object to be accomplished that is to be looked at. If we are faithful to ourselves we do not leave them without the necessary coercive means. The end to be accomplished is obedience and submission —the doing right. If you can bring it about by encouragement and persuasion and love, so much the better. If you cannot, you must resort to fear, because the end is too valuable to be sacrificed.

Mr. President, I believe greatly in the tribute which the honorable Senator has paid to the character of the American sailor; but permit me to say that the honorable Senator does not exactly, as I think, meet the question presented by this petition. He says the American sailor is a noble specimen of a man. As a general remark what he says is true. He says that such a man as that ought not to be degraded. I admit it; but is it proposed to degrade him? Is this a petition that Congress shall pass a law compelling the officers who have charge of the public ships of the country to whip all the men, those who behave well and those who behave ill? It does not propose that commanders shall do as our old friend Caleb Quotem, the schoolmaster in the farce, did. He had to leave his school to go to the review. He first went to the schoolhouse, and, not being able to remain long, he thought it best to whip the boys all round before he started, because, he said, he knew they would deserve it during the day. There is no proposal of that kind. These petitioners simply wish to restore that discipline in virtue of which a man who offends—a man who, by his conduct, soils this fair and excellent character which belongs to the American sailor—shall be made to suffer, and to suffer by punishment sufficient to restrain him, if possible, and, if not, at least to warn others whose virtue and whose principles may not be very strong from falling into a like error.

Suppose that a man should come forward and call upon society to abolish all punishments, and trust to the genial influence of moral suasion to prevent those who have a disposition to put their fingers into their neighbors' pockets and take their neighbors' pocketbooks, or those who desire to steal horses getting over their neighbors' hedges, or those who are bloodthirsty from cutting their neighbors' throats, it seems to me that he might offer precisely the same argument for abolishing all punishments. He would take up the criminal calendars which show how many men were punished for stealing, how many were punished for murder, and say: "These punishments are of no avail—they have done no good, and therefore no punishment should be inflicted." No man supposes for one moment that any institutions of society would ever prevent the occurrence of crime. But, before we come to the conclusion of the Senator, we must ascertain what would have been the condition of things in the navy and the condition of things in society in the case I have taken if all legal restraint were removed. Now the spirit of evil would rise refreshed, like a giant refreshed with wine. It would go forth for destruction and ruin upon all the best interests of society and social order. The Senator's argument proves this—if it proves anything—that the system of punishment, severe as it was, was not more than adequate to preserve a tolerably sound and healthy condition in the naval branch of the service, and, in my opinion, it proves nothing more.

Sir, I should be extremely glad to see a state of things in which the marine service is carried on always, and in all circumstances, by free and willing minds; and where, under the stars and stripes, there shall never be a necessity for resorting to any punishment. We would all rejoice at it.

I should be extremely glad to believe that the particular punishment alluded to can be dispensed with; but it does not help forward the consideration whether or not it ought to be dispensed with to say that it is treating the sailor like a slave. That, I admit, conveys to the mind something shocking and terrible. Why, the honorable Senator would not at all object to confining the sailor who had been guilty of misbehavior in irons or in double irons. I think it would be extremely difficult to show how a man could exhibit more the appearance of slavery than with his hands and legs manacled with double irons, and he himself locked up in prison on board ship. It would not be thought right, if I objected to that punishment, to say that putting a man in irons was treating him like a slave. In one sense of the word, whenever we seize an offender and restrain him in the exercise of his liberty we are treating him like a slave, but we are treating him like a slave because he has shown himself to need such treatment. We take from him that liberty which he has abused—he shows that he is not worthy to exercise the freedom of heaven, and we are obliged to take away some of his privileges.

Doubtless there have been men who have been so happily constituted in the command of an armed force as to be able to lead about their troops, as it were, by a charm. There may have been men under whose command punishment was unnecessary. The poet has told us, of the gallant General Wolfe, that "his example had a magnet's force, and all were swift to follow whom all loved." Still, if the general who commands the army be not that attracting magnet which induces his men to follow him from love, the interest, not of the officers, but of the country, requires that the men should be made to follow him from fear. Why, the poets tell us that the herds voluntarily followed Orpheus when he moved through the fields; but the ordinary herdsmen of that day were under the necessity of carrying goads to drive before them their reluctant steers.

We cannot argue from these particular instances; we must adapt our law to the general condition and character of mankind; and I think it would as unwise to speculate upon the capacity of officers of the navy superseding stringent and effectual punishment by attracting the love of their sailors toward them, as it would be if any fortunate herdsman in ancient times had said he would take a flute or a fiddle, throw away his thong, go out into the fields, and endeavor by piping to induce his cows and kine to follow him home to their pasture.

The petition in favor of restoring flogging was not granted.

CHAPTER VIII

A GREAT NAVY [1887]

Liberal Naval Policy of William C. Whitney, Secretary of the Navy under President Cleveland—Debate in the House on the Increase of the Navy: In Favor, William McAdoo [N. J.], Thomas B. Reed [Me.]; Opposed, William S. Holman [Ind.], Richard P. Bland [Me.], William C. Oates [Ala.]; Bill Is Enacted.

AFTER the Civil War interest in the navy languished. The President, as a rule, utilized the position of Secretary of the Navy in his advisory council as a place for an influential member of his party whose opinions on political policy in general might be of value, but whose conduct of his special department partook of the nature of routine.

When Grover Cleveland became President, however, he chose a vigorous man-of-affairs, William C. Whitney, as secretary of this department, who took most energetic steps to build up the navy at least to the rank of the naval establishments of the second-class European powers.

In 1887, in response to the urging of President Cleveland and Secretary Whitney, Congress in its appropriations for the Navy Department provided for the completion of ships authorized by the acts of 1885 and 1886, and for the building of seven new war vessels and their equipment.

INCREASE OF THE NAVY

HOUSE OF REPRESENTATIVES, FEBRUARY 26, 1887

This appropriation was opposed on February 26, 1887, in the House by William S. Holman [Ind.], the "Watch-Dog of the Treasury."

240

OUR EFFICIENT NAVY DEPARTMENT

Admiral Porter. THE QUEEN HAS TAKEN YOUR JACK. YOU NEVER *could* PROTECT YOUR JACK, MR. SECRETARY

(And they go on with their little game, never heeding the signal of distress from the Oneida)

From the collection of the New York Historical Society

Mr. Chairman, there is an extraordinary demand at this time in certain sections of the country for the appropriation of large sums of money for the construction of ships of war, the building of forts, the manufacture of guns and torpedoes. Our present navy is above the standard of our navies for many

IX—16

years. It is greatly beyond the strength and capacity of our navies of former years in time of peace.

Mr. Holman here presented statistics of the cost of the navy, including that which would be occasioned by the passage of the bill. The fourteen war vessels and four monitors already contracted for within three years involved an expenditure of $21,319,000. The seven new war vessels proposed by the bill would cost, exclusive of equipment, $4,950,000, making a total of $26,269,000.

And the gentleman from Maine [Charles A. Boutelle] comes forward with a further amendment to add ten steel cruisers and proposing to appropriate outright $15,000,000 for that purpose and $4,800,000 for the armament of the vessels, in all $19,800,000.

We are moving rapidly. Last year the entire appropriation for the navy, including $452,695 embraced in the sundry civil bill, only reached $15,070,837, but the enormous increase is seen in the fact that only twenty-eight years ago the entire annual cost of our navy was only $10,000,000.

And yet twenty-eight years ago we had as large a field for the employment of a navy as we have to-day, and, indeed, larger, for then the power and resources of our Government were not so well known, especially to remote nations, as they are to-day. This is rapid progression. Ingenuity itself is being exhausted for methods to reach the surplus in the treasury and maintain the present high rate of taxation. Within a few days bills have been reported to us from the Senate providing for the expenditure of $51,000,000 for war ships, fortifications, and munitions of war. If we were actually on the verge of war with a great naval power gentlemen could not display a greater solicitude for warlike preparation; this $51,000,000 equals the entire cost of the Government thirty-five years ago.

The Senate is demanding the expenditure of vast sums of money on fortifications which the experience of the late war shows would be of no value if an emergency for their employment should arise. It seems to be taken for granted that our people will tolerate these vast expenditures because they are demanded in the name of patriotism and for the public safety. Yet the experience of every war in which we have been engaged has demonstrated the fact that, when the calamity of war comes, our people are fully equal to the emergency, and that the sup-

posed preparations made were of little or no value in actual war.
Commodore Perry won his great victory with vessels which had
been hewed from the forests in ninety days and after the tocsin
of war sounded. In the late war it was the earthworks thrown
up in the emergency, and not costly fortifications, that were of
value. The vast accumulations of munitions of war were thrown
aside and your army in the main fought with arms furnished on
the spur of the occasion by the resistless energy of our people.

When this Republic was still feeble and all of Europe and the
continent of America, except our own portion of North America,
was under kingly power and every crowned head viewed with
jealousy and alarm the growth of free institutions, the then
maxim, "In time of peace prepare for war," was an expression
of prudent statesmanship. But, with the United States now
the foremost of the nations and guaranteed by Providence and
the laws of geography of the earth from a great invasion, with
no occasion for unfriendly relations with remote powers, that
maxim is a term of unseemly timidity, not of patriotic solicitude.

But gentlemen cry out: "The work of creating a formidable
war navy must not be delayed. We must have such a navy
at once, forts must be erected, munitions of war must be at once
provided," and the metropolitan press points with alarm to
the defenceless condition of our coasts—defenceless since the
days of the Revolution!

During the last sixty years on several occasions the relations between the United States and Great Britain have been in
sharp antagonism. The Northeastern and the Northwestern
boundary questions gave rise to fierce controversies. On the latter question the demand of our people was "54° 40′ or fight."
Public indignation against Great Britain was intense; that government was then, as now, a great naval power, and yet on
neither occasion did our people display the least anxiety in case
hostilities should occur!

When we demanded of France and other European powers
the abandonment of their scheme to give an imperial government to Mexico we were weakened by four years of intestine
war, and yet actually disbanding our army. There the Government displayed its old-time confidence in its resources for any
emergency; yet now, at a period of profound peace, there is a
pretence of danger from abroad demanding prompt preparation!

Now, sir, what is the meaning of all this? It cannot be
pretended that our commerce requires the protection of a war
navy. The protection of commerce is the common interest of

all nations. Our restricted policy has ruined our carrying trade.
That is a cosmopolitan employment in which those who carry
the cheapest monopolize the trade, yet our commerce reaches
every shore.

Our nation, having no "entangling alliances" with other
nations, and being only related to them by the peaceful ties
of commerce, and occupying such a commanding position
not only on account of the number and intelligence of our people and the vastness of our resources, but on account of the high
sense of honor and justice which has, from the beginning, characterized our Government in its intercourse with the nations,
that, without an army or navy, our people and our commerce
are secure in every quarter of the globe.

If we imitated the policy of monarchies and impoverished
our people by supporting the costly luxury of a great navy it
would not add one particle to the honor and respect which
gather around our flag floating in peaceful security over our
consulates from the ports of the half-civilized people of Corea
to the most enlightened capital of Europe. Gentlemen who believe that a powerful navy would add to the respect and honor
of the American flag abroad and our security at home underestimate the standing of their Government among the nations.

The mutterings of war between Germany and France recall
an event which illustrates the moral power of a people too great
and powerful to require the parade of armies or navies to command the respect of the world. In the closing hours of the
death struggle between those powers over an issue which the
petty ambition of kings had transmitted from age to age, when
government was overthrown and the despotism of the commune
overawed the capital of France, the flags of the nations supported by armies and navies went down and their representatives
fled, while your flag floated over the ministerial residence of
your ambassador, Elihu B. Washburne, in the midst of the
storm of rebellion, as secure from insult and dishonor as it does
from the dome of this Capitol. You had then three wooden
ships in the European waters.

A feeble government may find it necessary to win respect
by a display of power; this our fathers never did, even in the
infancy of the Republic. It was not in harmony with their
theory of government. The Republic they established rested
and must ever rest on the moral power of a free and enlightened
people.

The traditions of this Government are against a great military force. A few regiments to guard the frontier against

savage tribes, and to form the nucleus of an army when an occasion for an army should arise, a small and respectable navy to keep up the traditional courtesies between ours and other nations and furnish the Government with officers and men skilled in naval warfare for any emergency have been the extent of our war preparations in time of peace for a century—to this extent, following the practice of all the former years of our history, I think both army and navy should be maintained. Our present army and navy are now full up to the requirements of prudent statesmanship. Great Britain is the only naval power with which, by any reasonable possibility, serious complication can arise so long as we adhere to the traditional policy of this Republic of standing aloof from political relations with other governments, and this alone can result from our relations to the dependencies of Great Britain on this continent; and yet the most improbable event in the history of the times that are coming is a war between us and Great Britain.

The events of centuries have so adjusted the relations between us and Great Britain that a war could only be fatal to her. We hold as guaranties for her fair dealing, and as a bond to keep the peace with us, her vast possessions on this continent north of us. Every year increases the value of the security. Her people have hundreds of millions of dollars of wealth invested in the Canadian Pacific Railway and other public works in her North American possessions. She has Jamaica and other valuable islands on our coasts.

Does any human being doubt that, in the event of war between these governments, every vestige of British possession on this continent would be wiped out within a year? Within sixty days of the first tap of the drum announcing war between the United States and Great Britain an army which could not be resisted by all the force that the combined navies of Europe could bring to these shores would occupy the British possessions' from the Gulf of St. Lawrence to Puget Sound and Jamaica and every other British island on the American coast. I do not speak extravagantly, but in moderation. Besides, such a war would be fatal to her carrying trade—her commercial navy. It would disappear from the ocean.

No, sir. We hold the highest guaranties ever held by a nation that Great Britain will not break the peace with us. Talk about a fleet entering the Northern lakes by the Welland Canal! We would occupy at once both sides of the line from the Welland Canal to the entrance of Lake Superior, and on west to Puget Sound. It is absolutely absurd to talk about a nation sending a navy into the absolute possession of its enemy. We would not destroy the Welland Canal in such an event, but hold it by an irresistible force. Gentlemen greatly underestimate the resources of their Government.

Our torpedo system will see to it that no enemy's vessel ever enters our ports; every year renders it the more efficient. Again, let me ask, what is the meaning of this extraordinary solicitude for the creation at once of a great war navy, building forts, and laying up munitions of war? I need not say it is a proceeding in striking contrast with the policy of our fathers and of the statesmen of modern times even down to a recent period. The European governments, still overmastered by the traditions of centuries, traditions from which even France, after the fierce struggle of a hundred years, cannot escape, are armed to the teeth, not only to resist the aggression of neighboring States, but to overawe their people. So that Europe to-day, as in the past centuries, bristles with arms. Besides, the nobility and privileged class, which give strength to monarchy, could only be maintained by permanent military power. So that every state of Europe, except perhaps the free Swiss in their impregnable mountain fastnesses, leans on the sword, and armies and navies eat up the fruit of labor and fill the Continent with poverty and wretchedness.

On every frontier of the nations armies watch each other, and every coast is patroled by ships of war. War navies are the police of the colonies held by European powers. No nation of Europe has a large war navy unless it has outlying possessions as well as cities on its own coasts to overawe. Great Britain, with a monarchical establishment to maintain at home and wide-extended colonial possessions, has the greatest of the war navies of the world. Have gentlemen who are moving in this effort to arm America and place this free Republic on a war footing considered the wonderful contrast between European states accursed by military government and this blessed land of ours, resting in safety on the patriotism and manhood of its people?

The history of the world presents no other such contrast. The despotism of feudalism formed the governments of Europe; peaceful industry laid the foundation of the States of this Union. In Europe the petty ambition of kings, the mean ambition of conquest and dominion, organized armies and navies; the fruits of this in the course of centuries are kings, nobles, and serfs—in America the recognized natural equality of men and the dignity of labor, organized government, its fruit free institutions, a free, intelligent, and prosperous people, who, in the course of a few generations, have developed the foremost nation on the face of the globe.

And now, in a time of profound peace, with every guaranty of security from foreign interference increased beyond that ever known in the former years of our history, with no outlying possessions to require a war navy, it is proposed by gentlemen in the Senate and House to enter upon a system of naval and military preparation—ships, forts, and munitions of war—as if a formidable enemy was actually threatening our shores. Now, sir, I ask again what is the meaning of all this? The expenditure of the vast sums of money proposed to be expended in ships, fortifications, torpedoes, and military supplies, suggested by the surplus in our treasury—a surplus that excites the cupidity of the great multitude of men who seek to live off of the labor of our people—is an incidental and purely mercenary motive for this extraordinary movement, but this is but the impulse of the hour, the result only of sordid motives. If this was all, it would simply involve the useless expenditure of millions of money for the benefit of the great capital interest of the East with inconsiderable benefit to labor. Nothing less, nothing more.

But, sir, there is no disguise as to the real meaning of all this. The unexampled accumulation of great fortunes during the last quarter of a century—the outgrowth in a large degree of partial and vicious legislation, for, in the natural course of events and without favoritism in legislation, no such result was possible—threatens an entire change in your system of government. Through all the former years your Government has rested securely on the patriotism of your people and their devotion to your free institutions. Occasional public disorders and the natural unrest of multitudes of your people, conscious of unjust legislation which has created and centralized the wealth of our Government to an extent never before known in history, have alarmed the great capital interests, naturally timid and un-self-reliant.

The vast and dishonoring surplus in the treasury excites the cupidity of that great and ever-growing number of men who are resolute in their determination to live off of the labor of other men. Besides these influences, the press of the country, always eager to create a sensation by cries of alarm for the public safety, excites the fears of the well-meaning and timid.

Here, sir, are the underlying forces which are precipitating this Congress into an unprecedented expenditure for warlike preparation. But the most powerful of all these forces is the silent and effective movements of the men of overgrown estates, the controllers of great monopolies and of centralized wealth, who have lost faith in the people and free institutions and seek the shelter of a strong Government, and the wealth drawn from labor is sought to be employed in vast sums to place your Government, in imitation of the governments of Europe, on a military foundation. Our Government, in the opinion of the new statesmanship, must lean for safety upon the sword— not upon the patriotism, the intelligence, and the manhood of our people.

This extraordinary movement has been for several years silently pressing its theories upon Congress, and now bills involving vast millions of the wealth of our people are demanding a hearing and forcing their way through the Houses of Congress. Warlike supplies, forts, ships of war! Can any man doubt that the ingenious methods by which the public mind has been prepared to accept these measures will soon enlarge your standing army as well as man your enlarged naval establishment? I protest against these measures. Your army as it is—although the occasion for it when established by our fathers, that of protecting our frontiers from the Indian tribes, has, in the main, gone by—I am willing to keep up, and a small and respectable navy, according to the traditional policy of our Government, to meet an emergency that might possibly arise—and such an emergency, according to our experience, may arise at remote intervals—and to keep up the occasional courtesies between our Republic and other nations—a cheap imitation of the customs of feudalism. In this way our small navy has, in our long periods of peace, been heretofore mainly employed.

But I protest even against the beginning of the revolution, silent as it may be, that aims at placing this Republic on a military footing—a revolution involving a change in our system of government, of which even many of the chief actors are, or seem to be, unconscious. If our people, in the dream of peaceful security, shall permit this vast accumulation of wealth in the national treasury to be the pretext and the occasion for entering upon this scheme of military power to bolster up the Government, instead of the old reliance on the patriotism of the people, a reliance sanctified by a century of prosperity and peace such as elsewhere the world has never witnessed, it will be the greatest misfortune that ever befell the human race. The day should be forever accursed that witnessed its beginning.

William McAdoo [N. J.] replied to Mr. Holman.

Mr. Chairman, I deeply sympathize with the efforts of the gentleman from Indiana [Mr. Holman] to be consistent in his efforts in saving the treasury. I wish to say to him that I am as jealous of the growth of military power as the gentleman himself, and if this were a question of the increase of the regular army of the United States beyond what it should be in time of profound peace I would join in protest with him against the passage of the bill.

But there is no man on this floor who knows better than the gentleman from Indiana that the statesmen of the infant Republic, including such men as President Monroe, always drew a clear line of demarcation between a standing army and a navy. The guns of our navy frown over the waters of the Atlantic and Pacific and our Northern and Southern borders, but never imperil the rights or liberties of any citizen of New Jersey or Indiana. It was the remark of one of the most profound of our earlier statesmen that the guns of a navy had never been turned against the liberties of a country and a people, and every dollar of these appropriations for the building of a navy and for the making of guns is for an armament which will be turned not against the country itself but against its invaders. Never against republican institutions, but against foreign aggression—in protecting our coast or defending our citizens abroad.

I believe, with the gentleman from Indiana, that this country never will be successfully invaded by an alien army. But the gentleman from Indiana must himself know that, while our soil may never be polluted by the foot of an invader, the cities on our coast are now at the mercy of the smallest navies in the world.

The gentleman from Indiana says why this great cry from the financial centers (meaning the sea and lake board cities), from the centers where great wealth and population have aggregated there comes up the demand for a navy. The gentleman from Indiana must know that the cause of that cry is because the financial centers and great cities are mostly located at exposed points for naval attack. It is not, for instance, because the capital in New York is threatened by the citizens of New York, but it is because all the people of New York, without regard to conditions, know that the city of New York is exposed to bombardment and destruction by naval powers, which we could neither oppose nor punish. The gentleman says he views with alarm the growth of military power in these efforts to defend our coast and to increase naval armament.

The gentlemen who occupied this House in 1859, and for many years prior to that time, who were true Republican-Democrats in the universal sense and stanch defenders of liberty, and as careful of the rights of man as the gentleman from Indiana, did not express any alarm—and we then had about the greatest naval power on earth—that the liberties of the citizens of the Republic were imperiled.

The gentleman from Indiana says we have already made vast appropriations. Well, we have made vast appropriations for numerous new post-offices and river improvements in his own and other States for instance. Does not the gentleman from Indiana know we have reached a crisis in the history of the American navy, that within a few years, and it may be months, about forty-five wooden vessels will, under the 20 per cent. dead line, be cut off the naval register?

A MEMBER.—That is the thing the Government ought to bless.

MR. McADOO.—Yes, but we want something to be put upon our naval list to replace them. We have, to replace them now, only four completed cruisers. Is that a monstrous and improper thing to do? Does that endanger the liberties of the country? If we had thirty new vessels not one additional fighting man would be enlisted. All that is contemplated by the gentleman from Texas is two additional cruisers and four gunboats to those already authorized by law, making eleven vessels of modern design to uphold the dignity of the Republic abroad and its safety at home and provide for the moderate *personnel* of officers and men of the American navy.

It may be that the gentleman from Indiana is making up in his discussion on the floor in behalf of economical expenditure for some lapses from virtue of a very recent date. [Mr. Holman had voted for expensive public buildings and internal improvements in Indiana.]

And when he brings to the aid of an argument against this very moderate increase of the armament of the navy of the United States an attempt to prejudice the minds of the members of the House by appealing to them as representatives against military power he is doing that which, in my opinion, with all deference and the greatest respect for him, is unfair to the House and calculated to mislead the country. The people of this country have during our whole history stood by the naval establishment, and they are earnest now in demanding its rehabilitation.

No man in these United States, however humble and however

RIP VAN WINKLE AWAKES AT LAST

Cartoon by *Victor Gillam*

great, and no State of this Union will be in any peril or his or
their rights and liberties by this increase of the navy. We are
not building up the navy for the purpose of foreign aggression.
Our flag, I trust, will never be floated over any foreign soil by
way of conquest. God made our country to bless, not curse
and oppress, mankind. It is not the policy of this Government
to interfere with outside nations, save when they infringe our
domestic rights.

But unhappily for us, and unhappily for all mankind, we
have not yet arrived at that latitudinarian condition of universal
politics wherein wars and rumors of wars have ceased; and
when the gentleman from Indiana appeals to this House to arm
the defences of the country with nothing more formidable than
delusive rhetoric, as if we were in the millennium period, he
forgets the divine edict that until the end of time (unfortunately
on account of our weak and wicked human nature and the irrepressible conflict between good and evil, and because of the
selfishness of nations), the hand of man will be raised betimes
offensively or defensively against his fellow-man.

Within the limits of my own country I believe in the doctrine
of the fullest individual and local liberty, but I have not yet
arrived at that period where I can indorse the sentiment that
the nations of the earth have joined together in the bonds of
fraternal love and friendship, and that all envy, and hatred,
and selfishness, and evil have been eliminated from the heart
of man.

It is unfortunate, but it is true, that the selfishness and
the cupidity of nations are like the selfishness and cupidity
of individual man himself; and that as an undefended country,
though the richest in the world, we are exciting the cupidity as
well as the jealousy of all the nations of the earth.

As earnestly as any man who loves his kind I deprecate war
even when necessary and just under existing conditions as cruel
and brutal, and trust that as intelligence and modern civilization advance it may become infrequent and finally cease. On
the other hand, the sword has frequently made way for liberty
and afterwards defended its existence against its enemies; and
as against universalism in politics I am deeply impressed that
the spirit of nationality has elevated and ennobled our advanced
mankind and secured the freedom and prosperity of people
against the incursions of their more ignorant, debased, or vicious
neighbors. The mission of nations and races has not yet ceased,
much as we may desire the consummated fraternity of all mankind.

Richard P. Bland [Mo.] came to the support of Mr. Holman.

Mr. Chairman, there are always pretexts for taxing the people. Especially do we find pretexts here for the continuation of excessive taxation upon the American people. All this cry about a "new navy," "great guns," and "armaments," by which we are to be prepared for war in time of peace, comes from a spirit, sir, that desires to perpetuate in this country an onerous system of taxation, the burdens under which the people of the country yet groan, and which have ground them down into poverty. I believe, myself, that in time of peace is the time we should prepare for war. But how is that to be done? I reply that it is by reducing our national debt. That is the first step.

Why Germany to-day, in order to hold her people in bondage and subject to taxation, is making the pretext of war against France, and France is taxing her people to death to prepare for war under the pretence that it is defending against Germany. We are called upon here to further burden the American people on the plea that the whole world may dump their armaments down upon us and destroy some seaboard city. I repeat, sir, that the proper way and the only way to prepare for war in time of peace is to build up the citizens of the country in their wealth and prosperity, wipe out national and State debts, and then, when war comes, we will be in a situation to meet it; for at last all success in war depends upon the financial ability of the people to carry it on; and, in order to be prepared, financially, for any war that may come, we want in time of peace to stop this infamous policy of imposing burdens upon the people to continue taxation for the purpose of perpetuating the public debt.

We are in no danger of war, and this whole bill, for the purpose of building fast cruisers and war ships, is simply an excuse to tax the people of the country in order to squander in a few large cities the amount of the appropriation—a perfectly useless expenditure of money, as has been shown by the operations of twenty years past, during which time, as I have said, five hundred millions have been expended—squandered—in such useless protection as these ships are said to afford.

THOMAS B. REED [Me.].—This country has 4,000 miles of seacoast lined by great cities filled with wealth which is almost incalculable. No nation at any time in the history of the world has been free from danger of war; and this generation and many more will pass away before the fear of war will pass away from the earth.

There never has been since the foundation of the world any other time to prepare for war than the time of peace, and the truth of that maxim is more impressive to-day than it ever was before. In the time of our fathers it required but rude fortifications and rude artillery to protect any nation against invaders. One single fact will show and one single sentence will demonstrate the tremendous change which the last thirty years alone have given rise to.

In 1856 the largest cannon that was built in France cost 2,600 francs. To-day it will cost twice that sum to fire once the biggest cannon in France. Twice the cost of the largest cannon of thirty years ago is the price of the single discharge of the greatest cannon of to-day.

Years ago the preparation of ordnance was a matter of but short time, and I venture to say that I shall surprise some members even of this House when I say that the utmost skill of our mechanics or of the mechanics of any nation on the earth can give us an 8-inch gun only at the expenditure of eighteen months of time; and that a manufacturer with the best equipped plant in Europe will not dare to promise you a 16-inch gun in a less period than three years, and nobody dares to promise it with certainty in this country in less than four.

Now, every man who has noticed the fortifications along our coast knows that we have not a single fort which can stand for one single day the impact of a ton of cold cast-steel flung with a velocity which can send it 11 miles through the air.

Under those circumstances, and with the additional facts staring us in the face that of all these great guns we have but two, and those only of 8-inch caliber, while it takes 18 months to build the smallest and four years to build the largest, and that we have cities along our shore the ransom of which would be worth the whole empire of Rome—under those circumstances to this terrible ordnance the gentleman from Indiana [Mr. Holman], with the simplicity of the earlier and better days, would oppose "free hearts and free foreheads!" What an amazing statement is this for a man to make to three hundred intelligent men, that to-day of all the days we need no preparation for war! Why, to-day we need it more than we ever did.

We all know that against modern guns, against modern armored ships, we are in precisely the condition of helplessness which ought to awaken the attention of every citizen, and is awakening the attention of every citizen outside of Congress, and inside where they have no other schemes on hand.

Why do we hesitate to build these ships? Is it because we are poor, while a surplus that threatens to burst the vaults of the Treasury exists in the revenues of the United States to-day? Never was there a time when we needed more to do this work. Never in the history of the country was there a time when we could afford to do it as we can now.

The gentleman from Missouri [Mr. Bland] says that this is a scheme to spend the money of the people. Who is it that is presenting this scheme? Look in every newspaper, look at every expression of public sentiment, and you will find that it is the people of the United States who demand that this disgraceful situation shall end. And have not the people of the United States a right to expend their own money when it is overflowing the treasury? The gentleman from Missouri does not want all the other money of the country to keep company with his silver dollars as they are hoarded in the treasury vaults. We should expend it for the needs of the people. Is that economy? Is it honest economy? I stand here to say that it is.

Why do we raise money? For what purpose? For what object? What excuse have we for filling the treasury except that the money is to be used for the purposes for which the people demand expenditure? Is it the right thing to buy a dollar's worth for a dollar when you have got the dollar? That is our situation. We want fortifications; we want guns; we want a navy; and, thanks to the wise administration of the Republican party for twenty-five years, we have got the money in the treasury to pay the bills for the things which we want and which the nation demands. [Applause on the Republican side.] And I say to this House to-day that it is not going to be the fault of the Republican party if the nation does not have what it wants and what its necessities demand.

WILLIAM M. SPRINGER.—Why did not you give it to them in the Forty-seventh Congress, when you had full control?

MR. REED.—Look at the gentleman from Illinois. [Laughter.] He is the only man that does not appreciate the gravity of the situation. [Renewed laughter.] He is the only man in this House that interposes with the frivolous, the threadbare, the worn-out objection of "Why didn't somebody else do this in times past?" Why, the gentleman never got within a decade of the present in his life, and his party surrounds him where he stands. [Laughter.]

WILLIAM C. OATES [Ala.].—From an infant republic of four

million population one hundred years ago we have grown to
sixty million, and are keeping abreast with the foremost nations
of the earth in all that develops and marks national greatness.
The martial tread of soldiery drowns not the hum of industry,
for we have no army except a skeleton, and need none except
a few regiments to prevent Indian depredations in our Western
Territories.

We have no navy and no coast defences, yet the flag protects
our commerce, which mounts up into the millions annually in
value, just as securely as though we had the finest navy afloat.
And now, sir, when this country is in a state of profound peace
and amity with all other powers, when there is not the slightest
probability of a rupture of those relations, nor the most remote
prospect of war, it is gravely proposed to expend $25,000,000 for
the building of ships of war and floating batteries, and twenty-
one million more for coast defence.   These expenditures are
proposed in addition to the increase in our naval establishment
already provided for at the last session and the present, which
I regard as ample.   A few swift-sailing cruisers as a nucleus for
a navy in case of war are all the vessels that we need.

The nations of Europe maintain great navies and immense
standing armies which they are constantly increasing; they watch
each other like gladiators in the prize ring, ready to strike
for supremacy and conquest the moment any prospect of success
is discovered; while the United States, as a nation content with
her own, presents to the world in strong contrast at once a
theme for the philosopher, the statesman, and the historian,
which can but add to the greatness of the American name.

The people of the old monarchies of Europe, in addition to
the unrest of constant apprehension, are loaded down with
burdens of taxation almost unbearable to keep on a war footing
the armies and navies of their royal masters, who may at any
moment plunge into war to support their imperiled dignities,
titles, or possessions.   Hundreds of thousands of those unhappy
people, over whose future hangs like a funeral-pall the eternal
black cloud of war, despairing of peace and rest in their father-
land, have annually flocked to our peaceful country, which is not
only the asylum for the oppressed of every land, but also by our
too liberal policy for their paupers and criminals as well.   Now,
sir, under whatever pretext measures are seriously urged which
in my judgment will inaugurate a policy of maintaining a large
and expensive naval establishment I shall oppose them.

If that were accomplished a demand would soon follow for
a corresponding increase of the standing army, all of which

would of course impose new and permanent burdens of taxation upon the people. They have to foot the bills, and I am not willing to impose upon them a dollar's expense for that which is unnecessary. I contend, sir, that we need no navy except that which has been provided for during the present Congress. I contend, sir, that a large naval establishment, like a large army, is inconsistent with the spirit and genius of our Government, inconsistent with economy, and dangerous to the liberty of the people. I deny that any necessity exists for the naval establishment proposed by the two Senate bills. There is nothing in the foreign policy of this country which renders it necessary.

Our isolation—the great oceans intervening between this and every other powerful nation—relieves us from complications in the quarrels of others, and of itself frees us from the necessity of being prepared for war in time of peace. When other considerations are also weighed, it is next to impossible that this country can be involved in war if her people and the Government do not turn their attention to preparations for it.

But, sir, whenever a nation, like an individual, is weaponed—armed to the teeth—and prepared for war, that nation will soon find some pretext for it. Belt a pistol around the most peaceable citizen and let him never go among men without it, and ere long that man's character will undergo a change, and he will shoot some one or be involved in personal rencontre with his fellow-man.

The character of a nation is always indicated by if not identical with the individual character of the people who compose it.

Again I ask from what source is there any danger to be apprehended? Have we anything to fear from Great Britain? The relative situation of the two countries furnishes a complete answer in the negative. English bottoms transport to and from this country nearly all our commerce, which amounts to hundreds of millions annually.

Can she afford to lose such an immense carrying trade? When, in all her history, except when insanity pervaded her counsels and caused her to lose her American colonies, did Great Britain ever go to war if it was pointedly against her commercial interests? By a war with the United States her commerce would be practically destroyed. Look at her possessions stretching entirely across the continent on our northern border. These we hold as hostages for the empire's good behavior. She will never sacrifice them.

IX—17

Is there any danger of a war with Spain? The Queen of
the Antilles and her sister islands with her depleted coffers
and heavy debt furnish us absolute security against danger
from that direction. There is no friction between this country
and France, Germany, or Russia. Wherein can there arise any
cause for war between this country and any other? It has been
said by some whose apprehensions had obtained ascendency
over their judgment that owing to the defenceless condition of

RIDING THE HIGH HORSE

Cartoon by Victor Gillam

From the collection of the New York Public Library

our seaboard we were liable to be humiliated at any time. That
the little South American state of Chili might send one of
her ships of war into New York Harbor and lay that city under
contribution or in ashes. Let the possibility of that assertion
be granted. What of it? Will it ever occur? Are the rulers of
Chili idiots seeking self-destruction? May we not assume that
they are men of some sense and some knowledge of the history,
numbers, and resources of this country?

Have they not heard of a war among ourselves which occurred a quarter of a century ago and continued four years,
in which the total enlistment of soldiers on each side exceeded
thirty-three hundred thousand, and which cost more than
$3,000,000,000? Do they not know that if they were to assault
one—even the smallest—of our defenceless seacoast cities that

before many months elapsed Chili would have no place on the map of nations except as an outlying territory of the United States?

It is utterly reckless to assert even the possibility of such a course upon the part of Chili or any power similarly weak, and hence that illustration of the necessity for numerous ships of war or coast defences has no force. Sir, it is utterly impossible for a sufficient number of nations ever to combine or form an alliance and bring men enough to our shores to whip us. With all the States united in defence of the flag, as they now happily are, the Union is invincible and can defy the world in arms.

Mr. Chairman, upon the subject of coast defence it does seem to me that the lessons we learned in our late civil war should not be forgotten. Was it not demonstrated time and again that no masonry—brick and mortar and stone, however skillfully put together—can resist the heavy projectiles which powerful guns can hurl against it? Nothing has yet been discovered which can resist them but earthworks, and these can be constructed with comparative rapidity and upon an emergency.

A very few first-class heavy guns may, and, I think, should, be constructed for coast defence and placed in New York Harbor and a few other important points. But as there is no prospect of early need for them, and as the inventions and improvements in gunnery and engines of war which are constantly going on render at the end of every decade all those previously cast almost or entirely useless, I am unwilling to vote any large sum for this purpose.

To use the mildest term applicable to a greater appropriation, I say it would be recklessly improvident. For twenty years we have had no coast defences and no navy worthy to be called such, and yet no nation has had the temerity or insanity to molest our commerce, insult our flag, or violate our rights. Whence comes the clamor now, in the face of this long experience and profound peace, for both coast defence and a navy? Some New England fisherman has lost his bait.

I do not like, when I can avoid it, to question the motives of others, but most obviously these three Senate bills providing for the expenditure in the aggregate of $46,000,000 originated and are advocated in obedience to either a mere sentiment of national ostentatiousness, a fear of invasion which is ridiculous because baseless, or they are the result of a well-devised scheme to take advantage of that unsubstantial and transitory popular idea in favor of building a navy, to make a permanent disposition of the surplus revenue, and thereby dispense with the necessity of revising the tariff and reducing taxation.

One small but well-equipped gun factory, where experiments in the construction of a few first-class heavy guns may be made and subjected to the severest tests, is all that we need, and all that I will vote for in that direction.

We are often reminded of the injunction of the Father of his Country, "In time of peace prepare for war." That was full of wisdom when uttered. But the United States was a different country then from the United States of to-day. Then we were weak in numbers and resources, could scarcely stand alone, vast and powerful only in future possibilities. To-day, taking into the count all our advantages of numbers, resources, extent, and situation of territory, intelligence, courage, and patriotism of our people, this is the most powerful nation of the earth.

Money and credit are the real sinews of war, and that nation which in time of peace secures the most money and the best credit makes the best possible preparation for war. Pay our debts with the surplus revenue and stop the interest from running against the people. It is better for them that the surplus should be buried in mid-ocean than devoted to placing the country upon a war footing.

War is the greatest calamity to which a nation can be subjected. Let the people continue their peaceful pursuits. Let this great country continue to depend for its defence upon the affections of the people. Like a great giant, in the consciousness of his strength, let this nation, with no unrighteous schemes of diplomacy or conquest, unarmed but defiant in the maintenance of its rights, remain a marvelous example of peace and prosperity.

What need is there for such a naval establishment as the bills I have referred to provide for? Can we hope to compete with Great Britain, and in this respect become the rival of the mistress of the seas? That would involve this country in an annual expenditure which no administration could survive. Large appropriations and reduction of taxation are utterly antagonistic propositions. The true friend of the people, who honestly desires to reduce the amount of taxes collected from them, cannot be the friend and supporter of these propositions, involving such large expenditures.

Gentlemen should be consistent and get on the one side or the other of this question. You cannot ride both horses at once. Sir, I prefer to take the side of the people and lower taxes. This country has no use for coast defences, a navy, and an army. Their maintenance would add many millions to the annual expenditure, and they might be used to overawe the people and diminish the individual liberty of the citizen.

Wherever a great navy and a standing army are established in time of peace they have always become permanent institutions of the nation and are never reduced. Let gentlemen consider well of the probable consequences before they vote to saddle such burdens upon those who are to succeed us.

Sir, there is too much of a disposition among some of our people to imitate European countries even in our legislation as well as in habits and manners. It is un-American and I despise it. Our Government is unlike every other in the world, and consequently the conduct of others should be of no force as precedents here. Let the burdens of this Government and its restraints of natural liberty rest so lightly upon the citizen that he scarcely feels them and contentment and comfort will be constant visitors to the poor and will knock with even hand at the doors of the palace and the cottage.

For the defence of such a Government in case of invasion a million of the best soldiers that ever enlisted in any cause would, in less than sixty days, be on the march to meet our country's foes. The seas would swarm with our privateersmen, and with our exhaustless resources and limitless credit the best ships of war would appear under our flag as though constructed by the hand of magic. Let us so legislate as to maintain a healthy sentiment within our own country; we have nothing to fear from without.

The amendment providing for the construction of the seven new vessels was passed by a vote of 151 to 72. The bill passed the House by a vote of 107 to 28. The Senate passed the bill with amendments. A joint conference was appointed, whose report was accepted by both Chambers, and President Cleveland approved the act on March 3, 1887.

CHAPTER IX

PENSIONS

ON April 29, 1830, Robert Y. Hayne [S. C.] delivered in the Senate a lucid narrative of the pension acts of the Government from the time of the Revolution to date, a forcible presentation of the principles which should govern such legislation, and a shrewd interpretation of a "general service pension bill" which was then before Congress, applying virtually to all who were in any way connected with military service during the Revolutionary War. The purpose of this bill, the distinguished Senator claimed, was to justify the continuance of the exorbitant taxes of the "American system" by opening up new means of extravagant expenditure of the revenue accruing therefrom, and he charged that the manufacturers and politicians of the North had devised the measure for their selfish interest.

Although no serious attempt was made by the advocates of the bill to refute the argument of Senator Hayne, the bill was passed by the votes of the National Republicans and a number of Democrats who had regard to the "old soldier vote" in their constituencies.

"GREED, NOT GRATITUDE"

SENATOR HAYNE ON THE ANIMUS OF THE GENERAL SERVICE PENSION BILL

Mr. Hayne said this was a bill similar in its character to that which was brought forward during the last session of Congress, and which was then known by the significant appellation of the Mammoth Pension bill. Under the specious pretext of paying a debt of national gratitude to the soldiers of the revolution, it was calculated to empty the treasury, by squandering away the public treasure among a class of persons, many of whom, said Mr. Hayne, I do verily believe, never served in the Revolution at all, and others only for such short periods as hardly to entitle them to praise. I will yield, sir, to no gentleman here in a deep and abiding sense of gratitude for revolutionary services. Brought up among Revolutionary men, I imbibed in my infancy, and have cherished through life, a profound reverence and affection for the whole race—feelings which will descend with me to the grave.

But, sir, when the attempt is made to thrust into the company of the war-worn veterans of the Revolution, a "mighty host," many of whom, probably, never even saw an enemy; when a door is to be opened wide enough to admit mere sunshine and holiday soldiers, the hangers-on of the camp, men of straw, substitutes, who never enlisted until after the preliminaries of peace were signed; when, after having omitted to pay the debt of gratitude really due to the honest veterans who toiled through all the hardships and dangers of the great contest, you now propose to scatter the rewards earned by their blood with so profuse a hand as to enable all who ever approached the camp to share them; I must be permitted to say that neither my sense of justice, nor my devotion to Revolutionary men, will suffer me to lend my aid to the consummation of the injustice.

Sir, I know that deep as have been the wounds inflicted by the chilling neglect experienced by many of these gallant officers of the army who fought your battles throughout the war of the Revolution; keenly as they have felt the injustice which delayed, until a recent period, to satisfy their just demands, founded upon contract, none of these things, nor all combined, have inflicted so deep a wound upon their feelings, as the admission, to all the honors and rewards of the Revolution, of persons who shared few of the hardships, and none of the perils, of the war. He who toiled through the heat of the day has found the evening feast spread out for those whom he knew not in the camp, or on the field of battle, and whom he never saw till he found them at the festive board provided by the gratitude of the country.

It has been my pride and pleasure, on all proper occasions, to manifest my gratitude for the heroes of the Revolution, not merely by professions, but by the most unequivocal acts. Here and elsewhere, my efforts have not been wanting to manifest the sentiments by which I am animated. But, in refusing to support such a bill as this, I am conscious I am only doing that of which the veterans of the Revolution themselves, if they were here present, would cordially approve. In doing justice to the country, I am also doing justice to them.

In the further examination of this subject, I propose, said Mr. Hayne, to take a brief review of the pension system in this country, and to point out the new, extravagant, and alarming provisions which it is proposed, by this act, to introduce into that system.

The people of the United States, even before the Revolution, had imbibed a deep-rooted and settled opposition to the system of pensions.

In the country from which they had emigrated, they found it operating as a system of favoritism, by which those in authority made provision, at the public expense, for their friends and followers. In Great Britain pensions have long been used as the ready means of providing for the "favored few," at the expense of the many. This system affords the most convenient means of appropriating the industry and capital of the laboring classes for the support of those drones in society, the *"fruges nati consumere,"* who occupy so large a space in all refined, civilized, and Christian countries. Our ancestors had seen, and severely felt, the effects of such a system, which necessarily converts the great mass of the people into the "hewers of wood and drawers of water" for the privileged orders of society. When our Revolution commenced, therefore, a deep, settled, and salutary prejudice against pensions almost universally prevailed. On the recommendation of General Washington, however, Congress had found it necessary to provide that the officers of the regular army who should continue to serve to the end of the war should be entitled "to half pay for life." So strong, however, was the prejudice against pensions that the officers entitled "to half pay for life" found it necessary so far to yield to public opinion as to accept of a "commutation," in lieu thereof, of five years' full pay.

In 1806 provision was made by law for pensions to all persons disabled in the military service of the United States during the Revolution; and in 1808 the United States assumed the payment of all the pensions granted by the States for disabilities incurred in the Revolution. And from that time to 1818 the principle was settled that all persons disabled in the course of military service should be provided for at the public expense. Here, then, was the American pension system established on a fast and sure foundation. The principle assumed was not merely gratitude for services rendered, for that principle must have embraced civil as well as military pensions, and is broad enough to admit all the abuses that have grown up under the pension system even of Great Britain. Our principle was that pensions should be granted for disabilities incurred in military service—a measure deemed necessary to hold out those inducements to gallantry and deeds of daring which have been found necessary in all other countries, and which we have, perhaps, no right to suppose can be safely dispensed with in ours.

Here, then, we find, that, up to the year 1818, the principle of our pension system was disability, a wise and safe principle, limited in its extent, and almost incapable of abuse.

In 1818, however, the Representatives of the people, in Congress assembled, seem to have been seized with a sudden fit of gratitude for revolutionary services; an act was accordingly passed which provided for pensioning all who served in the army of the Revolution "for the term of nine months, or longer, at any period of the war," and "who, by reason of reduced circumstances, shall stand in need of assistance from their country for support." Here it will be seen that the principle which limits pensions to disabilities incurred in the service is abandoned, and length of service and poverty are made the conditions on which pensions are hereafter to depend. The history of that bill, as I have heard it from the lips of those who were actors in the political scenes of that day, is not a little curious. All agreed that the operation of the bill was to be confined to those who had, during the Revolution, given up their private pursuits, and devoted themselves exclusively to military service. No one imagined for a moment that any person who had rendered casual services merely; men who had only shared, in common with all the other citizens of the country, the dangers and sacrifices of the times, were to be the objects of public bounty. The original proposition, therefore, was to confine the provisions of the bill to those who had served in the regular army, either during the war or for a term of three years, and who stood in need of assistance from their country for support. But, sir, in the progress of that bill it was discovered that in a certain quarter of the Union a number of soldiers had been enlisted for a term of only nine months, and, to cover their case, "three years" was stricken out, and "nine months" inserted. Sir, no one foresaw the consequences of that measure. It was supposed that even this provision would include only a few hundred men. The whole charge upon the treasury was estimated at one hundred and sixty thousand dollars. And, seduced by this expectation, and by the popular cry of "Justice to the old soldiers," Congress were persuaded to pass a bill which they were assured could not make any very considerable addition to the pension list, which would be lessened from year to year, and would soon cease to exist. And what, sir, was the result? What a lesson does it read to legislators! How forcibly does it admonish us to weigh well the provisions of this bill before we undertake to enlarge or extend the pension law of 1818.

The number of applicants for pensions, under the act of 1818, considerably exceeded thirty thousand!—a number greater than that of General Washington's army at any period of the war; exceeding the whole number of soldiers that could be supposed to be alive in 1818. Notwithstanding the "rigid rules" laid down by the Department of War, it was found impossible to exclude the applicants. Upward of eighteen thousand were admitted and placed on the pension roll, one-third of whom at least (as it afterwards appeared) had no claim to be there. The claims of upward of twelve thousand of the applicants were found, even at the first examination, to be entirely groundless, and were accordingly rejected. The money required to pay the pensions was found to be not one hundred and sixty thousand dollars as had been estimated, but three millions, one hundred and eight thousand, three hundred and three dollars! And no one can tell to what extent these appropriations would have been carried if Congress had not interposed to correct the evil. The whole country had become alarmed. No one doubted that an immense number of persons were receiving pensions who had no claim to them whatever. Men who had never served at all, or for very short periods; men who had given away their property to their children, or conveyed it in trust for their own benefit; in short, everyone who was old enough to have served in the Revolution found little difficulty (notwithstanding the rigid rules of the War Department, of which we now hear so much complaint) in getting themselves placed upon the pension list.

To rescue the country from this enormous evil, the act of May 1, 1820, was passed, which, without changing the terms and conditions on which pensions were to be granted (still requiring service "for a term of nine months," and "indigent circumstances"), yet provided guards against frauds by requiring every applicant to submit "a schedule of his property," and to take the necessary "oaths," etc. Sir, under the provisions of this act, intended only to prevent frauds, upward of six thousand persons were stricken from the pension roll. Two thousand, three hundred and eighty-nine never even presented a schedule, or made an application under this act; and the Treasury was thus relieved from a charge of a million of dollars per annum.

Now, sir, with the experience afforded by this case one would really suppose that the very last thing that any statesman would propose would be still further to enlarge and extend the provisions of the act of 1818, again to unlock the treasury, which was wisely closed by the act of 1820, and subject it to a charge similar in character, and probably much greater in amount than was imposed by that law, and to open a wide door to all the evils, aye, and much greater evils, than were experienced by the country under the operation of that act.

What will be the effect of this bill? While the law required "a term of service of nine months or longer," although persons might be admitted who had rendered no efficient service, yet you had some security against abuse by requiring specific proof of a continuous service under one enlistment, with the power, in most cases, of referring to the original muster rolls and thereby detecting all attempts at imposition. Now, however, that the most casual service, and for the shortest periods, is to be taken into the account, who can fail to perceive how much the chances of imposition will be multiplied? Resort must be had to oral testimony. And what more uncertain than the memory of man as to the duration of another's service half a century ago? Who is there that ever served a month in the army, or who was even a follower of the camp, that will not be able to adduce certificates to show that he served for just so long a time as he may choose to lay claim to?

But, sir, there is a stronger objection to this measure even than its liability to abuse. It is that it rests on no sound principle applicable to military pensions. If there be any principle recognized and fully established in this country it is that pensions must be confined to those who were separated by the nature of their service from the great mass of the community and who devoted themselves exclusively to military duties. It is a palpable absurdity to talk of giving pensions to all the people. Those who, in the course of the Revolution, performed only in common with the rest of their countrymen the military service required of every citizen stand upon an equal footing. He alone who, in the strictest sense, put off the citizen and became a soldier, and who, in abandoning the pursuits, relinquished also the habits of private life, can have any just claim to be provided for at the public expense. If we once depart from the rule I have laid down and declare that mere casual service for short periods and at long intervals shall entitle a man to a pension, you cannot stop short of pensioning all who rendered any service whatever in the course of the Revolution. All the State troops will be embraced within this principle, and this bill, accordingly, proposes to provide for them. The militia will come next, for what true-hearted Whig was there in all America who did not, in the course of the seven years' war, render, from time to time, services equal in the whole to the period of "nine months"? I think I may very confidently assert that there was not, in the State of South Carolina, one genuine patriot of '76 capable of bearing arms who did not, in the course of the Revolution, spend more than nine months in the camp, and I should be glad to be informed on what principle they can be excluded, if these nine months' men are to be embraced? But I shall be told that the militia will all in due season be provided for, a proposition to that effect having already been submitted in the other House. It comes, then, to this, that all are to be pensioned who rendered military service of any description during the war. But were not services equally valuable rendered by men in civil stations? All these must of course be included, and it will finally come to this, that pensions must be provided for everyone who lived at the period of the Revolution; you cannot stop short of that, if the principle embraced in the bill is to be sanctioned.

But, sir, there are higher considerations connected with this question than any I have yet urged. I consider this bill as a branch of a great system, calculated and intended to create and perpetuate a permanent charge upon the Treasury with a view to delay the payment of the public debt and to postpone indefinitely the claims of the people for a reduction of taxes when the debt shall be finally extinguished. It is an important link in the chain by which the American system party hope to bind the people, now and forever, to the payment of the enormous duties deemed necessary for the protection of domestic manufactures. The point aimed at is to create demands upon the treasury equal at least to the whole amount now annually absorbed by the public debt. The great effort will be to accomplish this fully in the course of the ensuing four years, so that when the debt shall be paid the whole twenty-four millions of dollars now collected under our present unjust, unequal, and oppressive impost laws may still be found necessary to meet the demands upon the treasury created by law.

It is impossible, sir, it seems to me, for any man to look around him and see what is going on in both Houses of Congress without perceiving that this is a fixed and settled policy, to which the attention of the party to which I have alluded is constantly and steadily directed. We witness the astonishing spectacle in a free, popular government of constant and persevering efforts to increase the public expenditures; to spend money merely for the sake of having it expended; and we find the representatives of the people devising and contriving innumerable schemes to rivet upon them a system of taxation which both in its character and amount is almost without a parallel in history. All the popular topics of the day are eagerly seized upon and pressed into the service. Under the pretext of promoting the internal improvement of the country gigantic schemes are brought forward and the aid of the Government obtained for them to enormous amounts. The execution of all the plans of internal improvement proposed even during the present session of Congress would absorb the whole amount now annually applied to the public debt. But the advocates of this system are unwilling to rely on one class of measures only. We have schemes for colonization, education, distribution of surplus revenue, and many others, all admirably calculated to promote the great end—the absorption of the public revenue. But, sir, of all the measures devised for this purpose, this grand pension system got up last year and revived during the present session is by far the most specious, the most ingeniously contrived, and the best calculated for the accomplishment of the object. Here gentlemen are supplied with a fine topic for declamation. "Gratitude for revolutionary services!" "the claims of the poor soldiers!"—these are the popular topics which it is imagined will carry away the feelings of the people and reconcile them to a measure which must unquestionably establish a permanent charge upon the treasury to an enormous amount, and thereby furnish a plausible excuse for keeping up the system of high duties.

How comes it that this spirit of gratitude for revolutionary services should have slumbered for fifty years? Why is it that, without a single petition praying for such an addition to the pension system as this bill proposes, we should be seized with such a sudden and inveterate fit of gratitude to the old soldiers that we seem determined to seize them by force, and, taking no denial, to insist on their receiving our bounty, whether they will or no? Sir, the reason is obvious. The period for the final extinction of the public debt is at hand. Colonization has not yet been sanctioned; internal improvement advances too slowly; the distribution of the revenue meets but small favor; the existence of a surplus must, by some means or other, be prevented, and this must be accomplished without any reduction of duties. The friends of the system have therefore gone forth upon the highways, and "all are bidden to the feast."

There is another great object collateral to this, and having, I do verily believe, an important bearing on this measure. Sir, it is not to be denied that this country is divided into two great parts, the paying and the receiving States, or, as they have been sometimes called, "the Plantation States" and "the Tariff States," the former paying by far the greater portion of the duties which supply the treasury, and the latter receiving nearly the whole amount expended by the Federal Government. The present system operates so as to lay the taxes chiefly on one portion of the country and to expend them on another, and while, therefore, it is the interest of the former to diminish the expenditures and to lessen the taxes it is manifestly the policy of the latter to increase both.

I do not know that a more striking illustration of the unequal action of this Government can be adduced than is furnished by the operation of the pension system. Sir, no one can doubt that the sacrifices and services during the Revolution of the Southern were in no respect inferior to those of the Northern States. But when the pensions came to be distributed, how did the account stand? Of the twenty millions paid to pensioners, about fifteen millions have gone North, and only five millions have been expended in the South and West, and three millions out of every four hereafter to be applied to pensions will be expended north of the Potomac. Sir, although we know that the revolutionary services of the North did not surpass those of the South, we never complained of this inequality in the expenditure so long as the pension system was confined to the proper objects of national bounty. But, when it degenerates into a mere scheme for the distribution of the public money, we have a right to complain of the gross inequality of the system. It is the fact (well known and understood at least in one quarter of the country) that the Southern States pay by far the greater portion of the taxes, while they receive hardly any part of the expenditures, which leads to that lavish distribution of the public treasure which, we are told, has now become "the established policy of this country." The parents of the American system are unequal taxation and unequal appropriations; to them it owes its being, and without their sustaining influence it would be destined, after dragging out a brief and precarious existence, to "perish miserably."

The United States Government, in the time of the Civil War, and in the years following it, enacted most liberal laws for the payment of pensions, not only for disability and dependency growing out of the war, but also in recognition of service therein.

Notwithstanding these laws and their liberal construction by those in charge of their execution, many applicants for pensions were disqualified for inability to present the required evidence of disability, dependence, or service. As time passed such applicants, in increasing number, resorted, through their local Representatives, to Congress to have that body pass "private pension" bills in their favor. It became the habit of Congress to pass, and the President to approve, these bills without examining into the merits of the applications.

Upon his accession to the presidency Grover Cleveland determined to combat this abuse, as he considered it, so far as lay in his power. Of the private bills presented him during his first term he vetoed or "pocketed" 297, and during his second term 116, making a total of 413. These he considered were, on their face, mere raids on the Treasury.

Meeting with a great deal of criticism, interested from the old soldiers and Republican politicians, and disinterested from many citizens belonging to neither of these classes, President Cleveland, in his annual message of December 6, 1886, dwelt somewhat extensively upon the subject of pensions in general and private pension bills in particular.

Private Pension Bills

President Cleveland

On the 30th day of June, 1886, there were 365,783 pensioners on the rolls of the bureau.

The total amount paid for pensions since 1861 is $808,624,-811.57.

The number of new pensions allowed during the year ended June 30, 1886, is 40,857—a larger number than has been allowed in any year save one since 1861.

From January 1, 1861, to December 1, 1885, 1,967 private pension acts had been passed. Since the last-mentioned date, and during the last session of the Congress, 644 such acts became laws.

It seems to me that no one can examine our pension establishment and its operations without being convinced that through its instrumentality justice can be very nearly done to all who are entitled under present laws to the pension bounty of the Government.

But it is undeniable that cases exist, well entitled to relief, in which the Pension Bureau is powerless to aid. The really worthy cases of this class are such as only lack by misfortune the kind or quantity of proof which the law and regulations of the bureau require, or which, though their merit is apparent, for some other reason cannot be justly dealt with through general laws. These conditions fully justify application to the Congress and special enactments. But resort to the Congress for a special pension act to overrule the deliberate and careful determination of the Pension Bureau on the merits or to secure favorable action when it could not be expected under the most liberal execution of general laws, it must be admitted, opens the door to the allowance of questionable claims and presents to the legislative and executive branches of the Government applications concededly not within the law and plainly devoid of merit, but so surrounded by sentiment and patriotic feeling that they are hard to resist. I suppose it will not be denied that many claims for pension are made without merit, and that many have been allowed upon fraudulent representations. This

has been declared from the Pension Bureau, not only in this, but in prior administrations.

The usefulness and the justice of any system for the distribution of pensions depend upon the equality and uniformity of its operation.

The American people, with a patriotic and grateful regard for our ex-soldiers—too broad and too sacred to be monopolized by any special advocates—are not only willing, but anxious that equal and exact justice should be done to all honest claimants for pensions. In their sight the friendless and destitute soldier, dependent on public charity, if otherwise entitled, has precisely the same right to share in the provision made for those who fought their country's battles as those better able, through friends and influence, to push their claims. Every pension that is granted under our present plan upon any other grounds than actual service and injury or disease incurred in such service, and every instance of the many in which pensions are increased on other grounds than the merits of the claim, work an injustice to the brave and crippled, but poor and friendless, soldier who is entirely neglected, or who must be content with the smallest sum allowed under general laws.

There are far too many neighborhoods in which are found glaring cases of inequality of treatment in the matter of pensions, and they are largely due to a yielding in the Pension Bureau to importunity on the part of those, other than the pensioner, who are especially interested, or they arise from special acts passed for the benefit of individuals.

The men who fought side by side should stand side by side when they participate in a grateful nation's kind remembrance.

Every consideration of fairness and justice to our ex-soldiers, and the protection of the patriotic instinct of our citizens from perversion and violation, point to the adoption of a pension system broad and comprehensive enough to cover every contingency, and which shall make unnecessary an objectionable volume of special legislation.

As long as we adhere to the principle of granting pensions for service, and disability as the result of the service, the allowance of pensions should be restricted to cases presenting these features.

Every patriotic heart responds to a tender consideration for those who, having served their country long and well, are reduced to destitution and dependence, not as an incident of their service, but with advancing age or through sickness or misfortune. We are all tempted by the contemplation of such a

IX—18

condition to supply relief, and are often impatient of the limitations of public duty. Yielding to no one in the desire to indulge this feeling of consideration, I cannot rid myself of the conviction that, if these ex-soldiers are to be relieved, they and their cause are entitled to the benefit of an enactment under which relief may be claimed as a right, and that such relief should be granted under the sanction of law, not in evasion of it; nor should such worthy objects of care, all equally entitled, be remitted to the unequal operation of sympathy, or the tender mercies of social and political influence, with their unjust discriminations.

The discharged soldiers and sailors of the country are our fellow-citizens, and interested with us in the passage and faithful execution of wholesome laws. They cannot be swerved from their duty of citizenship by artful appeals to their spirit of brotherhood born of common peril and suffering, nor will they exact as a test of devotion to their welfare a willingness to neglect public duty in their behalf.

As an indication of the attitude of other recent American statesmen on the question of pensions, the following debate has been selected from the many that have taken place in Congress since the close of the Civil War.

On December 4, 1889, Cushman K. Davis [Minn.] introduced in the Senate a bill granting pensions to ex-soldiers and sailors who are incapacitated for the performance of manual labor, and providing for pensions to dependent relatives of deceased soldiers and sailors.

It was referred to the Committee on Pensions, which reported it on January 10, 1890. It came up for discussion in the Committee of the Whole on February 28.

PENSIONS FOR DISABLED EX-SOLDIERS AND SAILORS

SENATE, FEBRUARY 28–MARCH 31, 1890

Senator Davis explained the bill. It granted pensions of $12 a month to all soldiers and sailors of the Civil War who were incapacitated for earning their living by mental or physical disabilities, not the result of their own vicious habits. The bill had been indorsed by the grand encampment of the Grand Army of the Republic, the voluntary association of the military and naval veterans of the Civil War.

The principal reasons for this bill, outside of and apart from its natural justice, inhere in the fact that in the lapse of time since the war the mode of proof prescribed by the pension bureau, and by the law as it now is, and indeed any mode of proof by which it is required to attribute and trace the disease or the death by force of pathological connection to the casualties or hardships of the service, has become so difficult that in the majority of cases it is impossible to procure it. Among the people who favor this liberalized legislation an absolute conviction has arisen, strengthened by the undoubted fact that not a man went into the war and served through its infinite casualties and hardships and came out as well as he was before and without the seeds of disease in his constitution, that the technical bar in the way of proof to entitle a disabled soldier to the liberality and bounty of his country should be removed. This bill will call for the following items of expenditure additional to any items of pension expenditure under legislation as it now exists:

As to invalid soldiers..............................$14,400,000
As to the increase of pensions of those soldiers who
  are now drawing pensions below the sum of $12
  per month 5,908,800
As to those soldiers now unpensioned, dying annually and leaving widows.................... 1,728,000
As to those having pensions dying annually and
  leaving widows who would not be pensionable
  under present legislation, but who are pensionable, of course, under this bill, the annual expense
  is estimated to be............................ 864,000
As to the widows whose claims are now pending or
  have been rejected, the bill calls for an expense of 10,800,000
As to the children of widows in cases heretofore
  allowed, or whose claims are pending and will
  be allowed, the increase of from $2 to $4 per
  month raises an item of....................... 1,632,000
As to the children who will become pensionable under
  the pending bill and who are not pensionable
  under present legislation, the increase is........ 576,000
    Making a total of...........................$35,908,000

Mr. President, I have very little to say in terms of advocacy
at present of this measure. It received the very careful and
considerate attention of the Committee on Pensions. All of the
committee who attended (and that was all but one; one member
was prevented from attending any of our conferences) were
unanimous upon this measure. It comes here without dissent
from the members of either party on either side.

To my mind the great merit of this bill is, first, that it will
relieve the suffering soldiers of this country who are dependent
upon their labor for support from that never-ending, heartless,
and despairing pursuit of their claims in the pension office, in
which they are brought to eventual failure by a necessary application of the present rule that there must be, by a strict
method of testimony, an establishment of the pathological connection between death or disability and the military service.
I think it is a generally conceded fact—it is the result of the
personal experience of nearly every man who was engaged in
the privations and hardships of that tremendous struggle—that
no person ever came from it, after any length of service, the
same man physically or as to health that he was before. I
have no doubt that every man who went into the army and
served for any length of time discounted health and length of
years in the course of his service, and to erect between him and
the bounty which the Government in its hour of need promised
the barriers of an artificial proof with which he cannot comply,
because in the lapse of years his companions have been scattered
and many of them have died, is to work under the forms of law
a most substantial injustice.

The bill stops this ever-broadening and this ever-deepening
stream of pension legislation in special cases—yes, and in
general cases, too—which is rolling in upon us here from year
to year, and unnecessarily, for the want of general and practical
and comprehensive legislation, taking up so much time of the
national legislature.

Preston B. Plumb [Kan.] introduced an amendment
granting pensions ranging from $4 to $24 a month,
according to the disability, and eliminating inquiry into
the applicant's financial ability, and the cause of his
physical disability.

Mr. President, whatever the Government is to do it ought
to do ungrudgingly. Let it do nothing if it will, but if it does
anything at all let it do it in such a way that no man who up-

held the honor of the flag shall be required to make statements requiring the assent and the concurrence of his neighbors which put him upon a footing that must necessarily be, if not degrading, at least compromising to a degree among his neighbors.

If we are going to say that we will limit the benefits of this proposed act to a class, let it be to such a class as can bring themselves within its purview without making exhibitions of this kind. If we intend that it shall be a fair reward for disability actually existing and which we think ought to be presumed to have occurred during the military service of the applicant, then let us remit this inquiry into the financial condition and give to everyone who is disabled according to the degree of his disability or withhold it entirely.

There has been no theory of the administration of the pension laws, or of the obligation of the Government under them, which ever limited the pension to the man only who was financially disabled; it was to the man who was physically disabled, and the rich, as well as the poor, have had out of the treasury that which, measurably at least, made up to them the result of their physical incapacity by reason of their service; and it is not proper that the Government at this late day, or at any day, should draw new lines and say that, in the plethora of our resources, having given pensions to the rich and the poor and having given pensions of hundreds of dollars a month to rich widows, and to rich men because they had rank, we now draw the line on the private soldier, who is left, and say, "We will give you a pension only if you prove by the affidavits of your neighbors that if you do not get this aid you will go into the poorhouse." It overturns, it destroys, it uproots the entire theory of the pension laws as heretofore enacted and administered, and there ought to be some good reason for it if this change is to be made.

But, Mr. President, this amendment of mine commends itself to me chiefly because it is definite and certain. Every Union soldier will know, when this bill passes so amended, by the mere fact of a medical examination, just exactly what he is entitled to, and he will not be subjected to the mercy of an unfriendly administration of the law at headquarters. All he need to do will be only to make his application and through the methods and under the instrumentalities known to the Pension Office exhibit the degree of his disability in order to enable him to go upon the pension roll at a rate which he will understand and know as well as the Commissioner of Pensions himself.

I have made no calculation as to the amount that this amendment will cost. I do not think that enters into the case, as we are either going to provide for men who are disabled or we are not going to provide for them. If we are obligated to one, we are obligated to all. If we are not obligated to all, then we are obligated to none. Logically the situation requires the enactment of a bill which will respond to every man according to the degree of his disability.

The pensions we gave to the Mexican war veterans and the veterans of 1812 related not at all to disability, but took them by the arm, rich and poor, loyal and disloyal, North and South, East and West alike, and billeted them upon the national bounty.

HENRY W. BLAIR [N. H.].—Mr. President, to those who have been long in this chamber it will occur that the idea of the dependent-pension bill, as it has been called, originated some four Congresses ago; that for a long time I advocated that proposition against much opposition on both sides of the chamber; and that finally, in the Forty-ninth Congress, Senate bill 1886 was passed, which went to the other House, and in the other House it was amended very much according to the provisions of the present bill, and there became liable, if this bill be liable at all, to the criticisms which have been suggested by the Senator from Kansas. As the Senate passed that bill it was sent to a Democratic House, which amended it, and even in that form it was vetoed by the President.

I certainly would not be willing that this Senate and this Congress and this Administration should go to the soldiers of the country with a tender of any such bill as that which was vetoed by the Executive in the last Administration.

We give in the committee's bill a sum of money that goes at once without possibility of controversy or of those inaccuracies and those injustices which are perpetrated by the examinations of medical boards. One board will give the total amount; another board, under precisely the same circumstances, will not give to the soldier more than one-half or one-fourth; and thus great and gross inequality and partiality are manifested in the administration of the law.

Gideon C. Moody [S. Dak.] of the committee said:

My views are not in accord with those of the Senator from Kansas [Mr. Plumb] as to the construction of either the bill reported from the committee or of the proposed amendment.

This bill being merely a dependent-pension bill, the very theory and nature of it is that the recipient of the bounty of the Government must be a dependent person.

The amendment proposed by the Senator from Kansas, it seems to me, is in the nature of a service-pension bill. All that it requires different from a mere service-pension bill is that the party claiming the benefit shall show by the evidence that he is incapacitated from performing manual labor. No matter whether he is dependent upon his daily labor or not, though he may be worth millions, he is entitled under the amendment, it seems to me, to this pension, if he is physically disabled from the performance of manual labor.

It was not the theory of the original bill, and it is not the theory of the bill as amended by the committee, that one who is not dependent upon his daily labor, one who has sufficient means of support outside of that, shall receive this bounty of the Government. Two things must combine in order to entitle him to receive it: First, he must be without means of support except his daily labor, or, as the section has been amended, he must be dependent upon the charity of some one who is not legally bound for his support. Secondly, he must be incapacitated from performing such daily labor.

The difference between the proposition as submitted by the Senator from Kansas and this bill is then plainly this: His proposition is to give the soldier the benefit of this pension, if he is disabled, without requiring him to show that he is dependent upon his daily labor or that he is a needy person who needs the pension that is proffered him. This bill requires that he shall show he does need the pension.

The bill as it came to the committee did admit of the construction that it required the showing of a total incapacity for the performance of manual labor to entitle the applicant to the benefit of the proposed act, but as reported by the committee that is not necessary. All that is necessary is to show that he is incapacitated for the performance of labor. To what extent? In such a degree as to render him unable to earn a support. What would any commissioner with brains enough to occupy the position with credit to himself or the Government construe that to mean? Would it be that if a man could earn the bread he put into his mouth alone, and not the raiment that clothed him, he could earn a support; or if he could earn his clothing, and not his food, that he could earn a support; or that, if he could pay for the shelter over him and procure neither raiment nor food, he could earn his support? Certainly no. He would hold necessarily that the support of a man meant something more than mere food alone, raiment alone, or shelter alone; that it meant what was necessary to the maintenance of the man, not only the food, but the clothing, and not only the clothing, but the shelter; and therefore, if he was not able to earn a full support, he was not (within the meaning of the provisions of this bill) able to earn a support, and would be entitled to the benefit of the act.

The theory of the bill is simply that no man who has served his country faithfully shall be permitted to go to the poorhouse and be counted as a pauper; that the Government shall, so far as it is able to do so, sustain him, and that when he has passed away his widow, dependent as she was upon him, shall be taken care of, and that his minor children shall also be cared for by the Government.

GEORGE G. VEST [Mo.].—Mr. President, I take it for granted, with the past experience we have had on the subject of pension legislation, that this bill will pass in any sort of shape that meets the most extreme views upon the opposite side of the chamber, and I am simply discharging what I conceive to be my duty to the people who have sent me here when I point out to the friends of this measure (for I am not one of them) some glaring defects in the construction of the bill.

As I understand the meaning of this dependent-pension bill, it is that any soldier who served three months in the Union army and afterward becomes dependent by accident or disease entirely disconnected with his military duty is to receive $12 per month from the bounty of the Government, but when we come to his parents that idea is utterly ignored, and instead of being dependent we find that the parent who is independent receives the bounty of the Government as the soldier would receive it who had become dependent by reason of disease or accident.

Suppose a man by his own labor is earning $10,000 or $20,000 a year; suppose he is in robust health; is he entitled to $12 a month out of the taxation imposed upon my constituents, because his son was three months in the Federal army and has died? Is that a dependent pensioner? Why, sir, it is a monstrous proposition upon the very face of it, and yet it was deliberately inserted in this bill, and the very word "manual" was stricken out of the original bill, so as to include a man who was not working with his hands for his support, but was working as a clerical laborer or with his brain.

Now we come to the section which is proposed to be amended by the Senator from Kansas [Mr. Plumb], and we encounter the very same difficulty we had in the consideration of this bill when it was vetoed by President Cleveland. The chairman of the Pensions Committee of the other House then gave it one construction and the chairman of the Pensions Committee of the Senate gave it another. Now we are told in one direction it is total disability, that a man must be unable to earn a living, to make his own support, and we are told by the Senator from New Hampshire [Mr. Blair] that it means a man whose ability to earn as full a support as he could before he went in the army is impaired—that is, if he has only four-fifths of the ability, instead of five-fifths, his ability is impaired. I repeat, are we to leave this to the uncertain discretion of the Commissioner of Pensions? We all know what that means. We know that you might as well throw open the doors of the treasury and say "Walk in, gentlemen, and help yourselves" as to leave it in any such condition as that. President Cleveland saw this same objection and made it to this bill, and I am glad to see that my friend from Kansas has now profited by that statement.

The friends of the bill do not know what it means; they do not agree upon this floor; they do not agree before the two Houses of Congress; they do not agree in the committee, and because the President vetoed it "liberty lay bleeding in the streets" and the Grand Army of the Republic nearly took up arms about it; and yet, if the bill is passed now, the chairman of the committee does not know how much money it will take. He says it is a very indefinte subject. We all know, when we had the arrears-of-the-pension bill here, it was guessing every time; we did not know how it would turn out, and no man can tell within millions and millions of dollars how much money is to come out of the treasury by reason of this legislation; and yet we must have it without asking a question as to even the meaning of a single section.

If the Senator from Minnesota be correct, then this is simply a service-pension bill, for every man that served in the Federal army had his faculties or ability to labor more or less impaired.

JOHN R. MCPHERSON [N. J.].—The three-month soldiers, scarcely one of whom went to the front at all or was ever in the presence of an enemy, thousands and tens of thousands of them, who were subjected to no hardship, who received no wound, who suffered no illness, are placed upon an exact equality with those who fought during the entire war. The man who has lived until to-day and is about to die of old age will have the consolation of knowing under this bill that, while he rendered but three months' service, in other words, while he was for three months only connected with the military or naval organization of the Government and in reality never saw any service at all, his children are to have $4 a month, while the children of the honest and willing soldier who did bear all these burdens have to put up with only $2 per month.

The more I look at it the more I am convinced that the bill ought to be recommitted to the Committee on Pensions and that a bill should be reported here that does in reality grant a pension to the dependent parents or the dependent children of soldiers who are justly entitled to pensions, but it should cut off all these rights and privileges which the bill seems to give them where they are not dependent at all.

SENATOR DAVIS.—It is a new idea, brought to light for the first time by the Senator from New Jersey, that the question of pensioning a widow or the children of a soldier should be made to depend at all upon the dependence of either. In all the history of this Government, in all of its pension legislation from the beginning, I venture to say that the idea or condition precedent of dependence as to the widow or child of a deceased soldier was never introduced.

When the bill passed, and passed willingly, without a call of the yeas and nays, putting the widows and children of the survivors of the Mexican war upon the pension list, the question was not raised then that it should be made to appear that those widows and children were dependent. Nobody then supposed the impossible case that some widow or child might be found who had inherited a million dollars from a deceased ancestor or a deceased husband.

SENATOR McPHERSON.—There always comes a time in the history of this Government when it is proper to grant a service pension to soldiers of a late war, but that time has not yet arrived for the soldiers of the Civil War. It will be at that period of time when, in the general order of nature and the order of things, a man is supposed to have reached an age in which it is impossible for him, if not possessed of a sufficiency of this world's goods, to support himself. When that time comes, then give a service pension, if you please, and I will join the Senator in giving it, to the survivors of the late war.

But the pension here provided for is said to be a dependent pension. Dependent upon what? How can any man of a proud and manly spirit who served three months in the war of the late rebellion, a man of sufficient wealth to enable him to leave millions of dollars to his children—how can he go to the treasury of the United States, if he has any shame about him at all, and ask the treasury to give his children after his death the pittance of $4 a month? No, I would make no such legislation.

There are thousands of men who served in the ranks of the Union army who were entitled, by reason of disability, of wounds, of sickness, to pensions under the law and never asked for them. The presumption is, when a man applies for a pension, that he needs it; and the presumption further follows that, as he has received a pension, his children are also entitled to it. I would not throw one single obstacle in the way of the widow or the minor child of any soldier now receiving a pension, provided they were dependent, and in like manner with the parents of the soldier.

James H. Berry [Ark.] opposed Senator Plumb's amendment.

I have been told that during the last campaign, throughout the Northern States, it was promised the Union soldiers that if the Republican party controlled this Congress they should all be placed upon the pension roll; that the surplus which is in the treasury was theirs, and they had a right to have it divided among them. If that be the purpose, then I ask the Senator from Kansas to come forward and say so in direct terms, and not seek, under the pretence of an amendment for those who are disabled and unable to take care of themselves, to put them all on the pension roll.

There is no man, I take it, who served in the Union army, or perhaps but very few, who is to-day under forty-four or forty-five years of age. Bear in mind this amendment does not require that the disability shall have been incurred during the service, but if it exists to-day they will be entitled to a pension, and there are 95 per cent. of them who can come forward and prove that they are to some extent incapacitated for manual labor and suffering under certain disabilities.

If the Senate is ready to pass a bill giving a service pension to the Union soldiers, let it be put in plain and direct words, and do not mislead the people of the country by saying that we are trying to keep the old soldiers out of the poorhouse when the object and purpose is to put them all upon the pension roll.

If this is to be done, I think we ought to hear something about the probable cost of an amendment of this character. Already we are paying between $90,000,000 and $100,000,000 annually for pensions, and still the cry is for more. It was said by the Senator from Minnesota, I think, that some eight hundred thousand soldiers are not yet upon the pension roll. I want to know where the revenue is to come from, with the enormous expenditures that we are making, if you pass an amendment of this character, which practically puts all upon the pension roll.

Mr. President, I for one do not believe that is just or fair. I do not believe that the time has come when the soldiers have a right to be quartered upon the other people of the United States of America. While I honor as much as any man the Union soldiers, those who fought for their country and those who were wounded in time of battle, yet there are other citizens whom it is our duty to care for. As was said by the senior Senator from Kansas [Mr. Ingalls] a few days ago, distress exists throughout this country among the farming and laboring classes, and we are standing here to-day and having read statements from the Department of Agriculture giving a reason for this distress among the farmers of the country; yet the appropriation goes on under every pretence whatever to increase it from year to year, and the taxes go on, and there is no relief and no diminution.

On March 31 General Joseph R. Hawley [Conn.] opposed the Plumb amendment.

It is not agreeable to say no to what is supposed to be the request of soldiers of the Republic. But I do not believe that the American soldiers ask for this amendment. I will stake whatever little my political salvation is worth that I can meet five thousand old soldiers and get a heavy majority vote against this amendment after an hour's argument.

This headlong extravagance will bring men into power who will scrimp and squeeze and deny the soldier. A silent conservatism in the Republic that will be glad to stay with the Republican party, and will stay with it if it can be permitted to do so, will utter no loud word against the soldier nor against the old party, but it will quietly stay away from the polls.

There is a limit to this. I appeal to every old soldier to permit us to be reasonable and to be just. God knows the American nation is not stingy in this matter. Including the present fiscal year and what is proposed for the next, the appropriations for pensions since the war will by June, 1891, amount to nearly $1,300,000,000. I do not complain so far as a dollar of it was necessary to relieve real distress, nor do the American people complain. But no nation in the world ever appropriated a sum that could be compared with it. All that they have done for their soldiers in their distress sinks into utter insignificance in comparison with what we are doing for ours.

I beg the old soldiers to remember that, if we are threatened with war again, that which will scare the people who pay taxes will be, not the cost or the blood of the war, but the consequences of it. I beg them to remember that it is pauperizing and degrading them to constantly insist in their behalf that they have claims and claims and claims. So they have in a sense, but they know—no man knows better than that gallant body of survivors—that we owe every cent we have and every drop of blood to the Republic, and they offered it all proudly. Let them remember that these enormous sums to be paid come out of the pockets very largely of people as poor as themselves. You may lay the tax upon the rich man, but it filters down and down, and a large portion of it finally comes out of his tenant in the tenement house, or out of the subfarmer, or out of the mechanic. Remember the other people in the country who pay taxes.

When General Grant last visited this building, with his characteristic modesty he kept out of this chamber, and sat in that cloak room in the spot I am pointing at. Nearly every Senator of both parties visited him before he left, manifesting in the most gratifying manner their personal respect. He sat with his accustomed cigar and talked freely upon any question that anybody proposed. I will try to relate as if I were on the witness stand what he said à propos of this question. "Now," said he, "I will tell you what I would do if I were President. I would sign any reasonable bill seeking to relieve the distress of an honest old soldier, or his widow, or his children, but I would not vote one dollar to the able-bodied man."

I live up to that statement. That is my platform. I would not care to see an old soldier going to the almshouse. If he goes to the almshouse, either his State or the nation must pay the cost, and I would as lief the nation should pension him.

You had a great deal better, if you are going to spend this $500,000,000, take it and divide it *pro rata* among the men who actually need the money. Do not throw out $500,000,000 or $100,000,000 or $50,000,000 at random, and to a considerable extent to strong men who are in comparative health and have a little property or who did not suffer enough to induce them to apply till from fifteen to twenty-five years after the war. Perhaps the man can get along pretty well without it. Aim as sharply as you can at the actual necessity and take care of the old soldiers, and do not—I was about to say something that is not polite—do not be stampeded by claim agents. Do exactly what you think is generous and right. The country will sustain you, and it will not otherwise.

HENRY M. TELLER [Col.].—Mr. President, there never was such a war in the history of the world as ours. There never was a contest in all the long line of history that had any comparison to it. No other people ever fought their equals as we fought ours—a national affair, with the very pick and flower of the world on both sides, the men of the highest intellectual standing and culture on the face of the earth. When we got through with that conflict we had lost one-half of the accumulated wealth of the country for two hundred years and we had incurred a debt that the great majority of men in this country and all over the world believed was past the possibility of being paid. We have paid it. We have paid $2 of interest to the men who advanced money to carry on the war where we have paid a single dollar to the soldier.

I do not complain of that, although they bought their bonds at a discount. They bought them when everything was high, and they made money on them, but it was the plighted faith of the Government they trusted. We said, "We will pay this public debt," and we are paying it. That is right; we ought to pay it. But we said more than that. We said to the soldiers and to the sailors of this country that if they incurred disabilities we would pay them a pension. We said more than that. We said in every public place in the North, we said it on the rostrum, we said it from the pulpit, that there was a merit in going into the American army; that we would ever hold its members in grateful remembrance; and that there was nothing they could demand of this Government that they should not receive. When we can pay the great debt of $3,000,000,000 and pay it within a generation and less, we can afford to do justice to the soldier; and whenever it shall be made to appear to me that there is a just and proper demand I shall respond to it without reference to the amount.

The Senator from Connecticut [Mr. Hawley] undertook to demonstrate that we could not do certain things because there was not enough money and that is the cry every time it is proposed that we shall do something for the soldier. At this hour, right now, to-day, we could call on the treasury for $300,000,000 for any purpose that we might desire and the money is there, and it could be taken without detriment to the public interest. If it is necessary to do justice, either to pay our debts, whether they be represented by a bond or whether they be represented by our obligation to the soldier, we can in an hour's notice raise more money, and millions more money, than is in the treasury. We have the power to make legal-tender notes, if that be necessary, which we made in the hour of our distress, and which we made these men take when they were worth 40 cents on the dollar and when they were working at $13 a month. While the bondholders and the business men who the Senator from Maine says are to rise up in arms against our legislation were piling up their money by the millions, these men were working for $13 per month, many of them, and taking their pay in paper money worth 40 cents on the dollar only.

Senator Plumb's amendment was rejected by a vote of 9 to 46. The bill was passed by a vote of 42 to 12. The negative votes were all cast by Senators from the ex-slave States. Wilkinson Call [Fla.], James Z. George [Miss.], Randall L. Gibson [La.], and E. C. Walthall [Miss.] voted in the affirmative.

The House amended the bill by giving it a service-pension character, and passed it on April 30 by a vote of 179 to 71. The Senate refused to concur in the House amendments, and, after two conferences, these were abandoned, and various other amendments were agreed upon, the chief being the substitution for the uniform rate of $12 of a pension of from $6 to $12, varying according to the extent of disability.

The House passed the bill on June 11 by a vote of 145 to 56. The Senate passed it on June 23 by a vote of 34 to 18. President Harrison approved the bill on June 28, 1890.

CHAPTER X

CIVIL SERVICE REFORM

Lyman Trumbull [Ill.] Introduces in the Senate Bill to Make Recommendations by Senators or Representatives of Persons for Office Unlawful—Debate: In Favor, Sen. Trumbull, John Sherman [O.]; Opposed, Oliver P. Morton [Ind.], James W. Nye [Nev.], Simon Cameron [Pa.]—Carl Schurz [Mo.] Moves as a Substitute Examinations for Civil Service—Debate: In Favor, Sen. Schurz; Opposed, Jacob M. Howard [Mich.]; No Action Taken on Either Bill—George H. Pendleton [O.] Introduces in the Senate a Civil Service Reform Bill—Speech of Senator Pendleton—Bill Becomes Law—Pendleton's Subsequent Career.

ON January 4, 1871, Lyman Trumbull [Ill.] brought forward in the Senate a bill from the Judiciary Committee "to relieve members of Congress from importunity and preserve the independence of the departments of the Government" by making it unlawful for any member of Congress or territorial delegate to solicit or influence in any way the appointment of any person to a Government office, and for the President or any head of a department to make any appointment so solicited, if the appointee were privy to the solicitation. The penalty for the infraction of the act was a fine not exceeding $1,000. The act did not apply to actions by Senators upon nominations made by the President to the Senate.

RECOMMENDATIONS TO OFFICE

SENATE, JANUARY 4-27, 1871

SENATOR TRUMBULL.—It is unnecessary to recapitulate the evils of the present system; they are known to all. It is known that in the departments in Washington there are a great many more clerks than would be needed if those there were capable, efficient, and faithful officers; and it is known that many of them are put in merely as a reward for political services.

288

If Congress divests itself of this subject, the responsibility is then upon the head of the department. He will be held responsible for the persons he appoints to office, and there will be no political influence here to compel him to keep incompetent men in and no political influence here to compel him to appoint incompetent men. If the duties are not properly performed, if more clerks are there than are needed, Congress will hold the proper secretary responsible.

Senator John Sherman [O.] supported the bill. At first he said he had been opposed to it on the ground that it changed the custom established from the beginning of the Government, but now he believed it necessary to relieve not only Senators, but the President.

Members of Congress, especially of the House of Representatives, claim the right to dictate local appointments, and if their wishes are not yielded to in every case it creates at once a cause of quarrel, which finds its outlet in some legislation or other. The legislative and executive departments of the Government should be as distinct and marked as if they were separated by a broad river. The only connection between the executive and legislative departments, so far as appointments are concerned, should be between the President and the Senate.

The President ought to have the right to seek information everywhere, not only from members of Congress, but in the selection of officers he ought not to be embarrassed by the demands of persons upon whose votes he is daily subject, in the course of ordinary legislation, and over whom he might wish by patronage to establish a control.

I have regarded this measure for the last year as being not a complete civil service reform in itself, but as being an entering wedge indispensably necessary to bring about a civil service reform separating the civil service in the executive departments entirely from the legislative until the unconstitutional habit that has sprung up in this country of allowing members of Congress to control appointments is broken up. Unless we ourselves abdicate, surrender, give up that power of control over the executive appointments, we cannot expect to agree upon a civil service reform.

OLIVER P. MORTON [Ind.].—The bill, in my opinion, is unconstitutional from beginning to end, and proceeds upon false principles. I undertake to say that this Government could not be readily nor safely administered upon this bill.

Why, sir, what does the bill propose to do? It makes it a penal offence for me to exercise a right that belongs to every citizen of the United States. Every person in these galleries, every postmaster has the right to recommend to the President for appointments to office; but this bill proposes to make it a criminal offence for a Senator to do so. And then the President is a criminal if he dares to make an appointment that has been advised by a Senator, if it is done with the knowledge of the person whose appointment is advised. Have we a right to make the President a criminal for doing that?

Why, sir, what is the effect of it? If a Senator recommends a man with his knowledge he becomes ineligible. Have we a right to establish a qualification for office of that kind? It would be a clear violation of the Constitution of the United States. It has been decided by the Senate that where a State constitution provided that a man holding a State office was not eligible during his term of office to be elected to the Senate of the United States, such provision was a nullity, and no State constitution had the power to fix an additional qualification for office.

I know there are some people in this country who believe that everybody in Congress is corrupt, and if we pass this bill they will have a right to believe that we think so; that we ourselves are willing to legislate on the idea that we cannot safely be trusted to recommend men for appointments.

Why, sir, I should be glad to be relieved of this labor. It is particularly afflicting to me in my present state of health. But what right have I to be relieved of it? If I take the office of Senator I take it with its burden. Senators want to make the place entirely pleasant, relieved of all responsibilities and of all disagreeable features. Sir, when a man accepts the office of Senator, or the office of Representative, he takes it with its responsibilities and with its annoyances.

Now, let us suppose it to be the law that the President has a right to call on members of Congress for information in regard to appointments, but they have no right to give an opinion without it; how much are they relieved? Would not the President at least feel under political and moral obligation, ordinarily, to consult his political friends in either House as to appointments from their States? Would not that be expected as a matter of course, and would it not be regarded as unfriendly if he did not do it? Every man who wanted to be a district attorney or a marshal in his State would understand that the Senator would be called upon to give his opinion, and so he would send his application to the President and refer the President to the Senator from Illinois; and that is the way they would all do, and the Senator would not be relieved at all.

Now, Mr. President, I come to the principle of the bill, and insist that it is false in itself. I undertake to say that the greatest security an executive can have, who can know but a very small number of the American people, is the fact that he can rely upon members of Congress, his political friends, for recommendations to office. Take a member of the House. He is expected to recommend, if he is a political friend of the President, for the local offices in his district. The people understand that, and if there is a bad appointment made, if there is a bad postmaster, if a horse thief is appointed postmaster, they hold the member of Congress directly responsible for it. Therefore, it becomes his interest at once to recommend good men for these offices; his reëlection depends upon it.

JAMES W. NYE [Va.].—Suppose by some chance a Senator should find out that a most unworthy man, some horse thief say, was being recommended and likely to receive an appointment to office; would he be subject to this penalty if he should tell the President of that fact?

SENATOR MORTON.—I do not know whether opposing a nomination would come within the penalties of this bill; but I will state what would come within it.

SENATOR NYE.—If you cannot recommend, you cannot oppose. I simply desire to know whether I should be put in the penitentiary for doing that act, instead of the thief? [Laughter.]

SENATOR MORTON.—I suppose *prima facie* you would, under this bill. [Laughter.]

The discussion was resumed on January 10.

SENATOR TRUMBULL.—The only interference that Congress or any member of Congress legitimately has with the appointment of officers is in giving the advice and consent of the Senate to the nominations that are made by the President. With that exception this whole executive power is vested in the executive department, and, so far from its being unconstitutional to prohibit interference by members of Congress with appointments, it is carrying out the very spirit of the Constitution to prohibit such interference, and it is an encroachment on the rights of the Executive whenever appointments are made or dictated by members of Congress from either House.

And such, Mr. President, was the early understanding. For

the first forty or fifty years of the Government members of Congress did not interfere with appointments.   It was regarded at

OUR STUMBLING-BLOCK

Cartoon by Thomas Nast

From the collection of the New York Public Library

that time as exceedingly indelicate and improper for a member of Congress to go to the President, or to any head of a department, and suggest the name of a person for office.   The practice that now obtains is of modern origin.   The principle that "to the victors belong the spoils'' was not announced until Jackson's administration, some forty years ago; and when first promulgated it shocked the country, but it never went any further than to fill the offices of the country with the friends of the Administration. The practice was not carried to the extent at that day of allowing a member of Congress to dictate among the friends of the Administration who should and who should not hold office in his district.

Now, Mr. President, it is that very custom which is an infringement upon the Constitution, and which, I think, should be corrected.

In view of these abuses, which were apparent to President Grant, in his annual message he called our attention to the subject in this language:

"Always favoring practical reforms, I respectfully call your attention to one abuse of long standing, which I would like to see remedied by this Congress. It is a reform in the civil service of the country. I would have it go beyond the mere fixing of the tenure of office of clerks and employees who do not require 'the advice and consent of the Senate' to make their appointments complete. I would have it govern, not the tenure, but the manner of making all appointments. There is no duty which so much embarrasses the Executive and heads of departments as that of appointments; nor is there any such arduous and thankless labor imposed on Senators and Representatives as that of finding places for constituents. The present system does not secure the best men, and often not even fit men, for public place. The elevation and purification of the civil service of the Government will be hailed with approval by the whole people of the United States."

What is the remedy for this state of things? A civil service system has been proposed, one where there should be competitive examinations, and under which appointments should be made without regard to politics, and the best men should be sought to discharge the duties of the respective offices to which they might be appointed. I think if a system of that kind could be devised it would be very desirable that we should adopt it.

The remedy suggested by the late Secretary of the Interior, General Jacob D. Cox, in a recent article in the *North American Review*, is:

"To apply to the civil service, completely and thoroughly, the plain principles of common business administration; to separate the public offices, absolutely and forever, from all favoritism, nepotism, and 'influence'; to declare patronage in all its forms to be anti-Republican and dangerous to the State; to find and practice upon a principle of selection for office which shall give every citizen of the country a perfectly equal chance to prove his capacity and fitness for the public service; and to obtain a position in it when he has made the proof, with thorough independence of President, Secretary, or Congressman, and simply and solely because of his citizenship and his fitness.

"The entire separation of the civil service from the control of politicians would secure a thorough and impartial congressional criticism of all the administrative bureaus and their operations. The sloth and incompetence found in any department now are known by the members of Congress to be in no small measure due to the fact that their own friends and dependents have been forced into places. They know, also, that the pruning-knife would reach their own scions as quickly as another's if retrenchment under a better system were begun; and it requires no ordinary character to pass a 'self-denying ordinance' of that kind. There have not been wanting demagogues who would declaim in favor of reducing the clerical force, and march straight to a department with an earnest appeal to crowd in one more clerk for them; but few men have the assurance for this."

It was not to be expected that any measure of reform would pass this body without opposition. Any bill which is calculated to destroy an abuse will always encounter the opposition of those who profit by its continuance.

Members will not support this bill who owe their nominations and elections to the offices that they have farmed out in their respective districts, to the promises they have made to put this man in as assessor and that one as collector in their districts, to appoint one person postmaster at this crossroads and another in that village, to make one an inspector and another a gauger of whisky in their districts.

The measure which I have introduced does not go as far as recommended by Mr. Cox; it does not go as far as the measures which have been adopted in Great Britain, which have secured such substantial and beneficial reforms; but it is one step in the right direction. We can probably pass no thorough bill, a bill establishing competitive examinations, a bill separating the appointment of subordinate officers from politics, until we shall have first separated Congressmen from all participation in appointments, and then we shall be in a condition to go to work and frame a bill that shall accomplish a thorough reform in the civil service.

The Senator from Indiana denies the right of Congress to declare that persons recommended by members of Congress shall not be appointed to office.

Has the Constitution of the United States fixed qualifications for clerkships, for assessors, for whisky inspectors, for postmasters? Surely not. All these are the creatures of law, and the Congress of the United States has a right to prescribe any qualifications it pleases.

Congress may, in its discretion, take away from the President the power to appoint all inferior officers, every postmaster in the United States; may not only tell him that he shall appoint no man that is not qualified, no man that cannot read and write, no man that is recommended to him by a member of Congress, but they may say to the President of the United States, "You shall not appoint a postmaster throughout the United States."

SENATOR MORTON.—In making that argument I was speaking of those appointments that are by the Constitution vested in the President of the United States.

SENATOR TRUMBULL.—It is just as competent to control those that are vested in the President as those that are vested in the heads of departments or the courts. Are not most of the appointments in the army and the navy made by regular promotion, in pursuance of a law of Congress?

But the Senator from Indiana objects to this bill that it makes it criminal for members of Congress to make recommendations to the President; in other words, to dictate appointments. He says that is degrading. Why, sir, the law will have no operation upon anyone who does not violate its provisions. There is an old couplet somewhere, in "McFingal" I think, which says:

> "No man e'er felt the halter draw
> With good opinion of the law."

Very likely those who propose to violate the law do not want a law that shall impose a penalty for so doing. A law prohibiting Senators and Representatives from making recommendations to office will affect no Senator or Representative who does not violate its provisions. What is there about a Senator or Representative that puts him above the criminal code? Suppose he is guilty of bribery, or corruption, or larceny, or robbery, or murder, is he not to be punished? Is there any divinity that hedges a man because he happens to be elected a Senator or Representative? Why, this is the old story of the divine right of kings: "The king can do no wrong."

It is the law now that if any Senator or member of Congress receives a present or any consideration, with a view of obtaining an office for another, he is liable to punishment by imprisonment in the penitentiary.

I am as tenacious, I think, of the privileges of this body and of its individual members as any Senator; but I am not for degrading the office of a Senator or Representative by making him the mere instrument for procuring offices contrary to his duty and to the Constitution.

This bill, if passed, will have the effect to render the departments independent. It will make the head of every department responsible for the appointments which he makes, and no secretary will then venture to have in his employ double the number of clerks required. Congress will hold him responsible when the responsibility is put upon him. It will make members of Congress independent also, and it will relieve them from obligations to the President and heads of departments. It will take away a source of temptation; and in cases where bad and corrupt men occupy positions in Congress (not an impossibility) it will impair their power to corrupt and debauch the public service.

And it will restore appointments to the executive department, where the Constitution places them, and to the people, where they belong.

On January 12 Senator Morton replied to Senator Trumbull.

The Senator seems to consider that we can enter upon an administration of the civil service which would require perfection in human nature, require men to be destitute of ambition, of jealousy, of all the passions which ordinarily interfere with the proper administration of government. Sir, we shall never have such an administration. It is not possible. We must take human nature as it is. Plato's dream of a republic can never be realized.

The Senator says that he is in favor of organizing the civil service so that officers shall be appointed without regard to politics. Now, sir, to have appointments made without regard to politics will suit our Democratic friends remarkably well while they are not in power, but it would not suit them one moment after they came into power.

The Senator went on to state some of the abuses which required this interference. He said that there are here in the departments of this Government more than twice as many clerks as are needed to do the business. I regard that as a very injurious statement. It is one that will excite and alarm the country. It will lead the country to believe that everything is corrupt; that everything is rotten in the administration of this Government in this capital. I submit that the Senator is mistaken; that it is not true. There is not, in my opinion, five per cent. of it true; the evidence cannot be found to establish its truth. If the Senator can produce the evidence of this, let the country have it, and let those men who are placed in charge of these departments be held responsible, and be condemned by Congress and by the people.

SENATOR TRUMBULL.—I read from the article of the ex-Secretary of the Interior, in which he states the fact that a moiety of the clerks could perform the duties.

SENATOR NYE.—Is not the number of clerks in the departments prescribed by law?

SENATOR TRUMBULL.—I suppose it is; but the Senator will understand that the pressure of Congressmen makes it necessary to increase the number beyond the necessary amount; Congressman after Congressman asks for one more, and in that way we provide for twice as many as are necessary.

SENATOR NYE.—Would it not be better to strike out from the law the requisition as to the number of clerks, and leave it discretionary with the heads of departments to employ as many as were needed? Would not that be a better remedy than to provide for putting us in prison?

SENATOR TRUMBULL.—I think the Senator from Nevada will probably be able to keep out of the penitentiary. He has been able to do so thus far, and I think he is in no particular danger now in that respect.

SENATOR NYE.—My apprehension was not for myself, but for my distinguished friend from Illinois. [Laughter.] I think if the files of the departments were consulted quite as many of his recommendations would be found there as of anybody else's.

SENATOR TRUMBULL.—Let me say that I have adopted the plan I propose for myself. I think the Senator cannot find within a year or two a recommendation of mine for a clerk in any department.

SENATOR MORTON.—"A year or two!"

SENATOR TRUMBULL.—I do not pretend to be better than other people. If I made recommendations while this system prevailed it would be a mere personal matter; and it would not change the force of the argument if I had recommended a thousand.

SENATOR MORTON.—The Senator from Illinois praises the civil service system of Great Britain. A system that might be appropriate to Great Britain would not be appropriate here; our institutions are different. In England the tenure of office in the civil service is for life. They hold their offices during good behavior; that is to say, during life. Can we adopt the life tenure here?

Why, sir, ten thousand men in this city holding office for

life would form a privileged class that would revolutionize the very foundation principle of this Government. We have but one life tenure under our Constitution, and if we had it to make over again we would not have that. I refer to the Supreme Court of the United States. An experience of seventy-five years has shown that the reason which induced the incorporation of the life tenure in the organization of that court is not a good one; it has failed; and we would not now reëstablish it. Certainly we would not apply the life tenure to seven or ten thousand men in the employment of the Government, and place them beyond the ordinary responsibilities that men in office are placed under. If a man has an office for life it takes a very serious cause to get him out. An ordinary delinquency, an ordinary neglect or abuse or failure is never sufficient to oust a man who holds an office for life. No, sir, we cannot afford to adopt the English system under any circumstances; it is anti-republican; it is contrary to the fundamental principles of this Government; and yet the Senator held up to us the beauties of the English system!

Sir, what is the fact there? Are the English clerks better qualified than those in our departments are? From the evidence I have, they are not; but they have one quality that our clerks have not got; that is, they have "the insolence of office" that results from a life tenure. I could refer to facts on this point. You have all read "Little Dorrit," by Charles Dickens, where he described the Circumlocution Office and the Somerset House.

I am not arguing against competitive examinations; I am in favor of them; but they are not infallible by any means. Men may pass an examination, and a first-rate examination, and yet be utterly unqualified for the position. How does it happen so often that the young men who graduate at law schools and carry off the first prizes fail in the practice of the law? So in regard to medicine. And how often does it happen that those who take the honors of the class at West Point do not succeed upon the field of battle or in the army? You can adopt no system that will guard again exceptional cases.

This system of competitive examinations is not new. We have had it ever since 1853, though a good many people do not seem to know that fact. I will read from the act of March 3, 1853:

"No clerk shall be appointed in either of the four classes until after he has been examined and found qualified by a board, to consist of three examiners, one of them to be the chief of the bureau or office into which he is to be appointed, and the two others to be selected by the head of the department to which the said clerk will be assigned.''

For seventeen years the departments have been administered under the operation of this law; and yet under this very system incompetent and worthless clerks, it is said, exist in great numbers in the departments. Against the statement of the Secretary of the Interior I put his own practice. According to his statement there were twice the number of clerks in the Interior Department when he went there than were required. And yet there was but one less when he left than when he entered the department.

The Senator from Illinois said that for the first fifty years of this Government members of Congress did not recommend appointments to the President. I confess I was astonished to hear that statement. This practice of recommendations by members of Congress has existed from the very beginning of this Government. The number of officers to be appointed was very small then compared with what it is now, but the practice was the same. Our Fathers, for whom I have great reverence, were governed by the same motives that govern men in these days. Sir, they recommended appointments just as we do; but they had not nearly so many to recommend.

But the Senator refers to the crowd of office-seekers that haunt members of Congress and that haunt the anterooms of the White House. I ask him, if he changes the system, if he makes it a penal offence for a member of Congress to recommend anybody for office, how that will diminish the number of office-seekers? Will that cut off the ambition of men all over this country? Certainly not. And if they cannot apply to a Senator or Representative they will come here themselves; and the crowd of office-seekers will be greater than it is now. Why, Mr. President, this Government has got to be carried on; and the thousands of offices have got to be filled. There will be competition for them, as there always has been. Men will come in droves just as they always have done. If they cannot present their applications through members of Congress they will go up in an army to the White House and seek to do it themselves; and, if they cannot get admission, they will seek to do it through gentlemen who open brokers' offices here for the purpose of securing appointments, and who secure appointments for money, just as lawyers secure patents for fees.

But the Senator says that officers ought to be appointed without regard to politics. Whenever you can carry on this

Government without regard to politics that doctrine will do. But this is a Government of the people and a Government of public opinion, in which the mass of the people take a deep interest, as they do not in England and in countries on the continent of Europe. Just so long as the character of this Government continues as it is, appointments will continue to be made with reference to politics; and no system can be devised that will prevent it. I do not care how many competitive examinations you institute, or whether you make the tenure for life or a tenure for ten years, you cannot change that thing unless you change the character of the Government. But what propriety is there in it? A man high in office, who has climbed up the political ladder, may then turn around and slap the faces of his friends who helped him up, if they should want appointments, and call that virtue! Would it make it virtue?

The amendment suggested by the Senator to his bill is that the President may, in writing, call upon a member of Congress to answer in writing in regard to a recommendation to office. That is the establishment of a circumlocution office—''how not to do it.'' The Senator from Illinois may be with the President of the United States, and the President may choose to consult him about an appointment; but the President must sit down and put his question in writing in due form, signed, sealed, and delivered, I suppose in the presence of witnesses, and then the Senator, in writing in due form, may answer that question!

But it is said the member of Congress will recommend his own friends. He has to recommend somebody's friends, and, if he recommends his own, provided they are as well qualified as another man's friends, what is there wrong about it? The point I make is that, as the thing stands now, a Senator or a member of Congress is held responsible at the bar of public opinion for an appointment, it being supposed that he recommended it, and therefore, if he does recommend his friend, the President has the assurance that he will recommend a good friend, one that is qualified and respectable, because, if he fails to do it, the responsibility for it will fall upon him, in common with the Administration.

I would say to the Senator that his intimation that those who oppose this bill oppose it because they are interested in having those appointments made does not hit me. I have been in the Senate now nearly four years, and there have been but three clerks appointed upon my recommendation. As far as I am personally concerned, I would be glad to be relieved of all this labor; but what right have I to be relieved? My friends have the same right to call upon me that I have had in times past to call upon them, and, if they are respectable, and capable, and honest, why should I refuse to give them that legitimate aid which may be within my power? Why, sir, men act upon this principle in all conditions of life, whether in regard to politics or in regard to business; and you cannot change it by any enactment which you can make.

SENATOR NYE.—The character of this legislation, in my opinion, tends to belittle the office of Representative, either in the other House or in this body, in the eyes of an intelligent people. I was pleased a good many years ago to see that it was said by Henry Ward Beecher that when it made him any the less a man to be a minister he would quit the business. I repeat that remark here: when it makes me any the less a man to be a Senator of the United States I shall resign my position.

Now, sir, it seems to me that the appointing power, so cast as it necessarily is and must forever continue to be in a Government like our own, turns as naturally toward the Representative for counsel and advice as the child turns to its mother for sustenance. Who else is there that the President can consult? My honorable friend from Illinois says he can consult other people away from here. So he can. But where are those people? How does he know them? What means has he of knowing whether their judgments are right or wrong when he does consult with them in a State as distant as my own or as California? Sir, the impossibility of avoiding this responsibility is too palpable to legislate upon.

I accept for good or for evil, with my party friends at home, my full responsibility for advising who is a proper man to hold this position or that position in the State which I have the honor in part to represent. I shrink from none of that responsibility; and I claim that I have advantages for knowing who are best fitted to hold those positions far superior to the appointing power. My advice is not always heeded, nor is that of the honorable Senator from Illinois; but when it is not heeded the appointing power does not generally get quite as good a man as it would have got if it had taken the one I recommended. I have seen it tried. I assume that this is a part of the responsibility of a Representative. I undertake to represent a district in my State in Congress; I undertake to do all its representative duties. What are those duties? My first duty is to see to it that no officer is appointed by the appointing power

who is not worthy and capable of filling the place. That is
my duty as a man.

Now, what is my duty as a politician? It is to see that
nobody but a good Republican fills an office. I hold that nobody but a good sound Republican is fit to hold office. I am
not going to be mealy-mouthed about this subject. Why, sir,
you and I have labored with the masses until our locks were
wet with the drops of the night to convince them that nobody
but Republicans were fit to hold office. We have echoed that
cry on every hilltop and in every valley until a large majority
of the people believe it. We tried the Democrats; we weighed
them in the balance and they were found wanting; and the
people said, ''Turn them out''; and they were turned out, and
stayed out and browsed out until their hair is as long as that
of him who browsed of old. [Laughter.]

The honorable Senator from Illinois in his zeal is going to
make it a penal offence for me, a Senator, to say what I have
said on every stump in almost every State in the Union. I
repudiate all such doctrines as that. I believe that nobody but
a person who has honestly imbibed and carries out Republican
doctrines is fit to hold office. I do not mean to say that everybody else is dishonest; but I mean that for the harmony and
well-being of the whole it is best that those who believe in the
great principles espoused by the Republican party should hold
the offices of the country. They have won them not only upon
a thousand fields of blood, but on a thousand fields that were
not so bloody but quite as important in their results.

I have observed since I have been here, now more than six
years, a tendency of things that has occasioned me painful reflection. We are assailed at one time from one department,
saying that we must not frank letters, because the members of
Congress are dishonest; and a hue and cry is got up from
ocean to ocean to abolish the franking privilege; and a bill
for that purpose runs, like fire through the prairies, through
the House. It is brought here, where men sometimes reflect
before they vote, and it is brought to a little stand. What was
the object of it? To establish the fact to the world that Congressmen were dishonest. Why, sir, I cannot get a sheet of
paper in my committee-room unless I send a written order with
a seal on it as big as that of a surrogate. I cannot get a box
of matches to light my cigar unless I send a written order for
it. And I am to account to a Committee on Contingent Expenses—I believe that is what they call it. I cannot get a knife
to make a pen without a written order. We are going to keep

Congressmen honest! [Laughter.] Great God! When did ever a Congressman steal a sheet of paper, or a knife, or a pen, or a box of matches? [Laughter.]

All this character of legislation, this estimate that is put upon the honorable Senators on this floor, has tended to degrade them in the eyes of an intelligent people. I repudiate the necessity of such legislation for my brethren, and I hope some one will rise and say he will do it for me, that I did not come here to establish a penknife store, nor a match store, nor a stationery store. I came here, in my humble way, to represent the best interests of the State that honored me with its commission. The people of that State did not believe that I would steal paper at home. If they had they would not have sent me here. [Laughter.]

Sir, this is a part of the same species of legislation. You are not to be trusted because you are clothed with the senatorial mantle. Mr. President, from my earliest boyhood I looked up with reverence to a United States Senator, and I should have felt insulted in my own person if anyone dared to assail the integrity and the fidelity of a Senator to his trust. If we do not feel so now, we ought to do so. If we indorse this mean, dirty suspicion that pervades the public mind, we deserve all the opprobrium that we get. Away, then, with this character of legislation!

We must not frank; we must not have the chance to use all the paper we want without accounting for it; and now my friend from Illinois, in stepping to the music of the time, is going to put us in the penitentiary for advising or not advising the nomination of a man to office! Well, sir, I think we had better go home. I am so constituted, I will tell you the honest truth, that I am afraid I shall get into the penitentiary if this bill should become a law, and I have not time to go [laughter]; because, if I should see the President or any of these departments putting in one whom I knew to be a bad man, I should commit this offence to a dead moral certainty. [Laughter.] I could not help it. My friend from Massachusetts [Mr. Sumner], with his honest impulses, would be there, too. Such a company would hardly ever be seen in the penitentiary. "What is your offence, gentlemen? You have advised the President not to appoint a bad man, or you have advised him to appoint a good man without any request of his!"

But gentlemen say that they want a civil-service bill. I do not; and we may as well meet this question at once. There is nothing on this earth so unendurable to a sensitive man as "the insolence of office"; there is nothing that becomes so odious in every government as "the insolence of office," where the officers have life tenures. Sir, a thousand-fold would I rather take the chances of changing these clerks as often as the political control of the Government changes in this country than to have them there by law whether they do their duty or not, and becoming insolent with age and defying all power to eject them. I say that under a republican form of government such a bureaucratic system of office-holding is repugnant to the genius of our free institutions. Let it prevail in monarchies and empires if you please, but let it never gain an entrance in republican America.

I like to see young men enter the race of competition for these offices. I like to see from every State a class of young men moved by the ambition and the incentive to some day fill these places; and by daylight and dark they toil to obtain the necessary acquirements, and, when they have obtained them, by every rule of our institutions and every law of right, they have a right to enter into competition for them. Fill them once and shut the door for thirty years, only opening it on funeral occasions, and the incentive to qualify for such places becomes very small indeed.

Mr. President, what will come next in the way of legislative hamper or shackle upon Senators and Representatives is yet to be seen. You have got them cornered now so that they must have "eyes right" and "faces to the front," or it is a penal offence. If they say so and so, it is unlawful. Sir, I said once what had well-nigh cost me more than I should like to have this saying cost me. I said it in an unfortunate latitude, when the Fugitive Slave law was in existence, that there was not power enough in this Government to make me chase a negro. I assert here now that there is not power enough in this Government to make me hold my tongue if I see them putting a rascal into office. I could not. It would be sinful in me if I did, for I may have knowledge that nobody else possesses. When the time comes that I cannot join my poor recommendation to that of nobler and better citizens, then I think it is time I took my departure from this place, from a place that needs laws to correct the ordinary moral duties of life.

Mr. President, I have opposed a steady opposition to this whole character of legislation. It serves to belittle the Senate in our own estimation and in the estimation of a gazing world. At the proper time, after my friend from Illinois has had a full chance at his bill, I shall move, unless some one else does so, to lay it upon the table, to sleep, as I hope, the sleep that never wakes.

SIMON CAMERON [Pa.].—Senators talk about not taking care of your friends. A man who has no heart may have no friends, and he may have no feeling of friendship; but when I cease to have regard and friendship for those who are my friends I will pray God to take me from the earth immediately. If a man is ambitious of getting a place in this free Government of ours, of which he is a part, why should he not come here and ask for it? And why should not I, whom he has helped to my position, assist him in getting that which he desires? I have never in my life recommended to the President a man for office whom I did not believe better fitted than anybody else who had been presented for the place; and I shall continue to do so.

Sir, look at the history of all parties with reference to this subject. The elder Adams commenced by saying that men who were peculiarly fitted for places ought not to be removed, and should not be; and Mr. Jefferson pursued that course, removing very few men. There were not many offices then to be filled, but whenever vacancies occurred he put in his own friends. Was not that right? Will not the friends of an Administration be likely to be more faithful to it than its enemies So it was in the time of Mr. Madison; so it was in the time of Mr. Monroe; none but the supporters of the Administration were then put into office. When General Jackson came in he was a little more liberal toward his friends. He made removals of those whom he thought dishonest; but no man peculiarly fitted for a place was removed by him. Why, sir, there yet remain in office men who were appointed before General Jackson went into the presidency. No Administration has ever thought of removing a man who was better fitted than anybody else by his experience for the place that he occupied.

When this measure was introduced I was glad of it, because it was an admonition to people not to come here and ask for office. I have thought, from the beginning of my experience here, that the greatest misfortune a man could have put upon him was to get a place in Washington City. I know men in these departments who are fit to fill the highest places in the Government who are now fourteen hundred or sixteen hundred dollar clerks, and who have not means enough to educate their children or to clothe their wives. I have had many appeals to assist them in getting bread in this city of Washington; men who, if they had remained at home and had aspired to office, could have the highest that the State had to give, and who, if

IX—20

they had turned half the industry and half the energy they
employ here in any capacity at home, even as mechanics or
laborers, would have been able to support themselves much
better than they do now.

I am for leaving this thing as it has been in the past and
let Nature work out its own way. Some men will be prosperous and some will not; some will do wrong and some will not.
But you can make no laws here which will regulate this thing
upon utopian doctrines.

On January 27 Carl Schurz [Mo.] moved a substitute to the bill, which provided that after its passage
all appointments of civil officers, with certain exceptions,
such as postmasters, should be made from those persons
found qualified therefor by open examinations or other
tests of fitness. To aid in the execution of the act a
paid Civil Service Board of nine commissioners was to
be appointed. The board was to investigate the character of all applicants, including postmasters, etc., not
examined. Appointments were to be made and vacancies
filled in order of merit. Promotions were to require
examinations for the new grade. In special cases the
board could call for assistance upon experts in the office
for which appointments were to be made and upon civil
and military and naval officers. Appointments of present officers were to be made for five years, and of new
officers for eight years, the first being a year of probation, during which the officer could be removed at the
pleasure of the President; thereafter, he could not be
removed except for cause. The board was to establish
the causes and rules of removal, etc., and act as a court
in the specific cases, reporting its findings to the President for action. Judges and clerks of the Federal
courts, members of the Cabinet, ministers plenipoten-
tiary, and officers of Congress were to be exempt from
the provisions of the act.

Senator Schurz supported his bill in a long and able
speech. He imagined each of his hearers to be a
foreigner who, admiring our Republican institutions, had
come to this country to see them in operation. He represented him as a spectator at the inauguration of a
President, and depicted the scene—"grand, simple, and

in imposing harmony with the nature of our institutions''—which would impress him.

So far your mind receives impressions corresponding with the convictions you had previously formed. But you spend some time at Washington, after having viewed this interesting and grand spectacle. Presently it strikes you that upon the avenues, and in the hotels, and at all public places you meet a motley throng with anxious eyes, nervous movements, a curious expression of countenance. Gradually you learn to understand what it means. After a few days you desire to pay your respects to the President. With something akin to awe you enter the White House to visit the Chief Magistrate of this grand Republic. Of course you expect to find him surrounded by his council of state, and, being new to the duties of his great office, diligently and earnestly studying those great problems which it will be his mission to solve. But how do you find him? In the midst of the same anxious faces, the same eager eyes, the same nervous countenances which have already attracted your attention before, and man after man pressing upon him, pouring hurried tales into his ear, or pressing papers upon him with the vehemence of extreme urgency. What do they ask for? They all want office, and want it quickly. You see the President bewildered, confused; and after a little while you come to the unwelcome conclusion that the great chief of the American Republic, in his present situation at least, is an object of pity. From him you go to visit the ministers of state, the heads of the departments, and what do you find there? You expect, of course, to see them at least, if the President is otherwise occupied, engaged in an arduous study of their great duties, for to them also these duties are new. But you find the same spectacle there; a pressing multitude asking for office. You visit Senators and Representatives, and how do you find them? Engaged in the consideration of the great political questions whose solution the situation of things demands of them? No; you find them surrounded by the same crowd, dogged from place to place, marching along the avenue at a hurried step, followed by a long train of anxious pursuers, running to the President, running to the departments—nay, you may follow them even to another place in some of these splendid public buildings of ours—a side office, where they pay their respects to a young gentleman who at first must appear to you one of the high dignitaries; and you are somewhat astonished when you hear that he is the appointment clerk, who very graciously receives the representatives of the people, with their hats in their hands, and condescendingly dispenses his favors upon them, or with polite regret assures them that he cannot accommodate them all.

What does this spectacle of frantic hurry and pressure mean? It means nothing more nor less than that the President, the members of the Cabinet, Senators, and Representatives, and the whole multitude which fills the capital are busy in taking to pieces the whole machinery of the Government immediately after the accession to power of the new Administration, then to recompose it again out of new materials.

Now, sir, what is to guide the appointing power in this fearful and perplexing task? Is it personal knowledge? Impossible. They do not know the men who are applying for office. They are required to act on recommendations, and those recommendations are put on paper. The applicant for office is represented to be the model man of the age in point of character, of intelligence, of capacity, and of political merit; he is just the man for such a place, and it would inflict serious damage on the country not to appoint him.

Now, sir, how are these recommendations made and how are they obtained? Look at the Congressman who is to distribute the offices in his district. Laboring under the pressure coming from those who exercise political influence among his constituents, he is not permitted to follow his own judgment. He is bound to a great many of his "political friends" by what he considers honorable political obligations, and he is forced to take their judgment in a great many cases for his own.

But as to offices not local, you witness the interesting spectacle of Senators and Representatives coöperating. It is the organization of a mutual insurance society: "You sign this recommendation of my friend, I sign that recommendation of yours." It is a matter of mutual accommodation. And here the element of personal knowledge enters but rarely. What must the consequences be? Suppose we find that we have recommended an improper man. What should we do when called upon to confirm or reject the nomination? Reject the nomination we ourselves had induced the President to make? Or confirm it against the dictates of our own consciences? Do you perceive the conflict between duty and fairness which the present way of doing things is so apt to bring upon us?

And, sir, this is not the worst feature of the business. I have known instances where a regular office brokerage was established, and where a member of this Senate, not now here, a gentleman of the most honorable character, was induced by a so-called friend to sign a recommendation for a third individual, by which that third individual was to obtain an appointment in one of the departments, the "friend" having exacted and obtained a fee of $100 to procure the signature of the Senator. The Senator would have kicked that friend out of his presence had he had any suspicion of the dishonorable traffic. But I ask you, can you tell, or can I tell, if we are facile enough to sign papers at the request of outside friends, that we have not fallen into the same snare, and that your and my signature have not been sold by an office-broker for money?

Now, sir, a glance at the absurdities that are occurring under this system. There is that most formidable of men, "the man to be provided for"; a man who must necessarily have an office; a man who has "claims" that cannot be disregarded and who cannot be neglected with impunity; a man to be put in position at all hazards.

I will tell you of the case of a man to be provided for that came under my own personal observation. He aspired to a post-office, a pension agency, a minister residentship, a full mission, and finally landed in the governorship of a Territory; and the appointing power, yielding to the peculiar pressure character-. istic of the existing system, declared him fit for all these places consecutively. And all this in seven days.

Must it not be clear to every observing mind that our present mode of making appointments is a blindfold game, a mere haphazard proceeding? Was Mr. Lincoln very wrong when once, in a moment of despair, he said, with grim humor, "I have discovered a good way of providing officers for this Government: put all the names of the applicants into one pepper-box and all the offices into another, and then shake the two, and make appointments just as the names and the offices happen to drop out together"?

The other day the Senator from New Hampshire [Mr. Patterson] showed you that, as the investigations of the Retrenchment Committee prove, the New York Custom House, too, suffers from men to be provided for, for whom offices must be created, even if the service does not need them.

You notice officers there called inspectors; officers whose duties are of the very highest consequence. They, in fact, to a very great extent, hold the revenue of the custom house in their hands; for they have to watch the unloading of ships and see to it that no goods are smuggled into the city from the vessels arriving in that port. What class of people are those inspectors taken from? We heard it said the other day by the Senator from New Hampshire that they, as they themselves confess, are in the habit of accepting bribes of fifteen to fifty dollars for each vessel that is unloaded under their supervision; that they accept those bribes as a rule, not as an exception. And those officers are selected from that class of people of whom the Senator from New York told us that, yielding to the frailties of human nature, they would naturally drift into the habit of taking presents or bribes, and you would not expect anything else. If you cannot expect anything else, what becomes of the revenue? But, I will admit, under the present system of distributing offices, you have, indeed, no right to expect anything else. If you cannot expect anything else, what becomes of the revenue? But, I will admit, under the present system of distributing offices, you have, indeed, no right to expect anything better.

Go to San Francisco and you will find exactly the same system working there, leading to similar results. You will be told there that under the prevailing system five collectors went out of office as defaulters to the Government. You will be told that under the law officers are to be examined before they are appointed, and yet the very heads of those establishments will, at the same time, inform you that the examination is a mere farce; that, as soon as the examining board knows whom the collector wants appointed, the favored candidates will pass the examination without the least difficulty.

Senator Schurz, reverting to the laying aside of important business to settle applications for office at the beginning of an Administration, said it continued throughout the Administration.

Mr. President, I ask you, in all candor and soberness, is not this something like Bedlam? Look over all the civilized countries of the world: do you discover anything equal to it?

Under such a system it cannot be otherwise but that inexperience should follow inexperience and rascality should follow rascality in rapid succession. There is nothing unnatural to your mind now in the needless and expensive multiplication of offices. There is nothing surprising to you now in the frequency and magnitude of embezzlements and defalcations. You understand now perfectly well that when the whiskey tax was fixed at two dollars it was absolutely impossible to enforce the law with the machinery of the public service we had. You are no longer surprised at the frequency of mail-robberies which are perpetrated in post-offices. You see the smugglers in our ports lying in wait to watch their opportunity when, taking advantage of the inexperience of new officers, or with the aid of dishonest ones, they can rush whole cargoes into the ports of the United States. It is no longer surprising to you henceforth when you read in the reports of the Committee on Retrenchment that from this source losses have occurred for many years amounting to from twelve to twenty-five million dollars annually at the port of New York alone. Nor is it surprising to you to learn, as is calculated by gentlemen of experience in that institution, that each change of a collector in the Custom House at New York costs the country an average of ten million dollars, in consequence of the confusion and disorder which necessarily follow.

No, sir; there is nothing astonishing in all this, for you have learned that the offices of the Government are mere "spoils," "public plunder"; that, instead of being regarded as the places of duty, they are regarded as conquests, the conquest of a party; as "berths" into which men are put, not to use the best of their energies, not to look with anxiety after the interests of the Government, but to make it comfortable for themselves and to serve their friends. And you have learned more: how current these words "spoils" and "plunder" have become in the mouths of the people, so that we have lost all sense of their fearful meaning.

Sir, when a man receives an office as a reward for political services rendered, or as an incentive for further political work; when he feels himself sustained, less by his own energy and efficiency than by political influence, is he not naturally led to rely upon that political influence instead of his own fidelity and efficiency to sustain him in office? Is it not a matter of experience that even well-intentioned men who go into office honest and industrious frequently become dishonest and lazy there, feeling that political influence is more potent than the appreciation of dutiful conduct?

Let us look further. Is not the short and uncertain tenure of office a very severe temptation to a man burdened with the ordinary frailties of human nature to make the most of short opportunities, or at least to have the greatest possible benefit from the least possible work? Hence the formation of "rings" in the public service.

Now, sir, observe the effect which this system is calculated to produce upon the character of those who are under its influence. Officers being party servants, have they not to sacrifice to a very great extent the independence of their own opinions?

Is it not true that their very position breeds hypocrisy, sycophancy, and venality, and that this is apt to result in a deterioration of manhood?

Is it not also natural that, in consequence of this, the public service should not stand as high in public opinion as it ought to do; that men who aspire to office do so not infrequently at a sacrifice of self-respect? There is the destruction of that *esprit de corps* which preserves the morality of the civil service in other countries, and which here distinguishes the army and navy in point of personal honor and integrity. Render our public servants proud of the dignity of their position, and most of the immoral practices will disappear from which the public service is now suffering.

But, sir, the effect upon the efficiency of the civil service itself is not the worst evil we have to deplore. Follow a Congressman into his State or District. Look at him as a candidate. Some of them rely for success upon their ability, their character, their merits; others do not. These others speculate upon the frailties of human nature among their constituents. Observe one of the latter; how he attempts to build up the machinery of his influence at home; and for this the patronage offers him the ready means. He makes promises of office for the purpose of obtaining support, sometimes promiscuously, recklessly, in duplicate and in triplicate—promises impossible to be kept. Look at the situation of such a man. He is covered all over with fraudulent mortgages, and he stands before himself as a dishonorable deceiver before he is elected. By his promises he may have endeavored to buy others; he has certainly succeeded in demoralizing himself.

But now he is elected, and he commences to distribute offices. The Senator from Indiana [Mr. Morton] says that the system by which a Congressman is to distribute local offices is a guaranty for conscientious recommendations, for a Congressman would make himself unpopular by recommending unworthy men to public place. In some cases that may be so; but is it not frequently otherwise? Does not a Congressman frequently make recommendations for office merely for the purpose of paying old debts, discharging political obligations, or preparing for a new campaign with a view to his own reëlection?

But, sir, when he commences to distribute the offices, those duplicate and triplicate promises come down upon him; and what then? Then you will find those cases which are referred to in the essay of ex-Secretary Cox, where he describes honorable Senators and members of the House of Representatives standing before a member of the Cabinet with recommendations in their hands and with the candidates for office on their arms, abounding in expressions of good will and friendship for their *protégés*, presenting them as the worthiest of mortals, whose appointment they most ardently, anxiously advocate, while the Cabinet minister has in the drawer of his table confidential notes from the same honorable Congressmen requesting him not to pay any regard to the recommendation which they are just so eloquently and affectionately urging. What will you say of a system which brings forth such results among the Representatives of the people, who make the laws of the country?

Let us proceed. The machinery of the home influence is now constructed, and the Congressman thinks he has accomplished what he needs for his future prospects. But something new intervenes. It happens that the Executive has a pet scheme of which the Congressman conscientiously disapproves. Here is a complication. Does he insist upon his opposition? Then the Executive may threaten to withdraw his favor from him and to remove his appointees. If, on the other hand, he yields, the Executive may promise not only to keep those in office who were appointed upon his recommendation, but to grant new favors to him. There, sir, is that great struggle between conscience and interest which has brought so many a man to his fall. Will such things happen? They may happen; nay, sir, they have happened; and the spoils system invites them with such power of seduction that they certainly will happen again. Here the system develops its full effects upon the frailties of human nature.

The temptation to the Executive is certainly great. It is that temptation which is always connected with power; a temptation which but few men, if any, have been able to withstand. But the temptation to the Congressman is still greater. His interest is potently working upon his mind. The Congressman, losing favor with the appointing power, loses his power also to keep that machinery of home influence, upon which in a great measure he depends for success, in working operation. His chances at the next election are constantly before his eyes. His own appointees, if he persists in his opposition to the Executive, may turn against him, for the Executive has means to work upon the frail human nature of office-holders. Thus the Congressman may suddenly find himself deserted by the very friends upon whose gratitude he counted. The clamor of new aspirants for office will be still stronger.

Sir, we have all experienced that kind of pressure upon us.

Do you remember at the commencement of this Administration, when we were asked to repeal the tenure of office act, how the clamor of office-seekers arose around us to influence our decision; how they denounced those who resisted the repeal of that law as the enemies of the President at the very beginning of the Administration; and how they vociferously demanded that we should fling the laws at the feet of him who sits at the fountain-head of favor?

Thus the spoils system, with the vast ramification of its influences, works upon the independence of the legislator.

But the same temptation presents itself in another shape. A Congressman discovers abuses in a department. If he attacks them he is in danger of having his clerks removed; he may be informed that he is no longer entitled to the favors of that department. Shall he give up his appointees or violate his duty in ignoring the abuses?

The thing has sometimes been turned the other way. I am reliably informed that Congressmen have gone to a head of department and threatened him that unless he appointed their particular *protégés* they would vote against the appropriations for the department. To appoint supernumeraries would have been a grave violation of duty on the part of the head of the department. And yet, under the pressure of the spoils system, a Congressman demands it, with the threat that unless it be done he will violate his duty in a manner equally gross, by voting against a necessary appropriation.

But it appears in still another shape. A Congressman has procured an appointment for one of his friends, an appointment of great responsibility. He has, so to say, pledged his honor for the honor of the officer. That man commits gross misconduct; under his management serious abuses develop themselves. Is not that Congressman sorely tempted to cover up or white-wash that delinquency instead of fearlessly exposing it and bringing the guilty man to punishment? Is not there again the interest of the Congressman, under the influence of the spoils system, working directly against the interest of the public good?

And now, sir, we arrive at a very interesting and somewhat startling question: Can a Congressman, under the present system, be entirely honest? That question has been addressed to me by an intelligent observer, and my first impulse was at once to say certainly he can. Yes, I believe he can; but I declare, sir, when you survey the whole field, when you study the influences of the present system upon the frailties of human nature, you will admit that it is exceedingly difficult for him to be so.

The system is a hotbed of that peculiar kind of corruption which is the more dangerous as it does not appear in the palpable, gross, and unequivocal form of money, but appears in the seductive shape sometimes of an apparently honorable political or personal obligation. It insinuates itself like a subtle poison into those crevices of the human conscience which are opened by the expansion of generous feelings. And when that poison finds in an individual already the least corrupt tendency to work upon, it will develop it with wonderful rapidity.

Now look at the effect upon the workings of the Government. It is said that, by the patronage as it is now dispensed, a part of the executive functions is transferred to the legislature. This is true. But at the same time the independence of the legislature is seriously endangered by the corrupting power of the Executive. The true statement of the case seems to be this: by the so-called right of recommendation, as it is at present practiced, members of the legislature encroach beyond the point foreseen in the Constitution upon what the Executive ought to be most independent in and responsible for, namely, the administrative functions; and, on the other hand, by the power of giving and withholding patronage, the Executive exercises control over what the legislature ought to be most independent in, namely, the law-making function. Thus the system weakens and demoralizes both ways. It is a disturbance of the constitutional balances; it is a perversion of the powers of the Government.

But, sir, on the whole, it strengthens the Executive in the worst sense by giving him power over the meaner instincts of human nature. See how it works. The Representative of the people stands before the Executive in the attitude apparently of an adviser, but in fact of a petitioner—an attitude always improper, and not seldom degrading. The appointments to office he asks for, even if they are calculated to promote the public good, are granted to him as favors, favors that can be withheld just as well as they can be granted. If such favors are necessary to him to keep up the machinery of his influence at home, then he feels himself, as he really is, in the power of the Executive.

The temptation is terribly strong, therefore, to buy those favors, even at the expense of his convictions and of his manhood. Thus it is that this system weakens the backbone and makes supple the knees of public men before the great dispenser of gifts. Thus it creates and nourishes that fawning servility which stifles the voice of honest criticism; and it requires very great emergencies indeed, like Andrew Johnson's glaring tergiversation, to break that dangerous spell.

But, on the other hand, the system is a source of peculiar dangers to the Executive also. Those who ascend the presidential chair do not leave all the frailties of human nature behind them. The voice of interested sycophancy is apt to fill their ears and to befog their judgment. Even their errors find some who will applaud them. Even their follies will meet with obsequiousness. The servility which cringes before them is apt to lower their general estimate of manhood. They will form the dangerous conclusion that they can wield the people as readily as they can wield those individuals who live and thrive on the presidential smile. They are not seldom easily persuaded that, whatever a few factious critics may say, the country is fairly aglow with delight over its ruler. Why, sir, even Andrew Johnson, when he arrived at that point where those of his friends who respected themselves turned their backs upon him, was firmly convinced that his popularity with the people was omnipotent; and Presidents of better sense are not exempt from the danger of falling into errors of similar significance. They are not unfrequently led to despise an unpleasant truth because it appears so lonesome and forlorn in the crowd of agreeable fictions gotten up for the purpose of pleasing and propitiating the presidential fancy. And thus Presidents, seduced by the picture of popular admiration which is constantly held up before them, are apt to drop from mistake to mistake, to dare one blunder after another, until finally the verdict of the people, unmistakably expressed, wakes them up from the dangerous and deceptive dream of invincible popularity.

And why all this? The reason is very simple: because the spoils system has made the atmosphere of the Executive mansion so thick with favor-seeking flattery that the sound waves of an independent public opinion can no longer penetrate it. Thus even Presidents are apt to become the victims of the spoils!

And yet this is not the worst feature of the system. You extend your observations further. A new presidential election is coming on; a great contest of principles and policies, but at the same time a great contest for "public plunder." There are the spoils ahead, with the prospect of "a new deal." Men of patriotic and pure motives enter the arena; but also the speculators rush to the front, with whom all patriotic motives are overshadowed by mercenary impulses. They are ready for what is called "dirty work," and their presence will create it where they do not find it.

The periodic recurrence of a "new deal" of the spoils has created a greed for office which is raging like an epidemic disease and is continually growing worse. There is a desire, unfortunately spreading among the young men of the country, to live either without work or with as little work as possible, and that desire is stimulated to a morbid degree by the seductive opportunities of political life. Many good men, young and old, are drawn off from honest and remunerative labor, because they are told that it is so easy to get an office and so pleasant to enjoy a living at the public expense. A political proletariat is forming itself in consequence, which is recruited from men who, following that morbid infatuation, are drawn away from productive pursuits. That proletariat is pressing upon candidates, not infrequently forming their bodyguard. The most reckless politicians become very important in the fight, voluntarily undertaking the work which sometimes candidates would shrink from advising. And these men will be the most clamorous for reward; and, being the most persistent and the most dangerous, they will not unfrequently be also the most likely to receive it. Thus a class of camp-followers, caring for nothing but the spoils, fastens itself upon political parties.

You ask, Why cannot political parties preserve their purity? Mainly because the spoils system attracts to them, and makes prominent and important in them, impure elements. On the other hand, men of a higher tone, disgusted with this spectacle, will sometimes fall to the rear; and thus we deplore the loss of some of the most valuable elements of the population from active political life.

Now, sir, the presidential election being over, the same spectacle, as I have described it, is repeated, whatever party may have carried the day. Another question presents itself: the spoils system being carried on under the auspices and responsibility of political parties—can a political party be honest? Sir, I look upon it as almost, I might say entirely, impossible. The reason is simple: the party in power being held responsible for the conduct of partisan officers, will always be irresistibly tempted, in order to save itself, to conceal and whitewash the dishonest practices and abuses carried on by such officers, instead of fearlessly exposing, punishing, and correcting them. Party interest, as now understood, exercises a terrorism over the members of political organizations which but few are able to resist. He who honestly and fearlessly denounces abuses is considered not only a dangerous character, but he is considered a bad party man; and it may interest the Senate to know that a member of this body, who but a few days ago spoke about the abuses carried on in one of the offices of the country, was approached by anxious political friends and blamed for having made a speech against his party!

Sir, it is in vain while the spoils system prevails to look to any party for a thorough reform of abuses. It is in vain, because those very abuses have become an integral part of the machinery through which parties obtain and wield power.

But by far the worst and most dangerous effect of the spoils system is the demoralization of the public sentiment. We know that on certain frontiers smuggling, robbing the revenue, is not considered an entirely dishonorable business. Now I ask you, sir, is it not true that here it does not render a man generally infamous if he robs the United States, provided he does it cleverly? Is it not true that things are considered fair in politics which would be looked upon as positively dishonorable in private life? Has not the taking dishonest advantage of political power and influence for the acquisition of wealth become a thing which is judged by a great many with alarming leniency? When the offices of the Government are looked upon as spoils to be enjoyed, instead of duties to be performed, is it a wonder if in certain quarters the atrocious notion has gained currency that he is a fool who in a political position is not knave enough to steal? Is it a wonder that under the spoils system the pursuit of politics should be looked upon as a trade of somewhat tainted character; that in explaining the actions even of the most honorable men the suspicion of impure motives should, in preference of all others, be resorted to by the multitude, not with proper indignation, indeed, but with stolid levity and with resigned indifference, an indifference still more demoralizing?

Is it a wonder if professional politicians, sensible of the tainted character of their business, sometimes ask themselves, "Why should we be better than the reputation of our trade? Why should we not enjoy the benefits of dishonest dealings if they are imputed to us all the same?" Is it a wonder that even well-meaning men drift into corrupt practices without knowing it, since long habit and the general example have dulled their moral apprehension of the true character of such practices, and since public opinion has become so indifferent to them?

Thus, sir, the demoralization nourished by the system of spoils has filtered through the whole body-politic from top to bottom, even to the lowest strata of the population; and you cannot fail to feel the deep significance of the words once uttered by Mr. Lincoln, to which the Senator from Massachusetts [Mr. Wilson] has already alluded. One day, shortly before his death, after the commencement of his second Administration, he pointed out to a friend the crowd of office-seekers besieging his door, and said to him: "Now we have mastered the Rebellion; but there you see something that in the course of time may become far more dangerous to this Republic than the Rebellion itself." And indeed, sir, he had a prophetic mind.

I have endeavored to describe the evil; what now is the remedy? Is there any probability that the evil will correct itself? I doubt it. A revolution in public sentiment ever so decided would hardly have lasting effect unless clothed in the form of law. We have to deal with a system of temptations which will work the same results as long as it exists at all. Let us see, then, whether legislative means are available and bid fair to be effective.

The present practice of distributing office in the way of patronage being the root of the evil, the problem consists in reaching that without running against the spirit of the Constitution. I desire to move the bill to reform the civil service which I introduced at the beginning of the last session as a substitute for the bill introduced by the Senator from Illinois [Mr. Trumbull]. I have changed it in only one essential point.

I do not indulge in the delusion by any means that the substitute I offer has any claim to perfection; on the contrary, I am painfully sensible of its shortcomings; but at any rate it may serve well as a basis for discussion. As I have already stated, the weak point in the bill of the honorable Senator from Illinois is this: that, if he renders it impossible for the appointing power to derive information about the appointments to be made from members of Congress, another source of information must be substituted, which his bill fails to do. This source of information is supplied in my bill. The bill establishes a civil service board before which all the applications for office are to go. This board is not to be in any sense a partisan engine. The mode of appointment and the tenure which it is to have will give it a certain independence of party government. It is to be renewed one-third by every successive Administration, and will soon have a mixed political character, as one Administration succeeds upon another, probably under the auspices of different parties. The members of the board shall not be removed except for cause, according to the provisions of the tenure of office act before it was amended by this Congress at its first session. But they may be removed for cause deemed sufficient by the Senate. The salary of the commissioners is to be ample enough to command a respectable degree of ability and acquirements, and the value of the salary is enhanced by a long tenure. I will add that the number of commissioners composing the board, as the bill fixes it, is not essential. It ought not to be too small at first, for there will be a great pressure of work. It might be reduced afterward, when the machinery is in successful operation.

The officers of the Government are divided into two classes; first, the subordinate officers, whose appointment is now by law vested in the heads of the different departments, the routine men, the clerks; and, secondly, the executive officers, who are now appointed by the President of the United States by and with the advice and consent of the Senate. The subordinate officers are to be appointed after competitive examination.

The fitness of candidates for presidential appointments shall also be examined by the board. There are certain offices the discharge of the duties of which requires special knowledge, experience, and skill; and candidates for such offices are fit subjects for regular examination. There are other offices—for instance, country post-offices—in connection with which the examination of a candidate would hardly be deemed necessary and proper. The distinction is to be fixed by the regulations of the board. Where no examination is considered necessary the board shall institute such inquiries as may be necessary to ascertain the character, antecedents, standing in society, and general fitness of candidates. The results of such examinations shall be reported by the board to the President and to the Senate, to guide the Executive in making nominations and the Senate in confirming or rejecting them. The interference of Congressmen will then no longer be required.

You will notice that in the case of presidential appointments the President is to choose freely from the whole number found fit, and that those only are to be excluded from his choice who are found unfit for the office for which they present themselves. Thus the choice is by no means to be made by the board, but by the President.

One of the most important features of the substitute is the change in the tenure of officers. The section of my bill touching subordinate officers, as it originally stood, provided that those subordinate officers who are appointed by the heads of departments, except postmasters, should be appointed on good behavior. The current objection to this was that it would create a distinct and aristocratic class among our population. I, for my part, must confess that I never feared any such result. In fact, the idea of a class of aristocrats, consisting of departmental clerks at Washington and of custom house and post-office clerks at New York and other cities, seems to me somewhat ludicrous.

WILLARD WARNER [Ala.].—Would not this system prevent the President from appointing to office any man who did not apply?

SENATOR SCHURZ.—No, sir; it would not. The President may select a man whom he wishes to appoint to office, and then send him before the civil service board, to ascertain whether he is fit. If that man does not want to go before the civil service board, the presumption is that he does not want to go into office.

I was just remarking that, in my opinion, the tenure on good behavior of those subordinate officers would, in my opinion, by no means be productive of the dangers which have been pictured in such glaring colors. I do not believe that these dangers exist in a country which is ruled by public opinion, and where the administration of affairs changes so frequently. And yet it is so obvious that a proposition like this could not carry in either House of Congress, or perhaps even before public opinion, that it has been abandoned. This, however, is not the only reason why it was given up. I believe that free competition and a rigid competitive examination before a board composed of conscientious examiners, as a condition of appointment, will prevent the frequent occurrence of removal without sufficient cause. At any rate, when vacancies in the departments are to be filled only with men having issued best from a competitive examination, the service will not suffer by the change, removals and appointments on partisan grounds will cease, and greater stability will be secured without the elasticity of the system being sacrificed.

It is provided that the regular term of office shall be eight years, and whenever a vacancy occurs it shall not be filled merely for the balance of the unexpired term, but the officer filling the vacancy shall be appointed for another full term of eight years. The object is this: in the first place, regular rotation with every successive Administration shall cease. Officers being removable only for cause, and officers appointed by one Administration holding through the term of another, we shall accustom ourselves to the practice of having men in office belonging to another party than that which controls the Administration. And as vacancies gradually occur, by death, resignation, or

IX—21

removal for cause, to be filled for full terms of eight years, the expiration of the terms of the different officers will no longer occur at one time, but be scattered over the period of eight years, thus giving the civil service board sufficient time to conduct their examinations and inquiries as they successively become necessary to fill vacancies, and enabling the Executive, as well as the Senate, to act leisurely and intelligently upon all the cases coming before them.

That the regular term should be just eight years I do not deem absolutely essential. It would, indeed, give the public service the benefit of more experienced officers. But to attain the other objects described it would be sufficient to fix a term of five, six, or seven years as well. I admit that the practical capacity of a candidate for office, his executive ability, cannot be with sufficient certainty ascertained by examination. This might lead to embarrassments, as the officer is not to be removed during his term except for cause to be tried. It is therefore provided that the first year of service of an officer belonging to this class shall be his year of probation, during which his practical ability may be well ascertained. And during that year of probation the Executive shall have power to remove the officer at pleasure, without assigning or proving a cause. It will thus be seen that no distinct and privileged class of Government officers, no bureaucracy is to be created, but the elasticity of the present system is to be preserved, improved, however, by a system of selection, which will secure a better class of officers, and by a longer and more secure tenure, which will remove the partisan character and raise the moral standard of the service.

Finally, sir, certain officers are excluded from the operation of this bill. As far as the judges of the United States are concerned, it may be presumed that no other than men universally recognized as being eminent in the law would be selected for such places by any Administration; and, as to members of the Cabinet and diplomatic officers, representing, as they do, not only a public duty but in a certain sense also the political views of the Administration, it is proper that the Administration should have the free disposal of those places.

JACOB M. HOWARD [Mich.].—I would ask the honorable Senator why he excepts the judges of the Supreme Court from the category of persons to be examined before their appointment? Is there not greater necessity for the examination of applicants for judicial station than for any other position in the civil service?

SENATOR SCHURZ.—As I have already stated, it may fairly be presumed that no Administration would select any other but men very eminent in their profession to fill such positions.

SENATOR HOWARD.—Is not the eminence of the station the strongest reason that can be conceived for subjecting the applicant to an examination as to his fitness?

SENATOR SCHURZ.—It might there with propriety be asked who is to examine the candidates for such places as judgeships on the supreme bench? There are examinations in the army for a number of grades. We might just as well ask who is to examine a candidate for the position of general-in-chief.

CORNELIUS COLE [Cal.].—Would not that reason apply to all offices?

SENATOR SCHURZ.—It would not. In the nature of things, it may fairly be presumed that the applicants will exclusively belong to the small class of those who are eminent enough to be mentioned in connection with such places.

AARON H. CRAGIN [N. H.].—The Senator, I presume, has not forgotten that these appointments are for life, and therefore there would be greater necessity of having exactly the right men.

MR. SCHURZ.—I have certainly not forgotten that. But, on the whole, I think the experience of the people of the United States has been that but very few mistakes in the history of this country have been made in the selection of members of the Supreme Court of the United States. As to the diplomatic officers of the Government, there, I admit, this question might be asked with much greater propriety. But as diplomatic officers of the Government are to represent not only a public duty, but also the political views of the Government, it is proper that the Administration should be left free in their choice; and I believe also that when no longer any danger exists that a man will be appointed minister-resident or minister-plenipotentiary because he fails in obtaining a post-office, we shall have a better set of diplomatic officers than now.

Now, sir, I repeat, I do not pretend that this plan is in any way perfect. On the contrary, I feel its shortcomings. Let us regard it as a suggestion that may call out others. I invite the Senate to consider the benefits arising from some such system. It would, of course, not at once remove all the evils complained of; but it would certainly secure greater efficiency in the civil service. It would certainly procure for it men of higher capacity, even by deterring ignorance and men of low reputation. It would certainly raise the respectability of the service; and a certificate of fitness issued by the civil service board would be a mark of distinction and serve as a passport in all the walks of private life everywhere. It would certainly inspire a sentiment of honorable pride among officers. It would secure more efficient control by putting by the side of an officer one belonging to another party, instead of making the whole one great partisan ring. It would abolish the absurd practice by which an Administration is pressed to take to pieces and rebuild at the start the whole machinery of the Government. It would relieve the President, Cabinet, and Congressmen from importunity, and give them time to attend to their legitimate duties. It would restore the independence of the different departments of the Government. Offices ceasing to be party machinery, political parties would be relieved of responsibilities and would be encouraged in the freedom of criticism. Then a thorough retrenchment and reform of abuses would finally be attainable.

But, more than that, the spoils system once destroyed, a healthier moral feeling in political life will be rendered possible; the corrupt temptations working in all spheres of the body-politic will be greatly lessened; the standard of morality in political life will be raised; political contests will once more be contests of principles and policies, instead of being scrambles for spoils; the political proletariat, with its demoralizing practices and influences, will gradually be broken up, and all the best elements of the population will again be attracted to political life. Politics will then become once more what they always ought to have been, a most honorable occupation engaging the noblest aspirations.

I know some of the objections that are currently brought to a system like this. It is said that the reform proposed would be obnoxious to the theory of our Government. I maintain that in its effects it would be in strict accordance with the original intentions as exemplified by the early practices of the Government. The Senator from New Hampshire a few days ago quoted a passage from "The Federalist," in which Alexander Hamilton states most strongly the intention of the makers of the Constitution to prevent the interference of members of Congress in the appointment of officers and to secure stability in the civil service.

GEORGE H. WILLIAMS [Ore.].—Does it not appear from the early history of this Government that it was held that officers were subject to removal at the will of the Executive?

SENATOR SCHURZ.—It does; but it appears also that the

power of the Executive in that direction was but very rarely exercised. It appears from the teachings of the fathers, as well as the early practice of the Government, that nothing was further from the minds of the statesmen of those times than that there should be a general breaking up of the administrative machinery every four years, to be accompanied and followed by the scandals which we now witness. Who of them ever thought of it, that a competent and worthy officer should be removed as long as he was competent and worthy? Nay, let me say to the Senator: if the great Fathers of the Republic, if Washington and Adams and Jefferson and Madison and Hamilton could rise up from the dead and look at the spectacle which now so frequently presents itself to our eyes, they would stand aghast at the perversion which the beautiful fabric of the Government, as they designed it, has suffered at the hands of subsequent generations.

SENATOR WILLIAMS.—I wish to ask the Senator if the system which he is now assailing was not established by the fathers of this Republic, and if all the evils of which he complains may not be remedied by electing a man President of the United States who will return to the early practices of the Republic?

SENATOR SCHURZ.—Have we not elected more than once men to the presidency of the United States upon whose integrity and sagacity and wisdom we built the highest hopes? Can the Senator recollect within the reach of his memory a single President of the United States who ever dared to attempt the sweeping reform of which he speaks? Does he expect, as long as the present system prevails, if a change of party control should occur, that then a President would have the strength to rise up and say, "I will have no longer a partisan organization in the public service"? Does he think that such a President could thus control the greed of his partisan followers? Does he expect any party that may follow ours in the control of affairs to abstain from grasping the spoils if there is no impediment in the way? To produce such a result would require a tremendous revolution in popular sentiment. I certainly would hail with delight such an event; but have we a right to expect a moral revolution so powerful unless we prepare the way for it by removing the temptations which are now operating on the minds of the politicians and the multitude?

We are told that there is a popular notion prevailing in this country that every American citizen is entitled to public office. Yes, so he is; but would it not be well to create the additional popular notion that then every American citizen shall fit himself for public office in point of intelligence, acquirements, and character? Thus office may even become an educational element in society.

"Are we to do nothing for our friends who helped send us here?" we are sometimes asked. "Shall we say to them when they come to us asking for an office, 'No, you shall not have it'?" Sir, I am willing to do much for my friends; they shall command my best endeavors. But I think we can do something vastly better for them and their children and their children's children than giving them post-offices and places in custom houses; and that is to pass laws which will secure to them good government.

Again, the objection is made that a reform of this kind would be incompatible with republican institutions. Sir, it seems to have become fashionable with some, whenever a great abuse is attacked that has worked itself into our political habits, to say that this is one of the evils inseparably connected with republican government, and that we must not touch it lest we touch republican government itself.

I, sir, have a far higher idea of republican government. I do not believe that true republican government is in any sense necessarily wedded to organic disorder and demoralization. I certainly do not indulge in the delusion that all the frailties and weaknesses of human nature can be abolished by an act of Congress; but I do not think that republican government will suffer if we repress ignorance and mercenary motives, and thus open a wider practical field for the intellectual and moral elevation of man. I am sure that republican government can endure the examination of candidates for public office before they are intrusted with public responsibilities; and that it can endure also the exclusion of those who are intellectually and morally unfit for public station.

Republican government, it seems to me, does not depend upon an official tenure of four years. I think it will not suffer by an extension of that tenure to six or eight. I maintain that republican government will rather gain than lose, and gain immensely, by a reform which takes from the machinery of the public service its partisan character, and which will remove from our political life that most dangerous agency of corruption and demoralization which consists in partisan patronage; which will restore to political activity again all the best elements of our population, and to predominance the loftiest and most patriotic feelings of the human heart. I therefore repel that cry, as a slander upon the beneficent institutions under which we live and as an insult to the good sense of the American people.

It is said also that the country cannot be governed, that parties cannot be sustained under any but the existing system. Why, sir, such assertions are almost as old as history. There never was an absolutist, there never was a devotee of despotism who did not strenuously affirm that if you limited the power of kings the whole world of morals and civilization would fall into chaos. If you had asked Walpole, he would have told you that it was impossible to govern England without a corruption fund. If you had asked the Duke of Wellington, he would have insisted upon it that the constitution of Great Britain would be ruined beyond redemption if you abolished the rotten boroughs. Why, have we become so imbecile as to declare ourselves incapable to conceive and act upon a new idea which is to do away with existing abuses? Has republicanism really arrived at its wit's end? Nay, sir, we are not permitted to stand still in this matter; we must go either forward or we shall be driven backward. We must control these evils or these evils will control us.

It has been said that a practice like the one proposed might have been proper when the Republic was young and small, when the interests it had to deal with were limited, and when the number of offices was insignificant; but that now, since the Republic has grown great, since the functions of the Government have become complicated and the number of officers immense, it is entirely out of the question. Is that so? I affirm that just the reverse is the case. When the machinery of government was simple and when the eyes of the Executive and his chiefs could be everywhere, then rotation in office might have been endurable; it might not have left these dangerous consequences behind it. But now, since the interests we have to deal with have grown so tremendous, since the number of officers has risen to the dimensions of an army, and since the machinery of government stretches its arms into every relation of life, now, sir, is it not evident that the evils springing from the demoralizing tendency of the existing system increase a thousandfold as we go on, and that a reform is imperatively commanded by this very circumstance?

On previous occasions I have alluded to the dangers threatening from the growing power of great moneyed corporations; how that power is already felt in State and national politics, and bids fair to exercise a controlling influence, dangerous even to our free institutions. Can we afford to disregard that danger?

Is it not time to consider what will become of our political life when such a power takes possession of political parties, whose very discipline is enforced by continual appeals to mercenary motives, and by practices in their very nature corrupting? Is it not time to consider what, under the influence of such a power, a government will become which is surrounded by demoralizing temptations on all sides, and which holds in its hands means of corruption penetrating all spheres of society? And considering this, in the face of such dangers, is it not high time that those temptations should be removed, that the means of corruption should be curtailed, and that a moral spirit should be infused into our body politic capable of resisting such sinister influences?

Sir, this is no mere fancy. The demand for civil service reform is not a mere cry of croakers who are constitutionally dissatisfied, or of restless innovators who want to achieve a little cheap notoriety. It springs from the patriotic anxieties of serious-thinking men, who, with profound solicitude, watch the growth of evils threatening the future of the Republic which they love. That demand cannot be laughed out of the way; it will not be put down by jests and sneers. That demand will become stronger every day; and I predict the time is not far when no political party can disregard it with impunity.

It was to me a hopeful sign when the President had a favorable word for civil service reform in his message. Why should we hesitate to act upon that suggestion? Do we not know that the older the evil grows the more difficult will be its eradication? Do we not feel that every session, every day lost is an opportunity lost? It is in this spirit that I have submitted to the Senate the plan I have explained. I repeat that I have no pride of opinion about it. On the contrary, no man would be happier than I if the wisdom of the Senate should discover and furnish one which is better. But let us at last approach this important problem with that fearlessness of thought which will enable us to be candid with ourselves, and with that determination of purpose which is necessary to arm us for the struggle with inveterate habit, prejudice, and the corrupt influences developed to such alarming power in our political life.

Senator Howard closed the debate with a speech in opposition to Senator Schurz's proposition.

I have no confidence in the civil service bill whatever. I look upon it as a mere dream of a political millennarian, who entertains the hope that the political millennium will some time or other come, when nobody will be recommended or appointed to office except such as may be entirely fit for it. Sir, we shall see no such day. Our Government is a republican-democratic government. The theory of it is that the representative shall be as near the constituent as possible. It is the constituent that is ultimately responsible for the use of the political power which

"CHILDREN CRY FOR IT"

U. S. G. "IF YOU CAN STAND IT, I CAN"

Cartoon by Thomas Nast

From the collection of the New York Public Library

he bestows upon his representative; and the nearer you keep the representative to the constituent the better, and the more perfect is our republican representative system. But if you undertake to separate the representative from the constituent, and place the former above the latter at such a height that he cannot approach to him or speak to him, you have taken the first step toward converting a representative republican government into that more simple and dignified government known as a despotism.

There are evils connected with all governments. It is undoubtedly true that, on the inauguration of every new President, Washington is filled with visitors, many of whom resort hither for the purpose of securing offices. Sir, they are part and parcel of the sovereigns of the country. They have a right to come here, and to ask the President or a secretary or the head of a bureau for an office. They have a right to express their wishes and to represent themselves as persons fit for and wanting an office. Who doubts it? Is this a crime? Is it even a fault?

The honorable Senator from Missouri spoke of the crowd of visitors who attend inaugurations here as a "motley crowd," intending, doubtless, to cast odium upon those visitors who happen to come here on that occasion for office-seeking. As a general thing, the crowd who assemble here are not a "motley crowd." The most respectable and intelligent portions of the people of the United States ordinarily compose this crowd of visitors. Is it the purpose of the honorable Senator from Missouri to debar the people of the United States from making these visits to Washington, whether they come for office or not? Does his fanciful and imaginary republican form of government exclude all contact between the people and the persons they elect to office?

Now, sir, I am opposed to this civil service bill because its direct tendency is to build up a privileged class, a sort of office-holding aristocracy in the country; and I tell you, sir, enact this bill, put it into operation, and say to the masses of the people of the United States, "You shall not be eligible to an office under the Government of the United States unless you have placed yourself within this charmed circle of persons who have been examined before a board of examiners," and your statute will not remain the period of one single Congress upon the statute book. Have we not schools in this country? Have we not institutions of learning where persons may fit themselves for the discharge of official duties? And what magic is there in a "board of examiners"? How will this board of examiners ascertain the fact better than the friends of the parties who are not members of the board as to the fitness of the applicants?

Sir, intending no disrespect to the honorable Senator from Missouri, I must say that this is one of the emptiest visions that I have ever seen, one of the most impracticable projects; and, if it were practicable, one of the most objectionable and odious. I hope that the amendment of the honorable Senator from Missouri will meet with the fate which in my judgment it so richly merits, and that it will be rejected.

The Senate took no action this session upon the bill either of Senator Trumbull or of Senator Schurz.

In the fall of 1882 the Democrats won a sweeping victory in the Congressional elections chiefly on the issues of tariff and civil service reform.

Early in the session of 1882-83 the Senate Committee on Civil Service and Retrenchment reported a bill framed by George H. Pendleton [O.], of the committee. Senator Pendleton supported the bill on December 12, 1882.

CIVIL SERVICE REFORM

SENATOR PENDLETON

I beg the Democratic party throughout the country not to mistake this result of last fall as a purely Democratic triumph. It was achieved by the Democratic party with the assistance of men of all parties upon whom their love of country sat heavier than their love of party. It was a protest made by an awakened people who were indignant at the wrongs which had been practiced upon them. It was a tentative stretching out of that same people to find instrumentalities by which those wrongs could be righted.

The people demanded economy and the Republican party gave them extravagance. The people demanded a reduction of taxation and the Republican party gave them an increase of expenditure. The people demanded purity of administration and the Republican party reveled in profligacy; and when the Republican party came to put themselves on trial before that same people the people gave them a day of calamity.

I beg that my colleagues on this side of the Chamber may remember, I desire that our party associates throughout the country shall remember, that the people will continue to us their confidence and increase it, that they will continue to us power and increase it, just in the proportion that we honestly and fairly and promptly answer to the demands which the people have made, and which were thus responded to by the Republican party. They asked revenue reform and they received none. They asked civil-service reform and they obtained none. They asked that the civil service of this Government should not either as to its men or its expenditures be made the basis upon which political contests were to be carried on, and they received for answer that that was an old fashion and a good method of political warfare.

I beg gentlemen upon this side of the Chamber to remember that, if they desire to escape the fate which now seems to be impending over their adversaries, they must avoid the example which those adversaries have set them.

Mr. President, the bill which I have the honor to advocate to-day, and which is reported by a committee of the Senate, is the commencement, in my humble judgment, of an attempt to answer one of the demands which the people have authoritatively made. I speak advisedly. It is the commencement of an attempt to organize a system which shall respond to one of the demands which the people have made.

I suppose the most enthusiastic supporter of this bill will not pretend that it is perfect. I suppose he will not pretend that upon the adoption of this bill a system will immediately spring into life which will perfect and purify the civil service of the Government. But it is the commencement of an attempt to lay the foundations of a system which, if it shall answer in any reasonable degree the expectation of those who by experience and faithful study have framed it, it will in the end correct the abuses to which I have alluded, and which have been delineated by no enemy of the Republican party or of the Administration in the report which I have read to the Senate.

The bill has for its foundation the simple and single idea that the offices of the Government are trusts for the people; that the performance of the duties of those offices is to be in the interests of the people; that there is no excuse for the being of one office or the paying of one salary except that it is in the highest practicable degree necessary for the welfare of the people; that every superfluous office-holder should be cut off; that every incompetent office-holder should be dismissed; that the employment of two where one will suffice is robbery; that salaries so large that they can submit to the extortion, the forced payment of two or ten per cent., are excessive and ought to be diminished. I am not speaking of purely voluntary contributions.

If it be true that offices are trusts for the people, then it is also true that the offices should be filled by those who can perform and discharge the duties in the best possible way. Fidelity, capacity, honesty were the tests established by Mr. Jefferson when he assumed the reins of government in 1801. He said then, and said truly, that these elements in the public offices of the Government were necessary to an honest civil service, and that an honest civil service was essential to the purity and efficiency of administration, necessary to the preservation of republican institutions.

Mr. Jefferson was right. The experience of eighty years has shown it. The man best fitted should be the man placed in office, especially if the appointment is made by the servants of the people. It is as true as truth can be that fidelity, capacity, honesty are essential elements of fitness, and that the man who is most capable and most faithful and most honest is the man who is the most fit, and he should be appointed to office.

These are truths that in their statement will be denied by none, and yet the best means of ascertaining that fitness has been a vexed question with every Administration of this Government and with every man who has been charged with the responsibility of its execution. We know what is the result. Pass examinations have been tried; professions have been tried; honest endeavors have been tried; a disposition to live faithfully up to these requirements has been tried; and yet we know, and the experience of to-day shows it, that they have all made a most lamentable failure. We do not know that so great has been the increase of the powers of this Government and the number of officers under it that no President, no Cabinet, no heads of bureaus, can by possibility know the fitness of all applicants for the subordinate offices of the Government. The result has been, and under the existing system it must always be, that the President and his Cabinet and those who are charged with the responsibility have remitted the question of fitness to their own partisan friends, and those partisan friends have in their turn decided the question of fitness in favor of their partisan friends. The Administration has need of the support of members of Congress in carrying on its work. It therefore remits to members of Congress of its own party the questions of appointment to office in the various districts. These gentlemen, in the course of their political life, naturally (I do not find fault with them for it) find themselves under strain and pressure to secure a nomination or a renomination or election, and they use the places to reward those whose friends and families and connections and aids and deputies will serve their purpose.

I put it to gentlemen, particularly to my friends on this side of the Chamber, because you have not the opportunity to exercise this patronage as much as our friends on the other side, whether or not the element of fitness enters largely into the questions of appointment in your respective districts and States? It cannot be. The necessities of the case prevent it. The pressure upon men who want to be elected prevents it. The demands that are made by partisan friends and those who have been influential and potent in securing personal triumph to gentlemen who may happen to be in such relation to the appointing power that they have the influence to secure appointment prevent it. The result is, as I have stated, that, instead of making fitness, capacity, honesty, fidelity the only or the essential qualifications for office, personal fidelity and partisan activity alone control.

When I came to the Senate I had occasion more than ever before to make some investigation upon the subject, and found, to my surprise, the extent to which the demoralization of the service had gone. I saw the civil service debauched and demoralized. I saw offices distributed to incompetent and unworthy men as a reward for the lowest of dirty partisan work. I saw many men employed to do the work of one man. I saw the money of the people shamefully wasted to keep up electioneering funds by political assessments on salaries. I saw the whole body of the public officers paid by the people organized into a compact, disciplined corps of electioneers obeying a master as if they were eating the bread of his dependence and rendering him personal service. I saw these evils were fostered, encouraged, stimulated very largely by Senators and Representatives. They had their friends who lent them a helping hand; and, regardless of the fitness of these friends, of the necessity of their employment, they insisted on the appointment and had the power which, on consideration, was found sufficient to secure it.

I believed then, and I believe now, that the existing system, which, for want of a better name, I call the "spoils system," must be killed or it will kill the Republic. I believe that it is impossible to maintain free institutions in the country upon any basis of that sort. I am no prophet of evil, I am not a pessimist in any sense of the word, but I do believe that, if the

present system goes on until 50,000,000 people shall have grown
into 100,000,000, and 140,000 officers shall have grown into
300,000, with their compensation in proportion, and all shall
depend upon the accession of one party or the other to the
presidency and to the executive functions, the presidency of
the country, if it shall last in name so long, will be put up
for sale to the highest bidder, even as in ancient Rome the imperial crown was awarded to those who could raise the largest
fund.

I beg gentlemen to believe that, whatever I may have said

UNCLE SAM'S LUNCH COUNTER

From the collection of the New York Public Library

as to the relation of parties, I do not approach the question of the form of the civil service in any mere partisan spirit. It was because I thought I saw this danger, because I believed that it was imminent, because I believed then, as I do now, that it is destructive of republicanism and will end in the downfall of republican government, that I felt it my duty to devote whatever ability I had to the consideration of this subject. It was that which induced me a year or two ago to introduce a bill which, after the best reflection, the best study, the best assistance that I coud get, I did introduce in the Senate, and which, in some degree modified, has come back from the Committe on Civil Service Reform, and is now pending before this body.

The purpose of this bill is merely to secure the application of the Jeffersonian tests—fidelity, honesty, capacity. The methods are those which are known and familiar to us all in the various avocations of life—competition, comparison.

Mr. President, it is because I believe the "spoils system" to be a great crime, because I believe it to be fraught with danger, because I believe that the highest duty of patriotism is to prevent the crime and to avoid the danger, that I advocate this or a better bill if it can be found for the improvement of the civil service.

There has been great misapprehension as to the methods and the scope of the bill. I desire the attention of the Senators while I briefly state them. The bill simply applies to the executive departments of the Government here in Washington and to those offices throughout the country—post-offices and custom houses, which employ more than fifty persons. I am told, and I am sure that I am not far out of the way, if I am not exactly accurate, that the number of such offices does not exceed thirty, or perhaps thirty-five, and that the number of persons who are employed in them, together with those in the departments here, will not exceed 10,000.

I said that this was a tentative effort; that it was intended to be an experiment, and it is because it is tentative, because it is intended to be an experiment, that the committee thought it advisable in its initial stages to limit it, as they have limited it, in the bill. The bill does not apply to elective officers, of course, nor to officers appointed by the President, by and with the advice and consent of the Senate, nor to the military, nor to the naval, nor to the judicial establishment. It applies simply now to those officials who are employed in the departments here and in the large offices of the Government elsewhere, first, because as an experiment it was thought that it gave scope enough to test its value and labor enough to employ all those who are engaged in putting it in operation until its merits shall be fairly tried and it shall commend itself either to the approval or condemnation of the American people.

There was another reason. The heads of offices and bureaus where the number of employees is small can themselves personally judge of the fitness of persons who are applicants for appointment, knowing, as they do, more or less in their narrow communities their antecedents, their habits, and their modes of life.

The bill does not touch the question of tenure of office or of removal from office. It leaves those questions exactly where the law now finds them. It concerns itself only with admission to the public service; it concerns itself only with discovering in certain proper ways or in certain ways—gentlemen may differ as to whether they are proper or not—the fitness of the persons who shall be appointed. It takes cognizance of the fact that it is impossible for the head of a department or a large office personally to know all the applicants, and therefore it provides a method by which, when a vacancy occurs by death, by resignation, by the unlimited power of removal, a suitable person may be designated to fill a vacancy. It says in effect that when a vacancy occurs in the civil service everybody who desires entrance shall have the right to apply. Everybody, humble, poor, without patronage, without influence, whatever may be his condition in life, shall have the right to go before the parties charged with an examination of his fitness and there be subjected to the test of open, regulated, fair, impartial examination.

The preamble expresses fully the philosophy of the bill. Read it carefully. It sets forth what common justice demands for the citizen and for the Government. It sets forth what the economy, efficiency, and integrity of the public service demand.

Whereas common justice requires that, so far as practicable, all citizens duly qualified shall be allowed equal opportunities, on grounds of personal fitness, for securing appointments, employment, and promotion in the subordinate civil service of the United States; and

Whereas justice to the public likewise requires that the Government shall have the largest choice among those likely to answer the requirements of the public service: and

Whereas justice, as well as economy, efficiency, and integrity in the public service, will be promoted by substituting open and uniform competitive examinations for the examinations heretofore held in pursuance of the statutes of 1853 and 1855.

I have heard it said that this system of examination proposes to present only a scholastic test; that it proposes only to give advantage to those who are college-bred, and have had the advantage in early life of superior education. The committee investigated that subject to some extent, and I have here the result in the city of New York. Says Mr. Burt:

About two-thirds of the appointees had a common school education; had not even an academic education.

Of course these examinations must be proper; of course they must be regulated upon common-sense principles; of course they must be conducted to test the fitness of the men who are to be appointed to particular offices. You have tests everywhere. To-day the law requires that there shall be a test of examination in the various departments here in Washington. They are pass examinations; they are imperfect; they are insufficient; they are not thorough. Mr. Graves himself says that the only examination in his case was that the superior in the department looked over his shoulder while he was writing and said, "I think you will pass." That was when he entered the service twenty-odd years ago.

If you have examinations why not have competitive examinations? If you have private examinations, why not have open examinations? If examinations are made in the departments by subordinates of the departments, why not have them made by responsible examiners amenable to the authority of the President under a system devised by the best intelligence that can be supplied?

I hear the system of competitive examination spoken of as if it were something extraordinary. Within the last fifteen years it has gotten to be a custom that I might almost say is universal that when a member of Congress has the right to appoint a cadet to West Point or to the Naval Academy he asks his constituents to compete for it. Formerly it was never done; it was looked on as the mere perquisite of a member of Congress.

Nor are there any aristocratic tendencies about this system, as I have heard suggested; for while it does not in any wise create an official caste it does in words and in effect open up the possibility of the public service to the poorest and the humblest and least influential in the land.

It has been said that the abandonment of the spoils system will exclude Democrats from office when the day of our victory shall come. I do not think it. On the contrary, I believe that the adoption of this policy as our party creed will hasten the day of the victory of our party and its adoption as a law will under any administration fill many offices with Democrats. I think it will bring to our aid very many men not hitherto of our political faith who believe this reform a vital question in our politics. I think it will disarm and disorganize and neutralize the trained bands of officeholders who have wrested from us at least two presidential elections.

The bill was passed by the Senate on December 27 by a vote of 38 to 5, the minority all being Democrats. The House passed the bill on January 5, 1883, by a vote of 155 to 47. Thirty-nine of the minority were Democrats. President Arthur approved the bill on January 16.

The Democratic opponents of the bill were of the Jacksonian school which held that "to the victors belong the spoils." In 1885, when Pendleton's term as Senator expired, this element in Ohio put forward as his successor General Durbin Ward, known as the "War-Horse" of the old "Moss-back" Democracy. The young reform element, known as the "Kids," endeavored to reëlect Senator Pendleton. The legislature was Democratic. Pledges were secured from the Democratic legislators in favor of one or the other of these candidates; and it seemed as if one or two votes would decide the contest, and that only at the end of a long "deadlock." However, on the first ballot, a millionaire, Henry B. Payne, was elected, to the great surprise of everybody, including the legislators themselves who voted for Payne. It was charged by responsible newspaper editors in the State, of both parties, that the election was brought about through the "influence" of the Standard Oil Company, of which Mr. Payne's son, Oliver, who had been active in his father's support, was a prominent officer. Each legislator voting for Payne had been "persuaded" to cast a "complimentary" vote for the heretofore unmentioned candidate in recognition of his "services" to the party, being kept in ignorance of the fact that a majority of the legislators had promised to do the same. After the vote quite a number of these men found excuses not to return to their constituents until the indignation of these had cooled down.

The Senate ordered an investigation into the election. The committee found in favor of allowing Mr. Payne to retain his seat. Senator Pendleton was appointed by President Cleveland Minister to Germany, which office he held until his death in 1889.

Murat Halstead, editor of the Cincinnati *Commercial,* was named by President Harrison as Minister Pendleton's successor, but owing, it is said, to his having denounced the Payne investigation as a "whitewashing" process, the Senate refused to confirm the nomination.

WHY THEY DISLIKE HIM [CLEVELAND]—HE WILL NOT PROVE HIMSELF A

CAT'S-PAW IN THE ENTERPRISE

Cartoon by Victor Gillam

From the collection of the New York Public Library

CHAPTER XI

The Speaker as "Czar"

Autocratic Rulings of Thomas B. Reed [Me.], Speaker of the House, in Disputed Election Cases—Committee on Rules Introduces a New Code—Joseph G. Cannon [Ill.] Presents Majority Report; John G. Carlisle [Ky.], and Samuel J. Randall [Pa.], Present Minority Report—Debate: In Favor, Mr. Cannon, Elijah A. Morse [Mass.], Edward P. Allen [Mich.], David B. Henderson [Ia.], Leonidas C. Houk [Tenn.], William D. Kelley [Pa.]; Opposed, Charles F. Crisp [Ga.], Roger Q. Mills [Tex.], Benton McMillin [Tenn.], William S. Holman [Ind.], William McAdoo [N. J.], Amos J. Cummings [N. Y.], Asher G. Caruth [Ky.], Benjamin F. Shively [Ind.]; the Rules Are Adopted.

IN the session of 1889-90 the Republicans of the House had a rather slender majority with which to carry through their measures, and it was therefore of partisan advantage for them to unseat a number of Democratic Representatives. This they set about doing, disclaiming, however, that there was any animus in their action other than the maintenance of purity in national elections; indeed, they produced a vast amount of evidence tending to show that gross fraud and intimidation had been perpetrated in the contested cases.

The Democrats insisted that the charges of the Republicans were trumped up for partisan purposes, and they felt justified, on this account, in resorting to "filibustering" to enable the Representatives in question to retain their seats as long as possible.

In order to prevent the filibustering, Thomas B. Reed [Me.], Speaker of the House, exerted his official powers to discriminate in favor of Republicans as against Democrats by recognizing speakers who should have the floor and by counting members who were present but not voting as present for quorum purposes—a violation of long established custom.

J. B. Reed

The Democrats were roused to extreme anger by the Speaker's course; at times they rose and advanced toward his chair with shouts of menace and denunciation, and on one or two occasions indicated their protest by leaving the hall in a body.

The newspapers of the country made much of this interesting "copy." Julius Chambers, of the New York *Times,* wrote a graphic description of the arbitrary action of Speaker Reed. The copy editor of the paper used the word "autocrat" in the headline, and the composing office complained that it was too long. The matter being brought to Mr. Chambers's attention, he substituted the word "czar." This was at once adopted by the press of the country, and as "Czar" Reed the Speaker was permanently enrolled in at least the parliamentary, if not also political, history of the country.

In order to make the procedure of Speaker Reed the established rules of the House the Committee on Rules presented a new code. The majority which made this report consisted of Messrs. Reed, William McKinley [O.], and Joseph G. Cannon [Ill.]. Ex-Speakers John G. Carlisle [Ky.] and Samuel J. Randall [Pa.] made a minority report against the new code.

On February 6, 1890, Joseph G. Cannon [Ill.] submitted to the House the majority report. On February 10 it came up for discussion.

RULES OF THE HOUSE

HOUSE OF REPRESENTATIVES, FEBRUARY 10-14, 1890

Mr. Cannon explained the difference between the new rules and the old ones.

The committee believe that there should be radical changes touching the manner and the conduct of the business of the House, and the changes recommended in this report are so radical and so proper in our opinion that some gentlemen upon the other side have denounced them as "revolutionary." Before I refer to these rules particularly I want to say that for many Congresses I have sat in my place as a member of the House and have seen, under the rules of former Houses, the Speaker, frequently without the aid of even a minority of one, but frequently with the aid of a minority of one or at least of a small minority, absolutely hold at arm's length the great majority of the Representatives of the people upon both sides of the House. So far as former Congresses are concerned, especially those of recent date, you may search the whole range of parliamentary history and nowhere in any English-speaking country will you find such instances of absolute power as that exercised by the Speakers of those Congresses, under the code of rules which then prevailed, with or without the aid of a minority of the House of Representatives.

Do you ask for instances and cases? I will give them. In the Forty-ninth and Fiftieth Congresses the Senate of the United States passed what was known as the Blair educational bill. That bill came to this House, was referred to a committee, and there, under the rules of the House, at the will of the Speaker, although a great majority of the House upon both sides desired to consider it, it slept the sleep of death in each of those Congresses, and the majority was, as I have said, held at arm's length by the will of the Speaker. Do you want other instances? Political campaigns were made in North Carolina and in Virginia in which Democratic Representatives excused themselves for not repealing the internal tax upon tobacco by saying that the Speaker of the Forty-ninth Congress and of the Fiftieth Congress, under the rules of the House, would not allow the consideration of a bill for that purpose, and that, too, although the great majority of the members of the House desired its consideration. Do you want other instances? Within the recollection of every member of the last Congress, one man, the gentleman from Iowa [James B. Weaver], stood for three days against 324 Representatives here and said to them, ''You shall not consider any matter of legislation unless you first agree with me that the Oklahoma bill shall be considered.''

What was the result of that exercise of the Speaker's power? The result was that the business of sixty millions of people piled up on the calendars, and not more than 5 per cent. of it could receive consideration, and, in fact, under former codes of rules, almost as much time was given to obstruction by the minority as was given to the consideration of the business of sixty millions of people. The consequence was that there came to us, from right-thinking members of the last Congress and of this, in their cooler moments, and from conservative public sentiment throughout the country, a demand that we should reverse the engine and should so construct a code of rules as to enable a majority of the representatives of the people, in the shortest possible time consistent with fair debate and consideration, to register the will of the people in the shape of law.

The Committee on Rules have attempted to do this in the code which they have reported here. And the material matters about which there will be difference of opinion are, I take it, first, the provision which cuts up dilatory motions by the roots; second, the provision under which gentlemen present in the House of Representatives to prevent legislation shall (if they be in fact present) be counted as part of the quorum under the Constitution to aid legislation; third, the provision of the rules by which 100 shall constitute a quorum in the Committee of the Whole; and, fourth, the daily order of business.

Now, first, as to dilatory motions, I desire to read the report of the committee touching clause 10 of Rule XVI, which provides—

No dilatory motion shall be entertained by the Speaker.

The report of the committee on this point is terse and direct, and covers the ground upon which this rule is recommended, and is as follows:

This clause is merely declaratory of parliamentary law. There are no words which can be framed which will limit members to the proper use of proper motions. Any motion the most conducive to progress in the public business or the most salutary for the comfort and convenience of members may be used for purposes of unjust and oppressive delay. The majority may be kept in session for a long time against reason and good sense, sometimes at the whim of a single member, and sometimes for a still longer period, at the will of one-fifth who are misusing the provision of the Constitution for yeas and nays, by the aid of simple motions proper in themselves, but which are improperly used.

In the early days such prostitution of legitimate motions caused by anger, wilfulness, and party zeal was not so much as named among legislators. To-day the abuse has grown to such proportions that the parliamentary law which governs American assemblies has found it necessary to keep pace with the evil, and to enable the majority, by the intervention of the presiding officer, to meet, by extraordinary means, the extraordinary abuse of power on the part, sometimes, of a very few members. Why should an assembly be kept from its work by motions made only to delay and to weary, even if the original design of the motion was salutary and sensible? Why should one-fifth, even, be entitled to waste a half hour of themselves and of four other fifths by a motion to adjourn, when the majority manifestly do not want to adjourn?

If the suggestion should be made that great power is here conferred, the answer is that as the approval of the House is the very breath in the nostrils of the Speaker, and as no body on earth is so jealous of its liberties and so impatient of control, we may be quite sure that no arbitrary interruption will take place, and, indeed, no interruption at all, until not only such misuse of proper motions is made clearly evident to the world, but also such action has taken place on the part of the House as will assure the Speaker of the support of the body whose wishes are his law. So that in the end it is a power exercised by the House through its properly constituted officer.

Now, motions made in this House if used to forward legislation or for legitimate purposes are perfectly proper; but the moment motions proper in themselves, framed to assist the House in shaping legislation, are used not for the purpose of consideration, but by a minority of one or more to hold the majority at bay and say that legislation shall not be had, that moment they are perverted from the legitimate use for which they are made, they become dilatory, and would fall within the clause of this general rule.

There is no legislative body on this earth so jealous of its privileges and power as the House of Representatives. The Speaker is a member, as you and I are. We made him, and a majority of this House can unmake him at any time, because it is the privilege of the House, and not of the Speaker. So no Speaker would dare to refuse to entertain a motion until it becomes patent to all the House that it is a dilatory motion, and then he ought to refuse to entertain it.

You have come to the point where you must lodge this power with the Speaker subject to the revision of the House or the Speaker and a majority of four-fifths of the House must abdicate power, one and all, and let a minority of one or of a handful of members run the House and the country.

Gentlemen say this is "tyrannical." I deny it. But if it be tyrannical, then the "tyranny" is exercised by the Speaker sustained by the majority of the House; and on the other hand the tyrannical minority that has controlled heretofore fails to control now. If I must choose between the "tyranny" of a constitutional majority, responsible to the people, or the "tyranny" of an irresponsible minority of one, I will stand by the Constitution and our form of government, and so act as to let the majority rule.

Now, Mr. Speaker, I pass on to discuss clause 3 of Rule XV in the proposed code. It is as follows:

3. On the demand of any member, or at the suggestion of the Speaker, before the second roll-call is entered upon, the names of members [sufficient to make a quorum] in the hall of the House who do not vote shall be noted by the clerk and recorded in the Journal, and reported to the Speaker with the names of the members voting, and be counted and announced in determining the presence of a quorum to do business.

I call attention to the general parliamentary law, to adjudications of courts, both State and national, and the practice of general legislative assemblies in the several States in harmony with this rule.

Here the speaker cited a number of cases.

The doctrine is well established that "those who are present and who help to make up a quorum are expected to vote on any question, and their presence alone is sufficient, whether they actually vote or not." If eighteen are present and nine vote, all in the affirmative, the measure is carried; the refusal of the other nine to vote being construed as a vote in the affirmative, so far as any construction is necessary. The highest parliamentary authority is explicit and uniform to the same point. In discussing this question a few days ago in the House, I read from "Principles of Procedure in Deliberative Bodies," by Hon. George Glover Crocker, president of the Massachusetts senate, a statement of the well-established principle touching this matter.

I state now, Mr. Speaker, not *in extenso*, that the universal practice under English and American parliamentary law and the practice of nearly all parliamentary assemblies except this, heretofore, has been to hold under law or constitution similar to ours that a majority shall constitute a quorum to do business; that the presence of that quorum is sufficient, although less than a quorum votes.

The gentleman from Virginia [Charles T. O'Ferrall], who seems to me at times to rise up to leadership, closed his speech a few days ago with a whole page of sentences like this:

Let the finger of autocratic power in this House direct the way to those who will follow it. Let the voice of autocratic power sound through these halls and command those who may obey it; but as for me and my people—

He is sweet on *my people*—

but as for me and my people I protest against this usurpation, against this outrage, against this violation of the sacred rights of the weak, against this cruel and wicked and unconstitutional violation of the rights of the minority. [Applause on the Democratic side.]

I say to the gentleman from Virginia that for years and years the Democratic House of Representatives in the State of Virginia has counted a quorum which was present and did not vote, and, where the yeas and nays were not called, has counted and voted them, too, in the negative. And yet my friend from Virginia gets up here on this floor and gives notice that in these, the last days of this unheard-of proposition, when liberty is tottering upon her throne, when war, pestilence, and famine are abroad, the gentleman from Virginia, with flaming eye, uplifted arm, and flowing hair, will lead the column and defend to the last the liberties of the country as the brave three hundred defended the Pass of Thermopylæ. [Laughter.]

Now, gentlemen, we have counted a quorum in this House and entered their names on the Journal when they were present, through the Speaker, and the action of the Speaker has been ratified time and time again by the House; and in placing this rule in the code we do it as a matter of convenience, so that the clerk may perform that duty under the eye of the Speaker and hand the names when the vote is handed to the Speaker. If gentlemen on that side want to go to the country upon the principle contained in this rule, we are ready to go and let the people choose between us. But as sure as we remain here and remain in a majority during this Congress, after due consideration and debate, a majority of the House of Representatives in the Fifty-first Congress will perform the function that the Constitution and the people make it their duty to perform.

Now, the gentleman from Georgia [Henry G. Turner] and his worthy colleague from Georgia [Charles F. Crisp], when this question was under consideration a few days ago, had much to say about czarism and tyranny. What! Tyranny to count gentlemen present under the Constitution when they were present? Oh! that will break up the country! Let us see about that.

Take the district of the gentleman from Georgia [Mr. Crisp]. Now, the gentleman has probably 30,000 votes in his district, and yet only 1,700 of those 30,000 went to the polls and chose him as a Representative of 30,000 voters in this House. Now, then, I will ask the gentleman if he indorses the principle that will allow 28,300 electors to silently sit by in his district and protest against any election, while 1,704 vote for and elect him. Why, if you carry this principle to a legitimate conclusion, that it requires a vote one way or the other (a majority of a quorum), then by analogy no man is justly entitled to a seat in this House unless a majority of the voters in his district did vote.

MR. CRISP.—A word merely in answer to my friend from Illinois in regard to Representatives here and business: The Constitution of the United States provides that it shall require a majority of the Representatives here to do business; but there is no such provision as to a popular election before the people.

MR. CANNON.—My friend, we talk about the Constitution. In that same Constitution I find rights given to every citizen of the United States. I will not make further comment. I only said by analogy, and upon correct principle, that the logic which requires a majority of all this House to vote in addition to being present would require a majority of the electors in a congressional district to vote.

BENTON McMILLIN [Tenn.].—Does not my friend know that, on the contrary, the Constitution and laws which govern a popular election provide specifically that the candidate getting the highest number of votes, whether that be a majority or a mere plurality, shall be entitled to the certificate?

MR. CANNON.—I will answer frankly, yes; and in answering I will state further that in every State in this Union with constitutions similar to the Constitution of the United States the law is the same, as interpreted by the Supreme Court of the United States, which provides that, a quorum being present, a majority of those that vote legislate; and that law is as great and high as the law to which the gentleman refers. I was speaking only by way of illustration of the case of the gentleman from Georgia to show that if a correct principle would require non-action in one case it would in the other.

There is not an honest laboring man, in my opinion, there is not a man of culture throughout the length and breadth of this country, but knows in his heart, when free from passion or partisan bias, that our construction of the Constitution is right and that it is absolutely necessary to be asserted and defended or the Republic ceases to be a government of the majority and becomes a government of a minority, a mere aristocracy. I will never stand here when this question is presented and a precedent is to be made helping to do that thing. If the people want to revolutionize our form of government, let them do it after they directly have discussed and taken action as the Constitution provides.

Now, sir, I come to speak of another rule proposed. Clause 2 of Rule XXII provides in substance that a quorum in the Committee of the Whole shall consist of 100 members.

The reasons for making the quorum 100 in the Committee of the Whole are so tersely and clearly given in the report of the Committee on Rules that I read the same, as follows:

The Constitution provides, article I, section 5, clause 1, that "a majority of each House shall constitute a quorum."

Neither House of Congress has ever had a rule fixing the number of a quorum in the Committee of the Whole, but from the First Congress to the present the practice has been to require the same number as in the House. The quorum of the House of Commons (consisting of 670 members) is 40. The Committee of the Whole, like a standing or select committee, has merely advisory powers and jurisdiction. Its action concludes nothing, and must be reported to the House, which approves or rejects, as it pleases. The same principle is true with respect to a quorum of standing and select committees. The House has never adopted a rule on this subject, and it has been a common practice for such committee, in arranging its days of meeting, order of business, etc., to fix the number of its quorum, which is less than a majority of its whole number. So far, therefore, as the constitutional or legal question is concerned, it has never been denied or questioned that it was entirely competent for the House to select any number it might please as a quorum of the Committee of the Whole. The only question involved is one purely of legislative expediency and propriety.

The reason that the issue has never heretofore been presented is due entirely to the fact that until recent years members have not sat in their seats in the House and refused to vote when their names were called.

The House, for convenience, commits temporarily its jurisdiction to standing and select committees. It never parts with or permanently surrenders it. That jurisdiction so committed is returned to the House with the bill or proposition, and is again referred by the House for convenience to a Committee of the Whole. That the action of that committee is purely preliminary and advisory is demonstrated by the facts that no proposition pending therein can be laid upon the table, that the previous question can not be ordered therein, that a motion to reconsider can not be made, that the yeas and nays can not be taken, and, finally, that it can not adjourn.

The action of the Committee of the Whole being, therefore, purely advisory and concluding nothing, it is clear that this provision can not be in contravention of the Constitution—which is silent on the subject—and is in harmony with the well-recognized principles and practice of the English Parliament, the original sources of our parliamentary rules and practice and of modern constitutional governments.

I pause merely long enough to say that many men have heretofore advocated this. That great parliamentarian, once a member of this House and afterward Vice-President, noted everywhere for his intelligence and his conservatism—William A. Wheeler—favored a provision similar to this. It was favored by many great commoners from time to time. Mr. Garfield introduced a resolution like this. The gentleman from Iowa, Mr. Kasson, and the gentleman from Kentucky [Mr. McCreary] and another gentleman from Kentucky, not in this Congress, Mr. Willis, and other gentlemen from time to time have advocated this provision.

After sixteen years of service in this cause, I am satisfied that at the sessions of the Committee of the Whole there are not present one-half of the time one hundred members. I have stood by this desk hour after hour in charge of appropriation and other bills, begging gentlemen not to make the point of "no quorum." I have time and again accepted amendments and bought the poor privilege of going on with the consideration of bills by accepting amendments upon condition that gentlemen would abstain from making the point of "no quorum." What does the Committee of the Whole do? It considers matters committed to it by the House, just as the Appropriations Committee or as the Ways and Means Committee considers matters committed to it. The Committee of the Whole consists of all the members of the House, if they want to be present, as they ought to be, and after that committee considers the business then it reports it back with a recommendation, and then, for the first time, the House acts and accepts or rejects the recommendation of the Committee of the Whole.

ROGER Q. MILLS [Tex.].—The code of rules which the majority of the committee have reported to the House for its adoption is a new departure in parliamentary law. It is a proposition to reverse the legislative engine and to run back on the track upon which we have been running forward for a whole century. It is a code based upon a newly discovered idea, that in this country minorities have no rights, and that majorities are all-powerful, that they speak by inspiration, that their utterances are infallible and their actions impeccable. It is the resurrection of the old, exploded idea of centuries ago that the king is the divinely appointed agent of the Almighty, and of course "the king can do no wrong."

It is not, Mr. Speaker, the theory upon which our fathers built this great temple of free government. It is not the theory upon which our Government has been administered for a century. The great object of our Government, as proclaimed in the Declaration of Independence, is to secure the inalienable rights of the citizen.

Upon this broad declaration has been erected the great family of American constitutions—this, the Federal Constitution, the central one of the whole, and those of the States, conforming to this great principle, that our governments are instituted to secure the rights of the citizen.

How are these rights to be secured? Certainly not by subjecting them all to the caprice and whim of a majority. Oh, no; our fathers never meant to do anything of that sort. Why, sir, they knew that power when vested either in a million of people or in one man, without any limit upon its exercise, is a tyrant. Hence our Government is a government of checks and balances. It is a government of limitations, delegations, and prohibitions.

Within the jurisdiction of the majority the majority is supreme. When it speaks within its rightful limits there is no power beyond it; there is no appeal from its decision; its judgment is final and conclusive.

Yes, Mr. Speaker, majorities within their limits as defined by the Constitution are supreme. But there are some powers that our fathers thought it dangerous for majorities to have, and they said that majorities should not have them. They put majorities under the ban of suspicion. They surrounded them with limitations. They directed the vigilant and watchful eye of the citizen on all their movements. A majority can raise and support an army, but it cannot raise and support a church. It can create a court, but it cannot create an establishment of religion. In that the minority is superior to the majority.

A majority can create a navy, but it cannot create a military commission to try any citizen in time of peace. A majority can close our ports, but it cannot close our mouths. Free speech is one of the rights which are safely secured within the bolts and bars of the Constitution; it is far beyond the reach of the strong arm of the majority. A majority may suppress an insurrection, but it cannot suppress the freedom of the press. The press, though it be in a small minority, is still more powerful than the majority. A majority may prevent the assembling of a hostile army, but it cannot prevent the peaceable assembly of the people to petition the Government for a redress of their grievances. A majority may make a rule or a law, but it cannot suspend the habeas corpus unless in time of war, when the public safety is endangered. A majority can levy taxes on imports, but it cannot levy taxes on exports. A minority of a thousand or of ten thousand can send out of the country and all over the world what they please, and a majority of sixty millions cannot prevent it. A majority cannot pass bills of attainder or *ex post facto* laws.

Why is this? Among the people from whom we came majorities did all these things. In England the Parliament is the seat of supreme power. It can do what it wills, and no minority can obstruct or prevent it. It can crown and uncrown the king at pleasure. It can make and unmake the British constitution. It has not only passed bills of attainder and *ex post facto* laws, but it has declared what is orthodoxy and prescribed the religious belief of the people. It has butchered the people, broken them on wheels, burned them at stakes, and dyed the land with English blood to compel the minority to think, speak, feel, and act as the majority wished them to do.

Unfortunately for England and for humanity she had no written constitution as our fathers gave to us to protect us; yes, to "secure" us in the enjoyment of the inalienable rights with which we were endowed by the Creator. To avoid these great crimes for which unrestricted majorities in the English Parliament are responsible, our fathers established this Government to secure—remember the word "secure"—to themselves and their posterity the rights with which nature and nature's God endowed them. They said in many things majorities should be supreme and in many others that minorities should be supreme. In all matters of religion the minority is absolutely supreme over themselves and absolutely beyond the reach of political government as long as they do no injury to others.

We see again in the Constitution an interdiction against the power of the majority over the personal right of the citizen. It is prohibited from making any law to try him for an infamous crime except on the indictment of a grand jury. It cannot deprive him of trial by jury. It cannot deny him the compulsory power of the Government to bring his witnesses to testify in his behalf. It cannot deny him the right to be confronted with his accusers face to face. In all these cases the power of the majority is declared by the Constitution to be dangerous to the liberty of the citizen. Here the citizen, though the humblest in the land, can sit within the fortress of the Constitution, and, sheltered by its power, bid defiance to the will of legislative majorities.

But, Mr. Speaker, it is not only in our national Constitution we see these limitations thrown around majorities. It is so in every State constitution in the Union. What is it for? It is to protect the minority; that is what it is for. It is a check to the madness of the majority, or its caprice, or its wantonness, to use the word employed by Mr. Jefferson. It is to take away from it that power which all history shows it has so grossly abused.

The Constitution of the United States prescribes the rules for the government of the great body of the people of the United States. The constitution of each State prescribes the rules for the government of the people of each State. The Constitution of the United States confers the powers on this House to prescribe the rules for its government.

The rules prescribed under the power conferred by the Constitution of the United States are for the protection of the minority, and they have done it from the foundation of the Government. That is one of the objects of making rules. It is not alone to facilitate business. Of course rules are intended to se-

IX—23

cure the orderly procedure of the business of this body, but at the same time they are intended to cause the House to halt, to pause, to reflect, and in some instances, where it may become necessary, to go back and inquire of the sober second thought of the people again. It is on the sober second thought of the people our Government rests. The people themselves may become mad. They may become wanton with power, and the very security of our free institution rests on the fact that the sober second thought, in the language of one of our illustrious forefathers, will bring them back to a sense of their duty to their fellow citizens and themselves, and thus preserve the blessings of free government for themselves and their posterity.

My friend on the other side felicitates himself upon the wonderful triumph that he and his party gained in the struggle of the last six or eight days, and said that a minority has been setting itself up against the will of the majority, and that the majority of the House on that side had said that they would unseat J. M. Jackson, of West Virginia, and they did unseat him, that they could do it, and they would do it, and they did do it, and he congratulates himself and the majority of the House upon the splendid victory achieved in the struggle thus ended.

Mr. Speaker, what we have done on this side of the House was simply to call the attention of the people of the United States to the fact that the majority in this House had broken the bounds assigned to it by the Constitution of the United States, and that it was ravening like a wolf in the fold at night, that it was coming into the House in defiance of the constitutional mandate to make rules for the government of its procedure, rules for the protection of the minority as well as rules for the expression of the will of the majority in the prosecution of the business before the House.

Mr. Speaker, we have appealed to the sober second thought of the people with the claim that the majority shall first make rules for the conduct of the business of the House, and, having done that, then try the case presented upon its merits. If, in that event, the contestant was entitled to his seat, award it to him; but if, on the other hand, the contestee was admitted to have the right to the seat, let him hold it. But instead of that they said they intended to empty the seat, that they had the power and the manhood to do it, and that they would do it. And so, Mr. Speaker, they did. But I once heard of a story that is applicable here, a story of a little bull that had the hardihood to get in front of a locomotive running at sixty miles an hour and boldly challenged its advance. He did not stay very long, it is true. After the train passed there was nothing left of the belligerent little bull but his horns and hoofs; and some one standing by and watching the result of the contest said, "Little fellow, I admire your courage, but damn your judgment." [Laughter.]

I call the attention of the House to the words of Mr. Jefferson in his manual of parliamentary law. This manual is the first code of procedure adopted by Congress, and from the beginning it has been the general parliamentary law of the House until rules are adopted by each succeeding House. This code was prepared by Mr. Jefferson when, as Vice-President, he was presiding over the Senate. That body made some rules, but they referred to the decision of their presiding officer without debate or appeal all questions of order arising under their own rules or where their rules had made no provision. The tribute to his ability and impartiality was something like that paid by our friends on the other side to the ex-Speaker [John G. Carlisle], who sits by my side. Such a manifestation of the esteem of a legislative body was a high compliment, and one which was highly appreciated both by Mr. Jefferson and Mr. Carlisle. In seeking for information to enable him to prepare his manual where did he go? He had to go somewhere. But he did not go to the State legislatures nor to the Continental Congress. Both of these had obtained their information from the British Parliament. It was then the greatest legislative assembly in Christendom.

Here was the correct source of parliamentary law; here was the great body which for five hundred years had been in existence. It is true it had been guilty of the grossest excesses in its early history; it had beheaded kings and filled the land with the blood of their subjects; but it was at that time the fountain of parliamentary law. It had been presided over by a long line of the ablest men who ever presided over any legislative assembly in the world. And this was the body to which Mr. Jefferson went to ascertain what was the general parliamentary law. Mr. Jefferson says:

Mr. Onslow, the ablest among the speakers of the House of Commons, used to say it was a maxim he had often heard when he was a young man, from old and experienced members, that "nothing tended more to throw power into the hands of the administration and those who acted with the majority of the House of Commons than a neglect of or departure from the rules of proceedings—

The very thing you gentlemen have been doing for two months—

that these forms, as instituted by our ancestors, operated as a check and control on the actions of the majority, and that they were in many instances a shelter and protection to the minority against the attempts of power.''

That is what Speaker Onslow says. What does Mr. Jefferson say in regard to that?

So far the maxim is certainly true, and is founded in good sense, that, as it is always in the power of the majority, by their numbers, to stop any improper measure proposed on the part of their opponents, the only weapons by which the minority can defend themselves against similar attempts from those in power are the forms and rules of proceeding which have been adopted as they were found necessary, from time to time, and are become the law of the House, by a strict adherence to which the weaker party can only be protected from those irregularities and abuses which these forms were intended to check and which the wantonness of power is but too often apt to suggest to large and successful majorities.

This, Mr. Speaker, is what we have been contending for. We have been contending for rules—rules which provide the mode of procedure in the orderly dispatch of the business of the House, rules which have been provided for the protection and preservation of the rights of the minority, whether that minority be 1 or 160. We have asked for a code like that of our fathers. We have asked for the old institutions of our fathers. We have stood here and remonstrated with the majority on that side of the House against sweeping that code out of existence, a code which we have had for a century, a code under which our nation has grown from 3,000,000 to 65,000,000 of people, under which we have grown to be the most prosperous, the most powerful, and most intelligent people on the earth.

But it is now proposed to tear down all the barriers interposed by our fathers for the protection of the rights of the citizen and permit the majority to make rules to pass bills in violation of the Constitution, to pass them practically without opposition, without consideration, without mature deliberation.

Pass these rules and there remains no limitation on the power of the majority. Pass the rules as you have reported them, tear down the barriers, and enthrone arbitrary power.

It is true that a little filibustering has occasionally occurred. But are all these great barriers that were intended for the preservation of the inalienable rights of the citizens to be removed? Are the obstructions interposed for the protection of the treasury to be removed out of the way? Our friends are so alarmed at the scandal of filibustering that they forget the part they have played in its performance. They forget who introduced it into congressional legislation.

When did it start here and who started it? Mr. Speaker, it is the legitimate offspring of the Republican party. The two motions which your committee have reported to eliminate from our rules—the motion to adjourn and the motion to fix a day to which the House shall adjourn—have been in our code for a hundred years. They came from the British Parliament. They are in Jefferson's Manual. They have been adopted by the House of Representatives and the Senate, and are hoary with age; and yet these two motions were never used to obstruct legislation until 1854, when a Republican minority in the House of Representatives alternated them 128 times to prevent the passage of the Kansas-Nebraska bill. But it did not ruin the country by their obstruction; they appealed from the House to the public judgment whether that bill ought to pass. They called upon the legislative assembly to pause, to deliberate, to re-examine again while they made an appeal to the sober second thought of the people.

There is no reason why these motions should be used for obstructing legislation. The fact is they are never used except on most extraordinary occasions and when some extraordinary measure is being proposed to be enacted into law. And when that occurs it is not an unmixed evil to delay the legislation till the public mind can be consulted and the public judgment had.

It is sometimes used to prevent one man from getting into Congress or to prevent another from being turned out; but in all these cases where it has been used in my experience (and I am one of the oldest members of the House; only a few others have been here longer than I have, and only three or four as long as I have) I have never seen filibustering tactics resorted to in the House except when one side or the other thought the majority was being guilty of a flagrant wrong.

The Speaker, elsewhere, has referred to the fact that filibustering was never known in election contests before 1882. But there had never been any occasion for it before that time. The Republicans had control of the Government in all its branches prior to that time and since 1861. They had created returning boards for the Southern States that certified their candidates into the House, whether they were elected or not. The minority could not filibuster against their admission when they were already in.

My predecessor was elected to the Forty-second Congress by five or six thousand majority, but the certificate was given to

his opponent and he took the seat the voters had given to another. When my friend from Illinois [Mr. Cannon] and myself came into the Forty-third Congress, two Republican members sat here through the whole term of two long years, until the
last night of that term, and after the sun had gone down and
it was dark and the lamps were lighted the Republican Committee on Elections called up and had adopted their unanimous report that neither one of them had been elected. That was the
action of a majority that we are now told can do no wrong.
We have been told by the Speaker in another place that there
were scandals in filibustering in 1882. Was there no scandal
in this?

In 1882, when parliamentary obstruction was first resorted to
in election cases, the Republicans again had control of the
House; but the returning boards had passed into history and
the Representatives elected by the people were given the certificates of their election, and on those certificates they had been admitted to the House, and the majority again tried, though by a
different method, to disfranchise the constituencies by unseating
the elected members and seating those not elected, and that pro-
voked the minority to use parliamentary tactics to defend
the right of electors to choose their own Representatives.

In 1882 a Republican Congress turned out one Democratic
member who had a majority of 8,036 votes, another who had a
majority of 5,272 votes, and reported in favor of turning out
another who had a majority of 8,468 votes, and the report would
have been adopted, but the Congress expired before the report
could be adopted and the defeated contestant sworn in. It was
to prevent these flagrant wrongs that filibustering first made its
appearance in election cases.

But to come down to more recent times. In the last House
of Representatives we saw the perpetration of this same ''scandal'' by the Republican minority. The very mention of filibustering nauseates their stomachs now, but it was a labor of love
to them then. They are now wrestling with penitential agonies
over our sins, but they feel no compunctious visitations of conscience over their own. Who was it that from day to day refused to permit the House to consider the report of the committee in the contested election case of Sullivan against Felton?
Who was it that resorted to dilatory motions every time the committee called up that case? Who was it that prevented the
House till the last moment of the term from acting on that report? It was the very gentlemen who are now denouncing dilatory motions as scandalous. And, Mr. Speaker, you and the ma-

jority on the floor to-day, who, after the elections in the fall of 1888 had given you this House, began your crusade against the rules because they permitted dilatory motions, yet in February and March of 1889 were using dilatory motions to keep in one of your members and are now condemning dilatory motions, to enable you to unseat our members in the present House.

There is another feature of the proposed code to which I want to call the attention of the House and the country. It is proposed to invest the Speaker with power to contradict the record provided by the Constitution. The Constitution declares that in a certain contingency a recorded vote shall be had and at all times a majority shall be required to constitute a quorum. It is now proposed that the Speaker may add to, vary, or contradict that record, and that against the uniform ruling of all the Speakers that have ever presided over the House from the beginning of the Government. The record of this House is like the record of a court, it imports absolute verity. No man can attack the record of a court in a collateral inquiry. No man can say its records are not true or that the record does not contain all the facts, and supplement it by the statement of a bystander.

The judge cannot do it, when it is collaterally called in question. The clerk cannot do it, and no party can. The record is conclusive. The Constitution has provided that a record of the yeas and nays shall be made in certain cases, and the record shall decide whether a quorum has voted and which side has the majority. In the face of this plain provision, the Speaker decides, and the majority sustain him, that he can look out over the assembly and write down as present anybody that he pleases, whether he is present or not. He is to be the judge, not the record, not even the House. The record is made by the answer of the member under the supervision of the whole body, taken down by the clerk, read to the House, vouched for as accurate and then approved. But all this is abrogated and the voice of one man is substituted in its stead, and he is authorized to make the Journal say what he wants it to say, whether that be correct or not.

If it were in the power of the House to confer this authority it should not be conferred on any man. What we contend for is this unbroken line of decision by all the Speakers of the House. The rule proposed is condemned by the public opinion of the country. Instead of expediting legislation, the country is erecting checks and barriers against it in every direction. In all the later constitutions adopted by the States it is declared in unequivocal and unmistakable terms that bills shall be passed only by an affirmative vote of the majority of all members elected to the legislature, and the vote taken by yeas and nays.

Now, Mr. Speaker, why has the change been made? Here is the evidence of a great reform in public sentiment. We never see a change of this kind without there has been a mischief which the law is intended to remedy. In the interpretation of a law a court will always look to the old law, the mischief, and the remedy.

The old law was that State legislatures had railroaded legislation to the public injury. The old law had permitted the perpetration of numerous and great wrongs, and the old law was changed to prevent the continuance of that evil, and the constitutions of these States which have been adopted in recent years have adopted a check on railroading legislation. They have, for the protection of the people and in the interest of honest and wise legislation, required a yea-and-nay vote and the affirmative vote of a majority of all members elected to pass a bill.

This has been the rule in Congress, where the yea-and-nay vote is called, without interruption, from the beginning, and now, when the public have become disgusted with the wrongs occurring in State legislatures and have changed State constitutions to make representative bodies conform to the rule held in Congress, we are abandoning the rule of our fathers and taking up the discarded and condemned code of the older State legislatures, this very condemned and reprobated rule which Speaker James G. Blaine said had led to the greatest legislative frauds ever committed.

Mr. Coburn, of Indiana, in the Forty-third Congress, wanted the majority to do the very thing that the gentleman from Illinois [Mr. Cannon] wants them to do now. He wanted the majority to rule, and rule right or wrong. He wanted them to exhibit "their manhood" and show what they could do, and he pointed out substantially the same way to the Speaker now pointed out by the Speaker and his Committee on Rules. But what said Speaker Blaine, one of the most distinguished parliamentarians now living? He said:

> There can be no record like that of the yeas and nays, and from that there is no appeal. The moment you clothe your Speaker with power to go behind your roll-call and assume that there is a quorum in the hall, why, gentlemen, you stand on the very brink of a volcano.
>
> The very principle enunciated by the gentleman from Indiana has been the foundation probably for the greatest legislative frauds ever committed. Where a quorum in the judgment of the Chair has been declared to be present in the House against the result of a roll-call, these proceedings in the different legislatures have brought scandal on their names.

I am no prophet, nor am I a prophet's son, but I venture to predict that if you adopt the old, reprobated, and discarded rules that have produced frauds and scandals in State legislation you will see the same cause producing the same effect in national legislation. "An evil tree cannot bring forth good fruit." Break down the barriers, silence the voice of the minority, crush out all opposition, expedite and accelerate the speed of all bills as they move through the House, and you will wish before the Fifty-first Congress expires that you had permitted the minority to challenge your measures, to put you on guard, and cause you to give more thought and more careful examination to all proposed legislation.

You will wish you had kept the House abreast of the public opinion of the day. You will wish, instead of going to bad precedents in State legislatures, you had kept in the beaten path of congressional precedents. Even before the adoption of rules the general parliamentary law was well established that we should keep in the line marked out by the rules of preceding Houses. Mr. Blaine, on this point, said in the Senate, in the Forty-sixth Congress:

What has been held by the gentlemen who have occupied the [Speaker's] chair has been that, in the absence of an existing House adopting rules, instead of falling back on what has been loosely termed general parliamentary law—and I never knew any yet who was able to determine what that was—the House fell back on the rules of the nearest analogous body pending any discussion on new rules, and the nearest analogous body was the preceding House. That has been uniformly held by persons holding the chair of the House.

Now, if that has been uniformly held by all the Speakers of the House from Speaker Muhlenberg to Speaker Carlisle, if it had been the unbroken current of decision of the greatest parliamentary body on earth, why did Speaker Reed go to Tennessee to inquire what was general parliamentary law?

BENTON McMILLIN [Tenn.].—And to a decision already overruled.

MR. MILLS.—And to a decision twice overruled, as I am informed by the public press. He could have found decisions to the contrary in the other States. He could have found a decision in the State of Illinois, made by a Republican speaker, that he could not go behind a roll call.

But that was not the decision the Speaker wanted. He had determined to silence the minority. He had determined that Democrats should be railroaded out of the House. He had determined that certain measures should be expedited through the House. He was not looking for correct decisions. He was looking for something to throw in the faces of the minority when they complained of his usurpation. He was hunting for something, for anything, to help him in the position he had resolved to take. Now, if the Speaker of the House can make the Journal as he pleases, if he can make the quorum as he says he can and as he has done, why did he not continue to make the quorum on the vote to vacate Jackson's seat?

There has not been a constitutional quorum in the House since the day of its organization last December till the vote was taken on unseating Mr. Jackson and seating Mr. Smith. Yet on that vote the Speaker was careful to vote himself and the majority were careful to have the constitutional quorum present. Why was this? It was a confession that the decision of the Speaker in counting a quorum outside of the record could not stand a judicial examination. On that question Mr. Jackson could have gone to the courts; on the other rulings he could not.

You delayed the vote until you brought here your sick men, in order to make a constitutional quorum of your own number. Why, sir, that was a confession that your decision was wrong. Having confessed the wrong, as you have done by your vote, you ought to have renounced and abandoned it and taken up the right. But, instead of that, you are going on again in the same course where we have no way to review your decision, where the question cannot be taken to the courts. When the occasion arises again when you want to unseat some member who has been duly elected, you will again take care that the decision shall not be in such a shape as to be taken to the courts; you will have here your 166 members. You will not risk an appeal to the courts of the country in such a way as to secure a review of the decision of the Speaker.

Mr. Speaker, my friend from Illinois [Mr. Cannon] says that he is in favor of removing all impediments out of the way; that it is the policy of his party to "expedite legislation," to expedite the execution of the will of the majority, to railroad your measures through the House. That, Mr. Speaker, is not in accordance with the views of our fathers. If you will look at your constitutions you will see in every line and between the lines delay, debate, consider, pause. Why do the constitutions of nearly all the States require a bill to be read on three several days? That is the provision in nearly all the States. In some of them the constitution refuses to let a bill be passed at all by unanimous consent until it has been read on three several days. That is not expedition; that is not railroading.

The people want deliberation and calm investigation of all questions. They do not want a great library of laws passed. Our fathers built this Government upon the theory that the people who are least governed are best governed; that the fewer the laws the better; that the larger the amount of liberty allowed to the citizen the better it is for him. They believed the Creator knew best how man should be governed. He knew better than any man can know how the happiness of the human race could be best promoted. Hence they thought that laws to protect people in the enjoyment of life, liberty, and the pursuit of happiness were enough. We believe with our fathers that we do not want many laws and we do not want them rapidly made. One of the greatest authors that ever wrote in the English language, second only, in my judgment, to Shakespeare, I mean Henry Thomas Buckle, who wrote the "History of English Civilization," was so disgusted with the constant interference of government with the rights of the citizen that he laid it down as a rule that there is but one wise act that any legislative assembly can pass, and that is an act to repeal a former law.

It was not the idea of our republican fathers that we wanted a government to be passing laws every hour of the day, interfering constantly with the liberties of the people. We want to have as little law as possible, as little intermeddling as possible with the affairs of the people. We want to protect and preserve the natural rights of the citizen; and, in order to do this, these checks and balances have been provided in the constitutions of all the States, as well as in the Federal Constitution, and in the rules of proceedings of all legislative bodies, the object of which, as I have said, is to compel legislative assemblies to go slow, to deliberate, to debate, to reflect, to pause, to examine the pending question in all its aspects, to let party passion and party madness die, to let judgment resume its sway. These are the things that wise legislation demands; and this is all we have asked.

In challenging the ruling of the Speaker, in challenging the will of the majority as it has been placed before us, we have only appealed to the intelligent judgment of the country. We have only said that we want rules in this House which will protect the people against rash, ill-advised, and unwise legislation. We want mature consideration given to every question. We want the right defended. We want the wrong prevented. And where measures are dictated by partisan considerations and filled with injustice we want the right to check them and to require the majority party to pass them by their own votes. We are not charged with the responsibility of legislation. The majority party have been charged by the people with that duty.

We are in the opposition to that party and to its measures. We claim the right to discharge the duties placed on us by our constituents in the way that seems to us the most effective. We say you should pass your own measures by your own votes. You have no right to compel us to assist you in accomplishing that to which we are opposed. Why should we be compelled to aid you in making a quorum? If, in our judgment, that is the proper course for us to pursue in discharge of the trust confided to us, you should not compel us to act against our interests and the interests of our people.

You have the majority. Keep them in the House and attend to your own business, and do not put any part of it on our shoulders. You show that you can have a majority when it is absolutely necessary, why can not you have it all the time"

We only want the safeguards our fathers have thrown around the rights of the people in the Constitution. We simply pause here to emphasize to the country the wrong you are doing. We refuse to vote. We stop and invoke the public judgment on the conduct of the majority. From their judgment we appeal to the judgment of the people of the country, and by that judgment we are perfectly willing to abide. [Applause.]

William S. Holman [Ind.] spoke on "filibustering."

This general purpose and method of obtaining delay in legislation is nothing new, sir. It is as old as the Constitution of the United States. It will be found in all legislative bodies where there are manhood and independence. It will be found on the other side of the ocean, whence we derived, in the main, in the beginning our system of parliamentary rules, even in constitutional monarchies. It will be found in every stage of the history of the Anglo-Saxon race, except where arbitrary rule has suppressed it by superior power, and it will continue as long as there are virtue and manly sentiment among representatives of the people and the majority is either arbitrary, profligate, or corrupt.

The statement made that, until recent years, the minority of the House of Representatives patiently submitted, and that without resorting to every means in their power to defeat unjust and vicious measures of legislation of the majority, is a libel on our fathers and a falsification of history. Just think of the men who, by counsel or by arms, aided in securing liberty to the American people submitting to a rule in legislation by which less than one-sixth of the members of the House of Representatives (51 out of 330, as now proposed) could cut off debate in the Committee of the Whole, and a bare majority in the House cut off all debate in the House, thus forcing a measure, no matter how important, through without consideration or debate.

What would John Adams or Thomas Jefferson or Robert Morris or John Rutledge have said of such a rule which ignored in your legislation the judgment of a minority, which might, as in the case of the minority in this House, represent a majority of the American people?

What would those great champions of liberty say of such a rule? They would say, judging from the record of their great lives, that such a rule in legislation was worthy only of a petty tyrant, for even a despot would despise the false pretence the rule involves; for, if 51 men can close debate and report the bill to the House, all men know that moving the previous question in the House cuts off all further consideration, and the subservient majority at once passes the bill. So the people of this country will understand that the millions of dollars drawn annually from their labor by remorseless taxation is at the mercy of a "rump" committee of 100 of their House of Representatives of 330 members, and that the minority of this House can only, at the pleasure of that committeee, obtain even the poor privilege of protesting against the injustice done to their constituents.

Now, gentlemen, let us consider the character of dilatory motions and the expedients for time in legislation of which gentlemen of the majority now, for the first time in our history, complain. I select instances which have occurred within the last thirty years which I can call to mind. In 1864 Elihu B. Washburne, of Illinois, one of the ablest and most valuable men that ever sat on the floor of this House, a man who was worthy of the highest gift of the American people, made use of every parliamentary stratagem ever known to this House to prevent the passage of the extraordinary measure which gave the mortgage of the Union Pacific Railroad system priority to that of the Government, which made the Government the guarantor of bonds to the amount of more than $128,000,000, nearly twice the sum necessary to complete the system. Is there a gentleman

on the other side of the House or on this side of the House
who does not regret that Mr. Washburne failed in that honorable effort to prevent the passage of that measure? Every expedient was resorted to by him to defeat it. It passed at midnight. If he had succeeded in its defeat, which all men know
now would not have delayed the completion of the Pacific railroads one hour, the temptation to fraud which that legislation
suggested could never have occurred, and two venerable men,
long honored in this House, would not have left this hall with
bowed heads, with dishonor resting upon them, leaving this hall
overwhelmed with the consciousness that the judgment of this
House, condemning their connection with the employment of
the vast resources thus furnished by the Government to influence the actions of members of Congress, was just, to seek
solitude and the grave.

Several years later, I think in the Forty-second Congress, the
Hon. George F. Hoar, then in the House and now the distinguished Senator from Massachusetts, with gentlemen from both
sides of the House, for a whole night and more resisted legislation that proposed to commit Congress to the policy of paying
for all property destroyed in the States in insurrection during
the late war, and the contest defeated the measure—a measure
which now would not, I think, receive a single, solitary vote in
this House. It involved, as you see, gentlemen, hundreds of
millions of dollars. Yet Senator Hoar and his associates would
now be condemned as "obstructing proper legislation." When
the "Pacific Mail subsidy" was pending in this House—a half
a million a year, I believe, for ten years—when this hall was
actually crowded with lobbyists, when Samuel J. Randall stood
up and declared to the Speaker of the House in a loud, ringing
voice that reached every nook in this great chamber that the
very atmosphere was loaded with bribery, had he succeeded in
his brave and manly effort to defeat that wicked and vicious
measure of legislation, this House would not have been humiliated within a year after that contest by a report from a Republican committee that $750,000 had been used by the Pacific Mail
Steamship Company to bribe members of Congress to secure
the passage of that bill; a member would not have left this hall
with the brand of infamy upon his brow; another would not
have fled to Canada for the purpose of escaping punishment;
an officer of your House would not have been hunted down as
a felon.

Show me an instance, sir, where what is known as filibustering movements for the purpose of delaying and defeating un-

just and improper legislation have ever operated injuriously to the people of the United States. Further on, in the Forty-eighth, Forty-ninth, and Fiftieth Congresses, a measure growing out of that same bill which Mr. Washburne failed to defeat—the Pacific railroads came in here and demanded that the debt they owe to the people of the United States of over $113,000,000 shall be postponed at a nominal rate of interest for fifty years. Now I ask any member of this House, no matter what may be his views on the general subject, if he failed to admire the position of the gentleman from Kansas [John A. Anderson], on the other side of the House, in his honorable and manly effort during three Congresses to defeat the passage of that measure? One hundred and thirteen million dollars of the people's money sought to be virtually given to these Pacific corporations, for, if ever you extend at 3 per cent. for fifty years that debt, the people of the country will realize nothing for the extraordinary advances they have made to those corporations, out of which Mr. Gould, Mr. Huntington, and others have amassed their imperial fortunes.

Where is Mr. Anderson now? What has become of my friend and coworker? He has heretofore been so manly, courageous, determined, and resolute that I and others have, with confidence, followed his movements. I fear that, like the proverbial Arab, he has "folded his tent and silently stolen away." [Laughter and applause.] Does he abandon his constituents and permit these great corporations to steal from the people of the United States at their pleasure? I hope I am mistaken, and that, notwithstanding the new rules for "easy legislation," my friend will stand by the people. But can he under the new rules?

In the Forty-third Congress, when this House was presided over by one of the best parliamentarians who ever honored the Speaker's chair, and certainly the ablest man of whom the great party now controlling the Government can boast—permit me to say one of the greatest men of our age, whom history may pronounce the greatest [1]—when Samuel J. Randall and his associates here, day after day and night after night, stood up and, by parliamentary methods, recognized for one hundred years, postponed the passage of what was known as the "force bill"— a bill that proposed to ignore the States and place the elections of members of Congress under the control of the Federal Government—when the Democrats, under the lead of Samuel J. Randall, defeated that revolutionary measure (for such was the

[1] James G. Blaine is referred to.

purpose and effect of those almost countless motions which were made) did a measure go down that ought to have become a law? It was the greatest parliamentary contest of our period. The Forty-seventh Congress came with a Republican House, a Republican Senate, and a Republican President, yet no man in either House of Congress proposed to revive that measure. The public judgment was against it. Yet the majority was for it in the Forty-third Congress. Its defeat was the crowning glory of the great life of Samuel J. Randall, and will be associated with his memory, in honor, as long as the records of Congress shall endure. [Loud applause on the Democratic side.]

When Senator Fessenden, in a small minority, resisted by every means in his power (and this parliamentary resistance belongs to the same class of resistance to Congressional action of which the other side of the House complain) the measure that would have driven the then President of the United States from his honored office, setting a precedent the effect of which no man could foresee, presaging vicissitude and instability to our Government; when that great Senator, the greatest of our time, unless Stephen A. Douglas should be excepted, threw parliamentary obstacles in the way of inconsiderate action, will men on the other side say now that he did an improper thing? Yet that was of the same character of resistance, the parliamentary procedure recognized for a hundred years, which has been deemed proper for securing the "sober second thought" of Congress, as well as of the people, the source of congressional power.

Again, sir, calling to mind an incident in the Forty-second Congress bearing on this question. A most unexpected and questionable measure came to the House from the Senate, the more extraordinary for it was ascertained that if it passed the House it was to be followed by a succession of bills of the same character: "A bill to revive the lapsed grant of land to the St. Croix and Bayfield Railroad Company in Wisconsin," a tract of land of great value. The revival of the grant would give an imperial possession to a corporation of wealthy gentlemen. If it passed other similar bills were to follow.

Mr. Schenck, of Ohio, I think, controlled the bill and sought to put it on its passage without a moment's debate. Mr. Cox, of New York, of ever-honored memory, Mr. Van Wyck, then of New York, and others resisted its passage; lands worth millions of dollars should go to the corporation or to the settlers. It was the most animated contest I have ever seen on this floor. At first the members who opposed the bill could scarcely command the number necessary to call the yeas and nays, but they grew stronger, and, after two days of fierce contest, the opponents of the bill gained control of it, and I had the honor to move a substitute to the bill declaring the land open to homestead set-tlers only—homesteads instead of corporate monopoly of public land. The Senate, of course, refused to accept our substitute, and all men know of the extraordinary decision rendered after-ward by the Supreme Court affecting this question. But the value of this precedent in this House must convince all honor-able and fair-minded men that, if the rights of the people are to be maintained, this arbitrary and despotic rule that strikes down and ignores the rights of the minority and the rights of the people ought to be resisted to the last extremity. I am limited to half an hour, but, if I had the time, I could point out a multitude of instances where, during the last twenty-five years and before that time, inconsiderate, corrupt, and fraudulent measures have been defeated by the persistent efforts of the minority, the minority which is ignored and rendered powerless by the infamous rules which are to be adopted by the House.

Now, sir, I challenge gentlemen on the other side of the House to point to a single instance in all our history where delays, no matter how brought about, no matter by what means, whether in the Congress under the Articles of Confederation or in Con-gresses under our Constitution, where men sometimes abandoned their seats for the purpose of postponing measures, down to the present time—I defy any gentleman on this floor to point to a single instance where public interests have suffered by resistance on the part of a minority to the passage of a measure. There have been many instances, undoubtedly, where delays have, in the current business of the House, been occasioned by improper and unjustifiable motions; but shall such instances, which did no harm, justify rules that ignore the minority and leave the majority without any restraint whatever? It is only the lobby that could demand such a state of the rules.

This is not properly a party question, for it must be borne in mind that gentlemen on the other side have joined in these ob-structive proceedings; the minority has not been composed ex-clusively of one party. I have seldom known a filibustering movement touching a matter of current legislation when the minority was not composed of gentlemen on both sides of the House. Upon the single question of elections, filibustering has occurred from time to time on both sides of the House. It is always a temporary matter and always disposed of. These con-tests never affect the current business of legislation. But in current legislation gentlemen must remember that resistance to a legislative measure is seldom confined to one side of the House, but embraces gentlemen on both sides. During the last thirty years methods of delay have been as frequently resorted to by gentlemen on the other side of the House, and no public injury has ever resulted from such delay. If it secured an appeal to the people, who could complain?

Why should gentlemen on the other side who, in manfully standing by their constituents, have exhibited some of the manhood displayed by the Republican party when it first came into power in this House—why should they meekly submit to a system of rules that dwarfs them and renders it hardly creditable that a gentleman should be a member of this House if he has the spirit of his ancestors and desires to act like a man? [Applause.] This submission to power of gentlemen on the other side of the House is most extraordinary.

There never has been a time in my experience in Congress, not excepting the extraordinary period when that Pacific Mail Steamship Company subsidy passed through, when a greater number of schemes of plunder were seeking access to your treasury than now. Three hundred and fifty million dollars, not for the present moment, but to be fixed and settled for early expenditure for ships of war and fortifications, and that, too, in time of profound peace; millions for subsidies, millions for irrigation, by which a few men are to be made rich at the expense of the laboring masses of our people, and cartloads of old Southern war claims that have been examined and rejected by the proper department of Government—these measures are all crowding upon us. The public bills alone now pending involve in the aggregate a sum exceeding the public debt. Go into your corridors. Have you ever seen so many syndicates and organized lobbies here before? Have you ever seen such manifest preparations for an onslaught on your public treasury as now? Have you ever known of as many schemes and projects to draw money from the treasury as are to be found among the bills already introduced?

These new rules of procedure meet the unanimous approval of the syndicates and lobbies. These well-dressed and courteous gentlemen who live off the labor of other men and acquire fortunes by acts of Congress naturally despise the wretched old rules of the House which for a hundred years have been employed, at least in some degree, to protect the public treasury and maintain the purity and honesty of the Government. These new rules will leave the public treasury absolutely without protection so far as this House is concerned, which is made by the Constitution its especial guardian. They manacle the watchman and arm the lobby with crow-bars!

Mr. Speaker, I hope that the gentleman from Illinois [Mr. Cannon], who I see scents even now the perils of the hour, when he comes forward with his appropriation bills, will be able to maintain some check upon the expenditures even under rules which will invite profligate extravagance. It may be that under the pressure of the coming elections some degree of moderation in appropriations will, at least during this session, be displayed. I am sure he will have the cordial support of this side of the House. But, sir, so surely as this code of rules is adopted, so surely as you vest, as contemplated by these rules, the whole power of the House in the Speaker and chairmen of committees, the growth and profligacy of expenditures of this Government will, at an early period, alarm all honest and patriotic men, and the record you are making will be condemned as unworthy of the representatives of the American people. Great estates are being created by our system of taxation and methods of public expenditures, on the one hand and impoverished families, on the other, fast enough even under the present order of things, and why, in the name of justice, should you enlarge facilities for such results?

Gentlemen, you need not talk about revising your revenue system, tariff, or the internal taxation if you adopt these rules. I venture to say your revenues at an early period will have to be enlarged to meet the growing demands on your treasury. The taxation that is creating a fearful gulf betwen the wealth and poverty of our people will not be reduced, but enlarged.

No man can misunderstand—I think no gentleman does misunderstand—exactly what this change of rules means. It means that the Speaker, instead of being, as for the past one hundred years, the servant of the House, shall be its master; that the Speaker and the chairmen of committees shall be a petty oligarchy, with absolute control of the business of the House. It means the striking down of the manhood and proper influence and control, in legislation, of every other member of the House on your side, gentlemen, as well as ours. It means more than all that: it means a great navy, an enlarged army, a great zoölogical park, and other embellishments in this city, and all else that creates a splendid government and gives a sense of security to the owners of overgrown and imperial estates who have no faith in the people and long for a stronger government.

It means that the wealthy gentlemen, men of imperial fortunes, who have been made millionaires by acts of Congress
and now own the Pacific railroad system, shall receive a further
gift of over one hundred and thirteen million dollars from the
United States; for the extension of their debt to the Government
for fifty years means that and nothing less. It means millions
of dollars in subsidies to the capitalists of Europe and America
engaged in your carrying trade. It means all this and more, a
splendid government and an impoverished people!

Will I be told that the Senate may intervene! When has
the Senate in the last twenty-five years interposed any objection to any profligacy of the House?

It gives every scheme of expenditure an assurance of obtaining success without giving the minority an opportunity to appeal to the people in order to secure a sober second thought.
[Applause.]

Permit me to say to you gentlemen who are framing this
despotic code of rules that manacle the minority that the next
House of Representatives will wipe out these arbitrary rules
you are ingrafting upon an honored code approved by the experience and wisdom of a century, with the same spirit that
animated our fathers when they struck the Alien and Sedition
laws from the statute-books of the United States. [Great applause.]

William McAdoo [N. J.] opposed the rules.

In the brief time allotted I would like to make a short
comparison between the methods of obstruction in this House
and the Parliament which our fathers largely had in view in
framing this Government.

It would be supposed that there would be more advantage
given to the individual member on this floor and that his rights
in this body would be more assured and that his influence
would be more felt than under the monarchical system. But
such is not the case. Why, sir, under the old rules, arraigned
and indicted before the country as obstructive of public business,
there was less power to obstruct it than under the rules of the
British House of Commons. The mode of obstruction in that
body is as follows: Every member of the British House of
Commons has the absolute right to be recognized the moment
he rises. The speaker of that assemblage has no privilege to
ignore the claim for the floor of any individual member who
rises to obtain it.

He must recognize the man who rises first, he may be of the ministerial party or he may be of the bitterest in opposition, but he must be recognized in the order in which he rises. When two members arise simultaneously in that body the question is put to the House which of them shall be recognized first. That places the individual member with the inherent constitutional right to be heard in a free assembly. No wall-eyed speaker for one side of the house; no winkers or blinders such as are put on horses for this side or that. The speaker looks with the eyes of impartial fairness. He is obliged to recognize a member as a constitutional right, and when a member of that body once obtains the floor he is privileged to hold it as long as he discusses the subject to which he addresses himself. The humblest and newest member is not a mere effigy to fill a seat and ejaculate at intervals "Ay" and "No," like a patent doll.

Well, this right, they claimed, was abused in the Commons. Mr. Parnell and his followers, judging that very extreme, coercive measures were to be applied against the dearest rights and liberties of their people and their outraged nationality, organized an opposition.

Mr. Gladstone, the greatest and best of men, then in the wrong, as he now admits, was then Prime Minister of England, and he proposed to stop this form of obstruction which was greater and larger in every degree than that exercised by members of this House under the former rules. When this determined and patriotic obstruction threatened the "supply" or appropriation bills for England, he proposed what was called "procedure." He notified the House of Commons on the 20th of February, 1882, that he would move for this change of "procedure." That was on the 20th of February. Now mark the difference between the deliberation in this House and that. The whole English-speaking people in England and her colonies were stirred to their depths by the proposition to restrict the rights of members of Parliament. The great English democracy was moved as never before. For ten long months that question was debated at frequent intervals in the House of Commons. You propose by these rules a more radical change of procedure in this House than that which is called "clôture" in the House of Commons. But it took the English nation ten months in a thoroughly deliberative assembly to determine that matter, and you have said that these rules shall be discussed and the minority silenced in this assembly in less than forty-eight hours. And yet this is a republic, and England is a limited monarchy. Let debating societies hereafter argue whether there would have been more liberty under your predecessors, the Federalists, or under the old system.

Now, what was that procedure, that clôture? That clôture, bad and unfair, was in nowise as restrictive, was not in anywise as despotic and tyrannous as the proposed rules which you bring into this House. You have given to the Speaker of this House the right to judge the conscience of every Representative and to say to him when he makes a motion, "That is not made in good faith." He impugns his personal honor as well as restricts his representative rights. In the House of Commons there is no such power given in a monarchial government to the Speaker. He is elected, not by a party, but he is held to be as fair as a judge on the bench. He makes no political suggestions. He generally rules and holds the balances as fair as the Chief-Justice of your Supreme Court, and the only right of clôture given him was this: That when a member has discussed a great public question for an inordinate length of time the Speaker says that he must restrict himself to it, and finally "names him" when he has exhausted the patience of the House. One-third of the House must sustain this ruling, that is, 200 members. That rule was adopted only aften ten months of deliberation.

It is said that there has been some abuse of the old rules. There has never been an instance of mere personal and factitious filibustering under the old rules by the eminent gentleman at whose seat I stand, who now lies on a bed of sickness, the distinguished statesman from Pennsylvania [Mr. Randall], or by the distinguished and "Grand Old Man" and veteran from Indiana [Mr. Holman]. Whenever they applied the constitutionally obstructive features of the old rules they were, I may say, by an overwhelming majority of the popular vote at the next election, ratified, indorsed, encouraged, and lauded by the masses of our people, and to-day there are no men more beloved and confided in by millions of American freemen than these guardians of the treasury and of popular rights. They have stood for liberty, they have been the shield of honesty against fraud, and their names are written in the hearts of their countrymen. Like the burglars that ply by night, muzzle the honest watch-dogs, as befits you.

Now, Mr. Speaker, we hear a great deal about reform of the rules. I will tell you where, in my opinion, true reform lies. Adopt this code of rules. You, sir, can go back to your constituency; you can make a canvass upon a bill pending or to be brought into this House; you can pledge them on every stump that you will oppose that bill when you come back into the next House; you can go back in the next House, if continued as it is now [turning to the Democratic side]—confidentially, it will not be; you can go back to the next House, and you can sit here from day to day, manacled, bound, fettered, gagged, and mummified by these rules, and you will never get an opportunity to even vote on the bill, let alone discuss it. What course will that bill pursue? It will be introduced on bill day and put in the private box, under the proposed rules, in charge of the Clerk, taken by the Speaker to his room, if he chooses, in his satchel, and distributed by him as he sees fit, with the poor privilege of being here in time the next morning to move to have it recommitted to another committee or make a useless noise about it. It goes, under our system, to the little secret imperial congresses that you have created here called committees.

It is digested and debated and disposed of with closed doors. The theosophy of the East is not more mysterious and exclusive. The star chamber and the executive meetings of the Senate are not more secretive. If you are not a member of that committee you do not know what action is to be taken upon it. It is brought in here by the chairman of the committee, who will, if these rules are adopted, become endowed with great power, and with the help of the Speaker under this proposed code it can be hurried through in the Committee of the Whole with a quorum of a hundred and the previous question ordered on the passage of the bill, and you can go back to the constituency to whom you pledged undying opposition to that bill, and before them and your Maker truthfully declare that you never had an opportunity to even look at it. This is proclaimed here and elsewhere as reform, and its chief advocates in the light of opposition compare themselves to the martyrs and confessors of the early ages.

How restrictive even the old rules appeared to that distinguished and impartial foreign observer, Professor Bryce, whose great work supersedes that of De Tocqueville, let me quote:

Still true is it that Congressmen generally complain less of the procedure under which they live, and which seems to an English observer tyrannical, than do members of the English House of Commons of the less rigid methods of their own ancient and famous body. I know no better instance of the self-control and good humor of Americans than the way in which the minority in the House generally submit to the despotism of the majority—

So that, my friends, shows that we did not coin the word "despotism" as used in that connection—

consoling themselves with the reflection that it is all according to the rules of the game, and that their turn will come in due course.

Coming down to Mr. Bryce:

To use the power of closing debate as stringently at Westminster as it is used at Washington would revolutionize the life of the House of Commons. But the House of Representatives is an assembly of a very different nature. Like the House of Commons it is a legislating, if hardly to be deemed a governing body. But it is not a debating body. It rules through and by its committees, in which discussion is unchecked by any closing power; and the whole House does little more than register by its votes the conclusions which the committees submit.

How will you really reform this House? By restoring the individual rights of each member. Break down the imperialism of the committees. Do what they do in other free representative assemblages, bring each bill into the grand committee, the Committee of the Whole House. Let the bill be digested, not by thirteen men behind closed doors, with pass-words, signs, and sword-bearers in a committee-room; let it be digested, considered, deliberated upon in the light of day before the country in the whole House, each member having the right to voice his sentiments, to offer amendments, and finally to cast his vote, by yea or nay, on the record, for or against it.

Now, Mr. Speaker, in conclusion, we hear a great deal about law and order. This side of the House have been charged in the public prints with being disorderly. I would not have much respect for the manhood of one who was the willing and "orderly" victim of a highwayman. [Laughter.] Mr. Speaker, the most monstrous atrocities that have ever fallen upon helpless man have been committed under the names of law, order, and necessity. The noblest, greatest, and purest of men have fallen victims to this at times unholy triumvirate. Under these names the helpless and the innocent have often called to heaven for justice. The most cruel injustices have been perpetrated in the name of "law." Liberty has been outraged time and time again under the cry of "order," and "necessity," says the great genius of blind Milton, "is the devil's plea for tyranny." This is well illustrated by a most memorable career in the English-speaking world.

In 1648 there was born in the small town of Acton, Denbighshire, England, of somewhat obscure but respectable parentage, a man-child, who, as he grew up to be boy and man, displayed talents of a high order. He was the soul of good company. He was a wit, and in later years the court-room was frequently enlivened with guffaws of servile followers at his jests made even at the expense of his victims. He chose his political side with the cool calculation of a mathematician solving a problem. He assailed the government until he was bribed with a place on the bench, and from that place on the bench, literally on the bodies of his victims, under the guise of "law and order," he rose to the very pinnacle of state until he became the proud possessor of the Great Seal of England. He sent hundreds to the gibbet in one circuit following Monmouth's rebellion, and thousands in chains as slaves to the tropical plantations of the West Indies.

Under the name of "law and order" he browbeat witnesses, bullied counsel, and took from them every privilege and right which had belonged to them for a thousand years. He swam a sea of blood to gratify hellish ambition. His very smile was the blight of death. In the county of Dorsetshire, satiated with blood, "great alarm," says his biographer, "was excited, and not without reason, by his being seen to laugh in church, both during the prayer and sermon, which preceded the commencement of business in the hall—his smile being construed into a sign that he was about 'to breathe death' like a destroying angel and to sanguine his very ermine in blood." At last, when the weak and pusillanimous king whom he had served fled from England, the first impulse of the great masses of the people, as they rose, was to wreak vengeance upon this tyrannical Lord Chief-Justice and Lord Keeper of the Great Seal. He fled, disguised in the coarse habiliments of a sailor, to a collier ship, and was glad from there to seek refuge, pursued by the Furies, in the Tower, where he died a miserable death from his outraged countrymen.

The name of Jeffreys throughout the whole civilized world is synonymous to-day with tyranny and outrages upon liberty and constitutional right committed, under the name of "law and order," by him who presided over judicial tribunals. His pleasing quips, his jests that "set the table on a roar," his flashing repartee, his apparent courage, his savage audacity, his courtly demeanor, his great intellect, are forgotten, for they were but the mask that hid the man from public observation. He had great intellectual gifts; he had a powerful brain, but his intellect was perverted, his head was directed by no heart and checked by no conscience.

So, Mr. Speaker, let the majority pursue the course they have begun. Let this code become a part of the law of the land, and, while the man who occupies that chair some day in the very distant future, let us hope, may not be able to shed the blood of his countrymen, he can let loose a whole band of spoliators and brigands upon the public treasury. [Applause on the Democratic side.] He can break down the liberties of his countrymen.

Under the impulses of partisanship he can, with cold, calculating design, array one section against another. He can take from the people the liberty of free elections. He can pay back the mortgages that secured the power of his party. What is the meaning of these rules? You obtained power in this land in 1888 by a mere scratch. You are mortgaged; you pledged the public treasury; you promised every clique and class and interest in this land which helped you into power that you would pass legislation for their benefit, however nefarious, dishonest, or unconstitutional this might be, and you are smoothing the way to keep your promises because these interests threaten foreclosure of their mortgage.

We mark with sad confidence the course of your arranged extravagance, for, alas! you are helpless. The greedy and soulless speculators in our politics—the Mephistophelean "boodle" raisers, the base Shylocks in whose hands you are, will allow of no retreat on your part. They paid for the goods and you must deliver them. They will foreclose their mortgage unless you can suppress the minority, unless you can pass these rules, as you will, and then follow them up by paying back the "blocks of five" and the bills of twenty, as my friend from Missouri, William H. Hatch, has said, with which you carried the last presidential election.[1] [Applause on the Democratic side.]

But, Mr. Speaker, when you have paid them back, when you have paid back the banded interests which defeated the popular will and the popular candidate and outraged the liberties of our people, you will find yourself face to face with men whom you can neither bribe nor intimidate. The honest freemen, the unbought and unpurchasable millions of this land, will go to the polls at the next election and the succeeding election; they will change the majority of this House from that side to this, and they will repeal with great enthusiasm and soulful

[1] It was claimed by the Democrats that correspondence between Republican politicians had been discovered in which mention was made of buying voters in "blocks of five," at twenty dollars a block.

hurrahs the infamous code which you are now about to adopt. [Applause on the Democratic side.]

Elijah A. Morse [Mass.] supported the new rules.

Mr. Speaker, what means this large array of business men who are members of the Fifty-first Congress, many of them all unused to legislative halls? It means that the business men of the country are demanding business legislation and that the "do-nothing policy" of Congress for the last ten years shall change. And how shall you change it without amending the rules that bind the body hand and foot?

The business men of the country want a bankrupt law. We want, at least, radical amendments to the interstate commerce law. We want greatly needed public buildings in centers of population and business. We want life-saving stations, light-houses, and needed improvements to rivers and harbors, to keep pace with this great and growing country. We want laws regulating and restricting immigration. We want a wise revision of the tariff on protection lines.

The Union soldiers want the soldiers' dependent-pension bill, a bill that decrees that no soldier shall die in the poor-house, vetoed by Grover Cleveland.

Yes, we want a navy and coast defences that will command confidence at home and respect abroad. The country has been demanding this legislation for ten years, and the only way to reach it is to cut the chains that bind this body, as is proposed by these new rules, and make it a republican body, where the majority, who are responsible for its acts, can do business.

I claim as a Representative of the plain people to say that they do not understand this business, they do not understand by what hocus-pocus, by what trick of legerdemain the minority have been able to defeat the majority in Congress for the last twenty years. They have not read this old book of rules [shows Book of Rules, Fiftieth Congress], as big as the Bible, and, I grant, hoary with age and precedents, and which should have written in large letters on its cover, for a title, "How not to do it."

I say the plain people all over the country do not understand the process by which the minority of this body is able to defeat the majority, so as to prevent all business, and we are content to go before the people on this issue. [Loud applause on the Republican side.]

Edward P. Allen [Mich.].—Mr. Speaker, the Fifty-first

Congress met in orderly manner, under the Constitution and the laws, on the first Monday in December last, with no rules adopted by this body. Proceedings were conducted under what is known as parliamentary law, a system of rules which prevails in all popular assemblies until supplemented by others. The business of the House proceeded regularly and with no interruption until a question arose of the highest moment to the House, ranking in importance any other that can be considered by this body, to wit, the right of a member to his seat here. To prevent consideration of that question tactics known as "dilatory" were at once adopted by the Democratic members.

These dilatory tactics were adopted, not to further public business, not to prevent raids upon the treasury, such as gentlemen on the other side have been glibly talking about, not for the purpose of thwarting the consummation of some great wrong, but solely to prevent the consideration even of the question whether Mr. Jackson had a right to a seat upon this floor. Those dilatory motions were also, in their nature, revolutionary, because if, by such tactics, one man can be kept in a seat which is challenged, then a dozen or a hundred men can be kept in their seats in the same way, and it would be impossible ever to investigate, upon its merits, any question of this nature. How did the minority proceed? They had answered roll-calls regularly and promptly; they had been in their seats participating in the business of the House, but when the question was raised of considering the contested election-case of Smith against Jackson dilatory practices at once began, and they were promptly overruled by the Speaker, the mouthpiece of this House, the organ of the House, the man who stands for us and in our stead to make deliverances here. [Applause.]

These motions were overruled expressly upon the ground that they were dilatory and nothing else. The next step was what? Why, when questions were raised in their regular order the gentlemen upon the other side remained in their seats and kept silent. It was like the silence in heaven after the seventh seal was broken, as recorded by John of Patmos, and continued for about the same length of time, half an hour. [Laughter and applause.] Then it was broken, and broken in a way that no man present will ever forget. Why, sir, when those gentlemen who insisted that they were not present because they did not answer to their names arose *en masse* (when the Speaker announced that they were in their seats) and, with one voice, with a hundred voices, with the voices of mighty winds, as it were, rushed simultaneously upon the Speaker, no man, I say, who heard them will ever forget. [Renewed laughter.] They were here then. When opportunity offered to put a rail through the spokes of the wagon-wheel to stop it every man of them took hold of the rail. When opportunity offered to stop the business of this House they were all here, they were all here together, rushing down the aisles as if about to take the Speaker bodily from the chair where this House had placed him. Who can ever forget my friend from Indiana [William D. Bynum] as, with clenched fists and "form like old Goliath tall," he moved down the aisle with arms akimbo like a Dutch windmill, threatening dire disaster to the gentleman who occupied the chair? [Laughter.] Who did not stand with bated breath as the silver-tongued gentleman from Kentucky [William C. P. Breckinridge], with solemn mien and measured words, announced to the country and the world that this side of the House and the Speaker were "corrupt"? Who will ever forget my friend from Arkansas [John H. Rogers] as he stood transfixed with amazement and speechless as his eyes beheld the sun of liberty go down forever! [Laughter.]

But, Mr. Speaker, "the winds blew, the floods came" in vain; and, when the airy storm passed by this House, the country saw in that chair a "Reed" that was not shaken by wind. [Laughter and applause on the Republican side.] Why, sir, that yell has not been duplicated within twenty-five years. [Renewed applause.] Instantly came to my mind the words which Walter Scott puts into the mouth of the Last Minstrel upon a noted occasion, when

> At once there rose so wild a yell
> Within that lone and narrow dell,
> It seemed as if the fiends that fell
> Had pealed the battle-cry of hell!

[Laughter and applause.]

Well, Mr. Speaker, that passed by. The Speaker of this House found that these gentlemen were here and he told them so and told the country so.

But, sir, we are told that this is a dangerous precedent; we are told that we are overriding precedents. Do not gentlemen know that precedents sometimes become so cruel that they must be cut down and destroyed? Patrick Henry destroyed precedents when, in the Virginia house of burgesses, he dared to use language that was treasonable; but when he used it he broke the spell that bound the people about him, and from that time onward liberty received a new impetus. [Applause.] John Quincy

Adams broke precedents when, in this House, with the Clerk, a creature of the House, refusing to do certain things, he arose in his seat and said: "Gentlemen, I will put the question myself"; and he did it, bringing order out of confusion and wiping out a "precedent" forever.

Sir, the people of this country have grown impatient under the operation of rules that have been builded up in this House of Representatives. For years they have been complaining that this House, instead of attending to its duties, has simply been obstructing the business of the country, and doing it under forms of law. The people became uneasy, and not only uneasy, but impatient, and they determined that there should be a change. It is not true, sir, that this is a new question. It was foreshadowed years ago that the time would come when these rules must be changed so that the House could do its business properly. That question was discussed throughout the whole North in the last campaign, and the House of Representatives was denounced because of its obstructiveness and because of its determination, hedged about by rules, to thwart the will of the American people. [Applause on the Republican side.]

The country understands to-day that when the rules are changed and the chains are broken it means that the majority of the Representatives in this House elected by the American people shall take the responsibility of legislation and be held accountable for that legislation. And, when they return to their constituents, if they have done unwisely, others will be substituted in their places. But what the people desire and propose to have is work done. [Applause.]

Why, sir, all who were here in the last Congress saw the most important bill strangled, not by a committee, not by this House, but by the gentleman who occupied the chair at that time. When we remember these things, to accuse the present occupant of the chair of "tyranny" is mockery. Had it not been for the "tyranny" of one man, had it not been for the power that the rules gave him here, the State of Michigan to-day would have half a million dollars in her treasury that belongs to her, money that she took freely from her people in order to put down rebellion, money which she gave by virtue of a law which expressly provided that other States should contribute their share. But, instead of so doing, the States that neglected to pay their tax, claiming that the money now in the treasury belongs to all the people, refuse either to give us back what we contributed or to pay their own proper proportion. [Applause.]

Mr. Speaker, if gentlemen can sit in their seats silent and

refuse to vote or take any part in the proceedings, they might as well be entirely out of the House. But, sir, "the world moves." Thirty years ago gentlemen on that side, instead of sitting silently in their seats, would have walked out of the hall. The reason they do not now is because public sentiment would smite them for it. They were afraid to undertake to repeat that experiment; and, therefore, they staid in their seats and drew their salaries, at the same time claiming that they were absent—present in the body, but absent in the spirit. And I want to say further to gentlemen on the other side that, as public opinion prevented you from leaving the hall, so, within five years from this date, public opinion will so utterly condemn the man who undertakes to obstruct the public business here that the pernicious "precedent" will have passed away forever.

Gentlemen may say that this refusal to take part in the business of the House is parliamentary; they may say that they are simply exercising their rights when they sit silently here and refuse to act. But history will say that it is silent secession; that you are not doing your duty as your oath of office commands you to do; that there is no possible way by which a Representative of the American people, sworn to do his duty as a Representative, can by obstructive movements lawfully defeat the will of the people as represented by a majority of this House.

Heretofore the rules have been so constructed that one, two, or three men could control the action of this House. That time has gone by forever. [Applause.] The American people will no longer submit to one-man power. It is not submitting to one-man power to-day. What the Speaker has done has been in strict accordance with parliamentary law, has been in strict accordance with the demand of a majority of the Representatives of the American people.

It is useless to throw epithets at him. It were more manly to throw them at us, because, as you have learned from past experience, epithets do not scare him and wind does not affect him. [Laughter.] He is prepared to take the responsibility of his high place and go forward in the discharge of his duty. And the rainbow in this whole horizon that I see is this: That, when you take "the sober second thought" you will come and lay tributes of praise at the feet of the man whom you have maligned because of the fact that he has known his duty and, knowing it, has dared to do it. [Applause on the Republican side.]

On February 12 Amos J. Cummings [N. Y.] spoke against the rules.

Mr. Speaker, the 5th day of January, 1642, was a memorable day for the cause of both national and parliamentary freedom. On that day Charles I, King of England, appeared at the door of the House of Commons with an armed force. He entered the House with his nephew, Charles, the Prince Palatine of the Rhine. His brows were knit and his eyes flashed as he strode up the aisle. He glanced at the place where the patriot Pym was wont to sit and then walked directly to the chair occupied by the speaker. Speaker Lenthal sat with the mace before him. The King commanded him to sit still. But, as the monarch strode toward the desk, Speaker Lenthal rose with the other members of the House. As the King approached, Lenthal left the chair and dropped upon his knees. His Majesty ascended the steps leading to the speaker's desk.

The representatives stood with their heads uncovered in stern, respectful silence. In angry tones the king explained the object of his visit. On the previous day he had sent to the House commanding the arrest of Pym, Hampden, Strode, Hasselrig, and Hollis. The Commons did not respond. The five patriots remained free and the House determined to protect them. On this day the King himself came to arrest them. They were not in their seats. They had heard of his approach and at the urgent solicitation of their friends in the House, had withdrawn. Charles angrily asked the speaker where they were. Instead of meanly replying: "I saw Jack Hampden go into the cloakroom a few minutes ago and Dan Hollis is down in the restaurant," Speaker Lenthal resolutely replied: "May it please Your Majesty, I have neither eyes to see nor tongue to speak in this place but as the House is pleased to command me, whose servant I am here." [Applause on the Democratic side.]

The King replied: "My eyes are as good as another's. I will use them."

After a searching survey he said: "I see the birds have flown." Thereupon he turned and, with a shuffling apology, marched out of the chamber. From that day down to the opening session of this Congress no person occupying the Speaker's chair in either the House of Commons or the House of Representatives has ever presumed to use his eyes except as directed in advance by the House. [Renewed applause.]

Wherever, in minor legislative bodies, the presiding officer has assumed to use his eyes, it has always been after rules for the government of the body had been adopted. The rulings here, which preceded the report of the Committee on Rules, are not based upon the memorable ruling of Speaker Lenthal. Instead of uttering the voice of this House as its speaker, that functionary evokes that voice from silent members and then uses those silent members to stamp the subterfuge as genuine. No subsequent party sanction can make this ruling aught but an act of tyranny. From this ruling no appeal is permitted. A thousand quorums made up in the same way can not change its complexion. Every vote so taken only stamps it with deeper damnation. The Speaker himself makes the quorum, independent of the call of the House, and the minority is made the instrument of his tyranny.

Instead of acting as the Speaker of the House and declaring the voice it utters he evokes that voice with his eyes and utters what he has not heard, in defiance of parliamentary law. Instead of giving the House an opportunity to express its will, he takes upon himself to declare his own will as the will of the House, and makes his ruling good despite the fact that a yea and nay vote shows that it is sustained by a minority.

This is the ruling that it is proposed to sanction by this new code of rules. It is a ruling involving a clause of the Constitution. If constitutional, it needs no incorporation in the new rules. If unconstitutional, such an incorporation can not make it constitutional.

It has been said that it takes a score of lies to support one lie. It evidently takes nearly as many unparliamentary rulings to support one unparliamentary ruling. Wandering from the beaten track, the present Speaker seems to be lost in a wilderness. He orders tellers one day and refuses them the next, thus robbing the House of its undoubted right to revise his count.

The Speaker well said at the outset of his usurpation of authority that the American people are an eminently parliamentary people. They hold school meetings at nearly every cross-road and church meetings in nearly every house of God. They hold political primaries in nearly every block of every great city and assemble in mass-meetings to discuss nearly every question of public interest. In the smallest hamlet of the most obscure county of the least populated Territory you will find some one who has some knowledge of parliamentary rules. The simplest of these rules are stamped upon his memory. He has learned and he knows that a motion to adjourn is always in order; he has learned and he knows that an appeal from the decision of the chair is always in order. Yet, under this new dispensation, the Speaker refuses to entertain either a motion to adjourn or an appeal from a decision. He has done this daily and almost hourly.

He has assumed to question the motives of members in making a motion, independent of the opinion of the members of the House, for he refuses to allow an appeal. It is an assumption violative of the rights of all our constituencies.

Look at it. The Representative of the First Congressional district of Maine has taken it upon himself to determine the motives of the Representatives from the Third District of Georgia and elsewhere in making the simplest of parliamentary motions. If he has the right, why has he not the right to determine the motives of the gentleman from Georgia in introducing a bill or in presenting a report? And, if the Representative of the First Maine District has a right to determine the motives of the gentleman from Georgia in the exercise of any of his public duties, why has not the gentleman from Georgia the right to determine the motives of the gentleman from Maine in the exercise of any of his functions? It is such outrageous rulings as these that are to be perpetuated in this Congress by the adoption of these proposed rules.

But I will specify no further as to the butchery of the simplest parliamentary rules. Everything pales when we look upon the butchery of the individual rights of a member. He is bucked and gagged and wound in the web of committee privileges until you can hardly tell the color of his clothes. Possibly he has already learned that recognition is not based upon the rights of individual members, but upon favor. He will now learn that he has no rights at all, that all his rights and privileges are to be usurped by committees dominated by partisan majorities. Even the poor privilege of demanding the reading of a bill upon its introduction is refused. If he wants to know anything about reports of committees he must watch the Calendars. All the old avenues for information are closed. Committee rule, backed by all the pride of committee, is to be made paramount, and, were it not for the recording of his vote, the individual member might almost as well go back to his constituents, for he could serve them nearly as well at home as in this House under the proposed rules.

I appeal to thoughtful members not to remove the old buoys and tear down the light-houses that have made parliamentary navigation safe in the American Congress for a hundred years.

Stick to the broad channel. Cut-offs are dangerous. The old ship of state is sound and in good condition. Keep her so. Remorseless wreckers have their eyes upon her, and the men of her crew who throw her into their clutches will be held to a strict accountability by the passengers. [Loud applause on the Democratic side.]

Asher G. Caruth [Ky.] opposed the rules.

The Constitution says that the Congress shall legislate, and intends that the members who constitute the law-making body shall have their voice in its legislation. But practice has done away with this idea and the Speaker becomes the law-maker of the Congress. He ought to be denominated "General Legislator." [Laughter.] He has been known at this session of the House as "General Parliamentary Law." [Renewed laughter.] Now, if it was the intention of our fathers who framed the Constitution to place such arbitrary power in the hands of one man, why go to the trouble to have a House of Representatives at all? Why not elect a Speaker by a direct vote of the country and get rid of the necessity of paying salaries, mileage, and stationery accounts altogether and cover "the contingent fund of the House" into the national treasury instead of paying it out for extra help, printing, and the thousand and one things for which it is annually expended.

At first I thought that General Parliamentary Law might do well in command of the House. I thought I knew the general. I had been introduced to him at divers times, at various places—debating societies, conventions, and the like, by a man named Cushing, who was supposed to know him well. [Laughter.] I thought that the principle was that first come first served, and "recognition" a mere matter of promptness and voice. I was mistaken. General Parliamentary Law was a tyrant, a god; his will was supreme, and he would not see a Democrat on the floor or hear his "Mr. Speaker" when he so willed it, although he was evidently there and his voice was ringing through the House as loud as the tones of a calliope. [Laughter and applause.]

I thought it was some singular defect of vision which enabled the Speaker to see and note a Democrat when he was seated in his chair on the floor of the House with his mouth shut and be unable to see him when he stood on his feet and was calling attention to himself at the height of his voice. [Laughter and applause.] It looked to me as if he ought to be treated with

Mulberry Seller's [1] eye-water. [Laughter.] But I feared that he had the disease so bad and was so far gone that he would have to be dosed "externally, internally, and eternally." I have seen this General Parliamentary Law, acting in accordance with this usage, recognize a Republican before he came into view above his chair and before the first syllable of "Mr. Speaker" had left his lips.

It puts me in mind of the lieutenant-governor of a Western State who, during the session of the Senate, addressing the door-keeper, said: "Send out and hunt up Senator Johnson—he is somewhere about the capitol—and tell him that he has been recognized and has the floor." [Great laughter.] Never in any debating society, never in any convention, never in any deliberative body that I had ever attended has it been said that it was out of order to move an "adjournment" or to "appeal from the decision of the chair." Yet General Parliamentary Law, when he took charge of this House, proclaimed this to be the rule. The general was omnipotent, but differed from omnipotence in one respect: he was not the same yesterday, to-day, and forever. [Great laughter and applause on the Democratic side.]

General Parliamentary Law gave me personal offence, too, for he voted me against my will and miscalled my name, violating the rules of pronunciation recognized in my family for over a hundred years with as little compunction of conscience as he did the rules of deliberation in this House, which had been established for a century [laughter and applause on the Democratic side], and would not recognize me when I arose to a question of privilege, although I addressed him in my loudest and clearest tones.

At the end of the episode I felt like Bret Harte's man at the society who was hit in the abdomen.

> He kind of smiled a sickly smile and curled upon the floor,
> And the subsequent proceedings interested him no more.

[Laughter and applause.]
I became anxious to get rid of him or to have him define himself in some definite way. So I was a hearty friend of the resolution introduced by the gentleman from New York [Mr. Cummings] providing for the publication of 2,000 copies of the rules of general parliamentary law which were governing

[1] A character in "The Gilded Age," by Mark Twain and Charles Dudley Warner.

the House. He did not press the motion because it was known that the only thing which could be printed was a photograph of the present Speaker, and there was not a good negative of him in Washington. So I became anxious to have this arbitrary, tyrannical general superseded.

The new rules are called rules of proceedings, but they should be denominated "Rules to magnify the Speaker, glorify the committees, and repress the members of Congress." As a member of Congress who wags the tail end of the Committee of Expenditures in the Agricultural Department, and wrestles with the furious, impatient, and greedy Blair bill confined in the Committee on Education, I want to protest against the adoption of these rules. I do not want to magnify the Speaker; God knows he is big enough now, and great enough, under the old rules; but these rules will add to his weight, and size, and importance, and, when they are adopted, seated on his throne of power, he can well exclaim:

> I am Sir Oracle,
> And when I ope my lips let no dog bark!

[Applause.]

No; I do not want to magnify the Speaker. I do not want to glorify the committees of the House; but least of all do I desire to repress the individual member of Congress. He is little enough here in Washington. He may have been somebody at home; but he is less than nobody here, unless he has been "indorsed." I pity the new member. He is not recognized by the Speaker in the appointment of committees. He can not be a chairman. He can not get the floor, nor would he be likely to know what to do with it if he did get it.

But the people at home think he is somebody, and they are scanning the newspapers to see what he has done toward immortalizing himself, and expect him to do this before he has found out how to tell a Capitol car from one bound for the Baltimore & Ohio depot, or has fixed in his mind the northeast or the southwest portions of this beautiful and mystifying city, and before he has a chance or half a chance some ambitious individual who wants the seat he has hardly warmed by his presence pronounces him a "stick" and "a complete failure." Under the old rules he might, on Monday, rise in his place, under the call of States, and present his bill in the sight of the reporters and in view of the ladies in the gallery. But, alas! even this is denied him under the proposed rules.

He, too, being faithful in his attendance at his committee
meetings, might be selected to report some pet measure, and
then the people would see it telegraphed over the country that
he had made this report, and "the boys" in his district, gath-
ering at the country stores or waiting their turn at mill or bar-
ber-shop, might talk over the distinction which had been conferred upon him and unite in the opinion that he is "the best
Representative the district ever had"; but, under these proposed rules he does not stand up in the face of the House
and the country; he claps his hands for a page and has his report shoved in a box.

Do not these rules indeed repress him? And is it not practically treading on a man when he is down? What is a new
member to do? There is nothing left for him but to tread his
weary way from department to department, write letters, or
scatter "seeds" with a lavish hand over his district in the hope
that they will come forth and bear a rich harvest of votes at
the fall election. But he can "participate," says the gentleman
from Ohio [Benjamin Butterworth], by drawing his twelve or
thirteen dollars a day. But, alas! as we know to our sorrow,
he cannot always do that, for some renegade Republican from
the gentleman's State may creep into our confidence, worm his
way into office, and run off with our pay.

So I am opposed to repressing the individual member. I
am opposed to the policy which is tending to make him "small
by degrees and beautifully less." I am in favor of laws which
give all constituencies, through their Representatives, equal advantages on this floor, rules which recognize the rights of this
large minority, and which will not inaugurate in the American
Congress—

> . . . the good (?) old rule,
> . . . the simple plan,
> That they should take who have the power,
> And they should keep who can.

[Laughter and applause.]

DAVID B. HENDERSON [Ia.].—Mr. Speaker, this country in
the last few weeks has witnessed scenes unequaled in its history.
The Speaker of this House, backed by every Republican member on this floor, has been making a stand for the rights and
liberties of the people. That battle brought opposition from
the Democratic side exceeding in monstrous proportions, in
respect to brutality, anything that ever occurred in the national
Capitol. Only one picture stands out stronger in our legis-

lative history, and that was when a Democratic club laid the
immortal Sumner on the floor of the United States Senate.
This battle against reform has been made like the rioting of a
mob, presenting a disgusting and disgraceful scene to 65,000,000
people.

Epithets unbecoming manhood have been hurled from that
side of the chamber at the presiding officer of the House of
Representatives. "Tyrant," "usurper," "corrupt," "backed
by a mob," were the speeches to which the country was treated.
Language that would have expelled the user of it from the floor
of this or any other legislative body has been cast to the country
and flashed over the wires. We could not afford to call the gentlemen using it to account. To do so would involve a trial consuming weeks and weeks. This you well understood. We were
here for business, and we are here still for business. [Ap-
plause on the Republican side.]

The presiding officer, rising to the situation like our granite
mountains, not afraid of hissing, storms, frowning clouds, or
any other assault, met the occasion, and calmly and grandly
did the duty of the hour. As I passed by that central door,
after one of those exciting scenes, I heard a gentleman on that
side of the chamber say to another, "Did you hear the rebel
yell?" [Laughter.] Gentlemen, understand here and now that
the Northern "doughface" is an animal of the past. Understand that this country has passed through a fiery furnace that
has eliminated the Northern "doughface." [Applause on the
Republican side.]

You undertook and intend to control this country whether
you are in the majority or in the minority. You can not do
it, gentlemen. [Applause on the Republican side.] We mean
business; and it is to do business calmly, earnestly, bravely, and
patriotically that we are here. Assault after assault from great
and small of you has been hurled against the Speaker. You
were mighty chary of such burning and biting speeches when
he held a seat on this floor, armed with his fearless eloquence,
instead of being tied up as the presiding officer. [Applause on
the Republican side.]

Hosts of you have served by him and with him as Speaker
or as Representative from two to twelve years. You did not,
inside or outside of this Chamber, dare to insult him during that period. Is your present course chivalrous? Is this
brave? Is this an exhibition of what we have been told about
Southern chivalry, for men to stand here and in front of
that desk and hurl epithets at a gentleman who is no longer

on this floor? If he had been, you would not have dared do it. [Applause on the Republican side.]

Now, gentlemen, what is the real issue underlying this struggle?

It is this: Shall the election methods in certain States of this Union now boasted of by men high in recognized power be brought into this House of Representatives and be here protected and enjoyed?

Election cases and proposed election laws disturb you. Gentlemen, understand this here and now: If there is a member on this floor entitled to his seat, this side of the House will stand by him as the old Imperial Guard did around the First Napoleon, to defend him in his seat; but, if there is a man on this floor who holds his seat by black-hearted fraud or red-handed murder, we will unseat him if we have the power. [Loud applause on the Republican side.]

Election laws; yes, God knows we need them. The gentleman from Kentucky [Mr. Caruth], who just preceded me, said, with a splendid burst of eloquence, "we want a show for our 'white alley.' " The Republican party wants a show for its "black alley" [laughter and loud applause], and, under the Constitution, we intend to have it. These are the underlying questions of this mighty struggle. He who wants to make it the occasion for wit or for sarcasm may do so. Standing here, I feel myself in the presence of a mighty problem appealing to the patriotism of each Representative. Standing here with that conviction, I shall relax no effort that will make it impossible for the minority to throttle the expressed wishes of the majority in this country. The Constitution is my warrant, and I shall fight for the rules reported to this House. [Loud applause on the Republican side.]

Leonidas C. Houk [Tenn.] supported the rules.

My idea of coming here was that I, as a Representative, was to engage in trying to do the business of the country. It seems, though, that our Democratic friends have the exactly opposite idea about this matter. Your speeches [pointing to the Democrats], your conduct, and the whole course of your action since this controversy began show that you want a set of rules adopted that will enable you not to do business. [Laughter.] When you get back to your constituents and ask for a reëlection are you going to say: "My fellow-citizens, you ought to return me to Congress; I demand and am entitled to a reëlection because I have refused to do your business myself and done all in my power to prevent others from doing it for you?" No, no; you dare not talk that way to the people. You dare not say to them that you represent the "grandest party on earth"; that "our statesmanship has demonstrated to the people how not to do their business." [Laughter and applause.]

Gentlemen, there is no use in dodging this matter. You are either here to do business or not here to do business. Which did you come here for? [Laughter and applause.]

If you are right now, why in the name of all the gods at once did you not adopt this policy in 1861 and burst this Government into splinters by refusing to vote and by running backward—by imitating the crawfish? [Laughter and applause.] If you are correct now, you could have destroyed the Union then by a "dumb" rule; by sitting in your seats and refusing to vote, as you now claim to have a right to do under the Constitution. You had the power to destroy the Union in this way without firing a gun or shedding a drop of blood.

Now, there is another thing. There is a great affection and veneration for the old rules, especially that rule which allows you to play "crawfish" and not vote and not be counted. [Laughter.] Why, God bless your sweet souls, you have been miseducated on this subject. [Great laughter.] You have. You have been educated and seem to believe that it is improper to count those present and refusing to vote in order to make a quorum, and that, because there was no rule authorizing it to be done, it has become a sacred right to thus refuse to do business. But you never stopped to think why that system of rules was built up, and why the distinguished gentleman from Pennsylvania [Mr. Randall], who is now confined to his bed by illness and cannot be here, built it up. You never stopped to think why it was that he has been leading you along and building up a process of violating parliamentary principles under the old rules when you could not be counted.

Why, God bless your innocent souls [laughter], he did it, and the leaders of the party did it for the purpose of preventing the Democratic party from ruining the country [renewed laughter and applause], and they were right [applause], for that party is incapable of governing wisely or well in any branch of the Government. It can tear down, but it does not know how to build up; it can destroy, but it cannot create or restore. [Applause.]

I am amused at the great solicitude which you manifest. You are terribly alarmed about the country in general and the Re-

publican party in particular, for fear we will commit some sort
of *hari kari* and ruin ourselves. Why, God bless you, gentlemen,
why do not you let us ruin ourselves? [Laughter] Why, Mr.
Speaker, in all seriousness, if the Republican members of this
House are capable of the atrocities that you on that side of
the House ascribe to us, then every one of us ought to be in the
penitentiary instead of being here on this floor. [Laughter on
the Democratic side.]

I was amused again at the gentleman from Illinois [William
M. Springer] who entertained us to-night.

A Member on the Democratic side.—God bless your soul!

Mr. Houk.—No, the Lord will not hear a prayer from that
side of the House. [Laughter.] The gentleman from Illinois
[Mr. Springer] inveighed against the rulings of the Speaker,
and especially against that particular ruling which has created
all this antagonism and excitement, and pointed to the conduct
of the Republican party in the Fiftieth Congress in taking advantage of the old rules and filibustering to prevent the party
then dominant in the House from reaching the proper jury in a
contested election case.

I thank thee, Jew, for teaching me that word.

The very illustration which the gentleman has used is one
of the strongest, most forcible, and most logical reasons which
could be presented on this floor why the ruling of the Speaker
is right and why this rule should be adopted for the guidance
of this House in the performance of its duties in representing
and legislating for the American people. The gentleman's argument is this: "You Republicans took advantage of the ruling which then existed and prevented us from getting a case
before the proper jury, and now you are proposing to adopt
a rule by which you can reach the jury under all circumstances
at any time, and I am against that. You did wrong before, and
now, when you propose to do right, I will do wrong." That
is his argument. He denounces us for refusing to vote and thus
preventing the trial of a contested-election case, and yet he and
his party resort to the same bad habit for the same purpose,
and claim that we are tyrants if we do not make it lawful
for them to continue this wicked practice. "Consistency, thou
art a jewel." Indeed the gentleman from Illinois is "a jewel."
He deals in pearls and gems of sarcasm, from whose withering
touch I am bound to believe the Speaker fled and placed the
present occupant in the chair. [Laughter.]

But, gentlemen, you may possess your souls in peace. We are not going to hurt you. We are going to adopt this code of rules and make you behave yourselves, and, when you do not vote, we are going to count you to constitute a quorum unless you run away. [Laughter.] We are going to do it. [Renewed laughter.] We will do it as certain as the world stands. I did not vote for Reed in the caucus for Speaker, but I am in the habit of apologizing to him twice a day ever since I have seen how he has borne himself in the chair. [Great laughter and applause.]

And I am inclined to think our honored and worthy Speaker may yet survive, even though he has the frowns and is compelled to endure the disfavor of all the Democratic statesmen who have hitherto sought and obtained fame and a name by a dilatory use of the motion to adjourn [laughter], and who desire to preserve the right to make this motion hereafter as they have in the past, that their statesmanship may resound down through the corridors of time. [Laughter and applause.] Let me say to our Democratic friends, you may speak, you may use epithets, you may do what you will, but the country has intrusted the Republican party with the administration of the Government and with the control of legislation in this House of Representatives, as well as in the other end of the Capitol, and has put a Republican President in the White House, and we are going to run it for the time being, regardless of what you may think, say, or do in reference to our action. [Applause.]

There is no use of attempting to dodge this question. We intend to do the people's business, and we are going to do it our way, and not yours. [Renewed laughter.] The Republican party has not only taken care of itself, but its genius and patriotism and statesmanship have proved capable of taking care of the country in the past, and, by the help of Reed, we are taking care of it in the present, and, by the grace of God and the good-will of the American people, we propose to take care of it in the future. [Applause.] And what, then, is all this noise and confusion about? [Laughter.] What is it all about? It is all because the majority will not consent that the minority may not do the business for which they were elected. Well, gentlemen, you may just fold your arms and not do a thing if you do not want to, but we over on this side propose to work. [Laughter.]

Mr. Speaker, every court, so far as I have been able to investigate, where the direct question upon which Speaker Reed has been ruling here for several days has come before it, has unanimously sustained the principle upon which that ruling of the Speaker rests. The Supreme Court of Tennessee had this direct question before it at a recent term at Knoxville, and that Democratic court gave a unanimous decision sustaining the principle maintained by the Speaker in his rulings here.

The court held that a majority of a quorum must be present in order to make the action of the parliamentary body legal, its acts valid. Among the authorities quoted and approved is this: "So if a board of village trustees consists of five members, and all or four are present, two can do no valid act.

"But if three only were present they would constitute a quorum. Then the votes of two, being a majority of the quorum, would be valid. Certainly so, where the three are all competent to act." (2 Dill, Mun. Corp., section 217.)

The only possible way to avoid this law, as thus laid down by the Democratic Supreme Court of Tennessee, is for our Democratic friends who have all along been present here in their seats to insist that they are not "competent to act." That may be what they have been trying to prove by their conduct—that they are not competent to act! [Laughter].

BENJAMIN F. SHIVELY [Ind.].—Mr. Speaker, I believe that it will be generally admitted that the gentleman who just resumed his seat [Mr. Houk] presented the case of the majority report in the most prudent, logical, sober, and dispassionate manner thus far observed by that side of the House. [Laughter.]

The contention that this code is designed to enable the majority to control the public business is without foundation. The majority should control the public business within its legal limits, and it can do so now. This code is expressly intended to enable the minority, however small, with the assistance of the Speaker, to rush measures through the House. The old constitutional rule which compels the party which insists on controlling the public business to have its majority in the House is stricken down. A new rule is submitted in its place, under which a mere minority of 3, or even 1, as admitted by gentlemen on the other side, could, with the assistance of the Chair, carry bills through this House taking millions of dollars out of the public treasury. In brief, to provide that a minority of the Representatives elected by the people may control the public business is the very purpose and essence of the proposed code, and all the hysterical protestations of gentlemen to the contrary have not changed the fact.

It may not be amiss to recall the fact, Mr. Speaker, that

some of the obnoxious features in the proposed code were fully discussed in former Congresses. Mr. Blaine, when Speaker of the House, repudiated the proposition that the Speaker should count a quorum, as conducive to fraud and scandal, and predicted that the recognition and exercise of such a power would place the House "on a volcano." Garfield and Hawley and Conger and the present Speaker of this House, when in the Forty-sixth Congress, denounced the proposition that the Chair should "see" a quorum. The present occupant of the chair then denounced the proposition not only as vicious in parliamentary policy, but clearly unconstitutional, and in that view he was sustained by an overwhelming majority on both sides of the House. What was then denounced as vicious is now eulogized as virtuous. What was then pronounced clearly unconstitutional by our present Speaker is now held by him to be clearly constitutional. What was then characterized by him as a "valuable privilege" is now stigmatized as a "vicious practice." What was then denounced as unwise, reactionary, and revolutionary is now applauded as wise, parliamentary, and legal.

Indeed, sir, how irresistible must be the influence about this Capitol that can work such a complete change of opinion and such inexplicable inconsistencies in human conduct. But the public can hardly be deceived as to the secret power at work. The creatures of Government favor demand, among other things, that the time for the payment of the debt due the Government from the Pacific railroads shall be extended seventy years, the confirmation to the subsidized railroads of the title to their unearned land grants, additional legislation for favored banks, the refunding and perpetuation of the national debt for several generations, and these things can be accomplished only by Congress stealing a march on the public opinion.

The American people are to be chained still more securely to the chariot wheels of monopoly, and the old rules must be thrust aside as hampering and impeding that process. Under the old rules, parliamentary motions seldom, if ever, embarrassed good legislation; in many distinct instances they arrested doubtful legislation, and they certainly never facilitated the progress of bad legislation. To correct this tendency and effect is the patriotic and philanthropic purpose of the proposed code!

The rage of contending interests for priority at the public treasury is on. The clamor of the lobby rings out high above the voice of the people. Ninety-nine out of every hundred pledges so lavishly made to the soldier turn to ashes, while the gigantic combinations of steamship and other subsidy bandits storm this House and train their artillery on the exchequer of the Government. The subsidy and the fictitious claim offer large percentages, while the honest claim must wait tardy recognition of its merit. The beneficiaries of privilege sentinel the Capitol of the nation; the farmer and laborer, to whom so much was promised in the last campaign, are forgotten, and nothing is to flourish but the industry of raising and consuming taxes.

Mr. Speaker, this occasion will stand memorable in the parliamentary history of the country. Even the occupant of the chair admits in his report that some of the provisions in this code are "extraordinary," while we all know that they are radical and revolutionary. The authority of great names is disregarded. The precedents of a century are trampled under foot. The purse-strings of the nation are flung to the wind. The way is blazed, broad and plain and direct, for the lobby into the public treasury. That there are gentlemen on the other side of the House who are doubtful of the propriety of many of the innovations in these rules and have misgivings as to their effects there can be no question.

But no such speech on either side of the House will change a single vote. The word has been spoken. The decree has gone forth. The power that could suggest such a code of rules will find means for enforcing its adoption. Recognition and subserviency go hand in hand. Things may grow worse before they grow better. At all events, we are soon to see evidenced how comparatively short is the time which may elapse between the birth and the maturity of folly. [Applause on the Democratic side.]

William D. Kelley [Pa.] supported the rules.

Mr. Speaker, the only doubt that I ever had in regard to the policy and propriety of the proceeding now in issue was when the Speaker of the House referred to a Democratic precedent to show that it was right. I then began to have some doubt. But I was soon relieved of the doubt by the suggestion coming from the other side that David B. Hill [1] is not entirely orthodox in his democracy; that relieved me very much.

Now, sir, I know that the Speaker of this House is a very modest man; but, if he will permit me, I will suggest that, if, in

[1] As Lieutenant-Governor of New York, Mr. Hill adopted in the State Senate the practice now sought to be made the rule of Congress.

the course of human events, it comes to pass that the Republican party of this great country should put the name of Thomas B. Reed at the head of their ticket for President in 1892, and, if it should come to pass also that the Democratic party in their wisdom should put at the head of their ticket the name of David B. Hill as their Presidential candidate, I apprehend and I predict here that our Democratic friends who have been so strenuously and so violently opposing this measure will canvass the United States all over, claiming that David B. Hill is the man entitled to the credit for this great advance that has done so much, and by that time will have done so much, for liberty, and so much good for American legislation. [Applause on the Republican side.]

On February 14, 1890, the rules were adopted by a vote of 161 to 144.

CHAPTER XII

POPULAR ELECTION OF PRESIDENT AND SENATORS

The Jefferson-Burr Contest for the Presidency—William H. Crawford [Ga.] Nominated by a Caucus of Congressmen—Opposition to the Caucus System—Andrew Jackson [Tenn.] Receives Plurality of Electoral Votes—House of Representatives Elects John Quincy Adams [Mass.]—Was This a Violation of the Popular Will? Affirmative, George McDuffie [S. C.]; Negative, Louis McLane [Del.]—Sen. Thomas H. Benton [Mo.] on the Evils of the Convention System—Redfield Proctor [Vt.] Introduces in Senate Constitutional Amendment to Limit Each President to One Term of Six Years; Committed—William M. Stewart [Nev.] Introduces in Senate Constitutional Amendment Forbidding the President to Succeed Himself; Committed—William A. Peffer [Kan.] and John H. Mitchell [Ore.] Introduce in Senate Constitutional Amendments for Popular Election of President; Committed—Similar Resolutions in the House—David Turpie [Ind.] and Sen. Mitchell Introduce in the Senate Constitutional Amendments to Elect Senators by the People; Committed—Gen. John M. Palmer [Ill.] Introduces Similar Amendment in the Senate—Debate: In Favor, Gen. Palmer, Sen. Mitchell, Henry M. Teller [Col.]; Opposed, William E. Chandler [N. H.]—Resolutions of Same Purport Are Introduced in the House and Committed; Henry St. G. Tucker [Va.], of the Committee, Makes Majority Report Favoring Compulsory Popular Election of Senators; Allen R. Bushnell [Wis.] Makes Minority Report Favoring Option of Such Election—Majority Resolution Passed—Speech of Senator George F. Hoar [Mass.] against the Popular Election of Senators—William E. Borah [Ida.] Introduces in Senate Amendment to the Constitution for Popular Election of Senators—Debate: Varying Views by Sen. Borah, Isidor Rayner [Md.], Thomas H. Carter [Mont.], Norris Brown [Neb.], George Sutherland [Utah], Augustus O. Bacon [Ga.], Chauncey M. Depew [N. Y.], Joseph W. Bailey [Tex.], Henry Cabot Lodge [Mass.], Joseph L. Bristow [Kan.], Elihu Root [N. Y.]; Amendment Enacted.

THAT the Constitution cast serious obstacles in the way of a choice for President of a man who was clearly the favorite of the people was early and strikingly shown in the election of 1800. The revolt of the country against the undemocratic acts of the Federalists, particularly the Alien and Sedition laws, had unmistakably showed that a Republican would be elected in the contest, and all indications pointed to Thomas Jefferson, who, with James Madison, had led the fight against these laws, as the logical choice for the nation's Executive. However, Aaron Burr, of New York, the shrewdest political manipulator that had yet appeared in our history, who had made himself what would now be called the "boss" of his party [the Republican] in his State, determined to secure the position for himself.

According to the Constitution, at that time the Electoral College voted for two persons, without designating which was their choice for President and which for Vice-President. The person receiving the more votes got the higher office, and the other man the lower. Burr's power in his party was such that he received as many votes in the College as did Jefferson. This, by the rule of the Constitution, cast the election in the House of Representatives, where, in such a decision, each State has one vote, decided by the majority of its Representatives.

Here was Burr's opportunity. The Federalists hated Jefferson more bitterly than any other Republican because of his leadership in the successful fight against their policies, and, besides, were anxious to save as much as they could from the wreck in the way of political positions. Burr therefore, by making a bargain with the Federalist politicians that their party would be recognized in the dispensation of the offices, secured their co-operation in an attempt to have the House vote for him for President. To do this, control of nine States out of the sixteen then in the Union was necessary. The votes of eight States were secured by the Federalist Representatives voting for Burr. In two other States, Vermont and Maryland, the Burr-Federalist coalition was able to divide the vote equally with the Jefferson Republicans.

The balloting continued from February 11 to 17, 1801, amid the intense excitement of the country, many Republicans believing that it was the intention of the

IX—26

Federalists to prevent a decision until after March 4, when they would make John Marshall (who had recently been appointed Chief-Justice) the chief magistrate. However, Jefferson was finally chosen by a vote of ten States out of the sixteen. It was James A. Bayard, Sr., of Delaware, the Federalist leader in the House, who, having received assurances from Jefferson that he would support certain "strong" national policies, such as the maintenance of public credit and the navy, and would not remove minor office holders for political reasons, decided the contest by inducing the divided States to vote for the man who was overwhelmingly the choice of the country.

It was to prevent the recurrence of such "deadlocks" that the Twelfth Amendment to the Constitution was adopted in 1904 [see Vol. 1, pages 423, 426].

Nomination of the President by Caucus

For a quarter of a century after the first election of Jefferson the Republican Senators and Representatives selected the party's candidate for President in caucus. From the beginning of the practice objection had been made to it as defeating the intention of the Constitution in establishing the Electoral College, and as making the President practically, if not theoretically, the choice of Congress. However, since Jefferson's successors, Madison and Monroe, were also unmistakable favorites of the people no issue was made of the question until the election of John Quincy Adams.

Monroe's Administrations, especially the second, when he was elected President by 228 electoral votes to 1 (which was cast for John Quincy Adams by an elector who wished to have the distinction of a unanimous choice remain with President Washington), were distinguished by political harmony, the opposition Federalist party becoming extinct. The period was aptly known as the "era of good feelings." At the close of Monroe's second administration all the candidates for the succeeding presidency were classed as members of the same party, the Republican. These were William H. Crawford

[Ga.], General Andrew Jackson [Tenn.], John Quincy Adams [Mass.], Henry Clay [Ky.], and John C. Calhoun [S. C.]. From the number of contestants and the fact that none was of the preëminence that had characterized previous Presidents—all men of the Revolutionary era—the contest was called the ''scrub-race for the presidency.''

It was known that a majority of Congress were pledged to Mr. Crawford. Accordingly the supporters of the other candidates refused to enter the presidential caucus, and thereby, says Senator Thomas H. Benton, ''broke down both the system and the candidate.'' Only one-third (68) of the Congressmen met in the caucus and nominated Crawford. In a debate on the subject, in the Senate on March 18-19, 1824, Rufus King [N. Y.] and Robert Y. Hayne [S. C.] denounced the Congressional caucus as a legislative usurpation of the rights of the people.

The decision of the caucus in favor of Mr. Crawford had little effect upon the Electoral College, the vote of which stood: For President, Jackson 99, Adams 84, Crawford 41, Clay 37; for Vice-President, Calhoun (who had withdrawn from the presidential race) 182, the remaining votes being mostly complimentary. Calhoun was thus elected. The analysis of his vote, 114 votes from free States and 68 from slave, shows that the sectional feeling engendered by the Missouri affair had been thoroughly allayed by the Compromise.

No presidential candidate having received a majority of all the votes cast, the election was thrown into the House of Representatives. The House, following the constitutional rule, proceeded to ballot for the three candidates who stood highest. Clay, thus excluded, turned his influence in favor of Adams, who received the votes of thirteen States (seven voting for Jackson and four for Crawford), and thereby was elected.

Before the vote was taken in the House there was considerable debate over the doctrine advanced by George McDuffie [S. C.] of ''plurality preference,'' namely, that the House was morally bound to select the candidate (Jackson) for whom the people had shown a preference by a plurality vote. Louis McLane [Del.] replied to this view as follows:

THE REAL WILL OF THE PEOPLE

LOUIS McLANE

The theory of our Government is that all power is in the people and derived from the people—but they never act themselves, excepting in their electoral franchise. They act through the different organs and functionaries of the Government, appointed by the Constitution and the laws, and they have no proper right to act in any other way. These functionaries are always responsible for a wise and faithful discharge of their various duties, but cannot be instructed in their exercise. The Congress are authorized to pass laws; and the judicial power to execute them—the people give the power to both, but they cannot properly instruct either.

The gentleman from South Carolina argues that the will of the people is the paramount law, according to what he was pleased to term the philosophy of the Constitution—to this the Representative is bound to yield his judgment and conscience; and shame, and disgrace, and infamy are denounced as the portion of him who shall venture to obey his own sense of right in opposition to this will! Before he could recognize a power so absolute, Mr. McL. said, he was disposed to examine its source and character. He would make no lofty professions of regard for the will of the people, according to the phrase of the day. Nothing was more easy, however—nothing more common—it was the ordinary theme of all political declamation. It is the common price of power, and paid most liberally by those who most covet it. We scarcely read of a tyrant, the first page in whose history is not filled with hallelujahs to the people's will. Sir, said he, ambition seeks not to be governed, but to govern; to govern the people; and it flatters the people to put more power over them. But, it is the wild tumultuous will that is thus courted; that which springs from sudden excitements, irregular ebullitions, stirred up by practical causes, and confined to particular districts. Of this false image of the people's will he was no worshipper: while, for the real will of the people, he sincerely felt a profound reverence. I mean, said he, the will of a *majority* of the people, *constitutionally* expressed, in the mode prescribed by the laws. It is this will which is the great moral and political power on which the Government reposes.

It is this will which comes in the panoply of the Constitution, and should be a law to all. He would recognize no other will of the people than that so made manifest; everything else was but its counterfeit. For this constitutional will we manifest our respect by cherishing and sustaining the institutions of its creation.

The gentleman from South Carolina says the election of the President by the people is the best mode which human wisdom can devise. I may admit the position, but what follows? The Constitution supposes it the best and, therefore, resorts to it in the first instance; but it also supposes it may fail in its object. It requires a majority of the people in favor of some one candidate to make an election; it supposes this majority unattainable and, in such an event, which has now happened, directs a new mode of election and by a different power. I ask gentlemen to look into the Constitution and see what restrictions are imposed upon the exercise of this power. There is none but the number to which the choice is limited. Within this number it is in vain to shackle our discretion.

The Constitution meant, and for wise purposes, that the direct agency of the people in this election should cease after the result of the electoral votes, and that, in the new and further election, the federative principle of the Government should operate—rejecting all influence from numbers and the weight of population. It became absolutely necessary to resort to such a principle, to promote and ensure an election by disregarding the causes which had prevented it in the electoral colleges. It designed to remove us from that very influence which had defeated the will of the majority. By giving each State a vote, without regard to its population, the electoral combinations or disagreements are broken up and a new principle established. But the doctrine contended for by the gentleman from South Carolina brings the force of the population in the worst and most irregular form to operate on the election here and disappoint the great object of the change.

After 1824, in place of the caucus, the party convention plan was adopted, in which delegates were chosen by the people to nominate the party candidates for the Electoral College and instruct them, in case of their election, to vote for particular men for President and Vice-President. Of the new system Senator Benton thus remarked (in his "Debates of Congress"):

"The substitute worked well while its letter and its spirit were observed; but degeneration ensued. Instead of delegates, fresh from the people, knowing their will and doing it, the conventions became gorged with officeholders and officeseekers, generally appointed by intrigue and fraud, and wholly intent upon doing their own will for their own benefit; and also largely composed of delegates from States which could give no vote for the person nominated, but who could control the nomination, and, of course, control the election, so far as the party was concerned. These abuses became so glaring and flagrant in the course of the first twenty years of the convention system that one of the most instrumental in putting down the Congress caucus system (Mr. Calhoun) made a public protestation against it—declaring it to be *"an hundred times"* worse than the old caucus system! tending directly to corruption, to the centralization of Government; and the annihilation of the elective power of the people; and, therefore, he refused to suffer his name to go before the Democratic convention of that period (1844). In justification of his opinion of conventions, Mr. Calhoun published his reasons at large in an address to the people of South Carolina, and, strong as those reasons were at that time, it must be admitted that they have grown stronger with the sitting of every convention which has since sat.

PRESIDENTIAL PRIMARIES

In recent years the presidential convention has been essentially changed in character, though not in form, by the delegates in a number of States being selected at popular primary elections, with instructions to vote for particular candidates. The Democratic and Progressive platforms in 1912 declared for this principle.

With the climax of strength achieved by the People's Party in the early eighteen-nineties there came to the front among the more progressive statesmen of all parties one of the chief propositions of the new movement: the popular election of the President and Senators.

ONLY ONE TERM FOR PRESIDENT

Introductory to these measures was the proposition that the President should hold office for only one term. This had been advocated in his inaugural address

(March 5, 1877) by President Hayes, who recommended that the single term be for six years.

On February 18, 1892, Redfield Proctor [Vt.] introduced in the Senate a joint resolution providing that the Constitution of the United States be so amended that the President shall hold his office for one term of six years and shall not be eligible for reëlection. It was tabled.

On March 11 William M. Stewart [Nev.] introduced in the Senate a joint resolution proposing an amendment to the Constitution forbidding the reëlection of a President until after the expiration of at least four years, the article to take effect March 4, 1897.

Senator Stewart spoke in favor of the resolution.

The measure is not in the language of many joint resolutions of like character which have been introduced and which provide for lengthening the term. That, I think, would be objectionable, because the stake would be too strong and might produce revolution at some time. There have been contingencies in the history of the Government where there have been irregularities of which great complaint was made, where the people have willingly submitted in consequence of the fact that the term was only four years. I think it would be unwise to extend the term for a longer period, because elections are not an unmitigated evil; they are necessary for educational purposes and should come as often as once in four years.

The civil service organization is for the purpose of preventing political influence operating upon appointments. If it be important that the clerks and minor officers should be removed from political influence in their appointment, it is of much more importance that the executive head, who exercises the power and patronage of the whole Government, should be relieved from all temptation to use the power in his hands to reëlect himself to that office.

This measure is no criticism upon any particular administration. If a reform of this kind is to take place, it must take place during somebody's administration. It is not a sufficient answer that, heretofore, all Presidents have refrained from using the power in their hands to secure a reëlection, because the power of the President is increasing with the growth of the country, and there is a disposition to increase that power; our legislation is all tending in that direction. We passed a bill the other day—the pure food bill—which adds enormously to the power and patronage of the Executive, and bills of that character are pressing upon us constantly. The growth of the executive office is enormous in power and patronage, and no person should be placed in a position where the temptation would be to use that power for electioneering purposes. The White House should be entirely free from a political campaign. It should not be the head center, the storm center, so to speak, of contests that come every four years. If this temptation is removed we shall have the entire time and services of the Executive devoted to the discharge of his duties. His duties are growing more and more important, and his attention should not be distracted from the public service by a political campaign.

It will be further observed that, in this proposed amendment, I have relieved it of all personal application, so that it shall not affect any possible present aspirant. It is not proposed that it shall go into effect until 1897, so that none of the present aspirants will be affected by it. It does not deny to a private citizen, although he may have been President, the right to aspire to that high office, and I do not see why he should be denied that right. If he goes out among his fellow-citizens and takes the same chances that others do, it is no detriment to the cause of civil service reform to have him as a candidate. The only way to benefit the civil service is to remove from the administration of the Government the temptation to use the power and patronage of the Government for electioneering purposes.

I believe there is a general desire that an amendment of this kind should pass.

I think that the amendment should properly go to the Committee on Civil Service and Retrenchment, and I make that motion.

The motion was agreed to. The resolution was not reported.

Popular Election of the President

On January 18, 1892, William A. Peffer [Kan.] introduced in the Senate a joint resolution to amend the Constitution so as to elect the President and Vice-President by a direct vote of the people; it was referred to the Committee on Privileges and Elections, which did not report it.

On June 22 John H. Mitchell [Ore.] introduced in the

Senate a joint resolution proposing an Amendment to the Constitution of the United States providing for the election of electors of President and Vice-President of the United States by direct vote of the people of the several States. It was referred to the Committee on the Judiciary, which did not report it.

David A. DeArmond [Mo.] introduced a similar resolution in the House, which slumbered in committee.

POPULAR ELECTION OF SENATORS

SENATE, DECEMBER 10, 1891–APRIL 12, 1892

On December 10, 1891, David Turpie [Ind.] introduced in the Senate a joint resolution proposing an Amendment to the Constitution of the United States, providing for the election of United States Senators by a direct vote of the people of the several States. It was tabled for the present.

Senator Mitchell offered, on the same day, a joint resolution to the same effect. It was committed.

On December 17 Senator Turpie supported his resolution. He read a resolution of the Indiana State legislature in support of the popular election of Senators.

The question by whom Senators should be chosen does not seem to have been much considered by the framers of the Constitution or by the constituencies to whom it was submitted for adoption.

That they should be chosen by the legislatures of the several States was determined almost of course. Indeed, the State legislatures during the war for independence and for some time afterward were the favored and trusted depositories of a variety of delegated powers. It is not strange, therefore, that the part given them in the election of members of this body should have attracted little notice, elicited no dissent. The alternative of a choice by the people or the legislature of the States appears not even to have been presented.

The Fathers, however, did not omit to provide for the contingency that a matter then regarded as of minor moment might become, as this has in our age, of great concern. So such things were left by their provident wisdom to the disposal of future advisement and after amendment.

This is called a government of the people, republican in form, and very justly may it be so called in comparison with many others, especially those in vogue at the time of its establishment. Such a government ought to be one wherein the people should control and more immediately direct the management of public affairs. We are constantly repeating the maxim that the people are the real source of all authority, yet in the actual drift of events there is a tendency to slip away from this source—to deny and to disown it.

The distribution of powers was justly regarded by the framers of our fundamental law as one of the chief safeguards of liberty, and it is within the purview of their polity and by virtue thereof that tendencies to centralism or absolutism may, by this means, be checked and thwarted. A redistribution of power; that is what this amendment proposes. It relates to a readjustment of power as at present apportioned. There is a certain element in our system which to-day is demanding a larger share of power, as is evidenced by the action of the learned and honorable Senator from Wisconsin [William F. Vilas] in introducing the resolutions of his legislature this morning in favor of the popular election of Senators. They are demanding a larger share, and I may be permitted to say they deserve it. This decentralization is always competent by the voluntary suffrage of the people of the States, under the forms of law.

In accordance with this policy of distribution we have been provided with three departments of the Government, the legislative, executive, and judicial.

Of these three under the present form which is controlled by the people? Surely not the judiciary. This whole province of power touches but once its putative source and origin, at the time of appointment, and then only in the most indirect manner. Thereafter it is forever independent of, and, indeed, irresponsible to, the people as such.

Just as certainly it is not the executive. The head of this department is chosen by electors, who are themselves chosen by the people; but, when elected, and after his induction, the President and the chiefs of the great administrative sections appointed by him are not at all subjects of popular regulation or direction.

There remains, then, only the legislative, whereof the people have control of but one branch, the House of Representatives. It will be thus seen that in this triple distribution of powers now existing no division thereof is allotted to the people.

The amendment submitted by the general assembly of the

State of Indiana, if approved, would grant to them wholly **and** directly the control of the legislative department.

Ought not at least one department to be so ordered and bestowed?

It was said in the discussion, very elaborate, which attended the issue of the rejection or approval of our present Constitution that Senators in Congress were the representatives of the States, of the sovereignty of the States. No change is intended in this relation. The Senator would yet continue to be the representative in a special manner of his State. The only modification proposed is that of the electoral body which chooses the Senator. This would consist of the whole number of voters in the State, who would vote for United States Senators in the same manner as they now vote for governor and other officers.

The States as such would lose nothing of dignity, sovereignty, or power. That centripetal force indigenous to all forms of government, so alien to the spirit of a free democracy, has always been greatly favored by modes of communication such as those now existing between the Senate and the people, modes somewhat devious, indistinct, indefinite. To make the path of this communication straight, to make it a public highway, an open course, unbroken and uninterrupted from the polls to the Senate chamber, is to inflict a grievous wound upon centralism, and will help to drive monopoly from its noxious lair. To grant to the whole body of electors in a State this Senatorial franchise must induce and awaken an interest much enlarged, a sense of responsibility very much heightened in the heart and mind of every citizen.

Aggrandizement of the units in a free State is not that of the Federal head, but creates and subserves the condition of distinct, independent, personal thought, feeling, and action, the unassailable bulwarks of home rule and local sovereignty. The added influence, importance, and power of each individual voter at his home must diminish the means as it would lessen the opportunity for Federal aggression.

Very keen distrust has been sometimes expressed as to the action of legislative bodies in the choice of Senators. This is only one of the forms which the popular protest against the present method most frequently assumes. Consider how full, clear, and thorough would be the remedy for the mischief of such suspicion under the new mode of election. It is true added importance would be given to that class of conferences called State conventions, and their action might be obnoxious to as grave charges as that of the legislature. But the selection made by such conventions would not be final; it would only be primary, tentative; it would be subject to review and reversal at his leisure by every voter in the State. For that reason, no doubt, their action would be the more carefully guarded against the imputation of wrong, and yet, if found impure, might fail of acceptance.

Even upon the passage of this amendment the legislatures of the States will yet retain great functions in our Federal polity, the very greatest, far superior to those of Congress or any of the departments. The States may, at any time, upon a vote sufficiently unanimous of an adequate number, three-fourths thereof, resume any part of the powers granted to the executive, judicial, or legislative divisions, or without formal resumption the people may thus directly exercise through their legislatures the definitive functions of constitutional change and reformation. An enactment of the people through the States, in the form of a constitutional amendment, is in the nature of a decree legislative and judicial, unaffected by precedents, paramount to every other. Take the instance of the adoption of the recent amendments upon the subject of slavery. How fundamentally iconoclastic are these enactments! What a mass of ordinary statutes, State and national; what an innumerable series of judgments and decisions were overruled, repealed, and annuled thereby! Of rights vested, of rights corporate, long established, and recognized both by courts and lawgivers, relating to this subject, not a vestige remains.

There is a restriction upon the high prerogative of the people to make in this mode the law of the land; but that restriction is made for the benefit of the States, and it relates to the composition of this body.

Not even a constitutional amendment can deprive any State of its equal suffrage in the Senate without the consent of that State.

To correct the illegitimate tendencies in our system adverse to free institutions, to avoid the necessity of too frequent resort to extraordinary legislative action, the best method is now by this measure suggested, an increase of direct popular representation in the national legislature.

This would cause the character of the people to be transposed more perfectly into the modes of government. This would cause the needs, wants, aims, and aspirations of the masses of men in our free communities to be more faithfully reflected, more clearly imaged forth in the laws of the country and their administration.

Congress, in the two branches thereof, would be thus brought closer to the people, and this immediate proximity would have the most wholesome effects not only upon the legislative but upon every other bureau and department of the public service.

Such a change would purify the air in the slumbrous cavern dwelt in of old by those stalagmites, the perpetual placemen of routine; it would leaven the whole lump of official autocracy; it would cut away the entail of false prestige and unfounded pretensions; it would greatly lessen the evil of illicit departmental interference with congressional legislation, an evil which has increased, which is increasing, and which ought to be extinguished.

Under the beneficent environment of this new senatorial franchise even those classes most averse to popular influences would by degrees recognize the ultimate political truth. All legislative grants and franchises, as well as public offices, are public trusts. Those who hold them are not owners or proprietors; they are only trustees; they are merely tenants, tenants at will, at the will of the people.

And thus it may be known of all men that the founders of this Republic did give to the purely democratic element an indisputable ascendency; that they granted to this popular tribunal a jurisdiction from which there can be no appeal; that, in fullest faith, in confidence unshaken, they have committed the destinies of their country to the arbitrament of the conscience and the judgment of a free people. What is said above relates to rights granted; it has no relation to natural rights, sometimes called inherent—rights belonging to the citizen as a man, a person, or human, common to all. These rights, as they are not conferred, neither can they be taken away by any legislation.

Under the provisions of this amendment there would be an actual approach—a contact; not a partial sympathy; not an oblique connection or relationship between the servant and those served.

The nearer a governmental agency is to the real source of power the greater will be its value, probity, and efficiency. Direct responsibility breeds honesty, and good faith sustains the wavering, encourages the timid, and, what is of fully as much consequence, it detects and defeats the unworthy, the incompetent, and the corrupt.

Members of this body are now chosen by political agents, acting for the people. Why should not the principals themselves make that choice? Were this amendment in effect to-day the constituencies of the members of the two Houses of Congress would yet be quite different, if that be a condition worthy of attention. For more than fifty years, under the early practice, members of the House were chosen by the people of the whole State upon a single ticket, but this no longer obtains. Wherefore, were this amendment in force, the Senator would be chosen by and would represent the whole mass of voters; the Representative would, as he now does, in a special sense represent the people of the district or portion of the State from which he is sent, and wherein he usually resides.

Government for the people is a phrase easily flexed and much abused. Ivan the Terrible, the White Czar, first of the Romanoffs famous in history, claimed that his administration of affairs was a government for the people.

Government by the people is an expression more stable, standing for a practice and policy which have been greatly aggrandized since the era of 1776, both here and elsewhere.

At the time of the adoption of the Federal Constitution, in 1789, none of the States gave to their citizens the unqualified right to vote, and very few of them afforded the opportunity of its exercise as to any considerable number of official positions. Nearly every office in the States was filled by appointment either by the legislature or the chief executive. Even the voting for members of the legislature was not general, as may be well enough inferred from the clause concerning the election of members of the House of Representatives.

The electors in each State shall have the qualifications requisite for electors of the most numerous branch of the legislature.

At present all public offices, including the judicial, in the States, and even in the smaller subdivisions of counties and townships, have become for the most part elective. Manhood suffrage has everywhere become general, almost unqualified.

During the lapse of time since the surrender of Yorktown there have been a vast increase in the body of electors and a great enlargement of the use of the ballot made by these organic changes in the law of the States. So that, although this cause has been elsewhere well promoted, yet in the States of this Union the principle of popular sovereignty has made much greater advancement.

The whole mass of governments in the Old World and the whole family of commonwealths in this Republic have, within the last century, moved toward the people. This movement has been quiet, gradual, but continuous, persistent, not to be impeded; there has been no retrograde or recession; with no thought of return, without haste, without rest, it has gone always forward. The history of this movement, as has been said of another, was like that of the enchanted well in the Irish legend, which lay for centuries shrouded in darkness in the midst of a gorgeous city, till some careless hand left open the door that had inclosed it and the morning sunlight for the first time flashed upon its waters. Immediately it rose responsive to the beam; it burst the barriers that confined it, submerged the city that had surrounded it, and, in resistless waves, chanting music to heaven, rolled over the temples and over the palaces of the past.

Sir, there is nothing in the history of the people of these States which should induce us to check this movement, to distrust it, or to disallow its just influence in modification of the original terms of the Federal compact. The spirit of liberty which has led to the rise, progress, and consummation of the dominion of the ballot in the States should have somewhat of its free course in the nation.

Shall we, who have knowledge of these marvelous transformations, stand motionless upon the shore of the last century, taking no note of the tidal surge which has risen around us, which awaits, yet may not always await, our action?

The passage of this amendment would be in accord with the law of our growth; it would bestow upon the people a gift entirely worthy of their acceptance and of our proffer.

Sir, we are preparing for the exhibition of a splendid international pageant [the Columbus celebration] commemorative of the discovery and settlement of this continent. In the imperial commercial metropolis of the great lakes, that urban miracle of the century, we are to show from our own country, we are to behold from others, whatever is most excellent in nature, art, or industry. Many a medal will be cast, many a souvenir will be designed in honor of this event so notable. It would be most felicitous should we signalize it by the submission and adoption of this amendment, thus publishing to this grand ecumenical council of the world's commerce and exchanges that the great Republic of the West had given to its people direct control of the legislative department of the Government.

Such an act would be a monument of the age, worthy of its genius and fortunes; more enduring than the Eiffel tower, more imperishable than the column of Trajan or the arch of Titus, which have for centuries marked and adorned the site of the Eternal City. Herein the right, truly divine, of self-government, the sovereign rule and dominion of the people, would be proclaimed, vindicated, justified, glorified in the eyes of all earth's inhabitants to the latest posterity.

Senator Turpie's resolution was referred to the Committee of Privileges and Elections.

Cn February 2, 1892, General John M. Palmer [Ill.] introduced a similar resolution. It came forward for discussion on February 18. Senator Palmer said that the people of Illinois called for such a constitutional amendment.

The election of a Senator by a popular vote, which, by common consent, should control members of the legislature, was not novel to the people of Illinois, for they were familiar with the history of the great contest of 1858, when Douglas and Lincoln were spontaneously chosen to represent opposing opinions upon subjects which, by their gravity and importance, interested and excited every intelligent voter in the State.

The State committee of the Democratic party of Illinois, in 1890, in connection with a call for a State convention, submitted to the electors attached to that party two propositions to be considered and determined by them in their primary conventions.

These propositions were, in substance, first, the propriety of a nomination by the proposed State convention of a candidate for Senator, to be voted for by the people at the next election, as directly as is possible under the provisions of the Constitution; and, secondly, the selection of a candidate for Senator if it should be determined that a candidate be nominated.

Mr. President, I am here to-day the Senator thus elected by the free people of the State of Illinois, and my duty to them and my own sincere and well-matured convictions alike require me to urge upon the Senate the submission to the legislatures of the several States of an amendment to the Constitution of the United States which will provide that Senators shall be elected by the direct vote of the people of the States.

It is not a sufficient answer to the popular dissatisfaction with the present mode of electing Senators to say that it is the method provided by the Constitution.

It is manifest that there prevailed in the convention which adopted the Constitution the most profound distrust of popular elections.

It was conceded, indeed, that an election, of one branch at least, of the proposed legislature by the people immediately was a clear principle of free government.

The organization of the Senate was, for more than one reason, a matter of difficulty; the small States demanded equal representation in the Senate, and this was, as we know, ultimately yielded.

But it is probable that the general purpose of the convention in the organization of the Senate and in the mode of electing Senators was expressed by John Dickinson, who said he wished "the Senate to consist of the most distinguished characters, distinguished for their rank in life and their weight of property, and bearing as strong a likeness to the English House of Lords as possible," and he thought "such characters more likely to be selected by the State legislature than by any other mode."

James Madison, sharing the same feeling, said: "The use of the Senate is to consist in its proceeding with more coolness, with more system, and with more wisdom than the popular branch." And on another occasion he said he was "an advocate for refining popular appointments by successive filtrations," but thought it "might be pushed too far." He wished "the expedient to be resorted to only in the second branch of the legislature, and the executive and judiciary branches of the Government."

Considerations like these largely influenced the convention to confide the election of Senators to the legislatures of the States. Perhaps it will excite surprise to persons who are familiar with existing conditions to be reminded that another of the objects intended to be accomplished by confiding the election of Senators to State legislatures was that of protecting the commercial and moneyed interests. It was argued in the convention "that the commercial and moneyed interests would be more secure in the hands of the State legislatures than of the people at large. The former have more sense of character, and will be restrained by that from injustice." And then, to illustrate their incapacity, it was added, "The people are for paper money, when the legislatures are against it." In Massachusetts the county conventions had declared a wish for a "depreciating paper that would sink itself."

At that time the planting States, as they were termed, were the wealthiest, and their influence was dreaded by the commercial States of the East and North. What marvelous changes time has produced! The "commercial and moneyed interests" are now most potent. They have representation in every department of the Government.

IX—27

I do not concede that the framers of the Constitution properly estimated the intelligence and capacity of the then people of the several States. Most of the members of the convention were themselves still under the influence of inherited aristocratic ideas, and were without experience of the successful workings of popular institutions.

The inefficiency of the Articles of Confederation led to the calling of the convention, and the object of the leading members of the convention was to provide a new government founded on popular rights, which should at the same time possess stability and strength. Having these objects in view in the formation of the new government, it is not surprising that the framers of the Constitution feared that to allow other people a large participation in the direct control of the Government would be to introduce into the system a new element of weakness.

In this apprehension, no doubt, the authors of the Constitution were mistaken, for experience has demonstrated that whenever any portion of the American people have been intrusted with political power they have been equal to its responsibility. They enter and occupy new Territories in multitudes, and at once improvise governments and establish order. The Americans of that day would, like their descendants, have been equal to their responsibilities and have added strength to the fabric of the Government, of the Constitution. They were brave, patriotic, and self-denying; they were not instructed in the learning of the schools, but they loved liberty and order, and were masters of the arts of self-help and self-care, which is the most useful, if not the noblest, education.

If, however, it was conceded that the framers of the Constitution properly estimated the intelligence of the people of that day, we cannot be blind to the changes produced by a century of progress.

It is not in material respects alone that the United States have within the century accomplished so much; for in 1787 liberal culture was the exception; in 1892 it is the rule. Now the schoolhouse dots every neighborhood; useful libraries are found in every village; institutions for higher culture are open to the humblest student, and the newspaper, with its many million sheets, reaches daily the most obscure settlements, and the telegraph and telephone have annihilated time and distance, and steam, a comparatively new force, is almost obsolete now that the lightning is made subject to the requirements of human necessities.

But few public men can be found who do not recognize the

intelligence of those who control the instruments of modern industry, and those who are engaged in what were once the sober and quiet pursuits of agriculture, quickened by the consciousness that the products of their acres are by the modern means of communication and transportation brought in competition with every productive acre on the globe, are asserting their right to participate in the direct control of the Government. It may be lamented, but it is true, that the peaceful contentment of farm life is no longer found anywhere, since the farmers are but the manufacturers of the raw material of commerce, and have become necessarily restless students of political and social economy.

From what I have said the conclusion is inevitable that none of the reasons which led the framers of the Constitution to deprive the people of the direct control of the executive department and of the Senate now exist.

Experience long ago demonstrated the uselessness of the electors as agents for the selection of President and Vice-President. Electors are now but counters for the enumeration of the votes of the States, the John Does and Richard Roes of our political system.

The propositions I repeat and seek to maintain are that the Constitution should be so amended that the election of Senators should be taken from the State legislatures and conferred upon the people, to be exercised by them directly.

Specific proof of the incapacity of the legislature to exercise electoral functions and of the capacity of the people to do so will be found on examination of the revised and amended constitutions of the older States and of the new States modeled after them.

It will be sufficient for my purposes, and tend to brevity, for me to refer to the constitutions of the State of Illinois.

Under the constitution of 1818 the legislature was omnipotent, and it is difficult to describe the extent to which it abused its powers. It established a visionary system of internal improvements and elected commissioners to execute the contemplated public works, with authority to sell the bonds of the State in domestic and foreign markets, by which means a public debt was created so enormous that when the people in 1847 called a convention to revise the constitution poverty and distress prevailed on every hand.

The convention of 1847 made many valuable changes in the existing constitutions. It prepared and submitted to the people a provision for the payment of the State debt, which the people, with that sturdy, rugged honesty and courage which has always characterized the people of Illinois, adopted by their direct vote, and saved themselves and their posterity from the shame of repudiation.

The convention of 1847, however, did more, for it deprived the legislature of all electoral power; it provided for the election of governor and all the executive officers of the State and the justices of the supreme court and the judges of the inferior courts by the direct vote of the people, and further provided that no officer, whether created by the constitution or the laws, should thereafter be elected by the legislature.

Mr. President, if it was possible it would be wise to incorporate in the Constitution of the United States many of the reforms to be found in the improved constitution of Illinois and other States for the protection of popular rights.

It is true that it has been charged at different times that the votes of State legislatures have been controlled by Federal patronage, and instances have occurred where Federal appointments were given to members of the legislature very soon after they had voted for the successful candidate. If the Constitution is amended to permit the election of Senators by the direct vote of the people then the "gerrymander" will no longer influence the choice of Senators, but will in that respect, at least, pass into "innocuous desuetude." [1]

I will not assert, but I confess that I doubt whether the legislative districts in any State are so adjusted as to allow a fair and just expression of the popular will in the selection of representatives in either branch of the State legislature. I do not, by this, intend to assail the conduct of any political party, for, while States are "gerrymandered to serve the purposes of political parties," other causes have operated to produce unfair apportionment in State legislatures.

The elections for the choice of presidential electors; the election of members of the legislature, who elect Senators; the election for members of the House of Representatives in Congress are alike influenced and often controlled by the unfair arrangement of districts.

If the amendment to the Constitution which I propose is

[1] By "gerrymander" the Senator alluded to the practice, said to have been originated by Elbridge Gerry [Mass.], of the party in control of a State legislature reforming the congressional districts of the State, by concentrating the vote of the opposing party into a few districts, so as to give themselves as many Federal Representatives as possible. In time the term was broadened to include any unfair apportionment for political purposes. "Innocuous desuetude" was a phrase made current by President Cleveland's use of it in a message.

adopted the members of the Senate of the United States will be chosen by the direct vote of the free people of the several States, and will be, what it never yet has been, the popular branch of the Congress of the United States.

There is one additional consideration to which I call the attention of the Senate. In 1787 the property of the country was of small value; in 1892 its value cannot be expressed in terms which can be comprehended by the ordinary mind. In 1787 it was believed by many that the security of property would be endangered by the direct participation of the people in the election of Senators; now the rights and the liberties of the people are threatened by the overwhelming and all-pervading influence of property.

It is not necessary in order to make myself understood that I should assail or denounce those who control the enormous aggregates of either fixed or speculative property; it is enough to point to the irresistible logic of existing conditions, the property, or, to use more expressive words, the wealth invested in commerce, in manufactures, in the railways, the forests, the mines, and in the myriad forms of organized activity demands legislation for its protection or its benefit, and its political power, whether employed in the Congress of the United States or in the State legislature, rarely fails of success. Organized as it is, it is so related that it can direct its influence to the attainment of any desirable end.

Mr. President, the property to which I have alluded has now nothing to fear from the aggressive action of the people or from their direct influence upon the Government. All that they can gain by the amendment to the Constitution I have proposed will be enlarged powers of self-defence. Senators hereafter to be elected by the people by their direct votes will be their true and exact representatives, and will defend their homes and their property from unequal and excessive burdens. They will dignify the States, for the people are the States.

They will recognize their responsibility to the people who elect them, and they will find their reward in the approval of their fellow-citizens whom they have faithfully served.

On April 12, 1892, William E. Chandler [N. H.] opposed the resolution.

I regard the extension of the system of popular elections to the choice of Senators of the United States as certain to result in the taking possession of the Federal elections in the States by

Federal officials appointed by the National Government, and I call the attention of Senators to the fact that the amendment which is now proposed immediately extends the Federal power over popular elections in the States to an extent which the Constitution does not now permit.

The Constitution provides (section 4 of Article I) as follows:

> The times, places, and manner of holding elections for Senators and Representatives shall be prescribed in each State by the legislature thereof; but the Congress may at any time by law make or alter such regulations, except as to the places of choosing Senators.

The provision as to the election of Senators is:

> Section 3, Article I. The Senate of the United States shall be composed of two Senators from each State, chosen by the legislature thereof for six years, and each Senator shall have one vote.

If, then, this amendment, which the Senator from Illinois proposes, is adopted, and Senators are hereafter to be elected directly by the people, it follows immediately and conclusively that the powers given to Congress to make regulations are extended to the popular elections of Senators, and in my judgment just as soon as it comes to be seen that Representatives and Senators both are to be elected by the people there will be a demand for the enactment of a Federal election law which it will be impossible to resist.

If the joint resolution is reported to the committee or to the Senate in the form determined upon by the Senator from Oregon and the Senator from Indiana I shall move to amend the same by striking out the provision that the electors shall have the qualifications requisite for electors in the most numerous branch of the State legislature and by providing that they shall have "such qualifications as may be prescribed by Congress," to the end that it shall be within the power of Congress, when both its Senators and its Representatives are chosen by the people, to determine who shall be the electors in the several States and in order that the States may not be allowed to make such discriminations that the qualifications of the electors in one State shall be different from the qualifications of the electors in another.

Moreover, Mr. President, there is another reason why the adoption of this amendment will result in the passage of a Federal election law, and that is that increasing the number of popular elections will not stop with committing to such elections the choice of Senators. It is almost certain that this amendment, if adopted, will be followed by provisions for the choice of

President and Vice-President by the people. I regard that result as inevitable.

Whenever the President and Vice-President are chosen by popular elections it will be entirely possible for one State, by enormously swelling its vote by fraudulent methods, or by other unfair means not absolutely fraudulent, wholly to overcome the exact and honest votes of other States. Assume that we make the change that I have proposed, that Congress shall fix the qualifications of the voters of the several States so that they may be the same in all the States, yet even then there is the possibility that the State of New York will swell its vote by improper and fraudulent methods 50,000 more or less and overcome the true votes of the other States.

I challenge the attention of the three Senators who advocate this measure to this prediction: I am confident that, first, the election of Senators by the people will be followed by the election of President and Vice-President by the people, and that, whenever those two changes are made, there will be of necessity a national election law, which will not only fix the qualifications of the electors of Representatives, Senators, and President and Vice-President in the several States, but will also take complete possession of the electoral machinery therein, and our Representatives, Senators, President, and Vice-President will be chosen at popular elections called by Federal officials, with the voting lists made up by Federal officials, and with the count and the declaration and certificate of election made by them.

Do the Senators who advocate this measure desire this result? I cannot believe that they do. At all events I shall certainly feel that, if after these two amendments of the Constitution are adopted a movement is made by those who believe in and have advocated a Federal election law, we shall be sustained by many Senators and many Representatives who have bitterly denounced such an election law.

SENATOR MITCHELL.—I cannot conceive how this amendment would give Congress any more power in regulating the election of Senators of the United States than it has now.

SENATOR CHANDLER.—Congress can now only regulate, as it does by the law of 1866, the proceedings which take place in the halls of the legislature; but when Senators are elected by the people *ipso facto* the power of Congress to regulate the whole process of choosing Senators is enlarged, and it will be just as competent for Congress to provide Federal officials to conduct the elections of Senators as it now is to provide such officials for the elections of Representatives in Congress and to fix the time, place, and manner of holding such elections.

SENATOR MITCHELL.—In one case Congress is simply regulating the election of one set of electors, and in another case is regulating the election of another set of electors; but will it follow that they will have power to go into all this machinery to which the Senator has referred without some grant?

SENATOR CHANDLER.—Unquestionably it follows from the amendment, as the Senator reports it, that the Congress can proceed to pass a Federal election law applicable to the popular election of Senators just as now it has power to pass a Federal election law applicable to the election of Senators by the legislatures.

Mr. President, my second objection to the passage of this amendment at this time is that it is the very beginning of radical innovation. It will be absolutely the first fundamental change in the Federal Constitution concerning our frame of government. It may seem strange to Senators to hear the statement made that this will be the first change when the fifteen amendments to the Federal Constitution are recalled, but a brief consideration of those amendments will prove the truth of my assertion, that this will be the first change during a hundred years in the framework of the Federal Government.

Mr. President, I am conservative on this subject. I am inclined to canvass with care and prudence the first suggestion of a change and to challenge its advocates to prove their case beyond a doubt and beyond a peradventure. It is characteristic of the Anglo-Saxon race, so Mr. Macaulay says, that it changes its laws slowly; that it legislates with great caution.

The wisdom of the proposed constitutional amendment may be tested by Mr. Macaulay's propositions. He says: "Never remove an anomaly merely because it is an anomaly"; and for that reason we should hesitate to provide for any change of the election of President and Vice-President; "never innovate, except when some grievance is felt; never innovate, except so far as to get rid of the grievance"; and there has been no grievance shown by the Senators who have addressed the Senate on this subject. It has not been established that this country has suffered in the slightest degree from the method of choosing United States Senators by the legislatures of the various States.

Take the speeches of the three honorable Senators which I now hold in my hand, take the report which the Senators have drawn up for presentation to the Senate, and you may search them through and through without finding any demonstration whatever of any grievance, of any harm, or of any injury that has happened to this country by reason of the existing system of choosing Senators.

Mr. President, do the Senators pretend that if there had been a system of popular elections of Senators this body of which we have the honor to be members would have contained more distinguished men than have reached it? Can there be found in the galaxy of great men belonging to any nation brighter stars than those which have illuminated the American firmament from the Senate of the United States? We will not speak of the members of the present Senate, who, I judge, will find no fault with the methods which brought them here. Take the Senate for a hundred years down to our time and look at the distinguished men of whom it has been composed, and declare if you can that if there had been a system of elections by the people there would have been greater men, better men, or nobler men as its members.

Mr. President, the grievance is not shown; the necessity for action is not demonstrated. There are wants of this people no doubt, there are improvements possibly that may be made in our Federal Constitution, but there has been absolutely no injury resulting from the present method of electing Senators.

There is one exception to the general criticisms which I have made of the Senators who advocate this amendment. When I say that they have indicated no injury, that they have pointed out no grievance, although you may search their speeches from one side to the other, there remains to be specified the exception that they do suggest that under the present system of elections rich men may improperly get into the Senate: and when they say this I take it for granted that they mean that wealthy men have so reached the Senatorial office heretofore, not that the Senators are merely apprehensive that if we do not change the Constitution these rich men will so reach the Senate; because, if we have gone on for a hundred years and no wealthy man has by objectionable means yet reached the Senate, it will be safe for us to continue in the ways of the fathers until some case has happened which proves that there is real danger to the country from the invasion of the Senate by wealthy men, so that we must change the Constitution in order to prevent them from getting here.

But, Mr. President, I do not believe that the people of the United States have hitherto suffered because rich men have forced their way into this body who would not have come here if Senators had been elected by the people, which is of course the issue now made. Have no millionaires been elected governors of States? Have there been more rich Senators elected to this body than have been elected governors? The governors are chosen by the people. They are chosen precisely as the three Senators say the United States Senators should be chosen; and yet I do not think complaint has been made that millionaires have improperly taken possession of the governorships; and if they have so taken possession of the governorships they are just as likely and just as sure to take possession of Senatorships under a system of popular elections as they are under a system where the legislatures choose the Senators.

Rather than pass this amendment solely on the ground that rich men purchase their way into the Senate I would prefer to take steps to limit the wealth of our millionaires, and I have drawn up an amendment which I commend to the Senators and which I am willing to support, which I think would be, on the whole, a great deal better than to go through this form of sending out to the States an amendment of the Constitution which we admit we adopt simply because we are afraid plutocrats will buy up State legislatures and get into the Senate when they ought not to come here.

ARTICLE XVI

The excessive accumulation of wealth by individuals and corporations shall not be allowed. Congress may enforce this article by appropriate legislation, and shall prohibit the issue by corporations of stock certificates or bonds or other evidence of indebtedness unless the sums expressed therein have been paid into the treasuries of the corporations; and shall prohibit the payment of excessive dividends.

That is an amendment which is an amendment.

HENRY M. TELLER [Col.].—I should like to suggest to the Senator from New Hampshire that the general complaint is not that those people have got too much, but that the rest of us have got too little.

SENATOR CHANDLER.—There is an amendment that will remedy the whole evil.

SENATOR TELLER.—I do not think it reaches the point we are more particularly interested in.

SENATOR CHANDLER.—If Congress is allowed by law to prevent excessive accumulation of wealth in the hands of individuals or corporations it can provide that when an individual becomes too rich and we are afraid he will break into the Senate with his excessive riches they shall be taken away from him. The natural provision would be that the excess should be paid into the public treasury, but there would be no constitutional objection under such a law to dividing it among needy individuals like the Senator from Colorado.

SENATOR TELLER.—That would meet with our approval. [Laughter.]

SENATOR CHANDLER.—I believe this is the way to do it. I will support this amendment with pleasure. I believe that it is competent for a great nation, when it is in danger of being corrupted by enormous fortunes, to check the growing evil, and I think this is the best way to do it.

This amendment has this merit, to which I wish to call special attention, that it strikes at the root of these great fortunes by controlling the corporations through which alone the great fortunes have been accumulated.

Mr. President, you cannot point to any one of these vast fortunes without seeing that it has been secured by the aid of corporations and corporate powers, and I believe further that you cannot point to one of them that has not resulted from watered stock in corporations. Where is there an enormous fortune that has been accumulated by private individuals using only the means and powers which belong to private individuals for the purpose of accumulating wealth? With possibly one exception of a fortune from large landed property these great fortunes have arisen in this country through the aid of corporations; and corporations which ought to be an unadulterated blessing to a community have in many cases become a curse, because stock and bonds have been allowed to be issued which did not represent money paid into their treasuries.

Mr. President, my amendment will reach the difficulty, and if it is adopted and Congress legislates accordingly there will be no necessity of having the amendment to the Constitution proposed by the Senator from Illinois in order that our rich men may not force their way corruptly into the Senate.

There is, however, a history of this amendment which I will venture to state, which illustrates some of the difficulties that we shall find in getting it adopted. A few years ago a member of the House of Representatives, who came from a farming district, said to me that he wished to introduce some measures that would popularize him with his constituents, and he asked me if I could not draw up something for him. I told him I would think of it, and the next day I sent him this amendment, which I told him I thought would make him strong and popular with the farmers of his district.

I supposed he would at once introduce it, but I did not see that he did. I met him a week or two later, and I said, ''Why did you not introduce that amendment? You told me that your district was wholly a farming district, and that you wished to introduce measures which would strengthen you with the farmers, and I cannot conceive of anything that would be any more beneficial to you with your constituents than that amendment." He said: "That is so; it would help me with the farmers; but let me tell you a little obstacle in the way of my introducing it. Every time I run for reëlection there is a millionaire in my district who always gives me a couple of thousand dollars to help my canvass, and I am afraid it would hurt his feelings if I should introduce it." [Laughter.]

So the amendment has rested until this time, and now I offer it to my friend from Illinois as something on which I think we might all compromise upon this question. If the object of introducing these amendments to the Constitution and making these speeches is to satisfy the Farmers' Alliances—and I see they are passing resolutions for it, and I have no doubt that my friend from Oregon and my friend from Illinois and my friend from Indiana want to stand strong with the Farmers' Alliances—it is a great deal better to go the whole figure and just grapple directly with these rich men, take their excessive wealth away from them and make a good use of it, and not deal with them in a cowardly way by saying we mean at least to keep them out of the United States Senate by providing for senatorial elections by the people.

Now, Mr. President, another reason why I am not in favor of submitting this amendment to the States is that I do not conceive that it is necessary to do this in order to show that we do not distrust the people. That is the argument, the knock-down club with which Senators and others are to be met who do not want to vote for this amendment, who think it is a dangerous beginning of innovation, who think there is no need of it, the argument that we distrust the people when we refuse to adopt this amendment.

I do not think it indicates that we distrust the people by standing upon the Constitution of the fathers. Did they distrust the people? At the close of the Revolutionary war there was perfect unity of sentiment on one thing, irrespective of the question whether a government wholly republican in form should be adopted, or a government with an executive head for life. It was that the people should in fact rule America, and so the rich and the poor alike who had contributed of their substance and their labors to fight the battles of the Revolution became thoroughly democratic and there was no distrust of the people. All knew that in every government to any considerable extent republican sooner or later the people would have their own way; that there would be no institution connected with the government which the people could not change if they wished to change it and continued persistently of the mind to change it.

But although the framers of the Constitution did not distrust the people, they did distrust the sudden temper of the people. They were afraid that waves of excitement might sweep over the country, and that for the moment, for the day, or for the month, or for the year, the people would grow hot with desire to proceed to some extremity. Therefore the wisest men whom the world has ever seen undertook to frame a constitution which should guard against mutability in legislation and sudden changes in the Government.

I am unable to see how we are to begin to tear down these barriers and then to stop. If it shows a distrust of the people to continue to elect Senators by the legislatures of the States, does it not show a distrust of the people to elect them for six years instead of two? Does it not show a distrust of the people to elect a President for four years by electors instead of electing a President directly by the people and for two years only? The system of electing judges by the people has been adopted in many of the States.

It is in the direction of popular government, and it has been found to work well, I am told by the residents of the States where the judges are so elected, and yet the judges of the Supreme Court of the United States and all other Federal judges are appointed and hold office for life. If an amendment were to be proposed for the election by the people of the Federal judges would it not be as good an argument to say to the opposer of such an amendment, "you distrust the people," as it is to say that it implies a distrust of the people to oppose the radical change which is now suggested in the proposition to elect United States Senators by the people?

I have prepared an amendment which proceeds in the direction in which the Senators propose that we shall go, and I cannot see how any Senator who advocates the election of Senators by the people can consistently oppose this amendment. It will be said to him that he distrusts the integrity and the good sense of the people of the United States.

ARTICLE XVII

The President, Vice-President, and heads of departments; the Senators in Congress; the justices of the courts, each within his own judicial circuit or district; and the postmasters and collectors of revenue, shall be elected every two years at the times and places and in the manner provided for electing Representatives. Congress shall make rules and regulations for such elections and for temporarily filling vacancies.

Mr. President, in that amendment is the voice of the people. There the people are enabled to govern for themselves. There the people are notified that if they have a President they do not want they can get rid of him at the end of two years. If they find that they have Senators whom they do not love, whether they are millionaires or are poverty-stricken Senators like the Senator from Colorado, they can get rid of them at the end of two years. I am unable to see how we can have popular government, real, true, and complete, that shall satisfy the arguments of the Senator from Oregon, the Senator from Indiana, and the Senator from Illinois which have been made on this floor, and that shall meet their desires as expressed in those arguments, and give us that kind of popular government which our great and virtuous and intelligent people are entitled to, unless we adopt the amendment.

In this business of popularizing the American Government and making it more beneficial to the American people who have lived under it, struggled for it, fought for it, and praised it for a hundred years exactly as it is, and have never discovered any grievance involved in it, and have never discovered any necessity for amending it, if it is best now to begin to amend the Constitution so as to make this Government of ours a more popular government than it has been, then let us elect every officer every two years and you will have the grandest popular government that the world ever saw. How long it will last I do not predict.

I am entirely certain that popular elections by conventions will not give us any better Senators than come here under the existing system. I find the idea expressed in a paragraph in the St. Louis *Globe-Democrat*, published in the Chicago *Inter-Ocean* of February 21, 1892:

> A State convention can be bribed as readily as a legislature, and can be made to do the bidding of the boodlers. Indeed, the convention offers less difficulty than does the other body to this sort of work, for the members of the convention are in the public eye for a day or two only, and consequently are under less restraint than are the individual legislators whose service lasts a year or two.

Twenty joint resolutions were presented in the House to amend the Constitution in order to provide for the direct election of Senators by the people. Many of these were referred to the Committee on Election of President and Vice-President, the majority of which, on February 16, 1892, through Henry St. G. Tucker [Va.], reported a joint resolution requiring the popular election of Senators. Allen R. Bushnell [Wis.] made a minority report giving each State the option of such election. It came up for discussion on July 12.

The debate was naturally repetitions of the arguments in the Senate, and will not be reported here.

The joint resolution was passed by the House. The Senate referred it to the Committee on Privileges and Elections.

It was reported on April 2, 1893, during the next session.

On April 3 George F. Hoar [Mass.] submitted the following resolutions in opposition:

AGAINST THE POPULAR ELECTION OF SENATORS

SENATOR HOAR

Resolved, That it is inexpedient that the resolution sent to the Senate by the House of Representatives during the last Congress, providing for an amendment of the Constitution securing the election of Senators by the people of the several States, be adopted.

Such a method of election would essentially change the character of the Senate as conceived by the convention that framed the Constitution and the people who adopted it.

It would transfer practically the selection of the members of this body from the legislatures, who are intrusted with all legislative powers of the States, to bodies having no other responsibilities, whose election cannot be regulated by law, whose members act by proxy, whose tenure of office is for a single day, whose votes and proceedings are not recorded, who act under no personal responsibility, whose mistakes, ordinarily, can only be corrected by the choice of Senators who do not represent the opinions concerning public measures and policies of the people who choose them.

It requires the substitution of pluralities for majorities in the election.

It will transfer the seat of political power in great States, now distributed evenly over their territory, to the great cities and masses of population.

It will create new temptations to fraud, corruption, and other illegal practices, and in close cases will give rise to numerous election contests which must tend seriously to weaken the confidence of the people in the Senate.

It will absolve the larger States from the constitutional obligation which secures the equal representation of all the States in the Senate by providing that no State shall be deprived of that equality without its consent.

It implies, what the whole current of our history shows to be untrue, that the Senate has during the past century failed to meet the just expectations of the people, and that the State legislatures have proved themselves unfit to be the depositaries of the power of electing Senators.

The reasons which require this change, if acted upon and carried to their logical result, will lead to the election by the direct popular vote, and by popular majorities, of the President and of the judiciary, and will compel the placing of these elections under complete national control.

It will result in the overthrow of the whole scheme of the Senate and, in the end, of the whole scheme of the National Constitution as designed and established by the framers of the Constitution and the people who adopted it.

On April 6-7 Senator Hoar supported his resolutions.

Four important States have sent to us resolutions of their legislatures favoring such a change in the Constitution. Three Senators have advocated it in elaborate speeches. The House of Representatives, without a debate, has passed resolutions for submitting the change to the States. The careless and thoughtless dealing with this subject is shown by the proposal to take from Congress all power over the manner of electing Senators— a step which would go far, in my judgment, to change this country from a nation into a league or confederacy.

I am not sure whether it is the good fortune or the ill fortune of our American political system that our controversies so often relate to matters which are vital, not only to the well-being, but to the very existence of the Republic. The English take their constitution for granted. They can change anything in their state by a simple act of legislation. But it has been very rarely in their history that great constitutional changes have been brought about by the action of legislative bodies. They have never been brought about by the direct action of the people. Although our constitutions, State and national, are all in writing, there are constant attempts to make changes of the most radical and vital character, and to bring them about suddenly and without deliberation or discussion by popular action.

If the Senate as at present constituted is to be defended it is to be defended here. If the great reasons which moved our fathers to establish this Chamber, which they hoped would last in unbroken succession until time shall be no more, to give its members a tenure of office more enduring than that of any other department of the Government save the judiciary alone, to remove it from the operation of the fleeting passions of the hour, to lay its foundation below the frost, and to remove the appointment of the men who are to compose it, as far as may be, from the temporary excitements which so often move the people to their own harm, are understood anywhere, those reasons must be understood by the men who fill these seats. If this great part of the structure of our body politic is to be maintained it must be maintained by the confidence of the American people in the character of their Senators and by the strength of argument which those Senators must themselves at least help to furnish.

This is clearly, Mr. President, a question of centuries, and not of years. In determining it we must appeal to our experience of a hundred years, and not merely to that of yesterday or the day before. A present impatience is not only no good reason for making a change, but its existence seems to me an especial reason for postponing it. If we listen only to present complaints we must make radical changes also in the manner of electing the President, in the constitution of the State legislature, in our judiciary, in the House of Representatives, in the management of our great corporations, of our railroads, our schools, our universities, the church, the law, and the private habits of the people. Complaint, impatience, uneasiness attend upon everything which depends upon human instrumentality for its administration. They are the sign of vigorous health, and if soberly and thoughtfully dealt with are the conditions of all life and growth.

We must judge the Senate, as I have said, by the experience of a century, and not by a few recent failures. Whatever there may be of existing evil may be corrected by the intelligence and good sense of the people, as other evils quite as great have been corrected in the past.

The sufferings of the people have been mostly from their apprehensions, never from any actual misgovernment. Even our civil war itself came through the people of one section of the country anticipating evils arising from the abolition of slavery, yet the very men who waged the war against the Government now think that abolition was an unmixed good. Our political history seems to be almost made up of popular movements which are the result of the fears of the people—of evils apprehended from legislation which in fact are never experienced.

The history of the United States for a hundred years has been the history of marvelous prosperity and growth, which reads, even in the pages of soberest historians, like an Oriental tale. Yet our political journals have been constantly filled with prediction of disaster and ruin. If anybody need confirmation of this statement let him read the political platforms of the party conventions of the minority. It is marvelous to see how safe, conservative, and beneficent has been our national legislation in spite of all the violence and all the extreme utterances of the journals and the platforms. This quality in our legislation is derived largely, though not wholly, from the character of the Senate under the existing method of choosing its members.

The dangers of the country are the dangers to the elective franchise—violence, fraudulent voting, fraudulent counting, intimidation, corruption, gerrymandering, and unseating of legislators with unquestioned title to their seats for the accomplishment of political objects by unscrupulous men, the use of weapons intended to protect our institutions to subvert them. These things—not mistakes in finance, or an erroneous fiscal policy, or unwise laws of succession, or even rash and violent projects of social extremists—are the things that menace the permanence of our institutions to-day.

Every generation since the dawning of civilization seems to have been gifted with its own peculiar capacity. The generation which accomplished the American Revolution had a genius for framing constitutions which no generation before or since has been able to equal or to approach. The features of the State constitutions framed in that day have been retained with little changes in substance, and have been copied since by every new State.

I do not of course claim that the people cannot now amend, or that they cannot now improve, our Constitution. That Constitution itself would be a failure if the experience of a hundred years under its operation found the people unfitted to improve it. But the descendants of the fathers of the Republic must bring to the problems before them the same wisdom and courage and virtue. They must dare to tell the people plain truths. They must possess the wisdom of deliberate action, and rise to the austere virtue of self-restraint.

Mr. President, wherever there can be found an expression of admiration for the American Constitution in the works of any great writer or thinker at home or abroad it will be found that the admiration is based upon that part of its mechanism which secures the deliberate and indirect action of the popular will instead of its immediate, rapid, inconsiderate, and direct action. The parts of it which are everywhere the most praised and by which its framers sought especially to commend it to the confidence of the people were the constitution of the Senate and the constitution of the Supreme Court.

I think it can be established to their satisfaction that the proposed change in the method of electing Senators is in itself a change in principle and essence of the most vital character, and that its logic will lead to other changes equally vital and essential. And for that reason I have no apprehension of the success of this scheme when deliberately considered and discussed.

I am not afraid to say to the American people that it is dangerous to trust any great power of government to their direct or inconsiderate control. I am not afraid to tell them, not only that their sober second thought is better than their hasty action, but that a government which is exposed to the hasty action of a people is the worst and not the best government on earth. No matter how excellent may be the individual, the direct, immediate, hasty action of any mass of individuals on earth is the pathway to ruin, and not to safety. It is as true to-day as it was when James Madison, the great advocate of the rights of the people in his time, one of the foremost among the framers of our Constitution, first said it, "That, although every Athenian citizen might be a Socrates, every Athenian assembly would still be a mob."

Our fathers were profound students of history. They found that no republic, although there had been many examples of other republics, ever lasted long without a senate. The term senate implied to their minds, as to ours, a body of men of mature age and of a tenure of office which was removed from all temptation of being affected by temporary currents of public sentiment. The word senate is a misnomer when applied to any legislative body of whom these things are not true.

My friend from Oregon [John H. Mitchell] said the other day that the framers of the Constitution distrusted the people. He said that one of them who declared in the convention that legislation ought to be removed as far as possible from the immediate action of the people would be remanded to private life nowadays with a promptness that would be almost grotesque. Why, Mr. President, that Senator represents a State—one of the new States of the Union—that has incorporated the doctrine of that utterance into every department and arrangement of her constitution more completely, I think, than any other State in the American Union. The Senator overlooks what the author of the utterance with which he finds fault had so profoundly studied—the difference between the immediate action of the people upon legislation and administration and the expression of the sober and deliberate will of the people through instrumentalities whose own sobriety and deliberation are thoroughly secured.

Does my friend really think that the authors of the opening sentences of the Declaration of Independence, who rested their cause on those sublime and eternal truths in their great controversy with the mother country, who placed those truths at the very foundation of their new Government, who pledged their lives and fortunes and sacred honor to maintain them, distrusted the people? They trusted the people when they made those great declarations of natural right. They trusted the people when they declared the equal right of every human being without exception of race or color or nationality or rank or fortune. But they trusted them also with as profound and implicit a trust when they submitted to them constitutions, both State and national, filled with restraints which alike secure minorities and individuals against injustice and oppression from majorities, and secure the whole people against their own hasty and inconsiderate action.

No, Mr. President, it is not because the framers of our Constitution distrusted the people; it is because they trusted the people that they confidently asked their adoption of a Constitution which compelled them to deliberation, to sober thought, to delegated power, to action through selected agencies and instrumentalities, to thinking twice before acting once. It was not Madison or Hamilton, it was the people of the United States who ordained and established the Constitution.

I have no respect for the notion that the people of the United States need to be flattered or cajoled, or that they are impatient of the necessary restraints of constitutional liberty. Truth, frankness, and courage are the avenues to their confidence. There is but one way to discover what will be popular in this country, and that is to discover what is right. There is but one road to the enjoyment of the confidence of the people, and that is to counsel them to wise, honest, and safe policies. The public man who appeals to temporary opinion or who flatters temporary passion will find his hold upon power as temporary and short-lived as are the instrumentalities by which he seeks to obtain it.

It has been said in this discussion that the Constitution needed and received amendment as soon as it was adopted. This is true; but all the amendments were in the direction of placing checks on the power of the people and declaring that there were certain things the people should not be permitted to do. The great statesmen who framed the Constitution placed in it certain checks and safeguards against the popular will. The greater people to whom they submitted it perfected it by inserting other safeguards still.

I stated just now that the term senate implied to the apprehension of every studious man certain essential conditions; but the Senate of the United States, as established by our Constitution, implied something more than this.

First, our fathers wished to secure a dual legislative assembly. With the exception of Dr. Franklin and his associates in the Pennsylvania delegation, who are understood to have cast a formal vote out of deference to him, it was thought best to provide a dual representative assembly. Every act of the legislature was to be twice considered and have the approbation of two different, separate houses.

Second, these two houses were to have a different constituency. So every proposed law must run the gauntlet of two diverse interests and be judged from at least two points of view. Every State in the construction of its legislature has maintained these two principles. The American people, I suppose, are now agreed upon them with substantial unanimity.

Third, the Senate is expected to represent the equality of the States. This is the one principle which would never have been yielded by a majority of the States when the Constitution was made, and which has been made eternal as far as possible by the provision that it shall not be changed without the consent of every State.

Fourth, the Senate was to represent deliberation in the expression of the popular will by the length of the term of office of Senators and by its removal from the direct popular vote in the method of choice. It is this point at which the Senate is now attacked.

The constitution of the Senate secures the application of all these principles in the four great constitutional functions of the National Government—in legislation, in the making of treaties, in the appointment of the great executive officers, and in impeachment. The last of these powers has happily not often been resorted to in our history, but was regarded by the framers of the Constitution as essential for the security of the whole. As James Monroe well said:

> The right of impeachment and of trial by the legislature is the mainspring of the great machine of government. It is the pivot on which it turns. If preserved in full vigor and exercised with perfect integrity, every branch will perform its duty.

Each of these the Senate shares with other departments of the Government, and to each of them it contributes the great and conservative principle which our fathers thought essential to secure to all generations and amid all popular temptations and excitements the Government they framed against the evils by which all former republics had perished.

The Constitution also carefully provides in the case of the Senate, as in the case of the House, that the manner of the election shall be prescribed by the authority of the nation for whom the persons selected are to legislate.

It will be seen, I think, very clearly that the change proposed destroys the essential character of the Senate in each of these particulars.

It substitutes a direct election by the people for an election by the legislature.

For a selection by public officers to whom the great public duty of State legislation is intrusted there is to be a selection and nomination by conventions composed of persons without other responsibility. This, in most cases, will be the mode in which the majority, practically, will make its choice.

For a selection by men who are themselves selected under strict legal provisions there is to be, therefore, practically a selection by men who are not chosen in pursuance of any law.

Instead of selection by men under oath of office there must be a choice by men upon whom no oath is imposed.

For a selection by men of whose action there is a record the choice is practically to be made by men of whom no record exists.

For a choice by men acting under personal responsibility the selection will be made by men who may act by proxy.

For a choice by a permanent body there must be a choice by a body lasting but a day.

For a choice in a manner prescribed by national authority there must be a choice in a manner prescribed in no authority whatever.

For a choice by a body acting by majorities there must be substituted, in the end, a choice by a plurality.

For a choice by a body representing all localities in a State where different local interests are fairly represented there must be a choice by sheer force of numbers, where the popular masses in great cities will have an undue and disproportionate weight.

Instead of representing different constituencies to secure the different interests in legislation the Senate and the House are to represent constituencies of the same kind, differing only in size.

From the change in the manner of election will surely and inevitably, in my judgment, follow the destruction of the equality of the States in the Senate. It is true the Constitution now provides that no State shall be deprived of its equal vote in the Senate without its consent. But this provision relates to a Senate to be constituted and selected in the old constitutional manner, and will never be long tolerated, in my judgment, by the large States under the proposed arrangement.

The State legislatures are the depositories of the sovereignty of the States. They are, in theory, and I believe in general in fact, composed of the picked and chosen men of the communities from which they come. The men who make up the State legislatures are chosen by their neighbors. They are chosen by men who know them, or can know them. There have been exceptions, but in general they have been honest, wise, faithful, and just. The pages of the statute books of the forty-four commonwealths are in general without a stain. They can be read by the patriot without a blush. I am not afraid to compare them with the two hundred and fifty parliaments through which, for eight hundred years, the freedom of England

> Has broadened slowly down,
> From precedent to precedent.

There have been many things we might well wish were otherwise. In the chambers where all men are equally represented what is worse, as well as what is best, of humanity will sometimes find its representative. The ambition, the love of power, the party spirit, the private greed, the popular passion, injustice, and tyranny will occasionally appear there as elsewhere. In what spot in human history are they not found? But I am willing to take the legislation of any American State which is a quarter of a century old and compare it with the legislation of any government possessing a legislature in any period of its history. Why, in the British House of Commons Disraeli said that long after the close of the American war, and within the memory of men who heard him, a member of the government stood below the gangway at the final adjournment of the parliament and gave a £500 note to every member who had supported the administration.

You and I can well remember when bribery was a common and necessary method of getting a seat in the English House of Commons. But English constitutional liberty and English constitutional government have not proved a failure.

Do you propose to strip the State legislatures of any other function of their sovereignty? Can you not trust the men who make all the laws upon which the safety of property, the marriage relation, the security of the home, the administration of the schools, taxation, freedom of religion, the punishment of crime, and everything else which enters into the comfort and honor of private life are depending with the choice of Senators because my honorable friend from Illinois thinks that, in the experience of the people of that excellent State, the selection of Senators under existing conditions has been unsatisfactory?

What is the alternative, and what must be the alternative? What is the alternative proposed? What must be the necessary and only alternative that can be proposed for the exercise of this great function of local sovereignty? The State legislature is a failure, we are told, and is not fit to be trusted any longer. Who are to nominate our Senators? To whom is the practical selection to be intrusted? Whatever may be the theory, the practical choice of the Senator must be made by nominating conventions. Are not these bodies quite as likely to be susceptible to mistakes or to corrupt manipulation as a State legislature?

Cicero, in his oration for Lucius Flaccus, attributes the decay of Roman and the destruction of the Grecian liberty to the substitution of the turbulent popular assembly for the deliberative chamber in wielding the political power of the State. He has left his terrible picture of the popular assemblies of his time as a pregnant lesson for all mankind.

It may be said that governors and State officers and Representatives in Congress are selected in this way now. That is true. But have all nominations of governors and Representatives in Congress been on the whole more satisfactory to the people than the selection of Senators for one hundred years? I think that when any one of us wishes to arouse the State pride of the people he represents by enumerating the great men who have adorned their history, we find that the names of the men who have sat in these seats arise to our lips quite as naturally as the names of the governors or the Representatives in Congress, however illustrious. The people, who by any constitutional method of choice will in any generation send to this Chamber an ignoble or unworthy Senator will, I will venture to say, be found to have at the same time no better timber in their executive chair or in the House of Representatives.

But it is said that the choice of a nominating convention is but the first step. Any mistake it may make will be corrected by the people. But, Mr. President, except in most extreme cases, the correction must be worse than the evil which is to be cured.

At what cost are the people to vote down the nomination made by the convention of the party which is in the majority because of their disapproval of a man who is its candidate for the Senate? Of course the plurality system will be applied to this as to every popular election. The people, then, must manifest their disapproval of an unworthy candidate regularly nominated only by transferring their support to the candidate of another party. It is not likely that any man who would get the nomination of his party convention will be so unpopular that substantially the whole membership of his party will refuse to support him. What will happen will be the choice of the candidate of another party.

Now, what does this mean? It means that the people of a State are to give their support to doctrines, measures, policies, political principles of which they disapprove solely because of their opinion as to the individual character of the man who represents them.

In other words, the correction of the mistake made by the political convention is only to be made at the cost of destroying the character of the country because of the character of the candidate.

Mr. President, the experience of our first century has, it seems to me, most amply vindicated the constitutional purpose which resulted in the Senate. It is not expedient to have two Houses both directly dependent on the popular will. I would not speak with disrespect of the House of Representatives. Every American who knows the history of his country must feel a just pride in that great assembly, which has been and will hereafter be the direct representative of the people's will. The names of its great leaders—of Clay, of John Quincy Adams, and of Thaddeus Stevens—rise to the lips when we would stir in the hearts of any American assembly the emotion of national pride or the love of constitutional liberty. But the constitution of that House has compelled it to resort to many devices and to submit to many inconveniences. We should all be sorry if we were compelled to submit to them in the Senate. The freedom of debate in the House of Representatives is gone. What I sometimes think is even of more importance, the freedom of amendment is gone also.

Both these great essentials to wise and honest legislation exist only to a very limited extent, and then at the pleasure of the majority. It is here only that the freedom of debate is secure.

From all this has grown up the most pernicious of unconstitutional practices, that of filibustering, which was introduced originally to prevent hasty or arbitrary action by the majority, but is now used to prevent or overthrow the rule of the majority altogether. So that the course of legislation in that House to-day is this: A few great measures, to which the party in the majority is agreed, are carried through by special rules adapted for the purpose, the minority being deprived of all rights of reasonable debate or reasonable amendment.

All other measures, however important, however salutary, however much desired by the majority of the House and a majority of the people, are at the mercy of a small and resolute minority. This condition of things is unrepublican and undemocratic, and if continued long must result in the overthrow of republican government itself.

Another evil of like character and of equal magnitude has grown up from the necessities, or the fancied necessities, in the transaction of business in the House of Representatives.

The question whether an important measure shall be submitted to the House for consideration has to be determined, not by individual members, not by chosen committees, not by the majority of the House itself, nor even by its unanimous consent in many instances, but by the will of the presiding officer alone. He determines, at his sole volition, what members shall be recognized and what measures the House shall be asked to consider.

It is notorious that many measures of vast importance, many measures of relief demanded by justice and by the national good faith, abide session after session and Congress after Congress, having received the support of this body, and which would have received the unanimous consent of the other if they could be taken up, which never can be heard in that House because of the refusal of its presiding officer to submit them.

Now, Mr. President, habits like this in the conduct of legislation do not grow up and keep their place without some grave public reason, or at least some grave public necessity. It may be that a body which represents, as does that House, a temporary and sometimes fleeting popular purpose requires such restraints and chains and fetters as these for the public safety. I think we may well pause before we give to this body a character which will require such obstacles to be placed in the path of its free action. The time may come—some of us thought that it was near at hand—when it may be necessary to introduce even here a rule for a limited and carefully guarded clôture in debate.

Every member of this body would regard that as a most painful necessity. If that time ever comes, it will be because rules established for the protection of freedom of action in the Senate have been abused to prevent and subvert it. But I hope and believe the time will never come when any question will be taken in this Senate in regard to which every Senator shall not have an opportunity to express fully and freely his opinion in debate, and in regard to which he shall not have the fullest opportunity to offer amendments as seem to him desirable.

I suppose there have been a few instances of corruption of State legislatures in the election of Senators. In a few cases such attempts have been exposed and failed in the legislatures themselves. In a few cases they have been detected here. In very few, indeed, they have probably been successful. I thought the Senate touched its low-water mark when a few years ago it refused to investigate one of them. It is a great mistake to suppose that nominating conventions will be much more easily dealt with, or that popular elections have been or will hereafter be any more exempt from such influences. Have popular elections in ancient republics, or in England, or here, been freer from corruption than elections through delegated and chosen assemblies? Mr. President, there will never, for any length of time, be venal legislatures without a corrupt people behind them.

Besides, there are, unhappily, other modes of destroying the freedom of elections, to which popular elections are exposed, from which legislative assemblies are free. The great prize of the office of Senator is, if this amendment be adopted, to be added to the temptations which, unless many a report in the other House be without foundation, have induced in very many instances in our history false counts, fraudulent naturalization, personation of voters, fraudulent residences, forged returns, intimidation, and mob violence. These attend elections in great cities and in States where race differences still add their bitterness to the struggle for political power.

There have been, it is estimated, more than three hundred and twenty contested election cases in the House of Representatives. They have been the scandal and reproach of our political history. Excepting a very few creditable examples, they have been decided for partisan considerations, as like cases were decided in the British House of Commons until jurisdiction was transferred to the judges.

Until now the contested election cases in the Senate have in general depended upon constitutional or legal questions, or upon facts easily ascertained and established. But if this change be made, the Senate, in every close election, must undertake investigations which will range over an entire State. There will never be a close election without a contest here. Unless human nature shall change, the result of these contests will depend on partisan considerations, and will shake public confidence in the Senate to its very foundation.

Let no man deceive himself into the belief that if this change be made the Senate of the United States will long endure. Another legislative system will take the place of that which our fathers devised for us, and which for a hundred years has been the admiration of mankind. The method of election is indispensable to secure the peculiar quality of the body to be elected. The change will lead to an attempted overthrow of the equality of the Senate.

In twenty years the State of New York will have two million voters. Do you think they will long endure to submit to equality in legislation, in the making of treaties, in the appointment of great executive officers, in the power to punish and remove great offenders, in the making of war, and in the making of peace, with the 8,000 voters of dwindling Nevada, when the two States are simply two representative districts, whose only difference is that one is two hundred and fifty times as large as the other?

New York submits to this loyally to-day. She has pledged her eternal allegiance to the Constitution. She can not change it without the consent of every other State. It is so nominated in the bond, and is the price she pays for being the Empire State of an imperial nation. She can not escape it without a revolution. But open to her this door. Tell her that the Senate, as Hamilton and Jay conceived it, is gone. Tell her that it is no longer to be made up of chosen men, selected by chosen men, to be removed one degree from public impulse and passion, and representing the deliberate, sober, and instructed will of the people. She will tell you that her constitutional obligation has gone also, and that the equality of the States in the Senate may henceforth be abolished or modified like other provisions of the instrument. "I never promised," she will tell you, "to submit to it forever, under your new arrangement." "*Non in hæc fœdera veni,*" or, as my great predecessor [1] on this floor used to translate it, "I made no such bargain, and I stand no such nonsense."

How many instances there have been in our history in which an immediate popular vote would have led to disastrous consequences, but the sober second thought of the people has led to the path of safety. How many times great waves of delusion have swept over the land, whose force was broken by the sober discussions of deliberate assemblies. The great anti-Masonic movement of 1835, the Know-Nothing movement of 1854 and the years that followed, are but two out of many examples.

Neither Charles Sumner nor Salmon P. Chase could have been elected by a popular vote when they were first chosen. Mr. Sumner certainly would have gone down before the Know-Nothing movement, which he so bravely breasted, if the question of his reëlection had been submitted to a popular vote in Massachusetts in 1855. It is quite doubtful if Mr. Webster himself would have been chosen by a direct vote of the people of Massachusetts at any time after 1850.

This proposed amendment requires the voice of the State to be uttered by masses of its citizens, and removes political power to the great masses who are collected in our cities. Chicago is to cast the vote of Illinois, New York City of the State of New York. The farmer class, which now have their just weight, will be outweighed by the dwellers in the great towns where the two extremes meet—great wealth and great poverty—and combine to take possession of the affairs of the Government.

Second, plurality must take the place of the majority. The opportunity for third parties to have a just and reasonable weight will be destroyed.

Besides, there will be larger opportunities for fraud and crime in elections. These will be easy to commit and hard to be inquired into.

It is no affront to the American people to require that they shall be asked to secure that deliberation, that caution, that putting aside of hasty impulse and passion in their important affairs that every wise man practices in his own. This Republic is no mushroom growth. It is an oak which adds ring to ring through many a summer's heat and winter's cold. Its glorious gains come slowly that they may come surely. The deliberate

[1] Charles Sumner.

will of the people is, however, sure and certain of accomplishment. And our present constitutional forms and mechanisms have always proved abundantly sufficient for its accomplishment. And it is hardly too much to say that the great beginnings of popular movements for liberty have been in the Senate.

Mr. President, it is not true that the Senate, in the sober judgment of the American people, has failed to meet the just expectations of the generation who framed and adopted the Constitution. It has responded quite as speedily and quite as directly to the sober conclusion of the popular judgment and to the settled desires of the popular heart as has the other House or as has any State legislature.

It has originated far more than its proportion of the great measures in our legislative history, for the benefit of the people, which are found in our statute books.

It has resisted what is evil, but it has also initiated and accomplished what is good. This was never more true than in recent years. It is not too much to say—and I assert it without fear of successful contradiction—that—

If any private citizen want justice;

If any executive officer want to improve administration;

If any man desire new and wholesome laws;

If any man want the public mind awakened by discussion— he seeks and he finds what he desires in the Senate. Why, even the friends of this amendment to the Constitution come here for its first serious discussion.

It is said the recent elections of Senators in States lately admitted have been attended with some occurrences that tend to bring the present method of choosing them into disrepute. There has been no investigation into this matter. No man here can say how much truth there may be in these reports, in the charges or suspicions which appear in the columns of the newspapers. The fact that those elections have resulted in a way some of us do not like is of little importance.

The only questions are whether whatever evil may have attended them is likely to be permanent, and whether the same evils would not have existed if the choice had been by popular election, and have not existed to an equal degree in the choice of governors and Representatives in Congress.

Never before has there been proposed, so far as I know, a change which is to affect the great balance of political power which our fathers adjusted with so much care. I quite agree with the Senator from Oregon [Mr. Mitchell] that the principle of this change will lead to the choice of the President, the choice of the Senators, and in the end to the choice of the judges by the mere brutal force of numbers. I do not agree with him in thinking such a change is desired by the American people. When it shall be accomplished, the American Constitution is gone.

It is said the Senate has not responded to the popular will. When has it failed to respond to the popular will when the popular will itself had become settled? The gentlemen who make this complaint are impatient. They must remember that the Senate has to act for the interests of a people of 65,000,000 and for a nation whose life is to be measured, not by years or by generations, but by centuries. Sessions of Congress, terms of Presidential office, generations of men count but as minutes, are but as the pulsation of an artery in this mighty national life. But whenever the American people has made up its mind, when its judgment is formed, when its will is determined, that will is sure to be carried into effect. Whether through Senates or over States, through courts or over courts, through Presidents or over Presidents, through constitutions or over constitutions, the irresistible current will make its way.

Mr. President, I have no patience with the spasms of dismay which seem now and then to affect some worthy philosophers, and the effects of which are occasionally seen in the Senate Chamber. One day there is a fear that a few speculators in cotton or corn will diminish the price to the seller and raise it to the buyer; and so we are asked to overthrow and sweep away all of the rights of the States by a single legislative act, and a majority of this body and the other House lose their heads and are taken off their feet. They think all our existing constitutional resources are powerless before a few speculators. So, because a few millionaires clink their money bags about our State legislative halls, it is proposed to overthrow the Constitution of our fathers and build up a pure democracy in its place.

The American people have dealt with dangers that were serious before. They have put down rebellion, they have abolished slavery, they have thrown off the yoke of foreign tyranny by strictly constitutional processes, and, with the weapons in their hands that have served them so well in the past, they have no occasion for apprehension of these new dangers.

Contempsi Catilinea gladios, non pertinescum tuos.[1]

[1] "I have despised the swords of Catiline's band; I shall not tremble at yours."

We have had one great civil war. But yet it is our glory, as it is the glory of the country from which our ancestors came, that we determine the differences which cause revolutions elsewhere by debate and not by arms. We reason them out, and do not fight them out. This Chamber has been the most conspicuous arena of these conflicts. Here the champions have encountered and measured their strength. There have been chieftains in the Senate Chamber whose names and memory the American people cherish with pride and gratitude, as they cherish the names and memory of the men who marshaled the forces at Saratoga, or Yorktown, or New Orleans, or Appomattox.

The great conquests which gave the Union and Constitution their empire over the reason and affection of our countrymen have been achieved here. Here Webster hurled the weighty projectiles of his irresistible argument. Here the voice of Clay taught his countrymen North and South the great lesson of reconciliation. Here Calhoun was borne in his dying hours, his great heart overcoming the weakness and infirmities of his sinking body, sitting, as his colleague said, like "a wounded eagle, with his eyes turned to the heavens to which he had soared, but into which his wings could never carry him again." Here the blood of Sumner was shed—the baptismal water of our newer liberty. Here Seward summoned his countrymen to that irrepressible conflict from whose issue the vanquished gained even more than the victors. Victories in arms are common to all ages and to all nations. We do not excel, and it may be we do not equal, other people in these things. But the greatest victories of constitutional liberty since the world began are those whose battle ground has been the American Senate and whose champions have been the Senators who for a hundred years, while they have resisted the popular passions of the hour, have led, represented, guided, obeyed, and made effective the deliberate will of a free people.

The joint resolution was not acted upon by the Senate.

The advocates of the popular election of Senators were, however, not discouraged by the failure to secure the constitutional amendment; they set to work to achieve their purpose in another manner (by State action), with the result that in a number of States a senatorial primary is held, the legislatures accepting the choice of the people as morally, if not legally, binding them to elect the persons thus designated.

On January 11, 1911, William E. Borah [Idaho], from the Committee on Judiciary, introduced in the Senate a joint resolution proposing an amendment to the Constitution, providing that Senators be elected by the people of the several States.

The subject came up for discussion on January 19.

ELECTION OF SENATORS BY DIRECT VOTE

SENATE, JANUARY 19-FEBRUARY 28, 1911

Senator Borah spoke as follows:

Mr. President, will the mere change of the mode of selecting United States Senators effect or bring about any fundamental or incidental change in the scheme or plan of government as submitted to us by those who framed it? Will it not rather precisely bring about that which they desired, but which, owing to changed conditions, can not under the present system be realized?

Our fathers understood the science of government as no other single group of men has ever understood it. It is altogether probable that, if the plan upon which they built fails, with it will pass the hope of a democratic-republican form of government. But it will not fail if, studying closely the changed conditions brought about by our marvelous industrial progress and great economic changes, we make only such changes and modifications in government as will prevent those industrial conditions and economic changes from themselves working in subtle and silent ways modifications and changes in our institutions. We do not want to find ourselves in the attitude of a people who are satisfied with the shell of a government from which all real power has departed. We want the substance at all times, and not the shadow. We want the real power and the real responsibility to remain precisely where the fathers placed it, with the people.

We agree fully, too, with the proposition that the sober second thought is always safest in the important affairs of government. When matters of such vast moment depend upon human conduct, it is well indeed to have such checks and balances as will insure reflection and mature consideration before final action. This is simply transferring a wise rule

IX—29

of human conduct to affairs of government. In this the fathers showed great wisdom. No one would in this respect work a change. But, while the fathers wanted to have reflection and consideration, time for investigation and for passion to subside, while they wanted the sober second thought of the people, there could be no doubt but they wanted action when finally taken to be the action of the people and not the action of special influences or unfriendly forces. While they wanted the people to be induced to reflect and consider, they wanted a form of government which would insure the faithful recording of the result after the people had reflected and considered. It was never their intention to leave room for some sinister influence or power to interpose between the people's deliberate judgment and its achievement and realization. If by reason of conditions which they could not foresee that interposition is now possible, then it devolves upon those who have the great burden of preserving these institutions in their original integrity to modify our Constitution, if we can do so, so as to prevent these things from happening.

No complaint can be had at this time as to haste or lack of consideration in regard to this amendment. James Wilson of Pennsylvania presented and urged the matter in the constitutional convention itself. As early as 1826 a resolution was submitted to Congress looking to this change in the manner of electing Senators. It has been before Congress session after session for eighty-five years. It has met the approval of the first branch of Congress many times. It has received serious discussion here upon different occasions by some of the ablest men who have occupied seats in this Chamber. At least thirty-two States have declared in favor of the amendment or the principle. It has been the subject for years of discussion by editors and publicists. Literature on the subject is very extensive. And now after nearly a century of discussion and consideration the sober second thought of the people upon which the fathers so implicitly relied is greatly in its favor. If government of the people, by the people, and for the people has any bearing this record ought to be made now and the judgment of the people here entered in accordance with this earnest and long standing demand.

It is argued by the opponents of the resolution that by changing the mode or manner of electing Senators we will change the nature of the organization of our Government and of the relation of the States to the Federal Government and of the relation of the Senators to the States. What possible structure of our Government will be affected by the fact that a Senator appears in this body as a result of the direct vote of the people rather than by the vote of an agent selected by the people to cast that vote? Is it reasonable to assert that by changing the mode of selecting a State officer you change his attitude toward the State, assuming that a correct attitude is one of faithful representation? There are at least a dozen Senators upon this floor who as a practical fact were elected by the direct vote of the people. The people selected them and elected them. The legislature but recorded the decree already rendered. Do they stand in any different relation to their States; are they less regardful of its interests or hampered more in representing it than those who were elected by the legislatures? If the rights of these States are invaded, are their Senators less sensitive to that fact? Does the current of political power flow any better by flowing in a roundabout way through a legislature than when it flows directly from the source of power to one who is to exercise that power?

The constitutional recognition of sovereignty remaining in the State is recognized in the principle of equal representation and not in the manner of selecting that representation. The national and Federal principle is still preserved, combined and unimpaired, by the equal representation in the Senate and the proportional representation in the House. In like manner the check of one body upon the other is preserved. The object of having two branches of Congress or of any legislative body is to have the representation made by the different constituencies, different interests. Thus we still have, in the language of Mr. Story—

The Senate represents the voice not of a district, but of a State; not of one State, but all; not of the chosen pursuits of a predominant population in one State, but all the pursuits of all the States.

Would the distinguished Senators from the great State of Texas in any different degree represent the broad and diversified interests of that entire State—the trading and shipping interests upon one side and the vast stock-raising interests upon the other? Would not the Senators from the State of Massachusetts still represent not only the manufacturing interests, but the agricultural interests? It would still be true, also, that no law could be passed without a majority of the people and then a majority of the States. The supposed quickness of action under impulse and passion that was sought to be avoided is still avoided. The long service of six years still begets the profound

sense of responsibility and guards against unwarranted yielding
to passing political gales, which it is so often urged the fathers
had in view. None of these fundamental principles are changed
by changing the mode of electing. Rather does the change
guard against the possibility, and in these times the probability,
of securing those who do not represent the State, but interests
or particular forces.

It does not destroy the check intended to guard against
influence exerted through the passion or prejudice of an hour,
while it does tend to guard against sudden changes superinduced
by causes more sinister and destructive to democracy, more
disintegrating and demoralizing than political upheaval or turmoils. Influences far more to be feared than the hasty and
inconsiderate action which the fathers feared are to be dealt
with by our present civilization. If our fathers were wise to
guard against the one, will not their children display something of the same wisdom if in preserving the one they guard
against the other?

One of the most conclusive arguments in favor of taking
the election of Senators away from the State legislatures is that
these lawmaking bodies may be relieved of an exceptional and
unnatural and incongruous duty. Not only is it aside from
any duty or function naturally attaching to legislative bodies,
but it works to the great and almost constant embarrassment
of such a body in its important and natural work. It has
demoralized State legislatures more than any one single matter
with which they have had to deal. The members of the legislature should be elected upon the sole question of their fitness
for the duties of State legislation. After they are elected they
should be permitted to perform that important work with an
eye single to the moral and industrial interests of the State,
disentangled of the purely political task of performing the
duties of an elector. Our States are coming to be almost as
important in the field of legislation, if they do what they should
do, as was Congress in the beginning of the Government. When
measured by their varied interests and population, their moral
and industrial growth, individual States are now equal to the
thirteen States when Congress first assembled. Unfortunately,
and to the disturbance of everyone who reflects deeply upon
the question, many of the duties of the States are being shifted
and subtly attached to the National Government. If there is a
gospel of political salvation which ought to be preached in these
days with the fire and zeal of Peter the Hermit, it is that of
arousing the States to action in these matters of vast and purely

local concern. They ought to claim the right to do that which under the Constitution it was expected they would do.

And then, having the right allowed them, they ought to perform their duty with energy and pride, with intelligence and courage, and with the support of every man who loves our form of government. Just in proportion as you withdraw from the people the responsibility of caring for and the zeal in guarding matters of local concern, just in proportion as you take from them the right and relieve them of the duty of looking after those matters peculiarly belonging to local communities, just in that proportion you unfit the citizen for the duties of citizenship, shut the door of the great school of experience in his face, and deprive him of his training. When you do so you are undermining the pillars of the Federal Union. The man who would see the States stealthily shorn of their responsibility, as that power is defined, responsibility as placed by the great terms of the charter, is either grossly uninformed as to the history of the rise and reign of the people and the underlying principles of representative government or he is in his nature and make-up an enemy of the Federal form of government. There can be no such thing as a great Federal Union without great and powerful States upon which that Union may rest. There can be no such thing as a free and powerful people without a virile, independent, and self-governing citizenship. The only school in God's world for such training is local self-government. It was the great principle upon which our Government was founded. It is just as essential to-day as it was a hundred years ago. It was a great and fundamental truth stated by De Tocqueville when he said:

I maintain that the most powerful and perhaps the only means of interesting men in the welfare of their country which we still possess is to make them partakers in the government.

Equally impressive is the statement of one of the most profound students of our system of government, James Bryce, to the effect:

To the people we go sooner or later; it is upon their wisdom and self-restraint that the stability of the most cunningly devised scheme of government will in the last resort depend.

Mr. President, we need not fear to put a little decentralizing influence into our legislatures or our Government. It will not by any means neutralize the centralizing influence which from day to day we plant. We need not fear nor apologize for going back occasionally and connecting up the sources of political power directly with the people. Immediate, direct, constant contact will not hurt us. It will prove wholesome even if it is somewhat ancient and out of style. It will by no means recompense the people for the rights of sovereignty stolen away under the constant asseveration of public welfare. We have traveled a rapid pace since the Civil War. The dynasty of the bureau was born shortly thereafter. It has grown to wonderful proportions. It is now arrogant and imperious, hungry and insatiable for power. It may be possible that there is a worse form of government than a bureaucratic form of government, but if there is it has yet to be born, for it has never appeared upon the face of the earth.

I might cite a great many instances in which the rights of the citizens have been frittered away before these bureaucratic powers. But it is not my purpose at this time to do other than call attention to the matter. We can afford, very well afford, to reach back as an offset to such movements and get close to the people. Those who feel disturbed because of the democratic tendencies of to-day, of the disposition to liberalize in some directions, will find plenty of consolation in the more rapid and universal march in the other direction. If we are to maintain somewhat the equilibrium between the Federal and the National Government, we must make up in certain directions for the Federal Government what we are doing in other directions for the benefit of the National Government.

In the last twenty years there have been a great many prolonged contests in State legislatures which illustrate one of the great evils of the present system. The entire session of the legislature was occupied in the electing of a Senator, to the exclusion of everything else for which they were called together. In some instances special sessions were called at great expense. In some fourteen instances States have gone without full representation here because of deadlocks in the legislature. In other instances bribery and corruption have been charged and corruption and scandal have attached to the session. It is not alone that direct and open bribery sometimes prevails, but that which is equally as bad more often prevails—bills and measures are traded up or killed, the public interest is sacrificed or actually bartered away, patronage and office enter into the deal and the whole affair becomes a disgrace and is of itself sufficient condemnation of the present system.

Mr. President, the legislature is the arena, narrow and confined, wherein selfish and corrupt influences can successfully operate. The members are few. The chance for combination and approach is always at hand. Why keep that arena for this work? Why give selfish and corrupt influences such strategic advantage? Why not send the fight to the open forum upon which beats the fierce light of public opinion? Why not leave it where it will be settled upon merit, where candidates may appeal to the honor and patriotism of the masses and not be compelled to fight the combinations and trickery of a caucus, where the candidates must also take the people into their confidence before the election certificate is issued? Why compel men to pass through the season of humiliation and shame through which the sitting member of Illinois [William Lorimer][1] is passing if he is guiltless? Why make it possible for men thus to come here if guilty? It is a system vicious and out of date, prepared for a different age and under different conditions than that in which we live. The times demand a different system, a different mechanism for selecting the members of this great body.

The framers of the Constitution had no conception of the election of a Senator as it now takes place. Their idea was that the legislature would get together, not hampered by previous pledges or party obligations, deliberately look over the State, pick out some conspicuously able and competent man, and elect him. The party spirit to-day, the dominancy of party in all such matters, was unknown to them. The party system—and, in saying this, I do not condemn political parties, for they are indispensable to our form of government—the party system has taken away all the virtues and left all the vices of the plan as it was left by the framers. Almost invariably the people have their choice of Senator previous to the meeting of the legislature. Through pledges and otherwise they communicate that choice to their agents, the members of the legislature. If the agent faithfully performs the trust reposed in him, he does nothing more than record the choice of the people who elected him. He simply acts as agent of the principal—the voter. So, in this way, the plan of the fathers falls. But, if the agent violates his trust and votes for some other than the choice of the people, then, and only then, is the election made without regard to instructions from the popular vote, as the fathers assumed it would be. So, under our party system, the ancient principle can only operate by reason of the violation of a trust

[1] Lorimer was later deprived of his seat on the charge that State legislators had been bribed to vote for his election.

or a pledge. That is one of the very conditions which demand
a change. Says Edmund Burke:

> A state without the means of some change is without the means of
> its conservation.

The whole thing may be summed up in this—the principal
has discharged the agent because the agent was incompetent,
and the principal will now do precisely what the agent was
authorized to do. Again I quote from Edmund Burke:

> Better to be despised for too anxious apprehension than ruined by too
> confident a security.

Finally, Mr. President, is it not our duty to give some consideration and some heed to the long-standing, well-sustained,
almost universal demand of the people for this change? I can
not get away from the belief that, in all these great matters
which involve, not technical knowledge, but rather a broad and
wholesome principle of clean and efficient government, the surest
and safest guide is the deliberately formed and long-sustained
judgment of the people. There is something more than rhetoric
in the declaration "that the accumulated intellect of the masses
is greater than the greatest brain God ever gave to a single
individual." Mr. Bryce, in the closing pages of his interesting
and instructive work on our institutions ["The American Commonwealth"] says:

> A hundred times in writing this book have I been disheartened by
> the facts I was stating; a hundred times has the recollection of the
> abounding strength and vitality of the nation chased away these tremors.

There are a vast number of things in this Government in
which the people can have practically no voice and upon which
they can therefore have but a most indirect influence. That
sphere of government activity is, unfortunately, constantly increasing. We are fast becoming a Government by commission.
Not a Congress sits, but a bureau must be created with its hundreds of retainers; not a Congress ends, but some part of the
Government has been pushed a little farther from those in whose
welfare we are supposed to work.

Now, of necessity, many of these things must be done in this
way. But there are some things which the people may do which
they ought to do and which we ought to afford them the most
convenient opportunity to do. They may select their political
servants who make their laws. They may select the constitu-

tional agents who execute the laws. This is a power which they can exercise and which it will be wholesome for them to continue to exercise. It is our duty to place this power in constant, direct, immediate touch with the people. Dismiss every agent that it is possible to be rid of and go direct to the principal. Give him the responsibility and his own sense of patriotism will appreciate in time that responsibility, and he will not abuse it. It is only under such a system that men may grow to the full stature of citizenship in a republic.

On January 20 Isidor Rayner [Md.] supported the resolution.

I want to call the attention of the Senate to the two amendments, one the amendment of the Senator from Utah [George Sutherland], and the other the amendment of the Senator from New York [Chauncey M. Depew].

The resolution reported by the committee provides:

The Senate of the United States shall be composed of two Senators from each State, elected by the people thereof for six years; and each Senator shall have one vote. The electors in each State shall have the qualifications requisite for electors of the most numerous branch of the State legislatures.

The Senator from Utah proposes to add to that:

But Congress may at any time by law make or alter such regulations, except as to the places of choosing Senators.

In other words, the Senator from Utah takes the provision that is now in the Constitution [Article I, § 4, par. 1] with reference to the election of Representatives and attaches that provision to the election of Senators by the people.

THOMAS H. CARTER [Mont.].—Is it not the understanding of the Senator from Maryland that, when Senators are elected by popular vote, just as members of the House of Representatives are elected by popular vote, the same rule as to control by the Federal Government should obtain as to both?

SENATOR RAYNER.—Not at all, Mr. President. I object to the rule; and, if the Senator from Montana asks me my own opinion, I will say that, if I had my way, I should like to take out of the Constitution the clause which gives Congress the right to change the regulations of the States, even as to the election of Representatives, because it was under that clause that the bill known as the force bill was attempted to be passed here in the Senate, and I am opposed to it; but there it is and we can not change it, because we are not providing now for the election of Representatives, but, now that we have a new proposition for the election of Senators, I am opposed to applying the objectionable clause to the election of Senators.

If you give Congress the right to override the regulations of a State as to the manner of electing Senators, then you give Congress the power to pass a bill like the force bill or any bill substantially similar. I object to putting that power in the hands of the Federal Congress.

Now, let me come to the amendment of the Senator from New York [Mr. Depew], because we must take both these amendments together. Here is the amendment of the Senator from New York:

> The qualifications of citizens entitled to vote for United States Senators and Representatives in Congress shall be uniform in all the States, and Congress shall have power to enforce this article by appropriate legislation and to provide for the registration of citizens entitled to vote, the conduct of such elections, and the certification of the result.

Of course that goes much further than the amendment of the Senator from Utah, and it goes much further than the force bill attempted to go, because the force bill attempted to draw its power from the Constitution. This draws the power away from the Constitution and takes away the right of suffrage that is resident in the States and transfers it to the Federal Congress, gives Congress the right to control not only the machinery of elections, but to control the right of suffrage in every State of the Union. In other words, it shatters the Constitution of the United States to fragments by depriving the States of the right to say who shall enjoy the right of suffrage. It would deprive a State of the right to pass an educational qualification. It would deprive a State of the right to pass a property qualification. It would take away the entire power of the State and transfer it to the Federal Government, so far as the suffrage and qualification of its citizens are concerned. As it stands to-day, the States can do anything, provided there is no interference with the Fourteenth and Fifteenth Amendments, or there is no discrimination on account of race, color, or previous condition of servitude.

Limited by that amendment, I apprehend that there is not anything that the State can not do with reference to the suffrages of its citizens. The Supreme Court has said so in an unbroken line of cases, from the case of Minor *vs.* Happersett, from which I will not quote, but which I have in my hand, and which is found in Twenty-first Wallace, up to the case of Williams *vs.* Mississippi. They have never yet said that suffrage rests in the Federal Government. They have never yet said that the right of suffrage is an immunity or a privilege under the Fourteenth Amendment. On the contrary, they have said the opposite. They held, in this case, when they were contending for woman's suffrage, that a woman was a citizen, but that suffrage was not an immunity, and that, while she had the right to enjoy the rights of citizenship, she did not have the right to vote under any provision of the Constitution of the United States, and the State, in denying her a vote, had a right to do so.

NORRIS BROWN [Neb.].—Before the Senator leaves that branch of his argument I would call his attention to the fact that this supervisory power of Congress against which he complains is already in the Constitution. It is found in section 4 of Article I.

The proposition in the joint resolution is not only to change section 1, to take away from the legislature the power to elect a Senator and confer it on the people, but it goes further and contains an additional amendment to the Constitution, taking away from Congress the power of supervision. Those are two distinct propositions. The effort of the Senator from Utah is to confine the joint resolution to one proposition, namely, to allow the people to have an opportunity to elect their Senators.

I wish the Senator from Maryland would suggest why he objects to giving the Senate an opportunity to vote on a single proposition. Why not give the people of the United States the right to vote on a single amendment—the one that has been discussed, the one that has been demanded by the American people, and that is the right to elect their Senators, and why is it necessary in this joint resolution to submit two separate and distinct amendments?

I will say to the Senator, so far as I am concerned, I am willing to vote for his proposition and let it be referred to the States. Our adoption of the joint resolution does not amend the Constitution, and, without regard to the merits of his proposition, I am willing to vote for it by itself and thereby give the people an opportunity to put it in the Constitution if they want it there.

SENATOR RAYNER.—Suppose the insertion of the amendment of the Senator from Utah defeats the resolution. Suppose every

Southern State votes against the amendment that Congress can control their elections. What would the Senator say then? Suppose every Southern State is in favor of the joint resolution the way we reported it, and that every Southern State is against it the way the Senator from Utah proposes to amend it; does the Senator think he would be justified in insisting on putting that amendment in the body of the joint resolution?

SENATOR BROWN.—The trouble with the Senator is that he assumes that we are insisting upon putting in the joint resolution two propositions. I am insisting on leaving the joint resolution with one proposition.

SENATOR RAYNER.—Then the Senator and I are in accord on our proposition.

SENATOR BROWN.—I am in accord with the proposition of leaving the Constitution, so far as this joint resolution goes, alone——

SENATOR RAYNER.—Oh!

SENATOR BROWN.—Except on the proposition of the election of Senators.

SENATOR RAYNER.—Then the Senator has not stated his position so that we can understand it. Let me state plainly what the Senator is in favor of: The Senator is dealing with a new proposition—the election of Senators by the people. He is dealing with a proposition that the Constitution does not refer to, because the Constitution does not apply to the election of Senators by the people.

The Senator proposes to take a clause of the Constitution, which applies only to election of Senators by the legislature, and make that clause applicable to the election of Senators by the people. Therefore he is embodying two propositions, and we are embodying one proposition.

SENATOR BROWN.—I propose to put nothing in the joint resolution except the proposition to give to the people of the State the right to elect by direct vote the Senators of that State.

Senator Rayner then turned his attention to the principle of the resolution.

The most formidable speech, perhaps, that was ever made in this body against submitting this question to the people was the one made by George F. Hoar, of Massachusetts. I want briefly just to refer to some of the objections that he urged, merely to show that most of them are now impractical and obsolete, and therefore do not apply to the present situation.

One of the objections pressed by the Senator was that—

Such a method of election would essentially change the character of the Senate as conceived by the convention that framed the Constitution and the people who adopted it.

I am very sorry that I can not acquiesce in this statement. I do not think that an election by the people will change the character of the Senate. The members of the House of Representatives are elected by the people, and, in my judgment, there is no parliamentary assemblage in the world that compares with it, both as to character and ability.

The next objection that he made was this:

It would transfer practically the selection of the members of this body from the legislatures, who are intrusted with all legislative powers of the States, to bodies having no other responsibilities, whose election can not be regulated by law, whose members act by proxy, whose tenure of office is for a single day, whose votes and proceedings are not recorded, who act under no personal responsibility, whose mistakes ordinarily can only be corrected by the choice of Senators who do not represent the opinions concerning public measures and policies of the people who choose them.

I answer that by saying that in a great many of the States now Senators are nominated at primary elections, and I believe the time will come when every State will adopt this system.

Senator Hoar then stated:

It will create new temptations to fraud, corruption, and other illegal practices.

How will there be any temptations to fraud, corruption, or other illegal practices, especially in the States where they have corrupt practice laws?

Here is a proposition that I have never been able to understand. Senator Hoar said:

It will absolve the larger States from the constitutional obligation which secures the equal representation of all the States in the Senate by providing that no State shall be deprived of that equality without its consent.

I can not see how it can possibly have this effect. This constitutional provision is not subject to amendment without the consent of the State that is affected, and it is, therefore, impossible for me to comprehend how the larger States can be absolved from a constitutional obligation which obligation is unamendable by the terms of the Constitution itself.

I ask Senators who are opposing the joint resolution, how will this proposition disturb the equality of the States? You can not disturb that equality, Mr. President, without the consent of the State itself. The Constitution provides that that equality can not be interfered with unless the States consent. If every State in the Union except the nonassenting State were to favor an amendment giving the larger States a greater representation in this body than the smaller States, it would be void, because the Constitution says it requires the acquiescence of the State whose representation is to be changed.

Then the Senator states:

The constitutional convention concluded that every act of the legislature was to be twice considered and have the approbation of two different, separate Houses.

Has it not the approbation of two different, separate Houses? Whether those separate Houses are elected differently or elected the same way, how does it interfere with the approbation of two Houses to have both elections by the people?

Then the Senator says:

These two Houses were to have a different constituency. So every proposed law must run the gauntlet of two diverse interests and be judged from at least two points of view. Every State in the construction of its legislature has maintained these two principles.

Is not that a mistake, Mr. President? Because in every State, as I understand it, the Senate and the House of Delegates are elected by the same constituency and not by different constituencies.

Then the Senator says:

The Senate was to represent deliberation in the expression of the popular will by the length of the term of office of Senators.

We are not doing anything here to affect the term of office of Senator.

Then the Senator concludes the learned and masterly presentation of his objections by saying: "I do not believe in the brutal force of numbers."

The Earl of Roscommon once said that the multitude is always in the wrong. It seeems to me that in reading this great argument of this lamented Senator, there were some distinguished persons in this Republic who had reached the same conclusion. I think that the intelligent and patriotic multitude is generally in the right.

SENATOR SUTHERLAND.—If we do not adopt my amendment then we shall have in the Constitution hereafter two separate and, in some respects, antagonistic provisions. There will be a provision in the Constitution giving the Congress full supervisory power over the election of Representatives by the people and absolutely removing the supervisory hand of the Federal Government over the election of Senators by that same people. What reason is there for making that distinction? Why should we permit Congress to supervise the election of Representatives by the people and decline to give Congress the power to supervise the election of Senators by the people?

AUGUSTUS O. BACON [Ga.].—I want to ask the Senator from Utah if, in his opinion, this amendment should be adopted, would it be within the province of the Federal Government to prescribe that the Federal Government should have agents at elections to supervise those elections at which Senators would be chosen, to see the manner in which the votes were cast, and to enforce what might be thought to be the rights of electors?

SENATOR SUTHERLAND.—I think Congress would have that power, Mr. President, but that does not frighten me. Congress has possessed that power over elections to the House for nearly 125 years, and it has never exercised it, in my judgment, in a way that was not justified by the circumstances which existed at the time the particular laws have been passed. We have passed laws providing for supervision of elections, but this was at a time when such laws were absolutely necessary, and when the occasion for them had gone those laws were repealed.

On January 24 Senator Depew supported his amendment to the joint resolution.

This resolution virtually repeals the Fourteenth and Fifteenth Amendments to the Constitution. It validates by constitutional amendment laws under which citizens of the United States, constituting in the aggregate more than one-tenth of the electorate, are to be permanently deprived of the right of suffrage. These laws have their origin in a fear of the negro vote in those States where it is equal to the white vote or larger than the white vote. But they are urged or passed for purely political purposes in States where there is no possible fear of the dominance of the negro vote. Maryland, with a small proportionate negro vote, has tried several times within the last few years to disfranchise the colored people within that State, and the avowed purpose of the Democratic party in the

State of Maryland, which is not denied, is to continue this effort until they have succeeded in disfranchising this vote.

It is a curious commentary upon our forgetfulness of the results of the war for the Union that we have grown indifferent to such an extent to these provisions which were made the permanent results of that struggle by being engrafted into the Constitution. It becomes a subject of earnest study and of serious reflection whether, if it were a mistake to adopt the Fourteenth and Fifteenth Amendments at the close of the Civil War, it is not a greater mistake 45 years afterward, when intelligence and education have made such progess among these people, to so impair as to virtually repeal those articles.

The title of this proposition is to allow the people to vote. The purpose and object of the resolution is permanently to prevent the people from voting in any State where a dominant power or oligarchy wishes to disfranchise a certain portion of the citizens of that State. Now, I have sympathized with the conditions of the people of the Southern States since the Civil War. I have persistently and consistently opposed all the drastic measures which have been presented to interfere with their affairs. I was not in favor of the force bill. I was not in favor of the bill which passed the House of Representatives to enforce the provisions of the Fourteenth Amendment for the reduction of membership in the House of Representatives in proportion to the reduction of the negro vote in several States. But, when it comes to deliberately voting to undo the results of the Civil War, when it comes by constitutional amendment to permanently taking from 10,000,000 people the rewards of education and intelligence, that reward being in a free government the right to vote, I can not assent to or be silent upon the proposition.

Six years ago this same question came up in the Committee on Privileges and Elections, of which I was a member, and I then proposed this same amendment to the resolution which I have offered here.

This amendment simply says that, if the people are to vote for the election of United States Senators, then all the people recognized as citizens under the Constitution of the United States shall be permitted to vote. At that time this proposition of mine was incorporated into the general resolution, and had the unanimous vote of every Republican member of the committee, even of those who were in favor of changing the method of electing United States Senators from the legislature to the people. When it was adopted the resolution was defeated by the unanimous vote of the Democratic members of the committee.

But when I offered it in our Committee on the Judiciary it commanded only one vote beside my own.

Every Senator knows that the votes which have been cast in the several States for this measure have been so given in obedience to supposed party expediency and without general discussion. This movement has received more impetus from the advocacy of William J. Bryan than from any other cause during the half century since the war. And yet, when Mr. Bryan, with the responsibilities of office upon him as a member of Congress, proposed his idea of an amendment to the Constitution for this purpose in 1894, he left it for each State to decide whether it would elect United States Senators by the old method or the new. All the States which framed the Constitution and all those that can reckon a quarter of a century to their lives, in selecting men who have shed the greatest honor upon their respective commonwealths, have invariably named them from the membership of the United States Senate. No method of electing Senators could add to that glorious list. It has been said that governors of States furnish an example to the contrary, but it is the history of governors that they are in for a short time. They rarely succeed themselves, and, if they do, only once. I do not know that there is on record a single instance of a governor who has been ten years in the service of his State. Every Senator knows that the value of a member of this body, if he is fit to be a member of it, increases with the years. Every Senator also knows that, in popular elections, taking the governor as an example, covering the whole State, the second term would be the limit of the senatorial life of anyone, no matter how distinguished. Our Websters, our Clays, our Calhouns, with all their genius for public life and popular leadership, owed their influence upon the policies of parties and the legislation of the Republic to long experience in the Senate. The results of the primary laws have demonstrated that the United States Senator who comes here under the new system would, in a vast majority of cases, be the choice of a plurality, and, therefore, a minority candidate. In States where one party is sufficiently in the ascendant to make an election certain candidates would be as numerous as the ambitions of the citizens, and the successful one on the plurality might represent only a tenth of the electorate. The favorite of the great cities would always prevent the success of a candidate from the country. In many States, where the party discipline and organization have been submerged by the primary, races or religions combine and, by their united force, as against the scattered results of the general electorate, secure the necessary plurality for one of their race or religion. There is not the slightest pretence that, during the long life of our Government, a Senator has ever been placed in this body because of race or religion. I do not share in this distrust of the legislatures. Our several commonwealths have wisely legislated for the interest of the family, of property, of liberty. I do not assent to the proposition that representative government has the distrust of the people.

The Athenian Assembly was the ideal of popular government. I stood once upon the rocky platform from which Demosthenes addressed the voters of Athens. There were 300,000 slaves and 10,000 citizens. Those 10,000 easily gathered upon the plain in front of the orator. He won from his audience the approval of the measures which he proposed against his antagonists because of his eloquence and his ability to fire the popular imagination, stir the popular enthusiasm, and, through them, influence for the moment popular judgment. By holding up the raw head and bloody bones of Philip of Macedon he swept away all opposition, while Philip of Macedon had no purpose such as Demosthenes charged. We all know the appeals which can move a popular audience. A war speech and the bloody shirt had their influence for 25 years after Appomattox. When the new generation of voters came upon the stage these appeals meant nothing to them, and the campaign orators had to write new speeches upon new issues or else retire from the platform, as many of them did, because they could not comprehend the new issues. For 25 years more the operation of the railroads was an effective rallying cry. But legislation has been perfected for the control of the railroads by providing penalties for abuse and conferring such absolute power upon the Interstate Commerce Commission and the Commerce Court that the Government is the paramount member of the directorate of every railroad in the United States, and that has ceased to be the rallying cry. Next, it was the corporations. Again, legislation has largely cured corporate evils. The Sherman anti-trust law, strengthened by the decisions of the courts, and the corporation-tax law, exposing ever secret of every corporation to the Government and, through the Government, to the people, furnishes power, on the one hand, to the Government and that publicity, on the other, which makes corporate iniquities exceedingly difficult and punishment swift and sure.

Now a Chautauqua audience can be raised to frenzied heights of rage by picturing to them that they are the slaves of the interests. The interests are vague, but the more shadowy, like the ghost, the more terrible. Of course, the Athenian example is impossible with 100,000,000 of people, but the whole theory of democratic government in its evolution in Europe and in America is to escape, on the one side, from the arbitrary power of the autocrat, backed up by control of the army, the navy, the treasury, and taxes, and, on the other hand, to devise processes by which the passions of the hour shall not crystallize into legislation without plenty of time for deliberation and calm judgment. In a sense, every form of representative government may be called distrust of the people. Wherever a measure must take its chances, first with the Lower House and then with the Upper House, and then, again, in running the gauntlet, must escape the club of the veto of the Executive, every step is distrust of popular government. But it is a false idea to say that such distrust means lack of confidence in the people, or means defying the popular will. It is simply that where the great mass of the population are engaged in industrial pursuits, which absorb their minds and time, they must necessarily select from among their own number those whom they think best fitted for the tasks upon whom they devolve, as President or as Senator or as Representative or as governor or as member of the legislature, the perfection of measures and the enactment of laws which are for the best interests of the people.

I have received many letters since I introduced my amendment indicating the trend of popular thought, and many editorials not proper to be read in the Senate. Some of them go to an extreme which ought to please that eloquent advocate of popular government, the distinguished Senator from Oregon [Jonathan Bourne], and his recently organized salvation army. [Laughter.] They say: "Abolish the Senate. It is no further of any use. It was all very well when there were no railroads, no telegraphs, and no telephones, or morning and evening papers to have a Senate to hold in check the House until the people could be heard from; but now, with all these means of instantaneous and intelligent information, the people are informed every day, can reach their immediate Representatives every hour, and they need no protection by a conservative and critical body elected for a longer term and with securer hold of office." Others say: "In amending the Constitution, so amend it that no representative of the interests can be a Senator." They define the interests as every man who, in his personal business or in any employment he may have, is interested in legislation. They bar out everyone who, directly or indirectly, may be affected by the tariff. They bar out all who are coun-

sel for those who may be affected by the tariff. They bar out
all stockholders, bondholders, and counsel of corporations. They
bar out labor unions. They reduce the opportunities for choice
by this process of elimination until, if they ultimately succeed,
the United States Senate will be composed entirely of under-
takers, whose profits are in the increasing number of those who
die. [Laughter.]

Two sets of States, though having entirely different interests,
are cordially united in pressing this legislation. They are the
new States with small populations compared with the older ones,
and what were formerly known as the slave States of the
Union. This is the only measure on which is unfortunately revived the "solid South." I warn each of them that they are
prying off the lid from Pandora's box. They are letting loose
the devils to pursue them with increasing aggressiveness, force,
and strength during the coming years.

Senator Depew then discussed the subject of disfranchisement of negroes in the South, and the likelihood of
this becoming a paramount political issue if the power
of disfranchisement were strengthened by the adoption
of the proposed constitutional amendment. He presented statistics on the subject.

Now, as to the qualifications or disqualifications, undoubtedly
nobody votes in those States except those who are qualified by
the State laws. But who are disqualified? We all know the
grandfather clause, which is still in existence in many of the
States. But there are others. For instance, there is the educational clause.

SENATOR BACON.—Found also in Massachusetts.

JOSEPH W. BAILEY [Tex.].—It ought to be found in all of
them.

SENATOR DEPEW.—But in its application very different in
Massachusetts. A very interesting story was told me, and sometimes an illustration shows the situation better than an argument. This story was told me by a friend of mine, a South-
erner, a Yale man, and, therefore, entitled to belief on all questions. He said that at a precinct in his county a negro preacher
came up to vote. The canvassing officer said: "You know under
our law you have to read and write." "Well," he said, "I was
educated at Howard University and at the Howard Theological
School; I can read and write." "Do you understand the Constitution of the United States? That is another requisite."

"Well," said the clergyman, "I know it by heart, and think I understand it." "Well," said the canvasser, "under the Constitution of the United States you must get out a writ of *habeas corpus* before you can be permitted to cast a vote, and do you know what a *habeas corpus* is?" The minister answered: "No, Mr. Canvasser; I do not know what a *habeas corpus* is, but I do know that a negro can not vote in the State of Mississippi." [Laughter.]

Parties are always seeking paramount issues. The great leader of the Democratic party made this question of changing the method of the election of United States Senators, as he thought, a paramount issue. It failed to materialize as he imagined it would, because there was no popular response, and there is none to-day. But the glaring inequality exhibited by the figures which I present of negro disfranchisement are a firm foundation for a paramount issue. The resistless cry from the stump and from the press will be: "Less than a million of people shall not be permitted to neutralize and possibly defeat the wishes of over 27,000,000 citizens. This is a government of the people, by the people, and for the people, and here is a small oligarchy blocking the progress and defeating the wishes of an overwhelming majority. We have paved the way for this reform. It took us, the people, one hundred and twenty-two years to get rid of the fetish of the sacredness of the Constitution. Now we have buried that bugaboo, and the people, having come into their own in part, must regain the whole of the power to which they are entitled." What are our friends who are so gaily and hilariously pushing this proposition going to answer before indignant multitudes to this natural sequence? The next slogan for popular appeal will be: "Mend the Senate or end it."

Every intelligent student of the present rapid trend toward popular government must see what would happen when this sentimental bar of the States being represented by two Senators instead of by the people in the United States Senate is thrown down. The initiative, the referendum, and the recall are but symptoms of the times. That the people will have their way, because they, and they alone, are the government, is the underlying spirit of our institutions, of our newest State constitutions, and of our progressive laws. Skillful agitation seizes upon every pretext and eagerly grasps and enlarges every opportunity for appeal to the passions in an advancement of its purposes. The next cry will necessarily be: "Why not elect the Supreme Court of the United States by popular vote?" Why not elect the Fed-

eral judiciary everywhere by a popular vote? Unless we admit
that the fathers made a mistake, and a grave one, in throwing
these restrictions upon the immediate expression of the passion
of the hour into legislation or decision, there is no legitimate
answer to such a proposition. A constitutional convention can
abrogate the promise of equality of the States in the Senate in
the present Constitution. Let the wave rise high enough and
thirty millions of people will not consent to have their will
thwarted and their laws enacted by five millions. Majorities
are never sentimental and, when they believe they are right,
never merciful. "The power is ours by nature and by right, and
we will come into our own," will be the cry of the majorities
in the future, and there is no logical answer to the claim.

On February 6 Henry Cabot Lodge [Mass.] made a
speech against the resolution in the tenor of the great
speech of his predecessor, Senator Hoar.

On February 9 Joseph L. Bristow [Kan.] spoke in
favor of the resolution.

We are warned not to depart from the wisdom of the Fathers
by changing the manner of choosing the members of this body.
Such an argument, in the light of modern development, is
without weight. The conditions that exist in the United States
to-day are vastly different from those that prevailed when the
Constitution was framed. In 1790 there was but one post-office
for every 52,000 people, while to-day we have one post-office for
every 1,500 people. There was not a single letter carrier on
the continent. Then the postage on a four-page letter from
Washington to Boston was $1; now you can send that same letter
from Porto Rico to Manila, more than half way around the
globe, for 2 cents. At that time there was published but one
copy of a newspaper or periodical per week for each 50 of our
population; now there are four copies per day for every family.
Such a state of society as we now enjoy was not within the
wildest dreams of the most ardent enthusiasts among the founders of the Republic. Yet Senators tell us that to change the
details or the manner of electing Senators is to reflect upon the
wisdom of the forefathers. Mr. President, I join with the Senator from Massachusetts [Mr. Lodge] in paying high tribute
to the great wisdom and patriotism of the framers of the Constitution. He can not hold them in deeper reverence than I,
though his great learning enables him to express that reverence
in more eloquent phrases. But, while I join him in paying

tribute to the wisdom of the Revolutionary fathers, I regret that he refuses to join me in expressing confidence in the judgment and wisdom of the people of our own times. Without reflecting in the slightest degree upon the ability of the members of Congress in any other age of our country's history, I assert that the average American citizen to-day has a better education, is more thoroughly informed on public questions, has a keener sense of the responsibilities of citizenship, and is better equipped to pass judgment as to the wisdom of governmental policies than was the average member of the House of Representatives a century ago. Then a college graduate in a community was a rare and distinguished individual. Now they are to be found by the dozen in almost every township.

For the first half century of our history the greed of commercialism, except as it related to the slavery question, was not developed; now it is a menace to the country's welfare. As the commercial spirit developed and opportunities increased to use the power of government to promote the selfish interests of financial and industrial institutions, such concerns became more anxious to control the Senate. This has brought about the numerous legislative scandals that have occurred in recent years, and such scandal not only will continue but will increase until there is a change in the method of electing Senators.

In this connection I desire to say that not only do I believe that opportunity should be given the people to vote direct for their Senators, and to elect them in the same manner as they elect their Congressmen and governors, but I believe that all delegates to our national conventions should be elected by a direct primary, and that, on the primary ballot, the voter should express his first and second choice for the nominees of his party. It then would be the business of the national conventions to carry out the will of the people as expressed in the primary election. The expression of a second choice, to show the general preference of the people of a State that might have a "favorite son" as a candidate, is necessary in order that the choice of the people independent of local favor may be ascertained. It has become customary for national conventions to be made up of a large number of Federal officeholders who want to perpetuate themselves in official power, or to be composed of ambitious men who hope to secure the Federal offices. In addition to these two classes there are a number of commanding delegates who represent the powerful financial and commercial institutions of the country, and who are there to look after the interests of such institutions. Trusts and combinations representing great

transportation and industrial companies seek to control the
State and national conventions of both the great political parties,
and, if they succeed, it makes little difference to them how the
election goes or which side wins. Their representatives contribute generously to both campaign committees, and, because
of such contributions, expect to secure certain appointments and
also to control the legislation in which they are concerned. These
selfish financial interests are exceedingly anxious, first, to control the appointment of Federal judges; second, to shape the
laws which affect their interests; and, third, to control the appointment of the executive officers who are to administer those
laws.

Mr. President, these great combinations of wealth, under the
system that now prevails, have acquired too much power in the
affairs of this Government, and they have used that power to
enrich themselves at the expense of the general public. Unless
a change is made, not only in the method of electing Senators,
but also in the manner of selecting delegates to the national
conventions, the rising tide of unrest and dissatisfaction that
prevails throughout the country to-day will rapidly increase.
Men will not become less greedy for wealth and power. The
great financial interests will not abate their efforts to control,
not only the business, but the politics of the country.

The Senator from Massachusetts declared that the political
power of gigantic combinations of wealth had been broken, and
that they are no longer endeavoring to control the politics of the
country. How can the distinguished Senator entertain such a
delusion when at this very hour there are in a number of States
deadlocks in pending senatorial elections, caused solely by the
dogged and persistent determination of certain powerful financial interests to control the election of Senators from those
States. There never has been a time when these interests were
more vigilant and grasping for political power and dominion
than now.

Sir, I believe we are approaching a crisis, not only in our
commercial and industrial life, but in our political affairs as
well. The development of modern times has made it necessary
to place more power directly into the hands of the people, that
they may not only protect the man of small business from the
greed of his great and powerful competitor, but that they may
also protect the integrity of our political institutions.

We are warned by those who oppose this resolution that
by this change in the manner of electing Senators we will make
them responsible to the will of the mob, and, therefore, sub-

servient to the passion and prejudice of the unthinking masses; that by such a change we will endanger the perpetuity of our institutions. I do not believe it. I am not afraid of the mob. The American people are not controlled by passion or prejudice. They are conservative and cautious; do not welcome change, and cling to precedent. You place in their hands great power, and they will exercise it with deliberation and care.

The stability of a free government depends upon the intelligence and patriotism of its people. It is one of the fundamental laws of human nature that great responsibility not only brings out the best efforts of man, but also develops the conservative elements of his character.

Give the people greater power and more direct responsibility for the administration of the Government, and you bring to its institutions the most careful thought and patriotic consideration of the great masses of our population. General Grant has been credited with the statement that all the people know more than any one man. This, I believe, can be broadened into a declaration that all the people know more than any set of men. The marvelous and unprecedented progress of modern times in every branch of human industry and every line of mental effort has been possible only because the intellect of the race had been unshackled and the mental energies of the entire population brought into action. This Government of ours will be better administered and more wisely governed by inviting every citizen to give his best thought to the solution of its problems. Place greater responsibility for its administration upon the average man, and it will develop in him the highest degree of patriotism. It will place upon him that deep sense of responsibility that goes with ownership. He will feel more that this is his Government, and that he is responsible for the welfare of its institutions. Instead of endangering such institutions it will be their greatest safety. It will intrench them in the affections of an intelligent, patriotic, and devoted citizenship.

Sir, the menace to our country's future is not in the mad fury and passion of the unthinking mob. The mob has no influence with the American mind. It is repulsive to that sense of stability and order which is fundamental in the Anglo-Saxon's nature. Our menace is not the mob, but the greed and avarice of men who seek to control legislation for personal gain. Resentment against the injustice and tyranny of the trusts and the combinations of modern commercial life is far more dangerous to the welfare of this Republic than the action of an unthinking or turbulent spirit.

On February 20 Senator Borah spoke on the Sutherland amendment.

I do not know, Mr. President, how long the North is going to play the hypocrite or the moral coward on this negro question. The North always assumes, when we come to discuss the negro question, that there is in the North a superiority of wisdom and of judgment and of virtue and of tolerance with reference to dealing with that question which is not found in other parts of the country.

The Northern States have exhibited the same animosity, the same race prejudice and race hatred that have been developed in the other parts of the Union. We burn the negro at the stake; our Northern soil is cursed with race wars; we push the negro to the outer edge of the industrial world; we exhibit toward him the same intolerance in proportion to his number in our part of the country as they do in every other part of the land, and in the same way. I have not a particle of doubt, Mr. President, if we had to deal with this subject in all its widespread ramifications as others have to deal with it, judging from what has happened in Colorado, in Illinois, and in numberless other States of the North, that we would exhibit the same qualities, and display the same weaknesses and the same intolerance that others have been charged with exhibiting or possessing.

I want to ask my friends who have raised this question of protecting the negro in the South, and who assert that we have the power under Section 4 of Article I to deal with the subject, why we do not exercise the power if we have it. Speaking for myself, I deny that the power extends where the exigencies of this debate have sent it, and I resent the proposition that for 40 years wrongs have been committed which we have had the power to deal with, and that we have cowardly refused to exercise that power.

It is a fine situation, Mr. President, in which the great Republican party finds itself in this debate. It has been practically asserted, indeed, sir, it has been asserted upon the floor of the Senate that, under Section 4 of Article I, we can deal with what is called the "grandfather clauses" of State constitutions.

Then the question arises: When are we going to deal with them? It is my deliberate opinion that we have not an iota of power under Section 4 to deal with the question of suffrage in any State of this Union so long as it complies with the

Fifteenth Amendment of the Constitution, and whether it has or not can always be tested under the provisions of that amendment alone and of itself.

It has been asserted deliberately upon the floor of this body that the repeal of Section 4 of Article I would embarrass, if not repeal, the Fourteenth and Fifteenth Amendments to the Constitution.

Section 4 of Article I deals alone with individuals. The Fourteenth and Fifteenth Amendments deal alone with the States. It might be true that if Section 4 were retained we could do some things which it has been contended we should do by those Senators who are supporting the amendment which was offered by the Senator from Utah [Mr. Sutherland]; but certainly it can never be contended that a provision in the Constitution which deals with individuals can impair in any respect the provision of the Constitution which deals alone with the action of the States.

Let me say to the negro, from my place in the Senate, that, after the exigencies of this debate are over, after this resolution has again been killed, if they should succeed, you will never again hear anything about the virtues or the power of Section 4. No measure will be offered here, no bill passed under it for the substantial advantage or benefit of the negro. Let me say to the black man of the South and to his black brother in the North, do not permit the anxious and restless and hopeful spirit to call you from the path you are pursuing of working out your own salvation.

No law will be proposed, no statute passed, no voice will be raised in this Chamber again for years. The silence of the last decade will be followed by the silence of the next decade. The negro should turn from these political contentions and political exigencies and find the truth in reading the plain terms of the Constitution and decisions of the great tribunal that has never trifled with his cause. There he will find the exact measure of the nation's power.

Yes; let the truth be told. Let the hard facts be known that the State, and the State alone, fixes the qualifications of the voter, and that, outside of the principle of no discrimination, we are powerless to do otherwise. This is the great law of equality upon which all republics are founded, and it is the great law of equality under which all races must work out their salvation, and under which we must all be content to live. The North and the South must be satisfied with the rule. [Applause in the galleries.]

On February 21 Isidor Rayner [Md.] replied to an argument which had been previously made by Elihu Root [N. Y.].

I want to read the colloquy between the Senator from Georgia [Augustus O. Bacon] and the Senator from New York, and I want to see whether I cannot convince the Senator from New York that he is wrong in the proposition that he stated in that colloquy. There is no one at the American bar for whose opinion I have a higher respect than I have for that of the Senator from New York; there is no one for whose professional and private and public character I have a greater admiration. I know that in the heat of conflict he is as fair a foe as anyone could encounter, and I believe that, if he states a proposition of law and makes what I consider to be a fatal mistake, when his attention is called to it he will retract the statement he has made upon further reflection and an examination of the authorities.

The Senator from Georgia [Mr. Bacon] said:

Mr. President, do I understand the Senator from New York to mean that if the States have now upon their statute books laws which regulate the suffrage in those States, such as the Senator speaks of as "the grandfather clause," though that is simply a term generic in its character which relates to a general class of legislation—does the Senator mean that, with the laws now upon the statute books of the several Southern States, if the proposed amendment of the Senator from Utah [Mr. Sutherland] should be adopted, and we should pass the joint resolution to amend the Constitution, and it should be ratified by three-fourths of the States, it would then be within the power of Congress, if it conceived that these grandfather clauses as they are called—all the body of laws with reference to the regulations and limitations of the suffrage in the Southern States— if Congress should conceive that they were unconstitutional, does the Senator mean that, in his opinion, Congress would have the power, under the amendment of the Senator from Utah, to annul those provisions and to make Federal laws to control the election of Senators in such a way as to insure the right to vote to all persons thought by Congress to be entitled to vote?

SENATOR ROOT. Without the slightest doubt.

SENATOR BACON. Well, Mr. President, it is well that we are given this notice of what the Senator does mean and what the Sutherland amendment means.

SENATOR ROOT. I meant to put you on notice, and I mean to put the whole country on notice if my words are able to do so.

With great deference to the Senator from New York, I say that he is mistaken in the proposition of law, entirely mistaken. He is at variance with the decisions of the Supreme Court, and I will proceed, within the space of a very few minutes, to attempt to demonstrate that he is wrong.

Mr. President, what is that proposition? Let us look at it a moment. Of course, I know the Senator from New York is perfectly honest and sincere. I know that the Senator is opposed to the popular election of Senators by the people. He has said that, and we know it. I do not believe for a moment that he wants the Sutherland amendment put into the joint resolution merely to obtain votes on our side against it; I believe he is earnestly in favor of the amendment; but he has stated a proposition which, if it were true, would concentrate the whole Democratic vote against the joint resolution. I purpose to show that, even if it be put into the joint resolution, it can not possibly have the effect that the learned Senator from New York gives to it.

The right of suffrage, my friends, is in the States. The right of suffrage is not embraced in the Constitution of the United States. Citizens derive their right to vote, subject to the Fifteenth Amendment, from the States; and Congress can not, except by a constitutional amendment, change the electoral systems of the South and take away their right to control the suffrage, because those systems, as announced in Williams *vs.* Mississippi, are in obedience to the Constitution, and have been upheld by the Supreme Court of the United States.

Therefore the Sutherland amendment will never give you the power to change the electoral systems of any Southern commonwealth. You can not take away the suffrage of its citizens. You can prevent discrimination, but the State is the judge of the qualifications of its electors. A State has a perfect right to adopt a property qualification; a State has a perfect right to adopt an educational qualification; and, if it applies to the negro as well as it does to the white man, then it is sanctioned by the Constitution of the United States and by the decisions that have been made in pursuance of it.

You could not, under the Sutherland amendment, register the negroes of the South in defiance of the laws of the States. Is it possible that under that amendment we can do anything that we could not do without the amendment? Is it possible, I ask the Senator from New York, that under that amendment we could, in the slightest degree, interfere with any of the electoral systems in any of the Southern States?

Senator Root.—I understand that the provision which authorizes the Congress to make or modify the regulations governing elections in respect of time and place and manner was not an empty form of words, but was included in the Constitution upon grave consideration and for a substantial purpose.

That provision in regard to the election of members of the House of Representatives it is proposed to continue, and the provision in regard to the Senate it is proposed to destroy by transferring the election from the legislature to the people without also transferring the power of regulation. The purpose for which I suppose these provisions were included corresponds with the purpose that practical observation of elections indicates. The naked right to make laws regarding the exercise of the right of suffrage is practically useless unless there be the power to so arrange the time, place, and manner of the election that the laws can be made practically applicable. The only way ever found by man to compel a fair election is through arranging the time and place and manner of the election beforehand in such a way that the decorations of the law will not be *brutum fulmen*.[1]

Now, sir, my understanding is that there are certain provisions of the Constitution, in respect of elections, conferring other power upon the Congress. There is the right to judge of the elections and qualifications of the members of the two Houses, and there are the Fourteenth and Fifteenth Amendments, which relate to the rights of suffrage.

My proposition is and has been from the beginning that the preservation of the constitutional authority of the Congress to arrange the regulations governing elections as to time and place and manner is a necessary condition precedent to the effective exercise of all the other powers.

The Senator from Georgia put a question to me the other day predicated upon the proposition that certain laws were found to be, in the opinion of Congress, in violation of the Constitution, and he asked me whether, in my view, the adoption of the Sutherland amendment would result in Congress having the power to compel a change in or an abandonment of those laws, and I answered him in the affirmative.

Now the Senator from Maryland says that I was mistaken, because the laws are not in violation of the Constitution.

SENATOR BACON.—If the Senator from New York will pardon me, what I endeavored to say was this: That, of course, there would have been no question if it had been based on the assumption that the law was unconstitutional. My question was based on the assumption that, in the opinion of the States, it was constitutional, and, in the opinion of Congress, it was unconstitutional; and what, under the Sutherland amendment, I inquired of the Senator from New York, would, in his judgment,

[1] "Idle thunder."

be the power of Congress in such a contingency, which I suppose the Senator understands.

SENATOR ROOT.—I understand it.

SENATOR RAYNER.—Mr. President, there is no doubt about the proposition that Congress can not change the right of suffrage in the States, Sutherland amendment or not.

Is there any Senator here now, let me ask, because I want to be fair about this—I am not arguing this as a partisan, I am arguing it as a lawyer—is there any lawyer in this body who will rise and say that by law we can take away from the States the right of suffrage?

SENATOR ROOT.—Does the Senator mean his proposition to cover a case in which the franchise is established in the State by laws that are in contravention of the provisions of the Constitution?

SENATOR RAYNER.—Undoubtedly not. That is where the difficulty occurs between us. If the State laws are unconstitutional, the Supreme Court will set them aside. But, in Williams vs. Mississippi, the Supreme Court held that the laws of Mississippi were constitutional, and that they did not operate as a discrimination under the Fifteenth Amendment.

We have now a case from Maryland that has gone to the Supreme Court, and I apprehend that they will again decline to reverse it, and that they will never touch an electoral system of a Southern State, because the Southern States do not disfranchise the negro. They can not disfranchise the negro as such. They can not discriminate against the negro, and the laws that they pass, whether it be a property qualification or an educational qualification, apply to the characteristics of the white race just as well as to the negro.

The sum and substance, therefore, of my argument is this:

First. The Sutherland amendment is not necessary to punish fraud, violence, or intimidation at the polls at Federal elections.

Second. Under the Sutherland amendment efforts might be made by a partisan Congress to appoint boards of registration and certification to supersede the boards of registration and certification appointed by the State. If these boards, however, acted in defiance of the laws of the State and registered voters who had no right to be registered under the laws of the State, then the law of Congress would be void, and you do not want to confer upon Congress the power to pass a law which would be declared to be unconstitutional by the courts. If these boards of registration and certification acted in accordance with the laws of the State, then there is no practical necessity for the Sutherland amendment, as the State regulations are sufficient. In other words, I admit that under the Sutherland amendment an attempt might be made to pass another bill similar to the force bill, but I deny the constitutionality of the force bill.

Third. No legislation can be enacted under the Sutherland amendment to deprive the States of their right of suffrage. Therefore the appeal to Republican Senators to vote for the Sutherland amendment in order to change the electoral systems of the Southern States should not prevail. The right of suffrage subject to the Fourteenth and Fifteenth Amendments is in the States, and we can not take away the right of suffrage from the States except by a constitutional amendment that shall expressly so provide.

On February 24 the amendment of Senator Sutherland was passed by a vote of 50 to 37.

The joint resolution came to vote on February 28— 54 yeas and 33 nays. The requisite two-thirds majority not being obtained, the resolution was defeated.

During the next session (on April 13, 1911) the House by a vote of 296 to 16 passed a joint resolution submitting to the States for ratification a constitutional amendment providing for the popular election of Senators, and leaving the determination of the "times, places, and manner of holding the elections" to each State. It was introduced by William W. Rucker [Mo.].

The resolution came up for discussion in the Senate on May 15, when Joseph L. Bristow [Kan.] moved to amend it by striking out the provision in regard to the determination of the times, etc., of holding elections.

The question was discussed at length, the chief issue being the Bristow amendment, until June 12, 1911, when the amendment was adopted by the casting vote of Vice-President James S. Sherman, and the bill was passed by a vote of 64 to 24.

The House disagreed to the Senate amendment and a conference was appointed.

No action was taken on the resolution during the session.

On May 13, 1912, the House concurred in the Senate

amendment by 238 ayes to 39 nays, (more than the necessary two-thirds majority). Two days later President Taft signed the bill.

On May 31, 1913, William J. Bryan, Secretary of State, made official proclamation of the ratification of the Amendment by three-fourths of the States. For text of the Amendment see Volume I, page 428.

CHAPTER XIII

DIRECT LEGISLATION

[THE INITIATIVE, REFERENDUM, AND RECALL]

Speech of Sen. Jonathan Bourne [Ore.] on "Popular *vs.* Delegated Government"—Reply by Representative Charles F. Scott [Kan.]

O N May 5, 1910, Jonathan Bourne [Ore.], speaking in the Senate *pro forma* on an interstate commerce bill, delivered a notable address on direct legislation in Oregon, which, printed as a public document, afterward had a wide circulation because of the interest in the subject throughout the Union. The introduction of his speech is here presented.

POPULAR VS. DELEGATED GOVERNMENT

SENATOR BOURNE

Successful and permanent government must rest primarily on recognition of the rights of men and the absolute sovereignty of the people. Upon these principles is built the superstructure of our Republic. Their maintenance and perpetuation measure the life of the Republic. These policies, therefore, stand for the rights and liberties of the people and for the power and majesty of the Government as against the enemies of both.

The people have been shocked by the number of business and political exposures which have been brought out in the last ten years.

At the time of Mr. Roosevelt's inauguration the tendency was to measure national prosperity by property rather than by personal liberty. The commercial force of society was rapidly throttling the police power of the Government. Political machines and bosses dictated the legislative and administrative destinies of many communities and States. Mr. Roosevelt, with his experience in practical politics, familiarity with governmental operations, inherent honesty, dynamic energy, and limitless courage, demonstrated that he measured up to the needs of the time, and assumed leadership for reinstatement of the police power of the Government in supremacy over the commercial force of society. To him belongs credit for reëstablishment of these two great forces in their proper relative positions. He awakened the public conscience, and the result is a struggle throughout the nation between the advocates of what I would term "popular government" and the advocates of delegated government.

In many instances the people have lost confidence in their public servants, the same as many stockholders have lost confidence in corporation management. The remedy in government is the direct selection by the people of their public servants, with the resultant accountability of the public servant to the people, and not to a political machine or boss. I purposely use the word "selection" rather than "nomination," for to my mind it more clearly expresses the idea of the responsibility of good citizenship. Selection implies the careful investigation of all and the resultant choice of one.

Much has been said in favor of representative government. I believe in a truly representative government, but where the selection of public servants is left to a political machine or boss, as is frequently the case under our convention system, the tendency is toward a misrepresentative, and not a truly representative, form of government, notwithstanding the election is supposedly by the people.

By popular government I mean direct legislation as far as practicable, popular selection of candidates, and such regulation of political campaigns as will secure fair and honest elections. Popular selection under the present stage of evolution of our Government can be obtained only by direct primary laws and complete elimination of convention and caucus nomination of public officers.

Time was when a few self-constituted leaders in Oregon politics arrogated to themselves the prerogatives of government and made their assumption effective through illicit combinations and the use of money in any and every quarter where necessary to their purposes of control—that is, they commercialized conventions, legislatures, and the administrative branches of the city, county, and State government.

Revolting against these conditions, the State which I have the honor, in part, to represent has evolved the best-known system of popular government, and, because of this conviction, I take this opportunity of presenting not only to the Senate, but to the country, a brief analysis of the Oregon laws bearing upon this question.

In a speech on the popular election of Senators, on February 14, 1911, Senator Bourne continued the presentation of the principle of direct legislation, which formed the foundation of the specific subject.

To insure good service, responsibility and accountability must go together. Whatever an individual is responsible for he should to the same degree be accountable for. Under delegated government he is accountable to the political boss, who in most cases is but the agent of the largest campaign contributor, at best a shifting accountability, because of the relative fluctuations of contributions and contributors. Under popular government like the Oregon system the accountability is always to the composite citizen—individual unknown—always permanent, never changing, the necessitated result being that the public servant must serve the composite citizen who represents general welfare or be recalled, where the recall exists, or fail of re-election where an efficient direct primary exists.

The greater the centralization of power the wider should be the distribution of accountability. Where the accountability is to the individual, the payment will be personal, meaning necessarily special privilege or serving a selfish interest. Where the accountability in government is to the composite citizen—that is to say, the electorate, or, in corporate business, to all the stockholders—the inevitable result is necessitated service for the general welfare of all, or the earliest possible elimination of the servant, whether public or corporate.

The securing of proper accountability of government and corporate officials is one of our greatest national problems. The solution is simple. In government, direct accountability of all public servants to party and general electorates. This can be secured only by the people selecting all their public servants through direct primaries and minimizing the misuse of money through comprehensive corrupt practices acts, with the ultimate absolute elimination of all political machines, conventions, and caucuses. In business, rigid responsibility of the commercial force to the police force of society. In corporation management, primary responsibility to government, equal obedience to laws, and equal accountability to stockholders, giving the Government and the stockholders the fullest publicity of its operations, including absolute honesty and simplicity of its accounts, thus protecting the rights of the people and insuring to all the stockholders proportional enjoyment in the fruits of successful management, resulting in far greater stability for values and an infinitely greater market for its securities.

Oregon has evolved and demonstrated the best-known solution of the governmental problem to date. It incorporates:

The Australian ballot, which assures the honesty of elections.

The registration law, which guards the integrity of the privilege of American citizenship—participation in government.

The direct primary, which absolutely insures popular selection of all candidates and establishes the responsibility of the public servant to the electorate and not to any political boss or special interest.

The initiative and referendum, which is the keystone of the arch of popular government, for by means of this the people may accomplish such other reforms as they desire. The initiative develops the electorate because it encourages study of principles and policies of government and affords the originator of new ideas in government an opportunity to secure popular judgment upon his measures if 8 per cent. of the voters of his State deem the same worthy of submission to popular vote. The referendum prevents misuse of power temporarily centralized in the legislature.

I unhesitatingly assert that under the initiative the people not only will not, but cannot enact legislation against general welfare. Self-interest is the dominant force of humanity. Probably in a majority of cases self-interest descends into selfish interest. No two people ever have been or probably ever will be exactly alike; consequently because of the difference of the personal equation of the individual units of society and the resultant difference in the self or selfish interest dominating each individual unit where they act collectively, as they do under the initiative, an immense number of different forces are liberated, each struggling for supremacy and thereby engendering friction, so that before any community action can be established this attrition must wear away the selfish interests, and general welfare, according to the majority view of the community, absolutely control the community action.

The initiative and recall must stand or fall together. If right in my assertion that the people under the initiative cannot legislate against general welfare, neither will they by the same process of deduction ever recall a public servant who serves general welfare. If they are qualified to select their judges, they must be equally qualified to recall them. Judges, like all other public servants, are elected because of anticipated good service and would be recalled only for demonstrated bad service.

The corrupt practices act is necessary as a complement to the initiative and referendum and the direct primary, for without the corrupt practices act these other features of popular government could be abused. The publicity pamphlet provided for by the corrupt practices act affords all candidates for nomination or election equal means of presenting before the voter their views upon public questions and protects the honest candidate against the misuse of money in political campaigns. Under the operation of this law popular verdicts will be based upon ideas, not money; argument, not abuse; principles, not boss and machine dictation.

Under the machine and political boss system the confidence of sincere partisans is often betrayed by recreant leaders in political contests and by public servants who recognize the irresponsible source of power to which they are responsible. If the enforcement of the Oregon laws will right these wrongs, then they were conceived in wisdom and born in justice to the people, in justice to the public servant, and in justice to the partisan.

Plainly stated, the aim and purpose of these laws is to destroy the irresponsible machine and to put all elective offices in direct touch with the people as the real source of authority—in short, to give direct and full force to the ballot of every individual elector and to eliminate dominance of corporate and corrupt influences in the administration of public affairs. The Oregon laws mark the course that must be pursued before the wrongful use of corporate power can be dethroned, the people restored to power, and lasting reform secured. They insure absolute government by the people.

On February 28 Senator Bourne continued his exposition of direct government.

Mr. President, the most important measure enacted or adopted by the people of Oregon at the recent election, and, in fact, next to the initiative and referendum the most important law enacted by any State in recent years, is the law permitting voters in party primaries to elect their delegates to national conventions and to instruct them through popular expression of choice for President and Vice-President. This law, when enacted in all States, will absolutely destroy the power of a Federal machine to renominate a President or determine who shall be his successor. The "steam roller" will be relegated to the political scrap heap, and its operators dismissed to the shadow of things forgotten, while fourth-class postmasters will, as they should, cease to be a political asset for anybody or any party.

In the light of past experiences it seems to me this plan should appeal to all patriotic citizens as well as to conscientious partisans. It is a well-recognized fact that nominations by national conventions are the exclusive work of politicians, which the electorate of the whole United States is permitted only to witness in gaping expectancy and to ratify at the polls in the succeeding November. As unrepresentative as this feature of the national convention is, its flagrancy pales into insignificance in the presence of that other abuse against partisan conscience and outrage upon the representative system, which is wrought by the Republican politician in hopelessly Democratic States, and by the Democratic politician in hopelessly Republican States in dominating the national conventions with the presence of these unrepresentative delegations that represent neither party, people, nor principle.

With the presidential preference law in force throughout the United States the Southern Republican delegations will no longer be the vest-pocket trading material of Republican bosses, nor will Democratic delegations from solid Republican States in the North be subject to the will of Democratic bosses. The voice of the people will be heard in the selection of candidates, and delegates will be made, as they should be, mere messengers, conveying the expressed wish of the people whom they profess to represent.

Mr. President, whenever this law becomes nation-wide in its application it will absolutely destroy the power of the Federal machine; prevent a President renominating himself, except by demonstration of good service; destroy the possibility of any President naming his successor, and relieve him of any obligations to political bosses, campaign contributors, national committeemen, or national delegates, thus transferring the obligation from any known individual to the composite citizen, where it belongs.

Mr. President, the charge that the President of the United States has used his appointing power to coerce members of Congress is the most serious of all attacks made by the press. The accusation was made in recent months that, in an effort to dictate to members of Congress in what manner they should exercise their legislative power, President Taft had granted them the privilege of recommending persons for Federal appointment in their respective States, if the members voted in Congress as he desired, and had refused them this privilege if they voted upon measures in such a manner as to displease him. In other words, it was charged that the President of the United States engaged in a systematic trading of patronage for votes in Congress.

Reduced to its simple element, the charge was, in effect, bribery or intimidation—bribery if patronage was extended as a reward for voting in accordance with the wishes of the Executive, and intimidation if patronage was withheld as punishment for refusal to yield unwilling obedience. The charge was a direct attack upon the honesty of the Executive, and indirectly a reflection upon the intelligence, independence, and courage of members of Congress. It would be difficult to believe such a charge without positive proof.

Here Senator Bourne read a letter to a Republican leader in Iowa, dated September 15, 1910, and signed by "Charles D. Norton, Secretary to the President," which said in part:

The President feels that the value of Federal patronage has been greatly exaggerated, and that the refusal to grant it has probably been more useful to the men affected than the appointments would have been. In the preliminary skirmishes in certain States, like Wisconsin and Iowa and elsewhere, he was willing, in the interests of what the leaders believed would lead to party success, to make certain discriminations, but the President has concluded that it is his duty now to treat all Republican Congressmen and Senators alike, without any distinction.

Since this letter was signed by the private secretary to the President, purports to have been written by his direction, and, although five months have elapsed, has not been repudiated, must it not be accepted as stating the facts?

On March 2, 1911, speaking *pro forma* upon a bill to amend the judiciary laws, Charles F. Scott [Kan.] delivered an address to the House in favor of representative government as opposed to direct legislation.

REPRESENTATIVE GOVERNMENT VS. DIRECT LEGISLATION

CHARLES F. SCOTT, M. C.

There is a question now before the country, particularly before the people of the State I have the honor to represent in part, upon which I entertain very positive convictions, and which, I believe, is a proper subject for discussion at this time and in this place. That question, bluntly stated, is this: Is representative government a failure? We are being asked now to answer that question in the affirmative. A new school of statesmen has arisen, wiser than Washington and Hamilton and Franklin and Madison, wiser than Webster and Clay and Calhoun and Benton, wiser than Lincoln and Sumner and Stevens and Chase, wiser than Garfield and Blaine and McKinley and Taft, knowing more in their day than all the people have learned in all the days of the years since the Republic was founded.

And they tell us that representative government is a failure. They do not put this declaration into so many words—part of them because they do not know enough about the science of government to understand that the doctrines they advocate are revolutionary, and the rest of them because they lack the courage to declare openly that it is their intention to change our form of government, to subvert the system upon which our institutions are founded. But that is in effect what they propose to do.

They graciously consent that the people shall continue to elect Representatives to a legislative assembly, but they proceed at once to discredit those Representatives—and incidentally to impeach the judgment or the honesty of the people who elected them—by proposing a fantastic scheme whereby legislation may be enacted entirely independently of them.

They will still permit judges to be chosen, but they propose a plan whereby the wisdom and justice of their decisions shall be passed upon at a popular election, thus preparing the way for a campaign in which we shall witness the edifying spectacle of a candidate for judicial position enthusiastically declaring from the stump that if elected he will render such and such a judgment. They will continue to elect administrative and executive officers, but, if one of them is charged with failure to do his duty or with malfeasance in office, he shall be tried, not by a judge and jury and upon the evidence of witnesses sworn to tell the truth, but in the newspapers and on the stump and by whatever testimony partisan rancor or personal malice may see fit to present.

Such, in brief, is the plan of redemption offered to us by the prophets of the new dispensation. Such is the scheme which they propose as a substitute for the system of government which was devised by the founders of the Republic and which has been reaffirmed in every State constitution that has been drawn from that day to this.

I said that it is revolutionary and subversive of our present system of government. Let us see.

The Constitution of the United States, Section 4, Article IV, provides that "the United States shall guarantee to every State in this Union a republican form of government." By the very terms of our original charter, therefore, the form of government under which we live is that of a republic and not that of a democracy.

Every schoolboy knows that in a pure democracy the people themselves perform directly all the functions of government, enacting laws without the intervention of a legislature, and trying causes that arise under those laws without the intervention of judge or jury; while in a republic, on the other hand, the people govern themselves, not by each citizen exercising directly all the functions of government, but by delegating that power to certain ones among them whom they choose to represent them in the legislatures, in the courts of justice, and in the various executive offices.

Now, it does not follow by any means that because a proposed change is revolutionary it is therefore unwise. Taking it by and large, wherever the word "revolution" has come into human history it has been only another word for progress. Because a nation has pursued certain methods for a long time it does not at all follow that those methods are the best, although when a nation like the United States, so bold and alert, so little hampered by tradition, so ready to try experiments, has clung to the same methods of government for 130 years, a strong presumption has certainly been established that these methods are the best, at least for that particular nation.

But a presumption, however strong, must give way before a demonstration, and if it can be demonstrated, either by reason or experiment, that the system of government proposed by our latter-day leaders is wiser than that which has thus far prevailed, not only in our own country, but in every other important nation in the whole world, then we would be most foolish to refuse to adopt it.

But is the new system wiser than the old—in the matter of making laws, for example? The old system vests the lawmaking power in a legislative body composed of men elected by the people and supposed to be peculiarly fitted by reason of character, education, and training for the performance of that duty. These men come together and give their entire time through a period of some weeks or months to the consideration of proposed legislation, and the laws they enact go into immediate effect, and remain in force until set aside by the courts as unconstitutional or until repealed by the same authority that enacted them. Under this plan no law of general application is likely to be brought forward unless there is a widespread demand for it, no measure of importance can be passed without critical examination and discussion, and when passed it presumably represents the judgment of a majority of the people.

The new system—taking the Oregon law, for example, and it is commonly cited as a model—provides that 8 per cent. of the voters of a State may submit a measure directly to the people, and if a majority of those voting upon it give it their support it shall become a law without reference to the legislature or to the governor. That is the initiative. And it provides that if 5 per cent. of the voters are opposed to a law which the legislature has passed, upon signing the proper petition the law shall be suspended until the next general election, when the people shall be given an opportunity to pass upon it. That is the referendum.

Now, there are several things about this plan which I believe the people of this country, when they come really to consider it, will scrutinize with a good deal of care and possibly with some suspicion.

It is to be noted, in the first place, that a very few of the people can put all the people to the trouble and expense of a vote upon any measure, and the inquiry may well arise whether the cause of settled and orderly government will be promoted by vesting power in the minority thus to harass and annoy the majority. In my own State, for example, who can doubt that the prohibitory amendment, or some one of the statutes enacted for its enforcement, would have been resubmitted again and again if the initiative had been in force there these past 25 years.

Again, it will be observed that still fewer of the people have it in their power to suspend a law which a legislature may have passed in plain obedience to the mandate of a majority of the people, or which may be essential to the prompt and orderly conduct of public affairs, and when they come to think about it the people may wonder if the referendum might not make it possible for a small, malevolent, and mischievous minority to obstruct the machinery of government and for a time at least to nullify the will of the majority.

In the third place, it is to be remarked that a measure submitted either by the initiative or the referendum cannot be amended, but must be accepted or rejected as a whole, and we may well inquire whether this might not afford "the interests" quite as good an opportunity as they would have in a legislature to "initiate" some measure which on its face was wholesome and beneficent, but within which was concealed some little "joker" that would either nullify the good features of the law or make it actively vicious, and which, through lack of discussion, would not be discovered. How often have we here in this House seen some measure which represented the most careful and painstaking effort of a skilled and experienced legislator metamorphosed in committee until its own author would hardly recognize it, and then when it was brought into this chamber as the fruit of the very best judgment of eighteen able and honest men how often have we seen it modified in its most essential features as the result of the refining fire of debate upon this floor? Every day we have new and incontestable proof that "in the multitude of counselors there is wisdom." But that wisdom can never be had under a system of legislation which lays before the people the work of one man's mind to be accepted in whole or rejected altogether.

Once more let us observe that under this system, no matter how few votes are cast upon a given measure, if there are more for it than against it, it becomes a law, so that the possibility is always present that laws may be enacted which represent the judgment or the interest of the minority rather than the majority of the people. Indeed, experience would seem to show that this is a probability rather than a possibility, for in the last Oregon election not one of the nine propositions enacted into law received as much as 50 per cent. of the total vote cast, while some of them received but little more than 30 per cent. of the total vote.

And finally and chiefly, without in the least impeaching the intelligence of the people, remembering the slight and casual attention the average citizen gives to the details of public questions, we may well inquire whether the average vote cast upon these proposed measures of legislation will really represent an informed and well-considered judgment. In his thoughtful work on democracy, discussing this very question, Dr. Hyslop, of Columbia University, says:

People occupied with their private affairs, domestic and social, demanding all their resources and attention, as a rule have little time to solve the complex problems of national life. The referendum is a call to perform all the duties of the profoundest statesmanship, in addition to private obligations, which are even much more than the average man can fulfill with any success or intelligence at all, and hence it can hardly produce anything better than the Athenian assembly, which terminated in anarchy. It will not secure dispatch except at the expense of civilization, nor deliberation except at the expense of intelligence. Very few questions can be safely left to its councils, and these only of the most general kind. A tribunal that can be so easily deceived as the electorate can be in common elections can not be trusted to decide intelligently the graver and more complicated questions of public finance or private property, of administration, and of justice. It may be honest and mean well, as I believe it would be; but such an institution can not govern.

As to the practical working of the referendum four years ago nearly every appropriation bill passed by the Oregon legislature was referred to the people for their approval or rejection before it could go into effect. As a result, the appropriations being unavailable until the election could be held, the State was compelled to stamp its warrants "not paid for want of funds," and to pay interest thereon, although the money was in the treasury. The university and other State institutions were hampered and embarrassed, and the whole machinery of government was in large measure paralyzed. In other words, under the Oregon law a pitiful minority of the people was able to obstruct and embarrass the usual and orderly processes of government, and for a time at least absolutely to thwart the will of an overwhelming majority of the people.

A system of government under which such a thing as that is not only possible, but has actually occurred, may be "the best system ever devised by the wit of man," as we have been vociferously assured, but some of us may take the liberty of doubting it. And, as evidence that the sentiment in regard to the system is not all one way even in the State which has adopted it, I wish to quote part of an editorial which recently appeared in the Portland (Ore.) *Oregonian*.

The statement that no proposal here has ever assailed private or corporate property is absurd and untrue. Many measures have had no other motive or purpose. What is the single tax but an attack on private property? What of the gross earnings tax, enacted in 1906, and now in the United States Supreme Court? What of prohibition? What about the proposal for the State to get into the railroad business? And others that might be mentioned.

The theory of the proponents of direct legislation seems to be that only good laws will be initiated and only bad laws will be referred; that the initiative will be used only when a recalcitrant legislature has refused to respond to the demand of the people, and the referendum will be invoked only when a stupid or corrupt legislature has enacted a law which violates the rights or jeopardizes the interests of the people. But is not that theory pretty severely jolted by the facts? Since this system was adopted in Oregon the people have rejected nearly one-half of the measures submitted under the initiative, and they have approved exactly one-half of the laws submitted under the referendum. Now, these facts can be interpreted in only two ways: Either bad laws were submitted by initiative and good laws by the referendum, or the people deliberately voted against good laws and voted for bad laws. But to accept either of these alternatives brings us in square antagonism to another theory which is fundamental in the doctrine of direct legislation, and that is that the people can do no wrong.

The truth is, of course, that it is perfectly easy for a bad law to be initiated, and, if it is skillfully drawn so that its iniquity is not branded upon its very face, it is perfectly easy for the most honest people in the world to be deceived into voting for it. And it is perfectly easy for a good law to be referred and its operation thus suspended for two years with a large chance that with the right kind of a campaign it could be repealed altogether. A distinguished citizen of one of the States in which this system prevails has told me that if he needed a vicious law in his business he would rather submit it by the initiative than to try to put it through a legislature. And he added that if he were a "special interest" against which a legislature had passed some righteous measure he would rejoice in a system by which at the least he could be relieved of its operation for two years, with a big chance that at the end of that time he could defeat it entirely.

This sentiment is not an impeachment of the honesty, the intelligence, or the patriotism of the people. But it is an impeachment of a system of government under which laws are made by votes which from the very nature of the case are cast without information and without opportunity for that consideration which can only come from face to face discussion.

But the initiative and referendum, subversive as they are of the representative principle, do not compare in importance or in possible power for evil with the recall. The statutes of every State in this Union provide a way by which a recreant official may be ousted from his office or otherwise punished. That way is by process of law, where charges must be specific, the testimony clear, and the judgment impartial. But what are we to think of a procedure under which an official is to be tried, not in a court by a jury of his peers and upon the testimony of witnesses sworn to tell the truth, but in the newspapers, on the street corners, and at political meetings? Can you conceive of a wider departure from the fundamental principles of justice that are written not only into the constitution of every civilized nation on the face of the earth, but upon the heart of every normal human being, the principle that every man accused of a crime has a right to confront his accusers, to examine them under oath, to rebut their evidence, and to have the judgment finally of men sworn to render a just and lawful verdict?

Small wonder that the argument oftenest heard in support of a proposition so abhorrent to the most primitive instincts of justice is that it will be seldom invoked and therefore cannot do very much harm. I leave you to characterize as it deserves a law whose chief merit must lie in the rarity of its enforcement.

But will it do no harm, even if seldom enforced? It is urged that its presence on the statute books and the knowledge that it can be invoked will frighten public officials into good behavior. Passing by the very obvious suggestion that an official who needs to be scared into proper conduct ought never to have been elected in the first place, we may well inquire whether the real effect would not be to frighten men into demagogy—and thus to work immeasurably greater harm to the common weal than would ever be inflicted through the transgressions of deliberately bad men.

We have demagogues enough now, heaven knows, when election to an office assures the tenure of it for two or four or six years. But if that tenure were only from hour to hour, if it were held at the whim of a powerful and unscrupulous newspaper, for example, or if it could be put in jeopardy by an affront which in the line of duty ought, we will say, to be given to some organization or faction or cabal, what could we expect? Is it not inevitable that such a system would drive out of our public life the men of real character and courage and leave us only cowards and trimmers and time servers? May we not well hesitate to introduce into our political system a device which, had it been in vogue in the past, would have made it possible for the Tories to have recalled Washington, the copperheads to have recalled Lincoln, and the jingoes to have

recalled McKinley? Above all, may we not well hesitate to introduce into our political system a device which would subject
to recall a judge whose decision happened not to accord with
the passion or the prejudice of the hour? Is it conceivable that
any jurist of integrity and self-respect could be found who
would accept a seat on the bench knowing that his tenure of
office might be challenged at any hour, that his judgments were
to be reviewed, not by a superior court, but by the newspapers
and upon the political platform?

In all the literature of the age-long struggle for freedom
and justice there is no phrase that occurs oftener than "the
independence of the judiciary." The great fact which this
phrase expresses is the foundation upon which rests the citadel
of individual rights and of national liberty. In every battle
that has ever been waged by the people against oppression and
tyranny the one achievement which attested the final triumph
was the establishment of a court that no despot could reach
or control. The founders of the Republic realized more keenly
than we do—for to them the tyranny of king-controlled courts
was modern and not ancient history, as it is to us—the absolutely vital importance of the separation of king and courts,
and so they safeguarded it, as they thought, for all time by
declaring in the organic law of the land that the judiciary
should be forever independent of the legislature and the executive. And all the world said that is well. Not one man could
be found now among all our ninety millions to declare that
our Constitution should be changed so as to permit the President in the White House or the Congress in the Capitol to
dictate to our judges what their decisions should be. And yet
it is seriously proposed that this power of dictation shall be
given to the crowd on the street. That is what the recall means
if applied to the judiciary: and it means the destruction of its
independence as completely as if in set terms it were made
subject to the President or the Congress.

It is the theory of the initiative that it will never be invoked except to pass a good law, and of the referendum that
it will never be resorted to except to defeat a bad law; but we
have already seen how easily a bad law might be initiated and
a good law referred. And so it is the theory that the recall
will be invoked only for the protection of the people from a
bad judge. What guaranty can you give that it will not be
called into being to harrass and intimidate a good judge?
There never yet was a two-edged sword that would not cut
both ways.

Mr. Chairman, I should be the last to assert that our present system of government has always brought ideally perfect results. Now and then the people have made mistakes in the selection of their representatives. Corrupt men have been put into places of trust, small men have been sent where large men were needed, ignorant men have been charged with duties which only men of learning could fitly perform. But does it follow that, because the people make mistakes in so simple a matter as the selection of their agents, they would be infallible in the incomparably more complex and difficult task of the enactment and interpretation of laws? There was never a more glaring *non sequitur,* and yet it is the very cornerstone upon which rests the whole structure of the new philosophy. "The people cannot be trusted with few things," runs this singular logic, "therefore let us put all things into their hands."

With one breath we are asked to renounce the old system because the people make mistakes, and with the next breath we are solemnly assured that, if we adopt the new system, the people will not make mistakes. You cannot change the nature of men, Mr. Chairman, by changing their system of government. The limitations of human judgment and knowledge and conscience which render perfection in representative government unattainable will still abide even after that form of government is swept away, and the ideal will still be far distant.

Let it not be said or imagined, Mr. Speaker, that, because I protest against converting this Republic into a democracy, therefore I lack confidence in the people. No man has greater faith, sir, than I have in the intelligence, the integrity, the patriotism, and the fundamental common sense of the average American citizen. But I am for representative rather than for direct government, because I have greater confidence in the second thought of the people than I have in their first thought. And that, in the last analysis, is the difference, and the only difference, so far as results are concerned, between the new system and that which it seeks to supplant.

At not one step in the long and shining pathway of the nation's progress has representative government failed to respond to the nation's need. Every emergency that 130 years of momentous history has developed—the terrible strain of war, the harassing problems of peace—representative government has been equal to them all. Not once has it broken down. Not one issue has it failed to solve. And, long after the shallow substitutes that are now proposed for it shall have been forgotten, representative government "will be doing business at the old stand," will be solving the problems of the future as it met the issues of the past, with courage and wisdom and justice, giving to the great Republic that government "of the people, for the people, and by the people" which is the assurance that it "shall not perish from the earth." [Prolonged applause.]

CHAPTER XIV

THE RECALL OF JUDGES

[REPEAL OF THE JUDICIARY ACT OF 1801]

Debate in the Senate on the Bill to Repeal the Judiciary Law of 1801: In Favor of Repeal, John Breckinridge [Ky.], James Jackson [Ga.], Stevens T. Mason [Va.], David Stone [N. C.]; Opposed, Jonathan Mason [Mass.], Gouverneur Morris [N. Y.], Uriah Tracy [Ct.]—Debate in the House on the Repeal of the Judiciary Bill: Partisan Speeches by Thomas T. Davis [Ky.], Philip R. Thompson [Va.], William B. Giles [Va.], John Randolph [Va.], Republicans, and Archibald Henderson [N. C.], Thomas Morris [N. Y.], Joseph Hemphill [Pa.], John Stanley [N. C.], James A. Bayard, Sr. [Del.], Federalists—Impeachment of Justice Samuel Chase—Constitutional Amendment Proposed by John Randolph (1805) for the Removal of Federal Judges.

ONE of the first subjects to claim the attention of the first Congress was the organization of the Federal judiciary. This was felt to be the weakest of the three departments of government, and every effort was made to give it power within the limitations of the Constitution, and to impart to it impressive dignity.

The first judiciary act became law on September 24, 1789. It provided for a Supreme Court consisting of a chief justice and five associate justices, and holding two sessions a year beginning, respectively, in February and August; for Circuit Courts holding two sessions annually within their several districts, one of the Supreme Court justices and the district judge presiding; for a marshal and an attorney for each district; for an Attorney-General of the United States; for forms of writs, etc.

Since then the number of Supreme Court justices has increased to nine, and a distinct class of circuit judges has been created, while, of course, the number of districts has vastly increased with the growth of the country.

THE MIDNIGHT JUDGES

The first organization of a distinct class of Circuit Courts took place in the closing days of John Adams's Administration, when the Federalists planned to create, for certain of the faithful of their party, positions from which they could not be removed by the incoming party. In this plan President Adams, who had taken no part in the scheme to elect Burr in order to provide places for Federalists [see page 400 ss.], now came to the aid of his party, probably being incited to the act by an impulse of anger at the election of Jefferson.

On February 18, 1801, the day following the decisive ballot for Jefferson in the House, Adams signed an act of Congress creating twenty-three new judgeships. That this act was intended to make places for supporters of the Administration is clearly shown by the fact that at the time there was insufficient business to occupy the attention of the existing Federal judiciary. Adams, however, postponed rather contemptuously the appointment of the new judges until the evening of the last day of his Administration, when he spent the time until midnight affixing his signature to the necessary papers, whence the appointees received the name of the "midnight judges." A few of them, whose papers he hastily gathered into his pocket as the representative of the new President, fearing Adams's action, was taking possession of the executive office on the stroke of twelve, were dubbed throughout their short judicial careers "Adams's pocket judges."

The new Congress, being overwhelmingly Democratic, was desirous of annulling these acts of the Federalists, but were somewhat at a loss how most safely to proceed, since the Constitution provides that the terms of all Federal judges shall be for life, or during good behavior. They finally decided that if they could not remove the man from the office they could accomplish the same result by removing the office from the man.

Accordingly, on January 8, 1802, John Breckinridge [Ky.], the Administration leader in the Senate, introduced in that body a resolution to repeal the Judiciary act of February 18, 1801. The measure met with great opposition from the Federalists, who retained much of their former power in the Upper House.

At this session the proceedings of the Senate began to be reported, and so we are able for the first time in the history of that body extensively to reproduce one of its debates.

Other supporters of the repeal than Breckinridge were James Jackson, of Georgia, Stevens T. Mason, of Virginia, and David Stone, of North Carolina. Leading opponents of the repeal were Jonathan Mason, of Massachusetts, Gouverneur Morris, of New York, and Uriah Tracy, of Connecticut.

REPEAL OF THE JUDICIARY ACT

SENATE, JANUARY 8-FEBRUARY 3, 1802

SENATOR BRECKINRIDGE.—Because the Constitution declares that a judge shall hold his office during good behavior, can it be tortured to mean that he shall hold his office after it is abolished? Can it mean that his tenure should be limited by behaving well in an office which did not exist? Can it mean that an office may exist although its duties are extinct? Can it mean, in short, that the shadow, to wit, the judge, can remain when the substance, to wit, the office, is removed? It must have intended all these absurdities, or it must admit a construction which will avoid them.

The construction obviously is that a judge should hold an existing office so long as he did his duty in that office; and not that he should hold an office that did not exist, and perform duties not provided by law.

SENATOR J. MASON.—The judges hold their appointments for life, unless they misbehave themselves. Why? For this reason: They are not the depositaries of the high prerogatives of government, such as are the President, the Senators, and the Representatives. They neither appoint to office, nor hold the purse-strings of the country, nor legislate for it. They depend entirely upon their talents, which is all they have to recommend them. They cannot, therefore, be disposed to pervert their power to improper purposes. What are their duties? To expound and apply the laws. To do this with fidelity and skill requires a length of time. The requisite knowledge is not to be procured in a day. These are the plain and strong reasons which must strike every mind for the different tenure by which the judges hold their offices, and they are such as will eternally endure wherever liberty exists.

On examination it will be found that the people, in forming their Constitution, meant to make the judges as independent of the legislature as of the Executive. Because the duties which they have to perform call upon them to expound not only the laws but the Constitution also; in which is involved the power of checking the legislature in case it should pass any laws in violation of the Constitution. For this reason it was more important that the judges in this country should be placed beyond the control of the legislature than in other countries where no such power attaches to them.

SENATOR MORRIS.—What will be the effect of the desired repeal? Will it not be a declaration to the remaining judges that they hold their offices subject to your will and pleasure? And what will be the result of this? It will be that the check established by the Constitution, wished for by the people, and necessary in every contemplation of common sense is destroyed. It had been said, and truly, too, that governments are made to provide against the follies and vices of men. For to suppose that governments rest upon reason is a pitiful solecism. If mankind were reasonable, they would want no government. Hence checks are required in the distribution of the power among those who are to exercise it for the benefit of the people. Did the people of America vest all power in the legislature? No; they had vested in the judges a check intended to be efficient—a check of the first necessity, to prevent an invasion of the Constitution by unconstitutional laws—a check which might prevent any faction from intimidating or annihilating the tribunals themselves.

SENATOR JACKSON.—We have been asked if we are afraid of having an army of judges? For myself, I am more afraid of an army of judges, under the patronage of the President, than of an army of soldiers. The former can do us more harm. They may deprive us of our liberties, if attached to the Executive, from their decisions; and from the tenure of office contended for we cannot remove them; while the soldier, however he may act, is enlisted, or, if not enlisted, only subsisted for two years; while the judge is enlisted for life, for his salary cannot be taken from him. Sir, it is said these evils will not happen. But what security have we for the truth of the declaration? Have we not seen sedition laws? Have we not heard judges crying out through the land sedition, and asking those whose duty it was to inquire, Is there no sedition here? It is true, the sedition law had expired with the last Administration, and he trusted it would not exist, or, at least, be acted on, under the virtuous Jefferson. But hereafter, if it should exist, your judges, under the cry of sedition and political heresy, may place half your citizens in irons. I thank God that no such law now exists or is likely to exist. I thank God that we are not now under the influence of an intolerant clergy, as is evident from their abuse of the President; and that we are not under dread of the patronage of judges is manifest from their attack on the Secretary of State [James Madison]. And I trust that we shall long keep this patronage off by not sanctioning the religious persecution of the clergy on the one hand nor the political violence of the judges on the other.

But, upon the principles of gentlemen, the law which creates a judge cannot be touched. The moment it is passed it exists to the end of time. What is the implication of this doctrine? To alter or amend what may greatly require alteration or amendment it is necessary to return to the creator, and to inquire what this creator is. My principle is that the creator is the people themselves; that very people of the United States whom the gentleman from New York had declared ourselves to be the guardians of, to save the people themselves from their greatest enemies; and to save whom from destroying themselves he had invoked this House. Good God! is it possible that I have heard such a sentiment in this body? Rather should I have expected to have heard it sounded from the despots of Turkey, or the deserts of Siberia, than to have heard it uttered by an enlightened legislator of a free country, and on this floor.

I am clearly, therefore, of opinion that, if the power to alter the judiciary system vests not here, it vests nowhere. It follows, from the ideas of gentlemen, that we must submit to all the evils of the present system though it should exhibit all the horrors of the Inquisition.

It has been remarked by a celebrated writer on the English Constitution that one of the greatest political evils that could befall a people was the existence of large judiciary bodies. To illustrate his ideas he had instanced the Parliaments of

France. If the spirit which last session gave existence to sixteen new judges continued, who could say by what number
they would be limited? They might indeed soon become, what
they had been likened to, an army of judges.

I do not wish to be severe in my remarks on the conduct
of the late Administration. I admire the private character of
Mr. Adams. But I do believe the succession of his political
acts tended ultimately to accumulate in and attach all powers
to a particular person or favorite family.

If I wished to bestow on Mr. Jefferson this mass of patronage which I contend this horde of officers bestows, I should be
in favor of the bill that is now moved to repeal; but, as a
political person, I am no more for Thomas Jefferson than for
John Adams. When he acts, according to my opinion, right I
will support him; when wrong, oppose him; and I trust a majority on this floor will act in the same way.

SENATOR TRACY.—Will it be said that, although you cannot
remove the judge from office, yet you can remove his office
from him? Is murder prohibited, and may you shut a man
up, and deprive him of sustenance till he dies, and this not be
denominated murder? The danger in our Government is, and
always will be, that the legislative body will become restive and,
perhaps, unintentionally break down the barriers of our Constitution. It is incidental to man, and a part of our imper-
fections, to believe that power may be safely lodged in our
hands. We have the health of the nation at command, and are
invested with almost irresistible strength; the judiciary has
neither force nor wealth to protect itself. That we can, with
propriety, modify our judiciary system so that we always leave
the judges independent is a correct and reasonable position;
but, if we can, by repealing a law, remove them, they are in
the worst state of dependence.

SENATOR S. T. MASON.—If the arguments now urged be correct, that a court once established cannot be vacated, we are
led into the greatest absurdities. For instance: Congress have
assumed jurisdiction over the Mississippi Territory, and have
established a court composed of three judges, which court is as
much an inferior court as the circuit or district courts. Of
this jurisdiction Georgia denies the validity. The contest is in
a train of settlement. Suppose it shall turn out that the
United States are convinced of the injustice of their claim,
relinquish it, and restore the Territory to Georgia, what becomes
of the judges? Their offices, their duties, are gone! Yet they
will tell you: We are vested with certain constitutional rights

of which you cannot deprive us. It is true the territory is no longer yours. You have no jurisdiction, we have no power; yet we are judges by the Constitution. We hold our offices during good behavior, and we will behave well as long as you will let us. Is not this a strange situation? You have judges in a territory over which you have no jurisdiction; and you have offices which are perfect sinecures, and officers who are pensioners for life. Such an absurdity I am sure the Constitution never meant to justify. It is an absurdity equally repugnant to the letter and genius of the Constitution.

I fear that, if you take away from these judges that which they ought officially to do, they will be induced, from the want of employment, to do that which they ought not to do. They may be induced, perhaps, to set about that work gentlemen seem so fond of. They may, as gentlemen have told us, hold the Constitution in one hand and the law in the other, and say to the departments of Government, So far shall you go and no farther. This independence of the judiciary, so much desired, will, I fear, sir, if encouraged or tolerated, soon become something like supremacy. They will, indeed, form the main pillar of this goodly fabric; they will soon become the only remaining pillar, and they will presently become so strong as to crush and absorb all the others into their solid mass.

Senator Mason then went into the history of the passage of the Judiciary act which it was proposed to repeal.

I will say that not an argument was urged in favor of the bill, not a word to show the necessity or propriety of the change. Yet we are told that there was great dignity, great solemnity in its progress and passage!

But there is something undignified in thus hastily repealing this law, in thus yielding ourselves to the fluctuations of public opinion! So we are told! But, if there be blame, on whom does it fall? Not on us, who respected the public opinion when this law was passed, and who still respect it; but on those who, in defiance of public opinion, passed this law after that public opinion had been decisively expressed. The revolution in public opinion had taken place before the introduction of this project; the people of the United States had determined to commit their affairs to new agents; already had the confidence of the people been transferred from their then rulers into other hands. After this exposition of the national will, and this new deposit of the national confidence, the gentlemen should have left untouched this important and delicate subject—a subject on which the people could not be reconciled to their views, even in the flood tide of their power and influence; they should have forborne till agents better acquainted with the national will, because more recently constituted its organs, had come into the Government. This would have been more dignified than to seize the critical moment, when power was passing from them, to pass such a law as this. If there is error it is our duty to correct it; and the truth was no law was ever more execrated by the public.

SENATOR STONE.—I take it to be a thing undeniable that there resides somewhere in the Government a power to declare what shall amount to misbehavior in office by the judges, and to remove them from office for the same, without impeachment. The Constitution does not prohibit their removal by the legislature, who have the power to make all laws necessary and proper for carrying into execution the powers vested by the Constitution in the Government of the United States. But, says the gentleman from New York [Mr. Morris], the judges are officers instituted by the Constitution, to save the people from their greatest enemies, themselves; and, therefore, they should be entirely independent of and beyond the control of the legislature. If such was the design of the wise men who framed and adopted the Constitution, can it be presumed they would have provided so ineffectual a barrier as these judges can readily be shown to be? It is allowed, on all hands, the legislature may modify the courts: they may add judges, they may fix the times at which the courts shall sit, etc. An understanding between the President and the Senate would make it practicable to fill the new offices with men of different views and opinions from those now in office. And what, in either case, would become of this boasted protection of the people against themselves?

What danger is there to the people from the legislature which the courts can control? The means of oppression nearest at hand to the legislature, and which afford the strongest temptation to their use, are the raising extravagant and unnecessary sums of money and the imbodying large and useless armies. Can the courts oppose effectual checks to these powers? I presume not. The Constitution permits their exercise to any extent within the discretion of the legislature.

The objects of courts of law, as I understand them, are to settle questions of right between suitors; to enforce obedience to the laws, and to protect the citizens against the oppressive use of power in the executive offices. Not to protect them against the legislature, for that I think I have shown to be impossible, with the powers which the legislature may safely use and exercise; and because the people have retained, in their own hands, the power of controlling and directing the legislature by their immediate and mediate elections of President, Senate, and House of Representatives.

It is not alone the sixteen rank and file which the gentleman from New York has so ludicrously depicted that I apprehend immediate danger from, but it is the principle which converts the office of judge into an hospital of incurables, and declares that an expiring faction, after having lost the public confidence, may add to those sixteen until they become sixteen hundred or sixteen thousand: and that the restored good sense of the legislature, the whole Government and Constitution, retains no means of casting them off but by destroying itself and resorting to revolutionary principles. The legislature may repeal unnecessary taxes, may disband useless and expensive armies, may declare they will no longer be bound by the stipulations of an oppressive treaty; and, if war should follow, the Constitution is still safe. But, if the construction which gentlemen contend for be correct, a band of drones, to any amount in number, under the denomination of judges, may prey upon the substance of the people, and the Government retains not the power to remove them but by destroying the Constitution itself.

SENATOR MORRIS.—The framers of the Constitution had seen much, read much, and deeply reflected. They knew by experience the violence of popular bodies, and let it be remembered that since that day many of the States, taught by experience, have found it necessary to change their forms of government to avoid the effects of that violence. The convention contemplated the very act you now attempt. They knew also the jealousy and the power of the States; and they established for your and for their protection this most important department. I beg gentlemen to hear and remember what I say: it is this department alone, and it is the independence of this department, which can save you from civil war. Yes, sir, adopt the language of gentlemen, say with them, by the act to which you are urged, "If we cannot remove the judges we can destroy them." Establish thus the dependence of the Judiciary Department, who will resort to them for protection against you? Who will confide in, who will be bound by their decrees? Are we then to resort to the ultimate reason of kings? Are our arguments to fly from the mouths of our cannon?

If we undertake to construe this Constitution to our purposes, and say that public opinion is to be our judge, there is an end to all constitutions. To what will not this dangerous doctrine lead? Should it to-day be the popular wish to destroy the First Magistrate, you can destroy him; and, should he to-morrow be able to conciliate to him the popular will, and lead them to wish for your destruction, it is easily effected. Adopt this principle and the whim of the moment will not only be the law but the Constitution of our country.

Do not, gentlemen, suffer the rage of passion to drive reason from her seat. If this law be indeed bad, let us join to remedy the defects. Has it been passed in a manner which wounded your pride or aroused your resentment? Have, I conjure you, the magnanimity to pardon that offence? I entreat, I implore you to sacrifice those angry passions to the interests of our country. Pour out this pride of opinion on the altar of patriotism. Let it be an expiatory libation for the weal of America. Do not, for God's sake, do not suffer that pride to plunge us all into the abyss of ruin. Indeed, indeed, it will be but of little, very little, avail whether one opinion or the other be right or wrong; it will heal no wounds, it will pay no debts, it will rebuild no ravaged towns. Do not rely on that popular will which has brought us frail beings into political existence. That opinion is but a changeable thing. It will soon change. This very measure will change it. You will be deceived. Do not, I beseech you, in reliance on a foundation so frail, commit the dignity, the harmony, the existence of our nation to the wild wind. Trust not your treasure to the waves. Throw not your compass and your charts into the ocean. Do not believe that its billows will waft you into port. Indeed, indeed, you will be deceived. Cast not away this only anchor of our safety. I have seen its progress. I know the difficulties through which it was obtained. I stand in the presence of Almighty God and of the world: and I declare to you that, if you lose this charter, never, no, never, will you get another! We are now, perhaps, arrived at the parting point. Here, even here, we stand on the brink of fate. Pause—pause! For Heaven's sake, pause!

The motion to repeal the Judiciary act passed in the Senate by a vote of 16 to 15.

When the bill came to the House it precipitated a

debate which was the most acrimonious that had ever been known in that body. The subject occupied the entire attention of the House from February 16 to March 3, when the act was passed by a strict party vote of 59 to 32. The main arguments relative to the measure had already been presented in the Senate, and it was a foregone conclusion that it would pass; therefore the speakers seized the opportunity to address the country in a series of stump speeches in which they discussed every political issue that had arisen since the inauguration of Washington, extolling the virtues of their own party and denouncing their opponents as the arch enemies of liberty and social order. About thirty Representatives made speeches, most of these long and rambling ones. There is space here to reproduce only a few passages of the most typical speeches. The Democratic speakers selected are Thomas T. Davis, of Kentucky, William B. Giles, of Virginia, and John Randolph and Philip R. Thompson, of Virginia. The Federalist speakers selected are James A. Bayard, Sr., of Delaware, Thomas Morris, of New York, Joseph Hemphill, of Pennsylvania, and Archibald Henderson and John Stanley, of North Carolina.

REPEAL OF THE JUDICIARY ACT

HOUSE OF REPRESENTATIVES, FEBRUARY 16-MARCH 3, 1802

MR. HENDERSON.—The construction which gentlemen on the other side of the House contend for tends to the concentration of legislative and executive powers in the same hands. If Congress, who have the power of making laws, can also displace their judges by repealing that which creates the offices they fill, the irresistible consequence is that whatever law is passed the judges must carry into execution or they will be turned out of office. Whatever the legislature declares to be law must be obeyed. The constitutional check which the judges were to be on the legislature is completely done away. They may pass *ex post facto* laws, bills of attainder, suspend the writ of *habeas corpus* in time of peace, and the judge who dares to question their authority is to be hurled from his seat. All the ramparts which the Constitution has erected around the liberties of the people are prostrated at one blow by the passage of this law. The monstrous and unheard of doctrine which has been lately advanced that the judges have not the right of declaring unconstitutional laws void will be put into practice by the adoption of this measure. New offences may be created by law. Associations and combinations may be declared treason, and the affrighted and appalled citizen may in vain seek refuge in the independence of your courts. In vain may he hold out the Constitution and deny the authority of Congress to pass a law of such undefined signification, and call upon the judges to protect him; he will be told that the opinion of Congress now is that we have no right to judge of their authority; this will be the consequence of concentrating judicial and legislative power in the same hands. It is the very definition of tyranny, and wherever you find it the people are slaves, whether they call their government a monarchy, republic, or democracy.

Mr. Chairman, I see, or think I see, in this attempt that spirit of innovation which has prostrated before it a great part of the old world—every institution which the wisdom and experience of ages had reared up for the benefit of man. A spirit which has rode in the whirlwind and directed the storm to the destruction of the fairest portion of Europe; which has swept before it every vestige of law, religion, morality, and rational government; which has brought twenty millions of people at the feet of one, and compelled them to seek refuge from their complicated miseries in the calm of despotism. It is against the influence of this tremendous spirit that I wish to raise my voice, and exert my powers, weak and feeble as they are. I fear, sir, on the seventh of December it made its appearance within these walls, clothed in a gigantic body, impatient for action. I fear it has already begun to exert its all-devouring energy. Have you a judiciary system extending over this immense country, matured by the wisdom of your ablest and best men? It must be destroyed. Have you taxes which have been laid since the commencement of the Government? Are they paid exclusively by the wealthy and the luxurious part of the community? And are they pledged for the payment of the public debt? They must be abolished. Have you laws which require foreigners coming to your country to go through a probationary state, by which their habits, their morals and propensities may be known, before they are admitted to all the rights of native Americans? They must be repealed, and our shores crowded with the outcasts of society, lest oppressed humanity then should find no asylum on this globe!

Mr. Thompson.—How long, Mr. Chairman, are we to be

imposed on by sound, how long are we to be entangled with the cobwebs of sophistry? The gentleman from North Carolina [Mr. Henderson] has warned us, solemnly warned us, against a violation of the Constitution. Why were not these sensations which he now experiences with such exquisite sensibility awakened a year ago, when he might perhaps have prevented an actual violation of the Constitution? I ask the honorable gentleman, sir, when with a sacrilegious hand this vital wound was inflicted on the Constitution if he raised the plaintive cry of, Spare, oh! spare the Constitution of my country? Yesterday, sir, the gentleman informed us, if the bill on your table should pass, he would heave no sigh, he would drop no tear over the expiring Constitution. When that law passed did he heave no sigh, did he drop no tear? Oh, no, sir, very different was the course which was then pursued. With cool, with cruel deliberation the devoted victim was immolated, and the blood which issued from the gaping wound will forever stain the pages of your statute book. The common law extends to all persons and all things. If the judges have the right of adopting this law, or such parts as they may deem applicable, they can annul your laws. If these powers are really contended for on the part of the judiciary, and if these powers should ever be conceded, they would without doubt possess an unlimited and uncontrollable power of legislation. I am free for my own part to declare that I had rather live under the government of a lenient despot than such a government of judges. And, if those powers are really contended for, I feel no hesitation in informing you, Mr. Chairman, that this is the tree where despotism lies concealed. And this, too, is the auspicious moment when those branches shall be pruned away which of late have vegetated with extraordinary luxuriancy. But, sir, nurture it with your treasure, stop not its ramifications, and suffer me seriously to inquire, What will be the consequence? It will overshadow your extensive Republic; your soil will become too sterile for the plant of liberty; your atmosphere will be contaminated with its poisonous effluvia, and your soaring eagle will fall dead at its root.

Mr. Hemphill.—The independence of the judges was a great point gained by the people of England. While the tenure of office depended on the nod of the Crown, they supported the arbitrary measures of the king; in one instance they decided that the king had a right to levy ship-money, without the consent of Parliament or people; and many an instance might be brought to the recollection of this honorable committee where they determined through fear and not from judgment. It is said they are not independent of Parliament. Why, sir, nothing is independent of Parliament; and there is not the same necessity there. There being no written constitution in England, the judiciary forms no check upon Parliament; and, besides, our Government is not a copy of the British Government; and this is not the only solitary instance where we have outstripped, as it is called, our too favorite prototype. There is not a leading feature in the Constitution that bears testimony of any servile imitation; it is our opponents who wish to test our Constitution by the principles of the British Government; it is they who wish that a construction be put upon the Constitution by Congress which shall be considered as the Constitution itself; and are unwilling that there should be any check to oppose it; and, of course, every construction put on it by the different legislatures will exhibit the appearance of a new Constitution, a Constitution to be tossed and blown about by every political breeze. The powers of Congress will be equal to the powers of the English Parliament, transcendant, splendid, and without control. I little expected that such lordly power would be grasped at by our plain Republicans, who have no ambitious desires and who wish rulers to be contented with humble prerogatives.

MR. DAVIS.—I found my opinion of the expediency of repealing the judiciary law, the power the judges declare they have, in the language of Judge Patterson, to "declare a law null and void." Never can I subscribe to that opinion. Never can I believe the judiciary paramount to both branches of the legislature. If it is, I have yet to learn it. There is an end to legislation. A knave or a fool can make void your best and most wholesome laws. In the present state of things, how will it affect us? The minority possessing one department of government completely frustrates the views of the other two, and governs the nation against the will of the people and the legislative and executive power. I am willing to admit the judiciary to be coördinate with the legislature in this respect, to wit, that judges thinking a law unconstitutional are not bound to execute it; but not to *declare* it null and void. That power rests alone with the legislature. But we are told this judiciary is necessary to check this House and the Senate, and to protect the people against their worst enemies. This is saying to the people, You are incapable of governing yourselves, your representatives are incapable of doing it; in the judiciary alone you find a safe deposit for your liberties; and saying also that the judiciary is the vitals of the nation, wherein all power, all safety dwells; that the legislature is subordinate thereto and a mere nominal thing, a shadow without substance, its acts perfectly within the control of the judiciary. I tremble at such ideas. The sooner we put men out of power whom we find determined to act in this manner, the better; by doing so we preserve the power of the legislature and save our nation from the ravages of an uncontrolled judiciary.

MR. MORRIS.—Gentlemen speak of the present as a very favorable moment for us to determine this great constitutional question. Sir, I believe that this is, of all moments, the most unfortunate for such a determination. I believe so because such have been the fatal effects of executive persecution that it has wrought up party spirit to its highest pitch of irritation. [Here there was a cry of order from different parts of the House.]

I did not mean to say anything that was disorderly, but, having occasion to allude to the present state of irritation of the public mind, I cannot help attributing it to what I believe to be the true cause of it. Sir, I am incapable of attributing to a majority of this House a settled determination of violating the Constitution of their country; but I do believe that, if they act from the impulse of the present moment, that valuable instrument will be sacrificed at the altar of resentment. And how can this belief be resisted when you hear so respectable a gentleman as the honorable member from Kentucky so far get the better of his usual discretion as to permit himself to say that he would vote for the bill because in no other way can judges be driven from their posts?

MR. STANLEY.—Popular assemblies are as much under the dominance of passion as individuals; they feel as sensibly and resent as malignantly. He who has not made this observation is a stranger to what has passed in all popular governments; and, I am sorry to add, a stranger to what has so lately passed in this country. By the exercise of this power, firm, upright judges, men of unbending virtue, are to be removed upon every change of administration, to make way for more pliant minions, the humble instruments of the legislature. The bulwark of our liberties against legislative encroachment, the independence and purity of our judiciary, is tumbled into ruins, and the rights of millions are crushed by its fall. The sacred altar of justice is polluted, the sword of justice becomes the rod of oppression. On the other hand, what danger is to be apprehended from that independence of the judges for which the friends of the Constitution contend? Not that bad and corrupt

IX—33

men will be fastened on us. No, the Constitution provides for their removal by impeachment. Not that they will viciously oppose the constitutional acts of the legislature. No, the legislature is a check upon them by the mode of impeachment, in which the House is the accuser and the Senate the judge. If the judge be corrupt, if he misdemean himself, he may be removed. If he continue pure and upright, he ought not to be removed; no earthly power but the mighty hand of the people, which formed the Constitution and can destroy it, can legally remove him. Should this measure be adopted and the independence of our judiciary be destroyed; should the administration of our Government unfortunately pass into the hands of men who feel power and forget right, our Constitution becomes indeed "a Lilliputian tie"; and this measure will be the first link in that chain of measures which will add the name of America to the melancholy catalog of fallen republics.

MR. GILES said: A great portion of the human mind has been at all times directed toward monarchy as the best form of government to enforce obedience and ensure the general happiness; whereas another portion of the human mind has given a preference to the republican form as best calculated to produce the same end; and there is no reason for applying improper motives to individuals who should give a preference to either of the principles, provided in doing so they follow the honest dictates of their own judgments. It must be obvious to the most common observer that, from the commencement of the Government of the United States, and perhaps before it, a difference of opinion existed among the citizens, having more or less reference to these two extreme fundamental points, and that it manifested itself in the modification or administration of the Government as soon as it was put in operation. On one side it was contended that in the organization of the Constitution a due apportionment of authority had not been made among the several departments; that the legislature was too powerful for the executive department; and to create and preserve a proper equipoise it was necessary to infuse into the executive department, by legislation, all artificial powers compatible with the Constitution upon which the most diffusive construction was given; or, in other words, to place in Executive hands all the patronage it was possible to create, for the purpose of protecting the President against the full force of his constitutional responsibility to the people. On the other side it was contended that the doctrine of patronage was repugnant to the opinions and feelings of the people; that it was unnecessary, expensive, and oppressive, and that the highest energy the Government could possess would flow from the confidence of the mass of the people, founded upon their own sense of their common interests. Hence what is called party in the United States grew up from a division of opinion respecting these two great characteristic principles. Patronage, or the creation of partial interest for the protection and support of Government, on the one side: on the other side, to effect the same end, a fair responsibility of all representatives to the people; an adherence to the general interests and a reliance on the confidence of the people at large, resulting from a sense of their common interests.

Here the speaker entered into a history of the Federalist Administration of John Adams, showing the growth of the system of executive patronage.

The general disquietude which manifested itself in consequence of these enterprising measures in the year 1800 induced the Federal party to apprehend that they had pushed their principles too far, and they began to entertain doubts of the result of the presidential election which was approaching. In this state of things it was natural for them to look out for some department of the Government in which they could entrench themselves in the event of an unsuccessful issue in the election, and continue to support those favorite principles of irresponsibility which they could never consent to abandon.

The judiciary department, of course, presented itself as best fitted for their object, not only because it was already filled with men who had manifested the most indecorous zeal in favor of their principles, but because they held their offices by indefinite tenures, and of course were further removed from any responsibility to the people than either of the other departments. Accordingly, on the 11th of March, 1800, a bill for the more convenient organization of the courts of the United States was presented to the House of Representatives. This bill appears to have had for its objects, first, the gradual demolition of the State courts, by increasing the number and extending the jurisdiction of the Federal courts; second, to afford additional protection to the principles of the then existing Administration by creating a new corps of judges of concurring political opinions. This bill, however, was not passed into a law during that session of Congress, perhaps from an apprehension that it would tend to increase the disquietudes which other measures had before excited, and therefore operate unfavorably to the approaching presidential election. At the next session, after the result of the late election was ascertained, the bill, after having undergone some considerable alterations, was passed into the law now under discussion. This law, it is now said, is inviolable and irrepealable. It is said the independence of the judge will be thereby immolated. Yes, sir, this law is now considered as the sanctuary of the principles of the last Administration, and the tenures of the judges as the horns of inviolability within that sanctuary. Gentlemen, discarding all generalizing expressions and the spirit of the instrument, tie down all construction to the strict letter of the Constitution.

Mr. Giles said it gave him great pleasure to meet gentlemen on this ground; and the more so because he had long been in the habit of hearing very different language from the same gentlemen. He had long been in the habit of hearing the same gentlemen speak of the expressions of "the common defence and the general welfare" as the only valuable part of the Constitution; that they were sufficient to obliterate all specifications and limitations of power. That the Constitution was a mere nose of wax, yielding to every impression it received—that every "opening wedge" which was driven into it was highly beneficial in severing asunder the limitations and restrictions of power—that the republicanism it secured meant anything or nothing. It gave him, therefore, great pleasure at this time to obey the injunctions of gentlemen in rallying round the Constitution as the ark of our political safety, and in interpreting it by the plain and obvious meaning and letter of the specified powers. But, he said, as if it was always the unfortunate destiny of these gentlemen to be upon extremes, they have now got round to the opposite extreme point of the political compass, and even beyond it. For, he said, they not only tie down all construction to the letter of the instrument, but they tell us that they see, and call upon us also to see, written therein, in large capital characters, "the independence of judges"; which, to the extent they carry the meaning of the term, is neither to be found in the letter or spirit of that instrument, nor in any other political establishment, he believed, under the sun.

Mr. Giles said he rejoiced that this subject was now to be discussed; he thought the crisis peculiarly auspicious for the discussion. He said the European world, with which the United States have the most relations, is now tranquilized.

The tremendous scenes of blood and revolution which had agitated that portion of the globe had at length subsided into profound peace; and had left mankind in silent amazement to retrospect the wonderful events which were passed; and he hoped, with calm deliberation, to improve the lessons they had furnished for the benefit of mankind in time to come. The interests and sympathies which the people of the United States felt in these events no longer turn their attention from their internal concerns; arguments of the highest consideration for the safety of the Constitution and the liberty of the citizens no longer receive the short reply, French partisans! Jacobins! Disorganizers! And, although the gentleman from North Carolina sees, or thinks he sees, the destructive spirit mount in the whirlwind and direct the storm, let him be consoled by the information "that all these, our actors, are mere spirits, and are dissolved into thin air." Yes, sir, these magical delusions are now vanished, and have left the American people and their Congress, in their real persons and original American characters, engaged in the transaction of American concerns.

Mr. Giles discussed at length the construction of the Constitution as to the judiciary, closing as follows:

Can so much inattention and folly be attributed to the framers of the Constitution as would result from the supposition that, if it was their intention that a law growing out of one of the specified powers, in contradistinction to all others, should be irrepealable when once passed, so extraordinary a principle would be left to mere implication? Such a supposition would be the highest injustice to the superior intelligence and patriotism of those gentlemen manifested in every other part of the instrument. No, sir, they would have made notes of admiration: they would have used every mark, adopted every caution, to have arrested and fixed the attention of the legislature to so extraordinary a principle.

They would have said, Legislators, be circumspect! Be cautious! Be calm! Be deliberate! Be wise! Be wise not only for the present, but be wise for posterity! You are now about to tread upon holy ground. The law you are now about to pass is irrepealable! Irrevocable! We are so enamored with the salutary and practical independence of the English judiciary system that, in infusing its principle into our Constitution, we have stamped it with the proverbial folly of the Medes and Persians! If this principle had been introduced into

the Constitution in express words it would have formed an
unfortunate contrast to all other parts of the instrument; yet
gentlemen make no difficulty in introducing that principle by
construction which would have appeared so stupid and absurd
if written in express words in the body of the instrument. But
there is no such language in the Constitution. Let us see what
is the language of that instrument. ''The judicial power of
the United States shall be vested in one Supreme Court and
in such inferior courts as Congress may from time to time
ordain and establish.'' Here, then, instead of cautioning the
legislature that a law for the organization of courts, when
passed, can never be repealed, it contains an invitation to a
revision from time to time. It contains an intimation that the
subject is new and difficult, and an injunction to ordain and
establish your courts from time to time, according to the results which an experience of the system alone could suggest.

MR. BAYARD.—Mr. Chairman, I must be allowed to express
my surprise at the course pursued by the honorable gentleman
from Virginia [Mr. Giles]. I had expected that he would have
adopted a different line of conduct. I had expected it as well
from that sentiment of magnanimity which ought to have been
inspired by a sense of the high ground he holds on the floor of
this House as from the professions of a desire to conciliate
which he has so repeatedly made during the session. We confided in the gentleman's sincerity, and cherished the hope that,
if the divisions of party were not banished from the House, its
spirit would be less intemperate. Such were our impressions,
when the mask was suddenly thrown aside, and we saw the
torch of discord lighted and blazing before our eyes. Every
effort has been made to revive the animosities of the House
and inflame the passions of the nation. I am at no loss to perceive why this course has been pursued. The gentleman has
been unwilling to rely upon the strength of his subject, and
has therefore determined to make the measure a party question.
He has probably secured success, but would it not have been
more honorable and more commendable to have left the decision of a great constitutional question to the understanding and
not to the prejudices of the House? It was my ardent wish
to discuss the subject with calmness and deliberation, and I
did intend to avoid every topic which could awaken the sensibility of party. This was my temper and design when I took
my seat yesterday. It is a course at present we are no longer
at liberty to pursue. The gentleman has wandered far, very
far, from the points of the debate, and has extended his ani-

madversions to all the prominent measures of the former Administrations. In following him through his preliminary observations I necessarily lose sight of the bill upon your table.

Whatever impression it might be the intention of the gentleman to make, he does not believe that there exists in the country an anti-Republican party. Insinuations of this sort belong not to the legislature of the Union. Their place is an election ground or an alehouse. Within these walls they are lost; abroad, they have an effect, and I fear are still capable of abusing the popular credulity.

We were next told of the parties which have existed, divided by the opposite views of promoting executive power and guarding the rights of the people. The gentleman did not tell us in plain language, but he wishes it to be understood that he and his friends were the guardians of the people's rights, and that we were the advocates of executive power.

I know that this is the distinction of party which some gentlemen have been anxious to establish; but this is not the ground on which we divide. I am satisfied with the constitutional powers of the Executive, and never wished nor attempted to increase them; and I do not believe that gentlemen on the other side of the House ever had a serious apprehension of danger from an increase of executive authority. No, sir, our views as to the powers which do and ought to belong to the general and State governments are the true sources of our divisions. I coöperate with the party to which I am attached because I believe their true object and end is an honest and efficient support of the general Government in the exercise of the legitimate powers of the Constitution.

I pray to God I may be mistaken in the opinion I entertain as to the designs of gentlemen to whom I am opposed. Those designs I believe hostile to the powers of this Government. State pride extinguishes a national sentiment. Whatever is taken from this Government is given to the States.

The ruins of this Government aggrandize the States. There are States which are too proud to be controlled; whose sense of greatness and resource renders them indifferent to our protection, and induces a belief that, if no general Government existed, their influence would be more extensive and their importance more conspicuous. There are gentlemen who make no secret of an extreme point of depression to which the Government is to be sunk. To that point we are rapidly progressing. But I would beg gentlemen to remember that human affairs are not to be arrested in their course at artificial points. The im-

pulse now given may be accelerated by causes at present out of
view. And when those who now design well wish to stop they
may find their powers unable to resist the torrent. It is not
true that we ever wished to give a dangerous strength to executive power. While the Government was in our hands it was
our duty to maintain its constitutional balance by preserving
the energies of each branch. There never was an attempt to
vary the relation of its powers. The struggle was to maintain
the constitutional powers of the Executive. The wild principles of French liberty were scattered through the country. We
had our Jacobins and disorganizers. They saw no difference
between a king and a president, and, as the people of France
had put down their king, they thought the people of America
ought to put down their President. They who considered the
Constitution as securing all the principles of rational and practicable liberty, who were unwilling to embark upon the tempest-
uous sea of revolution, in pursuit of visionary schemes, were
denounced as monarchists. A line was drawn between the Government and the people, and the friends of the Government
were marked as the enemies of the people. I hope, however,
that the Government and the people are now the same; and I
pray to God that what has been frequently remarked may not
in this case be discovered to be true, that they who have the
name of people the most often in their mouths have their true
interests the most seldom at their hearts.

A little experience will give the gentleman a new idea of
the patronage of this Government. He will find it not that
dangerous weapon in the hands of the Administration which he
has heretofore supposed it; he will probably discover that the
poison is accompanied by its antidote, and that an appointment of the Government, while it gives to the Administration
one lazy friend, will raise up against it ten active enemies.

Mr. Bayard then replied, point by point, to Mr.
Giles's indictment of the Adams Administration. At the
close he said:

There are the events of the general Government which the
gentleman has reviewed in succession and endeavored to render
odious or suspicious. For all this I could have forgiven him,
but there is one thing for which I will not, I cannot, forgive
him—I mean his attempt to disturb the ashes of the dead; to
disturb the ashes of the great and good Washington! Sir, I
might degrade by attempting to eulogize this illustrious character. The work is infinitely beyond my powers. I will only

say that, as long as exalted talents and virtues confer honor among men, the name of Washington will be held in veneration.

After, Mr. Chairman, the honorable member had exhausted one quiver of arrows against the late Executive, he opened another, equally poisoned, against the judiciary. He has told us, sir, that when the power of the Government was rapidly passing from Federal hands—after we had heard the thundering voice of the people which dismissed us from their service—we erected a judiciary which we expected would afford us the shelter of an inviolable sanctuary. The gentleman is deceived. We knew better, sir, the characters who were to succeed us, and we knew that nothing was sacred in the eyes of infidels. I believe these gentlemen regard public opinion because their power depends upon it; but I believe they respect no existing establishment of the Government; and, if public opinion could be brought to support them, I have no doubt they would annihilate the whole. I shall at present only say further on this head that we thought the reorganization of the judicial system a useful measure, and we considered it as a duty to employ the remnant of our power to the best advantage of our country.

The honorable member has thought himself justified in making a charge of a serious and frightful nature against the judges. They have been represented going about searching out victims of the sedition law. But no fact has been stated; no proof has been adduced, and the gentleman must excuse me from refusing my belief to the charge till it is sustained by stronger and better ground than assertion.

Do not say that you render the judges dependent only on the people. You make them dependent on your President. This is his measure. The same tide of public opinion which changes a President will change the majorities in the branches of the legislature. The legislature will be the instrument of his ambition, and he will have the courts as the instrument of his vengeance. He uses the legislature to remove the judges, that he may appoint creatures of his own. In effect, the powers of the Government will be concentrated in the hands of one man, who will dare to act with more boldness because he will be sheltered from responsibility. The independence of the judiciary was the felicity of our Constitution. It was this principle which was to curb the fury of party upon sudden changes. The first moments of power, gained by a struggle, are the most vindictive and intemperate. Raised above the storm, it was the judiciary which was to control the fiery zeal and to quell the fierce passions of a victorious faction.

We are standing on the brink of that revolutionary torrent which deluged in blood one of the fairest countries of Europe.

France had her National Assembly, more numerous and equally popular with our own. She had her tribunals of justice and her juries. But the legislature and her courts were but the instruments of her destruction. Acts of proscription and sentences of banishment and death were passed in the cabinet of a tyrant. Prostrate your judges at the feet of party and you break down the mounds which defend you from this torrent. I am done. I should have thanked my God for greater power to resist a measure so destructive to the peace and happiness of the country. My feeble efforts can avail nothing. But it was my duty to make them. The meditated blow is mortal, and from the moment it is struck we may bid a final adieu to the Constitution.

MR. RANDOLPH said that he did not rise for the purpose of assuming the gauntlet which had been so proudly thrown by the Goliath of the adverse party; but that he believed even his feeble powers, armed with the simple weapon of truth, a sling and a stone, capable of prostrating on the floor that gigantic boaster, armed *cap-à-pie* as he was; but that he was impelled by the desire to rescue from misrepresentation the arguments of his colleague (Mr. Giles), who was now absent during indisposition.

To the long catalogue of unpopular acts which have deprived their authors of the public confidence, the gentleman [Mr. Bayard] tells us he and his friends were "goaded" by the clamor of their opponents. He solemnly assures us that in the adoption of those measures they clearly foresaw the downfall of their power; but, impressed with a conviction that they were essential to the public good, and disdaining all considerations of a personal nature, they nobly sacrificed their political existence on the altar of the general welfare; and we are called upon now to revere in them the self-immolated victims at the shrine of patriotism. These are, indeed, lofty pretensions; and, although I shall not peremptorily deny, in this age of infidelity I may be permitted to doubt them; for I call upon this committee to decide whether, in this day's discussion, the gentleman has evinced that purity of heart or that elevation of sentiment which could justify me in clothing him with the attributes of Curtius or of the Decii?

I have long been in the habit of attending to the arguments of the gentleman from Delaware, and I have generally found, in their converse, a ready touchstone, the test of which they are rarely calculated to withstand. If you are precluded from passing this law, lest depraved men make it a precedent to destroy the independence of your judiciary, do you not concede that a desperate faction, finding themselves about to be dismissed from the confidence of their country, may pervert the power of erecting courts, to provide to an extent for their adherents and themselves? And that, however flagrant that abuse of power, it is remediless and must be submitted to? Will not the history of all governments warrant the assertion that the creation of new and unnecessary offices, as a provision for political partisans, is an evil more to be dreaded than the abolition of useless ones? Is not an abuse of power more to be dreaded from those who have lost the public confidence than from those whose interest it will be to cultivate and retain it? And does not the doctrine of our opponents prove that, at every change of administration, the number of your judges are probably to be doubled? Does it not involve the absurdity that, in spite of all constitutional prohibitions, Congress may exercise the power of creating an indefinite number of placemen, who are to be maintained through life at the expense of the community? But, when these cases are cited, you are gravely told that they suppose a degree of political depravity which puts an end to all argument. Here, sir, permit me to state an important difference of opinion between the two sides of this House. We are accused of an ambitious usurpation of power; of a design to destroy a great department of government, because it thwarts our views, and of a lawless thirst of self-aggrandizement which no consideration can restrain. Let us not be amused by words. Let us attend to facts. They will show who are contending for unlimited and who for limited power. The opponents of this bill contend that they did possess the power of creating offices to an indefinite amount; which, when created, were beyond the control of the succeeding legislature. They, of course, contend for the existence of such a power in the present legislature, for whose exercise there is no security but their self-respect. In other words that, if the present majority should incur the suspicion of the people, they may, as soon as there is any indication of their having forfeited the public confidence, on the signal of their dismissal from their present station, make ample and irrepealable provision for themselves and their adherents by the creation of an adequate number of judicial offices. Now, sir, this is a power which we reject, though it is insisted that we possess it. We deny that such an authority does exist in us. We assert that we are not clothed with the tremendous power of erecting, in defiance of the whole spirit and express letter of the Constitution, a vast judicial aristocracy over the heads of our fellow citizens on whose labor it is to prey. Who, then, are, in reality, the advocates of a limited authority, and who are the champions of a dangerous and uncontrollable power? In my estimation the wisest prayer that ever was composed is that which deprecates the being led into temptation. I have no wish to be exposed myself, nor to see my friends exposed, to the dangerous allurements which the adverse doctrine holds out. Do gentlemen themselves think that the persons whom I see around me ought to be trusted with such powers? Figure to yourselves a set of men whose incapacity or want of principle have brought on them the odium of their country, receiving, in the month of December, the solemn warning that on the fourth of March following they are to be dismissed from the helm of government; establish the doctrine now contended for, and what may we not expect? Yes, sir, the doctrine advanced by our opponents is that of usurpation and ambition. It denies the existence of one power by establishing another infinitely more dangerous; and this you are told is to protect, through the organ of an independent judiciary, the vanquished party from the persecution of their antagonists, although it has been shown that, by increasing the number of judges, any tone whatever may be given to the bench.

If gentlemen dread the act which we are about to pass they will remember that they have been the means of compelling us to it. They ought to have had the forbearance to abstain from such a measure at such a crisis. They have forced upon us the execution of a painful duty by their own want of prudence. If they wished the judges, like the tribe of Levi, to have been set apart from other men for the sacred purposes of justice, they should have considered well before they gave to publicans and sinners the privilege of the high priesthood.

Impeachment of Judge Chase

John Randolph made the control of the judiciary by the legislature a favorite measure. During the following year (1803) Samuel Chase, an associate-justice of the Supreme Court, delivered at his home in Baltimore, Md., what the Democrats considered a partisan harangue to the grand jury. For this and previous exhibitions of unjudicial temper by the justice, who was a very free speaking and irascible man, Randolph, in 1804, introduced in the House of Representatives a resolution that Justice Chase be impeached. This was passed in March, and the trial was set for the ensuing session of the Senate. The impeachment proceedings occupied the attention of this body from December 7, 1804, to March 1, 1805, when the accused was acquitted of all the eight charges brought against him, there being no constitutional majority (two-thirds) on any count, although on three there were bare majorities declaring him guilty.

The high position from which it was sought to remove the accused caused the proceedings to be memorable in the judicial and political annals of the country. The ablest legal and oratorical talent of the country was secured by both sides. Randolph led the prosecution. Chase's counsel were Luther Martin, Robert G. Harper, Charles Lee, P. B. Key, and Joseph Hopkinson.

This decision was valuable in the later history of American jurisprudence in discountenancing the impeachment of judges on frivolous grounds, and, at the same time, in warning judges to suppress all manifestations of partisanship while on the bench, for it was on charges of such conduct that Chase was found in fault by bare majorities, and for which he suffered odium throughout the remainder of his service on the bench, which was coterminus with his life.

The failure of the impeachment caused Randolph, on the day of Chase's acquittal, to introduce in the House the following amendment to the Constitution:

The judges of the Supreme and all other courts of the United States shall be removed by the President, on the joint address of both Houses of Congress requesting the same, anything in the Constitution of the United States to the contrary notwithstanding.

The motion came forward in one form and another and presented by various persons during the next six years, each time creating considerable discussion. On January 29, 1811, the House finally refused to consider it.

CHAPTER XV

THE RECALL OF JUDGES

[CONSTITUTION OF ARIZONA]

Debate in the Senate on the Admission of Arizona into the Union, with
Constitutional Provision for the Recall of Judges: Varying Views by
Robert L. Owen [Okla.], James P. Clarke [Ark.], Joseph W. Bailey
[Tex.], George Sutherland [Utah], George E. Chamberlain [Ore.], Jon-
athan Bourne [Ore.], William E. Borah [Ida.], Elihu Root [N. Y.];
Resolution Adopted; Veto Message of President Taft; Arizona Ad-
mitted without Recall, Which Is Then Adopted by State Legislature—
Ex-President Roosevelt Supports Recall of Judicial Decisions; President
Taft Opposes It—Joseph L. Bristow [Kan.] Introduces in the Senate
Constitutional Amendments for Such Recall.

THE subject of the recall of judges came forward
early in 1911 in connection with the admission
of Arizona into the Union.

On June 20, 1910, President Taft signed an act of
Congress enabling the Territories of New Mexico and
Arizona to form State constitutions and governments
preparatory to their admission into the Union.

On January 21, 1911, the people of New Mexico
adopted a constitution, and on February 7, 1911, the
people of Arizona adopted theirs. When these were
presented to Congress the radicals opposed the constitution of New Mexico as "reactionary," and the con-
servatives opposed the constitution of Arizona as "an-
archistic."

On March 4, 1911, Robert L. Owen [Okla.] spoke in
the Senate in defence of the Arizona constitution.

IN DEFENCE OF THE ARIZONA CONSTITUTION

SENATOR OWEN

Mr. President, the alleged offensive provisions of the constitution of Arizona are the initiative, referendum, and recall.

526

The people in Arizona, from whom all power flows, from whom comes all power, reserve to themselves this right of direct legislation. The Constitution makes it plain what these powers are:

Article IV, Sec. 2. The first of these reserved powers is the initiative. Under this power 10 per cent. of the qualified electors shall have the right to propose any measure, and 15 per cent. shall have the right to propose any amendment to the constitution.

Now we are told that Arizona may be admitted a little later on with this provision, but I call attention to the experience which we in Oklahoma had. We put this provision in our constitution, and our present National Chief Executive made an address in our State advising our people to vote down that constitution. One of his objections to it was that he regarded this provision as unwise. I know of no reason to believe that he has changed his mind with regard to it, although that is entirely possible. I deeply trust he may do so, but I greatly fear the reactionaries in the Senate will not vote to admit a progressive State, and I do not wish to leave the matter open.

(3) The second of these reserved powers is the referendum. Under this power the legislature, or 5 per cent. of the qualified electors, may order the submission to the people at the polls of any measure, or part of any measure, enacted by the legislature, except laws immediately necessary for the preservation of the public peace, health, or safety, or for the support and maintenance of the departments of the State government and State institutions.

Oklahoma has this provision in her constitution, and I am not willing to have Arizona affronted before the whole world and before this Republic because she has dared to write the initiative and referendum in her constitution. I do not think that right, and I am not going to submit to it. Why should the right be denied Arizona and the people of Arizona to write the organic law under which they live? There is no sound reason for it. Seventy-six per cent. of the people of Arizona have voted in favor of this constitution. It is all very well to say, "Let us have New Mexico admitted now and Arizona hereafter," but I do not believe the reactionaries or retrogressives intend to do anything of the kind if they can help it.

It is well known to everybody that the President is going to call an extra session. It will not be pretended that I am bringing about an extra session. The only thing which I am doing here is to emphasize this matter of the contest between delegated government and a government by popular sovereignty. That is the issue here, and I want to emphasize it as strongly as I can. It is the issue which is sweeping this nation; it is an issue which carried California in the last election, carried Washington, and which has controlled Oregon and has controlled Montana; which has become a part of the constitution of South Dakota; which is indorsed by both parties in North Dakota; which is written into the law of Nevada; which has been established as a principle in Arizona; which has been adopted by Colorado and Oklahoma and Missouri and Arkansas, and is about to be written into the laws of Nebraska. It is the issue in Michigan. It is an issue in Minnesota. It is the issue in Wisconsin, and is now about to be written on the face of the constitution of Wisconsin. It carried Illinois in the last election by four to one, and carried Governor Foss into the governor's chair in Massachusetts; and I think this notion of this being an "insane" doctrine is merely an evidence of the astonishing ignorance of some Senators of the United States of what is going on in this Republic.

Even the old State of Maine adopted it by a vote of two to one two years ago and wrote the initiative and referendum in her constitution.

JAMES P. CLARKE [Ark.].—The Senator is predicating his present address to the Senate upon the idea that it is necessary to defeat the adoption of the joint resolution proposing to admit New Mexico at this time because he thinks that thereby the prospect of the early admission of Arizona will be promoted. Is he not aware of the fact that, in the event this Congress shall fail to adopt the joint resolution admitting New Mexico, the President of the United States may do so, and that he has accomplished nothing in the interest of Arizona by the contest which he is making at this time?

SENATOR OWEN.—Now, it is true, as the Senator from Arkansas so forcibly points out, that, if Congress at its next regular session does not act or fails to disapprove, the President can and the President will admit. Why, then, this appeal to me to save New Mexico? Look at the astonishing constitution of New Mexico, with corporate control and machine politics written all over it, an ignorant electorate put in power and perpetuated so that an intelligence qualification is impossible.

THOMAS H. CARTER [Mont.].—I inquire of the Senator if he has prepared an amendment to this pending joint resolution proposing the concurrent admission of the Territories of New Mexico and Arizona?

SENATOR OWEN.—I have read it into the *Record* already, Mr. President.

Now, admitting Arizona and New Mexico together, it seems to me, might be a wise and proper method of proceeding if New Mexico had a decent constitution, but to admit New Mexico with a corporation constitution and allow the people of New Mexico to send two standpat Republican Senators to this floor, and deny the people of Arizona, with a people's rule constitution, the privilege of sending two Democratic Senators to this floor, I do not think a very good doctrine from a mere party standpoint, and I cannot consent to follow the leadership of the honored Senator from Texas [Joseph W. Bailey] in this proposal and demand, regardless of the merits of either constitution, for it will do the Republicans great service in the control of the next Senate and next presidential campaign, giving them four presidential electors, and will do the Democrats great harm by denying them two Democratic Senators and three presidential electors.

I do not like the direction of such Democratic leadership, and I cannot consent to follow it.

Now, perhaps the most obnoxious feature about the Arizona constitution to my distinguished opponents is the recall, and particularly as the recall applies to judges on the bench.

Article VIII, Section 1. Every public officer in the State of Arizona holding an elective office, either by election or appointment, is subject to recall from such office by the qualified electors of the electoral district from which candidates are elected to such office. Such electoral district may include the whole State. Such number of said electors as shall equal 25 per cent. of the number of votes cast at the last preceding general election for all of the candidates for the office held by such officer may by petition, which shall be known as a recall petition, demand his recall.

They say this will apply to a judge. So it does, and why should it not if the Arizona people want it? If a judge on the bench proves to be corrupt, proves to be unworthy and dishonest, or a brutal tyrant on the bench, imposing upon his fellow citizens by virtue of the power in his hands, why should he not be recalled by the Arizona people if they wish to have the law so? It is an easier method of dealing with him than by impeachment. The impeachment of a judge is done under circumstances most painful to the man who is impeached. Is not impeachment the right of recall? Impeachment puts a stigma upon him, however. It disgraces him to such an extent that men dislike to associate with him thereafter, whereas the right to recall is simply a matter of advising a man that he is not an acceptable public servant. The man who is defeated in a recall goes from his office without any necessary disgrace and without any deep stigma. It is simply a question of his being an unacceptable public servant. It has never been applied except for dishonesty. It has only been used three times on the Pacific coast—once in Los Angeles, where the mayor was believed to be corrupt. They simply nominated his successor and elected him, and the former mayor went out of office without any particular stigma except that of being a defeated candidate who was replaced by another man.

I want to quote from very high authority, our honorable ex-President, who has written upon this matter. In the *Washington Post* of March 4, 1911, this very morning, I find this item by our distinguished ex-President Theodore Roosevelt:

INTELLIGENT CRITICISM OF THE JUDGES AN ABSOLUTE NECESSITY
[Theodore Roosevelt, in the *Outlook*]

In the first place, it is absolutely necessary that there should be discrimination between, and therefore intelligent criticism of, the judges, who by their power of interpretation are the final arbiters in deciding what shall be the law of the land. Men ought not to be classed together for praise or blame because they occupy one kind of public office. The bonds that knit them in popular esteem or popular disfavor should be based not upon the offices they hold, but upon the way in which they fill these offices. Chief Justice Taney was, I doubt not, in private life as honorable a man as Chief Justice Marshall; but during his long term of service as Chief Justice his position on certain vital questions represented a resolute effort to undo the work of his mighty predecessor. If, on these positions, one of these two great justices was right, then the other was wrong; if one is entitled to praise, then the other must be blamed. Buchanan and Lincoln do not stand together in the popular eye because both were Presidents; on the contrary, they represent antipodal schools of thought. Andrew Johnson and Grant were as far asunder as Washington and Jefferson. There is no more ground for demanding that we refrain from differentiation between, and therefore from criticism of, Chief Justices than for adopting the same attitude as regards Presidents.

We must bear in mind the office; but we must also bear in mind the man who fills the office. This is a government of law, but it is also, as every government always has been, and always must be, a government of men; for the worth of a law depends as much upon the men who interpret and administer it as upon the men who have enacted it.

And Mr. Roosevelt in his recent Chicago speech asserted his belief that the right should not be denied Arizona to put the recall in her constitution as Massachusetts did in 1780.

It is not necessary to insist on the wisdom of the recall of judges, but I do insist that the people of Arizona have the right to establish their own organic law, if it be not in violation of the Constitution of the United States and of the principles of the Declaration of Independence.

The recall is not a novelty. It appears in the constitution of Massachusetts of 1780 and of to-day. The State of Massachusetts, moreover, elects its governor and other State officers only for one year, recalling them at the end of a year by a short tenure of office without reproach or reproof. If they are quite satisfactory, they are reëlected; if they are not quite satisfactory, they are automatically recalled by the short tenure.

If a governor were guilty of high crimes, they might impeach, which would be a recall in the form of a trial.

I can readily understand how an argumentative objection might be argued to the recall of judges on the ground that it would interfere with the independence of the judiciary. But it must be remembered that a judge on the bench, being only a human being, after all, may, under temptation, become corrupt, and corrupt in such a fashion that proof of his corruption is impossible, so that impeachment is impossible, while the recall, nominating his successor, is available.

Again, a judge upon the bench, being only a human being, after all, might become grossly intemperate, not sufficient to justify impeachment, but sufficient to justify recall.

Again, a judge upon the bench, being only a human being, after all, might become utterly tyrannical, overbearing, dictatorial, and offensive to the people over whom he has been trusted to discharge this function; not sufficient, perhaps, to justify impeachment, but yet sufficient to justify recall.

Moreover, a judge upon the bench, interpreting the law, may so interpret the law as to become a lawmaker instead of a law interpreter; may exercise, under the color of judicial power, legislative power. Not sufficient to justify impeachment, perhaps, but yet sufficient to justify recall.

Moreover, judges on the bench, being merely human beings, after all, are themselves controlled by their environment, by their professional education, by social, political, and business influences. They may lead a judge to a point of view which is extremely injurious to the common welfare. Not sufficient, perhaps, to justify impeachment, but yet sufficient to justify recall.

And, Mr. President, even Boston, the "Hub of the Universe," around which revolves all intellectual, moral, and ethical worth, two years ago adopted the doctrine of the recall in relation to the mayor and members of the municipal council.

Ex-Senator Henry W. Blair, of New Hampshire, advises me

that the power of removal of the judiciary by address of the two houses
of the legislature existed, and perhaps still exists, in the State of New
Hampshire, while the entire judiciary has been changed frequently by act
of the legislature whenever the public good seemed to require it, and the
courts, since I can remember, about four times.

Has not Arizona the right to write her own organic law if
Arizona is to be admitted on an equal footing with the other
States, as required by the Constitution of the United States?
If Arizona should be forced to expunge the initiative and referendum and recall from her constitution and was then admitted, could she not write those provisions into her constitution immediately afterward? Can you forestall it or prevent it? Or will you drive out of the Union the States of
Oregon, Montana, South Dakota, Maine, Arkansas, Oklahoma,
Colorado, California, Wyoming, and Nevada, who have already
adopted this provision?

The question answers itself.

The truth is self-evident. The initiative and referendum
and the recall are not contrary to the Constitution of the
United States. The Constitution of the United States was
adopted by a practical referendum of delegates pledged by the
people.

And the recall of the President of the United States is provided by impeachment proceedings, and the principle of recall
by impeachment is recognized in the Constitution of the United
States and of every State in the Union, as well as in the hundred municipalities who have recently directly adopted it.

On April 4, 1911, Henry D. Flood [Va.], from the
Committee on Territories, introduced a joint resolution
in the House approving the constitutions of New Mexico
and Arizona. It was referred back to the committee.
The committee, on May 16, reported it back with an
amendment suggesting to the voters of Arizona that, in
view of the objection of President Taft to the provision
for the recall of judges, in their constitution as submitted they eliminate this feature.

The subject was warmly discussed until May 23,
when the joint resolution was passed in the form that
the constitution submitted, "being republican in form
and not repugnant to the Constitution of the United

THE ARIZONA CONSTITUTION 533

States and the principles of the Declaration of Independence,'' was approved.

The resolution was referred in the Senate to the Committee on Territories, which, on July 11, reported it subject to amendment.

THE ARIZONA CONSTITUTION

SENATE, JULY 11-AUGUST 15, 1911

George Sutherland [Utah] opposed the resolution.

While I thoroughly disapprove of the initiative and the modern referendum and the recall as applied to executive and legislative officers, I could well subordinate my judgment to that of the people of Arizona if they had not gone further and provided that the recall should embrace the judiciary as well. The power to recall a judge who renders an unpopular judgment is to my mind so utterly subversive of the principles of good government that I can never get my own consent to withhold my condemnation and disapproval of it.

The Senator from Oregon—not the father of the "composite citizen" [Jonathan Bourne], but the junior Senator, George E. Chamberlain—in his speech of April 17 last, asks:

But, as an abstract proposition, why should a judicial officer be independent of the wishes of his constituents?

Ah, Mr. President, much of the vice and fallacy of the argument for the right to recall judges rests in this assumption that the judge, like a Congressman or a legislator, represents a constituency. What is a constituent? He is a person for whom another acts. A constituent implies, as a necessary corollary, a representative who speaks for him. A judge has no constituents; he is only in a restricted sense a representative officer at all. The people who elect him can with propriety make known their wishes only through the laws which they enact. The judge is the mouthpiece of the *law*. His constituents are the *statutes* duly made and provided. If his decisions are wrong, the remedy is to appeal to a higher court—not to the people. The scales of justice must hang level or there is an end of justice. The recall puts into the scale, upon one side or the other, in every case where strong public feeling exists, the artificially induced anxiety of the judge for the retention of his place. Bound by all the sacred traditions of his office to decide impartially between the parties according to the law and the evidence, he begins the discharge of his high duties with a personal interest in his own decision.

The judge represents no constituents, speaks for no policy save the public policy of the law. If he be not utterly forsworn, he must at all hazards put the rights of a single individual above the wishes of *all* the people. He has no master but the compelling force of his own conscience. Every circumstance which diminishes his independence and his courage, which closes his ears to the righteousness of the cause and opens them to the voice of clamor, makes for injustice.

If charged with incompetency, dishonesty, or corruption, common fairness demands that he should be tried in the open before an impartial tribunal, where he may be heard, not with a limitation of 200 words upon his defence, but in full, and where he may face his accusers and test the truth of their accusations by those orderly methods of procedure which the experience of centuries has demonstrated are essential to the ascertainment of truth. But the recall institutes a tribunal where everybody decides and nobody is responsible; where at least 25 per cent. of the membership have already, as the judge's accusers, prejudiced his case, and from whose arbitrary and unjust findings there is no appeal. In such a forum idle gossip and village scandal stand in the place of evidence; assertion takes the place of sworn testimony; and the foulest lie goes unchallenged by the touchstone of cross-examination. The voter will make up his verdict of vindication or conviction under the illuminating radiance of the torchlight procession, in the calm, judicial atmosphere of the brass band and the drum corps, and upon the logical summing up of the spellbinder and the campaign quartet.

Mr. President, I am not one of those who have become impatient at the restraints and checks and safeguards of the representative form of government and the written Constitution. I am not one of those who would launch the ship of state, with every sail set, upon the wide sea of tossing waters—with all its unsounded depths and unknown shallows, with here a whirlpool and there a half-submerged rock—without a chart or a compass or a rudder or an anchor, trusting alone to the merciful chance of wind and wave and the tumultuous efforts of an uncaptained crew to preserve it from disaster. I disagree utterly with the distinguished Senator from Oklahoma [Mr. Owen], who told us a few days ago, in that calm, judicial way of his, that the Constitution of the United States—for which some of us had conceived a rather high opinion—was all wrong; that it was not sufficiently democratic; that it was so drawn by Madison and those who were in the constitutional convention as to vest unfair power in the hands of the minority, and that this principle shows from one end of it to the other; that, among other things, to his deep regret, he had been unable to discover in that worn and antiquated document any provision for the recall of the Supreme Court of the United States. There are some individuals in this country who ought to be prosecuted for monopolizing so much of the wisdom that a discriminating Providence intended should be distributed in modest proportions among a somewhat extended number of people. I do not mean to say that the Senator from Oklahoma is one of these, but I feel sure that it was a distinct misfortune that he did not make his appearance at a date sufficiently early to give the fathers who framed the Constitution the benefit of his counsel and advice. I am not certain that in that event the Constitution would have been better, but I am sure it would have been longer.

For a century and a quarter the great names of Washington, who was the president of the convention; of Benjamin Franklin, Alexander Hamilton, James Madison, James Wilson, Charles Pinckney, and all the others of the immortal list, have occupied a shrine of glory in the hearts of the misguided multitude as the framers of a Constitution which, instead of being undemocratic "from one end of it to the other," is inspired "from one end of it to the other" with the thought that the day when the king commands and the people obey has gone, and that the new day has risen when the people shall command and the king obey.

But we have all been mistaken. The fathers, in framing the Constitution, were unpatriotic and undemocratic. They were engaged in turning over an amiable majority to the mercy of a ferocious minority; in setting up a government that could not be overturned by every breath of popular emotion; in creating a responsible and independent judiciary; and in other similar unholy and reprehensible enterprises, for which, I have no doubt, the enlightened "composite" citizenship of Oklahoma would, if they had the opportunity, commit them to the county jail as a gang of nonprogressive, standpat aristocrats.

Against these criticisms of the Constitution by this American Senator I would put the strong words of the great British commoner [William E. Gladstone], who described it as "the most wonderful work ever struck off at a given time by the brain and purpose of man.'' Against the petulant view of this American Senator, that this learned, courageous, and patriotic court should be made responsive, by means of the recall, to the changing moods of the majority, I would set the vigorous statement of another Briton, James Bryce, who said:

The Supreme Court is the living voice of the Constitution; that is, of the will of the people expressed in the fundamental law they have enacted. It is, therefore, as some one has said, the conscience of the people, who have resolved to restrain themselves from hasty or unjust action by placing their Representatives under the restriction of a permanent law. It is the guaranty of the minority, who, when threatened by the impatient vehemence of a majority, can appeal to this permanent law, finding the interpreter and enforcer thereof in a court set high above the assaults of faction.

To discharge these momentous functions the court must be stable, even as the Constitution is stable. Its spirit and tone must be that of the people at their best moments. It must resist them the more firmly, the more vehement they are. Intrenched behind impregnable ramparts, it must be able to defy at once the open attacks of the other departments of the Government and the more dangerous, because impalpable, seductions of popular sentiment.

Against all such wild and visionary demands for the popular recall of the judges I would print in letters of living light the strong words of Chief-Justice John Marshall:

The judicial department comes home, in its effects, to every man's fireside; it passes on his property, his reputation, his life, his all. Is it not to the last degree important that he should be rendered perfectly and completely independent, *with nothing to influence or control him but God and his conscience?*

Sir, I hope I am not given to overextravagant statement, but I declare my solemn conviction that, the moment a provision for the recall of the judges of the Supreme Court shall be written into the Federal Constitution, that moment will mark the beginning of the downfall of the Republic and the destruction of the free institutions of the American people.

And now, Mr. President, what is to be the next step in the onward march? Will it be to apply the referendum to judicial matters? Why not? If laws can be made by the simple formula of counting heads at the ballot box, why not laws construed and questions of fact unraveled by the same infallible method?

Such a device would seem to be the fitting complement of the recall. When a court is confronted with a particularly perplexing case in which there are great popular interest and warm

public feeling, where the precedents of the law and the sentiment of the people are both conflicting, and the poor judge is
driven to his wits' end to harmonize the one and accurately
interpret the other, instead of putting him to the uncomforta-
ble alternative of rendering a judgment which, however satisfactory to himself, may not meet the preponderating fancy of
the multitude, surely he might have the benefit of the ballot-box
opinion *before* instead of *after* he has decided. This *may* result in more or less disappointment to the losing litigant; it
will result in a good deal of uncertainty respecting the law, but
the judge will be saved and the power of the people will be
vindicated.

Sir, the suggestion is not so fanciful as it may at first appear. In the wild witches' dance which is only just beginning
the nimble feet of the "composite citizen" seem destined to cut
livelier capers and more bewildering pirouettes than even this.
An enterprising district attorney in San Diego, Cal., has already proposed to submit to the taxpayers of the county, if a
way can be found, the question as to whether he shall further
prosecute a case of arson in which the jury has already twice
disagreed.

Those who are so intemperately appealing to the people to
take over the *direct* management of their government, with its
multiplicity of detail and difficulty, the successful operation of
which demands concentration of effort and thoroughness of application, are preparing the way for future mischief. They are
advocating a political creed alluring to the imagination, but utterly impossible of successful realization, and which, if adopted,
will lead us more and more into the domain of the impracticable, with political chaos or political despotism as the ultimate result. It is the old contest between idealism and stubborn, matter-of-fact reality. It is the story of the philosopher's
stone over again—the dream of transmuting all the metals into
gold—the hunt for the master key that will open all locks,
however different in size and shape—the problem of fitting
square pegs into round holes—the puzzle of how to eat one's
cake and have it—the search for the chimera of perpetual motion—the quest for the mythical pot of gold at the foot of the
rainbow—and all the other impossible undertakings which have
vexed men's souls and turned their brains and filled the lunatic
asylums since mankind was divided into those who see facts
and those who see visions. Finally, this latest delusion of having everybody drive the horses and everybody ride in the coach
at the same time must share the fate of all the others, for it is

now as it has always been, that the pursuit of the unattainable
is the most profitless of human occupations.

On August 5 Jonathan Bourne [Ore.] replied to Senator Sutherland.

Mr. President, the Senator from Utah has seen fit to ridicule that portion of my address of February 27, 1911, in which
I expressed my conviction that the action of the composite citizen always tends to promote the general welfare. Let me repeat what I said:

> The people can be trusted. The composite citizen knows more and
> acts from higher motives than any single individual, however great, experienced, or well developed. While selfishness is usually dominant in the individual, it is minimized in the composite citizen. The composite citizen is
> made up of millions of individuals, each dominated in most cases by selfish
> interest. But because of the difference in the personal equations of the
> individual units making up the composite citizen, there is a corresponding
> difference in the interests dominating said units; and while composite
> action is taking place friction is developed, attrition results, selfishness is
> worn away, and general welfare is substituted before action is accomplished.

In my speech I demonstrated that under the initiative and
referendum the people cannot legislate against the general welfare, and by the same logic I assert that under the recall the
people will never recall a public servant, judicial or otherwise,
who serves the general welfare.

Mr. President, objection is made to the admission of Arizona
because its constitution contains the recall provision. The particular point of objection is that the recall applies to the judiciary as well as to executive, administrative, and legislative
officers. The great fear is that constant accountability to the
people of the State will exercise an improper influence upon
the courts.

To my mind this objection is untenable. As I said recently
in an article in the *Saturday Evening Post*, if the people of
Arizona or any other State are competent to elect their judges
and can be trusted to act fairly and honestly in the election,
they can also be trusted in the exercise of the recall power.
The Arizona constitution, like that of nearly every other State,
provides for the election of judges by the people. Those who
oppose the power of the people to recall a judge should—in
order to be consistent—also oppose the power to elect judges
in the first instance.

The people of a State or district elect a man to a judicial position, because they believe he will serve the general welfare. They elect him in anticipation of good service and they would recall him only for demonstrated bad service. The assumption that the people would recall a judge without reason—for the gratification of spite or while they were under the impulse of passion—is without justification. The American people never act in such a way when given an opportunity to act in a lawful and considerate manner.

Men who profess opposition to the recall as applied to the judiciary for fear judges will be improperly influenced by public opinion do not realize that they are offering a greater insult to the judiciary than the advocates of the recall could possibly offer. Advocates of the recall have confidence in the judiciary in general; but they recognize the fact, demonstrated by experience, that human frailty exists in judges as in other men.

To assert that judges are above corruption or improper prejudice and that they are always efficient public servants is too absurd for serious consideration. The men who sit on the bench to-day were boys when members of the legislative branch of government were boys. They were no better or worse on the average than we. In childhood and young manhood we mingled on an equality, enjoyed the same sports, received instructions in the same schools, were taught the same religious principles, were subjected to the same temptations, indulged in the same vices, and cherished the same ambitions. Upon what reasoning, then, can it be asserted that the boy who studied law and found such favor in the eyes of the political boss as to secure a nomination for the bench is superior in either efficiency or honesty to his brother who entered business and was slated by the same boss for a position in the executive or legislative branch of government? Let us look at this subject from a common-sense viewpoint.

There hangs no halo of sanctity around the head of the judiciary, except as unthinking men concede a sacredness which the legal profession has assumed for occupants of the bench. Judges, like all other men in public or private life, are generally honest. Their failure, in exceptional instances, to serve faithfully the people by whom they are employed is due to the same cause to which may be attributed similar failure on the part of other public servants. This cause is the unrepresentative system by which they are chosen.

Opponents of the extension of the recall to the judiciary profess great fear that judges will listen to what they call pub-

lic clamor and will render decisions against justice in order to
avoid public displeasure. How strange that this fear of improper influence has been so long suppressed! In every State
where the convention system is in vogue political machines exist, with political bosses in control. The political bosses maintain their machine organizations by means of funds contributed
by individuals having special interests to promote or protect.
Where the convention system exists the successful candidate for
nomination for judicial position must have the active or passive
support of the political boss. Special privilege is as much interested in the judiciary as in any other branch of government.
Though it may be true that in most cases there is no express
agreement between the political boss and the candidate for a
judicial nomination, any man with the least knowledge of human nature knows that the political boss will aid in securing
the nomination of the candidate who seems most likely to be satisfactory to his backers.

Under that same convention system the man once elected
judge must look to the political boss for his renomination for
a second term. Will anyone say that a judge who will listen
to popular clamor will not also yield to the wishes and interests
of the political boss? And, if the judge must be subject to influences controlling his election or retention in office, which presents the greater danger, the influence of popular will or the
influence of the political boss?

It is useless for men to hold up their hands in horror and
assert that the judiciary is above the influence of the political
boss. If the judiciary is above that influence it is certainly also
above the influence of popular clamor, and the argument against
the recall falls to the ground.

We have heard much in recent weeks about the "rule of
the mob" in connection with the initiative and referendum and
the recall. Now a mob is a body of men acting against law,
order, and justice. Legislatures sometimes do this—the people
never, if an opportunity is given to act in a lawful way. I
grant that where wrongs have been long imposed and remedies
have been denied the people finally resort to force to redress
their grievances, just as they did in the American Revolution.
To some this is mob action. I am disposed to give it a higher
characterization; and, though it is an overthrow of existing authority, I regard it as the establishment of law and order in the
highest sense.

The overthrow of a misrepresentative system, maintained by
political machines enjoying dictatorial powers, and the substitu-

tion of a truly representative system mean the attainment of higher standards of human justice and equality, and, consequently, of a more peaceful and more nearly perfect government. The voice of the people should be the law of the land, and since the initiative and referendum and the recall register the voice of the people they are the best mediums for the establishment of the best governmental principles.

The people of Arizona have the courage to assert themselves and the patriotism to sacrifice even statehood, if necessary, rather than yield their political principles. Their admission to all the privileges of American citizenship will be an honor to the Union; the refusal to admit them would be a national disgrace.

On August 7 William E. Borah [Idaho] supported the resolution, although he was opposed to the recall of judges.

The constitutions submitted by the respective Territories conform to the terms of the enabling act. They are also, in my judgment republican in form, as that term was used and is understood in the guaranty clause of the Federal Constitution. I propose to vote for their admission, therefore, notwithstanding there is one provision in the Arizona constitution to which, as a principle and policy of government, I do not subscribe. But the right of local self-government is an indispensable—and, to my mind, should be an inviolate—principle under our system, and notwithstanding my individual views and objections I must concede the right of the people of Arizona to settle that question for themselves. So long as their constitution is republican in form I feel that the proper rule is to leave the details to the people who are to live under it.

There is another reason which leads me to this conclusion, and that is that we would have no power to keep this provision out of the State constitution of Arizona if Arizona were once admitted to the Union. I think, therefore, that it serves no good purpose to demand temporarily that which we can not effect permanently.

But, in view of the fact that either or both of the resolutions require the submission of the question of the recall of judges again to the votes of the people, I want to submit some reasons why, in my judgment, the people should not retain it in their constitution. While it is not unrepublican in form, I believe it to be unwise in principle.

Senator Borah presented his argument largely in the form of quotations. Those from George Washington, John Adams, Alexander Hamilton, James A. Bayard, Sr., Daniel Webster, the great commentators on constitutional law, James Kent and Joseph Story, Edmund Burke, Benjamin Harrison, and Wendell Phillips, upheld the general principle of the independence of the judiciary. Those from Governor Woodrow Wilson [N. J.], and ex-President Theodore Roosevelt more specifically applied to the case in hand.

Dr. Woodrow Wilson has been quoted a number of times of late by reason of his peculiarly honorable and high position in public thought, and I call attention to a word from him upon this subject. He has given it his consideration, not only from the standpoint of a student, but of late undoubtedly, as he has other questions, of a man in the practical affairs of life. Governor Wilson says:

The recall is a means of administrative control. If properly regulated and devised, it is a means of restoring to administrative officials what the initiative and referendum restore to legislators, namely, a sense of direct responsibility to the people who choose them.

The recall of judges is another matter. Judges are not lawmakers. They are not administrators. Their duty is not to determine what the law shall be, but to determine what the law is. Their independence, their sense of dignity and of freedom, is of the first consequence to the stability of the State. To apply to them the principle of the recall is to set up the idea that determinations of what the law is must respond to popular impulse and to popular judgment.

It is sufficient that the people should have the power to change the law when they will. It is not necessary that they should directly influence by threat of recall those who merely interpret the law already established. The importance and desirability of the recall as a means of administrative control ought not to be obscured by drawing it into this other and very different field.

Colonel Roosevelt, speaking to the people of Arizona, said:

Speaking generally, and as regards most communities under normal conditions, I feel that it is to our self-interest, to the interest of decent citizens who want nothing but justice in its broadest sense, not to adopt any measure which would make judges timid, which would make them fearful lest deciding rightly in some given case might arouse a storm of anger, temporary but fatal. You should shun every measure which would deprive judges of the rugged indifference and straightforward courage which it is so preëminently the interest of the community to see that they preserve.

I know, Mr. President, that politics sometimes has its influence in the highest court. We all concede that the controversy is how to diminish the effect of it rather than how to increase it; and, in my humble judgment, the recall of judges, instead of diminishing, would increase it. I would necessarily bring it into politics; you could not prevent it. Merciful justice! have we not enough politics in our system already, such as it is? Shall we now include the courts? You are much mistaken if you think the people want more politics; they want less. If you will give me a law-making department which is intelligent and true to the people, and an executive department which is fearless and true, with the judicial system which we now have, I will show you the best governed and the happiest people in the world.

But, Mr. President, I am not only opposed to the popular recall, but I am opposed to private recall. I am opposed to the subtle, silent system which has grown up in this country to a remarkable extent unknown to most people—that of exercising an influence upon Federal judges through the executive departments of our Government. If there is going to be a recall, we want a popular recall. We want a people's recall. We want it in the open and not in quiet and subtle ways by devious and undiscovered methods. We want the privacy sought to be established between Federal judges and the heads of departments forever condemned and damned. It is vicious, indefensible, and ought to forever discredit the judge who would brook it or the department head which would seek it.

If the time ever comes in this country when the people of the country understand that there is any string attached to a' Federal judge which they do not through established laws hold, they will not only elect, but they will recall their Federal judges.

Senator Borah said in conclusion:

I sympathize fully, and I want to coöperate at all times, with those who would make the political side of our Government more responsive and more obedient to the demands of the people. I know that changed conditions demand a change in the details of our Government upon its political side. But the rules by which men who distribute justice are to be governed and the influences which embarrass them in this high work are the same now, and will always be the same, as they have ever been. Let us not impeach the saneness and the worth of our great cause by challenging the great and indispensable principle of an independent judiciary. Let us not mislead the people into the belief that their interests or their welfare lies in the direction of justice tempered with popular opinion. Let us not draw these tribunals, before which must come the rich and the poor, the great and the small, the powerful and the weak, closer, even still closer, than now, to the passions and turmoils of politics. Let us cling to this principle of an independent judiciary as of old they would cling to the horns of the altar.

Elihu Root [N. Y.] opposed the resolution.

The Supreme Court of the United States has decided in the Coyle case, the case relating to the right of the people of Oklahoma to change the location of their State capital, notwithstanding the provision of the enabling act which forbade that change, that, after a Territory has once been admitted as a State, the provisions of the enabling act do not control the action of the State. Therefore, in the consideration and action of the Senate upon this joint resolution, we speak the last word that it is competent for us to speak regarding the provisions of the State's constitution.

The question before the Senate is: Do we now approve the provisions of the Arizona constitution? Are we ready, Mr. President, to approve this provision of the recall of judges? If we are, we shall say so by our action upon this joint resolution. If we are not ready to approve this provision of this constitution, we are bound by the law we ourselves have enacted to make that known by our action, and we cannot escape the responsibility for, or the consequences of, that act.

Let me ask the Senate to consider for a moment what will be the necessary working of such a system? We all know that from time to time there arise in all courts cases which enlist great popular interest. Sometimes these are cases in which men are accused of crime and there is a well-founded and general public abhorrence of the crime. I submit to the experience of the members of the Senate the suggestion that the tendency of the public in their abhorrence of a great crime is to assume that the man who is declared by the police authorities to be responsible for it is responsible, to overlook questions of evidence as to whether he be the true criminal and questions as to the degree and character of his guilt, and to assume that the man who is charged is the man who is guilty. The more atrocious the crime the more general and customary is this tendency to condemn a person who is charged with its commission.

Sometimes questions which attract public interest are questions having a political bearing. In our complicated system of government it frequently happens that questions are submitted to the courts upon the determination of which must depend the success of one party or another in establishing its views or in securing the control of the machinery of government. There is great public excitement, intense interest, strong desire to have the decision in accordance with the views of political partisans, who naturally consider the view of their own party to be the correct view.

Sometimes such questions arise from the conflict of religious opinions. I have heard it said in this Hall to-day that courts can never pass upon religious questions. Ah, Mr. President, would any Senator say that no court can enforce the provisions of our Constitution in favor of religious liberty? New sects are continually arising in our country, and the votaries of the religious views of those sects are, at the beginning, small and insignificant minorities. Questions regarding their rights as religious bodies, questions regarding their rights to freedom of worship and of expression, are protected by the provisions of our constitutions, and against the wish, against the prejudice, against the passion of the vast majority of the people; the courts, and the courts alone, can maintain the rights of the few to pursue the dictates of their own conscience rather than the will of the majority.

Sometimes questions arise upon those limitations which our constitutions impose upon the action of legislatures and executive officers and people alike by those great rules that protect liberty and property against the power of government wherever it be vested.

Now, sir, picture to yourselves a judge before whom one of these cases is brought. A few people, a single man, is upon one side. The powers of a government are upon the other side. For the few and the weak there stand only the rules of law. Upon the other side stands the public desire to have a decision in accordance with the public interest or the public feelings. Picture to yourselves the judge who is called upon to decide one of those cases, and consider what his frame of mind and condition of feeling must be when he knows that if he decides against public feeling immediately a recall petition will be signed and filed, and the great body of the people against whose wish he has ruled will be called upon, will be required, to vote whether they prefer him to some man who has never offended public opinion.

IX—35

Upon all these cases, sir, so far as they depend upon evidence —and a vast majority of them do depend upon evidence—which is produced in the trial and which enters into the record of the case, the public does not see the record. It receives its information from the press. I beg the Senate to recall the reports of trials and arguments in our courts which they have been accustomed to see in the public press. The conditions of newspaper enterprise do not permit the publication of the full record of any trial. The gentlemen of the press, eager to secure items of news that will be interesting to the readers of their papers, catch upon the spectacular and interesting and startling incidents of the trial and reproduce them in their columns.

The judge is to pass upon the evidence that appears in the record, but he is to be judged upon the newspaper reports of the trial. And to whom, sir, will the judge try that case? To whom will counsel argue that case? What will become of that spirit which pervades every true court of justice, in which the facts as ascertained and the law interpreted and these alone form the basis of judgment? Is it in human nature that a judge, sitting under such circumstances as are exhibited by this provision which I have read, shall do other than try his case rather to the reporters than to his conscience, to his knowledge of the law, and to his understanding of the facts? For, at every step, the judge is on trial. His defence will not come when he has the opportunity to put 200 words of justification onto the ballot. His defence will begin with the first step in the trial of the cause. Human nature can not work otherwise. In all these great cases of public interest the judge will be on trial on the newspaper record, and in that trial he will take a far deeper interest than in the trial of the defendant or in the rights of the parties upon the record of the court.

Mr. President, there are many provisions in this constitution which I deeply regret to see incorporated in the constitution of any American State. But, for all that, I would not oppose the admission of Arizona as a State upon a constitution adopted by a vote of her people because it contained those provisions or because it contained any provision which did not seem to me to be fundamental in its character and to be in a considerable measure a negation of the true principles of our Government.

I conceive that this provision for the recall of judges is of that character. I think it goes to the very basis of our free Government. I have no quarrel with the gentlemen who extol the wisdom of the people. I believe that, in the long run, after mature consideration and full discussion and when conclusions are reached under such circumstances as to exclude the interests or the prejudice or the passions of the moment, the decisions of the American people are sound and wise. But, sir, they are sound and wise because the wisdom of our fathers devised a system of government which does prevent our people from reaching their conclusions except upon mature consideration, after full discussion, and when the dictates of momentary passion or self-interest are excluded.

Many of the framers of the Republic were men who inherited the traditions of a theocratic government, in which men were controlled as against their own impulses and passions by the dictates that were handed down in the revelation from the Divine Ruler. In a belief which we can not gainsay to-day they undertook to establish for this Government a code of fundamental principles of justice, of equality, principles formulated in specific rules of conduct to make practical their application. Those principles we describe as the constitutional limitations of the national and the State constitutions:

No man shall be deprived of his property except by due process of law.

And all the others, that great array of the fundamental and essential principles by which the American Republic has imposed restraints upon itself against its own interest of the moment, its own wishes of the moment, its own prejudice and passion of the moment. This is the great secret of the success of the American experiment in government, the maintenance of justice and order, individual liberty and individual opportunity in this vast continent, among these 90,000,000 people. And for the maintenance of those rules of justice our fathers provided that the government which may seek, under the interest or the passion of the moment, to override them shall be withheld by the judgment of a body of public officers separated from the interests and passions of the hour, with no pride of opinion because of having made a law, with no lust for power because of a desire to execute a law, with a strong hand according to individual opinion as to what may be best; but impartial, sworn only to the administration of justice, without interest, without fear, and without favor. They intrusted the maintenance of these rules to a body of judges, who were to speak the voice of justice without fear of punishment or hope of reward.

It is the establishment of this system of rules, fundamental rules, intrusted for their declaration and maintenance to a body of impartial judges, that is the great contribution of America to the political science of the world, the great contribution of America to the art of self-government among men.

The essential difference, sir, between the establishment of one of these great rules of right conduct in a constitution and the enactment of a law either by a legislature or by a people is that the fundamental rule is established upon considerations of abstract justice. The rule is established when no one has any concrete interest to be affected, when no one is desirous of doing the wrong thing that the rule prohibits or of undoing the right thing that the rule maintains. It is then, sir, that the voice of an intelligent people is the voice of God, when upon considerations of justice, when considering what is right and fair, and makes for justice and liberty, a people establish for their own control and restraint a rule of right; and the abstract rule is necessary because when the concrete interest comes into play, because when the passion of the moment comes into play, because when religious feeling is rife, when political feeling is excited, when the desire for power here or the desire to push forward a propaganda of views here comes into play, then the inherent weakness of human nature makes it certain that the great and fundamental principles of right will be disregarded.

Sir, we see every day legislatures of our States passing laws which are in violation of these fundamental rules. We see every day public officers exercising an arrogant power in violation of the fundamental rules, except as they are restrained by the cold and impartial voice of those tribunals that our people have established to assert the control of the principles of justice over the interests and the passions of the moment.

Mr. President, this provision for the recall of judges strikes at the very heart of that fundamental and essential characteristic of our system of government. It nullifies it; it sets it at naught; it casts to the winds that protection of justice that our fathers established and that has made us with all our power a just and orderly people. For, sir, when we say to the judge upon the bench, who is bound to assert the rules of justice established in a constitution long years before for the restraint of the people in their passion or their prejudice, you shall decide for the rules of justice at your peril; when we say to the judge if you maintain the abstract rule of justice against the wish of the people at the moment you shall be turned out of office in ignominy, we nullify the rule of justice and we establish the rule of the passion, prejudice, and interest of the moment.

So, sir, I say that this provision of the Arizona constitution strikes at the very heart of our system of government. It goes deeper than that. This provision, sir, is not progress, it is not reform; it is degeneracy. It is a movement backward to those days of misrule and unbridled power out of which the world has been slowly progressing under the leadership of those great men who established the Constitution of the United States. It is a move backward to those days when human passion and the rule of men obtained rather than the law and the rule of principles, for it ignores, it sets at naught the great principle of government and of civilized society, the principle that justice is above majorities.

I care not how small may be the numbers of a political faith or a religious sect, I care not how weak and humble may be a single man accused of however atrocious a crime, time was when the feelings and the passions and the wish of a majority determined his rights and oftentimes his right to life; but now, in this twentieth century, with all the light of the civilization of our times, after a century and a quarter passed by this great and free people following the footsteps of Washington, Hamilton, Jefferson, and Madison, now with all the peoples of the world following their footsteps in the establishment of constitutional governments, the hand of a single man appealing to that justice which exists independently of all majorities has a power that we cannot ignore or deny but at the sacrifice of the best and the noblest elements of government.

There is such a thing as justice, and, though the greatest and most arrogant majority unite to override it, God stands behind it, the eternal laws that rule the world maintain it, and if we attempt to make the administration and award of justice dependent upon the will of a majority we shall fail, and we shall fail at the cost of humiliation and ignominy to ourselves.

I do not envy the men who prefer the uncontrolled rule of a majority free from the restraints which we have imposed upon ourselves to the system of orderly government that we have now established. I do not envy the men who would rather have the French constituent convention, controlled by Marat and Danton and Robespierre, than to have a Supreme Court presided over by Marshall; who would rather have conclusions upon a question of justice reached by a popular election on the basis of newspaper reports than to have the impartial judgment of a great court. I do not envy the men who have no sympathy with Malesherbes and De Sèze pleading for the lawful rights of

Louis XVI against the dictates of the majority of the French capital in 1793.

I do not envy the men who see nothing to admire in John Adams defending the British soldiers against the protests of his neighbors and friends and countrymen after the Boston massacre. Rather, sir, would I feel that my country loves justice and possesses that divine power of self-restraint without which the man remains the child, the citizen remains the savage, and the community becomes the commune; that my country has carried into its system of law, and, whatever be its wish for the moment, whatever its prejudice, whatever its passion for the moment, will forever maintain as of greater importance than any single issue or any single man or any single interest that reverence for the eternal principles of justice which we have embedded in our fundamental law as our nearest approach to the application of the Divine command to human affairs.

The Senate passed the joint resolution on August 8, 1911, by a vote of 53 to 18.

On August 15, 1911, President Taft vetoed the joint resolution for the following reasons:

Veto of the Admission of Arizona

President Taft

This provision of the Arizona constitution, in its application to county and State judges, seems to me so pernicious in its effect, so destructive of independence in the judiciary, so likely to subject the rights of the individual to the possible tyranny of a popular majority, and, therefore, to be so injurious to the cause of free government, that I must disapprove a constitution containing it. I am not now engaged in performing the office given me in the enabling act already referred to, approved June 20, 1910, which was that of approving the constitutions ratified by the peoples of the Territories. It may be argued from the text of that act that in giving or withholding the approval under the act my only duty is to examine the proposed constitution, and, if I find nothing in it inconsistent with the Federal Constitution, the principles of the Declaration of Independence, or the enabling act, to register my approval. But now I am discharging my constitutional function in respect to the enactment of laws, and my discretion is equal to that of the Houses of Congress. I must therefore withhold my approval from this resolution if in fact I do not approve it as a matter of governmental policy. Of course, a mere difference of opinion as to the wisdom of details in a State constitution ought not to lead me to set up my opinion against that of the people of the Territory. It is to be their government, and, while the power of Congress to withhold or grant statehood is absolute, the people about to constitute a State should generally know better the kind of government and constitution suited to their needs than Congress or the Executive. But when such a constitution contains something so destructive of free government as the judicial recall it should be disapproved.

The Constitution distributes the functions of government into three branches—the legislative, to make the laws; the executive, to execute them; and the judicial, to decide in cases arising before it the rights of the individual as between him and others and as between him and the Government. This division of government into three separate branches has always been regarded as a great security for the maintenance of free institutions, and the security is only firm and assured when the judicial branch is independent and impartial. The executive and legislative branches are representative of the majority of the people which elected them in guiding the course of the Government within the limits of the Constitution. They must act for the whole people, of course; but they may properly follow, and usually ought to follow, the views of the majority which elected them in respect to the governmental policy best adapted to secure the welfare of the whole people. But the judicial branch of the Government is not representative of a majority of the people in any such sense, even if the mode of selecting judges is by popular election. In a proper sense, judges are servants of the people; that is, they are doing work which must be done for the Government and in the interest of all the people, but it is not work in the doing of which they are to follow the will of the majority except as that is embodied in statutes lawfully enacted according to constitutional limitations. They are not popular representatives. On the contrary, to fill their office properly they must be independent. They must decide every question which comes before them according to law and justice. If this question is between individuals, they will follow the statute, or the unwritten law if no statute applies, and they take the unwritten law growing out of tradition and custom from previous judicial decisions. If a statute or ordinance affecting a cause before them is not lawfully enacted, because it violates the constitution adopted by the people, then they must

ignore the statute and decide the question as if the statute had
never been passed. This power is a judicial power imposed by
the people on the judges by the written constitution. In early
days some argued that the obligations of the Constitution
operated directly on the conscience of the legislature, and only
in that manner, and that it was to be conclusively presumed
that whatever was done by the legislature was constitutional.
But such a view did not obtain with our hard-headed, courageous, and far-sighted statesmen and judges, and it was soon
settled that it was the duty of judges in cases properly arising
before them to apply the law and so to declare what was the
law, and that if what purported to be statutory law was at
variance with the fundamental law, *i. e.*, the Constitution, the
seeming statute was not law at all, was not binding on the
courts, the individuals, or any branch of the Government, and
that it was the duty of the judges so to decide. This power
conferred on the judiciary in our form of government is unique
in the history of governments, and its operation has attracted
and deserved the admiration and commendation of the world.
It gives to our judiciary a position higher, stronger, and more
responsible than that of the judiciary of any other country, and
more effectively secures adherence to the fundamental will of
the people.

What I have said has been to little purpose if it has not
shown that judges to fulfill their functions properly in our
popular Government must be more independent than in any
other form of government, and that need of independence is
greatest where the individual is one litigant and the State,
guided by the successful and governing majority, is the other.
In order to maintain the rights of the minority and the individual and to preserve our constitutional balance, we must
have judges with courage to decide against the majority when
justice and law require.

By the recall in the Arizona constitution it is proposed to
give to the majority power to remove arbitrarily, and without
delay, any judge who may have the courage to render an unpopular decision. Controversies over elections, labor troubles,
racial or religious issues, issues as to the construction or constitutionality of liquor laws, criminal trials of popular or unpopular defendants—these and many other cases could be cited
in which a majority of a district electorate would be tempted
by hasty anger to recall a conscientious judge if the opportunity were open all the time. No period of delay is interposed for the abatement of popular feeling. The recall is de-

vised to encourage quick action and to lead the people to strike while the iron is hot. The judge is treated as the instrument and servant of a majority of the people and subject to their momentary will, not after a long term in which his qualities as a judge and his character as a man have been subjected to a test of all the varieties of judicial work and duty so as to furnish a proper means of measuring his fitness for continuance in another term. On the instant of an unpopular ruling, while the spirit of protest has not had time to cool, and even while an appeal may be pending from his ruling, in which he may be sustained, he is to be haled before the electorate as a tribunal, with no judicial hearing, evidence, or defence, and thrown out of office and disgraced for life because he has failed, in a single decision, it may be, to satisfy the popular demand. Think of the opportunity such a system would give to unscrupulous political bosses in control, as they have been in control not only of conventions but elections! Think of the enormous power for evil given to the sensational, muckraking portion of the press in rousing prejudice against a just judge by false charges and insinuations, the effect of which in the short period of an election by recall it would be impossible for him to meet and offset! Supporters of such a system seem to think that it will work only in the interest of the poor, the humble, the weak, and the oppressed; that it will strike down only the judge who is supposed to favor corporations and be affected by the corrupting influence of the rich. Nothing could be further from the ultimate result. The motive it would offer to unscrupulous combinations to seek to control politics in order to control the judges is clear. Those would profit by the recall who have the best opportunity of rousing the majority of the people to action on a sudden impulse. Are they likely to be the wisest or the best people in a community? Do they not include those who have money enough to employ the firebrands and slanderers in a community and the stirrers-up of social hate? Would not self-respecting men well hesitate to accept judicial office with such a sword of Damocles hanging over them? What kind of judgments might those on the unpopular side expect from courts whose judges must make their decisions under such legalized terrorism? The character of the judges would deteriorate to that of trimmers and timeservers, and independent judicial action would be a thing of the past. As the possibilities of such a system pass in review, is it too much to characterize it as one which will destroy the judiciary, its standing, and its usefulness?

The argument has been made to justify the judicial recall that it is only carrying out the principle of the election of the judges by the people. The appointment by the executive is by the representative of the majority, and so far as future bias is concerned there is no great difference between the appointment and the election of judges. The independence of the judiciary is secured rather by a fixed term and fixed and irreducible salary. It is true that, when the term of judges is for a limited number of years and reëlection is necessary, it has been thought and charged sometimes that shortly before election in cases in which popular interest is excited judges have leaned in their decisions toward the popular side.

As already pointed out, however, in the election of judges for a long and fixed term of years, the fear of popular prejudice as a motive for unjust decisions is minimized by the tenure on the one hand, while the opportunity which the people have calmly to consider the work of a judge for a full term of years in deciding as to his reëlection generally insures from them a fair and reasonable consideration of his qualities as a judge. While, therefore, there have been elected judges who have bowed before unjust popular prejudice, or who have yielded to the power of political bosses in their decisions, I am convinced that these are exceptional, and that, on the whole, elected judges have made a great American judiciary. But the success of an elective judiciary certainly furnishes no reason for so changing the system as to take away the very safeguards which have made it successful.

Attempt is made to defend the principle of judicial recall by reference to States in which judges are said to have shown themselves to be under corrupt corporate influence and in which it is claimed that nothing but a desperate remedy will suffice. If the political control in such States is sufficiently wrested from corrupting corporations to permit the enactment of a radical constitutional amendment like that of judicial recall, it would seem possible to make provision in its stead for an effective remedy by impeachment in which the cumbrous features of the present remedy might be avoided, but the opportunity for judicial hearing and defence before an impartial tribunal might be retained. Real reforms are not to be effected by patent short cuts or by abolishing those requirements which the experience of ages has shown to be essential in dealing justly with everyone. Such innovations are certain in the long run to plague the inventor or first user and will come readily to the hand of the enemies and corrupters of society after the passing of the just popular indignation that prompted their adoption.

Again, judicial recall is advocated on the ground that it will bring the judges more into sympathy with the popular will and the progress of ideas among the people. It is said that now judges are out of touch with the movement toward a wider democracy and a greater control of governmental agencies in the interest and for the benefit of the people. The righteous and just course for a judge to pursue is ordinarily fixed by statute or clear principles of law, and the cases in which his judgment may be affected by his political, economic, or social views are infrequent. But even in such cases judges are not removed from the people's influence. Surround the judiciary with all the safeguards possible, create judges by appointment, make their tenure for life, forbid diminution of salary during their term, and still it is impossible to prevent the influence of popular opinion from coloring judgments in the long run. Judges are men, intelligent, sympathetic men, patriotic men, and in those fields of the law in which the personal equation unavoidably plays a part there will be found a response to sober popular opinion as it changes to meet the exigency of social, political, and economic changes. Indeed, this should be so. Individual instances of a hidebound and retrograde conservatism on the part of courts in decisions which turn on the individual economic or sociological views of the judges may be pointed out; but they are not many, and do not call for radical action. In treating of courts we are dealing with a human machine, liable, like all the inventions of man, to err, but we are dealing with a human institution that likens itself to a divine institution, because it seeks and preserves justice. It has been the corner-stone of our gloriously free Government, in which the rights of the individual and of the minority have been preserved, while governmental action of the majority has lost nothing of beneficent progress, efficacy, and directness. This balance was planned in the Constitution by its framers, and it has been maintained by our independent judiciary.

Precedents are cited from State constitutions said to be equivalent to a popular recall. In some, judges are removable by a vote of both houses of the legislature. This is a mere adoption of the English address of Parliament to the Crown for the removal of judges. It is similar to impeachment, in that a form of hearing is always granted. Such a provision forms no precedent for a popular recall without adequate hearing and defence, and with new candidates to contest the election.

It is said the recall will be rarely used. If so, it will be rarely needed. Then why adopt a system so full of danger? But it is a mistake to suppose that such a powerful lever for influencing judicial decisions and such an opportunity for vengeance because of adverse ones will be allowed to remain unused.

But it is said that the people of Arizona are to become an independent State when created, and even if we strike out judicial recall now they can reincorporate it in their constitution after statehood.

To this I would answer that in dealing with the courts, which are the corner-stone of good government, and in which not only the voters, but the nonvoters and nonresidents, have a deep interest as a security for their rights of life, liberty, and property, no matter what the future action of the State may be, it is necessary for the authority which is primarily responsible for its creation to assert in no doubtful tones the necessity for an independent and untrammeled judiciary.

The recall provision was omitted from the Arizona constitution, and a joint resolution was passed by Congress admitting that Territory and New Mexico into the Union. It was approved by President Taft on August 22, 1911.

The Arizona State legislature at its first session adopted the original recall provision as a part of its constitution.

Early in the next session of Congress (December 4, 1912) Joseph L. Bristow [Kan.], a Progressive, introduced in the Senate a joint resolution submitting to the States two constitutional amendments, the first permitting the President to submit to popular vote at a congressional election any measure he has recommended to Congress upon which no action has been taken for six months, and the second providing that, "if the Supreme Court shall decide a law, enacted by Congress, is in violation of the provisions of the Constitution of the United States, the Congress at a regular session held after such decision may submit the act to the electors at a regular congressional election."

Under each amendment it is proposed that the questions submitted to the people must have a majority of the popular vote in a majority of the States, as well as in a majority of the congressional districts.

The resolution was referred to the Judiciary Committee.

A new form of the recall was injected as an issue in both national and State politics by Theodore Roosevelt in the presidential campaign of 1912. This was the recall of judicial decisions. Colonel Roosevelt brought forward the issue early in his contest with President Taft for the Republican nomination and defended it through that contest and through the presidential campaign which followed. He gave it an important place in his speech at Chicago, August 6, 1912, before the Progressive national convention which nominated him as its candidate.

THE RECALL OF JUDICIAL DECISIONS

THEODORE ROOSEVELT

The American people and not the courts are to determine their own fundamental policies. The people should have power to deal with the effect of the acts of all their governmental agencies. This must be extended to include the effects of judicial acts as well as the acts of the executive and legislative representatives of the people.

Where the judge merely does justice as between man and man, not dealing with constitutional questions, then the interest of the public is only to see that he is a wise and upright judge.

Means should be devised for making it easier than at present to get rid of an incompetent judge; means should be devised by the bar and the bench, acting in conjunction with the various legislative bodies, to make justice far more expeditious and more certain than at present. The stick-in-the-bark legalism, the legalism that subordinates equity to technicalities, should be recognized as a potent enemy of justice.

But this is not the matter of most concern at the moment. Our prime concern is that in dealing with the fundamental law of the land, in assuming finally to interpret it, and therefore finally to make it the acts of the courts should be subject to and not above the final control of the people as a whole. I deny that the American people have surrendered to any set of men, no matter what their position or their character, the final right to determine those fundamental questions upon which free self-government ultimately depends.

The people themselves must be the ultimate makers of their own Constitution, and where their agents differ in their interpretations of the Constitution to the people themselves should be given the chance, after full and deliberate judgment, au-thoritatively to settle•what interpretation it is that their representatives shall thereafter adopt as binding.

Whenever in our constitutional system of government there exist general prohibitions that, as interpreted by the courts, nullify, or may be used to nullify, specific laws passed, and admittedly passed, in the interest of social justice, we are for such immediate law, or amendment to the Constitution, if that be necessary, as will thereafter permit a reference to the people of the public effect of such decision, under forms securing full deliberation, to the end that the specific act of the legislative branch of the Government thus judicially nullified, and such amendments thereof as come within its scope and purpose, may constitutionally be excepted by vote of the people from the general prohibitions, the same as if that particular act had been expressly excepted when the prohibition was adopted.

This will necessitate the establishment of machinery for making much easier of amendment both the national and the several State constitutions, especially with the view of prompt action on certain judicial decisions—action as specific and limited as that taken by the passage of the Eleventh Amendment to the national Constitution.

We are not in this decrying the courts. That was reserved for the Chicago convention in its plank respecting impeachment. Impeachment implies the proof of dishonesty. We do not question the general honesty of the courts. But, in applying to present-day social conditions the general prohibitions that were intended originally as safeguards to the citizen against the arbitrary power of government in the hands of caste and privilege, these prohibitions have been turned by the courts from safeguards against political and social justice and advancement.

Our purpose is not to impugn the courts, but to emancipate them from a position where they stand in the way of social justice, and to emancipate the people, in an orderly way, from the iniquity of enforced submission to a doctrine which would turn constitutional provisions which were intended to favor social justice and advancement into prohibitions against such justice and advancement.

We in America have peculiar need thus to make the acts of the courts subject to the people, because, owing to causes which I need not now discuss, the courts have here grown to occupy a position unknown in any other country, a position of superiority over both the legislature and the Executive. Just at this time, when we have begun in this country to move toward social and industrial betterment and true industrial democracy, this attitude on the part of the courts is of grave portent, because privilege has intrenched itself in many courts, just as it formerly intrenched itself in many legislative bodies and in many executive offices. Even in England, where the constitution is based upon the theory of the supremacy of the legislative body over the courts, the cause of democracy has at times been hampered by court action.

In a recent book by a notable English Liberal leader, L. T. Hobhouse, there occurs the following sentences dealing with this subject:

> Labor itself had experienced the full brunt of the attack. It had come, not from the politicians, but from the judges; but in this country we have to realize that within wide limits the judges are, in effect, legislators, and legislators with a certain persistent bent which can be held in check only by the constant vigilance and repeated efforts of the recognized organ for the making and repeal of law.

It thus appears that even in England it is necessary to exercise vigilance in order to prevent reactionary thwarting of the popular will by courts that are subject to the power of the legislature.

In the United States, where the courts are supreme over the legislature, it is vital that the people should keep in their own hands the right of interpreting their own Constitution when their public servants differ as to the interpretation.

I am well aware that every upholder of privilege, every hired agent or beneficiary of the special interests, including many well-meaning parlor reformers, will denounce all this as "Socialism" or "anarchy"—the same terms they used in the past in denouncing the movements to control the railways and to control public utilities.

As a matter of fact, the propositions I make constitute neither anarchy nor Socialism, but, on the contrary, a corrective to Socialism and an antidote to anarchy.

Many replies were made to Colonel Roosevelt on this issue by prominent statesmen and publicists. The common tenor of their arguments was virtually the same as that of the opposition to the recall of judges. This was expressed by President Taft in a speech at Toledo, O., on March 8, 1912[1]:

"I have examined this method of reversing judicial decisions on constitutional questions with care, and I do not hesitate to say that it lays the axe to the root of the tree of freedom and subjects the guaranties of life, liberty, and property without remedy to the fitful impulse of a temporary majority of an electorate."

[1] See introduction to the present volume.